Hockey Scouting Report 1996-1997

SHERRY ROSS

GREYSTONE
BOOKS

Douglas & McIntyre
Vancouver/Toronto

This book is dedicated to the memory of Dr. Katja Brackelmanns —
a gentle woman, but a fighter.

Greystone Books
A division of Douglas & McIntyre Ltd.
1615 Venables Street
Vancouver, British Columbia V5L 2H1

Editing by Anne Rose and Kerry Banks
Cover design by Peter Cocking
Cover photograph of Jaromir Jagr by J. McIsaac/Bruce Bennett Studios
Typesetting by MicroMega Designs
Printed and bound in Canada

The publisher gratefully acknowledges the assistance of the Canada Council and
of the British Columbia Ministry of Tourism, Small Business and Culture.

SHERRY ROSS

Yrs. of NHL service: 18
Born: Randolph, NJ
Position: in press box
Height: no way
Weight: you gotta be kidding
Uniform no.: DKNJ
Shoots: from the lip

LAST SEASON
Worked for *New York Daily News* as a beat reporter, covering the New Jersey Devils.

THE FINESSE GAME
The versatile Ross began her career in 1978-79, covering the New York Rangers as they reached the Stanley Cup finals. In addition to working as a sportswriter for 15 seasons for various newspapers, such as the *Bergen (N.J.) Record*, *Newsday* and *The National*, she became the NHL's first female team sportscaster in 1992 when she was hired as a colour commentator for the Devils' radio broadcasts on WABC-AM.

As a freelance writer, Ross has also contributed to *Sports Illustrated*, the *Hockey News*, the *Sporting News* and *Beckett Hockey Monthly*. She is the principal writer for Topps hockey cards, and serves as the secretary-treasurer for the Professional Hockey Writers Association.

THE PHYSICAL GAME
Ross has demonstrated the endurance necessary to travel the full 82-game schedule, but she charges her batteries with trail rides on her horse, Cody, and frequent trips to Walt Disney World. She is a terrible skater.

THE INTANGIBLES
Although her hand-eye coordination may have diminished in recent years, her passion for the game keeps Ross plugging away despite those snowy drives to Hartford.

ACKNOWLEDGEMENTS
Somehow, this book gets harder every year instead of easier. But one thing never changes, and that is the anonymous scouts, coaches, general managers and players whose input results in the assessments you will read in these pages.

Trying to predict team rosters three months before training camp requires even more gambling than Sandis Ozolinsh does on the ice, which is why in our last edition we overlooked players like Daniel Alfredsson (oh, like a rookie-of-the-year award is some big deal), Marcus Ragnarsson and Petr Sykora, but left in Steve Larmer and Chris Snell. This year, we have tried to include more potential up-and-comers, such as Jarome Iginla and Jamie Langenbrunner. That means a few old favourites, such as Kevin Lowe and Denis Savard, were left out of our pages, but if those gentlemen do play this season you should know them well enough by now anyway. If you don't, you must be reading this in Phoenix.

Many thanks are due. To all who helped with the analysis, your love for the game and your patience with me never ceases to amaze. Thanks to my former *Daily News* sports editor Kevin Whitmer and my current bosses Barry Werner and Dave Kaplan for allowing me back into the writing game. You still owe me for that Ireland trip.

Thanks to my *News* colleague Frank Brown for taping all those hockey games (someday I'll get ESPN2), and thanks to my friend Brad Fisher for the music.

Andy McGowan of the NHL and the member clubs provided invaluable data and assistance. Out west in Vancouver, computer genius Kelly Dresser helped me through numerous crises, and editors Kerry Banks and Anne Rose were stuck with proofreading my copy. Great job, all. Next year, maybe this will get easier.

CONTENTS

TOP 100

NHL Scoring Statistics 1995-96

RANK	POS.	PLAYER	GP	G	A	PTS	+/-	PP	S	PCT
1.	C	MARIO LEMIEUX	70	69	92	161	10	31	338	20.4
2.	R	JAROMIR JAGR	82	62	87	149	31	20	403	15.4
3.	C	JOE SAKIC	82	51	69	120	14	17	339	15.0
4.	C	RON FRANCIS	77	27	92	119	25	12	158	17.1
5.	C	PETER FORSBERG	82	30	86	116	26	7	217	13.8
6.	C	ERIC LINDROS	73	47	68	115	26	15	294	16.0
7.	L	PAUL KARIYA	82	50	58	108	9	20	349	14.3
8.	R	TEEMU SELANNE	79	40	68	108	5	9	267	15.0
9.	R	ALEXANDER MOGILNY	79	55	52	107	14	10	292	18.8
10.	C	SERGEI FEDOROV	78	39	68	107	49	11	306	12.7
11.	C	DOUG WEIGHT	82	25	79	104	-19	9	204	12.3
12.	C	WAYNE GRETZKY	80	23	79	102	-13	6	195	11.8
13.	C	MARK MESSIER	74	47	52	99	29	14	241	19.5
14.	C	PETR NEDVED	80	45	54	99	37	8	204	22.1
15.	L	KEITH TKACHUK	76	50	48	98	11	20	249	20.1
16.	L	JOHN LECLAIR	82	51	46	97	21	19	270	18.9
17.	R	THEOREN FLEURY	80	46	50	96	17	17	353	13.0
18.	C	PIERRE TURGEON	80	38	58	96	19	17	297	12.8
19.	C	STEVE YZERMAN	80	36	59	95	29	16	220	16.4
20.	C	VINCENT DAMPHOUSSE	80	38	56	94	5	11	254	15.0
21.	C	ADAM OATES	70	25	67	92	16	7	183	13.7
22.	C	PAT LAFONTAINE	76	40	51	91	-8	15	224	17.9
23.	R	ZIGMUND PALFFY	81	43	44	87	-17	17	257	16.7
24.	C	ROD BRIND'AMOUR	82	26	61	87	20	4	213	12.2
25.	L	VALERI KAMENSKY	81	38	47	85	14	18	220	17.3
26.	D	BRIAN LEETCH	82	15	70	85	12	7	276	5.4
27.	R	BRETT HULL	70	43	40	83	4	16	327	13.1
28.	C	MATS SUNDIN	76	33	50	83	8	7	301	11.0
29.	R	PAT VERBEEK	69	41	41	82	29	17	252	16.3
30.	D	RAY BOURQUE	82	20	62	82	31	9	390	5.1
31.	C	CRAIG JANNEY	84	20	62	82	-33	7	91	22.0
32.	C	MIKE MODANO	78	36	45	81	-12	8	320	11.3
33.	C	MICHAL PIVONKA	73	16	65	81	18	6	168	9.5
34.	R	PETER BONDRA	67	52	28	80	18	11	322	16.1
35.	R	TREVOR LINDEN	82	33	47	80	6	12	202	16.3
36.	C	BRIAN BRADLEY	75	23	56	79	-11	9	189	12.2
37.	L	BRENDAN SHANAHAN	74	44	34	78	2	17	280	15.7
38.	R	MARK RECCHI	82	28	50	78	20	11	191	14.7
39.	L	MARTIN RUCINSKY	78	29	46	75	18	9	181	16.0
40.	D	PAUL COFFEY	76	14	60	74	19	3	234	6.0
41.	C	VYACHESLAV KOZLOV	82	36	37	73	33	9	237	15.2
42.	C	IGOR LARIONOV	73	22	51	73	31	10	113	19.5
43.	C	DOUG GILMOUR	81	32	40	72	-5	10	180	17.8
44.	D	CHRIS CHELIOS	81	14	58	72	25	7	219	6.4
45.	R	CLAUDE LEMIEUX	79	39	32	71	14	9	315	12.4

GP = games played; G = goals; A = assists; PTS = points; +/- = goals-for minus goals-against while player is on ice; PP = power play goals; S = no. of shots; PCT = percentage of goals to shots; * = rookie

RANK	POS.	PLAYER	GP	G	A	PTS	+/-	PP	S	PCT
46.	R	TOMAS SANDSTROM	58	35	35	70	4	17	187	18.7
47.	R	SCOTT MELLANBY	79	32	38	70	4	19	225	14.2
48.	L	ZDENO CIGER	78	31	39	70	-15	12	184	16.8
49.	R	OWEN NOLAN	81	33	36	69	-33	16	207	15.9
50.	C	TRAVIS GREEN	69	24	45	69	-21	14	186	12.9
51.	L	LUC ROBITAILLE	77	23	46	69	13	11	223	10.3
52.	D	PHIL HOUSLEY	81	17	51	68	-6	6	205	8.3
53.	C	JEREMY ROENICK	66	32	35	67	9	12	171	18.7
54.	C	GERMAN TITOV	82	28	39	67	9	13	214	13.1
55.	C	CLIFF RONNING	79	22	45	67	16	5	187	11.8
56.	D	GARY SUTER	82	20	47	67	3	12	242	8.3
57.	D	NICKLAS LIDSTROM	81	17	50	67	29	8	211	8.1
58.	D	SERGEI ZUBOV	64	11	55	66	28	3	141	7.8
59.	L	GEOFF SANDERSON	81	34	31	65	0	6	314	10.8
60.	R	RUSS COURTNALL	81	26	39	65	25	6	205	12.7
61.	D	ROMAN HAMRLIK	82	16	49	65	-24	12	281	5.7
62.	L	DIMITRI KHRISTICH	76	27	37	64	0	12	204	13.2
63.	C	BRYAN SMOLINSKI	81	24	40	64	6	8	229	10.5
64.	C	BENOIT HOGUE	78	19	45	64	10	5	155	12.3
65.	C	JOE JUNEAU	80	14	50	64	-3	7	176	8.0
66.	R	TONY AMONTE	81	31	32	63	10	5	216	14.4
67.	C	ANDREW CASSELS	81	20	43	63	8	6	135	14.8
68.	C	ROB NIEDERMAYER	82	26	35	61	1	11	155	16.8
69.	L	STEVE THOMAS	81	26	35	61	-2	6	192	13.5
70.	R	*DANIEL ALFREDSSON	82	26	35	61	-18	8	212	12.3
71.	C	DALE HAWERCHUK	82	17	44	61	15	6	180	9.4
72.	D	AL MACINNIS	82	17	44	61	5	9	317	5.4
73.	D	LARRY MURPHY	82	12	49	61	-2	8	182	6.6
74.	R	RAY SHEPPARD	70	37	23	60	-19	14	231	16.0
75.	R	RICK TOCCHET	71	29	31	60	10	10	185	15.7
76.	C	RAY FERRARO	76	29	31	60	0	9	178	16.3
77.	R	SCOTT YOUNG	81	21	39	60	2	7	229	9.2
78.	C	BERNIE NICHOLLS	59	19	41	60	11	6	100	19.0
79.	C	JASON ARNOTT	64	28	31	59	-6	8	244	11.5
80.	C	ALEXEI ZHAMNOV	58	22	37	59	-4	5	199	11.1
81.	L	WENDEL CLARK	71	32	26	58	-5	8	237	13.5
82.	R	NELSON EMERSON	81	29	29	58	-7	12	247	11.7
83.	L	RANDY BURRIDGE	74	25	33	58	0	6	154	16.2
84.	R	ALEXEI KOVALEV	81	24	34	58	5	8	206	11.7
85.	L	ADAM GRAVES	82	22	36	58	18	9	266	8.3
86.	L	DAVE ANDREYCHUK	76	28	29	57	-9	14	241	11.6
87.	D	ROBERT SVEHLA	81	8	49	57	-3	7	146	5.5
88.	L	MARTIN GELINAS	81	30	26	56	8	3	181	16.6
89.	R	ANDREI KOVALENKO	77	28	28	56	20	6	131	21.4
90.	C	DEREK PLANTE	76	23	33	56	-4	4	203	11.3
91.	R	MARKUS NASLUND	76	22	33	55	20	4	144	15.3
92.	C	MICHAEL NYLANDER	73	17	38	55	0	4	163	10.4
93.	D	JEFF BROWN	76	8	47	55	8	5	177	4.5
94.	R	MIKE GARTNER	82	35	19	54	5	15	275	12.7
95.	R	JOZEF STUMPEL	76	18	36	54	-8	5	158	11.4
96.	D	JYRKI LUMME	80	17	37	54	-9	8	192	8.9
97.	D	SANDIS OZOLINSH	73	14	40	54	2	8	166	8.4
98.	D	MATHIEU SCHNEIDER	78	13	41	54	-20	7	191	6.8
99.	D	TEPPO NUMMINEN	74	11	43	54	-4	6	165	6.7
100.	D	GARRY GALLEY	78	10	44	54	-2	7	175	5.7

GP = games played; G = goals; A = assists; PTS = points; +/- = goals-for minus goals-against while player is on ice; PP = power play goals; S = no. of shots; PCT = percentage of goals to shots; * = rookie

ANAHEIM MIGHTY DUCKS

Players' Statistics 1995-96

POS.	NO.	PLAYER	GP	G	A	PTS	+/-	PIM	PP	SH	GW	GT	S	PCT
L	9	PAUL KARIYA	82	50	58	108	9	20	20	3	9		349	14.3
R	8	TEEMU SELANNE	79	40	68	108	5	22	9	1	5		267	15.0
R	28	ROMAN OKSIUTA	70	23	28	51	4	60	11		1		119	19.3
C	20	STEVE RUCCHIN	64	19	25	44	3	12	8	1	4		113	16.8
D	2	BOBBY DOLLAS	82	8	22	30	9	64		1	1		117	6.8
R	14	JOE SACCO	76	13	14	27	1	40	1	2	2	1	132	9.8
C	93	ANATOLI SEMENOV	56	4	22	26	-1	24			2		79	5.1
C	22	SHAUN VAN ALLEN	49	8	17	25	13	41			2		78	10.3
L	18	GARRY VALK	79	12	12	24	8	125	1	1	2		108	11.1
D	3	JASON YORK	79	3	21	24	-7	88					106	2.8
D	4	FREDRIK OLAUSSON	56	2	22	24	-7	38	1				83	2.4
C	32	ALEX HICKS	64	10	11	21	11	37			2	1	83	12.0
D	17	DAVE KARPA	72	3	16	19	-3	270		1	1		62	4.8
R	21	PATRIK CARNBACK	34	6	12	18	3	34	1				54	11.1
L	11	VALERI KARPOV	37	9	8	17	-1	10			1		42	21.4
R	16	PETER DOURIS	31	8	7	15	-3	9	2		3		45	17.8
L	12	*DAVID SACCO	23	4	10	14	1	18	2				26	15.4
R	46	*JEAN-FRANCOIS JOMPHE	31	2	12	14	7	39	2				46	4.3
L	42	*DENNY LAMBERT	33		8	8	-2	55					28	
R	36	TODD EWEN	53	4	3	7	-5	285			1		52	7.7
L	24	KEN BAUMGARTNER	72	2	4	6	-5	193			1		32	6.3
C	21	*JIM CAMPBELL	16	2	3	5	0	36	1				25	8.0
D	7	MILOS HOLAN	16	2	2	4	-12	24					47	4.3
D	29	RANDY LADOUCEUR	63	1	3	4	5	47					48	2.1
D	48	*DARREN VAN IMPE	16	1	2	3	8	14			1		13	7.7
R	24	STEVEN KING	7	2		2	-1	15	1		1		5	40.0
G	35	M. SHTALENKOV	30		2	2	0	2						
C	15	VIACHESLAV BUTSAYEV	7	1		1	-4						9	11.1
R	28	*DWAYNE NORRIS	3		1	1	0	2					3	
L	40	*JEREMY STEVENSON	3		1	1	1	12					1	
C	54	*SEAN PRONGER	7		1	1	0	6					3	
D	23	*JASON MARSHALL	24		1	1	3	42					9	
C	27	JOHN LILLEY	1				-1							
D	6	DON MCSWEEN	4				0	4					1	
D	44	OLEG MIKULCHIK	8				-2	4						
G	31	GUY HEBERT	59				0	6						

GP = games played; G = goals; A = assists; PTS = points; +/- = goals-for minus goals-against while player is on ice; PIM = penalties in minutes; PP = power play goals; SH = shorthanded goals; GW = game-winning goals; GT = game-tying goals; S = no. of shots; PCT = percentage of goals to shots; * = rookie

BOBBY DOLLAS

Yrs. of NHL service: 6
Born: Montreal, Que.; Jan. 31, 1965
Position: right defense
Height: 6-2
Weight: 212
Uniform no.: 2
Shoots: left

Career statistics:

GP	G	A	TP	PIM
374	30	60	90	257

1992-93 statistics:

GP	G	A	TP	+/-	PIM	PP	SH	GW	GT	S	PCT
6	0	0	0	-1	2	0	0	0	0	5	0.0

1993-94 statistics:

GP	G	A	TP	+/-	PIM	PP	SH	GW	GT	S	PCT
77	9	11	20	+20	55	1	0	1	0	121	7.4

1994-95 statistics:

GP	G	A	TP	+/-	PIM	PP	SH	GW	GT	S	PCT
45	7	13	20	-3	12	3	1	1	0	70	10.0

1995-96 statistics:

GP	G	A	TP	+/-	PIM	PP	SH	GW	GT	S	PCT
82	8	22	30	+9	64	0	1	1	0	117	6.8

LAST SEASON

Led team defensemen in scoring for second consecutive season. Career high in assists and points. One of two Mighty Ducks to appear in all 82 games.

THE FINESSE GAME

Dollas is an excellent skater with speed, mobility and agility, and he's strong on his feet. He doesn't like to get involved too much in the offense, preferring to make a smart, quick pass to start a teammate off. He makes poised plays out of the defensive zone, but has become more and more conservative.

Dollas gets a lot of ice time, and can handle it because he doesn't wear himself out racing up and down the ice. He will take the offensive chance when it is a high-percentage play, and he is skilled enough to handle point work on the second unit.

Dollas is being asked to be a number one defenseman, which is not his ideal slot, but until the Mighty Ducks acquire or develop a better defenseman, Dollas will do his best to handle the role. He has a strong shot from the point, but it takes him awhile to release it and more often than not the shot gets blocked.

THE PHYSICAL GAME

Because of his size, Dollas was thrust into the role of an enforcer with three different organizations. But he's not tough, doesn't like to fight and he got an unfair label as a soft player when the Red Wings (his last club before Anaheim) accused him of shirking while he had a back injury.

The Mighty Ducks knew what they were getting and didn't ask anything more of Dollas than to play steady two-way hockey. That he does. He uses his size to tie up rather than rub out players around the net. He doesn't scare people, but he won't be intimidated.

THE INTANGIBLES

Dollas is content in his role, and Anaheim seems happy with a defenseman who is a stabilizing force. Anaheim needs to find a strong offensive defenseman, who would make a fine partner with Dollas, but the team is thin at the position now.

GUY HEBERT

Yrs. of NHL service: 4
Born: Troy, N.Y.; Jan. 7, 1967
Position: goaltender
Height: 5-11
Weight: 180
Uniform no.: 31
Catches: left

Career statistics:

GP	MIN	GA	SO	GAA	A	PIM
187	10357	517	9	3.00	1	12

1992-93 statistics:

GP	MIN	GAA	W	L	T	SO	GA	S	SAPCT	PIM
24	1210	3.67	8	8	2	1	74	630	.883	2

1993-94 statistics:

GP	MIN	GAA	W	L	T	SO	GA	S	SAPCT	PIM
52	2991	2.83	20	27	3	2	141	1513	.907	2

1994-95 statistics:

GP	MIN	GAA	W	L	T	SO	GA	S	SAPCT	PIM
39	2092	3.13	12	20	4	2	109	1132	.904	2

1995-96 statistics:

GP	MIN	GAA	W	L	T	SO	GA	S	SAPCT	PIM
59	3326	2.83	28	23	5	4	157	1820	.914	6

LAST SEASON

Career high in wins. Career best in goals-against average. Fourth in NHL in save percentage.

THE PHYSICAL GAME

Hebert is technically solid in combining good angle play with quick reflexes. He stands up well and doesn't get flustered when he sees a lot of shots. He deadens pucks with his pads and doesn't leave big rebounds. Hebert challenges shooters but falls into lapses of staying too deep in his net. When he does, he struggles.

He uses his stick effectively around the net to control rebounds and deflect passes, but he doesn't handle the puck aggressively outside his net, and loses starts to backup goalie Mikhail Shtalenkov when the Mighty Ducks face a team with a strong forecheck. Hebert doesn't have to whip the puck up ice like Ron Hextall, but he should be secure enough to make little passes to avoid pressure and help his defensemen.

Hebert's lateral movement has gotten better. He takes away a lot of the net low and forces shooters to go high. Since he is a small goalie, shooters expect him to go down and scramble, but he stands his ground effectively.

THE MENTAL GAME

We really liked the way Hebert played down the stretch as the Mighty Ducks rallied in an attempt to reach the playoff for the first time. Hebert had some nagging injuries (notably a sore ankle) during the season which contributed to some of his slumps, but he proved himself to be a clutch goalie.

His weak stretches seldom last long. He has good intensity and concentration. His attitude and work ethic are sound. Playing for an expansion team can wear on a goalie, but Hebert maintains a positive attitude.

THE INTANGIBLES

Hebert has proven himself as Anaheim's number one goalie, but he can still upgrade his game (he's only 29, and John Vanbiesbrouck was able to step up another notch at 33). Hebert has few hockey miles on him and should get even better.

ALEX HICKS

Yrs. of NHL service: 1
Born: Calgary, Alberta; Sept. 4, 1969
Position: left wing
Height: 6-1
Weight: 195
Uniform no.: 32
Shoots: left

Career statistics:

GP	G	A	TP	PIM
64	10	11	21	37

1995-96 statistics:

GP	G	A	TP	+/-	PIM	PP	SH	GW	GT	S	PCT
64	10	11	21	+11	37	0	0	2	1	83	12.0

LAST SEASON

Signed as free agent, Aug. 23, 1995. First NHL season. Second on team in plus-minus. Played 13 games with Baltimore (AHL), scoring 2-10 — 12.

THE FINESSE GAME

Meet Pat Conacher, 10 years ago. After years of slogging through minor league games in Toledo and Las Vegas, Hicks finally got his NHL shot last season and made the most of the opportunity with his intelligence and work ethic.

Hicks drives to the net and gets his goals from his second effort. He has a decent shot but scores mostly from within 10 feet of the net. He excels at goalmouth scrambles. Hicks was a good scorer in the minors, but doesn't have the big-time speed and shot to make a serious splash in the NHL.

Hicks can be used to kill penalties, although he doesn't have great speed. He looks faster because he is always hustling.

THE PHYSICAL GAME

Hicks is strong and sturdy, and never quits trying for the puck along the wall or behind the net. If he had better hands, he could make things happen, but he can stir things up and is a very busy player who can rattle the defense into a bad pass.

THE INTANGIBLES

Hicks will be on the bubble, but unless the Mighty Ducks upgrade their talent level drastically, Hicks can find a spot on the third or fourth line as a checking centre who brings energy to his shifts. His top end is about 15 goals.

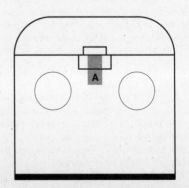

PAUL KARIYA

Yrs. of NHL service: 2
Born: North Vancouver, B.C.; Oct. 16, 1974
Position: left wing
Height: 5-11
Weight: 175
Uniform no.: 9
Shoots: left

Career statistics:

GP	G	A	TP	PIM
129	68	79	147	24

1994-95 statistics:

GP	G	A	TP	+/-	PIM	PP	SH	GW	GT	S	PCT
47	18	21	39	-17	4	7	1	3	1	134	13.4

1995-96 statistics:

GP	G	A	TP	+/-	PIM	PP	SH	GW	GT	S	PCT
82	50	58	108	+9	20	20	3	9	0	349	14.3

LAST SEASON

Won 1996 Lady Byng Trophy. Led team in goals, power play goals and shots for second consecutive season. Tied for team lead and tied for seventh in NHL in points. Tied for seventh in NHL in goals. Second on team in assists. Tied for second in NHL in power play goals. Led team in shorthanded goals. Fourth in NHL in shots. Tied for third on team in plus-minus. One of two Mighty Ducks to appear in all 82 games.

THE FINESSE GAME

A silky skater, so smooth and fluid his movement appears effortless, Kariya is also explosive, with a good change of direction, and he can turn a defender inside out on a one-on-one rush. His speed is a weapon, since he forces defenders to play off him for fear of being burnt, and that opens the ice for his playmaking options. He combines his skating with no-look passes that are uncanny. Teemu Selanne proved to be a perfect linemate for him, because the Finnish Flash breaks as soon as he sees Kariya with control of the puck. Kariya puts on a burst of speed and can lift his pass over the sticks of defenders just ahead of Selanne for him to skate into.

Kariya is smart; some would say cerebral. He is a magician with the puck and can make a play when it looks as if there are no possible options. Kariya likes to use the net for protection, like his idol Wayne Gretzky, and make passes from behind the goal line. His release on his shot is excellent. His overall positional play is well advanced for a youngster. He has been tested at high levels of competition and has excelled. He is defensively keen, but the Mighty Ducks need a two-way centre to play with him. That way, Kariya and Selanne can do their thing while the centre stays third man high.

THE PHYSICAL GAME

No doubt his size is a question mark because he can-not get into any physical confrontations at the NHL level, but his skill levels are so high it's worth the trade-off. Kariya has improved his strength in the last two seasons. He has very strong legs and has improved his upper body. Kariya is gritty in his own way and plays through minor nicks without a whimper.

THE INTANGIBLES

Kariya was doing it all by himself until Anaheim acquired Selanne. A complementary centre would improve the line. Anatoli Semenov played with them most of last season, but a Travis Green type would be ideal — someone defensively sound with enough skill to handle the puck and enough sense to stay out of Kariya and Selanne's way. Fifty goals and 100 points should be the norm for Kariya. We look forward to seeing how he fares in the playoffs.

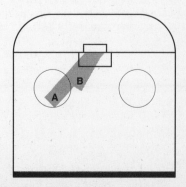

VALERI KARPOV

Yrs. of NHL service: 2
Born: Chelyabinsk, Russia; Aug. 5, 1971
Position: right wing
Height: 5-10
Weight: 190
Uniform no.: 11
Shoots: left

Career statistics:

GP	G	A	TP	PIM
67	13	15	28	16

1994-95 statistics:

GP	G	A	TP	+/-	PIM	PP	SH	GW	GT	S	PCT
30	4	7	11	-4	6	0	0	0	0	48	8.3

1995-96 statistics:

GP	G	A	TP	+/-	PIM	PP	SH	GW	GT	S	PCT
37	9	8	17	-1	10	0	0	1	0	42	21.4

LAST SEASON

Missed 29 games with fractured wrist.

THE FINESSE GAME

Karpov is an above average skater. He doesn't have outstanding breakaway speed, but he has a nice change of pace and handles the puck well. He has great hands. He goes to the net and gets his shots away quickly, more in the manner of Valeri Zelepukin than Pavel Bure.

Karpov fits nicely into a second-line niche now that the Paul Kariya-Teemu Selanne duo is established on the first line. Karpov plays with some grit and creates chances with his quickness. He has the hand skills and clever shots to put his opportunities away. His development was slowed by a wrist injury that sidelined him for two months.

THE PHYSICAL GAME

Karpov's size may hold him back, but he has gotten stronger since his draft year. He still doesn't have a great knack for handling physical play, and will try to play his game in open ice.

THE INTANGIBLES

Karpov went through a period of adjustment to the NHL and life in North America, and is just starting to feel comfortable. He could easily top the 20-goal mark this year if his progress continues.

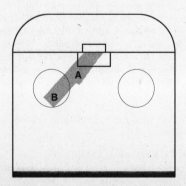

JASON MARSHALL

Yrs. of NHL service: 1
Born: Cranbrook, B.C.; Feb. 22, 1971
Position: right defense
Height: 6-2
Weight: 200
Uniform no.: 23
Shoots: right

Career statistics:

GP	G	A	TP	PIM
27	1	1	2	46

1994-95 statistics:

GP	G	A	TP	+/-	PIM	PP	SH	GW	GT	S	PCT
1	0	0	0	-2	0	0	0	0	0	1	0.0

1995-96 statistics:

GP	G	A	TP	+/-	PIM	PP	SH	GW	GT	S	PCT
24	0	1	1	+3	42	0	0	0	0	9	0.0

LAST SEASON

First NHL season. Played 57 games with Baltimore (AHL), scoring 1-13 — 14 with 150 penalty minutes.

THE FINESSE GAME

Marshall has borderline NHL skills. He skates well enough not to look out of place, but lacks the quickness and agility to get much done offensively. Playing for the Canadian Olympic team in 1994 helped his skating along as he was forced to work harder on the bigger ice surfaces.

Marshall doesn't have much of a point shot and isn't blessed with good hockey vision, so he prefers to simply wrist a shot on net, trying to get it to the front for a rebound or tip.

Marshall likes to hit, but has a tendency to start looking too hard for targets and stops playing positionally. He will have to be more disciplined, because his future is as a defensive defenseman. Marshall will get rattled under pressure.

THE PHYSICAL GAME

Marshall plays a strange, inconsistent game. He is impulsive, and some nights will seize the initiative and have an impact on the game. Other nights, he is quiet, hesitant and less of a factor.

THE INTANGIBLES

Marshall saw considerable ice time down the stretch for the Mighty Ducks and could get his last crack at being an NHL defenseman in this training camp. If he keeps the game simple, it will be much easier for him. He plays with enthusiasm and is probably a fifth or sixth defenseman.

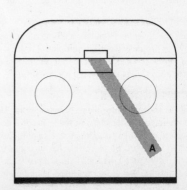

ROMAN OKSIUTA

Yrs. of NHL service: 2
Born: Murmansk, Soviet Union; Aug. 21, 1970
Position: left wing
Height: 6-3
Weight: 229
Uniform no.: 28
Shoots: left

Career statistics:

GP	G	A	TP	PIM
118	40	34	74	74

1993-94 statistics:

GP	G	A	TP	+/-	PIM	PP	SH	GW	GT	S	PCT
10	1	2	3	-1	4	0	0	0	0	18	5.6

1994-95 statistics:

GP	G	A	TP	+/-	PIM	PP	SH	GW	GT	S	PCT
38	16	4	20	-12	10	6	0	1	0	67	23.9

1995-96 statistics:

GP	G	A	TP	+/-	PIM	PP	SH	GW	GT	S	PCT
70	23	28	51	+4	60	11	0	1	0	119	19.3

games for Anaheim, so maybe he's gotten the message.

LAST SEASON

Acquired from Vancouver for Mike Sillinger, Mar. 15, 1996. Second on team in power play goals. Third on team in goals, assists and points, with career high in all categories. Missed eight games with groin injury. Missed four games with shoulder injury.

THE FINESSE GAME

Oksiuta has a long reach, and he needs it, because he is slow afoot. He is very powerful on his skates and once he is established in front of the net is extremely tough to budge. Oksiuta has very soft hands and good scoring instincts. He sees the ice well and moves the puck with assurance. The lumbering Russian could truly become a force on the power play because of his size and touch, but he doesn't indicate a consistent level of intensity.

Oksiuta's clunky skating makes him a liability defensively, and keeps him from getting any four-on-four time, although he thrives with the open ice on the power play.

While he is outstanding with the puck, he has to work on his game without the puck to be a factor.

THE PHYSICAL GAME

Oksiuta has never been known as a fitness nut, which is why his progress has been minimal. Oksiuta will take a beating, but doesn't retaliate or initiate. He needs to keep weight off, to help his mobility.

THE INTANGIBLES

Oksiuta has been on three teams in two seasons. He is a high-maintenance athlete who really needs a coach to ride herd on him to be more professional in his approach to the sport. Some of that has to come from Oksiuta. This may be his last chance to prove that he really wants an NHL job. He scored 12 points in 14

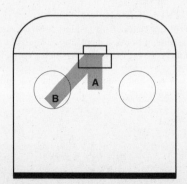

FREDRIK OLAUSSON

Yrs. of NHL service: 10
Born: Dadsejo, Sweden; Oct. 5, 1966
Position: right defense
Height: 6-2
Weight: 195
Uniform no.: 4
Shoots: right

Career statistics:

GP	G	A	TP	PIM
640	97	300	397	264

1992-93 statistics:

GP	G	A	TP	+/-	PIM	PP	SH	GW	GT	S	PCT
68	16	41	57	-4	22	11	0	3	0	165	9.7

1993-94 statistics:

GP	G	A	TP	+/-	PIM	PP	SH	GW	GT	S	PCT
73	11	24	35	-7	30	7	0	1	0	126	8.7

1994-95 statistics:

GP	G	A	TP	+/-	PIM	PP	SH	GW	GT	S	PCT
33	0	10	10	-4	20	0	0	0	0	52	0.0

1995-96 statistics:

GP	G	A	TP	+/-	PIM	PP	SH	GW	GT	S	PCT
56	2	22	24	-7	38	1	0	0	0	83	2.4

LAST SEASON

Acquired on waivers from Edmonton. Missed 26 games with irregular heartbeat, rib injury and colitis.

THE FINESSE GAME

Olausson is a power play specialist, and he (along with Teemu Selanne) helped the Mighty Ducks improve their power play late in the season. With the hand skills to cradle the puck when he is heading up-ice, Olausson has decent hockey vision. He plays the right (off) side at full strength and on the power play, where he worked the first unit with Paul Kariya on the left point.

Olausson gambles low on rare occasions, and usually stays at the point to prevent breakouts. He is adept at keeping the puck in at the point.

Olausson has some glaring defensive lapses, although his skating does help him to recover from some of his mistakes. He has pretty good jets, but is more determined on the attack than backchecking, when he tends to let an opponent go, leaving his defense partner outnumbered.

THE PHYSICAL GAME

Olausson's work ethic is more evident in the attacking zone than the defensive zone, but playing with former Jets teammate Selanne gave him some overall zip. He also had a tough year physically, but even at 100 percent he is not much of a factor.

THE INTANGIBLES

Olausson was besieged with health problems during the season, but the Mighty Ducks were so desperate for help on the point (due to Milos Holan's battle with leukemia and the trade of Oleg Tverdovsky) that he was added to their roster for the stretch drive. Unless the Ducks add another offensive-minded rearguard during the off-season, Olausson could start next season as the team's number one defenseman on the power play. Olausson scored 18 points in 36 games with the Mighty Ducks, and was a plus 7.

STEVE RUCCHIN

Yrs. of NHL service: 2
Born: London, Ont.; July 4, 1971
Position: centre
Height: 6-3
Weight: 210
Uniform no.: 20
Shoots: left

Career statistics:

GP	G	A	TP	PIM
107	25	36	61	35

1994-95 statistics:

GP	G	A	TP	+/-	PIM	PP	SH	GW	GT	S	PCT
43	6	11	17	+7	23	0	0	1	0	59	10.2

1995-96 statistics:

GP	G	A	TP	+/-	PIM	PP	SH	GW	GT	S	PCT
64	19	25	44	+3	12	8	1	4	0	113	16.8

LAST SEASON

Third on team in game-winning goals. Fourth on team in points. Missed 18 games with knee injury.

THE FINESSE GAME

Rucchin is an intelligent, versatile player who came out of nowhere (O.K., the University of Western Ontario) to win a job with the Mighty Ducks two seasons ago. A centre with good size and range, Rucchin shows constant improvement in his offensive game while not losing anything from his defensive job.

A bit in awe of the league at first, Rucchin has good hockey sense that makes the most of his above-average skating, passing and shooting skills. His knee injury affected his play last season, and he suffered a fractured finger in March that required post-season surgery (he didn't miss a game because of it). Despite his skating and his hands being affected, Rucchin still managed to finish fourth on the team in scoring.

Rucchin works well on the second line. He grinds and digs the puck off the wall, and has the vision and the passing skills to find on open teammate.

THE PHYSICAL GAME

Rucchin can become a real force. He's strong and balanced, willing to forecheck hard and fight for the puck along the boards and in the corners. When he wins the puck, he is able to create a smart play with it. He has long arms and a long reach for holding off defenders and working the puck one-handed, or reaching in defensively to knock the puck away from an attacker.

THE INTANGIBLES

Rucchin is an ideal number two centre for the Mighty Ducks. We thought Rucchin had a shot at 70 points last season (his prorated total was 56) and think he'll hit the 60-70 point range this season.

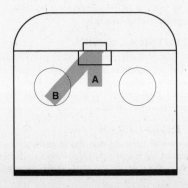

JOE SACCO

Yrs. of NHL service: 5
Born: Medford, Mass.; Feb. 4, 1969
Position: left/right wing
Height: 6-1
Weight: 195
Uniform no.: 14
Shoots: right

Career statistics:

GP	G	A	TP	PIM
261	53	53	106	138

1992-93 statistics:

GP	G	A	TP	+/-	PIM	PP	SH	GW	GT	S	PCT
23	4	4	8	-4	8	0	0	0	0	38	10.5

1993-94 statistics:

GP	G	A	TP	+/-	PIM	PP	SH	GW	GT	S	PCT
84	19	18	37	-11	61	3	1	2	1	206	9.2

1994-95 statistics:

GP	G	A	TP	+/-	PIM	PP	SH	GW	GT	S	PCT
41	10	8	18	-8	23	2	0	0	0	77	13.0

1995-96 statistics:

GP	G	A	TP	+/-	PIM	PP	SH	GW	GT	S	PCT
76	13	14	27	+1	40	1	2	2	1	132	9.8

LAST SEASON
Second on team in shorthanded goals.

THE FINESSE GAME
Sacco is a serviceable two-way forward. He got his training on the big international rinks with the U.S. Olympic Team in 1992. His outside speed is his greatest asset. A left-handed shot, Sacco played primarily on his off-wing and scored most of his goals driving to the net from the right side. There is nothing creative or dazzling about Sacco's moves. He just goes full-tilt. When he does score, it's highlight material.

Sacco is not a great finisher. He loves to shoot, but isn't always in the best spot to do so and doesn't have a quick release. If Sacco learned to use his teammates better, such as finding an open man after he has forced the defense back, he would be a more dangerous threat, but he has tunnel vision with the puck. Basically, he's just not a very smart player.

He has never been a prolific scorer at the pro level (minors or NHL). He is solid defensively, good in his own zone and keeps the game simple.

THE PHYSICAL GAME
Sacco does not play an involved game physically. He has a decent size to at least bang around a bit, but he is better with the puck than trying to obtain it.

THE INTANGIBLES
Sacco is becoming more aware of how he can use his speed as a weapon to drive the defense back and could be capable of 25 goals, though 20 is more likely his limit.

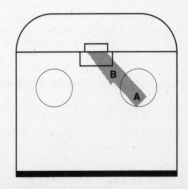

RUSLAN SALEI

Yrs. of NHL service: 0
Born: Minsk, Belarus; Nov. 2, 1974
Position: left defense
Height: 6-2
Weight: 190
Uniform no.: n.a.
Shoots: left

Career statistics (IHL):

GP	G	A	TP	PIM
76	7	23	30	123

1995-96 statistics (IHL):

GP	G	A	TP	+/P
76	7	23	30	123

LAST SEASON

Will be entering first NHL season. Drafted ninth overall by Anaheim in 1996.

THE FINESSE GAME

The Mighty Ducks pulled the surprise of draft day '96 when they went for immediate help in drafting the 21-year-old Salei out of the IHL instead of taking an 18-year-old prospect.

Salei played his first pro season in the minors last year and showed a taste for the North American game. He is a fairly agile skater, but doesn't have great breakaway speed. He skates well backwards and is not easy to beat one-on-one.

His defensive reads are very good, and he can kill penalties. There is a possibility he could see time on a second power play unit, because he moves the puck well and appears to have an NHL-calibre point shot. He shoots well off the pass and it is high velocity.

THE PHYSICAL GAME

Salei is mature and solidly built, and initiates a lot of contact. He is not afraid to hit anyone, and he has a little nasty streak that results in some cheap hits, but he can play it hard and clean, too.

THE INTANGIBLES

On a team that is strong in defense, Salei would be sent back to the minors for another year of conditioning, but he could step right in with the Mighty Ducks this season. He has some offensive upside, because he played behind more experienced offensive defensemen in Las Vegas and didn't get much prime ice time. His English is minimal, and he still needs some time to feel comfortable in North America.

Salei was banned from his junior league in Minsk for testing positive for what was believed to be a performance-enhancing substance, but the Mighty Ducks do not believe this is a chronic problem.

TEEMU SELANNE

Yrs. of NHL service: 4
Born: Helsinki, Finland; July 3, 1970
Position: right wing
Height: 6-0
Weight: 200
Uniform no.: 8
Shoots: right

Career statistics:

GP	G	A	TP	PIM
259	163	179	342	91

1992-93 statistics:

GP	G	A	TP	+/-	PIM	PP	SH	GW	GT	S	PCT
84	76	56	132	+8	45	24	0	7	0	387	19.6

1993-94 statistics:

GP	G	A	TP	+/-	PIM	PP	SH	GW	GT	S	PCT
51	25	29	54	-23	22	11	0	2	0	191	13.1

1994-95 statistics:

GP	G	A	TP	+/-	PIM	PP	SH	GW	GT	S	PCT
45	22	26	48	+1	2	8	2	1	1	167	13.2

1995-96 statistics:

GP	G	A	TP	+/-	PIM	PP	SH	GW	GT	S	PCT
79	40	68	108	+5	22	9	1	5	0	267	15.0

LAST SEASON

Finalist for 1996 Lady Byng Trophy. Acquired from Winnipeg with Marc Chouinard and a fourth-round draft pick for Chad Kilger, Oleg Tverdovsky and a third-round draft pick, Feb. 7, 1996. Tied for team lead and tied for seventh in the NHL in points. Led team in assists. Second on team in goals, game-winning goals and shots. Third on team in power play goals and plus-minus.

THE FINESSE GAME

Selanne has overcome knee problems and a career-threatening Achilles' tendon injury to regain the blinding speed that characterized his 76-goal rookie season. He has Porsche turbo speed. He gets down low and then simply explodes past defensemen, even when he starts from a standstill. He gets tremendous thrust from his legs and has quick feet. Acceleration, balance, it is all there.

Everything you could ask for in a shot is there as well. Selanne employs all varieties of attacks. He was reportedly not happy with the trade to Anaheim, but playing with the brilliant Paul Kariya quickly changed his outlook. Selanne plays off Kariya's puck control and exquisite lead passes. Selanne is constantly in motion. If his first attempt is stopped, he'll pursue the puck behind the net, make a pass and circle out again for a shot. He is almost impossible to catch and is tough to knock down because of his balance. He will set up on the off-wing on the power play and can score on the backhand. His shot is not especially hard, but it is quick and accurate.

Selanne doesn't just try to overpower with his skating, he also outwits opponents. He has tremen-dous hockey instincts and vision, and is as good a playmaker as a finisher. He is able to lift little passes to teammates over defenders' blades, so the puck hits flat for the recipient. Selanne has a reputation for being selfish with the puck, but he is more generous with Kariya and feeds him for one-timers.

THE PHYSICAL GAME

Anaheim is pretty much a one-line team, so Kariya and Selanne and whoever their centre might turn out to be will have to deal with checking pressure every night. Teams set out to bump and grind Selanne from the first shift, and he will have to fight his way through the junk. When the referees are slow on the whistle, he takes matters into his own hands, usually with his stick. He is one of the toughest young players in the league, European or otherwise. He is big and uses his strength along the wall.

THE INTANGIBLES

Selanne looks completely recovered from his physical problems and should be a consistent 50-goal, 100-point scorer. If the Mighty Ducks add a complementary centre, he could improve those numbers. He scored 16-20 — 36 in 28 games with Anaheim, which projects to 47-58 — 105. One more impressive stat: Before Anaheim acquired Selanne, the team's power play was operating at 11 per cent. After his arrival, the team went 29-149, a 19.5 per cent success rate.

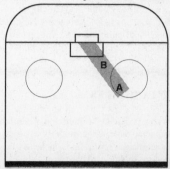

GARRY VALK

Yrs. of NHL service: 6
Born: Edmonton, Alberta; Nov. 27, 1967
Position: left wing
Height: 6-1
Weight: 205
Uniform no.: 18
Shoots: left

Career statistics:

GP	G	A	TP	PIM
365	57	80	137	459

1992-93 statistics:

GP	G	A	TP	+/-	PIM	PP	SH	GW	GT	S	PCT
48	6	7	13	+6	77	0	0	2	1	46	13.0

1993-94 statistics:

GP	G	A	TP	+/-	PIM	PP	SH	GW	GT	S	PCT
78	18	27	45	+8	100	4	1	5	0	165	10.9

1994-95 statistics:

GP	G	A	TP	+/-	PIM	PP	SH	GW	GT	S	PCT
36	3	6	9	-4	34	0	0	0	0	53	5.7

1995-96 statistics:

GP	G	A	TP	+/-	PIM	PP	SH	GW	GT	S	PCT
79	12	12	24	+8	125	1	1	2	0	108	11.1

LAST SEASON

Scored first career hat trick.

THE FINESSE GAME

Not much about Valk's game is pretty, but it is gritty. He is a defensive specialist, with a knock-kneed stance (the opposite of the many bowlegged skaters in the league). Through determination, Valk gets to where he has to go. He has a great deal of drive in his skating. He is strong on his skates but not fast.

Very streaky, he will go forever without getting a goal, then will pop home several in a week. Valk goes to the net hard, but he doesn't have great hands. Most of his goals come from second and third efforts around the net.

Valk is a defensive forward. He kills penalties well and has good jump forechecking. He keeps himself in excellent physical condition and mentally accepts his role as a checker.

THE PHYSICAL GAME

Valk has a strong work ethic and likes to get out on the ice and provide a spark for his team. He throws his body around with enthusiasm and will get into altercations. He can be very annoying to play against. Nothing Valk does is flashy, but he gets the job done in a blue-collar (well, OK, teal-collar) fashion.

THE INTANGIBLES

Valk was once a spare part on an established team (Vancouver), who found ice time and scoring chances in Anaheim and took advantage. Valk will find that as the team gets deeper he can find a niche as a third-line checking forward.

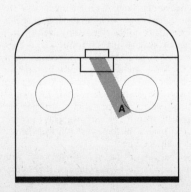

SHAUN VAN ALLEN

Yrs. of NHL service: 4
Born: Shaunavon, Sask.; Aug. 29, 1967
Position: centre
Height: 6-1
Weight: 200
Uniform no.: 22
Shoots: left

Career statistics:

GP	G	A	TP	PIM
197	25	67	92	143

1992-93 statistics:

GP	G	A	TP	+/-	PIM	PP	SH	GW	GT	S	PCT
21	1	4	5	-2	6	0	0	0	0	19	5.3

1993-94 statistics:

GP	G	A	TP	+/-	PIM	PP	SH	GW	GT	S	PCT
80	8	25	33	0	64	2	2	1	0	104	7.7

1994-95 statistics:

GP	G	A	TP	+/-	PIM	PP	SH	GW	GT	S	PCT
45	8	21	29	-4	32	1	1	1	0	68	11.8

1995-96 statistics:

GP	G	A	TP	+/-	PIM	PP	SH	GW	GT	S	PCT
49	8	17	25	+13	41	0	0	2	0	78	10.3

LAST SEASON

Led team in plus-minus. Missed 21 games with dislocated right thumb. Missed four games with back injuries.

THE FINESSE GAME

Van Allen always posted huge numbers in the minors, but like a lot of minor league stars, he couldn't transfer his scoring to the majors. The flaw in Van Allen's case is his skating, which is marginally NHL calibre and has forced him to change his strategy to that of a positional, defensive player.

When Van Allen does accomplish things offensively, like on the power play, it's because of his smarts. He is the best face-off man on the Mighty Ducks. If he controls the draw in the offensive zone, he knows how to set up an attack. Van Allen also kills penalties. He seldom plays a poor game because he is aware of his limitations.

THE PHYSICAL GAME

Van Allen's solid, intelligent play is enhanced by his work ethic. He's not a banger but he will get in the way. He knows he would have been a career minor leaguer but for this chance, and he doesn't forget what he has to do to stay in the NHL.

THE INTANGIBLES

Van Allen will always be on the bubble. Coaches will keep trying younger, more talented guys in his spot, but he'll probably keep getting back into the lineup because he's too valuable to sit in the press box. Van Allen was slowed by injuries last season, and is a third- or fourth-line centre.

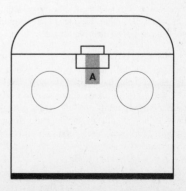

JASON YORK

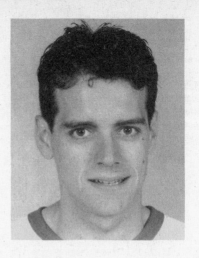

Yrs. of NHL service: 3
Born: Ottawa, Ont.; May 20, 1970
Position: right defense
Height: 6-2
Weight: 195
Uniform no.: 3
Shoots: right

Career statistics:

GP	G	A	TP	PIM
113	5	33	38	104

1992-93 statistics:

GP	G	A	TP	+/-	PIM	PP	SH	GW	GT	S	PCT
2	0	0	0	0	0	0	0	0	0	1	0.0

1993-94 statistics:

GP	G	A	TP	+/-	PIM	PP	SH	GW	GT	S	PCT
7	1	2	3	0	2	0	0	0	0	9	11.1

1994-95 statistics:

GP	G	A	TP	+/-	PIM	PP	SH	GW	GT	S	PCT
25	1	10	11	+2	14	0	0	0	0	28	3.6

1995-96 statistics:

GP	G	A	TP	+/-	PIM	PP	SH	GW	GT	S	PCT
79	3	21	24	-7	88	0	0	0	0	106	2.8

LAST SEASON

Second among team defensemen in scoring.

THE FINESSE GAME

York is about ready to hit his defensive prime. He is a smart, all-around defenseman who was able to put up some decent numbers at the AHL level, but is now concentrating more on his defensive play.

York's finesse skills are fine. He is a good skater with a very hard point shot, and can handle the point on the second power play unit although he isn't quite good enough to step up to the first five. York is a fine penalty killer. He reads plays well (his offensive reads are far superior to his defensive reads) and has the skating ability to spring some shorthanded chances.

THE PHYSICAL GAME

York is not very physical. He is not a big checker, but employs positional play to angle attackers to the boards, using his stick to sweep-check or poke pucks. Once he gains control of the puck, he moves it quickly with no panicky mistakes. He doesn't have a polished defensive game but he does work hard.

THE INTANGIBLES

York's offensive skills are not enough to compensate for his defensive shortcomings at the NHL level, and he must keep moving forward this season to earn a full-time job again with the Mighty Ducks. Anaheim gave him a lot of ice time during their stretch run and he responded well, which is a good sign.

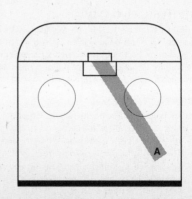

BOSTON BRUINS

Players' Statistics 1995-96

POS.	NO.	PLAYER	GP	G	A	PTS	+/-	PIM	PP	SH	GW	GT	S	PCT
C	12	ADAM OATES	70	25	67	92	16	18	7	1	2		183	13.7
D	77	RAY BOURQUE	82	20	62	82	31	58	9	2	2	1	390	5.1
R	22	RICK TOCCHET	71	29	31	60	10	181	10		3	1	185	15.7
R	16	JOZEF STUMPEL	76	18	36	54	-8	14	5		2		158	11.4
C	14	SHAWN MCEACHERN	82	24	29	53	-5	34	3	2	3		238	10.1
C	21	TED DONATO	82	23	26	49	6	46	7		1		152	15.1
R	8	CAM NEELY	49	26	20	46	3	31	7		3		191	13.6
C	20	TODD ELIK	59	13	33	46	2	40	6		2		108	12.0
L	17	DAVE REID	63	23	21	44	14	4	1	6	3	1	160	14.4
R	45	SANDY MOGER	80	15	14	29	-9	65	4		6		103	14.6
R	23	STEVE HEINZE	76	16	12	28	-3	43		1	3		129	12.4
D	32	DON SWEENEY	77	4	24	28	-4	42	2		3		142	2.8
D	46	*KYLE MCLAREN	74	5	12	17	16	73					74	6.8
L	42	TIM SWEENEY	41	8	8	16	4	14	1		2	1	47	17.0
R	11	JOE MULLEN	37	8	7	15	-2		4		1		60	13.3
D	34	RICK ZOMBO	67	4	10	14	-7	53			1	1	68	5.9
D	38	JON ROHLOFF	79	1	12	13	-8	59	1				106	.9
C	10	RON SUTTER	18	5	7	12	10	24		1			34	14.7
D	28	DEAN CHYNOWETH	49	2	6	8	-5	128					38	5.3
C	37	*CLAYTON BEDDOES	39	1	6	7	-5	44					18	5.6
D	41	PHIL VONSTEFENELLI	27		4	4	2	16					20	
G	30	BILL RANFORD	77		3	3	0	2						
D	6	ALEXEI KASATONOV	19	1		1	1	12					15	6.7
G	35	*ROBBIE TALLAS	1				0							
C	47	*RYAN HUGHES	3				0						2	
L	49	*ANDRE ROY	3				0							
C	26	CAMERON STEWART	6				-2						2	
D	40	*MARK CORNFORTH	6				4	4					1	
L	44	*DAVIS PAYNE	7				0	7					2	
L	19	*KEVIN SAWYER	8				-1	28					1	
G	39	*SCOTT BAILEY	11				0							
D	48	*STEVE STAIOS	12				-5	4					4	
G	31	BLAINE LACHER	12				0	4						
D	36	JOHN GRUDEN	14				-3	4					12	
G	1	CRAIG BILLINGTON	27				0	2						
R	29	MARC POTVIN	27				-2	12					14	

GP = games played; G = goals; A = assists; PTS = points; +/- = goals-for minus goals-against while player is on ice; PIM = penalties in minutes; PP = power play goals; SH = shorthanded goals; GW = game-winning goals; GT = game-tying goals; S = no. of shots; PCT = percentage of goals to shots; * = rookie

RAY BOURQUE

Yrs. of NHL service: 17
Born: Montreal, Que.; Dec. 28, 1960
Position: right defense
Height: 5-11
Weight: 210
Uniform no.: 77
Shoots: left

Career statistics:

GP	G	A	TP	PIM
1228	343	970	1313	935

1992-93 statistics:

GP	G	A	TP	+/-	PIM	PP	SH	GW	GT	S	PCT
78	19	63	82	+38	40	8	0	7	0	330	5.8

1993-94 statistics:

GP	G	A	TP	+/-	PIM	PP	SH	GW	GT	S	PCT
72	20	71	91	+26	58	10	3	1	1	386	5.2

1994-95 statistics:

GP	G	A	TP	+/-	PIM	PP	SH	GW	GT	S	PCT
46	12	31	43	+3	20	9	0	2	0	210	5.7

1995-96 statistics:

GP	G	A	TP	+/-	PIM	PP	SH	GW	GT	S	PCT
82	20	62	82	+31	58	9	2	2	1	390	5.1

LAST SEASON

Finalist for 1996 Norris Trophy. Tied for first among NHL defensemen in goals. Second among NHL defensemen in assists and points. Led team in plus-minus and shots. Second on team in assists, points and power play goals. One of three Bruins to appear in all 82 games.

THE FINESSE GAME

Bourque has tremendous defensive instincts, though his offensive skills usually get the headlines. His defensive reads are almost unmatched in the NHL, and he is an excellent transition player. He is not afraid to make the simple play, if it is the right one, instead of making a flashy play. If he is under pressure and his team is getting scrambly, Bourque is not too proud to simply flip the puck over the glass for a face-off.

As a passer, Bourque can go tape-to-tape as well as anybody in the NHL. He has the touch and the vision of a forward, and eagerly makes what for anyone else would be a low-percentage play, because his passes and skating are so sure.

Bourque is adept at keeping the puck in the zone at the point. He is a key performer on special team units. On the point, he has a low, heavy shot with a crisp release. He is an excellent skater who will also shoot from mid-range with a handy snap shot, or in close with a wrist shot. He does not squander his scoring chances and is a precise shooter down low. Bourque is able to go top shelf to either corner, which few other defensemen, let alone forwards, can match. Bourque's impressive point totals would be even higher if he had played with a talented partner on the point, but for the most part it is has been all Bourque all these years.

Willing to lead a rush or jump up into the play, he is a balanced skater, with speed, agility and awesome balance. It takes a bulldozer to knock him off the puck.

THE PHYSICAL GAME

Bourque's recovery time is astonishing. The Bruins do have some slowdown schemes to create extra face-offs that allow Bourque to grab a breather now and then, but considering all the ice time he logs, he should be dead on his feet by December. He is single-minded in his approach to fitness. Only twice in his 16 seasons has he failed to play more than 60 games a season (and one of those was an asterisk year, the 1994-95 lockout). He is no perimeter player, either. Bourque doesn't have cruise control.

He plays a physical game when he has to. It's amazing what kind of punishment he has been able to absorb over the years without missing time with a serious injury, since he is not very big by today's standards for defensemen (or forwards, for that matter). Most other teams try to eliminate him physically, and the Bruins superstar has paid a big price because of it.

THE INTANGIBLES

Bourque has got to show signs of decline at some point. Despite his exceptional conditioning, he will be 37 when this season ends, but trading him elsewhere would be like paving over Fenway Park. Still one of the top five defensemen in the league, he could go down in league history as the best player never to win the Cup . . . and this season, he might not even make the playoffs.

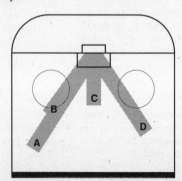

TED DONATO

Yrs. of NHL service: 4
Born: Dedham, Mass.; Apr. 28, 1969
Position: centre
Height: 5-10
Weight: 180
Uniform no.: 21
Shoots: left

Career statistics:

GP	G	A	TP	PIM
305	71	90	161	184

1992-93 statistics:

GP	G	A	TP	+/-	PIM	PP	SH	GW	GT	S	PCT
82	15	20	35	+2	61	3	2	5	0	118	12.7

1993-94 statistics:

GP	G	A	TP	+/-	PIM	PP	SH	GW	GT	S	PCT
84	22	32	54	0	59	9	2	1	1	158	13.9

1994-95 statistics:

GP	G	A	TP	+/-	PIM	PP	SH	GW	GT	S	PCT
47	10	10	20	+3	10	1	0	1	0	71	14.1

1995-96 statistics:

GP	G	A	TP	+/-	PIM	PP	SH	GW	GT	S	PCT
82	23	26	49	+6	46	7	0	1	0	152	15.1

LAST SEASON

Has not missed a game due to injury in the past three seasons (213 games). One of three Bruins to appear in all 82 games. Tied for third on team in power play goals.

THE FINESSE GAME

Donato is a small man who is able to survive in a big man's game because of his hockey sense. He is a good power play man on the second unit. When Donato gets the chance, he can work down low or use a shot from the point.

Donato has always had the knack for scoring big goals at every level he has played. He scored the winning goal in the NCAA Championship game when Harvard beat Minnesota, and he scored the winning goal for his high school to win the championships in Massachusetts.

He is also a strong penalty killer, especially working with Steve Heinze (they were teammates with the U.S. Olympic team in 1992 and began killing penalties together then). He can thrive as a forward on the shorthanded team because opponents are more concerned about getting the puck than hitting, and he is usually in the middle part of the ice. He gets a lot of defensive assignments but creates offense with his anticipation.

Donato is like a quarterback, very aware of what is going on around him and always communicating with his teammates so they know what is going on, too. He has good hands and makes hard or soft passes as the occasion warrants.

THE PHYSICAL GAME

Donato is cunning and doesn't allow himself to get into situations where he's close to the boards and could get taken out. He is a very elusive skater. Donato can be outmuscled, but he hustles for the puck and often manages to keep it alive along the boards.

THE INTANGIBLES

Donato exceeded our expectations last season, and if he continues to get significant power play time, he may top 20 goals again. His role is as a defensive forward, however. As a Group 2 free agent, rather moderately priced at that, there is a good chance another team may be interested in him.

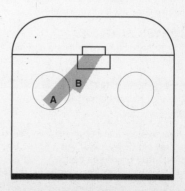

TODD ELIK

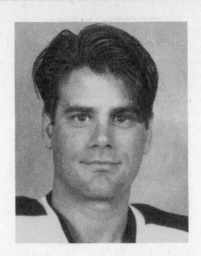

Yrs. of NHL service: 7
Born: Brampton, Ont.; Apr. 15, 1966
Position: centre
Height: 6-2
Weight: 195
Uniform no.: 20
Shoots: left

Career statistics:

GP	G	A	TP	PIM
417	107	206	313	400

1992-93 statistics:

GP	G	A	TP	+/-	PIM	PP	SH	GW	GT	S	PCT
60	14	27	41	-4	56	4	0	1	1	104	13.5

1993-94 statistics:

GP	G	A	TP	+/-	PIM	PP	SH	GW	GT	S	PCT
79	25	41	66	-3	95	9	0	4	1	185	13.5

1994-95 statistics:

GP	G	A	TP	+/-	PIM	PP	SH	GW	GT	S	PCT
35	9	14	23	+8	22	4	0	0	2	76	11.8

1995-96 statistics:

GP	G	A	TP	+/-	PIM	PP	SH	GW	GT	S	PCT
59	13	33	46	+2	40	6	0	2	0	108	12.0

LAST SEASON

Signed as free agent, Aug. 8, 1995. Missed five games with fractured wrist. Played seven games with Providence (AHL), scoring 2-7 — 9.

THE FINESSE GAME

Elik's hand skills aren't up to his skating speed, so he can't carry the puck or make many moves at high tempo. He often looks off-balance when he starts a rush because he is having trouble moving with the puck.

He has to work hard for his goals by going to the net. He doesn't shoot well in stride because he has to slow down to get the shot off. He has a decent wrist shot, which he uses at close range.

Elik will have an occasional night when everything is going his way offensively, and he can dazzle, but when his offensive contributions aren't forthcoming, he gets down mentally and does little to help his team in any other way. He makes high-risk plays, which can either pay off or kill a team.

THE PHYSICAL GAME

Elik has the size and speed to be more of an impact player physically. He will use his body fairly consistently in the offensive zone, and he has the agility to be a good forechecker. But he isn't very strong and he loses many of the one-on-one battles in traffic.

THE INTANGIBLES

Elik never seems to find a comfortable role anywhere for the long-term. Last season was a perfect example as he went from playing on the team's top line with Adam Oates and Cam Neely to being placed on waivers in February. By default, he is Boston's number one left wing and will get a lot of prime ice time as a result.

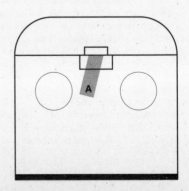

STEVE HEINZE

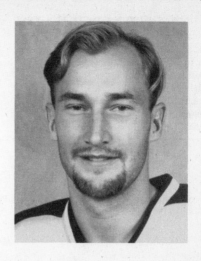

Yrs. of NHL service: 4
Born: Lawrence, Mass.; Jan. 30, 1970
Position: right wing
Height: 5-11
Weight: 190
Uniform no.: 23
Shoots: right

Career statistics:

GP	G	A	TP	PIM
276	54	49	103	128

1992-93 statistics:

GP	G	A	TP	+/-	PIM	PP	SH	GW	GT	S	PCT
73	18	13	31	+20	24	0	2	4	0	146	12.3

1993-94 statistics:

GP	G	A	TP	+/-	PIM	PP	SH	GW	GT	S	PCT
77	10	11	21	-2	32	0	2	1	0	183	5.5

1994-95 statistics:

GP	G	A	TP	+/-	PIM	PP	SH	GW	GT	S	PCT
36	7	9	16	0	23	0	1	0	0	70	10.0

1995-96 statistics:

GP	G	A	TP	+/-	PIM	PP	SH	GW	GT	S	PCT
76	16	12	28	-3	43	0	1	3	0	129	12.4

LAST SEASON

Tied for second on team in game-winning goals.

THE FINESSE GAME

Heinze is a traditional grinding Bruins forward who skates up and down his wing. Nothing special — which is probably why he was spent some time on the bench again last season. He has surprisingly good hands for a grinder, with a quick snap shot. He gets goals that go in off his legs, arms and elbows from his work in front of the net.

Heinze is smart at trailing plays along the way and digging out loose pucks, which he either takes to the net himself or, more often, passes off.

He has a good first step to the puck, which helps in his penalty killing as he forces the puck carrier. He was a big scorer at Boston College with David Emma and Marty McInnis (the HEM Line), but he succeeded at that level mainly because he was able to overpower people; he doesn't have that same edge in the pros. He plays an intelligent game and is a good playmaker with passing skills on his forehand and backhand.

THE PHYSICAL GAME

Heinze is hampered by his lack of size and strength. His probable future is as a third-line checking winger, but he doesn't have the power to line up against other teams' top power forwards. He is willing to get in the way and force people to go through him. The trouble is, they usually do.

THE INTANGIBLES

Heinze is a Group 2 free agent and the Bruins don't seem willing to open their wallets that wide for an-other checking winger (they have a glut of guys who can't score). Heinze could fit in very nicely elsewhere on a third line.

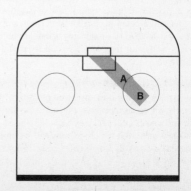

TRENT MCCLEARY

Yrs. of NHL service: 1
Born: Swift Current, Sask.; Oct. 10, 1972
Position: right wing
Height: 6-0
Weight: 180
Uniform no.: 20
Shoots: right

Career statistics:

GP	G	A	TP	PIM
75	4	10	14	68

1995-96 statistics:

GP	G	A	TP	+/-	PIM	PP	SH	GW	GT	S	PCT
75	4	10	14	-15	68	0	1	0	0	58	6.9

LAST SEASON

Acquired from Ottawa for Shawn McEachern, June 22, 1996. First NHL season. Missed two games with thumb injury. Missed two games with foot injury.

THE FINESSE GAME

McCleary was an unheralded player signed in 1992 by the Senators. He paid his dues for several seasons in the minors before bulling his way onto Ottawa's roster last season.

Rough around the edges, McCleary is a less talented version of Dirk Graham or Mike Keane. He has good foot speed and is very strong along the wall. He needs to get stronger for his one-on-one battles, and he seems very willing to work to improve. While he is not good enough to play on a first or second line, he has played with some skilled players, such as Geoff Sanderson in junior, and he complements better players as a safety valve. He doesn't do anything fancy, but if a team plays a dump-and-chase style he will excel.

McCleary is a dependable penalty killer. He is willing to learn and will adapt his style to follow the coaches' tactics.

THE PHYSICAL GAME

McCleary can't fight because of a detached retina, an injury that occurred in the minors, and he has to wear a tinted shield because of it. His vision is not a problem, but it's tough to be a tough guy and not be able to back it up with your fists, which McCleary would be willing to do.

THE INTANGIBLES

McCleary fits the mold of the grinding Bruins forwards. He will be a serviceable winger on the third or fourth line who can kill penalties because of his speed and hockey sense, but his production will be limited because his hand skills are average and he is not very creative.

KYLE MCLAREN

Yrs. of NHL service: 1
Born: Humbolt, Sask.; June 18, 1977
Position: left defense
Height: 6-4
Weight: 210
Uniform no.: 46
Shoots: left

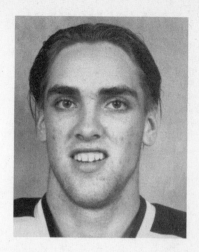

Career statistics:

GP	G	A	TP	PIM
74	5	12	17	73

1995-96 statisics:

GP	G	A	TP	+/-	PIM	PP	SH	GW	GT	S	PCT
74	5	12	17	+16	73	0	0	0	0	74	6.8

LAST SEASON

First NHL season. Tied for second on team and tied for NHL rookie lead in plus-minus. Named to 1996 NHL All-Rookie team. Missed seven games with bruised forearm.

THE FINESSE GAME

McLaren demonstrated precocious hockey sense as the biggest and best surprise of the Bruins' season. He can play either right or left defense and his advanced defensive reads allow him to adapt, which is very hard to do for a young player.

His puckhandling ability is much better than people give him credit for. He moves the puck out of the zone quickly and without panicking. McLaren can rush with the puck or he will make the cautious bank off the boards to clear the zone if that is his best option.

McLaren is a very good penalty killer because he is fearless. He blocks shots and takes away passing lanes. He can also play on the power play, and probably will improve in this area because he plays heads-up and has a hard and accurate slap shot with a quick release. As he gains more confidence, he will become more of an offensive factor.

THE PHYSICAL GAME

McLaren is tough and aggressive, but he doesn't go looking for fights and doesn't take foolish penalties. When he does get into a scrap, McLaren can go toe-to-toe and has already earned some respect around the league as a player you don't want to tick off. He is strong on the puck, strong on the wall and doesn't allow loitering in front of his crease.

THE INTANGIBLES

Sure, he got to play alongside Ray Bourque for much of last season, but not everything McLaren accomplished can be credited to his All-Star partner. He could become a dominant defensive defenseman and because of his skills with the puck, he has a huge offensive upside as well. McLaren is a budding star, and as Bourque's career winds down, he could well step into the role as the Bruins' number one rearguard. After nearly a decade of first-round draft disasters (Dmitri Kvartalnov, anyone?), the Bruins have gotten one right.

SANDY MOGER

Yrs. of NHL service: 1
Born: Vernon, B.C.; Mar. 21, 1969
Position: left wing
Height: 6-3
Weight: 200
Uniform no.: 45
Shoots: right

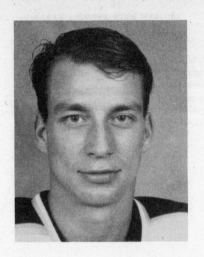

Career statistics:

GP	G	A	TP	PIM
98	17	20	37	71

1994-95 statistics:

GP	G	A	TP	+/-	PIM	PP	SH	GW	GT	S	PCT
18	2	6	8	-1	6	2	0	0	0	32	6.3

1995-96 statistics:

GP	G	A	TP	+/-	PIM	PP	SH	GW	GT	S	PCT
80	15	14	29	-9	65	4	0	6	0	103	14.6

LAST SEASON

Led team in game-winning goals in first full NHL season.

THE FINESSE GAME

Moger has been described by one scout as a "poor man's Tim Kerr." Or maybe the poor Bruins' Cam Neely, if injuries force Neely into retirement. Moger has a big body and he thrives on the power play. He has an excellent release on his shot and has sharp hand-eye coordination for deflecting pucks.

Moger has good hockey sense and in addition to his gifts around the net is very reliable killing penalties in his own end. He knows when to back off and protect the front of the net.

His downside is his foot speed. Moger is a marginal NHL skater but his diligence gets him where he has to go. He is well balanced on his skates for battles in the crease.

THE PHYSICAL GAME

Moger is a fearless, dangerous hitter who delivered a crunching check on big Eric Lindros last season. He is not afraid of taking abuse and will compete for any loose puck. He's a bit of a stringbean — tall but lean — and he could use some bulking up. Moger needs to get stronger because he does the dirty work in the trenches.

THE INTANGIBLES

Moger has made himself into an NHL player. Signed as a free agent by the Bruins in 1994, he was targeted as a career minor leaguer but has shown the desire to play in the bigs. He has an excellent work ethic and will probably get plenty of ice time again this season to improve himself. Moger has some upside but he really would have enjoyed himself on the smaller ice surface in old Boston Garden. Moger is a Group 2 free agent.

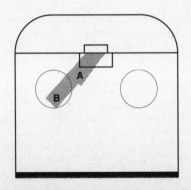

ADAM OATES

Yrs. of NHL service: 11
Born: Weston, Ont.; Aug. 27, 1962
Position: centre
Height: 5-11
Weight: 189
Uniform no.: 12
Shoots: right

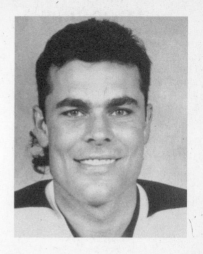

Career statistics:

GP	G	A	TP	PIM
746	236	678	914	249

1992-93 statistics:

GP	G	A	TP	+/-	PIM	PP	SH	GW	GT	S	PCT
84	45	97	142	+15	32	24	1	11	0	254	17.7

1993-94 statistics:

GP	G	A	TP	+/-	PIM	PP	SH	GW	GT	S	PCT
77	32	80	112	+10	45	16	2	3	0	197	16.2

1994-95 statistics:

GP	G	A	TP	+/-	PIM	PP	SH	GW	GT	S	PCT
48	12	41	53	-11	8	4	1	2	0	109	11.0

1995-96 statistics:

GP	G	A	TP	+/-	PIM	PP	SH	GW	GT	S	PCT
70	25	67	92	+16	18	7	1	2	0	183	13.7

LAST SEASON

Led team in assists and points for second consecutive season. Tied for second on team in plus-minus. Third on team in goals. Tied for third on team in power play goals. Missed 12 games with knee injury. Finalist for 1996 Lady Byng Trophy.

THE FINESSE GAME

Oates uses a shorter-than-average stick and a minimal curve on his blade, the result being exceptional control of the puck. Although he is a right-handed shooter, his right wings (Brett Hull, Cam Neely) have always been his preferred receivers. Oates can pass on the backhand, but also carries the puck deep, shields the puck with his body and turns to make the pass to his right wing.

Use of the backhand gives Oates a tremendous edge against all but the rangiest of NHL defensemen. He forces defenders to reach in and frequently draws penalties when he is hooked or tripped. If defenders don't harrass him, then Oates has carte blanche to work his passing magic. He will even drive to the net on his backhand.

The past two seasons, he has become less reluctant to shoot, although passing is still his first instinct. It doesn't matter how hard you shoot the puck when you have the jeweller's precision of Oates. Taking more shots makes him a less predictable player, since the defense can't back off and anticipate the pass. Oates is one of the best playmakers in the league because of his passing ability and his creativity. He is most effective down low where he can open up more ice, especially on the power play. He has outstanding timing and vision.

Yet, Oates isn't stubborn to a fault. He will also play a dump-and-chase game if he is being shadowed closely, throwing the puck smartly into the opposite corner with just the right velocity to allow his wingers to get in on top of the defense.

He is among the top five players in the league on face-offs, which makes him a natural on penalty killing because a successful draw eats up 10-15 seconds on the clock, minimum. He is not a great skater, but he is quick and agile enough.

THE PHYSICAL GAME

Oates is not a physical player, but he doesn't avoid contact. He's smart enough at this stage of his career to avoid the garbage, he plays in traffic and he'll take a hit to make the play. Oates is an intense player and has a wiry strength, but tends to wear down late in the season as his line receives all the checking attention. Unfortunately for Oates, the Bruins don't look to be any deeper.

THE INTANGIBLES

Oates has three years remaining on a U.S.$10-million contract, but reportedly will be seeking a renegotiation — which could mean his ticket out of Boston. Oates is a legitimate superstar. He scored nearly 100 points last season despite not playing with an elite finisher for the last 30 games. Like teammate Ray Bourque, Oates appears to be one of those ageless wonders, but he's 34 and has logged a lot of ice time. It would be nice to see him go out a winner, which won't happen in Boston.

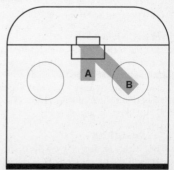

JEFF ODGERS

Yrs. of NHL service: 5
Born: Spy Hill, Sask.; May 31, 1969
Position: right wing
Height: 6-0
Weight: 195
Uniform no.: 36
Shoots: right

Career statistics:

GP	G	A	TP	PIM
334	48	34	82	1001

1992-93 statistics:

GP	G	A	TP	+/-	PIM	PP	SH	GW	GT	S	PCT
66	12	15	27	-26	253	6	0	0	0	100	12.0

1993-94 statistics:

GP	G	A	TP	+/-	PIM	PP	SH	GW	GT	S	PCT
81	13	8	21	-13	222	7	0	0	1	73	17.8

1994-95 statistics:

GP	G	A	TP	+/-	PIM	PP	SH	GW	GT	S	PCT
48	4	3	7	-8	117	0	0	1	0	47	8.5

1995-96 statistics:

GP	G	A	TP	+/-	PIM	PP	SH	GW	GT	S	PCT
78	12	4	16	-4	192	0	0	1	1	84	14.3

team (he was voted team captain while in San Jose), and will try to fill in at any role. Ideally, he is a third-line winger who won't score much more than 10-15 goals a season.

LAST SEASON

Acquired from San Jose with fifth-round draft pick for Al Iafrate, June 21, 1966. Led Sharks in penalty minutes for second consecutive season. Missed one game for personal reasons.

THE FINESSE GAME

Odgers is a meat and potatoes skater. He patrols up and down his wing with diligence, if not much style or creativity. Any scoring opportunities he generates come from his hard work off the forecheck.

He lacks the hands skills and the vision to be much of a playmaker, but anyone playing with him is wise to follow in his wake because he churns up a lot of loose pucks. And he's smart enough to play as a safety valve on a line with better offensive talent. He will drop back to cover high if the other winger and/or the defensemen move deep into the attacking zone.

Odgers has some good speed and balance, but only if he's travelling in a straight line without the puck. He lacks mobility and agility, but effort can compensate for a lot of finesse shortcomings.

THE PHYSICAL GAME

Odgers takes the body and plays tough. He loves to forecheck and finds it a special challenge to outwit goalies who are strong stickhandlers, getting in on top of them quickly to try to force a bad pass. He takes a lot of aggressive penalties, although he has cut down on the bad penalties that hurt his team.

THE INTANGIBLES

Odgers is one of those lunchpail types the Bruins prize so much. He will add toughness and leadership to the

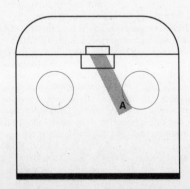

BILL RANFORD

Yrs. of NHL service: 10
Born: Brandon, Man.; Dec. 14, 1966
Position: goaltender
Height: 5-10
Weight: 170
Uniform no.: 30
Catches: left

Career statistics:

GP	MIN	GA	SO	GAA	A	PIM
518	29000	1659	12	3.43	22	54

1992-93 statistics:

GP	MIN	GAA	W	L	T	SO	GA	S	SAPCT	PIM
67	3753	3.84	17	38	6	1	240	2065	.885	10

1993-94 statistics:

GP	MIN	GAA	W	L	T	SO	GA	S	SAPCT	PIM
71	4070	3.48	22	34	11	1	236	2325	.898	2

1994-95 statistics:

GP	MIN	GAA	W	L	T	SO	GA	S	SAPCT	PIM
40	2203	3.62	15	20	3	2	133	1134	.883	2

1995-96 statistics:

GP	MIN	GAA	W	L	T	SO	GA	S	SAPCT	PIM
77	4322	3.30	34	30	9	2	237	2054	.885	2

LAST SEASON

Acquired from Edmonton for Mariusz Czerkawski, Sean Brown and a first-round draft pick in 1996, Jan. 11, 1996. Career high in wins. Missed five games with ankle tendinitis. Stopped Randy Burridge on penalty shot, Feb. 3, 1996.

THE PHYSICAL GAME

The athletic Ranford is notable for his great first-save capability. He is probably among the top five goalies in the league in that regard.

Ranford is a shining example of a goalie who made it to the NHL on his reflexes and continues there because he added elements of angle play and focus. He comes out of his net and, when he is on his game, he doesn't leave a lot of rebounds.

Very patient, Ranford hardly ever commits before the shooter does. He has good lateral movement and great confidence in his skating. He moves with the shooter well, keeping the five-hole closed. He doesn't drop down unless he has to; when he does, he bounces back up quickly. He uses his stick aggressively around the net to break up passes. He also stops hard-arounds and whips passes out to his teammates.

Ranford let in a number of soft goals last season, which is very much out of character and may have had more to do with his injuries than any lapse in concentration.

THE MENTAL GAME

The big question about Ranford's move to Boston was how he would handle being a goalie for a competitive team instead of toiling for an Edmonton club that had basically been a non-factor for the past four seasons.

Ranford responded adequately, but some scouts feel that his best days are behind him, and that he no longer ranks among the top 10 goalies. Still, he did upgrade Boston's goaltending dramatically.

THE INTANGIBLES

Knowing how much the Bruins relied on him to make the playoffs, Ranford kept dragging himself out into the crease on an apparently sore ankle, and before writing him off we'd like to see what a healthy Ranford can do. Unfortunately, the team in front of him won't be all that much better than the one he left behind in Edmonton.

JON ROHLOFF

Yrs. of NHL service: 2
Born: Mankato, Minn.; Oct. 3, 1969
Position: right defense
Height: 5-11
Weight: 220
Uniform no.: 38
Shoots: right

Career statistics:

GP	G	A	TP	PIM
113	4	20	24	98

1994-95 statistics:

GP	G	A	TP	+/-	PIM	PP	SH	GW	GT	S	PCT
34	3	8	11	+1	39	0	0	1	1	51	5.9

1995-96 statistics:

GP	G	A	TP	+/-	PIM	PP	SH	GW	GT	S	PCT
79	1	12	13	-8	59	1	0	0	0	106	0.9

LAST SEASON

Second NHL season.

THE FINESSE GAME

Rohloff is an older "young player," having completed four years at Minnesota-Duluth and a season in the minors before earning a spot with the Bruins two seasons ago. We have probably already seen the best he has to offer, which is a number six defenseman's role with some spot play in offensive situations, like a second-unit power play.

Rohloff has a mature, polished game. He is good enough to play on his off side, which is something few defensemen can handle.

Rohloff has a big shot. He has to develop more confidence in his shooting and scoring ability. He is also a smart passer. He can skate or move the puck out of his own end.

THE PHYSICAL GAME

Rohloff has come back all the way from major knee surgery. He is a fine skater and defends well one-on-one. He eliminates the body effectively and does a great job in his own end taking away space. He competes every night, every shift, but his game has its limitations.

THE INTANGIBLES

The Bruins had hopes of moving Rohloff into a top three position defensively, to ease the absence of Al Iafrate (now with San Jose), but Rohloff is not that gifted an offensive defenseman. He is on his way to becoming a solid two-way defenseman, but not one who will be on the ice at critical moments.

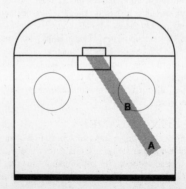

KEVIN SAWYER

Yrs. of NHL service: 0
Born: Christina Lake, B.C.; Feb. 18, 1974
Position: left wing
Height: 6-2
Weight: 205
Uniform no.: 19
Shoots: left

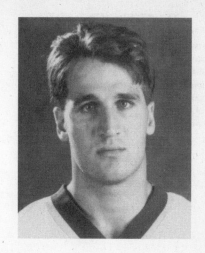

Career statistics:

GP	G	A	TP	PIM
8	0	0	0	28

1995-96 statistics:

GP	G	A	TP	+/-	PIM	PP	SH	GW	GT	S	PCT
8	0	0	0	-1	28	0	0	0	0	1	0.0

LAST SEASON

Acquired from St. Louis with Steve Staios for Steve Leach, Mar. 8, 1996. Will be entering first NHL season. Played 45 games with Worcester and Providence (AHL), scoring a combined 3-4 — 7 and 297 PIM with the two teams.

THE FINESSE GAME

Sawyer could become an effective role player if he can improve his skating. Right now it is marginal at best, but Sawyer was hampered by a serious groin injury most of last season, and if that problem persists it's unlikely he'll be able to develop the strength to power his skating more efficiently.

If he can contribute in some way, it will be as a forechecking winger who can pick up the team with a zesty shift now and then. His hand skills are minimal, but he can stir up loose pucks with some seek-and-destroy work in the corners.

THE PHYSICAL GAME

Sawyer will quite literally fight his way into the lineup every night. The new rule that causes a player to be ejected from the game for scrapping off the face-off will come as a real blow to him. He tangled with feared NHL heavyweight Chris Simon, and he is ready to take on all comers.

THE INTANGIBLES

The Bruins will not be a very talented team this season, so they will try to be a tough one, and Sawyer will be given every chance to make the team as an energy-generating fourth-line winger.

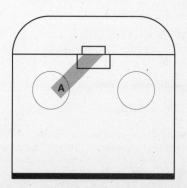

JOZEF STUMPEL

Yrs. of NHL service: 3
Born: Nitra, Czechoslavkia; June 20, 1972
Position: centre/right wing
Height: 6-1
Weight: 208
Uniform no.: 16
Shoots: right

Career statistics:

GP	G	A	TP	PIM
196	33	67	100	40

1992-93 statistics:

GP	G	A	TP	+/-	PIM	PP	SH	GW	GT	S	PCT
13	1	3	4	-3	4	0	0	0	0	8	12.5

1993-94 statistics:

GP	G	A	TP	+/-	PIM	PP	SH	GW	GT	S	PCT
59	8	15	23	+4	14	0	0	1	0	62	12.9

1994-95 statistics:

GP	G	A	TP	+/-	PIM	PP	SH	GW	GT	S	PCT
44	5	13	18	+4	8	1	0	2	0	46	10.9

1995-96 statistics:

GP	G	A	TP	+/-	PIM	PP	SH	GW	GT	S	PCT
76	18	36	54	-8	14	5	0	2	0	158	11.4

Despite the extra ice time, we don't see him scoring many more than 20 goals, although his assist total should be 30-40.

LAST SEASON

Third on team in assists with career high. Fourth on team in points with career high. Missed three games with fractured cheekbone.

THE FINESSE GAME

Stumpel was put in a position to succeed last season as the Bruins' number two centre and it proved to be the right spot for him, at least on this team. On a deeper team, Stumpel's lack of skating speed would drop him down farther on the depth chart.

Stumpel took advantage of the ice time with improved point production, finally living up to the promise that his hand skills had always indicated. Stumpel has a deft scoring touch and is also a passer with a good short game.

Stumpel has good hockey sense and is still adjusting to a full-time role. Given more time on the power play, he could respond to the responsibility, but he will never be a front-line player because of his skating.

THE PHYSICAL GAME

Stumpel is not an overly physical player and can be intimidated. He goes into the corners and bumps and he protects the puck with his body, but when the action gets really fierce, he backs off.

THE INTANGIBLES

Stumpel went from a bubble player at the start of the season to a regular on the second line under new coach Steve Kasper. He can hardly rest on one good season. Stumpel won't be pushed (there isn't much behind him in the system), so he will have to push himself.

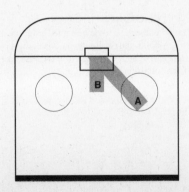

DON SWEENEY

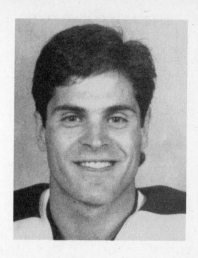

Yrs. of NHL service: 8
Born: St. Stephen, N.B.; Aug. 17, 1966
Position: left defense
Height: 5-10
Weight: 188
Uniform no.: 32
Shoots: left

Career statistics:

GP	G	A	TP	PIM
529	37	119	156	403

1992-93 statistics:

GP	G	A	TP	+/-	PIM	PP	SH	GW	GT	S	PCT
84	7	27	34	+34	68	0	1	0	0	107	6.5

1993-94 statistics:

GP	G	A	TP	+/-	PIM	PP	SH	GW	GT	S	PCT
75	6	15	21	+29	50	1	2	2	0	136	4.4

1994-95 statistics:

GP	G	A	TP	+/-	PIM	PP	SH	GW	GT	S	PCT
47	3	19	22	+6	24	1	0	2	0	102	2.9

1995-96 statistics:

GP	G	A	TP	+/-	PIM	PP	SH	GW	GT	S	PCT
77	4	24	28	-4	42	2	0	3	0	142	2.8

LAST SEASON

Tied for second on team in game-winning goals.

THE FINESSE GAME

Sweeney has found a niche for himself in the NHL. He's mobile, physical and greatly improved in the area of defensive reads. He has good hockey sense for recognizing offensive situations as well.

He mostly stays at home and out of trouble, but he is a good enough skater to get involved in the attack and take advantage of open ice. He is a good passer and has an adequate shot, and he has developed more confidence in his skills. He skates his way out of trouble and moves the puck well.

Sweeney is also an intelligent player who knows his strengths and weaknesses. He didn't get much playing time in his first two seasons in Boston, but, despite being a low draft pick (166th overall), he wouldn't let anyone overlook him.

THE PHYSICAL GAME

Sweeney is built like a little human Coke machine. He is tough to play against, and while wear and tear is a factor, he never hides. He is always in the middle of physical play. He utilizes his lower body drive and has tremendous leg power. He is also shifty enough to avoid a big hit when he sees it coming, and many a large forechecking forward has sheepishly picked himself up off the ice after Sweeney has scampered away with the puck.

Sweeney is the ultimate gym rat, devoting a great deal of time to weightlifting and overall conditioning. Pound for pound, he is one of the strongest defensemen in the NHL.

THE INTANGIBLES

Sweeney struggled through the first half of the season, probably because he no longer has Ray Bourque as his steady partner, but he righted his game in the second half. He is highly competitive and despite his small size a lot of teams would welcome him on their blueline. As his offensive skills are limited, we would expect him to stay in the 30-point range unless he gets more ice time with Bourque.

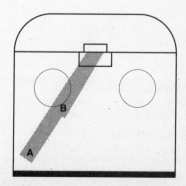

RICK TOCCHET

Yrs. of NHL service: 12
Born: Scarborough, Ont.; Apr. 9, 1964
Position: right wing
Height: 6-0
Weight: 205
Uniform no.: 22
Shoots: right

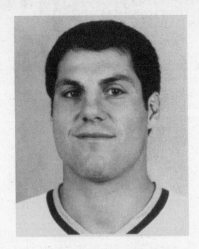

Career statistics:

GP	G	A	TP	PIM
788	338	598	736	2371

1992-93 statistics:

GP	G	A	TP	+/-	PIM	PP	SH	GW	GT	S	PCT
80	48	61	109	+28	252	20	4	5	0	240	20.0

1993-94 statistics:

GP	G	A	TP	+/-	PIM	PP	SH	GW	GT	S	PCT
51	14	26	40	-15	134	5	1	2	1	150	9.3

1994-95 statistics:

GP	G	A	TP	+/-	PIM	PP	SH	GW	GT	S	PCT
36	18	17	35	-8	70	7	1	3	0	95	18.9

1995-96 statistics:

GP	G	A	TP	+/-	PIM	PP	SH	GW	GT	S	PCT
71	29	31	60	+10	181	10	0	3	1	185	15.7

LAST SEASON

Acquired from Los Angeles for Kevin Stevens, Jan. 25, 1996. Led team in goals, power play goals and penalty minutes. Third on team in points. Tied for their on team in game-winning goals. Missed three games with suspensions. Missed five games with back injury. Missed two games with concussion. Missed two games with shoulder injury.

THE FINESSE GAME

Tocchet has worked hard to make the most of the finesse skills he possesses and that makes everything loom larger. His skating is powerful, though he does not have great mobility. He is explosive in short bursts and is most effective in small areas. He works extremely well down low and in traffic. Tocchet exceeded all expectations with his power play work last season. He drives to the front of the net and into the corners for the puck.

His shooting skills are better than his passing skills. He has limited vision of the ice for making a creative play, but he is a master at the bang-bang play. He'll smack in rebounds and deflections and set screens as defenders try to knock him down.

He has a strong, accurate wrist shot and gets most of his goals from close range, though he can also fire a one-timer from the tops of the circles. He'll rarely waste a shot from the blueline. He is a good give-and-go player because his quickness allows him to jump into the holes. He will beat few people one-on-one because he lacks stickhandling prowess.

THE PHYSICAL GAME

Tocchet gets about 20 shifts a game. That's like going 20 rounds with Joe Frazier, a heavyweight who comes at you again and again with everything he's got. There is no hiding from Tocchet. He is a tough hitter and frequently gets his stick and elbows up. He has long had a history of letting his emotions get the better of him, and although he has matured somewhat, he is acutely aware of his position as one of the few tough, physical forwards on a team of finesse players. Tocchet knows he has to play rugged to be effective and he can do that cleanly, but he will also get everyone's attention by bending the rules.

Tocchet has been plagued with a dodgy back for three seasons, and it causes him enormous pain at times, but there is never any letup in his effort.

THE INTANGIBLES

Without Tocchet, the Bruins would not have made the playoffs last season. He did everything he had to do to help the team win down the stretch, including picking fights. He scored 16 goals in 27 games in Boston. With Tocchet in the lineup, the team's enthusiasm skyrocketed. It's hard to imagine him keeping up that pace over an 82-game schedule, however.

Tocchet's work ethic is inspiring. He is always one of the last players off the ice, usually working on puckhandling drills. Before games, he's one of the first to the rink and is riding the bike; after games, he's lifting weights. He started his career as a goon, but has remade himself into a solid NHL player. Tocchet's health remains a huge question mark, but as long as he can stay on his feet he will be an impact player.

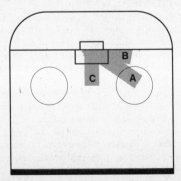

BUFFALO SABRES

Players' Statistics 1995-96

POS.	NO.	PLAYER	GP	G	A	PTS	+/-	PIM	PP	SH	GW	GT	S	PCT
C	16	PAT LAFONTAINE	76	40	51	91	-8	36	15	3	7	1	224	17.9
L	12	RANDY BURRIDGE	74	25	33	58	0	30	6		3		154	16.2
C	26	DEREK PLANTE	76	23	33	56	-4	28	4		5		203	11.3
D	3	GARRY GALLEY	78	10	44	54	-2	81	7	1	2		175	5.7
L	43	JASON DAWE	67	25	25	50	-8	33	8	1		2	130	19.2
L	10	BRAD MAY	79	15	29	44	6	295	3		4		168	8.9
D	44	ALEXEI ZHITNIK	80	6	30	36	-25	58	5				193	3.1
L	36	MATTHEW BARNABY	73	15	16	31	-2	335					131	11.5
C	27	MIKE PECA	68	11	20	31	-1	67	4	3	1		109	10.1
R	28	DONALD AUDETTE	23	12	13	25	0	18	8		1		92	13.0
C	19	*BRIAN HOLZINGER	58	10	10	20	-21	37	5		1		71	14.1
D	21	MARK ASTLEY	60	2	18	20	-12	80					80	2.5
D	8	DARRYL SHANNON	74	4	13	17	15	92					59	6.8
L	17	BRENT HUGHES	76	5	10	15	-9	148					56	8.9
D	34	*MIKE WILSON	58	4	8	12	13	41	1		1		52	7.7
L	18	MICHAL GROSEK	23	6	4	10	-1	31	2		1	1	34	17.6
R	24	*DANE JACKSON	22	5	4	9	3	41			1		20	25.0
L	32	ROB RAY	71	3	6	9	-8	287				1	21	14.3
R	25	ROB CONN	28	2	5	7	-9	18					36	5.6
L	33	SCOTT PEARSON	27	4		4	-4	67			1		26	15.4
R	15	DIXON WARD	8	2	2	4	1	6			1		12	16.7
D	6	DOUG HOUDA	38	1	3	4	3	52					21	4.8
D	38	*JAY MCKEE	1		1	1	1	2					2	
D	4	*BOB BOUGHNER	31		1	1	3	104					14	
G	39	DOMINIK HASEK	59		1	1	0	6						
L	9	*VACLAV VARADA	1				0						2	
G	31	*STEVE SHIELDS	2				0	2						
C	45	*SCOTT NICHOL	2				0	10					4	
C	76	*WAYNE PRIMEAU	2				0							
L	37	*BARRIE MOORE	3				0						3	
G	00	*MARTIN BIRON	3				0							
C	37	*CURTIS BROWN	4				0						1	
G	1	JOHN BLUE	5				0							
D	4	GRANT JENNINGS	6				1	28					3	
G	30	ANDREI TREFILOV	22				0	4						

GP = games played; G = goals; A = assists; PTS = points; +/- = goals-for minus goals-against while player is on ice; PIM = penalties in minutes; PP = power play goals; SH = shorthanded goals; GW = game-winning goals; GT = game-tying goals; S = no. of shots; PCT = percentage of goals to shots; * = rookie

DONALD AUDETTE

Yrs. of NHL service: 5
Born: Laval, Que.; Sept. 23, 1969
Position: right wing
Height: 5-8
Weight: 175
Uniform no.: 28
Shoots: right

Career statistics:

GP	G	A	TP	PIM
261	112	83	195	216

1992-93 statistics:

GP	G	A	TP	+/-	PIM	PP	SH	GW	GT	S	PCT
44	12	7	19	-8	51	2	0	0	0	92	13.0

1993-94 statistics:

GP	G	A	TP	+/-	PIM	PP	SH	GW	GT	S	PCT
77	29	30	59	+2	41	16	1	4	0	207	14.0

1994-95 statistics:

GP	G	A	TP	+/-	PIM	PP	SH	GW	GT	S	PCT
46	24	13	37	-3	27	13	0	7	0	124	19.4

1995-96 statistics:

GP	G	A	TP	+/-	PIM	PP	SH	GW	GT	S	PCT
23	12	13	25	0	18	8	0	1	0	92	13.0

LAST SEASON

Tied for second on team in power play goals. Missed two games with broken thumb. Missed 57 games with knee injury and reconstructive knee surgery.

THE FINESSE GAME

The above section should be entitled "lost season" for Audette, who underwent the third major knee operation of his career.

If he returns in good shape, Audette is a bustling forward who barrels to the net at every opportunity. He is eager and feisty down low and has good hand skills. He also has keen scoring instincts, along with the quickness to make good things happen. His feet move so fast (with a choppy stride) that he doesn't look graceful, but he can really get moving and he has good balance.

A scorer first, Audette has a great top-shelf shot, which he gets away quickly and accurately. He can also make a play, but he will do this at the start of a rush. Once he is inside the offensive zone and low, he wants the puck. His selfishness can be forgiven, considering his scoring ability.

Audette is at his best on the power play. He is smart enough not to just stand around and take his punishment, he times his jumps into the space between the left post and the bottom of the left circle.

THE PHYSICAL GAME

Opponents hate Audette, which he takes as a great compliment. He runs goalies, yaps and takes dives — then goes out and scores on the power play after the opposition takes a bad penalty.

He will forecheck and scrap for the puck but isn't as diligent coming back. He's not very big, but around the net he plays like he's at least a six-footer. He keeps jabbing and working away until he is bowled over by an angry defender.

THE INTANGIBLES

Audette lacks size, but not heart. He loves a challenge, and this latest setback may supply him with the biggest challenge of his career. How badly did the Sabres miss Audette? Just consider his production in a quarter of the season, while he was playing hurt. He could have a great second half this season, but expect a slow start.

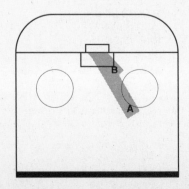

MATTHEW BARNABY

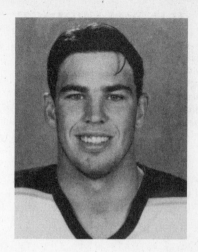

Yrs. of NHL service: 3
Born: Ottawa, Ont.; May 4, 1973
Position: left wing
Height: 6-0
Weight: 170
Uniform no.: 36
Shoots: left

Career statistics:

GP	G	A	TP	PIM
133	19	21	40	567

1992-93 statistics:

GP	G	A	TP	+/-	PIM	PP	SH	GW	GT	S	PCT
2	1	0	1	0	10	1	0	0	0	8	12.5

1993-94 statistics:

GP	G	A	TP	+/-	PIM	PP	SH	GW	GT	S	PCT
35	2	4	6	-7	106	1	0	0	0	13	15.4

1994-95 statistics:

GP	G	A	TP	+/-	PIM	PP	SH	GW	GT	S	PCT
23	1	1	2	-2	116	0	0	0	0	27	3.7

1995-96 statistics:

GP	G	A	TP	+/-	PIM	PP	SH	GW	GT	S	PCT
73	15	16	31	-2	335	0	0	0	0	131	11.5

LAST SEASON
Led NHL in penalty minutes.

THE FINESSE GAME
Barnaby's offensive skills are minimal. He gets some room because of his reputation, and that does buy him a little time around the net to get a shot away. He is utterly fearless and dives right into the thick of the action going for loose pucks.

But no one hires Barnaby for his scoring touch. His game is marked by his fierce intensity. He hits anyone, but especially loves going after the other team's big names. He is infuriating.

Barnaby skates well enough not to look out of place and he is very strong and balanced on his feet. He will do anything to win, and if he could develop a better scoring touch he would start reminding people of Dale Hunter.

THE PHYSICAL GAME
Barnaby brings a lot of energy to the game, and considering his size, it's a wonder he survived the season. He has to do some cheap stuff to survive, which makes him an even more irritating opponent. Big guys especially hate it, because it's a no-win when a Bob Probert or Randy McKay takes on the poor underdog Barnaby, but he's so obnoxious they just can't help it.

THE INTANGIBLES
Barnaby was a Group 2 free agent at the end of last season, but Sabres coach Ted Nolan appreciates Barnaby's toughness and the Sabres can expect to match any offer.

The key for Barnaby will be his ability to improve his skill level to become a more useful player, or else his willingess to just sit on the bench until the team wants to stir something up. Not all gunslingers can handle this role, but Barnaby appears to thrive on it.

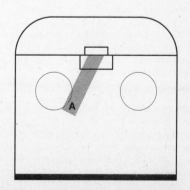

RANDY BURRIDGE

Yrs. of NHL service: 11
Born: Fort Erie, Ont.; Jan. 7, 1966
Position: left wing
Height: 5-9
Weight: 185
Uniform no.: 12
Shoots: left

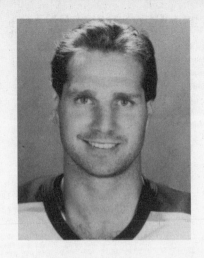

Career statistics:

GP	G	A	TP	PIM
621	185	224	409	438

1992-93 statistics:

GP	G	A	TP	+/-	PIM	PP	SH	GW	GT	S	PCT
4	0	0	0	+1	0	0	0	0	0	7	0.0

1993-94 statistics:

GP	G	A	TP	+/-	PIM	PP	SH	GW	GT	S	PCT
78	25	17	42	-1	73	8	1	5	0	150	16.7

1994-95 statistics:

GP	G	A	TP	+/-	PIM	PP	SH	GW	GT	S	PCT
40	4	15	19	-4	10	2	0	0	0	52	7.7

1995-96 statistics:

GP	G	A	TP	+/-	PIM	PP	SH	GW	GT	S	PCT
74	25	33	58	0	30	6	0	3	0	154	16.2

Burridge was rewarded with a new three-year, U.S.$2.5-million contract at the end of last season.

LAST SEASON

Second on team in points and shooting percentage. Tied for second on team in goals. Tied for third on team in assists. Missed five games with knee injury.

THE FINESSE GAME

Burridge's wrist shot is extremely quick and he packs plenty of power behind it. Goalies have trouble handling his shot on first try, so he creates a lot of rebound attempts for his linemates, or himself.

Despite a history of knee problems, Burridge still has pretty effective quickness, especially in the offensive zone. He gets a lot of his scoring chances by simply outworking the opposition. Burridge merits ice time on the power play because he will create openings and he can still bury the puck.

THE PHYSICAL GAME

Burridge makes the most of his physical assets and tries to play a bigger man's game with his heart and strength. Rather than suffer from limited size, he makes it work to his advantage. It isn't easy to knock him down because he has a low centre of gravity. He'll get to the boards or corners first, try to absorb the initial hit, then use his feet to keep the puck alive or move it to a teammate.

THE INTANGIBLES

Burridge is like one of those creatures in a horror movie. You think he's dead, but he keeps coming back. His character shows through in his comeback from a serious knee injury, and his effort and leadership will help the young Sabres players through what will probably be another very dark season.

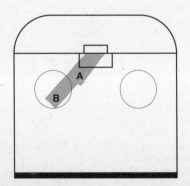

JASON DAWE

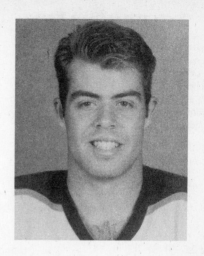

Yrs. of NHL service: 3
Born: North York, Ont.; May 29, 1973
Position: left wing
Height: 5-10
Weight: 195
Uniform no.: 43
Shoots: left

Career statistics:

GP	G	A	TP	PIM
141	38	36	74	64

1993-94 statistics:

GP	G	A	TP	+/-	PIM	PP	SH	GW	GT	S	PCT
32	6	7	13	+1	12	3	0	1	0	35	17.1

1994-95 statistics:

GP	G	A	TP	+/-	PIM	PP	SH	GW	GT	S	PCT
42	7	4	11	-6	19	0	1	2	0	51	13.7

1995-96 statistics:

GP	G	A	TP	+/-	PIM	PP	SH	GW	GT	S	PCT
67	25	25	50	-8	33	8	1	0	2	130	19.2

LAST SEASON

Tied for second in team in goals and power play goals. Played seven games with Rochester (AHL), scoring 5-4 — 9. Missed six games with fractured ribs.

THE FINESSE GAME

Dawe survived a shaky start, a demotion and a move from left wing to right to regain a spot among the Sabres' top six forwards last season.

Dawe is a skill player with the added element of being an eager forechecker. He is also intelligent enough to trail into the play if he is being used with faster forwards who are less alert defensively.

Dawe has a quick release on his shot, usually from the top of the left circle in. He has the good sense to read the play and knows when to back off and support the defense as the third man high.

Dawe is a good skater with a fluid stride and good balance. He's shifty and doesn't look out of place with the speedy Pat LaFontaine, although he played with Derek Plante on the second line late in the season. Dawe handles the puck well at high tempo (although he isn't much of a one-on-one threat) and in traffic. He is very effective on the power play.

THE PHYSICAL GAME

Dawe is willing to do the grunt work for his line. He is not big, but he is stocky and strong and will bang people off the puck. He is a diligent backchecker and has an aggressive streak.

THE INTANGIBLES

Dawe, who has been compared to Yvan Cournoyer, took a step backward last season. He needs a strong training camp and has to continue to compete to retain his spot on the top line. The only thing that could hold him back is his lack of size.

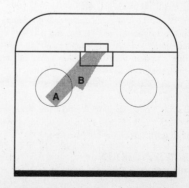

GARRY GALLEY

Yrs. of NHL service: 12
Born: Montreal, Que., Apr. 16, 1963
Position: left defense
Height: 6-0
Weight: 204
Uniform no.: 3
Shoots: left

Career statistics:

GP	G	A	TP	PIM
818	93	366	459	912

1992-93 statistics:

GP	G	A	TP	+/-	PIM	PP	SH	GW	GT	S	PCT
83	13	49	62	+18	115	4	1	3	1	231	5.6

1993-94 statistics:

GP	G	A	TP	+/-	PIM	PP	SH	GW	GT	S	PCT
81	10	60	70	-11	91	5	1	0	1	186	5.4

1994-95 statistics:

GP	G	A	TP	+/-	PIM	PP	SH	GW	GT	S	PCT
47	3	29	32	+4	30	2	0	0	0	97	3.1

1995-96 statistics:

GP	G	A	TP	+/-	PIM	PP	SH	GW	GT	S	PCT
78	10	44	54	-2	81	7	1	2	0	175	5.7

LAST SEASON

Led team defensemen in scoring for second consecutive season. Second on team in assists. Fourth on team in points.

THE FINESSE GAME

Galley is a puck mover. He follows the play and jumps into the attack. He has decent speed to keep up with the play, though he won't be rushing the puck himself. He is mobile and has a good shot that he can get away on the fly. He will pinch aggressively, but he's also quick enough to get back if there is a counterattack.

He works well on the power play. His lateral movement allows him to slide away from the point to the middle of the blueline, and he keeps his shots low. He is a smart player and his experience shows. Galley helps any younger player he is teamed with because of his poise and communication.

THE PHYSICAL GAME

Galley has added a physical element to his game over the past few seasons, but he is not and will never be a big hitter. He will take his man, but not always take him out, and more physical forwards take advantage of him. Galley gets in the way, though, and does not back down. But there are times when he is simply overpowered.

Galley has a quick stick and uses sweep- and poke-checks well. He will also get a little chippy now and then, just to keep people guessing.

THE INTANGIBLES

For the past four seasons (with Philadelphia and Buffalo), Galley led the team defensemen in scoring. He is not a true number one defenseman, but he served that role for the past three seasons and may have to again this season, though that is asking too much of him. He and Alexei Zhitnik will do some good things, but may have some nightmare evenings as well.

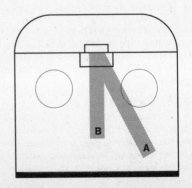

MICHAL GROSEK

Yrs. of NHL service: 2
Born: Vszkov, Czechoslovakia; June 1, 1975
Position: right wing
Height: 6-2
Weight: 200
Uniform no.: 18
Shoots: right

Career statistics:

GP	G	A	TP	PIM
50	9	6	15	52

1993-94 statistics:

GP	G	A	TP	+/-	PIM	PP	SH	GW	GT	S	PCT
3	1	0	1	-1	0	0	0	0	0	4	25.0

1994-95 statistics:

GP	G	A	TP	+/-	PIM	PP	SH	GW	GT	S	PCT
24	2	2	4	-3	21	0	0	1	0	27	7.4

1995-96 statistics:

GP	G	A	TP	+/-	PIM	PP	SH	GW	GT	S	PCT
23	6	4	10	-1	31	2	0	1	1	34	17.6

points in 22 games with Buffalo, a non-playoff team, and that is a promising sign for next season. Grosek could have a big breakout year, with the skill potential for 25 goals.

LAST SEASON

Acquired from Winnipeg with Darryl Shannon for Craig Muni and a first-round draft pick, Feb. 15, 1996. Played 39 games with Springfield (AHL), scoring 16-19 — 35.

THE FINESSE GAME

Grosek is a bundle of talent whose first shot at an NHL job was derailed by two serious injuries. He uses his speed and size to create some room, and he is genuinely tough.

He is still very young and has an eagerness to succeed at the NHL level. He is an excellent stickhandler, and he can be absolutely magical with the puck. He is good enough to play his off (left) wing as well as the right. He doesn't have a great shot, but he intimidates with his speed and drives to the net. With more confidence, his release may improve.

Defensively, Grosek's game needs work, but he also needs the ice time to improve, and he's just starting to get that.

THE PHYSICAL GAME

Grosek has gotten bigger and stronger in the past two seasons. He can be a little undisciplined, but once given a responsible role, he plays more intelligently. In the past, he has always had to fight for ice time. Once he started feeling more comfortable, his all-around game improved. He was a better player in Buffalo than he was in the minors. He's inconsistent in his gritty play, but when he sticks his nose in and plays hard, he is an impact player.

THE INTANGIBLES

Grosek looked like a different player once he was dealt to the Sabres and promoted to the first line with Pat LaFontaine and Brad May. He finished with 10

DOMINIK HASEK

Yrs. of NHL service: 5
Born: Pardubice, Czech.; Jan. 29, 1965
Position: goaltender
Height: 5-11
Weight: 165
Uniform no.: 39
Catches: left

Career statistics:

GP	MIN	GA	SO	GAA	A	PIM
211	11829	482	15	2.44	4	22

1992-93 statistics:

GP	MIN	GAA	W	L	T	SO	GA	S	SAPCT	PIM
28	1429	3.15	11	10	4	0	75	720	.896	0

1993-94 statistics:

GP	MIN	GAA	W	L	T	SO	GA	S	SAPCT	PIM
58	3358	1.95	30	20	6	7	109	1552	.930	6

1994-95 statistics:

GP	MIN	GAA	W	L	T	SO	GA	S	SAPCT	PIM
41	2416	2.11	19	14	7	5	85	1221	.930	2

1995-96 statistics:

GP	MIN	GAA	W	L	T	SO	GA	S	SAPCT	PIM
59	3417	2.83	22	30	6	2	161	2011	.920	6

LAST SEASON

Led NHL in save percentage. Missed 10 games with recurring abdominal strain. Missed three games with knee injury.

THE PHYSICAL GAME

Injuries and a porous defense caused Hasek to lose his spot among the league's goals-against leaders last season, but his save percentage was still remarkable, given the high quality shots he faces. Nobody has worse technique nor better leg reflexes than Hasek. His foot speed is simply tremendous. He wanders and flops and sprawls. But he stops the puck.

Usually what Hasek sees, he stops. He is adept at directing his rebounds away from onrushing attackers. He prefers to hold pucks for face-offs, and the Sabres have a decent corps of centres so that tactic works fine for his team. Hasek instructs his defensemen to get out of the way so he can see the puck, and they follow orders.

Hasek learned to come out of his net a little bit more, but he still doesn't cut down his angles well. He also has to work on his puckhandling. He has the single most bizarre habit of any NHL goalie we've seen in recent years. In scrambles around the net, he abandons his stick entirely and grabs the puck with his blocker hand. His work with the stick is brutal, which may be why he lets go of it so often.

THE MENTAL GAME

Hasek performed one of the more remarkable feats last season when he came into a game in relief of Andrei Trefilov and stopped Mario Lemieux on a penalty shot. That typifies Hasek's concentration in a nutshell.

Hasek is unflappable. He is always prepared for tough saves early in a game, and has very few lapses of concentration. His excitable style doesn't bother his teammates, who have developed faith in his ability.

THE INTANGIBLES

After receiving a contract extension a year ago, Hasek had that torn up and received a new deal for three years: U.S.$12.5 million. He's going to have to earn every penny behind this not very improved Sabres team this season, and his contract will make him difficult to trade down the road.

BRIAN HOLZINGER

Yrs. of NHL service: 1
Born: Parma, Ohio; Oct. 10, 1972
Position: centre
Height: 5-11
Weight: 180
Uniform no.: 19
Shoots: right

Career statistics:

GP	G	A	TP	PIM
62	10	13	23	37

1994-95 statistics:

GP	G	A	TP	+/-	PIM	PP	SH	GW	GT	S	PCT
4	0	3	3	+2	0	0	0	0	0	3	0.0

1995-96 statistics:

GP	G	A	TP	+/-	PIM	PP	SH	GW	GT	S	PCT
58	10	10	20	-21	37	5	0	1	0	71	14.1

LAST SEASON

First NHL season. Played 17 games with Rochester (AHL), scoring 10-11 — 21.

THE FINESSE GAME

Holzinger has a fine touch down low and patience with the puck to find the open passing lane. He will need to work with a grinder on one wing, because he is too small to do much effective work in the corners. It will help to have LaFontaine as a teammate; there is much Holzinger could learn from watching the veteran centre. Holzinger isn't quite as gritty as LaFontaine, nor does he have the latter's speed. He is more like Neal Broten (a former Hobey Baker winner, like Holzinger), crafty and deceptively quick.

Holzinger is not a natural scorer, but he has some speed that he can learn to use to his advantage.

The key to Holzinger's development will be adding the little things to his game to make him a complete player. He has to ask himself how he can contribute if he's not scoring. He can play, but can he win? Holzinger has a lot of raw talent, but at the moment he is an open-ice break player. He has a lot of hockey sense and may be adaptable. He certainly needs to learn better defense.

THE PHYSICAL GAME

Holzinger will have to work for his open ice in the NHL. He is not very big, nor very strong. Strength and conditioning work must figure in his summer vacation plans again.

THE INTANGIBLES

Expectations were high for Holzinger in last season's training camp, and he wasn't ready to live up to them. His season might have been salvaged by playing for a Calder Cup championship in Rochester. Holzinger scored the game-winning goal in Game 7, which will certainly be a confidence builder.

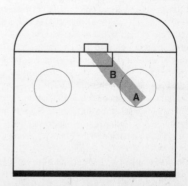

PAT LAFONTAINE

Yrs. of NHL service: 12
Born: St. Louis, Mo.; Feb. 22, 1963
Position: centre
Height: 5-10
Weight: 180
Uniform no.: 16
Shoots: right

Career statistics:

GP	G	A	TP	PIM
785	443	500	943	535

1992-93 statistics:

GP	G	A	TP	+/-	PIM	PP	SH	GW	GT	S	PCT
84	53	95	148	+11	63	20	2	7	1	306	17.3

1993-94 statistics:

GP	G	A	TP	+/-	PIM	PP	SH	GW	GT	S	PCT
16	5	13	18	-4	2	1	0	0	0	40	12.5

1994-95 statistics:

GP	G	A	TP	+/-	PIM	PP	SH	GW	GT	S	PCT
22	12	15	27	+2	4	6	1	3	1	54	22.2

1995-96 statistics:

GP	G	A	TP	+/-	PIM	PP	SH	GW	GT	S	PCT
76	40	51	91	-8	36	15	3	7	1	224	17.9

LAST SEASON

Led team in goals, assists, points, power play goals, game-winning goals and shots. Tied for team lead in shorthanded goals. Seventh season with 40 or more goals. Missed two games with concussion.

THE FINESSE GAME

Mario Lemieux deserved his Hart Trophy last season, sure, but we would hate to see where the Sabres would be without their Mr. Everything. Without LaFontaine, the Sabres are a minor league team.

If LaFontaine were a baseball player, he would be like the midget Bill Veeck once sent up to the plate. With LaFontaine's skating crouch, there is no strike zone. He's a ball of fire on the ice, low to the ground and almost impossible to catch or knock off stride. He gears up in the defensive zone and simply explodes.

Inexhaustible, he is double-shifted almost every night and doesn't miss a call. Nor does he float: he's like a shark, always circling and in motion. He has great quickness and acceleration, with deep edges for turns. Few players can get as many dekes into a short stretch of ice at high speed as LaFontaine does when he is bearing down on a goalie. His favourite move is "patented" but still almost unstoppable. He streaks in, moves the puck to his backhand, then strides right with the puck on his forehand. A goalie's only hope is for LaFontaine to lose control. Slim chance.

LaFontaine takes almost all of the Sabres' offensive-zone draws. He has quick hands and after winning the draw will burst past the opposing centre to the net.

On the power play, LaFontaine likes to lurk be-hind the cage, then burst out into the open ice at either side of the net for a pass and a scoring chance.

Opposing teams have to make the percentage play in their defensive zone against LaFontaine because of his anticipation and alertness in picking off passes.

THE PHYSICAL GAME

LaFontaine is much less of a perimeter player than people think. He goes into high-traffic areas and crashes the net. He won't knock people down and he won't run around making useless hits, but he will battle effectively in the neutral zone.

Strong on his skates and on his stick, LaFontaine will push off a defender with one arm and get a shot away one-handed. He is very disciplined and, despite the abuse he takes, spends little time in the penalty box.

THE INTANGIBLES

LaFontaine is among the league's elite forwards, but he is limited in some areas because he is not a power centre. Trade rumours were persistent last season, but the Sabres will probably wait to move him until after they sell enough tickets to fill their new building. LaFontaine is a marquee player, but Buffalo has little hope of improving much next season, and at 33, LaFontaine would like to play for a Stanley Cup instead of racking up 90-100 points for a non-contender.

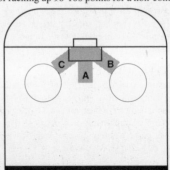

BRAD MAY

Yrs. of NHL service: 5
Born: Toronto, Ont.; Nov. 29, 1971
Position: left wing
Height: 6-1
Weight: 210
Uniform no.: 10
Shoots: left

Career statistics:

GP	G	A	TP	PIM
347	60	78	138	1104

1992-93 statistics:

GP	G	A	TP	+/-	PIM	PP	SH	GW	GT	S	PCT
82	13	13	26	+3	242	0	0	1	0	114	11.4

1993-94 statistics:

GP	G	A	TP	+/-	PIM	PP	SH	GW	GT	S	PCT
84	18	27	45	-6	171	3	0	3	0	166	10.8

1994-95 statistics:

GP	G	A	TP	+/-	PIM	PP	SH	GW	GT	S	PCT
33	3	3	6	+5	87	1	0	0	0	42	7.1

1995-96 statistics:

GP	G	A	TP	+/-	PIM	PP	SH	GW	GT	S	PCT
79	15	29	44	+6	295	3	0	4	0	168	8.9

LAST SEASON

Third on team in plus-minus and game-winning goals.

THE FINESSE GAME

May is better off trying to make the safe play instead of the big play, as more often than not, the safe play leads to the big play. He has more than brute strength on his side and possesses nice passing skills and good hockey sense.

He is not much of a finisher, though as he becomes more relaxed and confident (he was neither again last year) this may develop. He is certainly not a natural scorer; his goals will come off his hard work around the net.

May does have sound defensive instincts and was one of the few plus players on the Sabres. He is not a very fast or agile skater so he has to be conscious of keeping his position. He won't be able to race back to cover for an error in judgement.

THE PHYSICAL GAME

May is strong along the boards and in front of the net. A well-conditioned athlete, he is sturdy and durable. He has good balance and leg drive and is difficult to knock off his feet. He will take a hit to make a play and protects the puck well. He plays through pain.

THE INTANGIBLES

Even given the adage that power forwards need time to develop, May, now 25, is showing few promising signs. The Sabres keep giving him premium ice time, usually with Pat LaFontaine, but May is not elevating his game.

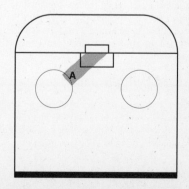

MIKE PECA

Yrs. of NHL service: 2
Born: Toronto, Ont.; March 26, 1974
Position: right wing
Height: 5-11
Weight: 180
Uniform no.: 27
Shoots: right

Career statistics:

GP	G	A	TP	PIM
105	17	26	43	99

1993-94 statistics:

GP	G	A	TP	+/-	PIM	PP	SH	GW	GT	S	PCT
4	0	0	0	-1	2	0	0	0	0	5	0.0

1994-95 statistics:

GP	G	A	TP	+/-	PIM	PP	SH	GW	GT	S	PCT
33	6	6	12	-6	30	2	0	1	1	46	13.0

1995-96 statistics:

GP	G	A	TP	+/-	PIM	PP	SH	GW	GT	S	PCT
68	11	20	31	-1	67	4	3	1	0	109	10.1

LAST SEASON

Tied for team lead in shorthanded goals. Missed seven games with sprained knee. Missed six games with back injury.

THE FINESSE GAME

Just call him "Peca the checka." Peca is a strong, sure skater who plays every shift as if a pink slip will be waiting on the bench if he slacks off. He's good with the puck, but not overly creative. Peca just reads offensive plays well and does a lot of the little things, especially when forechecking, that create turnovers and scoring chances. His goals come from his quickness and his effort. He will challenge anyone for the puck.

Although Peca is known for his grit, he can be a useful offensive player. Defensively, his game needs work, and he seems willing to learn. He is only average on face-offs. His hustle and attitude have earned him his NHL job.

THE PHYSICAL GAME

Peca plays much bigger than his size, and is always trying to add more weight (he has a tough time even keeping an extra five pounds on). He's among the best open-ice hitters in the league. Peca will also drop the gloves and go after even the biggest foe. He is fearless.

THE INTANGIBLES

Peca is an ideal third-line player. Although he lacks the size to match up with some of the league's bigger forwards, he is tireless in his pursuit and effort. He adds energy to the lineup, and may contribute 40 points, althogh scoring isn't his strong suit.

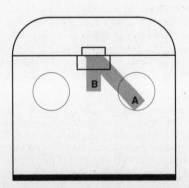

DEREK PLANTE

Yrs. of NHL service: 3
Born: Cloquet, Minn.; Jan. 17, 1971
Position: centre
Height: 5-11
Weight: 180
Uniform no.: 26
Shoots: left

Career statistics:

GP	G	A	TP	PIM
200	47	87	134	64

1993-94 statistics:

GP	G	A	TP	+/-	PIM	PP	SH	GW	GT	S	PCT
77	21	35	56	+4	24	8	1	2	0	147	14.3

1994-95 statistics:

GP	G	A	TP	+/-	PIM	PP	SH	GW	GT	S	PCT
47	3	19	22	-4	12	2	0	0	0	94	3.2

1995-96 statistics:

GP	G	A	TP	+/-	PIM	PP	SH	GW	GT	S	PCT
76	23	33	56	-4	28	4	0	5	0	203	11.3

LAST SEASON

Second on team in shots and game-winning goals. Third on team in points. Tied for third on team in assists.

THE FINESSE GAME

Plante has to compensate for his lack of stature with quickness and hand skills. He does not have blazing speed, but he can get the edge on a defender with a quick initial burst and he is very mobile with a change of gears.

It would obviously help Plante to play with a big winger who could convert his passes, but the Sabres didn't have anyone fitting that description last season. He is an excellent passer, with sharp instincts around the net, and works very well with the open ice on the power play. Plante would rather pass than shoot, but overcame that reluctance a bit more successfully last season.

Despite his good hand-eye coordination, Plante is average on draws and really loses an edge to bigger centres.

THE PHYSICAL GAME

Plante has a very slender frame and he's not very strong. He has always had trouble with the length of the pro season, tending to wear down if he gets too much ice time. He pays attention to conditioning, which helps, but he is limited by his physique. He will lose a lot of one-on-one battles.

THE INTANGIBLES

The Sabres were set to hand the number two centre's role to Brian Holzinger last season, but Plante had other ideas and played his way back ahead of the rookies. The Sabres already have a small-framed guy (Pat LaFontaine) as their number one, and will be looking to add size up the middle, so Plante will have to fend off challenges again, assuming he stays with Buffalo (he was a Group 2 free agent at the end of last season).

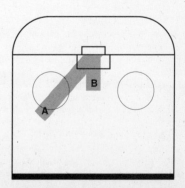

ROB RAY

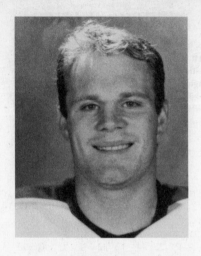

Yrs. of NHL service: 7
Born: Belleville, Ont.; June 8, 1968
Position: left wing
Height: 6-0
Weight: 203
Uniform no.: 32
Shoots: left

Career statistics:

GP	G	A	TP	PIM
424	24	27	51	1746

1992-93 statistics:

GP	G	A	TP	+/-	PIM	PP	SH	GW	GT	S	PCT
68	3	2	5	-3	211	1	0	0	0	28	10.7

1993-94 statistics:

GP	G	A	TP	+/-	PIM	PP	SH	GW	GT	S	PCT
82	3	4	7	+2	274	0	0	0	0	34	8.8

1994-95 statistics:

GP	G	A	TP	+/-	PIM	PP	SH	GW	GT	S	PCT
46	0	3	3	-4	173	0	0	0	0	7	0.0

1995-96 statistics:

GP	G	A	TP	+/-	PIM	PP	SH	GW	GT	S	PCT
71	3	6	9	-8	287	0	0	0	1	21	14.3

LAST SEASON

Second on team in penalty minutes. Missed 11 games with fractured orbital bone.

THE FINESSE GAME

Ray is a good skater for a big guy, very mobile and surprisingly quick. He is a solid forechecker and is learning to keep his gloves and stick down. There is nothing wrong with taking aggressive penalties, but Ray is big enough to check cleanly and effectively. His problem is one of the chicken-or-egg variety. Is Ray not getting enough ice time to allow him to improve his game, or is he merely a tough-guy winger that the team can't afford to have on the ice too often?

Ray has to work hard for his points. He has a nice wrist shot from in close and a hard slap shot. He doesn't do much creatively but patrols up and down his wing. He has good balance and can plant himself in front of the net, but he doesn't have really quick hands for picking up loose pucks.

THE PHYSICAL GAME

Ray is one of those hitters who can galvanize a bench and a building. A defender with the puck knows Ray is coming and either has to be willing to stand up to the check or bail out — either way, Ray has a good shot at loosening a puck and getting a turnover. The problem is that he can't do much with the puck once he gets it and needs a clever linemate to trail in and pick up the pieces.

A good fighter who doesn't get challenged much anymore, Ray was the player chiefly responsible for a rule change two seasons ago that penalized a player for shucking his jersey before an altercation. Ray continues to fight on half-naked, since he has gotten very good at making it look like the opponent has pulled off his jersey, which he wears large and loose and with the protective equipment sewn onto it. He's become hockey's version of Demi Moore, since he goes topless at every opportunity.

THE INTANGIBLES

There is still a place for a Rob Ray, especially on a team that has valuable small players such as Pat LaFontaine and Derek Plante. But the Sabres look to be adding talent to go with their toughness, and Ray may find himself on the bubble if the team has enough skaters who can take care of themselves.

RICHARD SMEHLIK

Yrs. of NHL service: 3
Born: Ostrava, Czechoslovakia; Jan. 23, 1970
Position: right defense
Height: 6-3
Weight: 208
Uniform no.: 42
Shoots: left

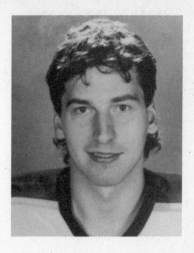

Career statistics:

GP	G	A	TP	PIM
203	22	61	83	174

1992-93 statistics:

GP	G	A	TP	+/-	PIM	PP	SH	GW	GT	S	PCT
80	4	27	31	+9	59	0	0	0	0	82	4.9

1993-94 statistics:

GP	G	A	TP	+/-	PIM	PP	SH	GW	GT	S	PCT
84	14	27	41	+22	69	3	3	1	1	106	13.2

1994-95 statistics:

GP	G	A	TP	+/-	PIM	PP	SH	GW	GT	S	PCT
39	4	7	11	+5	46	0	1	1	0	49	8.2

1995-96 statistics:

Did Not Play in NHL

LAST SEASON

Missed entire season with reconstructive knee surgery.

THE FINESSE GAME

It's always tough to judge players coming back off major knee surgery, especially those for whom skating is a major asset, and Smehlik is firmly in that category. Prior to the injury, Smehlik was a very agile skater with good lateral movement and was very solid on his skates. Because his balance is so good, he is tough to knock down.

If Smehlik is given more responsibility offensively, he will respond. He has good passing skills and fair hockey vision, and can spot and hit the breaking forward. Most of his assists will be traced back to a headman feed out of the defensive zone.

Smehlik is vulnerable to a strong forecheck. Teams are aware of his lack of experience and try to work his corner.

THE PHYSICAL GAME

Smehlik is still adapting to the North American game. He can use his body well but has to be more consistent and authoritative. He gained confidence through the season and was willing to step up aggressively, especially when killing penalties. He has to clean up his crease better but he's not a mean hitter. He prefers to use his stick to break up plays, and he does this effectively. He has a long reach and is able to intercept passes or reach in around a defender to pry the puck loose. His battles this season, however, will be mental until he tests his knee and is comfortable.

THE INTANGIBLES

Smehlik was planning to participate in the World Cup, which will be the first real test of his knee and will indicate at what level he will start off the season. Smehlik was on his way to becoming a reliable number three or number four defenseman with the Sabres before the injury.

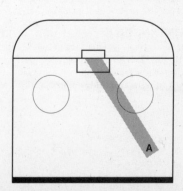

MIKE WILSON

Yrs. of NHL service: 1
Born: Brampton, Ont.; Feb. 26, 1975
Position: left defense
Height: 6-4
Weight: 195
Uniform no.: 34
Shoots: left

Career statistics:

GP	G	A	TP	PIM
58	4	8	12	41

1995-96 statistics:

GP	G	A	TP	+/-	PIM	PP	SH	GW	GT	S	PCT
58	4	8	12	+13	41	1	0	1	0	52	7.7

LAST SEASON

First NHL season. Second on team in plus-minus. Played 15 games with Rochester (AHL), scoring 0-5 — 5.

THE FINESSE GAME

Wilson is a stay-at-home defenseman with raw skills who needs to take another step up in his reads to become more effective. That is likely to come with experience.

He is an average skater, occasionally clumsy, and accordingly plays a very conservative positional game. He is very strong on his feet, and that's a factor along the boards and in the corners. He does not get involved in the attack to much extent, although he will make the rush now and again when space opens up. He has a long stride but is not very quick. Wilson does have a very capable first pass out of the zone, which at this stage is his best asset.

THE PHYSICAL GAME

Wilson is big, and playing in a small rink (the old Aud) helped him with his containment game last season. The Sabres will move into a new regulation-size rink this season, so Wilson will lose that home edge. He is not a heavy hitter, but he has a wide wingspan and makes players take the long way around him since it's not possible to plow through him.

THE INTANGIBLES

Wilson has a promising future as a defensive defenseman. He still has a lot of learning to do, but he is an intelligent player who could grow into a quietly effective Ken Morrow type. He is a hard worker with a good attitude.

ALEXEI ZHITNIK

Yrs. of NHL service: 4
Born: Kiev, Ukraine; Oct. 10, 1972
Position: left defense
Height: 5-11
Weight: 190
Uniform no.: 44
Shoots: left

Career statistics:

GP	G	A	TP	PIM
271	34	116	150	300

1992-93 statistics:

GP	G	A	TP	+/-	PIM	PP	SH	GW	GT	S	PCT
78	12	36	48	-3	80	5	0	2	0	136	8.8

1993-94 statistics:

GP	G	A	TP	+/-	PIM	PP	SH	GW	GT	S	PCT
81	12	40	52	-11	101	11	0	1	1	227	5.3

1994-95 statistics:

GP	G	A	TP	+/-	PIM	PP	SH	GW	GT	S	PCT
32	4	10	14	-6	61	3	0	0	0	66	6.1

1995-96 statistics:

GP	G	A	TP	+/-	PIM	PP	SH	GW	GT	S	PCT
80	6	30	36	-25	58	5	0	0	0	193	3.1

THE INTANGIBLES

Zhitnik was a Group 2 free agent at the end of last season, and despite his overall erratic play, the Sabres are expected to keep him as one of their top two defensemen. But, it wouldn't be surprising if he is dealt before this season's trade deadline to a team looking for some power play help that can afford his defensive lapses.

LAST SEASON

Third on team in shots. Second among team defensemen in scoring. Worst plus-minus on team.

THE FINESSE GAME

Zhitnik has a bowlegged skating style that ex-coach, Barry Melrose, once compared to Bobby Orr's. Zhitnik is no Orr, but he was born with skates on. He has speed, acceleration and lateral mobility.

He plays the point on the power play with Garry Galley, moving to the right point to open up his forehand for the one-timer. Zhitnik likes to rush the puck and shoots well off the fly. He uses all of the blueline well on the power play. He has a good, hard shot, but needs to work on keeping it low for tips and deflections in front.

Zhitnik sees the ice well and is a good playmaker. He can snap a long, strong headman pass or feather a short pass on a give-and-go. He can also grab the puck and skate it out of danger. Consistency continues to elude him, but he has the ingredients to put a great game together.

Defensively, Zhitnik can be a nightmare. He is a gambler who thinks offense first, and frequently leaves his defense partner outnumbered.

THE PHYSICAL GAME

Zhitnik has an undisciplined side to his game. He makes wild, leaping checks that are borderline charges, but for the most part he plays sensibly and doesn't take bad penalties. Teams often target Zhitnik physically and try to take him out of a game early, and the tactic will work as he wears out. He has to get stronger and pay more attention to conditioning.

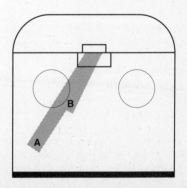

CALGARY FLAMES

Players' Statistics 1995-96

POS	NO.	PLAYER	GP	G	A	PTS	+/-	PIM	PP	SH	GW	GT	S	PCT
R	14	THEOREN FLEURY	80	46	50	96	17	112	17	5	4		353	13.0
C	13	GERMAN TITOV	82	28	39	67	9	24	13	2	2	2	214	13.1
C	92	MICHAEL NYLANDER	73	17	38	55	0	20	4		6		163	10.4
L	10	GARY ROBERTS	35	22	20	42	15	78	9		5	1	84	26.2
C	16	*CORY STILLMAN	74	16	19	35	-5	41	4	1	3		132	12.1
D	3	JAMES PATRICK	80	3	32	35	3	30	1				116	2.6
D	21	STEVE CHIASSON	76	8	25	33	3	62	5		2		175	4.6
D	33	ZARLEY ZALAPSKI	80	12	17	29	11	115	5		1		145	8.3
C	32	MIKE SULLIVAN	81	9	12	21	-6	24		1	1	1	106	8.5
C	34	COREY MILLEN	44	7	14	21	8	18	2		1	1	73	9.6
R	15	SANDY MCCARTHY	75	9	7	16	-8	173	3		1		98	9.2
L	18	PAVEL TORGAJEV	41	6	10	16	2	14					50	12.0
R	22	RONNIE STERN	52	10	5	15	2	111			1	1	64	15.6
L	12	PAUL KRUSE	75	3	12	15	-5	145					83	3.6
C	20	DEAN EVASON	67	7	7	14	-6	38	1		1		68	10.3
C	17	BOB SWEENEY	72	7	7	14	-20	65		1	1		62	11.3
D	5	TOMMY ALBELIN	73	1	13	14	1	18					121	.8
R	45	JOCELYN LEMIEUX	67	5	7	12	-19	45					90	5.6
D	7	JAMIE HUSCROFT	70	3	9	12	14	162			1		57	5.3
R	23	SHELDON KENNEDY	41	3	7	10	3	36			1		54	5.6
C	47	CLAUDE LAPOINTE	35	4	5	9	1	20		2	1		44	9.1
R	42	*ED WARD	41	3	5	8	-2	44					33	9.1
C	28	*MARTY MURRAY	15	3	3	6	-4		2				22	13.6
L	36	*YVES SARAULT	25	2	1	3	-9	8			1		26	7.7
D	8	TRENT YAWNEY	69		3	3	-1	88					51	
D	4	KEVIN DAHL	32	1	1	2	-2	26			1		17	5.9
G	31	RICK TABARACCI	43		2	2	0	8						
G	37	TREVOR KIDD	47		2	2	0	4						
R	46	*LADISLAV KOHN	5	1		1	-1	2					8	12.5
C	38	*CRAIG FERGUSON	18	1		1	-9	6					20	5.0
C	38	JARROD SKALDE	1				0							
R	35	*NIKLAS SUNDBLAD	2				0						3	
C	17	*TODD HLUSHKO	4				0	6					6	
D	5	*JOEL BOUCHARD	4				0	4						
L	19	*VESA VIITAKOSKI	5				-1	2					7	
D	27	*TODD SIMPSON	6				0	32					3	
D	29	*CALE HULSE	11				1	20					9	
D	39	DAN KECZMER	13				-6	14					13	

GP = games played; G = goals; A = assists; PTS = points; +/- = goals-for minus goals-against while player is on ice; PIM = penalties in minutes; PP = power play goals; SH = shorthanded goals; GW = game-winning goals; GT = game-tying goals; S = no. of shots; PCT = percentage of goals to shots; * = rookie

TOMMY ALBELIN

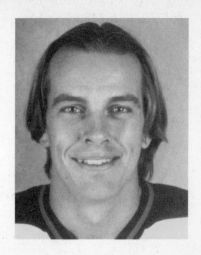

Yrs. of NHL service: 9
Born: Stockholm, Sweden; May 21, 1964
Position: defense
Height: 6-1
Weight: 190
Uniform no.: 5
Shoots: left

Career statistics:

GP	G	A	TP	PIM
473	29	135	164	313

1992-93 statistics:

GP	G	A	TP	+/-	PIM	PP	SH	GW	GT	S	PCT
36	1	5	6	0	14	1	0	1	0	33	3.0

1993-94 statistics:

GP	G	A	TP	+/-	PIM	PP	SH	GW	GT	S	PCT
62	2	17	19	+20	36	1	0	1	0	62	3.2

1994-95 statistics:

GP	G	A	TP	+/-	PIM	PP	SH	GW	GT	S	PCT
48	5	10	15	+9	20	2	0	0	0	60	8.3

1995-96 statistics:

GP	G	A	TP	+/-	PIM	PP	SH	GW	GT	S	PCT
73	1	13	14	+1	18	0	0	0	0	121	0.8

LAST SEASON

Acquired from New Jersey with Cale Hulse and Jocelyn Lemieux for Phil Housley and Dan Keczmer, Feb. 26, 1996. Missed six games with bruised thigh.

THE FINESSE GAME

Albelin is a strong skater, and agile enough to be used as a checking forward, which the Devils did for 13 games last season. He is fluid, with a big loping stride that covers a lot of ground with little wasted motion. Albelin skates backwards well and keeps his body positioned to break up passes. He can quickly turn an interception into a breakout pass as he sees his options well and doesn't panic with the puck.

Albelin doesn't like to carry the puck, preferring to use his teammates, but he can lug it if necessary. He has good hand skills for handling the puck if he goes in deep, although he usually stays at the tops of the circle (unless, of course, he is playing forward).

Albelin isn't a great power play quarterback because his shot is not overpowering, nor does it always get through to the net. He is a smart penalty killer.

THE PHYSICAL GAME

Albelin gets good drive from his powerful legs to take his man out along the boards. He isn't a big open-ice hitter. Albelin won't be intimidated and he is slow to rile, which is unpopular with some coaches who would prefer a bit more emotion.

THE INTANGIBLES

Albelin is like a white shirt; he goes with everything. He is versatile enough to play forward or defense, or play the right or left side on D. He can complement nearly any kind of player. He is like a utility infielder in baseball. Albelin may not have his own niche, but he can fill a lot of cracks in a team.

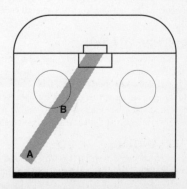

STEVE CHIASSON

Yrs. of NHL service: 10
Born: Barrie, Ont.; Apr. 14, 1967
Position: left defense
Height: 6-1
Weight: 205
Uniform no.: 21
Shoots: left

Career statistics:

GP	G	A	TP	PIM
547	75	225	300	948

1992-93 statistics:

GP	G	A	TP	+/-	PIM	PP	SH	GW	GT	S	PCT
79	12	50	62	+14	155	6	0	1	0	227	5.3

1993-94 statistics:

GP	G	A	TP	+/-	PIM	PP	SH	GW	GT	S	PCT
82	13	33	46	+17	122	4	1	2	0	238	5.5

1994-95 statistics:

GP	G	A	TP	+/-	PIM	PP	SH	GW	GT	S	PCT
45	2	23	25	+10	39	1	0	0	0	110	1.8

1995-96 statistics:

GP	G	A	TP	+/-	PIM	PP	SH	GW	GT	S	PCT
76	8	25	33	+3	62	5	0	2	0	175	4.6

He takes his leadership role to heart, and is an assistant captain.

LAST SEASON

Second among team defensemen in scoring. One of only five players to score on a penalty shot. Missed six games with hip injury and concussion.

THE FINESSE GAME

Chiasson's finesse game has improved along with his skating. The two go hand-in-hand (or foot-in-skate), and Chiasson has dedicated himself to improving in this critical area. He still has a bit of a choppy stride, but he's quick and better at getting himself into position offensively. He has a cannon shot. He saw more power play time last season, often on the second unit.

Chiasson is not afraid to gamble in deep, either, and has good instincts about when to pinch in. He handles the puck well down low and uses a snap or wrist shot. He is poised with the puck on the attack. Chiasson one-times a shot well.

Defensively, he plays a solid positional game and reads rushes well. While not great in any one area (save, perhaps, his shot), he has a nice overall package of skills.

THE PHYSICAL GAME

Chiasson is a competitor. He will play hurt, he will defend his teammates and he is prepared to compete every night. He lacked conditioning early in his career and it hurt him, but he has matured in his approach to his livelihood and it's paying off. Chiasson keeps his emotions under wraps and plays a disciplined game.

THE INTANGIBLES

Chiasson has become a solid two-way defenseman and is one of the game's more underrated blueliners.

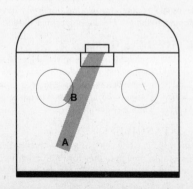

THEOREN FLEURY

Yrs. of NHL service: 8
Born: Oxbow, Sask.; June 29, 1968
Position: right wing/centre
Height: 5-6
Weight: 160
Uniform no.: 14
Shoots: right

Career statistics:

GP	G	A	TP	PIM
568	278	338	616	1103

1992-93 statistics:

GP	G	A	TP	+/-	PIM	PP	SH	GW	GT	S	PCT
83	34	66	100	+14	88	12	2	4	0	250	13.6

1993-94 statistics:

GP	G	A	TP	+/-	PIM	PP	SH	GW	GT	S	PCT
83	40	45	85	+30	186	16	1	6	0	278	14.4

1994-95 statistics:

GP	G	A	TP	+/-	PIM	PP	SH	GW	GT	S	PCT
47	29	29	58	+6	112	9	2	5	0	173	16.8

1995-96 statistics:

GP	G	A	TP	+/-	PIM	PP	SH	GW	GT	S	PCT
80	46	50	96	+17	112	17	5	4	0	353	13.0

LAST SEASON

Led team in power play goals for third consecutive season. Led team in goals, points and shots for second consecutive season. Third in NHL in shots. Led team in assists and plus-minus. Third on team in game-winning goals. Missed two games with eye injury.

THE FINESSE GAME

Fleury continues to prove that a small man can excel in a big man's game. Possessing great speed and quickness, he often seems to be dancing over the ice with his blades barely touching the frozen surface. He is always on the move, which is as much a tactic as an instinct for survival. You can't catch what you can't hit. He uses his outside speed to burn slower, bigger defensemen, or he can burst up the middle and split two defenders. He uses all of the ice.

A better finisher than playmaker, Fleury is not at his best handling the puck; he's much better at receiving the pass late and then making things happen. He always has his legs churning, and he draws penalties by driving to the net. He has a strong wrist shot that he can get away from almost anywhere. He can score even if he is pulled to his knees.

Fleury is an effective penalty killer, blocking shots and getting the puck out along the boards. He is very poised and cool with the puck under attack, holding it until he finds an opening instead of just firing blindly. His defensive play has improved, and he does a good job as a backchecker in holding up opposing forwards so his defensemen have extra time with the puck.

His hand quickness makes him very effective on draws, and he will take offensive-zone draws.

THE PHYSICAL GAME

Fleury can take a hit and not get knocked down because he is so solid and has a low centre of gravity. He uses his stick liberally and will take a lot of penalties sticking up for himself and his teammates.

THE INTANGIBLES

Only his size prevents Fleury from being among the NHL's elite forwards. We predicted he would flirt with the 100-point mark again, which he did in a dull Calgary season, but what was most impressive with Fleury's effort was the fact that he did it while being diagnosed with Crohn's Disease. Fleury underwent testing and experimentation with different kinds of medication while never missing a beat (the only two games he missed came as a result of getting hit in the face while he was sitting on the bench).

Fleury is a fiery leader who never backs down. Those Saddledome fans who booed him early in the season should hang their ten-gallon heads in shame.

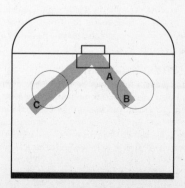

DAVE GAGNER

Yrs. of NHL service: 10
Born: Chatham, Ont.; Dec. 11, 1964
Position: centre
Height: 5-10
Weight: 180
Uniform no.: 15
Shoots: left

Career statistics:

GP	G	A	TP	PIM
717	265	318	613	850

1992-93 statistics:

GP	G	A	TP	+/-	PIM	PP	SH	GW	GT	S	PCT
84	33	43	76	-13	141	17	0	5	1	230	14.3

1993-94 statistics:

GP	G	A	TP	+/-	PIM	PP	SH	GW	GT	S	PCT
76	32	29	61	+13	83	10	0	6	1	213	15.0

1994-95 statistics:

GP	G	A	TP	+/-	PIM	PP	SH	GW	GT	S	PCT
48	14	28	42	+2	42	7	0	2	1	138	10.1

1995-96 statistics:

GP	G	A	TP	+/-	PIM	PP	SH	GW	GT	S	PCT
73	21	28	49	-19	103	7	0	3	0	215	9.8

LAST SEASON

Acquired from Dallas by Toronto with a sixth-round draft pick for Benoit Hogue and Randy Wood, Jan. 29, 1996. Acquired from Toronto for a third-round draft pick, June 22, 1996. Missed nine games with two concussions and a sprained shoulder.

THE FINESSE GAME

Gagner can score from just about anywhere except way out by the blueline. He can score off the rush or set up other players. He will pick up garbage goals, scoop up clean ones, finish off an outnumbered attack, or score off a drive down the wing with just his shot. He doesn't overpower goalies with his shot, but he has a quick and cunning release. Defensemen will sometimes back off him on a rush because he does have some moves to slip past them. On the power play he can work down low, though he works better coming off the half-wall.

Gagner's speed isn't as noticeable as his quickness. In a 20-foot radius, he's pretty quick, and he can throw in several dekes low as he drives to the net.

He is not a good defensive player. He is only average on face-offs.

THE PHYSICAL GAME

Gagner plays a tenacious, in-your-face offensive style. For a smaller player, he is pretty resilient. He stays in the traffic and doesn't get bounced out too easily. He can get overmatched one-on-one, but he tries to avoid battles where he can't use his quickness. Gagner's hard work is an inspiration to his teammates.

THE INTANGIBLES

Gagner will be reunited with Pierre Page (his former coach in Minnesota) in Calgary, and should get plenty of ice time on a team that is shaky up the middle. One caveat: Gagner suffered two concussions last season, and his play understandably suffered.

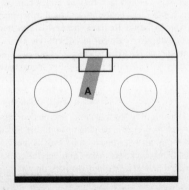

CALE HULSE

Yrs. of NHL service: 0
Born: Edmonton, Alberta; Nov. 10, 1973
Position: right defense
Height: 6-3
Weight: 210
Uniform no.: 29
Shoots: right

Career statistics:

GP	G	A	TP	PIM
11	0	0	0	20

1995-96 statistics:

GP	G	A	TP	+/-	PIM	PP	SH	GW	GT	S	PCT
11	0	0	0	+1	20	0	0	0	0	9	0.0

LAST SEASON

Acquired from New Jersey with Tommy Albelin and Jocelyn Lemieux for Phil Housley and Dan Keczmer, Feb. 26, 1996. Appeared in combined 55 games with Albany and Saint John of the AHL, scoring 6-30 — 36.

THE FINESSE GAME

Hulse has improved his puckhandling skills, which was one of his weakest areas, and has put together a solid two-way game that relies more heavily on his defensive ability and willingness to hit.

Hulse is a better than average skater. He doesn't have brilliant speed, but he has a long, strong stride with good balance. His agility is fine for a player of his size.

Hulse has a good shot from the point. He isn't too offensive minded, but he is smart enough to join the rush and could work on a second power play unit with more experience. Intelligent and steady, he may also develop into a mainstay on the penalty-killing squad.

THE PHYSICAL GAME

Hulse is tough, an outstanding fighter who doesn't go looking for trouble but won't back down from a challenge, either. He will hit hard along the boards and in the corners. Hulse is not a strong open-ice hitter, but he plays well positionally and makes attackers pay the price for coming into his piece of the ice. Hulse is intense and won't take a night, or a shift, off.

THE INTANGIBLES

Hulse is ready to step into the NHL, and was only reluctantly given up by the defense-deep Devils who had hoped Phil Housley would be the missing piece in their playoff run (wrong). Hulse's numbers may not ever be impressive, but his overall game will be. He could be among Calgary's top four defensemen by the midpoint of the season.

JAROME IGINLA

Yrs. of NHL service: 0
Born: Edmonton, Alberta; July 1, 1977
Position: right wing
Height: 6-1
Weight: 193
Uniform no.: 24
Shoots: right

Career junior statistics:

GP	G	A	TP	PIM
183	102	134	246	264

1995-96 junior statistics:

GP	G	A	TP	+/P
63	63	73	136	120

LAST SEASON

Acquired from Calgary with Corey Millen for Joe Nieuwendyk, Dec. 19, 1995. Second in scoring for Kamloops (WHL).

THE FINESSE GAME

Iginla is an ideal second-line player. In talent-starved Calgary, he will be asked to work on the first line and may be in a bit over his head, especially as a player fresh out of junior. He looked fine on a first line with Theo Fleury and German Titov (so long, Michael Nylander) in his two-game playoff trial, but adrenaline only goes so far.

Iginla doesn't have great speed but he is smart and energetic. His defensive play actually developed first in junior, and the scoring touch later, which is the reverse for most young players and is one of the reasons why Iginla is such a prized prospect. He may never be a great scorer and will have to work hard for his goals. Throw out Adam Graves' one 50-goal season and you are looking at Iginla's future.

Iginla does his best work in the corners and in front of the net. He is strong, and doesn't mind the trench warfare. In fact, he thrives on it.

THE PHYSICAL GAME

Iginla is gritty, powerful and aggressive. He will take a hit to make a play but, even better, he will initiate the hits. He has a mean streak and will have to control himself at the same time he is proving his mettle around the NHL; a fine line to walk.

THE INTANGIBLES

The key word to describe Iginla is character. He has played on winners in Kamloops (two Memorial Cups) and Team Canada (one World Junior Championship). He was not a bit player in those titles, either. Although much will be expected of him on a weak team, Iginla is a solid Calder Trophy prospect and will be an impact player in the NHL for years to come.

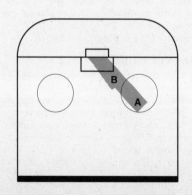

TREVOR KIDD

Yrs. of NHL service: 3
Born: Dugald, Man.; March 29, 1972
Position: goaltender
Height: 6-2
Weight: 190
Uniform no.: 37
Catches: left

Career statistics:

GP	MIN	GA	SO	GAA	A	PIM
123	6767	319	6	2.83	7	10

1993-94 statistics:

GP	MIN	GAA	W	L	T	SO	GA	S	SAPCT	PIM
31	1614	3.16	13	7	6	0	85	752	.887	4

1994-95 statistics:

GP	MIN	GAA	W	L	T	SO	GA	S	SAPCT	PIM
43	2463	2.61	22	14	6	3	107	1170	.909	2

1995-96 statistics:

GP	MIN	GAA	W	L	T	SO	GA	S	SAPCT	PIM
47	2570	2.78	15	21	8	3	119	1130	.895	4

LAST SEASON

Allowed penalty shot goal by Joe Sakic (Jan. 14, 1996).

THE PHYSICAL GAME

Kidd is a big goalie who loses his size advantage by going to his knees and staying there. He is a butterfly-style netminder who is good low, but he has an extremely awkward style. There are a lot of times when Kidd gets up so slowly from a skirmish that he looks as if he's been injured. His technique needs a great deal of work.

Kidd is a flopper, and since he is athletic, he is able to make his saves on sheer talent alone. He concentrates well to keep his attention on the puck through screens, but he often plays too deep in his net. Kidd will challenge shooters, but when he does he tends to lunge at them, rather than move out and keep himself square to the shooter.

Kidd is one of the better skating goalies in the league, and he is very quick at coming out to stop the hard-arounds behind his net. He has adapted well to the seamless glass in his home Saddledome rink. The puck can zip off the glass in a hurry, but Kidd plays it confidently.

THE MENTAL GAME

Kidd has won and lost the number one goalie role several times, and right now it is his by default. He is competitive, and he has not had the benefit of playing behind a very good team during the past two years.

THE INTANGIBLES

Kidd was drafted ahead of both Martin Brodeur and Felix Potvin in 1990, but both of those goalies are more accomplished and we don't think Kidd will ever be in their class.

PAUL KRUSE

Yrs. of NHL service: 4
Born: Merritt, B.C.; March 15, 1970
Position: left wing
Height: 6-0
Weight: 202
Uniform no.: 12
Shoots: left

Career statistics:

GP	G	A	TP	PIM
232	22	29	51	584

1992-93 statistics:

GP	G	A	TP	+/-	PIM	PP	SH	GW	GT	S	PCT
27	2	3	5	+2	41	0	0	0	0	17	11.8

1993-94 statistics:

GP	G	A	TP	+/-	PIM	PP	SH	GW	GT	S	PCT
68	3	8	11	-6	185	0	0	0	0	52	5.8

1994-95 statistics:

GP	G	A	TP	+/-	PIM	PP	SH	GW	GT	S	PCT
45	11	5	16	+13	141	0	0	2	0	52	21.2

1995-96 statistics:

GP	G	A	TP	+/-	PIM	PP	SH	GW	GT	S	PCT
75	3	12	15	-5	145	0	0	0	0	83	3.6

LAST SEASON

Third on team in penalty minutes. Missed games with pulled stomach muscle.

THE FINESSE GAME

Kruse is a prime example of a player who, with natural skating ability and a willingness to work and listen to his coaches, has developed an NHL career with just a modicum of skills. Kruse spent considerable time in the minors to work on his defensive game. He has become a player who won't make the big mistake. He will make the short outlet pass, or chip a puck off the boards if that is the safest play. He doesn't seek headlines, just playing time.

He understands defensive zone coverage and how to position himself for the outlet pass. He is fundamentally sound and gaining more confidence with increased playing time.

Kruse is fast in the flat and quick in the corners. A solid skater, he gets good leg drive to work the boards. He does not have great hands, and doesn't handle the puck well when moving, but is smart enough to know his limitations and doesn't try to do too much. Kruse's scoring chances come off forced turnovers and work around the net.

THE PHYSICAL GAME

Kruse is an agitator. Solid and sturdy, with a little mean streak, the rugged Kruse gets involved and is a player who has opponents looking over their shoulders. He has piled up the penalty minutes wherever he has played, so he has to learn to pick his spots. He is not a legitimate NHL heavyweight, but he will go toe-to-toe with the game's other big men and always ac-

quits himself well. His abdominal injury in February affected his last half of the season.

THE INTANGIBLES

Kruse's lack of production will keep him on the bench or on the bubble. He brings a lot of enthusiasm to the ice. He also has to bring some points.

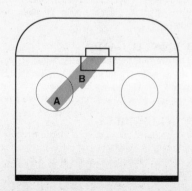

JOCELYN LEMIEUX

Yrs. of NHL service: 10
Born: Mont-Laurier, Que.; Mov. 18, 1967
Position: right wing
Height: 5-10
Weight: 200
Uniform no.: 45
Shoots: left

Career statistics:

GP	G	A	TP	PIM
566	76	81	157	713

1992-93 statistics:

GP	G	A	TP	+/-	PIM	PP	SH	GW	GT	S	PCT
81	10	21	31	+5	111	1	0	2	1	117	8.5

1993-94 statistics:

GP	G	A	TP	+/-	PIM	PP	SH	GW	GT	S	PCT
82	18	9	27	-3	82	0	0	2	1	151	11.9

1994-95 statistics:

GP	G	A	TP	+/-	PIM	PP	SH	GW	GT	S	PCT
41	6	5	11	-7	32	0	0	1	0	78	7.7

1995-96 statistics:

GP	G	A	TP	+/-	PIM	PP	SH	GW	GT	S	PCT
67	5	7	12	-19	45	0	0	0	0	90	5.6

LAST SEASON

Acquired from Hartford with a second-round draft pick by New Jersey for Jim Dowd and a second-round draft pick, Dec. 19, 1995. Acquired from New Jersey with Tommy Albelin and Cale Hulse for Phil Housley and Dan Keczmer, Feb. 26, 1996. Missed two games with bruised shoulder.

THE FINESSE GAME

If Lemieux had only half the scoring sense and shot that his brother, Claude, does, he would be any team's MVP. Lemieux skates with short, powerful strides. He is very well balanced and does not get pushed off the puck easily. He has good end-to-end speed, but is not real fancy and doesn't have a clever head. Lemieux is not creative enough to get much power play time, but his puck pursuit makes him a strong penalty killer.

His quick little strides serve him well along the boards and in the corners, and he keeps driving through traffic. He has a good wrist and snap shot.

Coaches love Lemieux's effort, but there is so little to show for it, and as a result he is relegated to checking roles.

THE PHYSICAL GAME

Lemieux is not coy. His theory is that the shortest distance between two points means eliminating one of the points, which he usually does with a flattening check. He loves to play through his checks and he makes opposing defensemen hesitant with his persistent pressure.

A bulldog with the puck or without it, Lemieux has little regard for his physical safety or, it seems, his lifespan, as he fearlessly throws himself in the face of bigger players with even meaner reputations than his. He leads by example and is unselfish. Lemieux knows that physical play is the key part of his game and he brings it to the ice almost every night. He keeps himself in phenomenal shape and can take increased ice time.

THE INTANGIBLES

Lemieux is consistently feisty and physical, but he's had nagging health problems and will probably have trouble getting much ice time. A 20-goal season would be a surprise.

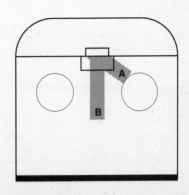

SANDY MCCARTHY

Yrs. of NHL service: 3
Born: Toronto, Ont.; June 15, 1972
Position: right wing
Height: 6-3
Weight: 225
Uniform no.: 15
Shoots: right

Career statistics:

GP	G	A	TP	PIM
191	19	15	34	447

1993-94 statistics:

GP	G	A	TP	+/-	PIM	PP	SH	GW	GT	S	PCT
79	5	5	10	-3	173	0	0	0	0	39	12.8

1994-95 statistics:

GP	G	A	TP	+/-	PIM	PP	SH	GW	GT	S	PCT
37	5	3	8	+1	101	0	0	2	0	29	17.2

1995-96 statistics:

GP	G	A	TP	+/-	PIM	PP	SH	GW	GT	S	PCT
75	9	7	16	-8	173	3	0	1	0	98	9.2

LAST SEASON

Led team in penalty minutes. Missed 17 games with rib injury.

THE FINESSE GAME

A surprisingly high draft pick in 1991 (52nd overall), McCarthy wasn't exactly singled out for his finesse skills. He does have some scoring instincts, however, enough to earn him a future role on the third line and some power play shifts on the second unit. McCarthy knows his job in the attacking zone is to drive to the net and screen the goalie. He is hard to budge from in front of the net and will take some abuse to fight for a loose rebound.

He has a decent shot but most of his chances will come from in close. As he becomes a better skater, he will be able to force the play off the forecheck. McCarthy will pressure more than a few defensemen into a hurry-up pass if he gets a good head of steam going.

McCarthy has to work more on his defensive game to become a better all-around player.

THE PHYSICAL GAME

McCarthy has taken a mature approach to improving his off-ice conditioning program. He is massive and he works on his leg strength to get more power out of his stride and to be more of a force around the net. McCarthy doesn't back down from any challenge, and he can throw 'em when the gloves come off.

THE INTANGIBLES

Enormous forwards who can also play are a rare and coveted commodity in the NHL; Calgary showed its faith in McCarthy with a three-year, $2.5-million contract after last season. His injury restricted his development. He will have to continue to take another stride forward. With good work habits, he could become a 10-15 goal scorer and an intimidating physical presence.

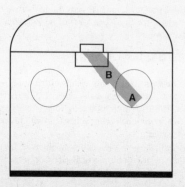

MICHAEL NYLANDER

Yrs. of NHL service: 3
Born: Stockholm, Sweden; Oct. 3, 1972
Position: centre
Height: 5-11
Weight: 190
Uniform no.: 92
Shoots: left

Career statistics:

GP	G	A	TP	PIM
211	41	103	144	88

1992-93 statistics:

GP	G	A	TP	+/-	PIM	PP	SH	GW	GT	S	PCT
59	11	22	33	-7	36	3	0	1	0	85	12.9

1993-94 statistics:

GP	G	A	TP	+/-	PIM	PP	SH	GW	GT	S	PCT
73	13	42	55	+8	30	4	0	1	2	95	13.7

1994-95 statistics:

GP	G	A	TP	+/-	PIM	PP	SH	GW	GT	S	PCT
6	0	1	1	+1	2	0	0	0	0	2	0.0

1995-96 statistics:

GP	G	A	TP	+/-	PIM	PP	SH	GW	GT	S	PCT
73	17	38	55	0	20	4	0	6	0	163	10.4

LAST SEASON

Led team in game-winning goals. Third on team in assists and points. Points matched career high. Missed three games with wrist injury. Missed one game with flu.

THE FINESSE GAME

Nylander is a one-way forward who isn't even consistent enough in his production to earn a spot on a number one line. Some nights Nylander will cut to the net with the puck and fight through checks; some nights he will hang on the perimeter.

An excellent skater with great composure with the puck, Nylander hangs onto the disk and looks at all the options to make a play. This is a gift — not a skill that a coach can teach. He holds the puck until the last split second before making the pass, a skill that has earned him some comparisons to Wayne Gretzky, but Nylander does not resemble the Great One in any other way.

Nylander can do things with the puck that are magical. The Swede knows all about time and space. He is an open-ice player, but still needs to improve his shot. If anything, he is guilty of hanging onto the puck too long and passing up quality scoring chances to force a pass to a teammate who is not in as good a position for the shot.

THE PHYSICAL GAME

Nylander is on the small side and plays even smaller. He will use his body to protect the puck, though he won't fight hard to get it away from the opposition.

THE INTANGIBLES

Nylander had a public spat with Pierre Page in Calgary and is likely to be on the trade block this season. He is still young and has great potential, but his situation is much like Alexei Kovalev's in New York. Nylander doesn't have the maturity to go with his talent. The young Swede has to realize that the game doesn't revolve around him.

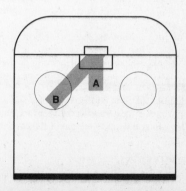

JAMES PATRICK

Yrs. of NHL service: 12
Born: Winnipeg, Man.; June 14, 1963
Position: right defense
Height: 6-2
Weight: 205
Uniform no.: 3
Shoots: right

Career statistics:

GP	G	A	TP	PIM
856	117	427	544	623

1992-93 statistics:

GP	G	A	TP	+/-	PIM	PP	SH	GW	GT	S	PCT
60	5	21	26	+1	61	3	0	0	0	99	5.1

1993-94 statistics:

GP	G	A	TP	+/-	PIM	PP	SH	GW	GT	S	PCT
68	10	25	35	-5	40	5	1	2	1	91	11.0

1994-95 statistics:

GP	G	A	TP	+/-	PIM	PP	SH	GW	GT	S	PCT
43	0	10	10	-3	14	0	0	0	0	43	0.0

1995-96 statistics:

GP	G	A	TP	+/-	PIM	PP	SH	GW	GT	S	PCT
80	3	32	35	+3	30	1	0	0	0	116	2.6

LAST SEASON

Led team defensemen in scoring. Fourth on team in assists. Missed two games with concussion.

THE FINESSE GAME

Coming off his most disappointing season (in 1994-95), Patrick accepted a $400,000 pay cut to play for the Flames last season, and was their most consistent defenseman.

Patrick is a gifted offensive defenseman, a wonderful, fluid skater. He skates backwards faster than many NHLers can skate forwards. He carries the puck out of the zone or makes the smart first pass and follows up on the play.

The criticism of Patrick over the years is that he makes everything look easy — so easy it looks like he isn't challenging himself, never pushing the envelope to see if there is another level to his game. The flip side of that — the conservative side — is that he is aware of his limitations and plays within them. There will always be two camps of opinion as far as Patrick is concerned.

There is no doubt that Patrick is a better support player than a star. He would rather pass than shoot, and if the pass isn't there he will take a stride over the redline and dump in the puck, always timing it well so that his mates are on the chase.

He plays the point on the power play and uses a strong, accurate wrist shot that he keeps low and on net. He will also cheat to the top of the circle for a one-timer.

THE PHYSICAL GAME

Patrick has never played to his size and isn't about to start now. He gets in the way. He bumps. He ties people up. But he doesn't bulldoze his crease or scrap one-on-one along the boards. He uses his finesse skills as his defense.

THE INTANGIBLES

Patrick is a class act and a gentleman, a grand addition to any team with young defensemen, since he will take the time and trouble to try to help their development. Patrick also goes out of his way to help the non-North Americans feel a part of the team.

Patrick has battled colitis for the past two seasons and is a bit fragile, but he played most of the season as a top four defenseman at a time when it looked like he was slowing down to a sixth or even a seventh. His days of big numbers are over.

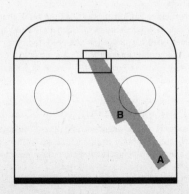

64

RON STERN

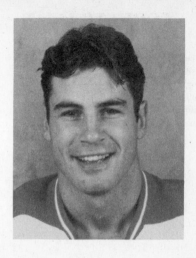

Yrs. of NHL service: 7
Born: Ste. Agathe, Que.; Jan. 11, 1967
Position: right wing
Height: 6-0
Weight: 195
Uniform no.: 22
Shoots: right

Career statistics:

GP	G	A	TP	PIM
414	57	62	119	1611

1992-93 statistics:

GP	G	A	TP	+/-	PIM	PP	SH	GW	GT	S	PCT
70	10	15	25	+4	207	0	0	1	0	82	12.2

1993-94 statistics:

GP	G	A	TP	+/-	PIM	PP	SH	GW	GT	S	PCT
71	9	20	29	+6	243	0	1	3	0	105	8.6

1994-95 statistics:

GP	G	A	TP	+/-	PIM	PP	SH	GW	GT	S	PCT
39	9	4	13	+4	163	1	0	0	0	69	13.0

1995-96 statistics:

GP	G	A	TP	+/-	PIM	PP	SH	GW	GT	S	PCT
52	10	5	15	+2	111	0	0	1	1	64	15.6

LAST SEASON

Missed 21 games with shoulder injury. Missed four games with suspension. Missed four games with back injury.

THE FINESSE GAME

Stern is a rugged, seek-and-destroy missile with modest skills. He is not a pretty skater or a good shooter, but he has the offensive instincts to make some smart plays in the attacking zone; his second effort often catches defenders napping. He has the quickness to get a jump on the defender, and looks for help from his linemates. He will drive to the cage and create his scoring chances off his physical involvement in front of the net.

Stern is not mesmerized by the puck. He doesn't make a lot of pretty plays but instead looks to get rid of the puck quickly with a pass or a shot.

He would be ideally suited as a checking winger but for his lack of skating ability. He also isn't as alert defensively as offensively, but he works hard at whatever task he is given.

THE PHYSICAL GAME

Stern makes his teammates feel a few inches taller and a few pounds heavier. He has no fear of anyone or any situation. He never bails out of a corner no matter what's coming. He's willing and able to go toe-to-toe with anybody. If he plays on a checking line, Stern is defensively aware and finishes every check. He can play in the crunch to protect a lead. If he plays on a fourth line, he will act as the catalyst, coming out with a strong shift to lift his bench.

THE INTANGIBLES

Stern's mission is to get momentum on the Flames' side. He is an effective fourth-liner. He plays with a sense of purpose. We thought 10 goals was his ceiling, but he surprised us by hitting that despite missing more than a quarter of the season due to injuries. If he can upgrade his production to 15 or so, that will be a fine contribution.

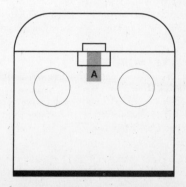

CORY STILLMAN

Yrs. of NHL service: 1
Born: Peterborough, Ont.; Dec. 20, 1970
Position: centre
Height: 6-0
Weight: 180
Uniform no.: 16
Shoots: left

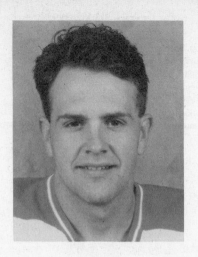

Career statistics:

GP	G	A	TP	PIM
84	16	21	37	43

1994-95 statistics:

GP	G	A	TP	+/-	PIM	PP	SH	GW	GT	S	PCT
10	0	2	2	+1	2	0	0	0	0	7	0.0

1995-96 statistics:

GP	G	A	TP	+/-	PIM	PP	SH	GW	GT	S	PCT
74	16	19	35	-5	41	4	1	3	0	132	12.1

LAST SEASON

First NHL season. Tied for fifth on team in points. Tied for ninth among NHL rookies in points. Missed one game with flu.

THE FINESSE GAME

An offensive specialist, Stillman was moved from centre to left wing, which is a more defensive position in the Calgary system. Although this may have hampered his offensive production, it will make Stillman a better all-around player in the long run.

Stillman brings a centre's playmaking ability to the wing. He is intelligent and has good hockey instincts, but may not have that extra notch of speed needed to be a quality player at the NHL level. Since he's not very big, he needs every advantage he can get.

Stillman has a good enough point shot to be used on the power play on the second unit. He has good hands and a keen understanding of the game. Dale Hawerchuk isn't a great skater, either, but possesses great patience and puckhandling skills, and is efficient in small areas. Stillman has the potential to be that kind of player, if he is supported by gifted forwards. He needs to play with finishers.

THE PHYSICAL GAME

Stillman is thick and sturdy enough to absorb some hard hits. He is not overly aggressive, but will protect the puck.

THE INTANGIBLES

Stillman played on a number two line with the Flames last season and was one of only two rookies to survive a freshman purge as Calgary went with an older lineup. He is a coachable type. He has some upside but won't be a real impact player.

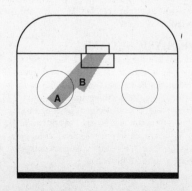

MIKE SULLIVAN

Yrs. of NHL service: 5
Born: Marshfield, Mass.; Feb. 27, 1968
Position: centre
Height: 6-2
Weight: 190
Uniform no.: 32
Shoots: left

Career statistics:

GP	G	A	TP	PIM
309	31	43	74	93

1992-93 statistics:

GP	G	A	TP	+/-	PIM	PP	SH	GW	GT	S	PCT
81	6	8	14	-42	30	0	2	0	0	95	6.3

1993-94 statistics:

GP	G	A	TP	+/-	PIM	PP	SH	GW	GT	S	PCT
45	4	5	9	-1	10	0	2	1	0	48	8.3

1994-95 statistics:

GP	G	A	TP	+/-	PIM	PP	SH	GW	GT	S	PCT
38	4	7	11	-2	14	0	0	2	0	31	12.9

1995-96 statistics:

GP	G	A	TP	+/-	PIM	PP	SH	GW	GT	S	PCT
81	9	12	21	-6	24	0	1	1	1	106	8.5

LAST SEASON

Career high in points. Games played matched career high.

THE FINESSE GAME

Speed, speed, speed. Sullivan is one of the flat-out fastest skaters in the league, but doesn't possess the hand skills to do much damage offensively. He is so much faster without the puck than with it.

Sullivan works hard and forechecks energetically. But his decision-making process is slow and he can't do much with the puck even when he forces a turnover. He can be asked to shadow some of the quickest forwards in the league.

He is effective killing penalties because of his speed and effort. He is fairly good on face-offs. He is able to bend low (he is a rather tall player) and tie up the opposing centre's stick.

THE PHYSICAL GAME

Sullivan does not play the body well. Considering his size, he would be so much more effective if he got involved. He could just flatten people because of his momentum, but he avoids contact.

THE INTANGIBLES

Sullivan is a blur when he is skimming impressively all over the ice, but he is not the asset he could be because of his bad hands.

GERMAN TITOV

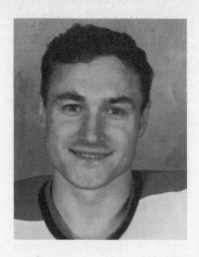

Yrs. of NHL service: 3
Born: Moscow, Russia; Oct. 16, 1965
Position: centre/left wing
Height: 6-1
Weight: 190
Uniform no.: 13
Shoots: left

Career statistics:

GP	G	A	TP	PIM
198	67	69	136	68

1993-94 statistics:

GP	G	A	TP	+/-	PIM	PP	SH	GW	GT	S	PCT
76	27	18	45	+20	28	8	3	2	0	153	17.6

1994-95 statistics:

GP	G	A	TP	+/-	PIM	PP	SH	GW	GT	S	PCT
40	12	12	24	+6	16	3	2	3	0	88	13.6

1995-96 statistics:

GP	G	A	TP	+/-	PIM	PP	SH	GW	GT	S	PCT
82	28	39	67	+9	24	13	2	2	2	214	13.1

LAST SEASON

Second on team in goals, assists, points and power play goals. Only Flame to appear in all 82 games.

THE FINESSE GAME

Titov uses a short stick and does a lot of one-handed puckhandling. This gives him good control and makes it harder for the defense to knock the puck loose without knocking him down and taking a penalty.

Titov was used primarily on the wing last season, but prefers playing centre and using all of the ice, weaving with his linemates (usually Michael Nylander and Theo Fleury). He will come down on his off-wing and cut to the net with a backhand shot. Titov shows great hockey sense in all zones. He is very creative, but is a streaky scorer. He was given the job on the top line due to Gary Roberts's absence, but didn't step up on a nightly basis.

Titov is an agile skater. Not outstandingly fast, he is very quick coming off the boards and driving to the circle for a shot. He has a good inside-out move and a change of gears. Strong on his skates, he is tough to knock down. He only adds to the Calgary Flames' depth on face-offs with his good hands on the draw. He kills penalties well and blocks shots.

THE PHYSICAL GAME

Titov uses his good size well. He takes a hit to make a play, blocks shots and sacrifices his body. He protects the puck in an unusual way, by getting his left leg out to kick away the stick of a defender so that he can sweep- or poke-check him. It's a move that requires superb balance.

THE INTANGIBLES

Titov needs to be combined with linemates who play a European style of weaving and puck control rather than dump-and-chase. Even though he played the left side — a defensive role under the Calgary left-wing lock system — he played the best hockey of his career, but wasn't consistent enough.

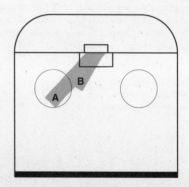

ZARLEY ZALAPSKI

Yrs. of NHL service: 8
Born: Edmonton, Alta.; Apr. 22, 1968
Position: right defense
Height: 6-1
Weight: 215
Uniform no.: 33
Shoots: left

Career statistics:

GP	G	A	TP	PIM
560	96	271	367	611

1992-93 statistics:

GP	G	A	TP	+/-	PIM	PP	SH	GW	GT	S	PCT
83	14	51	65	-34	94	8	1	0	0	192	7.3

1993-94 statistics:

GP	G	A	TP	+/-	PIM	PP	SH	GW	GT	S	PCT
69	10	37	47	-6	74	1	0	1	0	156	6.4

1994-95 statistics:

GP	G	A	TP	+/-	PIM	PP	SH	GW	GT	S	PCT
48	4	24	28	+9	46	1	0	1	0	76	5.3

1995-96 statistics:

GP	G	A	TP	+/-	PIM	PP	SH	GW	GT	S	PCT
80	12	17	29	+11	115	5	0	1	0	145	8.3

LAST SEASON

Missed two games due to illness.

THE FINESSE GAME

Zalapski is the ultimate tease. On any given night, he will elicit a "Wow!" and seem destined to be the next impact defenseman. The next night, he will make a mistake that costs his team the game. There is no level of consistency.

Zalapski has all-world offensive skills. He is a tremendous skater with speed and agility. He has great acceleration and scoring instincts to join or lead a rush, though his passing skills are overrated. The problem is that his vision of the ice is so weak that he might as well be hockey blind. He does not see any of his playmaking options, nor is he an intelligent shooter. He simply blasts away. He has a good enough shot to get by, but he could do so much more, and that is what is so frustrating. He could take something off his shot to make it more tippable. He could fake a slap and slide a pass into an open area of the ice. But he does not keep anyone guessing.

Zalapski is not a very good backskater, either. He doesn't read plays coming at him well, which makes him just a mess in the defensive zone. He hurries his hard-arounds without looking to see if the opposition is riding the boards waiting to pick off the pass.

THE PHYSICAL GAME

Zalapski adhered to a better fitness regime last season, which made his lack of consistent play all the more frustrating. One game in December illustrated the kind of force Zalapski could be, as he played tough around his net and rubbed his glove in the face of Mark Messier, of all people. He has the potential to be an absolutely dominating defenseman, but doesn't want to pay the price on a nightly basis.

THE INTANGIBLES

Zalapski played the last few months of the season with what proved to be an abdominal muscle tear. This probably contributed to his offensive falloff. Under normal circumstances, Zalapski is a 50-point producer, but seldom an impact defenseman.

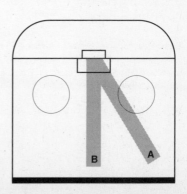

CHICAGO BLACKHAWKS

Players' Statistics 1995-96

POS.	NO.	PLAYER	GP	G	A	PTS	+/-	PIM	PP	SH	GW	GT	S	PCT
D	7	CHRIS CHELIOS	81	14	58	72	25	140	7		3		219	6.4
C	27	JEREMY ROENICK	66	32	35	67	9	109	12	4	2	2	171	18.7
D	20	GARY SUTER	82	20	47	67	3	80	12	2	4		242	8.3
R	10	TONY AMONTE	81	31	32	63	10	62	5	4	5		216	14.4
C	92	BERNIE NICHOLLS	59	19	41	60	11	60	6		2	2	100	19.0
L	55	*ERIC DAZE	80	30	23	53	16	18	2		2		167	18.0
R	17	JOE MURPHY	70	22	29	51	-3	86	8		3		212	10.4
C	18	DENIS SAVARD	69	13	35	48	20	102	2		1		110	11.8
L	32	MURRAY CRAVEN	66	18	29	47	20	36	5	1	7		86	20.9
R	24	BOB PROBERT	78	19	21	40	15	237	1		3		97	19.6
C	12	BRENT SUTTER	80	13	27	40	14	56			3		102	12.7
C	11	JEFF SHANTZ	78	6	14	20	12	24	1	2			72	8.3
D	4	KEITH CARNEY	82	5	14	19	31	94	1		1		69	7.2
R	25	SERGEI KRIVOKRASOV	46	6	10	16	10	32			1		52	11.5
D	2	ERIC WEINRICH	77	5	10	15	14	65					76	6.6
D	5	STEVE SMITH	37		9	9	12	71					17	
C	38	JAMES BLACK	13	3	3	6	1	16			1		23	13.0
L	19	BRENT GRIEVE	28	2	4	6	5	28					22	9.1
R	15	JIM CUMMINS	52	2	4	6	-1	180			2		34	5.9
D	39	ENRICO CICCONE	66	2	4	6	1	306					60	3.3
C	22	STEVE DUBINSKY	43	2	3	5	3	14					33	6.1
C	14	KIP MILLER	10	1	4	5	1	2				1	12	8.3
D	8	CAM RUSSELL	61	2	2	4	8	129					22	9.1
G	30	ED BELFOUR	50		2	2	0	36						
R	19	DANTON COLE	12	1		1	0						6	16.7
L	40	*ETHAN MOREAU	8		1	1	1	4					1	
G	31	JEFF HACKETT	35		1	1	0	8						
G	29	JIM WAITE	1				0							
D	6	*IVAN DROPPA	7				2	2					1	
D	3	BRAD WERENKA	9				-2	8					2	
R	23	*MIKE PROKOPEC	9				-4	5					5	

GP = games played; G = goals; A = assists; PTS = points; +/- = goals-for minus goals-against while player is on ice; PIM = penalties in minutes; PP = power play goals; SH = shorthanded goals; GW = game-winning goals; GT = game-tying goals; S = no. of shots; PCT = percentage of goals to shots; * = rookie

TONY AMONTE

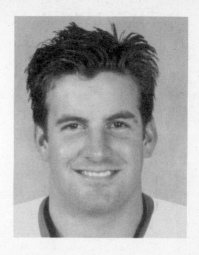

Yrs. of NHL service: 5
Born: Hingham, Mass.; Aug. 2, 1970
Position: left wing
Height: 6-0
Weight: 190
Uniform no.: 10
Shoots: left

Career statistics:

GP	G	A	TP	PIM
370	131	154	285	244

1992-93 statistics:

GP	G	A	TP	+/-	PIM	PP	SH	GW	GT	S	PCT
83	33	43	76	0	49	13	0	4	0	270	12.2

1993-94 statistics:

GP	G	A	TP	+/-	PIM	PP	SH	GW	GT	S	PCT
79	17	25	42	0	37	4	0	4	0	195	8.7

1994-95 statistics:

GP	G	A	TP	+/-	PIM	PP	SH	GW	GT	S	PCT
48	15	20	35	+7	41	6	1	3	1	105	14.3

1995-96 statistics:

GP	G	A	TP	+/-	PIM	PP	SH	GW	GT	S	PCT
81	31	32	63	+10	62	5	4	5	0	216	14.4

LAST SEASON

Second on team in goals and game-winning goals. Fourth on team in points. Tied for team lead in shorthanded goals.

THE FINESSE GAME

Amonte's work ethic was questioned early in his career, but he was Chicago's most consistent forward last season and his only question mark this year will be his recovery from a knee injury suffered in the playoffs.

Amonte is blessed with exceptional speed and acceleration. His timing is accurate and his anticipation keen. He has good balance and can carry the puck at a pretty good clip, though he is more effective when streaking down the wing and getting the puck late. Playing on the left side with high school teammate Jeremy Roenick, Amonte's forehand is open for one-timers. He has been called a young Yvan Cournoyer for the way he uses his speed to drive wide around the defense to the net. Eric Daze joined the line on the right side, and the rookie added size and power to the trio.

Amonte has a quick release on his wrist shot. He likes to go top shelf, just under the crossbar, and can also go to the backhand shot or a wrist shot off his back foot, like a fadeaway jumper. Amonte is a top power play man, since he is always working himself into open ice. He is an accurate shooter, but is also creative in his playmaking. He passes very well, and is conscious of where his teammates are and he usually makes the best percentage play.

Offensively, Amonte is a smart player away from the puck. He sets picks and creates openings for his teammates. He is an aggressive penalty killer and a shorthanded threat.

THE PHYSICAL GAME

Amonte's speed and movement keep him out of a lot of trouble zones, but he will also drive to the front of the net and take punishment there if that's the correct play. He loves to score, he loves to help his linemates score, and although he is outweighed by a lot of NHL defensemen, he is seldom outworked.

Amonte takes a lot of abuse and plays through the checks. He seldom takes bad retaliatory penalties. He just keeps his legs driving and draws calls with his non-stop skating.

THE INTANGIBLES

Amonte nearly made the 70 points we predicted last year, and if Roenick hadn't missed so much time due to injuries, Amonte would have scored more. His knee injury is troublesome, since so much of his game is based on his skating, but Amonte hoped to play in the World Cup and could be ready to start the season.

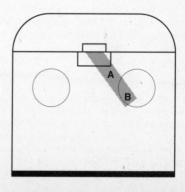

ED BELFOUR

Yrs. of NHL service: 6
Born: Carman, Man.; Apr. 21, 1965
Position: goaltender
Height: 5-11
Weight: 182
Uniform no.: 30
Catches: left

Career statistics:

GP	MIN	GA	SO	GAA	A	PIM
382	21713	959	29	2.65	15	216

1992-93 statistics:

GP	MIN	GAA	W	L	T	SO	GA	S	SAPCT	PIM
71	4106	2.59	41	18	11	7	177	1880	.906	28

1993-94 statistics:

GP	MIN	GAA	W	L	T	SO	GA	S	SAPCT	PIM
70	3998	2.67	37	24	6	7	178	1892	.906	61

1994-95 statistics:

GP	MIN	GAA	W	L	T	SO	GA	S	SAPCT	PIM
42	2450	2.28	22	15	3	5	93	990	.906	11

1995-96 statistics:

GP	MIN	GAA	W	L	T	SO	GA	S	SAPCT	PIM
50	2956	2.74	22	17	10	1	2.74	1373	.902	36

LAST SEASON

Led NHL goalies in penalty minutes. Posted 20 wins for sixth consecutive season. Missed eight games with recurring back injury. Missed one game with knee injury.

THE PHYSICAL GAME

Belfour's back injury made it difficult to truly judge his season. His style relies more on athleticism than technique. He is always on his belly, his side, his back. Belfour may be the best goalie with the worst style in the NHL.

Belfour has great instincts and reads the play well in front of him. He plays with an inverted V, giving the five-hole but usually taking it away from the shooter with his quick reflexes. He is very aggressive and frequently comes so far out of his crease that he gets tangled with his own defenders — as well as running interference on the opponents. He knows he is well-padded and is not afraid to use his body.

In fact, Belfour uses his body more than his stick or glove, and that is part of his problem. He tries to make the majority of saves with his torso, thus making the routine saves more difficult.

He tends to keep his glove low and the book on him is to shoot high, but that's the case with most NHL goalies and a lot of NHL shooters have trouble picking that spot. He sometimes gives up bad rebounds, but his defense is so good and so quick that they will swoop in on the puck before the opposition gets a second or third whack. When play is developing around his net, Belfour uses the odd-looking tactic of dropping his stick low along the ice to take away low shots and lunges at the puck. It's weird, but it's effective.

Belfour has a lot of confidence and an impressive ability to handle the puck, though he sometimes overdoes it. He will usually go for short passes, but can go for the home-run play as well. He uses his body to screen as he is handling the puck for a 15-foot pass.

THE MENTAL GAME

Belfour has to learn to channel his emotions, but it's difficult to put a lid on so intense a competitor. He takes matters into his own hands (and stick) around the net, and often takes bad penalties.

THE INTANGIBLES

The so-called "competition" between Belfour and Jeff Hackett was a bit overblown, since there was never any doubt who was number one in Chicago when healthy. Belfour had asked for a reduced workload at the start of the season (before his injuries started) to be fresher for the playoffs, but he was no doubt irked by the attention Hackett attracted with his solid play. Expect Belfour to train harder this summer, something he has gotten away from recently.

Belfour is heading into the last year of his contract, and will be the target of many trade rumours.

KEITH CARNEY

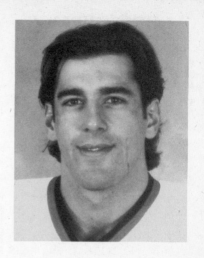

Yrs. of NHL service: 4
Born: Providence, R.I.; Feb. 3, 1970
Position: left defense
Height: 6-2
Weight: 205
Uniform no.: 4
Shoots: left

Career statistics:

GP	G	A	TP	PIM
181	13	28	41	217

1992-93 statistics:

GP	G	A	TP	+/-	PIM	PP	SH	GW	GT	S	PCT
30	2	4	6	+3	55	0	0	1	0	26	7.7

1993-94 statistics:

GP	G	A	TP	+/-	PIM	PP	SH	GW	GT	S	PCT
37	4	8	12	+14	39	0	0	0	0	37	10.8

1994-95 statistics:

GP	G	A	TP	+/-	PIM	PP	SH	GW	GT	S	PCT
18	0	1	1	-1	11	0	0	1	0	14	7.1

1995-96 statistics:

GP	G	A	TP	+/-	PIM	PP	SH	GW	GT	S	PCT
82	5	14	19	+31	94	1	0	1	0	69	7.2

LAST SEASON

Led team in plus-minus. One of two Blackhawks to appear in all 82 games.

THE FINESSE GAME

Carney was an offensive defenseman when he first tried to break into the league, but lacked the elite skills to succeed on that style alone. He has turned his finesse skills to his defensive advantage. Carney took advantage of Steve Smith's absence due to injury and proved himself as an everyday player.

Carney is quick and agile, and he positions himself well defensively. He is a smart penalty killer who worked on the first unit with Chris Chelios last season. He has good anticipation, reads plays well and moves the puck smoothly and quickly out of the zone.

THE PHYSICAL GAME

Carney is not a hitter, although he will get in the way of people. He will hit, but he's not punishing. He is a well-conditioned athlete who appreciates the second chance he's been given, and is about the last one off the ice in practice.

THE INTANGIBLES

Carney had been written off by the Sabres and nearly met the same fate in Chicago until the coaches made him a special project; Carney persevered to redefine his game. He is a capable fifth defenseman, and can even step up to a number four role in the right circumstances. His concentration on defense (and the roles of Chelios and Gary Suter as the offensive defensemen on the Hawks) will keep Carney's point total around 20-25.

CHRIS CHELIOS

Yrs. of NHL service: 12
Born: Chicago, Ill.; Jan. 25, 1962
Position: right defense
Height: 6-1
Weight: 186
Uniform no.: 7
Shoots: right

Career statistics:

GP	G	A	TP	PIM
848	143	529	672	1926

1992-93 statistics:

GP	G	A	TP	+/-	PIM	PP	SH	GW	GT	S	PCT
84	15	58	73	+14	282	8	0	2	0	290	5.2

1993-94 statistics:

GP	G	A	TP	+/-	PIM	PP	SH	GW	GT	S	PCT
76	16	44	60	+12	212	7	1	2	0	219	7.3

1994-95 statistics:

GP	G	A	TP	+/-	PIM	PP	SH	GW	GT	S	PCT
48	5	33	38	+17	72	3	1	0	0	166	3.0

1995-96 statistics:

GP	G	A	TP	+/-	PIM	PP	SH	GW	GT	S	PCT
81	14	58	72	+25	140	7	0	3	0	219	6.4

LAST SEASON

Won 1996 Norris Trophy. Led team defensemen in scoring for third consecutive season. One of two defensemen (with Phil Housley) to lead team in scoring. Fourth among NHL defensemen in scoring. Led team in assists. Second on team in power play goals.

THE FINESSE GAME

Chelios is among the top two-way defensemen in the league. Whatever the team needs they'll get from Chelios. He can become a top offensive defenseman, pinching boldly at every opportunity. He can create offense off the rush, make a play through the neutral zone or quarterback the power play from the point. He has a good, low, hard slap shot. He is not afraid to skate in deep, where he can handle the puck well and use a snap shot or wrist shot with a quick release. He and Gary Suter may have been the best power play point duo in the NHL last season.

If defense is needed, Chelios will rule in his own zone. He is extremely confident and poised with the puck and doesn't overhandle it. He wants to get the puck away from his net by the most expedient means possible. He is aggressive in forcing the puck carrier to make a decision by stepping up. Chelios also steps up in the neutral zone to break up plays with his stick.

Chelios is an instinctive player. When he is on his game, he reacts and makes plays few other defensemen can. When he struggles, which is seldom, he is back on his heels. He tries to do other people's jobs and becomes undisciplined.

He has excellent anticipation and is a strong penalty killer when he's not doing time in the box himself. He's a mobile, smooth skater with good lateral movement. He is seldom beaten one-on-one, and he's even tough facing a two-on-one. In his mind, he can do anything. He usually does.

THE PHYSICAL GAME

Chelios was already among the NHL's best in endurance, but the arrival of Gary Suter has made Chelios a more dedicated fitness advocate, and the two defensemen work out with a personal trainer.

Chelios doesn't seem to tire, no matter how much ice time he gets, and he routinely plays 30 minutes or handles four-minute shifts. He is not that big, but plays like an enormous defenseman. He is tough and physical, strong and solid on his skates, and has a mean streak the size of Lake Michigan. He is fearless. He has expressed an interest in playing a full 60 minutes some day. He could do it, too.

Chelios will someimes get frustrated and fight or take bad penalties, which is about the only way to get him off the ice. He plays with the heart and toughness of a much bigger player, and his pain threshhold is higher than the Sears Tower.

THE INTANGIBLES

Chelios won a Stanley Cup with Montreal, and desperately wants to do the same in Chicago. By adding some toughness (Bob Probert, Enrico Ciccone), the Blackhawks have made it a little tougher for opponents to run Chelios, and he should have an even better season this year with more freedom.

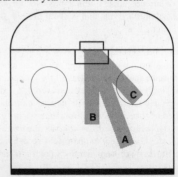

ENRICO CICCONE

Yrs. of NHL service: 4
Born: Montreal, Que.; Apr. 10, 1970
Position: left defense
Height: 6-4
Weight: 210
Uniform no.: 39
Shoots: left

Career statistics:

GP	G	A	TP	PIM
206	5	11	16	934

1992-93 statistics:

GP	G	A	TP	+/-	PIM	PP	SH	GW	GT	S	PCT
31	0	1	1	2	115	0	0	0	0	13	0.0

1993-94 statistics:

GP	G	A	TP	+/-	PIM	PP	SH	GW	GT	S	PCT
57	1	2	3	-4	226	0	0	0	0	33	3.0

1994-95 statistics:

GP	G	A	TP	+/-	PIM	PP	SH	GW	GT	S	PCT
41	2	4	6	+3	225	0	0	0	0	43	4.7

1995-96 statistics:

GP	G	A	TP	+/-	PIM	PP	SH	GW	GT	S	PCT
66	2	4	6	+1	306	0	0	0	0	60	3.3

THE INTANGIBLES

Ciccone may improve under Chicago's defensive system. He was obtained largely for his fierce reputation, and to protect teammates such as Chris Chelios.

LAST SEASON

Aqcuired from Tampa Bay for Patrick Poulin and Igor Ulanov, Mar. 20, 1996. Second in NHL and led team in penalty minutes. Missed 10 games with thumb injury.

THE FINESSE GAME

Ciccone's overall play is limited because of his skating. He has slow feet, and while he is well-balanced in tight quarters, he is at a disadvantage where any quick turn of foot is needed, even in corners or around the net. Chicago has a top six defense that is tough to crack, and Ciccone will have to add to his repertoire to get ice time. He has worked to improve his puck movement and positioning — two skills that can minimize his slow turn of foot.

Ciccone tends to overhandle the puck, especially in the defensive zone. He does block shots well, but he would be better off using bigger gloves (small ones come off more easily for fights) for defensive purposes. Ciccone has some skill and if he keeps working hard can earn a spot in the lineup.

THE PHYSICAL GAME

Ciccone doesn't back down from any challenge and often goes around issuing them himself. He can fight and he is a punishing checker. Coaches have tried to rein in his enthusiasm a bit, but they don't want to take away his physical presence. You can be tough without being dumb, and Ciccone has to learn the difference. He took some bad penalties in the the playoffs, which cost him ice time, and was involved in one particularly embarrassing incident on his way off the ice in Colorado.

MURRAY CRAVEN

Yrs. of NHL service: 14
Born: Medicine Hat, Alta.; July 20, 1964
Position: left wing/centre
Height: 6-2
Weight: 185
Uniform no.: 32
Shoots: left

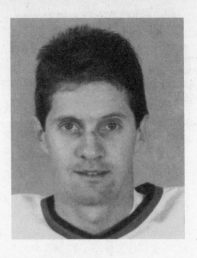

Career statistics:

GP	G	A	TP	PIM
867	242	437	679	465

1992-93 statistics:

GP	G	A	TP	+/-	PIM	PP	SH	GW	GT	S	PCT
77	25	52	77	-1	32	6	3	2	0	151	16.6

1993-94 statistics:

GP	G	A	TP	+/-	PIM	PP	SH	GW	GT	S	PCT
78	15	40	55	+5	30	2	1	3	0	115	13.0

1994-95 statistics:

GP	G	A	TP	+/-	PIM	PP	SH	GW	GT	S	PCT
16	4	3	7	+2	2	1	0	2	0	29	13.8

1995-96 statistics:

GP	G	A	TP	+/-	PIM	PP	SH	GW	GT	S	PCT
66	18	29	47	+20	36	5	1	7	0	86	20.9

LAST SEASON

Led team in game-winning goals. Tied for third on team in plus-minus. Missed 16 games with foot and back injuries.

THE FINESSE GAME

Craven is extremely versatile. He will check. He will score. He will play first unit on the power play or penalty killing. He will take draws. He will play right wing, left wing or centre.

Craven has never attained star status because, while he does a lot of things well, he isn't great at any one thing. He's a good skater, but doesn't have the hockey sense to use it as well he should. He isn't a natural scorer. He has to work hard for his 20 or so goals a season and scores most of them from close range. He does have a good slap shot, though, and can be used on the point on the power play in a pinch.

Craven is unselfish and, poised down low, he will confidently slide a backhand pass across the goal mouth to a teammate. He goes to the net with determination and has good hands for picking up loose pucks. He has a long reach and can beat a defender one-on-one by using his speed and dangling the puck away from his body but under control. He's no speed demon, but he plays well positionally.

THE PHYSICAL GAME

Craven is wiry but not very big. He loses some one-on-one battles in tight, but he uses his body effectively in the defensive as well as the offensive zone. He digs along the boards and in the corners for the puck.

THE INTANGIBLES

Craven has become a very good defensive role player who can also produce upwards of 20 goals a season — a pretty formidable combination. He is a complete hockey player, one who fits nicely into a role as a number two or number three centre, or winger.

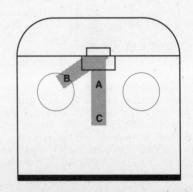

ERIC DAZE

Yrs. of NHL service: 1
Born: Montreal, Que.; July 2, 1975
Position: left wing
Height: 6-4
Weight: 202
Uniform no.: 55
Shoots: left

Career statistics:

GP	G	A	TP	PIM
84	31	24	55	20

1994-95 statistics:

GP	G	A	TP	+/-	PIM	PP	SH	GW	GT	S	PCT
4	1	1	2	+2	2	0	0	0	0	1	100.0

1995-96 statistics:

GP	G	A	TP	+/-	PIM	PP	SH	GW	GT	S	PCT
80	30	23	53	+16	18	2	0	2	0	167	18.0

LAST SEASON

Finalist for 1996 Calder Trophy. Named to NHL All-Rookie team. Led NHL rookies and second on team in goals. Second among rookies in points. Sixth among rookies in assists. Second among NHL rookies in shots. Led rookies in shooting percentage. Tied for rookie lead in plus-minus.

THE FINESSE GAME

Daze showed some sign of his NHL readiness when he joined the Blackhawks late in 1994-95, but he exceeded Chicago's hopes with an excellent rookie season.

While the most impressive thing about Daze is his size, it is his skating ability that sets him apart from other lumbering big men. He isn't a speed demon, but he skates well enough to not look out of place with linemates Tony Amonte and Jeremy Roenick.

Daze keeps his hands close together on his stick, and is able to get a lot on his shot with very little backswing. He has excellent hands for shooting or scoring, and is an adept stickhandler who can draw defenders to him and then slip a pass through to a teammate. Daze drives to the net and protects the puck, and may already be one of the best in the league at this. He sets screens on the power play. He has good hockey vision and an innate understanding of the game, and is also advanced defensively.

THE PHYSICAL GAME

Daze doesn't back down, but he doesn't show much initiative, either. That might develop this year as he becomes more comfortable in the league. He is very strong, and has a long reach so that he can pass or shoot the puck even when a defenseman thinks he has him all wrapped up and under control.

Daze slowed down drastically late in the season, with only seven goals in the last 36 games. That isn't uncommon for a player jumping to the NHL straight out of junior.

THE INTANGIBLES

Daze needs to play with forwards who will get him the puck. So as long as Chicago can provide the passers, Daze will provide the finish. He may not be a 50-goal scorer, but 40 isn't out of the question.

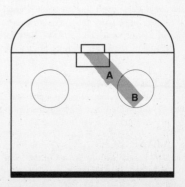

SERGEI KRIVOKRASOV

Yrs. of NHL service: 2
Born: Angarsk, Soviet Union; Apr. 15, 1974
Position: right wing
Height: 5-10
Weight: 174
Uniform no.: 25
Shoots: left

Career statistics:

GP	G	A	TP	PIM
100	19	17	36	71

1992-93 statistics:

GP	G	A	TP	+/-	PIM	PP	SH	GW	GT	S	PCT
4	0	0	0	-2	2	0	0	0	0	0	0.0

1993-94 statistics:

GP	G	A	TP	+/-	PIM	PP	SH	GW	GT	S	PCT
9	1	0	1	-2	4	0	0	0	0	7	14.3

1994-95 statistics:

GP	G	A	TP	+/-	PIM	PP	SH	GW	GT	S	PCT
41	12	7	19	+9	33	6	0	2	0	72	16.7

1995-96 statistics:

GP	G	A	TP	+/-	PIM	PP	SH	GW	GT	S	PCT
46	6	10	16	+10	32	0	0	1	0	52	11.5

LAST SEASON

Second NHL season. Played nine games with Indianapolis (IHL), scoring 4-5 — 9. Missed games with recurring knee injury.

THE FINESSE GAME

Krivokrasov is Russian for "exasperating." Every time the Blackhawks seem ready to give up on him — and he was mentioned prominently in several trade rumours last season — he comes up with a play like his overtime playoff goal against Colorado that makes everyone reconsider.

Krivoskrasov is highly skilled, but he's never been consistent despite getting prime ice time on the top line with Tony Amonte and Jeremy Roenick. Krivokrasov controls the puck well and reads offensive plays. He will shoot or pass and has good timing in both areas. He will draw defenders and open up ice for a teammate, before dishing off and heading to the net himself for a give-and-go. Sometimes he overhandles the puck, and doesn't shoot when he should.

His skating needs to get a hair quicker. He is strong and will drive to the net. Like New Jersey's Valeri Zelepukin, he will score a lot of goals from in tight.

THE PHYSICAL GAME

On most nights, Krivokrasov is not a physical player and can be intimidated, but other nights he breathes competitive fire and is a force on the ice.

THE INTANGIBLES

Krivokrasov has the skill to be one of the team's top six forwards, and this should be the year that determines whether or not he has the goods to be a big-time player. He has paid his dues in the minors and has had some problems with injuries. Since Chicago didn't re-sign Joe Murphy, Krivokrasov's golden opportunity looms.

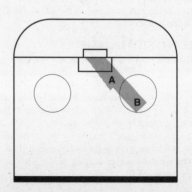

KEVIN MILLER

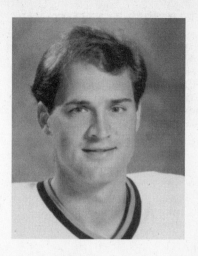

Yrs. of NHL service: 8
Born: Lansing, Mich.; Sept. 2, 1965
Position: right wing
Height: 5-11
Weight: 190
Uniform no.: 8
Shoots: right

Career statistics:

GP	G	A	TP	PIM
468	128	152	280	365

1992-93 statistics:

GP	G	A	TP	+/-	PIM	PP	SH	GW	GT	S	PCT
82	24	25	49	+2	100	8	3	4	2	163	14.7

1993-94 statistics:

GP	G	A	TP	+/-	PIM	PP	SH	GW	GT	S	PCT
75	23	25	48	+6	83	6	3	5	0	154	14.9

1994-95 statistics:

GP	G	A	TP	+/-	PIM	PP	SH	GW	GT	S	PCT
36	8	12	20	+4	13	1	1	2	0	60	13.3

1995-96 statistics:

GP	G	A	TP	+/-	PIM	PP	SH	GW	GT	S	PCT
81	28	25	53	-4	45	3	2	2	2	179	15.6

LAST SEASON

Acquired from San Jose for a fifth-round draft pick and future considerations, Mar. 20, 1996. Signed as a free agent by Chicago. Career high in goals and points. Tied for team lead in shorthanded goals.

THE FINESSE GAME

Like his older brother, Kelly, in Washington, Kevin Miller is a two-way forward with a tremendous work ethic. The role of checker was once limited to players who didn't have scoring skills, but players like the Miller brothers, who can create turnovers with their smart, persistent forechecking, and who have the finesse skills to produce points as well, have redefined the role.

Miller is an energetic skater who is all over the ice. He is a better playmaker than finisher. He's not overly clever and most of his scoring chances come from opportunities from the forecheck. He has fairly quick hands but lacks a soft goal scorer's touch.

He has succeeded at every level he has played — college, Olympic and minor league — and now has stamped himself as an NHL regular. He's small, but he plays much larger.

THE PHYSICAL GAME

The spunky Miller takes the body well, although he doesn't have great size. He is very strong and has a low centre of gravity, which makes it tough to knock him off the puck. He will get overpowered in heavy traffic areas, but that doesn't keep him from trying. Miller will frustrate opponents into taking swings at him and draw penalties.

THE INTANGIBLES

Miller has the unique ability to fill a checking or scoring role. He exceeded our 20-goal expectation last season, and we would expect him in the 20-25 range next season. Miller loves to play, and he was frustrated by his lack of ice time in Pittsburgh. He should see more playing time in Chicago.

ETHAN MOREAU

Yrs. of NHL service: 0
Born: Huntsville, Ont.; Sept. 22, 1975
Position: left wing
Height: 6-2
Weight: 205
Uniform no.: 40
Shoots: left

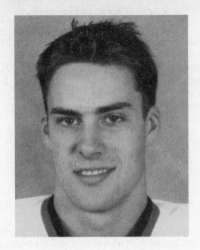

Career statistics:

GP	G	A	TP	PIM
8	0	1	1	4

1995-96 statistics:

GP	G	A	TP	+/-	PIM	PP	SH	GW	GT	S	PCT
8	0	1	1	+1	4	0	0	0	0	1	0.0

LAST SEASON

Will be entering first NHL season. Played 71 games with Indianapolis (IHL), scoring 21-20 — 41 with 126 PIM.

THE FINESSE GAME

Moreau's first pro season in the minors last year was very encouraging to the Chicago organization.

Moreau is a very intelligent player with good hockey sense. He can also play centre, although his future is clearly as a left wing. He is not a natural scorer but has to work for his goals, and with effort, his scoring touch improves. Funny how that works.

Moreau has a long reach and uses a long stick, which allow him to get his shots away around a defenseman who may think he has Moreau tied up. Defensively, he's on his way because he has an understanding of positional play.

THE PHYSICAL GAME

Moreau has good size and strength but needs to develop more of a presence around the net if he is going to scare off any NHL defensemen. He handled himself well in the minors, so there may be a latent aggressive streak that will emerge — especially if that's the difference between making the NHL or another year of riding the bus in the minors.

He is strong in the corners and will take a hit to make a pass.

THE INTANGIBLES

Patience is the key to developing a potential power forward, and the Blackhawks, who drafted Moreau in 1994, may give him more time in the minors at the start of the season. But the Hawks saw Eric Daze blossom last season, and will give Moreau a good long look in training camp.

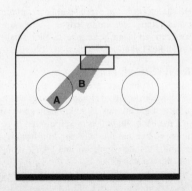

BOB PROBERT

Yrs. of NHL service: 10
Born: Windsor, Ont.; June 5, 1965
Position: right wing
Height: 6-3
Weight: 225
Uniform no.: 24
Shoots: left

Career statistics:

GP	G	A	TP	PIM
552	133	166	299	2327

1992-93 statistics:

GP	G	A	TP	+/-	PIM	PP	SH	GW	GT	S	PCT
80	14	29	43	-9	292	6	0	3	0	128	10.9

1993-94 statistics:

GP	G	A	TP	+/-	PIM	PP	SH	GW	GT	S	PCT
66	7	10	17	-1	275	1	0	0	0	105	6.7

1994-95 statistics:

P	G	A	TP	+/-	PIM	PP	SH	GW	GT	S	PC
					Did not play in NHL						

1995-96 statistics:

GP	G	A	TP	+/-	PIM	PP	SH	GW	GT	S	PCT
78	19	21	40	+15	237	1	0	3	0	97	19.6

LAST SEASON

Missed four games with knee injury. Second on team in penalty minutes.

THE FINESSE GAME

Probert is a slugger with a nice touch. He needs a little time to get away his shot, but let's face it, not too many brave souls play him that tight. In traffic, he can stickhandle and even slide a backhand pass down low. His shots aren't very heavy, but he is accurate and shoots mostly from close range. He is smart with the puck and doesn't give it away.

He doesn't have open-ice speed, but in tight he has one-step quickness and can even pivot surprisingly well with the puck. He can be used up front on the power play because he parks himself right in front of the net; the goalie looks like a bobble-head doll as he tries to peer around Probert's giant frame for a view of the puck. He gets some second-unit power play time because of this.

Probert has to play with linemates who get him the puck since he can't help out in pursuing the disk.

THE PHYSICAL GAME

Still one the scariest fighters in the NHL, Probert is strong, quick-fisted and mean, but he is slow to rile on some nights when the other teams decide it is best to let a sleeping dog lie. If he falls asleep on the ice, he is a non-factor. He will step up for his teammates and is strong along the wall.

THE INTANGIBLES

Probert had a great training camp and first few weeks, then the adrenaline rush wore off. After missing all of the previous season due to an NHL mandate, that was to be expected, Probert began playing well again and in December helped carry the team. He is still a solid contributor who works hard and knows his role.

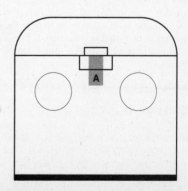

JEREMY ROENICK

Yrs. of NHL service: 7
Born: Boston, Mass.; Jan. 17, 1970
Position: centre
Height: 6-0
Weight: 190
Uniform no.: 27
Shoots: right

Career statistics:

GP	G	A	TP	PIM
524	267	329	596	570

1992-93 statistics:

GP	G	A	TP	+/-	PIM	PP	SH	GW	GT	S	PCT
84	50	57	107	+15	86	22	3	3	3	255	19.6

1993-94 statistics:

GP	G	A	TP	+/-	PIM	PP	SH	GW	GT	S	PCT
84	46	61	107	+21	125	24	5	5	1	281	16.4

1994-95 statistics:

GP	G	A	TP	+/-	PIM	PP	SH	GW	GT	S	PCT
33	10	24	34	+5	14	5	0	0	1	93	10.8

1995-96 statistics:

GP	G	A	TP	+/-	PIM	PP	SH	GW	GT	S	PCT
66	32	35	67	+9	109	12	4	2	2	171	18.7

LAST SEASON

Led team in goals. Tied for team lead in power play goals and shorthanded goals. Second on team in assists. Tied for second on team in points. Missed three games with thigh injury. Missed two games with broken jaw and concussion. Missed 11 games with sprained ankle.

THE FINESSE GAME

Roenick has great quickness and is tough to handle one-on-one. He won't make the same move or take the same shot twice in a row. He has a variety of shots and can score from almost anywhere on the ice. He can rifle a wrist shot from 30 feet away, or else wait until the goalie is down and lift in a backhand from in tight.

Roenick commands a lot of attention when he is on the ice, and draws the attention of the defenders to open up ice for his teammates. He has great acceleration and can turn quickly, change directions or burn a defender with outside speed. A defenseman who plays aggressively against him will be left staring at the back of his jersey as he skips by en route to the net. Roenick has to be forced into the high traffic areas, where his lack of size and strength are the only things that derail him.

Roenick would benefit from a solid number two centre being added to the team.

THE PHYSICAL GAME

Roenick plays with such a headlong style that injuries are routine. He has trouble keeping weight on, and generally loses 15-20 pounds between the start of training camp and the end of the regular season.

Roenick takes aggressive penalties — smashing people into the boards, getting his elbows up — and he never backs down. He plays through pain, and is highly competitive.

THE INTANGIBLES

Roenick was a Group 2 free agent after last season, and the Blackhawks will match any offer made for him. But unless the two sides come to a contract agreement early, Roenick could miss the start of the season. He will likely be in shape if he plays as expected in the World Cup. Roenick has always believed a player should earn his money, and if he plays up to the big salary he will soon be receiving, he could have a huge year.

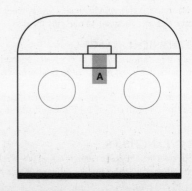

JEFF SHANTZ

Yrs. of NHL service: 3
Born: Duchess, Alta; Oct. 10, 1973
Position: centre
Height: 6-1
Weight: 195
Uniform no.: 11
Shoots: right

Career statistics:

GP	G	A	TP	PIM
175	15	39	54	87

1993-94 statistics:

GP	G	A	TP	+/-	PIM	PP	SH	GW	GT	S	PCT
52	3	13	16	-14	30	0	0	0	0	56	5.4

1994-95 statistics:

GP	G	A	TP	+/-	PIM	PP	SH	GW	GT	S	PCT
45	6	12	18	+11	33	0	2	0	0	58	10.3

1995-96 statistics:

GP	G	A	TP	+/-	PIM	PP	SH	GW	GT	S	PCT
78	6	14	20	+12	24	1	2	0	0	72	8.3

LAST SEASON

Games missed were coaches' decision.

THE FINESSE GAME

Shantz doesn't excel in many technical areas, but he is one of the best Hawk prospects in terms of hockey sense. He has good skills, but his game is heavily defense-oriented, and he played his best hockey as a right wing on the third line.

A good skater, Shantz is smooth in his turns with average quickness. He handles the puck well and sees his passing options. He won't be forced into many bad passes, preferring to eat the puck rather than toss it away.

He has a decent touch around the net but he won't score many highlight goals. He has a heavy shot but doesn't have a quick release. Most of his scoring will come from in tight off his forechecking efforts — perfect for Chicago's dump-and-chase style of attack. Shantz is very good on face-offs.

THE PHYSICAL GAME

Shantz doesn't have very good size and will need to keep up his conditioning and strength work. He had a shoulder operation in the 1995 off-season, which got him off to a slow start. Shantz is gritty, doesn't take bad penalties and plays hard but clean.

THE INTANGIBLES

Shantz was supposed to take over Brent Sutter's role as Chicago's best defensive centre, but by mid-December, Sutter was back in the lineup and Shantz was on the bench or on the fourth line. He is smart defensively but didn't seem up to the wear and tear of a full NHL season. Because he was a scorer in junior, Shantz should be able to upgrade his game and become more of a two-way player.

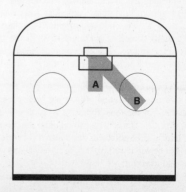

STEVE SMITH

Yrs. of NHL service: 11
Born: Glasgow, Scotland; Apr. 30, 1963
Position: left defense
Height: 6-4
Weight: 215
Uniform no.: 5
Shoots: left

Career statistics:

GP	G	A	TP	PIM
681	71	283	354	1971

1992-93 statistics:

GP	G	A	TP	+/-	PIM	PP	SH	GW	GT	S	PCT
78	10	47	57	+12	214	7	1	2	0	212	4.7

1993-94 statistics:

GP	G	A	TP	+/-	PIM	PP	SH	GW	GT	S	PCT
57	5	22	27	-5	174	1	0	1	0	89	5.6

1994-95 statistics:

GP	G	A	TP	+/-	PIM	PP	SH	GW	GT	S	PCT
48	1	12	13	+6	128	0	0	0	0	43	2.3

1995-96 statistics:

GP	G	A	TP	+/-	PIM	PP	SH	GW	GT	S	PCT
37	0	9	9	+12	71	0	0	0	0	17	0.0

THE INTANGIBLES

Smith returned to play a full-time role for the Blackhawks in the playoffs, but he has become a health risk due to his recurring injuries.

LAST SEASON

Finalist for 1996 Masterton Trophy. Missed 42 games with chronic back injuries. Missed three games with fractured fibula.

THE FINESSE GAME

Smith is a tower of strength on the blueline, an aggressive, smart and confident defenseman who probably doesn't get the credit he deserves because he is a complementary player who always makes his partner looks better. He has confidence to get involved in the attack, and knows his job in his own zone.

Smith is not a clever passer, but he's effective at getting the puck from point A to point B. He makes a great outlet pass from his defensive zone and can see the second option. He can carry the puck if he has to.

He does not have an overwhelming shot, but it is accurate and low from the point, and he can work on the power play. Defensively, Smith is tough to beat one-on-one. He has great balance, which allows him to drop to one knee, drag his back skate and place his stick flat along the ice while in motion. That shuts off a tremendous stretch of passing lane from the sideboards to the middle. He steps up in the neutral zone and plays aggressively to kill penalties.

THE PHYSICAL GAME

After suffering his second broken leg in three years, we have to wonder about Smith's loss of power from his leg drive. He can be a punishing hitter, but his mobility may also be affected. He doesn't get in many fights, but he will keep 90 per cent of the players wondering and worrying.

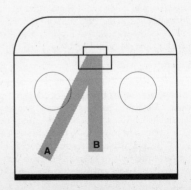

GARY SUTER

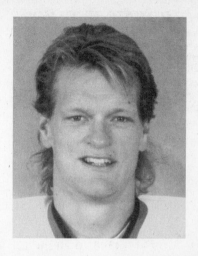

Yrs. of NHL service: 11
Born: Madison, Wisc.; June 24, 1964
Position: left defense
Height: 6-0
Weight: 200
Uniform no.: 20
Shoots: left

Career statistics:

GP	G	A	TP	PIM
763	160	514	674	1010

1992-93 statistics:

GP	G	A	TP	+/-	PIM	PP	SH	GW	GT	S	PCT
81	23	58	81	-1	112	10	1	2	1	263	8.7

1993-94 statistics:

GP	G	A	TP	+/-	PIM	PP	SH	GW	GT	S	PCT
41	6	12	18	-12	38	4	1	0	0	86	7.0

1994-95 statistics:

GP	G	A	TP	+/-	PIM	PP	SH	GW	GT	S	PCT
48	10	27	37	+14	42	5	0	0	0	144	6.9

1995-96 statistics:

GP	G	A	TP	+/-	PIM	PP	SH	GW	GT	S	PCT
82	20	47	67	+3	80	12	2	4	0	242	8.3

LAST SEASON

Tied for team lead in power play goals. Tied for lead among NHL defensemen in goals and power play goals. Tied for sixth among NHL defensemen in scoring. Second on team in assists and points. One of two Blackhawks to appear in all 82 games.

THE FINESSE GAME

Suter has great natural skills, starting with his skating. He is secure on his skates with a wide stance for balance. He has all of the components that make a great skater: acceleration, flat-out speed, quickness and mobility. He skates well backwards and can't be bested one-on-one except by the slickest skaters. He loves to jump into the attack, and he will key a rush with a smooth outlet pass or carry the puck and lead the parade.

Suter has a superb shot. It's not scary-hard, but Suter will keep it low. With his good friend, Chris Chelios, now working the points with him in Chicago, Suter was given free rein to quarterback the team's power play. He and Chelios comprised the best power play point duo in the league last season.

Not a great playmaker, his creativity comes from his speed and his dangerous shot. He can handle some penalty-killing time, though it is not his strong suit.

THE PHYSICAL GAME

Like Chelios, Suter is a marathon man who can handle 30 minutes of ice time a game and not wear down. He has a personal trainer that he, Chelios and several teammates work out with, and as a result Suter is exceptionally fit.

Suter can be a mean hitter (it was his check in the

1991 Canada Cup that was the start of Wayne Gretzky's back troubles). But he can get carried away with the hitting game and will take himself out of position, even when penalty killing. He doesn't like to be hit; he'll bring his stick up at the last second before contact to protect himself. His defensive reads are average to fair.

THE INTANGIBLES

Suter may be a notch below the league's elite defensemen, but he can handle a lot of responsibility. He has played his best hockey since coming to Chicago, and should continue to produce, but we don't expect him to top last year's excellent output.

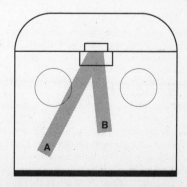

BRENT SUTTER

Yrs. of NHL service: 15
Born: Viking, Alta.; June 10, 1962
Position: centre
Height: 5-11
Weight: 180
Uniform no.: 12
Shoots: right

Career statistics:

GP	G	A	TP	PIM
1020	354	453	807	1008

1992-93 statistics:

GP	G	A	TP	+/-	PIM	PP	SH	GW	GT	S	PCT
65	20	34	54	+10	67	8	2	3	0	151	13.2

1993-94 statistics:

GP	G	A	TP	+/-	PIM	PP	SH	GW	GT	S	PCT
73	9	29	38	+17	43	3	2	0	0	127	7.1

1994-95 statistics:

GP	G	A	TP	+/-	PIM	PP	SH	GW	GT	S	PCT
47	7	8	15	+6	51	1	0	1	0	65	10.8

1995-96 statistics:

GP	G	A	TP	+/-	PIM	PP	SH	GW	GT	S	PCT
80	13	27	40	+14	56	0	0	3	0	102	12.7

34, but he can still play a key role on a team looking to take the next step up in the playoffs.

LAST SEASON
Two games missed were coaches' decision.

THE FINESSE GAME
Sutter is a superior two-way centre whose specialty is defense, but whose hand skills are sufficient to add some offense to a third line.

Sutter has great arm strength and can hold off a defender with one arm while shooting or passing with the other. He has a strong wrist shot and will pay the price in front of the net, plowing through traffic with the puck under control. He will pounce on loose pucks and create scoring chances off the turnovers forced by his forechecking.

Among the best in the league at draws (he cheats, and isn't usually caught), he is a solid penalty killer. In a pinch, he can still work on the second power play unit.

Sutter is not a gifted skater. He is a labourer and gets where he has to go by sheer force of will.

THE PHYSICAL GAME
Sutter plays much bigger than his size. He's wiry and deceptively strong. Anyone who wants the puck in Sutter's piece of ice will have to fight him for it. He always keeps himself in top condition.

THE INTANGIBLES
The Blackhawks looked to be phasing Sutter out in favour of centre Jeff Shantz, but when Shantz couldn't step up, Sutter stepped back in and was one of the most reliable Chicago forwards. An unrestricted free agent, Sutter may start this season in a new home (although the Blackhawks will try to re-sign him). He is

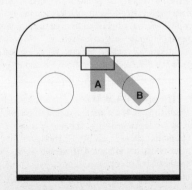

ERIC WEINRICH

Yrs. of NHL service: 6
Born: Roanoke, Va.; Dec. 19, 1966
Position: right defense
Height: 6-1
Weight: 210
Uniform no.: 2
Shoots: left

Career statistics:

GP	G	A	TP	PIM
439	32	139	171	323

1992-93 statistics:

GP	G	A	TP	+/-	PIM	PP	SH	GW	GT	S	PCT
79	7	29	36	-11	76	0	2	2	0	104	6.7

1993-94 statistics:

GP	G	A	TP	+/-	PIM	PP	SH	GW	GT	S	PCT
62	4	24	28	+1	35	2	0	2	0	115	3.5

1994-95 statistics:

GP	G	A	TP	+/-	PIM	PP	SH	GW	GT	S	PCT
48	3	10	13	+1	33	1	0	2	0	50	6.0

1995-96 statistics:

GP	G	A	TP	+/-	PIM	PP	SH	GW	GT	S	PCT
77	5	10	15	+14	65	0	0	0	0	76	6.6

THE INTANGIBLES

Weinrich has settled into a number four or five role with the Blackhawks, and his point totals from now on will probably hover in the 20-point range.

LAST SEASON

Missed five games with eye injury.

THE FINESSE GAME

Weinrich's skating is above average. He accelerates quickly and has good straightaway speed, but he doesn't have great balance for pivots or superior leg drive for power. He has improved his skating but needs to get even better. He is not sturdy on his feet.

He is strong on the puck, shooting and passing hard. He works on the point on the second power play unit, which doesn't get much ice time because Chris Chelios and Gary Suter play nearly the full two minutes. Weinrich has a low, accurate shot that he gets away quickly. He will not gamble down low, but will sometimes sneak into the top of the circle for a one-timer. His offensive reads are much better than his defensive reads.

Weinrich plays better with an offensive-minded partner. He is more useful when he is the support player who can move the puck up and move into the play.

THE PHYSICAL GAME

Weinrich is a good one-on-one defender, but doesn't take the body well in the crease area. He always has a high conditioning level and can play a lot of minutes. He is not a soft player (a criticism that dogged him early in his career). Weinrich will fight. It's not in his nature, but he won't get pushed around and will stand up for his teammates.

Lower-body strength and balance continue to be a weakness, causing him to lose some battles to smaller players.

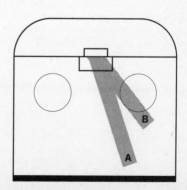

COLORADO AVALANCHE

Players' Statistics 1995-96

POS.	NO.	PLAYER	GP	G	A	PTS	+/-	PIM	PP	SH	GW	GT	S	PCT
C	19	JOE SAKIC	82	51	69	120	14	44	17	6	7	1	339	15.0
C	21	PETER FORSBERG	82	30	86	116	26	47	7	3	3		217	13.8
L	13	VALERI KAMENSKY	81	38	47	85	14	85	18	1	5		220	17.3
R	22	CLAUDE LEMIEUX	79	39	32	71	14	117	9	2	10		315	12.4
R	48	SCOTT YOUNG	81	21	39	60	2	50	7		5		229	9.2
D	8	SANDIS OZOLINSH	73	14	40	54	2	54	8	1	1	1	166	8.4
C	18	ADAM DEADMARSH	78	21	27	48	20	142	3		2		151	13.9
L	12	CHRIS SIMON	64	16	18	34	10	250	4		1		105	15.2
C	26	*STEPHANE YELLE	71	13	14	27	15	30		2	1		93	14.0
R	25	MIKE KEANE	73	10	17	27	-5	46		2	2		84	11.9
D	6	CRAIG WOLANIN	75	7	20	27	25	50		3			73	9.6
C	9	MIKE RICCI	62	6	21	27	1	52	3		1		73	8.2
C	10	TROY MURRAY	63	7	14	21	15	22			1		36	19.4
D	5	ALEXEI GUSAROV	65	5	15	20	29	56					42	11.9
D	7	CURTIS LESCHYSHYN	77	4	15	19	32	73			1		76	5.3
C	14	DAVE HANNAN	61	7	10	17	3	32	1	1	2		41	17.1
D	52	ADAM FOOTE	73	5	11	16	27	88	1		1		49	10.2
D	2	SYLVAIN LEFEBVRE	75	5	11	16	26	49	2				115	4.3
D	24	*JON KLEMM	56	3	12	15	12	20		1	1		61	4.9
L	20	RENE CORBET	33	3	6	9	10	33					35	8.6
L	16	WARREN RYCHEL	52	6	2	8	6	147			1		45	13.3
D	4	UWE KRUPP	6		3	3	4	4					9	
R	38	*PAUL BROUSSEAU	8	1	1	2	1	2				1	10	10.0
R	14	*LANDON WILSON	7	1		1	3	6					6	16.7
C	15	*JOSEF MARHA	2		1	1	1						2	
D	55	*ANDERS MYRVOLD	4		1	1	-2	6					4	
G	35	STEPHANE FISET	37		1	1	0	2						
D	31	*AARON MILLER	5				0						2	
G	33	PATRICK ROY	61				0	10						

GP = games played; G = goals; A = assists; PTS = points; +/- = goals-for minus goals-against while player is on ice; PIM = penalties in minutes; PP = power play goals; SH = shorthanded goals; GW = game-winning goals; GT = game-tying goals; S = no. of shots; PCT = percentage of goals to shots; * = rookie

ADAM DEADMARSH

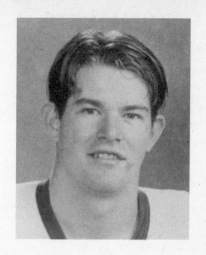

Yrs. of NHL service: 2
Born: Trail, B.C.; May 10, 1975
Position: right wing
Height: 6-0
Weight: 195
Uniform no.: 18
Shoots: right

Career statistics:

GP	G	A	TP	PIM
126	30	35	65	198

1994-95 statistics:

GP	G	A	TP	+/-	PIM	PP	SH	GW	GT	S	PCT
48	9	8	17	+16	56	0	0	0	1	48	18.8

1995-96 statistics:

GP	G	A	TP	+/-	PIM	PP	SH	GW	GT	S	PCT
78	21	27	48	+20	142	3	0	2	0	151	13.9

LAST SEASON

Second NHL season. Third on team in penalty minutes. Missed four games with hip flexor.

THE FINESSE GAME

Deadmarsh is a bigger version of Kevin Dineen. He's feisty and tough and can work in a checking role, but he can also score off the chances he creates with his defense. His game is incredibly mature. With barely two full seasons under his belt, he is reliable enough to be put out on the ice to protect a lead in the late minutes of a game, because he will do what it takes to win.

Deadmarsh doesn't have to be the glamour guy (Colorado is loaded with those types, anyway), but that doesn't mean he provides unskilled labour. Deadmarsh has dangerous speed and quickness. He has a nice scoring touch to convert the chances he creates off his forechecking. He can play centre as well as both wings, so he is versatile. He doesn't play a very creative game. He's a basic up-and-down winger, a nice complement to all of the flash and dash on the Avalanche. He excels as a dedicated penalty killer.

THE PHYSICAL GAME

Deadmarsh always finishes his checks. He has a strong work ethic with honest toughness. He never backs down from a challenge and issues some of his own. He isn't a dirty player, but he will fight when challenged or stand up for his teammates.

THE INTANGIBLES

Deadmarsh has a huge upside, and with more ice time (if he can get it on this stocked team) his production could soar. He will never be a 100-point player, but he is capable of leaping to the 60-70 point range. There just aren't enough good things scouts can find to say about this kid. He is the kind of player who will seldom be one of the three stars of the game, but will be one of the guys who found five ways to help win a game.

ADAM FOOTE

Yrs. of NHL service: 5
Born: Toronto, Ont.; July 10, 1971
Position: right defense
Height: 6-1
Weight: 202
Uniform no.: 52
Shoots: right

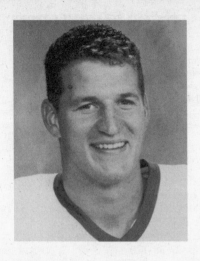

Career statistics:

GP	G	A	TP	PIM
280	13	40	53	419

1992-93 statistics:

GP	G	A	TP	+/-	PIM	PP	SH	GW	GT	S	PCT
81	4	12	16	+6	168	0	1	0	0	54	7.4

1993-94 statistics:

GP	G	A	TP	+/-	PIM	PP	SH	GW	GT	S	PCT
45	2	6	8	+3	67	0	0	0	0	42	4.8

1994-95 statistics:

GP	G	A	TP	+/-	PIM	PP	SH	GW	GT	S	PCT
35	0	7	7	+17	52	0	0	0	0	24	0.0

1995-96 statistics:

GP	G	A	TP	+/-	PIM	PP	SH	GW	GT	S	PCT
73	5	11	16	+27	88	1	0	1	0	49	10.2

Leschyshyn are three players who can play with anyone in their own zone.

LAST SEASON

Third on team in plus-minus. Missed five games with shoulder injury.

THE FINESSE GAME

Foote has great foot speed and quickness. Defensively, he's strong in his coverage and is a stay-at-home type. He is not creative with the puck, probably his major deficiency, but he was strong in that department as a junior player and there is hope he can recover some of that knack. Even if he doesn't, he is so competitive that he can always earn a spot on any team's roster.

Foote usually skates the puck out of his zone. He is less likely to find the man for an outlet pass. There are few defensemen in the league who can match him in getting the first few strides in and jumping out of the zone. He is an excellent penalty killer.

THE PHYSICAL GAME

Foote is big and solid and uses his body well. He is highly aggressive is his defensive zone, and anyone trying to get through Foote to the net will pay a price. He plays it smart and takes few bad penalties. He really stepped up his physical play — possibly a result of gaining confidence after back surgery in 1994 — and dished out some really powerful checks in the playoffs. Foote has good lower body strength and drives his body upwards, resulting in a heavy impact with his unfortunate target.

THE INTANGIBLES

Colorado didn't get much credit for its defense last season, but Foote, Sylvain Lefebvre and Curtis

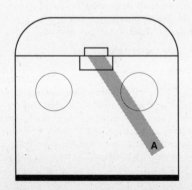

PETER FORSBERG

Yrs. of NHL service: 2
Born: Ornskoldsvik, Sweden; July 20, 1973
Position: centre
Height: 6-0
Weight: 190
Uniform no.: 21
Shoots: left

Career statistics:

GP	G	A	TP	PIM
129	45	121	166	63

1994-95 statistics:

GP	G	A	TP	+/-	PIM	PP	SH	GW	GT	S	PCT
47	15	35	50	+17	16	3	0	3	0	86	17.4

1995-96 statistics:

GP	G	A	TP	+/-	PIM	PP	SH	GW	GT	S	PCT
82	30	86	116	+26	47	7	3	3	0	217	13.8

LAST SEASON

Fourth in NHL in assists. Fifth in NHL in points. Led team in assists. Second on team in points. Tied for second on team in game-winning goals. One of two Colorado players to appear in all 82 games.

THE FINESSE GAME

There is nothing Forsberg can't do. Since he was traded to Quebec (now Colorado) in the Eric Lindros trade, it is frequently pointed out how much better Forsberg's game is than Lindros's. That's a bit unfair, since we would have to see Lindros playing with the same calibre of players that Forberg does before passing judgment.

Forsberg is used in all game situations: power play, penalty killing and four-on-four. His skill level is world class.

Forsberg protects the puck as well as anybody in the league. He is so strong that he can control the puck with one arm while fending off a checker, and still make an effective pass. His passing is nearly as good as teammate Joe Sakic's. In fact, Colorado now has two of the top four or five playmakers in the league in Sakic and Forsberg, which is joyous news to their wingers, but should depress the heck out of the rest of the NHL. The young Swede seems to be thinking a play or two ahead of everyone else on the ice, which was always Wayne Gretzky's great trait.

Forsberg is a smooth skater with explosive speed (think Teemu Selanne) and can accelerate while carrying the puck. He has excellent vision of the ice and is an outstanding playmaker. One of the few knocks on him is that he doesn't shoot enough. He works best down between the circles with a wrist or backhand shot off the rush.

THE PHYSICAL GAME

Forsberg is better suited for the North American style than most Europeans — or many North Americans, for that matter. He is tough to knock down. He loves the game and dishes out more than he receives. He relishes contact. Just try to knock him off the puck. He has a wide skating base and great balance. Forsberg can be cross-checked while he's on his backhand and still not lose control of the puck. Jaromir Jagr may be the only other player in the league who can do that.

Forsberg has a cockiness that many great athletes carry about them like an aura, and he dares people to try to intimidate him. His drive to succeed will help him handle the cheap stuff and keep going. He suffered only a slight slump in the playoffs when he appeared to hit the wall a bit — because 1994-95 was shortened by a lockout, Forsberg was unused to the long NHL season — but he finished with a powerful finals. Forsberg plays equally hard on any given inch of the ice.

THE INTANGIBLES

We predicted last season that Forsberg would be in the top 10 in the NHL in scoring. Now that looks too easy. So we'll put him in the top five, even with an anticipated team letdown that can be expected following the Cup win. Forsberg is the genuine article. He can easily take his place among the league's top three forwards. Over the next few seasons, it will be he, Lindros and Jaromir Jagr dominating All-Star games and trophy balloting.

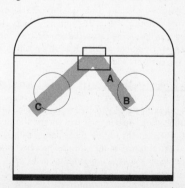

ALEXEI GUSAROV

Yrs. of NHL service: 6
Born: St. Petersburg, USSR; July 8, 1964
Position: left defense
Height: 6-3
Weight: 185
Uniform no.: 5
Shoots: left

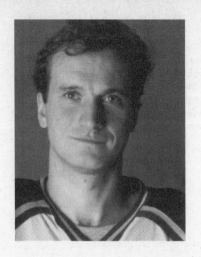

Career statistics:

GP	G	A	TP	PIM
338	27	86	91	191

1992-93 statistics:

GP	G	A	TP	+/-	PIM	PP	SH	GW	GT	S	PCT
79	8	22	30	+18	57	0	2	1	0	60	13.3

1993-94 statistics:

GP	G	A	TP	+/-	PIM	PP	SH	GW	GT	S	PCT
76	5	20	25	+3	38	0	1	0	0	84	6.0

1994-95 statistics:

GP	G	A	TP	+/-	PIM	PP	SH	GW	GT	S	PCT
14	1	2	3	-1	6	0	0	1	0	7	14.3

1995-96 statistics:

GP	G	A	TP	+/-	PIM	PP	SH	GW	GT	S	PCT
65	5	15	20	+29	56	0	0	0	0	42	11.9

LAST SEASON

Second on team in plus-minus. Missed two games with concussion.

THE FINESSE GAME

Gusarv has some impressive finesse skills, which he uses more in a defensive posture now than he did earlier in his career. Gusarov can still contribute to the attack, but he is not a top-flight offensive defenseman.

A shifty skater with a long reach and good range, Gusarov can handle the puck on the rush and will occasionally gamble deep in front of the net. He sometimes doesn't read the play well and will get trapped, although he was much more conservative in this facet last season.

Gusarov is confident in his skills and is aggressive in the neutral zone. He can kill penalties and work the point on the power play on the second unit.

THE PHYSICAL GAME

Gusarov does not play a physical game. He often fishes for the puck instead of bumping people. He is tall and lean and doesn't have the best centre of gravity for body work, but when he holds his position well he forces attackers wide.

THE INTANGIBLES

Gusarov was pushed down to a number five or six role on the depth chart by the development of other Avalanche defensemen, and was in and out of the lineup when healthy several times during the season. He did perform well in the playoffs, however, which may bump his stock back up a bit.

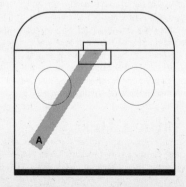

VALERI KAMENSKY

Yrs. of NHL service: 4
Born: Voskresensk, Russia; April 18, 1966
Position: left wing
Height: 6-2
Weight: 198
Uniform no.: 13
Shoots: right

Career statistics:

GP	G	A	TP	PIM
252	98	140	238	177

1992-93 statistics:

GP	G	A	TP	+/-	PIM	PP	SH	GW	GT	S	PCT
32	15	22	37	+13	14	2	3	0	1	42	16.0

1993-94 statistics:

GP	G	A	TP	+/-	PIM	PP	SH	GW	GT	S	PCT
76	28	37	65	+12	42	6	0	1	0	170	16.5

1994-95 statistics:

GP	G	A	TP	+/-	PIM	PP	SH	GW	GT	S	PCT
40	10	20	30	+3	22	5	1	5	0	70	14.3

1995-96 statistics:

GP	G	A	TP	+/-	PIM	PP	SH	GW	GT	S	PCT
81	38	47	85	+14	85	18	1	5	0	220	17.3

LAST SEASON

Led team in power play goals and shooting percentage. Third on team in goals, assists and points with career highs. Tied for third on team in game-winning goals.

THE FINESSE GAME

Injuries slowed Kamensky in his first few seasons — so much so that he changed his uniform number to avoid the jinx — but the fairly healthy left-winger finally fulfilled his promise with the Avalanche last season.

He is primarily a one-way forward. A gifted skater with speed and quickness, he is as dangerous without the puck as with it because of his sense for open ice. Kamensky is effective in four-on-four situations as he is a top transition player. His passes are flat and on the money, with just the right velocity. The recipient does not have to slow down but can collect the puck in stride.

Kamensky has quick hands and a good release on his wrist shot. He gets a lot of power play time, and excels at getting open in the left slot; he just rips his one-timer.

THE PHYSICAL GAME

Kamensky generally tries to avoid contact. He will venture into a spot where he might get hit if he believes he can zip out quickly before any damage is inflicted. Opposing teams generally make a point of hitting Kamensky early to throw him off his game.

THE INTANGIBLES

Kamensky finally had the kind of season people had been predicting for him for three or four years. He belongs in the 80-point range, and should continue to produce.

Trivia note: Kamensky has the distinction of scoring the first goal in Avalanche history.

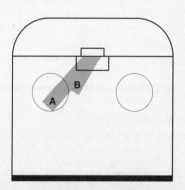

MIKE KEANE

Yrs. of NHL service: 8
Born: Winnipeg, Man.; May 28, 1967
Position: right wing
Height: 5-11
Weight: 185
Uniform no.: 25
Shoots: right

Career statistics:

GP	G	A	TP	PIM
561	90	189	289	536

1992-93 statistics:

GP	G	A	TP	+/-	PIM	PP	SH	GW	GT	S	PCT
77	15	45	60	+29	95	0	0	1	0	120	12.5

1993-94 statistics:

GP	G	A	TP	+/-	PIM	PP	SH	GW	GT	S	PCT
80	16	30	46	+6	119	6	2	2	1	129	12.4

1994-95 statistics:

GP	G	A	TP	+/-	PIM	PP	SH	GW	GT	S	PCT
48	10	10	20	+5	15	1	0	0	0	75	13.3

1995-96 statistics:

GP	G	A	TP	+/-	PIM	PP	SH	GW	GT	S	PCT
73	10	17	27	-5	46	0	2	2	0	84	11.9

score more than 15 goals a year with the Avalanche, but if injuries hit he can step in almost anywhere but in the net.

LAST SEASON

Acquired from Montreal with Patrick Roy for Jocelyn Thibault, Martin Rucinsky and Andrei Kovalenko, Dec. 6, 1995. Missed nine games with groin injuries.

THE FINESSE GAME

Keane is one of the NHL's most underrated forwards. There are few better on the boards and in the corners, and he's the perfect linemate for a finisher. If you want the puck, he'll get it. Not only will he win the battle for it, he'll make a pass and then set a pick or screen.

He is a good skater and will use his speed to forecheck or create shorthanded threats when killing penalties. He is not much of a finisher, though he will contribute the odd goal from his work in front of the net.

Keane can play all three forward positions, but is most effective on the right side. He is a smart player who can be thrust into almost any playing situation. Given the talent on the Avalanche, he sees little premium ice time, but he is a valuable role player.

THE PHYSICAL GAME

Keane is a physical catalyst. He is constantly getting in someone's way. He always finishes his checks in all three zones. He is aggressive and will stand up for his teammates, though he is not a fighter.

THE INTANGIBLES

Keane adds grit to a finesse-loaded Colorado lineup, and was a key ingredient in the team's championship mix. A former Canadiens captain, he is a natural leader. As a checking forward, he probably won't

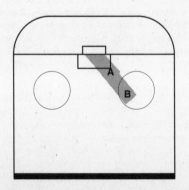

UWE KRUPP

Yrs. of NHL service: 10
Born: Cologne, West Germany; June 24, 1965
Position: right defense
Height: 6-6
Weight: 235
Uniform no.: 4
Shoots: right

Career statistics:

GP	G	A	TP	PIM
557	53	170	223	550

1992-93 statistics:

GP	G	A	TP	+/-	PIM	PP	SH	GW	GT	S	PCT
80	9	29	38	+7	67	2	0	2	0	116	7.8

1993-94 statistics:

GP	G	A	TP	+/-	PIM	PP	SH	GW	GT	S	PCT
41	7	14	21	+11	30	3	0	0	0	82	8.5

1994-95 statistics:

GP	G	A	TP	+/-	PIM	PP	SH	GW	GT	S	PCT
44	6	17	23	+14	20	3	0	1	1	102	5.9

1995-96 statistics:

GP	G	A	TP	+/-	PIM	PP	SH	GW	GT	S	PCT
6	0	3	3	+4	4	0	0	0	0	9	0.0

LAST SEASON

Missed 76 games with reconstructive knee surgery.

THE FINESSE GAME

Krupp made a remarkable recovery from early-season knee surgery to repair a torn anterior cruciate ligament in his knee. His comeback was capped when he scored the Cup-winning goal in triple overtime in Game 4 of the Stanley Cup Finals.

The key to his game is his awareness of his limitations. Not a quick skater even before the injury, Krupp was especially conservative, yet effective, after his return. He reads plays well both offensively and defensively. He positions himself well in his own zone, so he needs only one long stride to cut off the attacker.

Krupp has a hard shot, but it takes him far too long to get his big slapper underway and it is often blocked. Because he is so tall and uses such a long stick, he doesn't one-time the puck well, but instead must stop it and tee it up. He has a good wrist shot that he can use to better purpose, because he can get it away cleanly and with some velocity. He protects the puck well.

Krupp helps his team immeasurably by his ability to move the puck smartly out of the zone. He is a smooth passer and creates a lot of odd-man rushes by spotting the developing play and making the solid first pass.

THE PHYSICAL GAME

Krupp is enormous and takes up a lot of space on the ice, but doesn't use his body as a weapon. It's more of a roadblock, and it's one heck of a detour to get around. Krupp blocks shots willingly and is a very good penalty killer. He plays with restraint and takes few bad penalties. Checkers seem to bounce off him. On the rare nights when he gets physical, he can dominate, but he doesn't often play that way. It's just not his nature. Krupp worked extremely hard to rehab his knee injury and may have been in the best shape of his career aerobically by the playoffs.

THE INTANGIBLES

Krupp is reliable and sensible and can be used to protect a lead because he never takes unnecessary risks. He has been used with a lot of partners and complements all of them well, especially younger defensemen. He is a steadying influence, and now he's a champion as well.

ERIC LACROIX

Yrs. of NHL service: 2
Born: Montreal, Que.; July 15, 1971
Position: left wing
Height: 6-1
Weight: 205
Uniform no.: 28
Shoots: left

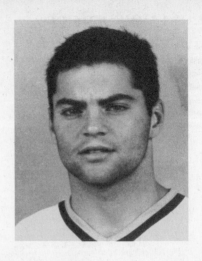

Career statistics:

GP	G	A	TP	PIM
120	25	23	48	166

1993-94 statistics:

GP	G	A	TP	+/-	PIM	PP	SH	GW	GT	S	PCT
3	0	0	0	0	2	0	0	0	0	3	0.0

1994-95 statistics:

GP	G	A	TP	+/-	PIM	PP	SH	GW	GT	S	PCT
45	9	7	16	+2	54	2	1	1	0	64	14.1

1995-96 statistics:

GP	G	A	TP	+/-	PIM	PP	SH	GW	GT	S	PCT
72	16	16	32	-11	110	3	0	1	0	107	15.0

LAST SEASON

Acquired from Los Angeles for Stephane Fiset and an exchange of first-round draft picks, June 20, 1996. Career high in goals, assists and points. Served five-game suspension.

THE FINESSE GAME

Lacroix brings zest and inspiration to every shift. There is nothing fancy to his game, but he didn't play with many skilled players in L.A. after Wayne Gretzky left town (Lacroix was a Gretzky favourite). Lacroix is a bigger, more skilled version of Edmonton's Kirk Maltby. It's hard to figure where he'll get ice time on a strong Stanley Cup championship team, but Lacroix can certainly complement some finesse players.

If Lacroix has the proper work ethic, he will become more than a big banger. Hitters and fighters like Rick Tocchet turned themselves into productive scorers first by earning room on the ice, then by practising shooting drills to make use of that extra space. Lacroix doesn't have great hands or a quick release, so any improvement will not come easy. He appears willing to work and is a good skater with balance and speed. He forechecks hard and forces turnovers.

THE PHYSICAL GAME

Lacroix hits to hurt, and some of his checks cross the line. He earned his suspension for checking Islanders defenseman Dennis Vaske, ending Vaske's season. Lacroix often makes such thunderous contact that he gets penalized because he leaves his feet and sometimes brings his elbows up.

With just a tad more control Lacroix could turn himself into a serious, clean checker who will scare puck carriers into coughing up the rubber, but he is undisciplined at this stage.

THE INTANGIBLES

Lacroix has a lot of upside. Improving to the 20-goal range would be a big step forward (we said this in last year's edition, and he nearly made it). There is a lot to like about him, starting with his heart. But talk about pressure: the GM of the team that just acquired him is his dad, Pierre.

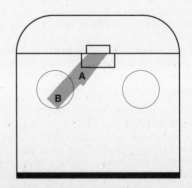

SYLVAIN LEFEBVRE

Yrs. of NHL service: 7
Born: Richmond, Que.; Oct. 14, 1967
Position: right defense
Height: 6-2
Weight: 205
Uniform no.: 2
Shoots: left

Career statistics:

GP	G	A	TP	PIM
488	22	85	107	417

1992-93 statistics:

GP	G	A	TP	+/-	PIM	PP	SH	GW	GT	S	PCT
81	2	12	14	+8	90	0	0	0	0	81	2.5

1993-94 statistics:

GP	G	A	TP	+/-	PIM	PP	SH	GW	GT	S	PCT
84	2	9	11	+33	79	0	0	0	1	96	2.1

1994-95 statistics:

GP	G	A	TP	+/-	PIM	PP	SH	GW	GT	S	PCT
48	2	11	13	+13	17	0	0	0	0	81	2.5

1995-96 statistics:

GP	G	A	TP	+/-	PIM	PP	SH	GW	GT	S	PCT
75	5	11	16	+26	49	2	0	0	0	115	4.3

a quiet leader, well respected by teammates and opponents. He made the perfect anchor for the roving Sandis Ozolinsh last season.

LAST SEASON
Missed six games with sprained ankle.

THE FINESSE GAME
Lefebvre is a good argument for instituting an NHL award for best defensive defensemen (as opposed to the Norris Trophy, which in recent years has gone to offensive defensemen). If there was such a piece of hardware, Lefebvre would be a finalist, if not a winner. He's one of the best at one-on-one coverage. He's always in position and always square with his man. He reads the play well, and makes good outlet passes from out of his own end.

Lefebvre plays his position the way any coach would try to teach it to a youngster. Safe and dependable, Lefebvre makes the first pass and then forgets about the puck. He couldn't be any less interested in the attack. If he has the puck at the offensive blueline and doesn't have a lane, he just throws it into the corner. His game is defense first, and he is very basic and consistent in his limited role. He does it all playing his "wrong" side on defense and matching up against the other team's top lines on a nightly basis.

Lefebvre actually has below-average skills in speed and puckhandling, but by playing within his limits and within the system he is ultrareliable.

THE PHYSICAL GAME
Tough without being a punishing hitter, Lefebvre patrols and controls the front of his net and plays a hard-nosed style. He plays a containment game.

THE INTANGIBLES
Lefebvre is a rock-solid defensive defenseman. He is

CLAUDE LEMIEUX

Yrs. of NHL service: 12
Born: Buckingham, Que.; July 16, 1965
Position: right wing
Height: 6-1
Weight: 215
Uniform no.: 22
Shoots: right

Career statistics:

GP	G	A	TP	PIM
715	261	258	519	1234

1992-93 statistics:

GP	G	A	TP	+/-	PIM	PP	SH	GW	GT	S	PCT
77	30	51	81	+2	155	13	0	3	2	311	9.6

1993-94 statistics:

GP	G	A	TP	+/-	PIM	PP	SH	GW	GT	S	PCT
79	18	26	44	+13	86	5	0	5	0	181	9.9

1994-95 statistics:

GP	G	A	TP	+/-	PIM	PP	SH	GW	GT	S	PCT
45	6	13	19	+2	86	1	0	1	0	117	5.1

1995-96 statistics:

GP	G	A	TP	+/-	PIM	PP	SH	GW	GT	S	PCT
79	39	32	71	+14	117	9	2	10	0	315	12.4

LAST SEASON

Acquired by Islanders from New Jersey for Steve Thomas; then acquired by Colorado for Wendel Clark on Oct. 3, 1995. Led team and tied for third in NHL in game-winning goals. Second on team in goals with second-best total of career. Second on team in shots. Third on team in power play goals.

THE FINESSE GAME

Lemieux challenged his Devils' contract at the start of last season, knowing the arbitration showdown would lead to his departure from New Jersey. And it did — landing him in Colorado, where he became only the fourth player in NHL history to win consecutive Stanley Cups with different teams. That's the way it always seems to go for Claude "Le Me," the squeaky wheel who always seems to roll into the right spot.

Lemieux is a shooter, a disturber, a force. He loves the puck, wants the puck, needs the puck and is sometimes obsessed with the puck. When he is struggling, that selfishness hurts the team. But when he gets into his groove everyone is happy to stand back and let him fly, and last season, on the talented Avalanche team, he fit right in.

When Lemieux is on, he can rock the house. He has a hard slap shot and shoots well off the fly. He isn't afraid to jam the front of the net for tips and screens and will battle for loose pucks. He has great hands for close-in shots. Although he wasn't asked to do much defensively for Colorado, he can kill penalties and check top forwards.

THE PHYSICAL GAME

Lemieux is strong, with good skating balance and great upper body and arm strength. He is very tough along the boards and in traffic in front of the net, out-duelling many bigger opponents because of his fierce desire. Because he is always whining and yapping, the abuse Lemieux takes is often ignored, but it's not unusual to find him with welts across his arms and cuts on his face. The satisfaction comes from knowing that his opponent usually looks even worse, but he still takes dumb penalties by jawing at the referees, who have little patience with him after all these years.

Lemieux was suspended twice during the playoffs for his overzealous work, and his reputation played a part in those rulings. Watch closely for Colorado's first game against Detroit, as Kris Draper was nailed from behind by Lemieux and injured when he went into the boards. Lemieux will be up for that one, too, as he is never intimidated by threats.

THE INTANGIBLES

Opponents hate Lemieux. Sometimes, his teammates do, too. But all was harmonious in Colorado last season as he stepped his play up to match his talented teammates. Lemieux might be due for a letdown this season, but even if he does slump, he'll be there in the playoffs. He is Mr. Spring.

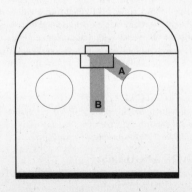

CURTIS LESCHYSHYN

Yrs. of NHL service: 8
Born: Thompson, Man.; Sept. 21, 1969
Position: left defense
Height: 6-1
Weight: 205
Uniform no.: 7
Shoots: left

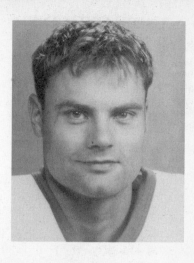

Career statistics:

GP	G	A	TP	PIM
516	33	100	133	503

1992-93 statistics:

GP	G	A	TP	+/-	PIM	PP	SH	GW	GT	S	PCT
82	9	23	32	+25	61	4	0	2	0	73	12.3

1993-94 statistics:

GP	G	A	TP	+/-	PIM	PP	SH	GW	GT	S	PCT
77	4	15	19	-7	143	0	2	1	0	66	6.1

1994-95 statistics:

GP	G	A	TP	+/-	PIM	PP	SH	GW	GT	S	PCT
44	2	13	15	+29	20	0	0	0	0	43	4.7

1995-96 statistics:

GP	G	A	TP	+/-	PIM	PP	SH	GW	GT	S	PCT
77	4	15	19	+32	73	0	0	1	0	76	5.3

THE INTANGIBLES

Leschyshyn is a solid two-way defenseman whose point totals will never rise much beyond the 25-30 point range. He has settled into using his finesse skills defensively.

LAST SEASON

Led team in plus-minus for second consecutive season. Missed two games with hip flexor.

THE FINESSE GAME

Leschyshyn has excellent skills for a big man, especially his skating, which is strong forward and backward. He has great lateral movement and quickness.

Leschyshyn has finely tuned stick skills. His passes are soft, and he will jump into the rush by skating the puck out of the defensive zone, moving it off his forehand or backhand. He is not as effective with his passes out of the zone, as he tends to get flustered, so he will usually lug it out when he gets the chance.

He has a nice point shot. It's low and accurate, and he gets it away quickly. He will also make a foray into the circle on occasion and can utilize his quick wrist shot. He knows the importance of getting the shot on target and would rather take a little velocity off the puck to make sure his aim is true.

Leschyshyn is not overly creative, and has become more defense-oriented in the past season. His reads are excellent.

THE PHYSICAL GAME

Leschyshyn is very fit. He made a successful comeback from a potentially career-threatening knee injury, a challenge that is more mental than physical. And he provides consistency and strong defensive-zone coverage.

Leschyshyn has become a more confident hitter, but he is not a big open-ice checker. He does make efficient take-outs to eliminate his man, and doesn't run around the ice trying to pound people.

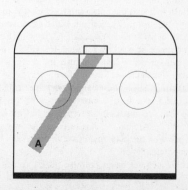

SANDIS OZOLINSH

Yrs. of NHL service: 4
Born: Riga, Latvia; Aug. 3, 1972
Position: left defense
Height: 6-1
Weight: 195
Uniform no.: 8
Shoots: left

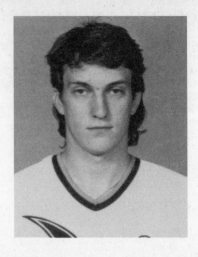

Career statistics:

GP	G	A	TP	PIM
239	56	110	166	148

1992-93 statistics:

GP	G	A	TP	+/-	PIM	PP	SH	GW	GT	S	PCT
37	7	16	23	-9	40	2	0	0	0	83	8.4

1993-94 statistics:

GP	G	A	TP	+/-	PIM	PP	SH	GW	GT	S	PCT
81	26	38	64	+16	24	4	0	3	0	157	16.6

1994-95 statistics:

GP	G	A	TP	+/-	PIM	PP	SH	GW	GT	S	PCT
48	9	16	25	-6	30	3	1	2	0	83	10.8

1995-96 statistics:

GP	G	A	TP	+/-	PIM	PP	SH	GW	GT	S	PCT
73	14	40	54	+2	54	8	1	1	1	166	8.4

LAST SEASON

Acquired from San Jose for Owen Nolan, Oct. 26, 1995. Led team defensemen in points. Missed two games with broken finger. Missed four games with shoulder separation.

THE FINESSE GAME

Ozolinsh is a pure "offenseman," but one who never knows when *not* to go. Unlike more intelligent rushing defensemen, such as Brian Leetch and Ray Bourque, Ozolinsh sees only one traffic light, and it's stuck on green.

Ozolinsh likes to start things by pressing in the neutral zone, where he will gamble and try to intercept cross-ice passes. His defense partner and the forwards will always have to be alert to guard against odd-man rushes back, because Ozolinsh doesn't recognize when it's a good time to be aggressive or when to back off.

When he does deign to visit his own zone, Ozolinsh will start the breakout play with his smooth skating, then spring a teammate with a crisp pass. He can pass on his forehand or backhand, which is a good thing because he is all over the ice. He will follow up the play to create an odd-man rush, trail in for a drop pass or drive to the net for a rebound.

Ozolinsh has good straightaway speed, but he can't make a lot of agile, pretty moves the way Paul Coffey can. Because he can't weave his way through a number of defenders, he has to power his way into open ice with the puck and drive the defenders back through intimidation.

He sometimes hangs onto the puck too long. He has a variety of shots, with his best being a one-timer from the off side on the power play. He is not as effective when he works down low. Ozolinsh does not stop and start well, especially when moving backwards.

THE PHYSICAL GAME

Ozolinsh goes into areas of the ice where he gets hit a lot, and he is stronger than he looks. He is all business on the ice and pays the price to get the puck, but he needs to develop more strength to clear out his crease.

THE INTANGIBLES

We said in last year's *HSR* that Ozolinsh was a sure bet for 50 points if he stayed healthy, and he managed to hit that mark despite losing some playing time to injuries. Few teams are as well-suited for his rushing style as Colorado, and this happy marriage may boost him into the top 10 of scoring defensemen next season.

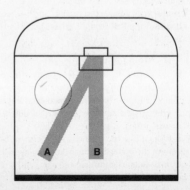

MIKE RICCI

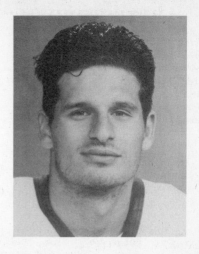

Yrs. of NHL service: 6
Born: Scarborough, Ont.; Oct. 27, 1971
Position: centre
Height: 6-0
Weight: 190
Uniform no.: 9
Shoots: left

Career statistics:

GP	G	A	TP	PIM
416	119	170	289	485

1992-93 statistics:

GP	G	A	TP	+/-	PIM	PP	SH	GW	GT	S	PCT
77	27	51	78	+8	123	12	1	10	1	142	19.0

1993-94 statistics:

GP	G	A	TP	+/-	PIM	PP	SH	GW	GT	S	PCT
83	30	21	51	-9	113	13	3	6	1	138	21.3

1994-95 statistics:

GP	G	A	TP	+/-	PIM	PP	SH	GW	GT	S	PCT
48	15	21	36	+5	40	9	0	1	1	73	20.5

1995-96 statistics:

GP	G	A	TP	+/-	PIM	PP	SH	GW	GT	S	PCT
62	6	21	27	+1	52	3	0	1	0	73	8.2

LAST SEASON

Missed 15 games with back injury. Missed three games with ankle injuries. Missed one game with sinus surgery.

THE FINESSE GAME

Ricci is a known quantity. He has terrific hand skills, combined with hockey sense and an outstanding work ethic. He always seems to be in the right place, ready to make the right play. He sees his passing options well and is patient with the puck. Ricci can rifle it as well. He has a good backhand shot from in deep and scores most of his goals from the slot by picking the top corners. His lone drawback is his speed. He's fast enough to not look out of place and he has good balance and agility, but his lack of quickness prevents him from being more of an offensive force.

Very slick on face-offs, he has good hand speed and hand-eye coordination for winning draws outright, or he can pick a bouncing puck out of the air. This serves him well in scrambles in front of the net, too, or he can deflect mid-air slap shots.

Ricci is a very good penalty killer, with poise and a controlled aggression for forcing the play.

THE PHYSICAL GAME

Ricci is not big, but he is so strong that it's not unusual to see him skate out from behind the net, dragging along or fending off a checker with one arm while he makes a pass or takes a shot with his other arm. He plays a tough game without being overly chippy. He is very strong in the corners and in front of the net. He plays bigger than he is.

Ricci will play hurt, and his injuries (especially the back injury) resulted in a sluggish second half for him last year, although his post-season performance more than atoned for his regular season. He pays attention to conditioning and has a great deal of stamina.

THE INTANGIBLES

Ricci proved his true value in the playoffs. When Claude Lemieux sat out with suspensions, Ricci stepped in as the antagonist. He drew penalties. He killed penalties. He made timely plays under pressure. Although he may never be as gifted offensively as Ron Francis is, he is similar to Francis in that he is a checking centre who can do so much more than just check.

Ricci's quality, character, leadership and dedication to the game and his teammates are impeccable. He is a throwback, and helps provide some grit in a finesse-laden lineup.

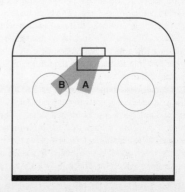

PATRICK ROY

Yrs. of NHL service: 11
Born: Quebec City, Que.; Oct. 5, 1965
Position: goaltender
Height: 6-0
Weight: 192
Uniform no.: 33
Catches: left

Career statistics:

GP	MIN	GA	SO	GAA	A	PIM
590	34223	1579	30	2.77	28	114

1992-93 statistics:

GP	MIN	GAA	W	L	T	SO	GA	S	SAPCT	PIM
62	3595	3.20	31	25	5	2	192	1814	.894	16

1993-94 statistics:

GP	MIN	GAA	W	L	T	SO	GA	S	SAPCT	PIM
68	3867	2.50	35	17	11	7	161	1956	.918	30

1994-95 statistics:

GP	MIN	GAA	W	L	T	SO	GA	S	SAPCT	PIM
43	2566	2.97	17	20	6	1	127	1357	.906	20

1995-96 statistics:

GP	MIN	GAA	W	L	T	SO	GA	S	SAPCT	PIM
61	3565	2.78	34	24	2	2	165	1797	.908	10

LAST SEASON

Acquired from Montreal with Mike Keane for Jocelyn Thibault, Martin Rucinsky and Andrei Kovalenko, Dec. 6, 1996. Became 12th NHL goalie to reach 300-win milestone. Stopped two penalty shots. Tied for third in NHL in wins. Sixth season with 30 or more wins.

THE PHYSICAL GAME

Roy is so cruel. He tempts shooters with a gaping hole between his pads, then when he has the guy suckered, snaps the pads closed at the last second to deny the goal. There is no one in the NHL better at this technique.

Roy is tall but not broad, yet he uses his body well. He plays his angles, stays at the top of his crease and squares his body to the shooter. He is able to absorb the shot and deaden it, so there are few juicy rebounds left on his doorstep.

A butterfly goalie, he goes down much sooner than he did earlier in his career. The book on Roy is to try to beat him high. Usually there isn't much net there and it's a small spot for a shooter to hit. He will get into slumps when he allows wide-angle shots taken from the blueline to the top of the circle, but those lapses are seldom prolonged.

Roy comes back to the rest of the pack in his puck-handling, where he is merely average. As for his skating, he seldoms moves out of his net. When he gets in trouble, he will move back and forth on his knees rather than try to regain his feet. His glove hand isn't great, either. It's good, but he prefers to use his body. If he is under a strong forecheck, Roy isn't shy about freezing the puck for a draw, especially since he plays with excellent face-off men in Colorado.

THE MENTAL GAME

If you have to win one game, this is the goalie you want in the net. As Roy proved in the 1996 playoffs, he still has the goods when a championship is on the line. Things worked out so well for Roy after the trade that, looking back, his outburst at Montreal president Ronald Corey — which precipitated Roy's quick trade — looks orchestrated.

THE INTANGIBLES

Given the supporting cast of young studs in front of him, Roy might be able to play effectively until he's 40. Even though Joe Sakic was a worthy Smythe Trophy recipient, don't believe for a minute that the Avalanche would have won the Cup with Jocelyn Thibault or Stephane Fiset in the net. Roy was the difference.

JOE SAKIC

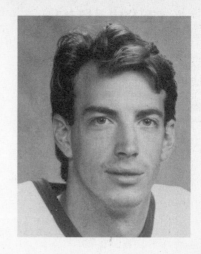

Yrs. of NHL service: 8
Born: Burnaby, B.C.; July 7, 1969
Position: centre
Height: 5-11
Weight: 185
Uniform no.: 19
Shoots: left

Career statistics:

GP	G	A	TP	PIM
590	285	461	746	227

1992-93 statistics:

GP	G	A	TP	+/-	PIM	PP	SH	GW	GT	S	PCT
78	48	57	105	-3	40	20	2	4	1	264	18.2

1993-94 statistics:

GP	G	A	TP	+/-	PIM	PP	SH	GW	GT	S	PCT
84	28	64	92	-8	18	10	1	9	1	279	10.0

1994-95 statistics:

GP	G	A	TP	+/-	PIM	PP	SH	GW	GT	S	PCT
47	19	43	62	+7	30	3	2	5	0	157	12.1

1995-96 statistics:

GP	G	A	TP	+/-	PIM	PP	SH	GW	GT	S	PCT
82	51	69	120	+14	44	17	6	7	1	339	15.0

LAST SEASON

Won 1996 Conn Smythe Trophy. Third in NHL and led team in points. Tied for fifth in NHL and led team in goals. Eighth in NHL and second on team in assists. Fifth in NHL and led team in shots. Led team and tied for second in NHL in shorthanded goals. Second on team in assists, power play goals and game-winning goals. Goals, assists and points all career highs. Fourth season with 100 points. One of five players to score on a penalty shot last season. One of two Colorado players to appear in all 82 games.

THE FINESSE GAME

We all knew Sakic could make plays, and we knew he could finish. The question was, when would Sakic ever get a little more selfish and shoot more? The answer came last season.

Sakic has one of the most explosive first steps in the league. He finds and hits the holes in a hurry, even with the puck, to create his chances. Sakic used a stick shaft with a little more "whip" in it last season, and that made his shots more dangerous. He has one of the best wrist shots and snap shots in the NHL.

Sakic's most impressive gift is his great patience with the puck. He will hold it until the last minute, when he has drawn the defenders to him and opened up ice, creating — as coaches love to express it — time and space for his linemates. This makes him a gem on the power play, where last season he worked mostly down low and just off the half-boards on the right wing. Sakic can also play the point.

Sakic is a scoring threat every time he is on the ice, because he can craft a dangerous scoring chance out of a situation that looks innocent. He is lethal trailing the rush. He takes a pass in full stride without slowing, then dekes and shoots before the goalie can even flinch.

Sakic is a good face-off man and if he is tied up, he will use his skates to kick the puck free.

THE PHYSICAL GAME

Sakic is not a physical player. He's stronger than he looks, and, like Wayne Gretzky, will spin off his checks when opponents take runs at him. He uses his body to protect the puck when he is carrying deep; you have to go through him to get it away. He will try to keep going through traffic or along the boards with the puck, and often squirts free with it because he is able to maintain control and his balance. He creates turnovers with his quickness and his hands, but not by initiating contact.

THE INTANGIBLES

The playoffs were one long coming-out party for Sakic, who may have been the league's best unknown player to that point. Sakic is a quiet leader, and a soft-spoken guy who doesn't draw much attention to himself. His game does that. We predicted 100 points for him last season, but never saw those goals coming. He should easily be in the top five in scoring again.

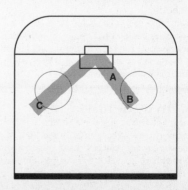

CHRIS SIMON

Yrs. of NHL service: 3
Born: Wawa, Ont.; Jan. 30, 1972
Position: left wing
Height: 6-3
Weight: 219
Uniform no.: 12
Shoots: left

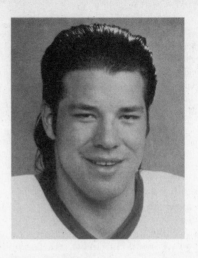

Career statistics:

GP	G	A	TP	PIM
146	24	32	56	555

1992-93 statistics:

GP	G	A	TP	+/-	PIM	PP	SH	GW	GT	S	PCT
16	1	1	2	-2	67	0	0	1	0	15	6.7

1993-94 statistics:

GP	G	A	TP	+/-	PIM	PP	SH	GW	GT	S	PCT
37	4	4	8	-2	132	0	0	1	0	39	10.3

1994-95 statistics:

GP	G	A	TP	+/-	PIM	PP	SH	GW	GT	S	PCT
29	3	9	12	+14	106	0	0	0	0	33	9.1

1995-96 statistics:

GP	G	A	TP	+/-	PIM	PP	SH	GW	GT	S	PCT
64	16	18	34	+10	250	4	0	1	0	105	15.2

THE INTANGIBLES

The door is open for him, since a team full of finesse players needs some balance in grit, but there are questions about how badly he wants it. There is much left to prove, and Simon has to concentrate on his conditioning and skating to improve.

LAST SEASON

Led team in penalty minutes for second consecutive season. Missed four games with shoulder injury. Missed two games with back spasms. Missed one game with flu.

THE FINESSE GAME

In many ways, Simon is the prototypical NHL fourth-line winger. He has made his reputation with his toughness, but has shown an added dimension in his ability to make plays that result in points. Whenever he does, jaws drop and observers wonder, "Where did that move came from?" But they shouldn't be so dumbfounded. After all, Simon gets a lot of room, which gives a player with modest skills more time to make a play.

What he doesn't get is a lot of ice time, and without it, Simon is not going to advance much. Unless he improves his skating — especially given the fact he plays on a very fast team — he'll spend a lot of time on the bench.

Simon has decent hands for a big guy, but all of his successes come in tight. Lack of quickness is a major drawback. If he gets a regular shift, he will answer the questions about his consistency and might produce some surprising numbers, but there are a couple of steps he has to take to reach that level.

THE PHYSICAL GAME

Simon is as tough as they come and has a wide streak of mean. He has already established himself as a player who can throw them when the time comes, and opponents have to keep a wary eye on him because they never know when he's going to snap.

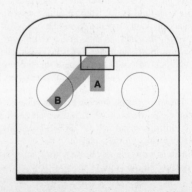

LANDON WILSON

Yrs. of NHL service: 0
Born: St. Louis, Mo; Mar. 13, 1975
Position: right wing
Height: 6-2
Weight: 202
Uniform no.: 14
Shoots: right

Career statistics:

GP	G	A	TP	PIM
7	1	0	1	6

1995-96 statistics:

GP	G	A	TP	+/-	PIM	PP	SH	GW	GT	S	PCT
7	1	0	1	+3	6	0	0	0	0	6	16.7

LAST SEASON

Will be entering first NHL season. Played 53 games with Cornwall (AHL), scoring 21-13 — 34 with 154 PIM.

THE FINESSE GAME

Wilson blends toughness and skill into a package that may be ready to be opened by the Avalanche.

A fine all-around athlete with good stamina, Wilson has developed a variety of shots. He can stick-handle around a defender and release a quick snap shot, or he can unload a powerful slap shot from the top of the circles. He has keen offensive instincts, and he is a finisher.

He doesn't have blazing speed, but he has good anticipation that buys him a step in a race, and he will power his way to the net with the puck or in pursuit of a rebound.

Wilson has an excellent work ethic (that might have something to do with his dad, Rick, being an NHL assistant coach) and has pushed himself to become a better player.

THE PHYSICAL GAME

Wilson is solidly built and strong on his skates, and competes for the puck in the high-traffic areas. There are some question marks about his intensity, but Wilson was fairly consistent in his physical effort last year after shaking off an early-season leg injury. He has not been able to dominate games in the pros the way he did as a younger player.

THE INTANGIBLES

Breaking into a Stanley Cup-winning lineup is no easy task, but if there is one spot where the Avalanche isn't exactly loaded, it's right wing, and Wilson could threaten for a job on the number two line. Because he played his minor hockey in Los Angeles, of all places, and played college hockey instead of major junior, this budding power forward has been brought along slowly, but he could be ready to step in.

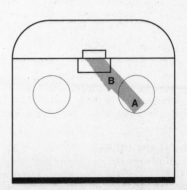

SCOTT YOUNG

Yrs. of NHL service: 7
Born: Clinton, Mass.; Oct. 1, 1967
Position: right wing
Height: 6-0
Weight: 190
Uniform no.: 48
Shoots: right

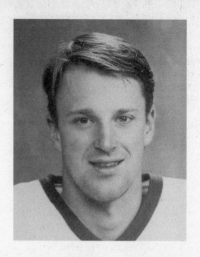

Career statistics:

GP	G	A	TP	PIM
527	155	220	375	215

1992-93 statistics:

GP	G	A	TP	+/-	PIM	PP	SH	GW	GT	S	PCT
82	30	30	60	+5	20	9	6	5	0	225	13.3

1993-94 statistics:

GP	G	A	TP	+/-	PIM	PP	SH	GW	GT	S	PCT
76	26	25	51	-4	14	6	1	1	0	236	11.0

1994-95 statistics:

GP	G	A	TP	+/-	PIM	PP	SH	GW	GT	S	PCT
48	18	21	39	+9	14	3	3	0	0	167	10.8

1995-96 statistics:

GP	G	A	TP	+/-	PIM	PP	SH	GW	GT	S	PCT
81	21	39	60	+2	50	7	0	5	0	229	9.2

model of consistency. Players with great wheels like his tend to last a long time, so expect him to display his veteran ability for many more seasons. His only problem is playing for the talent-rich Avalanche, because he doesn't always get a huge chunk of ice time. When he does, though, Young is ready.

LAST SEASON

Fifth on team in points. Tied for third on team in game-winning goals. Missed one game in contract dispute.

THE FINESSE GAME

Young is a hockey machine. He has a very heavy shot that surprises a lot of goalies. He loves to fire it off the wing or he can one-time the puck low on the face-off, or he will battle for pucks and tips in front of the net. Young is keen to score and always goes to the net with his stick down, ready for the puck.

With all of that in mind, his defensive awareness is even more impressive, because Young is basically a checking winger. He reads plays in all zones equally well and has good anticipation. Young played defense in college, so he is well-schooled.

Young is a very fast skater, which, combined with his reads, makes him a sound forechecker. He will often outrace defensemen to touch pucks and avoid icings, and his speed allows him to recover when he gets overzealous in the attacking zone.

THE PHYSICAL GAME

Young's lone drawback is that he is not a very physical player. He will do what he has to do in battles along the boards in the defensive zone, but he's more of a defensive force with his quickness and hand skills. He's not a pure grinder, but will bump and get in the way.

THE INTANGIBLES

A checking winger who can score 60 points is a rarity, and Young is that. He is a complete player and a

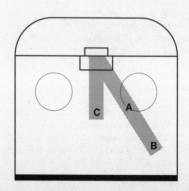

DALLAS STARS

Players' Statistics 1995-96

POS.	NO.	PLAYER	GP	G	A	PTS	+/-	PIM	PP	SH	GW	GT	S	PCT
C	9	MIKE MODANO	78	36	45	81	-12	63	8	4	4	1	320	11.3
C	33	BENOIT HOGUE	78	19	45	64	10	104	5		5		155	12.3
L	23	GREG ADAMS	66	22	21	43	-21	33	11	1	1		140	15.7
C	41	BRENT GILCHRIST	77	20	22	42	-11	36	6	1	2		164	12.2
D	4	KEVIN HATCHER	74	15	26	41	-24	58	7		3	2	237	6.3
L	20	BRENT FEDYK	65	20	14	34	-16	54	8				113	17.7
C	25	JOE NIEUWENDYK	52	14	18	32	-17	41	8		3		138	10.1
D	2	DERIAN HATCHER	79	8	23	31	-12	129	2		1		125	6.4
C	10	TODD HARVEY	69	9	20	29	-13	136	3		1		101	8.9
R	29	*GRANT MARSHALL	70	9	19	28	0	111				1	62	14.5
R	26	*JERE LEHTINEN	57	6	22	28	5	16			1		109	5.5
L	39	MIKE KENNEDY	61	9	17	26	-7	48	4		1		111	8.1
D	12	GRANT LEDYARD	73	5	19	24	-15	20	2		1		123	4.1
C	21	GUY CARBONNEAU	71	8	15	23	-2	38		2	1		54	14.8
D	24	RICHARD MATVICHUK	73	6	16	22	4	71			1		81	7.4
L	44	RANDY WOOD	76	8	13	21	-15	62	1				159	5.0
D	6	DARRYL SYDOR	84	3	17	20	-12	75	2				117	2.6
L	17	BILL HUARD	51	6	6	12	3	176					34	17.6
L	11	MIKE DONNELLY	24	2	5	7	-2	10					21	9.5
C	16	*JAMIE LANGENBRUNNER	12	2	2	4	-2	6	1				15	13.3
R	20	NIKOLAI BORSCHEVSKY	12	1	3	4	-7	6			1		22	4.5
L	43	JIM STORM	10	1	2	3	-1	17			1		11	9.1
D	18	MIKE LALOR	63	1	2	3	-10	31					46	2.2
D	3	CRAIG LUDWIG	65	1	2	3	-17	70					47	2.1
C	22	ROBERT PETROVICKY	5	1	1	2	1		1		1		3	33.3
C	28	BOB BASSEN	13		1	1	-6	15					9	
R	38	*MARK LAWRENCE	13		1	1	0	17					13	
D	32	*TRAVIS RICHARDS	1				-1	2						
G	31	*JORDAN WILLIS	1				0							
D	40	PAT MACLEOD	2				0						2	
R	37	*ZAC BOYER	2				0						3	
L	40	*PATRICK COTE	2				-2	5						
R	14	DAN MAROIS	3				0	2					1	
R	25	*DAN KESA	3				-1							
G	30	EMMANUEL FERNANDEZ	5				0							
D	14	PAUL CAVALLINI	8				-3	6					5	
G	45	ALLAN BESTER	10				0	2						
G	34	DARCY WAKALUK	37				0	6					1	
G	35	ANDY MOOG	41				0	28						

GP = games played; G = goals; A = assists; PTS = points; +/- = goals-for minus goals-against while player is on ice; PIM = penalties in minutes; PP = power play goals; SH = shorthanded goals; GW = game-winning goals; GT = game-tying goals; S = no. of shots; PCT = percentage of goals to shots; * = rookie

GREG ADAMS

Yrs. of NHL service: 12
Born: Nelson, B.C.; Aug. 1, 1963
Position: left wing
Height: 6-3
Weight: 195
Uniform no.: 23
Shoots: left

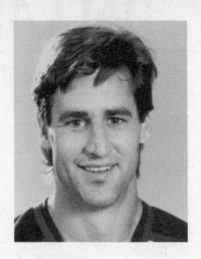

Career statistics:

GP	G	A	TP	PIM
753	271	292	563	254

1992-93 statistics:

GP	G	A	TP	+/-	PIM	PP	SH	GW	GT	S	PCT
53	25	31	56	+31	14	6	1	3	0	124	20.2

1993-94 statistics:

GP	G	A	TP	+/-	PIM	PP	SH	GW	GT	S	PCT
68	13	24	37	-1	20	5	1	2	0	139	9.4

1994-95 statistics:

GP	G	A	TP	+/-	PIM	PP	SH	GW	GT	S	PCT
43	8	13	21	-3	16	3	2	0	0	72	11.1

1995-96 statistics:

GP	G	A	TP	+/-	PIM	PP	SH	GW	GT	S	PCT
66	22	21	43	-21	33	11	1	1	0	140	15.7

LAST SEASON

Led team in power play goals. Second on team in goals. Third on team in points. Missed 11 games with fractured hand. Missed four games with broken toe.

THE FINESSE GAME

Adams is faster than he looks because he has a long, almost lazy stride, but he covers a lot of ground quickly and with an apparent lack of effort.

He can shoot a hard slap shot on the fly off the wing, but most of his goals come from within five feet of the net. He drives fearlessly to the goal and likes to arrive by the most expedient route possible. If that means crashing through defensemen, then so be it. Adams has good, shifty moves in deep and is an unselfish player. He played a lot of centre early in his career and is nearly as good a playmaker as finisher. One of the few knocks on him is that he doesn't shoot enough. One of his best scoring moves is a high backhand in tight. He always has his head up and is looking for the holes.

Adams has worked hard at improving his defensive awareness and has become a reliable player.

THE PHYSICAL GAME

Adams's crease-crashing style exacts a price; he is nearly always wearing an ice pack or getting medical attention for a nick or bruise. Yet he always comes right back for more. He is physical and tough without being aggressive. He does not fight and, considering the checking attention he gets, he remains remarkably calm and determined, seldom taking bad retaliatory penalties. He just gets the job done. Adams is stronger than he looks.

THE INTANGIBLES

Adams is an underrated player, but one who is always appreciated by his coach and teammates because of his attitude and work habits. He always shows up for the opening face-off and plays through the final buzzer. We predicted a big bounce-back season for Adams last season, and at age 32 and playing for a very bad Dallas team, 22 goals constitutes a pretty fair rebound. We don't expect much more out of him at this stage, but he has the hand skills to attain 20 again — more if he can ever stay healthy, which is unlikely.

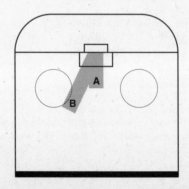

BOB BASSEN

Yrs. of NHL service: 10
Born: Calgary, Alta.; May 6, 1965
Position: centre/left wing
Height: 5-10
Weight: 180
Uniform no.: 28
Shoots: left

Career statistics:

GP	G	A	TP	PIM
569	76	130	206	816

1992-93 statistics:

GP	G	A	TP	+/-	PIM	PP	SH	GW	GT	S	PCT
53	9	10	19	0	63	0	1	0	0	61	14.8

1993-94 statistics:

GP	G	A	TP	+/-	PIM	PP	SH	GW	GT	S	PCT
59	11	17	28	+2	70	1	1	1	0	73	15.1

1994-95 statistics:

GP	G	A	TP	+/-	PIM	PP	SH	GW	GT	S	PCT
47	12	15	27	+14	33	0	1	1	0	66	18.2

1995-96 statistics:

GP	G	A	TP	+/-	PIM	PP	SH	GW	GT	S	PCT
13	0	1	1	-6	15	0	0	0	0	9	0.0

LAST SEASON

Missed 66 games with knee injury.

THE FINESSE GAME

Bassen has average straightaway speed, and with the playing time missed due to injuries (for the third consecutive season), he looked even slower after he returned to the lineup late last season. But he does have quickness and agility when healthy, which he puts to work in close quarters to avoid hits from bigger players. Don't get us wrong: if Bassen has to take a hit, he will, but he's also smart enough to avoid unnecessary punishment.

Bassen doesn't have great hands or a great shot to go with his work ethic. All of his finesse skills are average at best. His few goals come from going for the puck in scrambles around the net.

Bassen is only so-so on face-offs. He's not big enough to tie up most opposing centres, and he lacks the hand speed to win draws outright. He does try to scrunch himself low on draws to get his head under the opposing centre's to block the sight of the puck.

THE PHYSICAL GAME

Bassen plays much bigger than his size, aware every night that if he isn't scrapping along the boards or in front of the net, someone might take his job. He is extremely fit. There isn't an ounce of body fat on him. He hates to lose.

Bassen has a low centre of gravity, which makes it tough to knock him off his feet, and he's closer to the puck than a lot of skaters. He often wins scrums just by being able to pry the puck loose from flailing feet.

THE INTANGIBLES

Bassen is a blood and guts competitor, a throwback to hockey's glory days with the skills of a '90s player. A reliable team man, he's one of those players who always delivers an honest effort, which is why Dallas is counting on him this season despite his injury problems. He matches up night after night against most of the league's bigger, better forwards, and makes them work for what they get. He is a valuable role player, and a role model as well. Unasked, Bassen goes out of his way to help younger players.

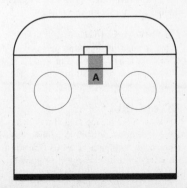

BRENT FEDYK

Yrs. of NHL service: 8
Born: Yorkton, Sask.; Mar. 8, 1967
Position: left wing
Height: 6-0
Weight: 195
Uniform no.: 20
Shoots: right

Career statistics:

GP	G	A	TP	PIM
403	93	106	199	278

1992-93 statistics:

GP	G	A	TP	+/-	PIM	PP	SH	GW	GT	S	PCT
74	21	38	59	+14	48	4	1	2	2	167	12.6

1993-94 statistics:

GP	G	A	TP	+/-	PIM	PP	SH	GW	GT	S	PCT
72	20	18	38	-14	74	5	0	1	0	104	19.2

1994-95 statistics:

GP	G	A	TP	+/-	PIM	PP	SH	GW	GT	S	PCT
30	8	4	12	-2	14	3	0	2	0	41	19.5

1995-96 statistics:

GP	G	A	TP	+/-	PIM	PP	SH	GW	GT	S	PCT
65	20	14	34	-16	54	8	0	0	0	113	17.7

LAST SEASON

Acquired from Philadelphia for Trent Klatt, Dec. 13, 1995. Tied for second on team in power play goals. Tied for third on team in goals. Missed one game with groin injury. Missed games with hamstring injury.

THE FINESSE GAME

Fedyk enjoyed some brief moments of glory in Philadelphia in the pre-Legion of Doom days as Eric Lindros's left wing, but that era is long gone. Fedyk finished last season as Joe Nieuwendyk's left wing, but he will be on the bubble there if any of the Dallas youngsters are ready to step up.

Fedyk was a successful scorer at the minor-league level but has never been able to convert that success in the NHL because of his limited skating skills. He will go to the net hard with the puck but isn't a true power forward because he doesn't convert his chances.

He is quite diligent defensively, having served mostly as a checking winger in Detroit's system. He kills penalties and is a shorthanded threat.

THE PHYSICAL GAME

Fedyk is not an imposing physical specimen and he is reluctant to make use of what size he has. He will not take a hit to make a play and his checks are half-hearted.

THE INTANGIBLES

Twenty goals is about the top range for Fedyk, which would be fine if he were back to being a third-line winger but it isn't enough of a contribution for a second-line forward who gets power play time.

BRENT GILCHRIST

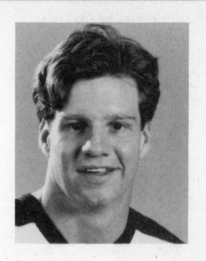

Yrs. of NHL service: 8
Born: Moose Jaw, Sask.; Apr. 3, 1967
Position: centre/left wing
Height: 5-11
Weight: 181
Uniform no.: 41
Shoots: left

Career statistics:

GP	G	A	TP	PIM
489	102	118	220	243

1992-93 statistics:

GP	G	A	TP	+/-	PIM	PP	SH	GW	GT	S	PCT
68	10	11	21	-12	49	2	0	0	0	106	9.4

1993-94 statistics:

GP	G	A	TP	+/-	PIM	PP	SH	GW	GT	S	PCT
76	17	14	31	0	31	3	1	5	0	103	16.5

1994-95 statistics:

GP	G	A	TP	+/-	PIM	PP	SH	GW	GT	S	PCT
32	9	4	13	-3	16	1	3	1	0	70	12.9

1995-96 statistics:

GP	G	A	TP	+/-	PIM	PP	SH	GW	GT	S	PCT
77	20	22	42	-11	36	6	1	2	0	164	12.2

LAST SEASON

Tied for third on team in goals. Fourth on team in points. Missed four games with groin injury.

THE FINESSE GAME

Gilchrist is a versatile forward who can play all three positions up front. He has the versatility to play on the top line in a scoring role in a pinch, but is better on the third line as a checker. Gilchrist has good knowledge of the ice. He anticipates well and is a smart and effective penalty killer.

Gilchrist was a prolific scorer in junior and in the minors, but hasn't shown the same touch at the NHL level and has become more of a defensive specialist. He actually spent time on a fourth line last season, and there are few fourth-line players who can give you 20 goals a season.

Gilchrist will work hard around the net and generates most of his scoring chances there. He has good balance and quickness in small areas, but is not a great finisher.

THE PHYSICAL GAME

Gilchrist is a strong player, though he doesn't take command of the ice. His good skating helps him move around and create a little more havoc, and he's not afraid to stand in and take a drubbing around the net. He won't back down from a challenge.

THE INTANGIBLES

Because Gilchrist is a hockey chameleon, he never seems to be given one definitive role. He can be slotted into so many situations. His 20 goals last season probably represents his top end.

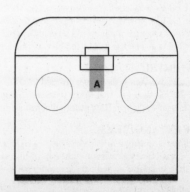

TODD HARVEY

Yrs. of NHL service: 2
Born: Hamilton, Ont.; Feb. 17, 1975
Position: centre/right wing
Height: 5-11
Weight: 200
Uniform no.: 10
Shoots: right

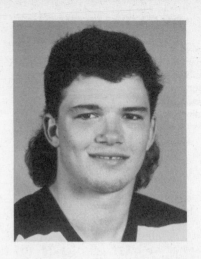

Career statistics:

GP	G	A	TP	PIM
109	20	29	49	203

1994-95 statistics:

GP	G	A	TP	+/-	PIM	PP	SH	GW	GT	S	PCT
40	11	9	20	-3	67	2	0	1	0	64	17.2

1995-96 statistics:

GP	G	A	TP	+/-	PIM	PP	SH	GW	GT	S	PCT
69	9	20	29	-13	136	3	0	1	0	101	8.9

LAST SEASON

Second on team in penalty minutes. Played in five games with Michigan (IHL), scoring 1-3 — 4. Missed two games with sprained knee. Missed one game with sore wrist.

THE FINESSE GAME

Chalk up Harvey's sophomore season as a real learning experience.

Everything came fairly easy for Harvey in his rookie year. Not much was expected of him, and despite some of the flaws in his game, he prevailed with his work effort. As a result, more was expected of him last season, and Harvey, thinking the game was easy, eased back on the throttle a bit. He lost an edge in his confidence and got a brief stint in the minors, which was probably an eye-opener for him. In hindsight, it probably would have helped him to go down earlier in the year.

Harvey's skating is rough. In fact, it's pretty choppy, and as a result he lacks speed. To make up for that, Harvey has good anticipation and awareness. He's clever and his hands are very good. When he gets the puck, he has patience and strength with it. Harvey went to a skating camp in the off-season to try to improve in that area.

Harvey's goals are ugly ones. He works the front of the net with grit. He goes to the net and follows up shots with second and third effort. He always has his feet moving and he has good hand-eye coordination.

THE PHYSICAL GAME

Size isn't everything, as Harvey learned in his rookie year. He has to regain that feisty style and get inside people's jerseys again. He's proven that he can do it.

THE INTANGIBLES

The Stars' acquisition of Pat Verbeek — a right wing, which was Harvey's position on the third line at the end of last season — and the development of Jere

Lehtinen does not bode well for Harvey. He will have to have a terrific camp, or he is destined for the third line. Harvey is such a character player that he should put up a fight.

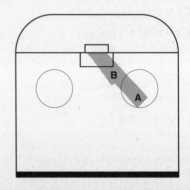

DERIAN HATCHER

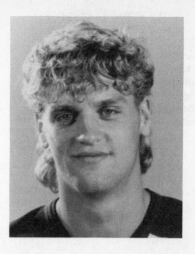

Yrs. of NHL service: 5
Born: Sterling Heights, Mich.; June 4, 1972
Position: left defense
Height: 6-5
Weight: 225
Uniform no.: 2
Shoots: left

Career statistics:

GP	G	A	TP	PIM
315	36	73	109	711

1992-93 statistics:

GP	G	A	TP	+/-	PIM	PP	SH	GW	GT	S	PCT
67	4	15	19	-27	178	0	0	1	1	73	5.5

1993-94 statistics:

GP	G	A	TP	+/-	PIM	PP	SH	GW	GT	S	PCT
83	12	19	31	+19	211	2	1	2	0	132	9.1

1994-95 statistics:

GP	G	A	TP	+/-	PIM	PP	SH	GW	GT	S	PCT
43	5	11	16	+3	105	2	0	2	0	74	6.8

1995-96 statistics:

GP	G	A	TP	+/-	PIM	PP	SH	GW	GT	S	PCT
79	8	23	31	-12	129	2	0	1	0	125	6.4

LAST SEASON

Second among team defensemen in scoring. Missed three games with shoulder injury.

THE FINESSE GAME

Sometimes the brother act works, sometimes it doesn't. Putting the big Hacher boys together seemed like a good idea at first, but Kevin struggled in Dallas, and as captain of the team, Derian was affected. Now that Kevin has been traded, it will be a relief, whether Derian recognizes it or not.

Hatcher plays in all key situations and is developing a confidence in his decision-making process. His skating is laboured (he has attended skating camps in the off-season to improve). So Hatcher lets the play come to him instead of, say, trying to chase Pavel Bure all over the ice. He is sturdy and well-balanced. The fewer strides he has to take, the better.

He has very good hands for a big man, and he has a good head for the game. Hatcher is fairly effective from the point on the power play — not because he has a big, booming slap shot, but because he has a good wrist shot and will get the puck on net quickly. He will join the rush eagerly once he gets into gear (his first few strides are sluggish) and he handles the puck nicely.

Hatcher makes fewer mistakes and his game is becoming more low-risk.

THE PHYSICAL GAME

Hatcher is a big force. He has a mean streak when provoked and is a punishing hitter, but has a long enough fuse to stay away from bad penalties. He plays physically every night and demands respect and room.

He is a big horse and eats up all the ice time Dallas gives him. The more work he gets, the better.

THE INTANGIBLES

Adding Sergei Zubov to the lineup will mean some defensive headaches for the Stars, but it will take a big weight off of Hatcher, who is expected to be an offensively oriented two-way defenseman. His offensive skills are overrated, but Hatcher is the kind of player the team looks to for consistent effort and intensity. He is a fine role model for the younger Stars and the veterans repect him as well. He is a quiet player who wants to make a big impact.

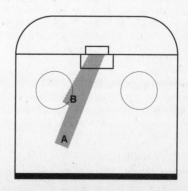

BENOIT HOGUE

Yrs. of NHL service: 8
Born: Repentigny, Que.; Oct. 28, 1966
Position: centre/right wing
Height: 5-10
Weight: 190
Uniform no.: 33
Shoots: left

Career statistics:

GP	G	A	TP	PIM
544	172	239	411	661

1992-93 statistics:

GP	G	A	TP	+/-	PIM	PP	SH	GW	GT	S	PCT
70	33	42	75	+13	108	5	3	5	0	147	22.4

1993-94 statistics:

GP	G	A	TP	+/-	PIM	PP	SH	GW	GT	S	PCT
83	36	33	69	-7	73	9	5	3	0	218	16.5

1994-95 statistics:

GP	G	A	TP	+/-	PIM	PP	SH	GW	GT	S	PCT
45	9	7	16	0	34	2	0	2	1	66	13.6

1995-96 statistics:

GP	G	A	TP	+/-	PIM	PP	SH	GW	GT	S	PCT
78	19	45	64	+10	104	5	0	5	0	155	12.3

two years, not a very good sign, but he played well in Dallas (27 points in 34 games) on the team's top line with Mike Modano, so he may be comfortable . . . for awhile.

LAST SEASON

Acquired with Randy Wood for Dave Gagner and a sixth-round draft pick, Jan. 29, 1996. Led team in plus-minus and game-winning goals. Tied for team lead in assists. Second on team in points.

THE FINESSE GAME

Hogue's chief asset is his speed. He is explosive, leaving defenders flat-footed with his acceleration. Add to that his anticipation and ability to handle the puck at a high tempo, and the result is an ever-lurking breakaway threat. Hogue is not a great puckhandler or shooter, but he capitalizes on each situation with his quickness and agility. He is a threat to score whenever he is on the ice.

Hogue plays primarily on the left side and even when playing centre will cut to the left wing boards as he drives down the ice. He is not a great playmaker, but he creates scoring chances off his rushes.

He is an excellent, aggressive penalty killer who is a shorthanded threat, and he can also be used on the power play, though he lacks the patience to be as effective as he could be. He is very good on draws.

THE PHYSICAL GAME

Hogue is a strong one-on-one player who will use his body to lean on an opponent. He is not a big checker, but he gets involved and uses his speed as a weapon to intimidate. He is a crunch-time player, whether a team needs to protect a lead or create one. He can get into ruts where he takes bad penalties.

THE INTANGIBLES

Hogue has changed uniforms three times in the past

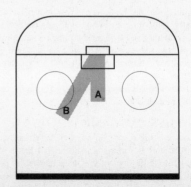

MIKE KENNEDY

Yrs. of NHL service: 2
Born: Vancouver, B.C.; April 13, 1972
Position: centre/left wing
Height: 6-1
Weight: 170
Uniform no.: 39
Shoots: right

Career statistics:

GP	G	A	TP	PIM
105	15	29	44	81

1994-95 statistics:

GP	G	A	TP	+/-	PIM	PP	SH	GW	GT	S	PCT
44	6	12	18	+4	33	2	0	0	0	76	7.9

1995-96 statistics:

GP	G	A	TP	+/-	PIM	PP	SH	GW	GT	S	PCT
61	9	17	26	-7	48	4	0	1	0	111	8.1

LAST SEASON
Second NHL season.

THE FINESSE GAME
Kennedy is deceiving in all aspects of his game. His skating is better than it looks and his puck work is better than his statistics indicate.

He has a good head for the game and good hands. He is very patient with the puck and is always involved in high-traffic areas to gain control. When he gets it, Kennedy has a fine short game with his passes or shot. He was moved back to the right side last season, and felt more comfortable there, but the Stars are looking deep on the right wing and he might have to go back on his off-side.

Kennedy is developing into a dependable two-way winger, along Mike McPhee lines. He plays hard no matter what the score is, and forechecks reliably and consistently.

THE PHYSICAL GAME
Kennedy isn't big, but he's strong in a rangy way. He's willing to go to war for the puck in the corners, along the boards and in front of the net. There can never be too many of these kinds of players in a team's system.

THE INTANGIBLES
Kennedy will be a bubble player again this year because his skill level isn't high enough to produce much more than 30-40 points. He is an earnest sort who is hard to keep out of the lineup because of his effort.

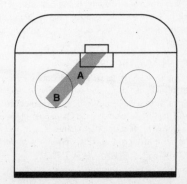

JAMIE LANGENBRUNNER

Yrs. of NHL service: 1
Born: Duluth, MN; July 24, 1975
Position: centre
Height: 5-11
Weight: 185
Uniform no.: 16
Shoots: right

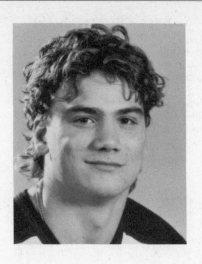

Career statistics:

GP	G	A	TP	PIM
14	2	2	4	8

1994-95 statistics:

GP	G	A	TP	+/-	PIM	PP	SH	GW	GT	S	PCT
2	0	0	0	0	2	0	0	0	0	1	0.0

1995-96 statistics:

GP	G	A	TP	+/-	PIM	PP	SH	GW	GT	S	PCT
12	2	2	4	-2	6	1	0	0	0	15	13.3

LAST SEASON

Will be entering first NHL season. Played 59 games with Michigan (IHL), scoring 25-40 — 65.

THE FINESSE GAME

Dallas has been patient with this promising blue chipper, allowing him to gain ice time and develop a more well-rounded game in the minors. He has progressed well and should start the season in Dallas.

Langenbrunner has terrific hand skills. He is intelligent and poised with the puck, and can play as a centre or a right wing. He has good hockey vision and can pick his spots for shots. He is also a smart passer on either his forehand or backhand.

He is only an average skater, so he won't be coming in with speed and driving a shot off the wing. He's not dynamic at all. Langenbrunner has a strong short game, with his offense generated within 15-20 feet of the net. He has a quick release on his shot.

THE PHYSICAL GAME

Langebrunner competes hard in the hard areas of the ice, to either get a puck or get himself into a space to get the puck. He is showing signs of being a tough, competitive forward. He lacks the size to be a power forward, but he may turn out to be one of the gritty types who are so annoying to play against, like Jeremy Roenick. He won't just hang on the perimeter. Langenbrunner won't back down and will even try to stir things up.

THE INTANGIBLES

Adjusting to the NHL game is tough enough. Doing it in as depressing an atmosphere as is likely to enshroud the Stars next season may preclude Langenbrunner from taking his place among the Calder Trophy candidates. One of his best qualities is his desire to succeed, and he has a history of playing well in big games under pressure.

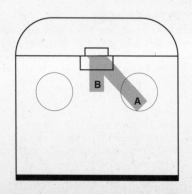

JERE LEHTINEN

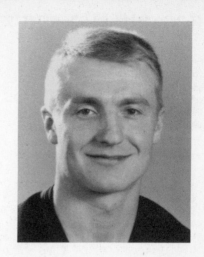

Yrs. of NHL service: 1
Born: Espoo, Finland; June 24, 1973
Position: right wing
Height: 6-0
Weight: 185
Uniform no.: 26
Shoots: right

Career statistics:

GP	G	A	TP	PIM
57	6	22	28	16

1995-96 statistics:

GP	G	A	TP	+/-	PIM	PP	SH	GW	GT	S	PCT
57	6	22	28	+5	16	0	0	1	0	109	5.5

LAST SEASON

First NHL season. Third on team in plus-minus. Missed seven games with groin injuries.

THE FINESSE GAME

Lehtinen stepped in last season and impressed his coaches and veteran teammates with his intelligent approach to the game. He has excellent hockey sense and vision.

His skating is well above adequate. He's not really top flight, but he has enough quickness and balance to play with highly skilled people, and was often used on a line with Mike Modano last season. Lehtinen controls the puck well and is an unselfish playmaker.

Lehtinen struggles only in his finishing. He appears to have a good shot with a quick release, but at times is reluctant to shoot. He endured some prolonged slumps last season, when he was lacking in confidence. He seemed to hit a lot of posts or catch bad breaks during the dry spells, and could just as quickly turn things around if some of those pucks start going in for him.

THE PHYSICAL GAME

Lehtinen is very strong on the puck, but he isn't a real physical force. He will protect the puck and won't be intimidated. Lehtinen competes along the boards. He completes his checks and never stops trying. He is very durable.

THE INTANGIBLES

Lehtinen never asked anything of the club, never complained, just asked what he could do or what he needed to do to become better. In short, a coach's dream. He received more and more ice time as a result of his effort and attitude, and was one of the few pleasant surprises of the season for Dallas. He was never a prolific scorer in Finland, but given his skills he could notch 25 to 30 goals and perform well defensively, which is a nice combination.

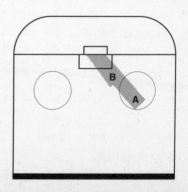

RICHARD MATVICHUK

Yrs. of NHL service: 4
Born: Edmonton, Alta.; Feb. 5, 1973
Position: left defense
Height: 6-2
Weight: 195
Uniform no.: 24
Shoots: left

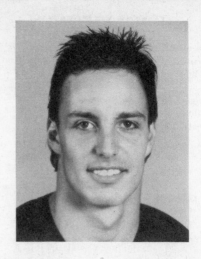

Career statistics:

GP	G	A	TP	PIM
165	8	24	32	133

1992-93 statistics:

GP	G	A	TP	+/-	PIM	PP	SH	GW	GT	S	PCT
53	2	3	5	-8	26	1	0	0	0	51	3.9

1993-94 statistics:

GP	G	A	TP	+/-	PIM	PP	SH	GW	GT	S	PCT
25	0	3	3	+1	22	0	0	0	0	18	0.0

1994-95 statistics:

GP	G	A	TP	+/-	PIM	PP	SH	GW	GT	S	PCT
14	0	2	2	-7	14	0	0	0	0	21	0.0

1995-96 statistics:

GP	G	A	TP	+/-	PIM	PP	SH	GW	GT	S	PCT
73	6	16	22	+4	71	71	0	0	1	0	7.4

LAST SEASON

Third on team in plus-minus. Missed four games with concussion.

THE FINESSE GAME

Matvichuk is starting to find his own niche as a mobile, defensive defenseman. Matvichuk is a good skater with a long stride, and he skates well backwards and pivots in either direction. He likes to get involved in the attack in a limited capacity. He has the hand skills and instincts to play with the offensive players to a point, but that is not a high priority with him. He uses his hockey skills defensively.

Matvichuk has a low, hard, accurate shot from the point. He makes smart, crisp passes and uses other players well. He can play either side defensively.

Matvichuk wants the ice time when the team needs a calm, defensive presence on the ice. He will kill penalties and block shots, and appears to be physically and mentally recovered from his knee surgery of a year ago.

THE PHYSICAL GAME

Matvichuk is aware of the importance of strength and aerobic training, and wants to add even more muscle to stay competitive at the NHL level, since he is a little light by today's NHL standards. He's added five pounds since his draft year and is very solid, and he's still growing. He's not mean, but he will stand in and use his body. Matvichuk occasionally gets into a mode where he starts fishing for the puck.

THE INTANGIBLES

Matvichuk has earned his place among the top four defensemen in Dallas. He could make a good partner for the daring Sergei Zubov, although we're not sure if he is up for that challenge.

MIKE MODANO

Yrs. of NHL service: 7
Born: Livonia, Mich.; June 7, 1970
Position: centre
Height: 6-3
Weight: 190
Uniform no.: 9
Shoots: left

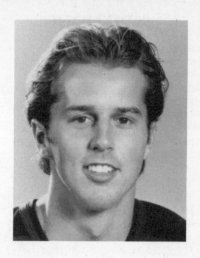

Career statistics:

GP	G	A	TP	PIM
501	221	291	482	400

1992-93 statistics:

GP	G	A	TP	+/-	PIM	PP	SH	GW	GT	S	PCT
82	33	60	93	-7	83	9	0	7	0	307	10.7

1993-94 statistics:

GP	G	A	TP	+/-	PIM	PP	SH	GW	GT	S	PCT
76	50	43	93	-8	54	18	0	4	2	281	17.8

1994-95 statistics:

GP	G	A	TP	+/-	PIM	PP	SH	GW	GT	S	PCT
30	12	17	29	+7	8	4	1	0	0	100	12.0

1995-96 statistics:

GP	G	A	TP	+/-	PIM	PP	SH	GW	GT	S	PCT
78	36	45	81	-12	63	8	4	4	1	320	11.3

LAST SEASON

Led team in goals, assists, points and shots. Tied for second on team in power play goals. Second on team in game-winning goals. Missed four games with a pulled stomach muscle.

THE FINESSE GAME

Modano was a fairly immature player when he broke into the NHL seven seasons ago, and while he has grown up a little bit more each year, he is going to fall short of being the elite, number one centre the Stars hoped for. Modano's skills rank with just about any-one but the top four or five players in the league, but he has never been able to take the next step to take his place among the great centres.

When there is a lot of open ice and a fairly tame game, Modano is a thrilling player to watch. He has outstanding offensive instincts and great hands, and he is a smooth passer and a remarkable skater in all facets.

Modano makes other players around him better, which is the mark of an elite player. His speed and movement with the puck mesmerizes defenders and opens up ice for his linemates. He hasn't found the ideal linemate yet.

Modano must better utilize players coming through the neutral zone and pick off an open lane to the top of the circle, as opposed to carrying it. His game is offense and he has to develop a complete repertoire. His defensive game has improved a great deal, and his anticipation and quick hands help him intercept passes. He needs work on his face-offs.

THE PHYSICAL GAME

Modano hasn't become the kind of leader who lifts a team with his effort. He doesn't dig in, like a Mark Messier or an Eric Lindros, and play hard in some of the hard areas. If he did, he could then look at his teammates and say, "There. Now you get your butt going. I'm busting mine." Whenever he leads, he leads with his skill and helps his team put points up, but the physical style is not his personality. He is not assertive, and the other facet of his game, the crucial facet that is needed to win championships in the NHL, may never develop.

Modano is also a bit of a whiner and an actor on mild penalty calls, to the point where he sometimes annoys his own teammates.

THE INTANGIBLES

Lacking his own reservoir of leadership, Modano has never played with anyone who could show him how to do so, either. When Messier retires, he should make inspirational instructional videos for the likes of Modano. Modano will get his points, but he hasn't shown that he will be a big-game player.

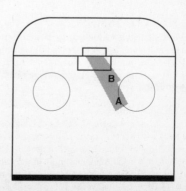

ANDY MOOG

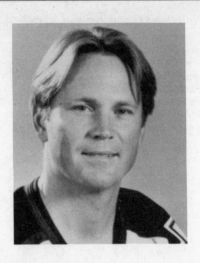

Yrs. of NHL service: 15
Born: Penticton, B.C.; Feb. 18, 1960
Position: goaltender
Height: 5-8
Weight: 170
Uniform no.: 35
Catches: left

Career statistics:

GP	MIN	GA	SO	GAA	A	PIM
623	35076	1902	22	3.25	23	214

1992-93 statistics:

GP	MIN	GAA	W	L	T	SO	GA	S	SAPCT	PIM
55	3194	3.16	37	14	3	3	168	1357	.876	14

1993-94 statistics:

GP	MIN	GAA	W	L	T	SO	GA	S	SAPCT	PIM
55	3121	3.27	24	20	7	2	170	1604	.894	16

1994-95 statistics:

GP	MIN	GAA	W	L	T	SO	GA	S	SAPCT	PIM
31	1770	2.44	10	12	7	2	72	846	.915	14

1995-96 statistics:

GP	MIN	GAA	W	L	T	SO	GA	S	SAPCT	PIM
41	2228	2.99	13	19	7	1	111	1106	.900	28

LAST SEASON

Recorded fifth season with GAA below 3.00. Missed 19 games with sprained knee. Missed two games with bruised knee. Missed one game with flu.

THE PHYSICAL GAME

Moog is a fairly good technical goalie who has relied on his reflexes for most of his career, but at this veteran stage he has improved his technique. He is a butterfly goalie who stays well on the top of his crease.

He is aggressive and comes so far out of his net that most teams know enough to come down the wing, fake a shot, go around him and pass to an open man for a lot of gimme chip-ins. His five-hole is not as good as it should be for a technically sound goalie, and he is now more vulnerable high than he was earlier in his career when he had such a good glove hand.

Moog scrambles back to his feet quickly when he is down, but he stays on his feet well and plays his angles.

THE MENTAL GAME

Moog had a difficult season playing behind an indifferent team defense, and at times his disgust with his teammates' play was visible even through his mask. Given that scenario, and his injuries, Moog's numbers look pretty impressive.

THE INTANGIBLES

It seems like every season Moog is surviving a challenge from another netminder, and this season it is expected that Roman Turek, who backstopped the Czech Republic to a World Championship, will provide the competition. The Stars signed Moog for one more year, which will probably be his last as a number one goalie.

JOE NIEUWENDYK

Yrs. of NHL service: 9
Born: Oshawa, Ont.; Sept. 10, 1966
Position: centre
Height: 6-1
Weight: 195
Uniform no.: 25
Shoots: left

Career statistics:

GP	G	A	TP	PIM
629	328	320	648	357

1992-93 statistics:

GP	G	A	TP	+/-	PIM	PP	SH	GW	GT	S	PCT
79	38	37	75	+9	52	14	0	6	0	208	18.3

1993-94 statistics:

GP	G	A	TP	+/-	PIM	PP	SH	GW	GT	S	PCT
64	36	39	75	+19	51	14	1	7	1	191	18.8

1994-95 statistics:

GP	G	A	TP	+/-	PIM	PP	SH	GW	GT	S	PCT
46	21	29	50	+11	33	3	0	4	0	122	17.2

1995-96 statistics:

GP	G	A	TP	+/-	PIM	PP	SH	GW	GT	S	PCT
52	14	18	32	-17	41	8	0	3	0	138	10.1

LAST SEASON

Acquired from Calgary for Jarome Iginla and Corey Millen, Dec. 19, 1995. Missed 30 games in contract dispute.

THE FINESSE GAME

Missing nearly half the season as he waited out his contract hassle before the trade to Dallas, leaving the only organization he had ever played for and undergoing a coaching change shortly after his arrival with the Stars made for a very tough go for Nieuwendyk.

If a "puck tipping" contest is ever added to the NHL All-Star game skills competition, Nieuwendyk would be one of the favourites. He has fantastic hand-eye coordination and not only gets his blade on the puck, he acts as if he knows where he's directing it.

He is aggressive, tough and aware around the net. He can finish or make a play down low. He has the good vision, poise and hand skills to make neat little passes through traffic. He is a better playmaker than finisher, but never doubt that he will convert his chances. Nieuwendyk has good anticipation in the neutral zone, and he uses his long reach to break up passes.

Those same hand skills serve him well on draws and he is defensively sound. Once a 50-goal scorer, knee surgery a few seasons ago robbed him of the necessary quickness to produce that total again. Nieuwendyk has become a better all-around player, though.

THE PHYSICAL GAME

He does not initiate, but he will take the punishment around the front of the net and stand his ground. He won't be intimidated, but he won't scare anyone else, either. Nieuwendyk would like to carry more weight, but recurring back and shoulder problems require him to stay on the lean side.

THE INTANGIBLES

We said in last year's *HSR* that Nieuwendyk would likely change postal codes, and he did — but he landed on a floundering team in Dallas. Nieuwendyk was a little lost and confused with the newness of his situation, but he is an intelligent player and will be in better shape when camp opens. He will likely be paired with a pure finisher in Pat Verbeek, and his points should be in the 70-80 range as he will get all the ice time he can handle.

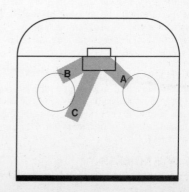

DAVE REID

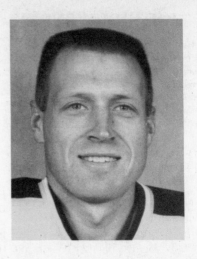

Yrs. of NHL service: 12
Born: Toronto, Ont.; May 15, 1964
Position: left wing
Height: 6-1
Weight: 217
Uniform no.: 17
Shoots: left

Career statistics:

GP	G	A	TP	PIM
603	122	145	267	164

1992-93 statistics:

GP	G	A	TP	+/-	PIM	PP	SH	GW	GT	S	PCT
65	20	16	36	+12	10	1	5	2	0	116	17.2

1993-94 statistics:

GP	G	A	TP	+/-	PIM	PP	SH	GW	GT	S	PCT
83	6	17	23	+10	25	0	2	1	0	145	4.1

1994-95 statistics:

GP	G	A	TP	+/-	PIM	PP	SH	GW	GT	S	PCT
38	5	5	10	+8	10	0	0	0	1	47	10.6

1995-96 statistics:

GP	G	A	TP	+/-	PIM	PP	SH	GW	GT	S	PCT
63	23	21	44	+14	4	1	6	3	1	160	14.4

LAST SEASON

Led Boston in shorthanded goals. Career high in goals and points. Tied for second on team in game-winning goals. Missed 16 games with fractured finger. Missed three games with abdominal strain.

THE FINESSE GAME

Reid took advantage of the lack of depth on Boston's left side by posting career numbers. And just in time, too, since Reid became a Group 2 free agent at the end of last season.

Under normal circumstances, Reid is a defensive forward and penalty-killing specialist. Opposition power plays always have to be aware of taking away Reid's space if they lose the puck, because he has the ability to blow the puck by the goalie from a lot of spots on the ice. Possessing an underrated, accurate shot with a quick release, he can freeze goalies with his unexpected shot.

Reid is a good skater with surprising straight-ahead speed, especially for a big player. He has proven he can play regularly in the NHL and contribute. All of his moderate skills are enhanced by his hard work and hustle.

THE PHYSICAL GAME

Reid can create a little maelstrom on the ice. A big guy who can get his skating revved up, he causes problems once he is in motion. He isn't a big hitter, though, and there is no nasty side to him. He is just an honest checker.

THE INTANGIBLES

Reid, who could have been picked up on waivers a few seasons back, signed a lucrative new contract with Dallas, and a million bucks a year isn't a bad paycheck for a third-line winger. Anyone expecting Reid to produce another 20-goal season will probably be disappointed, but he will contribute smart hockey and score some key goals.

DARRYL SYDOR

Yrs. of NHL service: 4
Born: Edmonton, Alta.; May 13, 1972
Position: right defense
Height: 6-0
Weight: 205
Uniform no.: 6
Shoots: left

Career statistics:

GP	G	A	TP	PIM
314	22	91	113	290

1992-93 statistics:

GP	G	A	TP	+/-	PIM	PP	SH	GW	GT	S	PCT
80	6	23	29	-2	63	0	0	1	0	112	5.4

1993-94 statistics:

GP	G	A	TP	+/-	PIM	PP	SH	GW	GT	S	PCT
84	8	27	35	-9	94	1	0	0	0	146	5.5

1994-95 statistics:

GP	G	A	TP	+/-	PIM	PP	SH	GW	GT	S	PCT
48	4	19	23	-2	36	3	0	0	1	96	4.2

1995-96 statistics:

GP	G	A	TP	+/-	PIM	PP	SH	GW	GT	S	PCT
84	3	17	20	-12	75	2	0	0	0	117	2.6

The offensive part has come naturally to him. Defense is a tougher proposition, and he seems preoccupied with it at times, but he should start to regain his game this season and be a 40-point man. It's a start.

LAST SEASON

Acquired from Los Angeles with a fifth-round draft pick for Shane Churla and Doug Zmolek, Feb. 17, 1996. Only Star to appear in all 82 games (played in additional games due to trade).

THE FINESSE GAME

Sydor lost some of his momentum towards becoming a good offensive defenseman in the muddled season in Los Angeles, then got stuck in another muddled situation in Dallas. The Stars see him as a project worth taking on.

Sydor is a very good skater with balance and agility and excellent lateral movement. He can accelerate well for a big skater and changes directions easily. He's not a dynamic defenseman, but he's better than average.

He has a fine shot from the point and can handle power play time. He has good sense for jumping into the attack, and controls the puck ably when carrying it, though he doesn't always protect it well with his body. He makes nice outlet passes and has good vision of the ice. He can rush with the puck or play dump-and-chase.

THE PHYSICAL GAME

Sydor wants and needs to establish more of a physical presence. He competes hard, but sometimes can't win his battles because he's physically outmatched or he'll overrun the play because he loses patience.

THE INTANGIBLES

Sydor has a real hunger to improve his game, but needs to develop confidence in his all-around game.

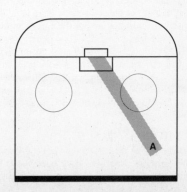

PAT VERBEEK

Yrs. of NHL service: 13
Born: Sarnia, Ont.; May 24, 1964
Position: right wing
Height: 5-9
Weight: 195
Uniform no.: 16
Shoots: right

Career statistics:

GP	G	A	TP	PIM
984	413	408	821	223

1992-93 statistics:

GP	G	A	TP	+/-	PIM	PP	SH	GW	GT	S	PCT
84	39	43	82	-7	197	16	0	6	2	235	16.6

1993-94 statistics:

GP	G	A	TP	+/-	PIM	PP	SH	GW	GT	S	PCT
84	37	38	75	-15	177	15	1	3	1	226	16.4

1994-95 statistics:

GP	G	A	TP	+/-	PIM	PP	SH	GW	GT	S	PCT
48	17	16	33	-2	71	7	0	2	1	131	13.0

1995-96 statistics:

GP	G	A	TP	+/-	PIM	PP	SH	GW	GT	S	PCT
69	41	41	82	+29	129	17	0	6	2	252	16.3

LAST SEASON

Signed as a free agent, July 3, 1996. Led Rangers in power play goals and tied for team lead in plus-minus. Second on Rangers in goals and game-winning goals. Third on Rangers in points. Missed two games with knee injury. Missed nine games with separated shoulder. Missed two games with back spasms.

THE FINESSE GAME

Verbeek has a choppy stride, so much of his best work is done in small spaces rather than in open ice. He is very strong on his skates and likes to go into traffic zones. Larger players think they can hit him, but he's so chunky with a low centre of gravity that he is nearly impossible to bowl over. He is very good at carrying the puck along the boards but is no stickhandler in open ice. He has no better than fair speed.

For a player who takes as many shots as Verbeek does, he is remarkably accurate; he wastes few quality scoring chances. Most of his shots come from in tight. Nothing brings out his competitive edge more than some serious crashing around the crease, most of which he initiates.

Verbeek's hands are soft and quick enough to surprise with a backhand shot. He feels the puck on his stick and looks for openings in the net instead of scrapping with his head down and taking poor shots. Verbeek is also effective coming in late and drilling the shot.

THE PHYSICAL GAME

Verbeek is among the best in the league at drawing penalties. He can cleverly hold the opponent's stick and fling himself to the ice as if he were the injured party, and it is an effective tactic. He also draws calls honestly with his hard work by driving to the net and forcing the defender to slow him down by any means possible.

Verbeek is tough, rugged and strong, with a nasty disposition that he is learning to tame without losing his ferocious edge.

THE INTANGIBLES

Verbeek has a history of having an off-year in the first year of a big new contract, which is exactly the situation now in Dallas. Buyer beware.

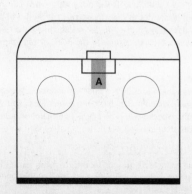

SERGEI ZUBOV

Yrs. of NHL service: 4
Born: Moscow, Russia; July 22, 1970
Position: right defense
Height: 6-1
Weight: 200
Uniform no.: 56
Shoots: right

Career statistics:

GP	G	A	TP	PIM
229	41	181	222	83

1992-93 statistics:

GP	G	A	TP	+/-	PIM	PP	SH	GW	GT	S	PCT
49	8	23	31	-1	4	3	0	0	0	93	8.6

1993-94 statistics:

GP	G	A	TP	+/-	PIM	PP	SH	GW	GT	S	PCT
78	12	77	89	+20	39	9	0	1	0	222	5.4

1994-95 statistics:

GP	G	A	TP	+/-	PIM	PP	SH	GW	GT	S	PCT
38	10	26	36	-2	18	6	0	0	0	116	8.6

1995-96 statistics:

GP	G	A	TP	+/-	PIM	PP	SH	GW	GT	S	PCT
64	11	55	66	+28	22	3	2	1	0	141	7.8

LAST SEASON

Acquired from Pittsburgh for Kevin Hatcher. Tied for seventh in scoring among NHL defensemen. Led Pittsburgh defensemen in scoring. Third on team in plus-minus. Missed 16 games with broken finger.

THE FINESSE GAME

Zubov has the ability to run a power play but he is not in the elite class of NHL point men, like his former teammate Brian Leetch. He is still very effective, despite his reluctance to shoot the puck.

He has some world-class skills. He skates with with good balance and generates power from his leg drive. He is agile in his stops and starts, even backwards. Zubov has a good slap shot and one-times the puck with accuracy, when he deigns to use it. He's not afraid to come in deep, either. Heck, sometimes he forechecks behind the goal line on a power play. He has very strong lateral acceleration, but he is also educated enough to keep skating stride for stride with the wing who is trying to beat him to the outside. So many other defensemen speed up a couple of strides then try to slow their men with stick checks.

When it comes to defense, though, it's not just a job, it's an adventure with Zubov. He is a high-stakes gambler, forcing the play at the blueline or skipping through his own crease with the puck, to the shock of his goalie. For every brilliant offensive pass, there is a nightmarish diagonal breakout pass that gets intercepted.

Zubov will use his reach, superior body positioning or his agility to force the play and compel the puck carrier to make a decision. He is a powerful skater who can accelerate on the glide and is capable of dropping to one knee on the glide to break up two-on-one passes. But he doesn't always search out the right man, or when he does, he doesn't always eliminate the right man. A team has to live with that, because Zubov's offensive upside is huge.

THE PHYSICAL GAME

Zubov is not physical, but he is solidly built and will take a hit to make a play. He can give a team a lot of minutes (he logged over 80 minutes in the four-overtime game against Washington in the playoffs) and not wear down physically.

His boyhood idol was Viacheslav Fetisov, and that role model should give you some idea of Zubov's style. He gets his body in the way with his great skating, then often strips the puck when the attacker finds no path to the net. He doesn't initiate much, but he doesn't mind getting hit to make a play.

THE INTANGIBLES

Last season was a big step-up year for Zubov. He handled a lot of minutes and absorbed being a target in the Rangers' playoff series when everyone was questioning his courage. His point totals probably won't be as high now that he has been dealt from the explosive Penguins to the less gifted Stars.

DETROIT RED WINGS

Players' Statistics 1995-96

POS.	NO.	PLAYER	GP	G	A	PTS	+/-	PIM	PP	SH	GW	GT	S	PCT
C	91	SERGEI FEDOROV	78	39	68	107	49	48	11	3	11	1	306	12.7
C	19	STEVE YZERMAN	80	36	59	95	29	64	16	2	8		220	16.4
D	77	PAUL COFFEY	76	14	60	74	19	90	3	1	3		234	6.0
C	13	VYACHESLAV KOZLOV	82	36	37	73	33	70	9		7		237	15.2
C	8	IGOR LARIONOV	73	22	51	73	31	34	10	1	5		113	19.5
D	5	NICKLAS LIDSTROM	81	17	50	67	29	20	8	1	1	1	211	8.1
L	55	KEITH PRIMEAU	74	27	25	52	19	168	6	2	7		150	18.0
R	22	DINO CICCARELLI	64	22	21	43	14	99	13		5		107	20.6
D	2	VIACHESLAV FETISOV	69	7	35	42	37	96	1	1	1		127	5.5
C	23	GREG JOHNSON	60	18	22	40	6	30	5		2		87	20.7
D	16	VLAD. KONSTANTINOV	81	14	20	34	60	139	3	1	3		168	8.3
L	21	BOB ERREY	71	11	21	32	30	66	2	2	2	1	85	12.9
R	25	DARREN MCCARTY	63	15	14	29	14	158	8		1	1	102	14.7
R	17	DOUG BROWN	62	12	15	27	11	4		1	1		115	10.4
C	37	TIM TAYLOR	72	11	14	25	11	39	1	1	4		81	13.6
C	33	KRIS DRAPER	52	7	9	16	2	32		1			51	13.7
R	11	*MATHIEU DANDENAULT	34	5	7	12	6	6	1				32	15.6
D	27	MARC BERGEVIN	70	1	9	10	7	33					26	3.8
R	20	MARTIN LAPOINTE	58	6	3	9	0	93	1				76	7.9
R	18	KIRK MALTBY	55	3	6	9	-16	67			1		55	5.5
D	15	MIKE RAMSEY	47	2	4	6	17	35					35	5.7
D	3	BOB ROUSE	58		6	6	5	48					49	
G	30	CHRIS OSGOOD	50	1	2	3	0	4					1	00.0
D	4	*JAMIE PUSHOR	5		1	1	2	17					6	
L	32	STU GRIMSON	56		1	1	-10	128					19	
D	34	*ANDERS ERIKSSON	1				1	2						
C	26	WES WALZ	2				0						2	
G	31	*KEVIN HODSON	4				0							
G	29	MIKE VERNON	32				0	2						

GP = games played; G = goals; A = assists; PTS = points; +/- = goals-for minus goals-against while player is on ice; PIM = penalties in minutes; PP = power play goals; SH = shorthanded goals; GW = game-winning goals; GT = game-tying goals; S = no. of shots; PCT = percentage of goals to shots; * = rookie

DOUG BROWN

Yrs. of NHL service: 9
Born: Southborough, Mass.; June 12, 1964
Position: right wing
Height: 5-10
Weight: 185
Uniform no.: 17
Shoots: right

Career statistics:

GP	G	A	TP	PIM
534	107	144	251	122

1992-93 statistics:

GP	G	A	TP	+/-	PIM	PP	SH	GW	GT	S	PCT
15	0	5	5	+3	2	0	0	0	0	17	0.0

1993-94 statistics:

GP	G	A	TP	+/-	PIM	PP	SH	GW	GT	S	PCT
77	18	37	55	+19	18	2	0	1	0	152	11.8

1994-95 statistics:

GP	G	A	TP	+/-	PIM	PP	SH	GW	GT	S	PCT
45	9	12	21	+14	16	1	1	2	0	69	13.0

1995-96 statistics:

GP	G	A	TP	+/-	PIM	PP	SH	GW	GT	S	PCT
62	12	15	27	+11	4	0	1	1	0	115	10.4

LAST SEASON

Games missed were due to coaches' decision.

THE FINESSE GAME

Brown's playing time was compromised by the creation of the five-man "Russian Unit." Brown had played as an honorary Russian with Sergei Fedorov and Slava Kozlov in 1994-95, but lost out with the addition of Igor Larionov to that line. As a result, Brown was shuffled around, which is something he's been quite used to throughout his career.

Brown is always hustling, giving the impression of being a fast skater. He's not, at least not straight ahead, though he does have real quickness side-to-side. He is sometimes too fast on his feet and wipes out frequently after losing his edges. Brown gets a lot of breakaways because of the quick jumps he gets on the opposition. The lack of a finishing touch prevents him from scoring as many goals as he should.

Brown offers a consistent effort night after night. He always attains his level of play but seldom surpasses it, which is why coaches often give younger players ice time ahead of Brown at the start of the season, then tend to go back to the old reliable redhead.

A determined penalty killer and shorthanded threat, he never quits around the net and comes up with tip-ins and stuffs. He blocks shots fearlessly and approaches the game with intelligence and enthusiasm.

THE PHYSICAL GAME

Brown is not a strong player, but he is one of the better grinders along the wall, since he will hang in there and not give up on a puck. He keeps the puck alive with his stick or feet. Brown won't fight, but he won't be intimidated, either.

THE INTANGIBLES

Brown is a chameleon. Despite lacking world-class skills, he fits in with world-class players. Or he does the grunt work on a checking line. He hustles and grinds and does all of the little things it takes to win a hockey game. Brown has spent most of his career on the bubble. He'll be there again this fall.

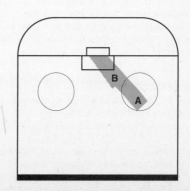

DINO CICCARELLI

Yrs. of NHL service: 16
Born: Sarnia, Ont.; Feb. 18, 1960
Position: right wing
Height: 5-10
Weight: 185
Uniform no.: 22
Shoots: right

Career statistics:

GP	G	A	TP	PIM
1079	551	549	1100	1212

1992-93 statistics:

GP	G	A	TP	+/-	PIM	PP	SH	GW	GT	S	PCT
82	41	56	97	+12	81	21	0	8	0	200	20.5

1993-94 statistics:

GP	G	A	TP	+/-	PIM	PP	SH	GW	GT	S	PCT
66	28	29	57	+10	73	12	0	1	2	153	18.3

1994-95 statistics:

GP	G	A	TP	+/-	PIM	PP	SH	GW	GT	S	PCT
42	16	27	43	+12	39	6	0	3	0	106	15.1

1995-96 statistics:

GP	G	A	TP	+/-	PIM	PP	SH	GW	GT	S	PCT
64	22	21	43	+14	99	13	0	5	0	107	20.6

LAST SEASON

Second on team in power play goals and shooting percentage.

THE FINESSE GAME

For a smallish player, Ciccarelli casts a big shadow. Yapping and jabbing, he plays few invisible games. His attitude and aggressive style enhance his skills, which are highlighted by his quickness and his scoring knack.

Ciccarelli has great hands for finishing plays. Although he has a big slap shot, he is more effective down low. He creates havoc for goaltenders, digging for loose pucks, deflecting shots and screening the goalie. His offensive game is straightforward. He's not a very creative playmaker, so he shoots first and asks questions later. Somehow, he always seems to get a piece of the puck.

A strong forechecker, Ciccarelli takes the body well despite his small size, and he can do something with the puck when it does squirt free. He doesn't have breakaway speed and dazzling moves, but he is a strong and well-balanced skater who is very quick in small spaces.

THE PHYSICAL GAME

"Dino the Disturber." Ciccarelli is starved for attention and isn't happy unless he's got a goalie in a tizzy or a goal judge pushing that red-light button. He isn't a very good skater, so he can't afford to be a perimeter player. He has to be parked right on the paint in front of the net, his heels on the crease, taking the punishment and dishing it out. Intimidation is a huge part of his game. He will check goalies out of their crease and try to get a piece of them while they're still in it.

Ciccarelli plays as if he has to prove his courage every night; pound for pound he's as strong as most bigger players. He has a low centre of gravity and is difficult to move. Defensemen may think, "No problem, I can move this guy," only to find Ciccarelli impossible to budge. Punish him as much as you want. He'll keep coming back.

THE INTANGIBLES

Early last season, someone asked Ciccarelli what his line should be called. "History," Ciccarelli replied. At the time, his linemates were Steve Yzerman and Ray Sheppard, and all three were prominently mentioned in trade rumours. Only Sheppard was gone by season's end, while Ciccarelli was one of the best Detroit performers in the playoffs.

With changes on the horizon after yet another Cupless spring, Ciccarelli could be moved, but he can still fill a niche on a team that needs some backbone and a power play specialist. He remains the quintessential hockey brat. He's slowed a bit, but Dino was never known for his speed anyway. With sufficient power play time, he should be productive again. His desire and competitive nature are big pluses.

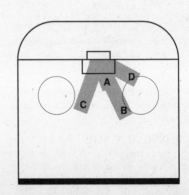

PAUL COFFEY

Yrs. of NHL service: 16
Born: Weston, Ont.; June 1, 1961
Position: right defense
Height: 6-0
Weight: 190
Uniform no.: 77
Shoots: left

Career statistics:

GP	G	A	TP	PIM
1154	372	1038	1410	1636

1992-93 statistics:

GP	G	A	TP	+/-	PIM	PP	SH	GW	GT	S	PCT
80	12	75	87	+16	77	5	0	0	0	254	4.7

1993-94 statistics:

GP	G	A	TP	+/-	PIM	PP	SH	GW	GT	S	PCT
80	14	63	77	+28	106	5	0	3	0	278	5.0

1994-95 statistics:

GP	G	A	TP	+/-	PIM	PP	SH	GW	GT	S	PCT
45	14	44	58	+18	72	4	1	2	0	181	7.7

1995-96 statistics:

GP	G	A	TP	+/-	PIM	PP	SH	GW	GT	S	PCT
76	14	60	74	+19	90	3	1	3	0	234	6.0

LAST SEASON

Third among NHL defensemen in points and assists. Second on team in assists. Third on team in points. Missed six games with back spasms.

THE FINESSE GAME

Coffey handles the puck while he is skating and whirling at top speed or changing directions. Few players are better at the long home-run pass, and Coffey has all the finesse skills of a forward when he works down low. He has tremendous vision to make a play, feather a pass or work a give-and-go. He understands the concept of time and space.

Coffey has a whole menu of shots, from wristers to slaps. He is a world-class point man on the power play, faking slaps and sending passes low, sliding the puck over to his point partner for a one-timer, or drilling the shot himself. He prefers to attack down the right side.

He has enough speed and skill to split the defense or beat a defender one-on-one. He is almost impossible to hit because he is so shifty and strong on his skates. He creates a lot of open ice for his teammates because he is intimidating as a skater.

Notice that all we've talked about is Coffey's offensive skills. No team has Coffey on its roster for his defense.

THE PHYSICAL GAME

Coffey has the size to hit and clear the slot, but he doesn't, and at this stage in his distinguished career that is not about to change. There will be times when he gets beaten coming out of the corner because he doesn't hit the opponent. He will block shots when it

counts (like in the playoffs), but most of his defense is based on his anticipation in picking off passes and his skill with the puck.

THE INTANGIBLES

Coffey put the points up on the board again last season, but we have a suspicion that this year will see the start of a downslide in his production, and while he may be in the top 10 in defense scoring, he won't rank in the top three.

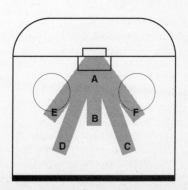

KRIS DRAPER

Yrs. of NHL service: 5
Born: Toronto, Ont.; May 24, 1971
Position: centre
Height: 5-11
Weight: 185
Uniform no.: 33
Shoots: left

Career statistics:

GP	G	A	TP	PIM
147	17	23	40	94

1992-93 statistics:

GP	G	A	TP	+/-	PIM	PP	SH	GW	GT	S	PCT
7	0	0	0	-6	2	0	0	0	0	5	0.0

1993-94 statistics:

GP	G	A	TP	+/-	PIM	PP	SH	GW	GT	S	PCT
39	5	8	13	+11	31	0	1	0	0	55	9.1

1994-95 statistics:

GP	G	A	TP	+/-	PIM	PP	SH	GW	GT	S	PCT
36	2	6	8	+1	22	0	0	0	0	44	4.5

1995-96 statistics:

GP	G	A	TP	+/-	PIM	PP	SH	GW	GT	S	PCT
52	7	9	16	+2	32	0	1	0	0	51	13.7

LAST SEASON
Missed 15 games with knee injuries.

THE FINESSE GAME
Draper has to work hard for his goals. They often come off his forecheck and his anticipation. When a linemate is doing the honours and forces a defender into a giveaway, Draper is there to jump on the free puck and get a good scoring opportunity away quickly.

But the strength of Draper's game is his defense. He plays his position well and is proud of his checking role. A good skater, he is strong on his feet and well balanced, but not fast. His clever play makes him seem much quicker than he is.

Draper is unselfish and is a good passer, especially in traffic. He is an effective penalty killer and can handle time on the second power play unit because of his intelligent work around the net, but he doesn't have a great finishing touch.

THE PHYSICAL GAME
Draper is not big, but he has wiry strength and uses his body well. He works the boards and corners and relishes physical play. He is intense and ready to play every night. Draper completes his checks and is a no-frills defensive centre with a strong work ethic.

THE INTANGIBLES
Heart seems to be in short quantity on Detroit's roster, but that's one thing that Draper has plenty of. He sees limited ice time, but is ready for every shift. His knee injury cost him playing time last season, but he had himself back in shape for the playoffs. Draper figures to be a role player for another season with the Red Wings thanks to his character, although Detroit may give a lot of (bigger) kids a long audition in training camp.

ANDERS ERIKSSON

Yrs. of NHL service: 0
Born: Bolinas, Sweden; Jan. 9, 1975
Position: defense
Height: 6-3
Weight: 218
Uniform no.: n.a.
Shoots: left

Career statistics (AHL):

GP	G	A	TP	PIM
75	6	36	42	64

1995-96 statistics (AHL):

GP	G	A	TP	+/-	PIM	PP	SH	GP
75	6	36	42	+26	64	3	0	0

LAST SEASON
Will be entering first NHL season.

THE FINESSE GAME
Eriksson is big, even by today's standards for NHL defensemen, but his strength lies in his mobility and puckhandling skills. He sees the ice well and his biggest asset is his ability to get the puck out of his own end fast. He is a heads-up passer who is poised with the puck.

Eriksson is improving his defensive reads and reactions. He will not jump into the play unless it is safe, and he won't pinch unless that is the correct play. Eriksson may err on the side of caution until he develops a little more confidence, but he has the skill level to provide some offense as a playmaker. He will probably limit his shots to the point.

Eriksson is a very good skater with balance and agility. He doesn't have a big turning radius and he accelerates well.

THE PHYSICAL GAME
Eriksson is not a big hitter, but he is strong and will tie up his man along the boards and in front of the net. He had some trouble adjusting to the drudgery of the minor-league schedule, but proved to be adaptable. His conditioning is very good, so the adjustment appeared to be more mental than physical. Eriksson should be able to handle the league's big power forwards because of his body positioning. He will force people to try to go through him.

THE INTANGIBLES
Last season's playoff disappointment should mean a lot of jobs will be up for grabs at Detroit's training camp, and Eriksson figures to nab one of them. He has been brought along slowly since the 1993 draft, in which he was a first-round pick. He played two seasons in Sweden and last year got a taste of North American play with a season in the AHL. He struggled early in the year, but improved steadily and is pencilled in to start the season with the Red Wings. He will be concentrating on learning defense, but may provide 35-40 points while he's doing it.

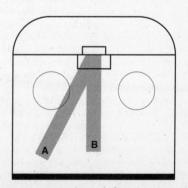

131

SERGEI FEDOROV

Yrs. of NHL service: 6
Born: Pskov, Russia; Dec. 13, 1969
Position: centre
Height: 6-1
Weight: 200
Uniform no.: 91
Shoots: left

Career statistics:

GP	G	A	TP	PIM
435	212	317	529	316

1992-93 statistics:

GP	G	A	TP	+/-	PIM	PP	SH	GW	GT	S	PCT
73	34	53	87	+33	72	13	4	3	0	217	15.7

1993-94 statistics:

GP	G	A	TP	+/-	PIM	PP	SH	GW	GT	S	PCT
82	56	64	120	+48	34	13	4	10	0	337	16.6

1994-95 statistics:

GP	G	A	TP	+/-	PIM	PP	SH	GW	GT	S	PCT
45	20	30	50	+6	24	7	3	5	0	147	13.6

1995-96 statistics:

GP	G	A	TP	+/-	PIM	PP	SH	GW	GT	S	PCT
78	39	68	107	+49	48	11	2	11	1	306	12.7

LAST SEASON

Won 1996 Selke Trophy. Led team in goals, assists, and points. Tied for ninth in NHL in scoring with second 100-point season. Led team in shorthanded goals and game-winning goals for second consecutive season. Second on team and in NHL in plus-minus. Third on team in power play goals. Missed four games with tonsillitis.

THE FINESSE GAME

After Detroit's acquisition of Igor Larionov, Fedorov played mostly left wing on the team's five-man Russian unit, and the quintet's skating and weaving was a wonder to behold. Fedorov is a tremendous package of offensive and defensive skills. He can go from checking the opponent's top centre to powering the power play from shift to shift. His skating is nothing short of phenomenal, and he can handle the puck while he is dazzling everyone with his blades.

He likes to gear up from his own defensive zone on the rush, using his acceleration and balance to drive wide to his right, carrying the puck on his backhand and protecting it with his body. If the defenseman lets up at all, then Fedorov is by him, pulling the puck quickly to his forehand. Nor is he by any means selfish. He has 360-degree vision of the ice and makes solid, confident passes right under opponents' sticks and smack onto the tape of his teammates. Fedorov will swing behind the opposing net from left to right, fooling the defense into thinking he is going to continue to curl around, but he can quickly reverse with the puck on his backhand, shake his shadow and wheel around for a shot or goalmouth pass. He does it all in a flash.

Fedorov also has the strength and acceleration to drive right between two defenders, keep control of the puck and wrist a strong shot on goal. He is an exceptional two-way forward, although he was probably not deserving of the Selke last season.

THE PHYSICAL GAME

Fedorov is wiry, and though he would prefer to stay in open ice, he will go to the trenches when he has to. Much of his power is generated from his strong skating. For the most part, his defense is dominated by his reads, anticipation and quickness in knocking down passes and breaking up plays. He is not much of a bodychecker and he gets most of his penalties from stick and restraining fouls. He gets exasperated by some of the tactics used against him and will retaliate with his stick. Fedorov also is a bit of an actor when it comes to drawing penalties.

THE INTANGIBLES

Word is that Detroit owner Mike Ilitch demanded that Fedorov be traded after his disappointing (two goals) playoff performance, but was talked out of it by Scotty Bowman. If that's true, then there will be more pressure than ever on the Russian this season. Fedorov is going into his option year, another stress factor to consider.

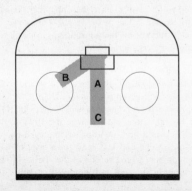

VLADIMIR KONSTANTINOV

Yrs. of NHL service: 5
Born: Murmansk, Russia; Mar. 19, 1967
Position: right defense
Height: 5-11
Weight: 190
Uniform no.: 16
Shoots: right

Career statistics:

GP	G	A	TP	PIM
369	42	94	136	687

1992-93 statistics:

GP	G	A	TP	+/-	PIM	PP	SH	GW	GT	S	PCT
82	5	17	22	+22	137	0	0	0	0	85	5.9

1993-94 statistics:

GP	G	A	TP	+/-	PIM	PP	SH	GW	GT	S	PCT
80	12	21	33	+30	138	1	3	3	0	97	12.4

1994-95 statistics:

GP	G	A	TP	+/-	PIM	PP	SH	GW	GT	S	PCT
47	3	11	14	+10	101	0	0	0	0	57	5.3

1995-96 statistics:

GP	G	A	TP	+/-	PIM	PP	SH	GW	GT	S	PCT
81	14	20	34	+60	139	3	1	3	0	168	8.3

LAST SEASON

Led NHL in plus-minus.

THE FINESSE GAME

Dynamic skating buoys Konstantinov's game. He is all over the ice, to the extent that he has to be calmed down or else he is too aggressive in the neutral zone and gets caught. He does not get overly involved in the attack, but when he does he'll make a good passing play rather than waste a shot when he is in deep, because he doesn't want to risk the shot being blocked before he has a chance to turn back up ice. In fact, he probably is too reluctant to fire. Konstantinov prefers to break out of the zone with a smart pass, but he can wheel the puck out of danger if under pressure.

Konstantinov is a fine skater with speed, agility, lateral movement, balance and strength. He is used on the first penalty-killing unit and will be on the ice to protect a lead late. He has good hand skills but sometimes is guilty of overhandling the puck in the defensive zone.

Konstantinov kills penalties although he does not block shots well. He has an occasional tendency to overcommit in the defensive zone when he gets mesmerized by the puck and forgets to play the man.

THE PHYSICAL GAME

Konstantinov is tough, mean, and plays much bigger than his size. If he gets the chance, he will put the hurt on an attacker. He will ride a skater into the boards, and he might use his stick high, too. People are always trying to swat him, but he's not afraid of retaliation.

THE INTANGIBLES

Konstantinov has quickly become the most hated defensemen in the West because he really doesn't care if he hurts people and he doesn't fight. He never drops his stick.

Konstantinov suffered a torn Achilles' tendon during the off-season, while playing tennis, of all things, so this big, nasty defenseman may have a slow start to the season.

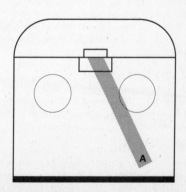

VYACHESLAV KOZLOV

Yrs. of NHL service: 3
Born: Voskresensk, Soviet Union; May 3, 1972
Position: centre/left wing
Height: 5-10
Weight: 180
Uniform no.: 13
Shoots: left

Career statistics:

GP	G	A	TP	PIM
229	87	99	186	181

1992-93 statistics:

GP	G	A	TP	+/-	PIM	PP	SH	GW	GT	S	PCT
17	4	1	5	-1	14	0	0	0	0	26	15.4

1993-94 statistics:

GP	G	A	TP	+/-	PIM	PP	SH	GW	GT	S	PCT
77	34	39	73	+27	50	8	2	6	0	202	16.8

1994-95 statistics:

GP	G	A	TP	+/-	PIM	PP	SH	GW	GT	S	PCT
46	13	20	33	+12	45	5	0	3	0	97	13.4

1995-96 statistics:

GP	G	A	TP	+/-	PIM	PP	SH	GW	GT	S	PCT
82	36	37	73	+33	70	9	0	7	0	237	15.2

Colorado in the team's big Western Conference final showdown, we question his crunch-time mentality.

LAST SEASON

Tied for second on team in game-winning goals. Third on team in goals. Only Red Wing to appear in all 82 games.

THE FINESSE GAME

Kozlov played the right side on Detroit's five-man Russian unit, but given the way all three forwards used all of the ice, it seems ridiculous to assign a position to any of them.

Kozlov fits in with the team's freewheeling offensive style. He doesn't just skate up and down his wing, but cuts and wheels and bursts into openings on the ice. He can split the defense if it plays him too close or drive the defense back with his speed and use the open ice to find a teammate. He has great control of the puck at high speed and plays an excellent transition game. He does not have to be coaxed into shooting, and has a quick release.

Kozlov stepped his game up to another level last season, and playing with his stylish countrymen probably helped that cause. Should the Red Wings play a more conservative style next season, that may not suit Kozlov as well.

THE PHYSICAL GAME

Kozlov is highly competitive and will fight his way through checks. He exceeded a lot of expectations in Detroit, but he is a stranger to the league no longer and draws considerable checking attention.

THE INTANGIBLES

Kozlov should be a consistent 80-point scorer with his skill level, but given the single goal he scored against

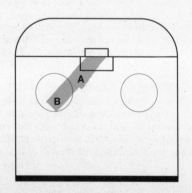

IGOR LARIONOV

Yrs. of NHL service: 6
Born: Voskresensk, Russia; Dec. 3, 1960
Position: centre
Height: 5-9
Weight: 170
Uniform no.: 8
Shoots: left

Career statistics:

GP	G	A	TP	PIM
376	95	201	296	176

1992-93 statistics:
Did not play in NHL

1993-94 statistics:

GP	G	A	TP	+/-	PIM	PP	SH	GW	GT	S	PCT
60	18	38	56	+20	40	3	2	2	1	72	25.0

1994-95 statistics:

GP	G	A	TP	+/-	PIM	PP	SH	GW	GT	S	PCT
33	4	20	24	-3	14	0	0	0	1	69	5.8

1995-96 statistics:

GP	G	A	TP	+/-	PIM	PP	SH	GW	GT	S	PCT
73	22	51	73	+31	34	10	1	5	0	113	19.5

LAST SEASON

Acquired from San Jose for Ray Sheppard on Oct. 25, 1995. One of five NHL players to score on a penalty shot last season.

THE FINESSE GAME

Among the best playmakers ever to come out of the old Soviet system, Larionov is an agile, elusive skater with marvellous hand skills and a creative mind. He waits for his wingers to get open, and he has an exceptional passing touch for finding the breaking man. He is tough to defend against. He looks so wispy and easy to take out of the play, but if challenged around the net, he dishes off the puck to someone for an easy tap-in or a one-timer.

Larionov does not shoot much, and a defender can always play the pass. Still, Larionov performs with such skill — and wingers Sergei Fedorov and Vyacheslav Kozlov provided such speed last season — that it is not always a serious flaw. He cannot over-power a goalie with his shot but prefers to work in tight, deking a defender, getting a step and using an accurate wrist shot.

Larionov is smart and plays well positionally. He can be used on both specialty teams and is a short-handed scoring threat because of his crafty play.

THE PHYSICAL GAME

Small and slightly built, Larionov will sometimes take a hit to make a play, but it doesn't make much sense to ask him to get into one-on-one confrontations. He is tough to knock off the puck, and is always aerobically fit. He has the type of muscles that give him explosive one-step quickness. Larionov will use his stick for protection.

THE INTANGIBLES

Larionov is a player of great intelligence who will probably be a terrific coach one day soon. Very soon. Given the failure of Detroit's "Red Wing Army" unit in the playoffs, Larionov's NHL days may be numbered if he doesn't fit into the team's plans. We think he still has a useful season left in him.

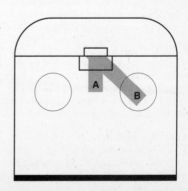

NICKLAS LIDSTROM

Yrs. of NHL service: 5
Born: Västerås, Sweden; Apr. 28, 1970
Position: left defense
Height: 6-2
Weight: 185
Uniform no.: 5
Shoots: left

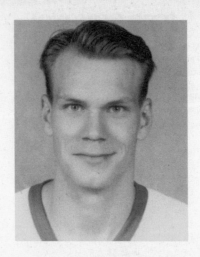

Career statistics:

GP	G	A	TP	PIM
372	55	195	250	102

1992-93 statistics:

GP	G	A	TP	+/-	PIM	PP	SH	GW	GT	S	PCT
84	7	34	41	+7	28	3	0	2	0	156	4.5

1993-94 statistics:

GP	G	A	TP	+/-	PIM	PP	SH	GW	GT	S	PCT
84	10	46	56	+43	26	4	0	3	0	200	5.0

1994-95 statistics:

GP	G	A	TP	+/-	PIM	PP	SH	GW	GT	S	PCT
43	10	16	26	+15	6	7	0	0	0	90	11.1

1995-96 statistics:

GP	G	A	TP	+/-	PIM	PP	SH	GW	GT	S	PCT
81	17	50	67	+29	20	8	1	1	1	211	8.1

best suited as a number two or three defenseman, similar to Calle Johansson. Lidstrom will not be an impact player, but will be a steady 50-60 point scorer as long as he doesn't have to be the number one guy.

LAST SEASON

Second among team defensemen in scoring.

THE FINESSE GAME

Lidstrom is an excellent skater and has good vision of the ice. He prefers to look for the breakout pass, rather than carry the puck, and he has an excellent point shot. Last season, he was moved to the point on the first power play unit with Paul Coffey, whose influence on Lidstrom's development cannot be overstated. Lidstrom is not an elite point man, because he does not always make smart decisions with the puck, but he has a hard and accurate point shot and he is more confident about moving down low.

Defensively, Lidstrom positions himself well and has improved his reads. He is tough to beat one-on-one, and sometimes even two-on-one, in open ice. He neatly breaks up passes with a quick stick. He kills penalties and willingly blocks shots.

Lidstrom seems to have trouble handling the puck in his feet, which is unusual for European skaters, who traditionally have some soccer training.

THE PHYSICAL GAME

Lidstrom does not take the body well, but he does take great pains to protect the puck with his body. He won't cough up the puck out of fear of getting hit, so it isn't quite accurate to call him a soft player. Let's call him a quiet one.

THE INTANGIBLES

At the start of his career, Lidstrom seemed poised to move into the top class of NHL offensive defensemen, but he doesn't have the goods for that next step. He is

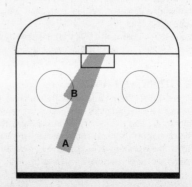

KIRK MALTBY

Yrs. of NHL service: 3
Born: Guelph, Ont.; Dec. 22, 1972
Position: right wing
Height: 6-0
Weight: 190
Uniform no.: 18
Shoots: right

Career statistics:

GP	G	A	TP	PIM
170	22	17	39	190

1993-94 statistics:

GP	G	A	TP	+/-	PIM	PP	SH	GW	GT	S	PCT
68	11	8	19	-2	74	0	1	1	0	89	12.4

1994-95 statistics:

GP	G	A	TP	+/-	PIM	PP	SH	GW	GT	S	PCT
47	8	3	11	-11	49	0	2	1	1	73	11.0

1995-96 statistics:

GP	G	A	TP	+/-	PIM	PP	SH	GW	GT	S	PCT
55	3	6	9	-16	67	0	0	1	0	55	5.5

THE INTANGIBLES

Maltby could produce 10-15 goals a season and provide smart checking if he can win a full-time job in Detroit.

LAST SEASON

Acquired from Detroit for Dan McGillis, Mar. 20, 1996. Missed 16 games with scratched cornea. Appeared in four games with Cape Breton (AHL), scoring 1-2 — 3.

THE FINESSE GAME

Possessing astute hockey sense, which has stamped him as a two-way winger, Maltby has good speed and just loves to flatten people with clean, hard hits. There are few nights when you don't notice when Maltby is on the ice.

Unless, of course, when he is on the bench, or on the sidelines, which is where Detroit kept him. Given their playoff failure, however, the Red Wings will be looking to add more toughness to their roster, and that's where Maltby fits in.

Maltby's skating helps keep him in position defensively. He is seldom caught up-ice and plays well without the puck. He understands the game well and is very coachable. He kills penalties well and blocks shots.

Maltby's size and offensive style resemble Kirk Muller's. He isn't overly creative, but he will work tirelessly along the boards and in the corners to keep the puck alive, as Muller does. He has an average wrist and snap shot.

THE PHYSICAL GAME

Maltby loves to check hard, and he is fearless. He is not very big but he is solid and won't back down from a challenge.

Maltby's power emanates from his lower-body drive. He is strong and balanced and will punish with his shots. His work ethic and conditioning are strong.

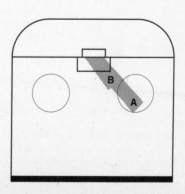

DARREN MCCARTY

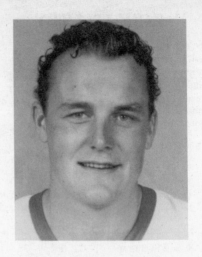

Yrs. of NHL service: 3
Born: Burnaby, B.C.; April, 1972
Position: right wing
Height: 6-1
Weight: 214
Uniform no.: 25
Shoots: right

Career statistics:

GP	G	A	TP	PIM
161	29	39	68	427

1993-94 statistics:

GP	G	A	TP	+/-	PIM	PP	SH	GW	GT	S	PCT
67	9	17	26	+12	181	0	0	2	0	81	11.1

1994-95 statistics:

GP	G	A	TP	+/-	PIM	PP	SH	GW	GT	S	PCT
31	5	8	13	+5	88	1	0	2	0	27	18.5

1995-96 statistics:

GP	G	A	TP	+/-	PIM	PP	SH	GW	GT	S	PCT
63	15	14	29	+14	158	8	0	1	1	102	14.7

LAST SEASON

Second on team in penalty minutes.

THE FINESSE GAME

McCarty has decent offensive skills to go along with his physical game, and will get the odd power play shift for the last 30 seconds or so. He led the OHL with 55 goals in 1991-92 while playing for Belleville. Although his totals at the minor league and NHL levels have not been as impressive, he has some potential to be a middling power forward.

Skating is McCarty's major drawback and the probable reason why he has not been productive as a scorer. He has an awkward stride and a slow first few steps. He has good hands, though, and will score the majority of his goals in tight. He is not terribly creative but plays a basic power game. He will try to generate a forecheck.

McCarty played in Sweden prior to last season and the experience might have enhanced his skill levels a bit.

THE PHYSICAL GAME

Mean, big, strong, tough and fearless. All the components are there, along with the desire to throw his body around and get involved. If a game is off to a quiet start, look for McCarty to wake everyone up. He is not a great fighter because his balance is only so-so, but he is willing.

THE INTANGIBLES

McCarty needs to take a big step forward in his development, especially in his skating, to have an NHL impact. The Red Wings, after their playoff disappointment, will be wanting to add some grit to their top two lines. The opportunity is there for McCarty.

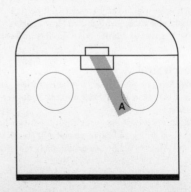

CHRIS OSGOOD

Yrs. of NHL service: 3
Born: Peace River, Alta.; Nov. 26, 1972
Position: goaltender
Height: 5-10
Weight: 175
Uniform no.: 30
Catches: left

Career statistics:

GP	MIN	GA	SO	GAA	A	PIM
110	6226	252	8	2.43	2	8

1993-94 statistics:

GP	MIN	GAA	W	L	T	SO	GA	S	SAPCT	PIM
41	2206	2.86	23	8	5	2	105	999	.895	2

1994-95 statistics:

GP	MIN	GAA	W	L	T	SO	GA	S	SAPCT	PIM
19	1087	2.26	14	5	0	1	41	496	.917	2

1995-96 statistics:

GP	MIN	GAA	W	L	T	SO	GA	S	SAPCT	PIM
50	2933	2.17	39	6	5	5	106	1190	.911	4

LAST SEASON

Finalist for 1996 Vezina Trophy. Led NHL in wins. Second in NHL in goals-against average. Tied for third in NHL in shutouts.

THE PHYSICAL GAME

Osgood plays his angles well and has very quick feet. His reflexes are excellent for close shots, and he stays on his skates and doesn't flop. He has a superb glove hand and is tough to beat high. Osgood is a small goalie, but by challenging shooters he makes himself look bigger in the net.

Osgood controls his rebounds well and as a result doesn't put himself into a position to scramble for too many second or third shots. His lateral movement is very good.

Osgood can handle the puck, and last season joined Ron Hextall as the only NHL goalie in history to score a goal. He isn't as active as Hextall is, though. Osgood doesn't have to be, because his teammates are so mobile and quick in coming back to get the puck. He uses his stick effectively to poke pucks off of attacker's stickblades around the net.

Osgood has to pay strict attention to nutrition and conditioning because he doesn't have the big body to get him through a busy schedule, and could easily wear down.

THE MENTAL GAME

Osgood concentrates well and keeps his head in the game. He doesn't defeat himself mentally. He has been brought along slowly and allowed to grow into the role of the team's top goalie.

THE INTANGIBLES

After two seasons of "Who's number one?" in Detroit, it's pretty clear that Osgood has deposed Mike Vernon in the nets. But Osgood couldn't help the highly favoured Red Wings win the Stanley Cup, although his playoff goals-against average (2.12) indicates Detroit's weakness this year wasn't between the pipes.

KEITH PRIMEAU

Yrs. of NHL service: 6
Born: Toronto, Ont.; Nov. 24, 1971
Position: left wing/centre
Height: 6-4
Weight: 220
Uniform no.: 55
Shoots: left

Career statistics:

GP	G	A	TP	PIM
363	97	135	230	781

1992-93 statistics:

GP	G	A	TP	+/-	PIM	PP	SH	GW	GT	S	PCT
73	15	17	32	-6	152	4	1	2	1	75	20.0

1993-94 statistics:

GP	G	A	TP	+/-	PIM	PP	SH	GW	GT	S	PCT
78	31	42	73	+34	173	7	3	4	2	155	20.0

1994-95 statistics:

GP	G	A	TP	+/-	PIM	PP	SH	GW	GT	S	PCT
45	15	27	42	+17	99	1	0	3	0	96	15.6

1995-96 statistics:

GP	G	A	TP	+/-	PIM	PP	SH	GW	GT	S	PCT
74	27	25	52	+19	168	6	2	7	0	150	18.0

LAST SEASON

Led team in penalty minutes. Tied for second on team in shorthanded goals. Tied for third on team in game-winning goals.

THE FINESSE GAME

Primeau has improved in two major areas in the past few seasons. First is his skating. With better skating has come more ice time, more confidence and more responsibility.

Second is his increasing versatility. Primeau has worked hard at all aspects of his game, and could have been used in almost any role by the Red Wings last season, including penalty killing and four-on-four play. His face-off work has improved dramatically.

Primeau has a huge stride with a long reach. A left-hand shot, he will steam down the right side, slide the puck to his backhand, get his feet wide apart for balance, shield the puck with his body and use his left arm to fend off the defenseman before shovelling the puck to the front of the net for a linemate.

Primeau is clever enough to accept the puck at top speed and make a move instead of wondering what to do with the puck. In tight, his backhand is as likely to be used as his forehand, and he will wade into traffic for loose pucks.

THE PHYSICAL GAME

It used to be that if Primeau had contact with someone, he would be the one to fall. Now, he has improved posture and balance, and can knock some pretty big men on their cans. He would rather go through you than around you.

Primeau has a fiery temper and can lose control.

Emotion is a desirable quality, but he has become too valuable a player to spend too much time in the penalty box. Primeau might have swung the pendulum back a little too far last season, though, and was too tame on some nights. He needs to wig out once in awhile to keep the opposition worried.

THE INTANGIBLES

One word on Primeau's playoff performance: Woof! He scored a single goal and was a non-factor. Primeau has shown he can be an impact player during the regular season (although his 27 goals fell below our projected 40), but he has had two dismal post seasons in a row. He is going into his option year, and playing for a new contract can either fire a player up or make him timid.

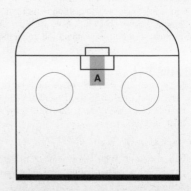

JAMIE PUSHOR

Yrs. of NHL service: 0
Born: Lethbridge, Alta.; Feb. 11, 1973
Position: right defense
Height: 6-3
Weight: 192
Uniform no.: 4
Shoots: right

Career statistics:

GP	G	A	TP	PIM
5	0	1	1	17

1995-96 statistics:

GP	G	A	TP	+/-	PIM	PP	SH	GW	GT	S	PCT
5	0	1	1	+2	17	0	0	0	0	6	0.0

LAST SEASON
Will be entering first NHL season. Played 65 games with Adirondack (AHL), scoring 2-16 — 18 with 126 penalty minutes.

THE FINESSE GAME
Pushor is a steady, stay-at-home type of defenseman with a mature game. He is a strong skater with average speed and accleration. He won't rush the puck up-ice, but he will move it sharply and smartly out of his zone with a pass. He has very good hockey sense.

Pushor reads plays well defensively. He uses his range to take away the passing lanes and force attackers to the boards. He also does the dirty work along the walls and in the corners. He knows his size is what will get him to the NHL and it will be his willingness to use his strength that will keep him there.

Pushor is a solid penalty killer. He doesn't get involved much offensively, but if the right spot opens up he will jump into the attack. Don't expect to see him stray in much beyond the blueline, however.

THE PHYSICAL GAME
Pushor takes the body well and finishes his checks. He isn't a big open-ice hitter because he lacks mobility, but he has good lower body strength for battles along the boards. He has a mean streak and will nail someone if the check is there.

THE INTANGIBLES
Pushor has paid his dues with three seasons in the minors and was close to making the team last season before the Red Wings opted to go with more veteran defenseman. Because of his years of service, Pushor would have to clear waivers to be sent to the minors again this year, so he will either find a job with Detroit or another NHL team. He's just a bit slow, which appears to be his only drawback, but could become a number five or six defenseman.

STEVE YZERMAN

Yrs. of NHL service: 13
Born: Cranbrook, B.C.; May 9, 1965
Position: centre
Height: 5-11
Weight: 185
Uniform no.: 19
Shoots: right

Career statistics:

GP	G	A	TP	PIM
942	523	738	1255	616

1992-93 statistics:

GP	G	A	TP	+/-	PIM	PP	SH	GW	GT	S	PCT
84	58	79	137	+33	44	13	7	6	0	307	18.9

1993-94 statistics:

GP	G	A	TP	+/-	PIM	PP	SH	GW	GT	S	PCT
58	24	58	82	+11	36	7	3	3	1	217	11.1

1994-95 statistics:

GP	G	A	TP	+/-	PIM	PP	SH	GW	GT	S	PCT
47	12	26	38	+6	40	4	0	1	0	134	9.0

1995-96 statistics:

GP	G	A	TP	+/-	PIM	PP	SH	GW	GT	S	PCT
80	36	59	95	+29	64	16	2	8	0	220	16.4

LAST SEASON

Led team in power play goals. Second on team in goals, points and game-winning goals. Tied for second on team in shorthanded goals. Third on team in assists.

THE FINESSE GAME

Yzerman is a model of consistency. His lapses during the season are few, and he seldom goes through a prolonged scoring slump, despite playing with a variety of linemates as he did last season. Considering how much ice time he gets and how active a skater he is, this is a great tribute to his devotion to conditioning and preparing himself for a game. Yzerman has always seemed mature beyond his years, even when he broke into the NHL at age 18.

He is a sensational skater. He zigs and zags all over the ice, spending very little time in the centre. He has great balance and quick feet, and is adroit at kicking the puck up onto his blade for a shot, in seamless motion. Yzerman is also strong for an average-sized forward. He protects the puck well with his body and has the arm strength for wraparound shots and off-balance shots through traffic.

Yzerman prefers to stickhandle down the right side of the ice. In addition to using his body to shield the puck, he uses the boards to protect it, and if a defender starts reaching in with his stick he usually ends up pulling Yzerman down for a penalty.

One Yzerman weakness is face-offs. He is only average for a centre of his skill and reputation. Defensively, he still has a few flaws, but he is a great penalty killer because of his speed and anticipation.

THE PHYSICAL GAME

Yzerman sacrifices his body willingly in the right circumstances. Detroit certainly doesn't want to see him going haywire and checking bigger players all over the ice. He will pay the price along the boards and around the net, and he's deceptively strong and durable.

THE INTANGIBLES

The only knock on Yzerman is his failure to achieve any playoff success in Detroit, and it happened again last year. Yzerman is one of three big-ticket Red Wings (along with Keith Primeau and Sergei Fedorov) who are heading into their option years. Trade rumours have hounded him nearly every season, and we expect them to surface again before the World Cup tournament ends.

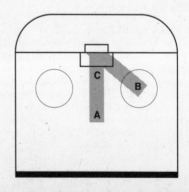

EDMONTON OILERS

Players' Statistics 1995-96

POS	NO.	PLAYER	GP	G	A	PTS	+/-	PIM	PP	SH	GW	GT	S	PCT
C	39	DOUG WEIGHT	82	25	79	104	-19	95	9		2	1	204	12.3
L	8	ZDENO CIGER	78	31	39	70	-15	41	12		3		184	16.8
C	7	JASON ARNOTT	64	28	31	59	-6	87	8		5	1	244	11.5
R	10	MARIUSZ CZERKAWSKI	70	17	23	40	-4	18	3		1		142	12.0
R	20	DAVID OLIVER	80	20	19	39	-22	34	14				131	15.3
C	26	TODD MARCHANT	81	19	19	38	-19	66	2	3	2	1	221	8.6
L	32	*MIROSLAV SATAN	62	18	17	35	0	22	6		4		113	15.9
D	2	BORIS MIRONOV	78	8	24	32	-23	101	7		1		158	5.1
D	6	JEFF NORTON	66	8	23	31	9	42	1		2		85	9.4
L	37	DEAN MCAMMOND	53	15	15	30	6	23	4				79	19.0
L	16	KELLY BUCHBERGER	82	11	14	25	-20	184		2	3		119	9.2
L	17	SCOTT THORNTON	77	9	9	18	-25	149		2	3		95	9.5
D	24	BRYAN MARCHMENT	78	3	15	18	-7	202					96	3.1
D	28	JIRI SLEGR	57	4	13	17	-1	74	1		1		91	4.4
L	15	*DAVID ROBERTS	34	3	10	13	-7	18	1		1		47	6.4
L	94	*RYAN SMYTH	48	2	9	11	-10	28	1				65	3.1
D	22	LUKE RICHARDSON	82	2	9	11	-27	108					61	3.3
L	19	KENT MANDERVILLE	37	3	5	8	-5	38		2			63	4.8
D	34	DONALD DUFRESNE	45	1	6	7	-4	20					21	4.8
D	5	*BRETT HAUER	29	4	2	6	-11	30	2		1		53	7.5
L	29	LOUIE DEBRUSK	38	1	3	4	-7	96					17	5.9
C	27	*RALPH INTRANUOVO	13	1	2	3	-3	4			1		19	5.3
D	25	*GREG DE VRIES	13	1	1	2	-2	12					8	12.5
C	64	*JASON BONSIGNORE	20		2	2	-6	4					13	
C	12	*TYLER WRIGHT	23	1		1	-7	33					18	5.6
G	31	CURTIS JOSEPH	34		1	1	0	4					1	
D	23	*NICK STAJDUHAR	2				2	4					1	
D	35	*BRYAN MUIR	5				-4	6					4	
G	40	FRED BRATHWAITE	7				0	2						
R	36	*DENNIS BONVIE	8				-3	47						
G	1	*JOAQUIN GAGE	16				0	4						

GP = games played; G = goals; A = assists; PTS = points; +/- = goals-for minus goals-against while player is on ice; PIM = penalties in minutes; PP = power play goals; SH = shorthanded goals; GW = game-winning goals; GT = game-tying goals; S = no. of shots; PCT = percentage of goals to shots; * = rookie

JASON ARNOTT

Yrs. of NHL service: 3
Born: Collingwood, Ont.; Oct. 11, 1974
Position: centre
Height: 6-3
Weight: 200
Uniform no.: 7
Shoots: right

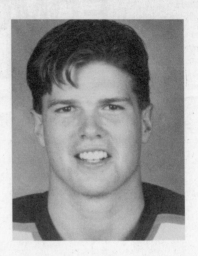

Career statistics:

GP	G	A	TP	PIM
184	76	88	164	262

1993-94 statistics:

GP	G	A	TP	+/-	PIM	PP	SH	GW	GT	S	PCT
78	33	35	68	+1	104	10	0	4	1	194	17.0

1994-95 statistics:

GP	G	A	TP	+/-	PIM	PP	SH	GW	GT	S	PCT
42	15	22	37	-14	128	7	0	1	0	156	9.6

1995-96 statistics:

GP	G	A	TP	+/-	PIM	PP	SH	GW	GT	S	PCT
64	28	31	59	-6	87	8	0	5	1	244	11.5

LAST SEASON

Led team in game-winning goals and shots. Second on team in goals. Third on team in assists and points. Missed nine games with knee injury. Missed seven games with facial injury and concussion.

THE FINESSE GAME

Injuries played a major role in derailing Arnott's steady progress since his rookie season three years ago. For a player of his size, he has tremendous skills. As a skater, he has speed, balance, a long stride and agility in turning to either side. And he has added muscle to his frame without losing any edge in his skating.

Arnott's biggest asset, though, is his hockey sense. As gifted as he is offensively, he doesn't overstay his welcome and is diligent in playing defensively.

Arnott is just as good a scorer as a passer, which makes it difficult for defenders who can't overplay him. His timing with his passes is fine, as he holds onto the puck until a teammate is in the open. If the shot is his, he will use an assortment — snap, slap or wrist — and is accurate with a quick release. He is fair on draws but will have to improve. Arnott played centre last year, but finished as the right wing on the Oilers' top line with Doug Weight and Zdeno Ciger.

Arnott works down low on the power play and is on the Oilers' first unit. He can also kill penalties.

THE PHYSICAL GAME

Arnott has serious grit. He has a mean streak, and he's honest as well. He loves to hit and gets involved, especially in the attacking zone. He has had fewer problems with inconsistency lately, and is learning to pay the price every night. A top-conditioned athlete, he gets a lot of ice time and can handle it.

THE INTANGIBLES

Arnott has been given a large amount of responsibility early in his career and for the most part, has handled his challenges well. Two things worry us as Arnott heads into his fourth season. His concussion last season was his third in two years, which raises health concerns. The other is the possible loss of Group 2 free agent Doug Weight, which would push Arnott into the role of carrying the team with a weak supporting cast. Should Weight return and Arnott stay healthy, we see him developing into a power forward capable of a 40-goal season.

Arnott was a Group 2 free agent at the end of the last season, which could either mean a healthy raise or an early season contract dispute.

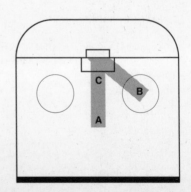

KELLY BUCHBERGER

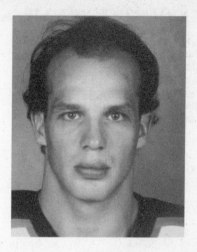

Yrs. of NHL service: 8
Born: Langenburg, Sask.; Dec. 2, 1966
Position: left wing
Height: 6-2
Weight: 200
Uniform no.: 16
Shoots: left

Career statistics:

GP	G	A	TP	PIM
580	64	107	161	1398

1992-93 statistics:

GP	G	A	TP	+/-	PIM	PP	SH	GW	GT	S	PCT
83	12	18	30	-27	133	1	2	3	0	92	13.0

1993-94 statistics:

GP	G	A	TP	+/-	PIM	PP	SH	GW	GT	S	PCT
84	3	18	21	-20	199	0	0	0	0	93	3.2

1994-95 statistics:

GP	G	A	TP	+/-	PIM	PP	SH	GW	GT	S	PCT
48	7	17	24	0	82	2	1	5	0	73	9.6

1995-96 statistics:

GP	G	A	TP	+/-	PIM	PP	SH	GW	GT	S	PCT
82	11	14	25	-20	184	0	2	3	0	119	9.2

LAST SEASON

One of three Oilers to appear in all 82 games; consecutive games-played streak is 216. Tied for second on team in shorthanded goals. Tied for third on team in game-winning goals.

THE FINESSE GAME

Buchberger is an ideal third-line player. Night in and night out, he faces other teams' top forwards and does a terrific shadow job, harassing without taking bad penalties.

He works hard and provides a consistent effort. He will grind, go to the net, kill penalties — all of the grunt work. He can finish off some plays now and then, but that is not his objective. The biggest change in Buchberger is that he has developed some degree of confidence in his finesse moves and is now willing to try something that looks too difficult for a "defensive" player. Sometimes it works, sometimes it doesn't.

Buchberger has some straight-ahead speed and will go to the net and muck, but this kind of player needs some luck to get goals. He has earned a great deal of respect for his work ethic.

THE PHYSICAL GAME

Buchberger's "shot heard 'round the NHL" was a check that gave former Oiler Wayne Gretzky a concussion. It wasn't an intentional hurt, of course, but Buchberger is a legitimately tough customer. Honest and gritty, he won't get knocked around and is a solid hitter who likes the physical part of the game. He is a very disciplined player. He's also very determined. He keeps his legs moving constantly, and a player who lets up on this winger will be sorry, because Buchberger will keep plugging with the puck or to the net.

THE INTANGIBLES

Buchberger was named captain of the Oilers, and as the last remaining Oiler from the 1990 Stanley Cup championship team, takes his leadership role to heart. Even after an unpleasant salary dispute prior to the season, Buchberger provided honest effort on a nightly basis. His offensive role is limited, but there are a lot of playoff-bound teams that will be asking for him in March if the Oilers are again out of the race.

MARIUSZ CZERKAWSKI

Yrs. of NHL service: 2
Born: Radomsko, Poland; Apr. 13, 1972
Position: right wing
Height: 5-11
Weight: 185
Uniform no.: 10
Shoots: right

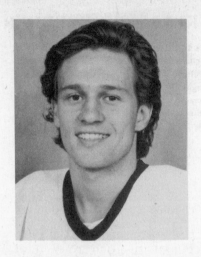

Career statistics:

GP	G	A	TP	PIM
121	31	38	69	49

1993-94 statistics:

GP	G	A	TP	+/-	PIM	PP	SH	GW	GT	S	PCT
4	2	1	3	-2	0	0	1	0	0	11	18.2

1994-95 statistics:

GP	G	A	TP	+/-	PIM	PP	SH	GW	GT	S	PCT
47	12	14	26	+4	31	1	0	2	0	126	9.5

1995-96 statistics:

GP	G	A	TP	+/-	PIM	PP	SH	GW	GT	S	PCT
70	17	23	40	-4	18	3	0	1	0	142	12.0

LAST SEASON

Acquired from Boston with Sean Brown and a number one draft pick for Bill Ranford, Jan. 11, 1996. Fourth on team in points. Missed 12 games with finger surgery and broken nose.

THE FINESSE GAME

While highly skilled, Czerkawski has still not shaken a common fault of gifted European puckhandlers. He will not make the simple play. Czerkawski often plays as if the objective is to dance through all five opponents on the ice before shooting or passing, leaving his teammates exasperated.

Czerkawski likes to use all of the ice, and will cut across the middle or to the right side to make the play. He is a shifty skater, not one with great straightaway speed, but he puts the slip on a defender with a lateral move and is off. Czerkawski is hard to defend one-on-one because of the jitterbugging his body does, all while in full control of the puck. Unfortunately, much of his energy goes to waste when he misses out on the prime scoring opportunities.

His quick wrist shot is his best weapon. With the extra room on the power play, he is at his best. He has soft hands for passes and good vision. He needs to play with someone who will get him the puck, since he will not go into the corners for it. Czerkawski was more reluctant to shoot last season.

THE PHYSICAL GAME

Czerkawski has to get better at protecting the puck and perform at least a willing game along the boards. He uses his body in the offensive zone, but in a perfunctory manner, and he doesn't like to get involved too much in the defensive zone. He is quick enough to peel back and help out with backchecking since he is very smart at anticipating passes, but he will rarely knock anyone off the puck.

THE INTANGIBLES

Because Czerkawski's talent is close to elite, the Oilers will be patient as his adjustment to the NHL continues. Czerkawski wasn't thrilled with the trade to Edmonton, but still scored 29 points in 37 games and managed to be a +7 in his Oilers stint. He should upgrade to a 60-point season in a role on the second line.

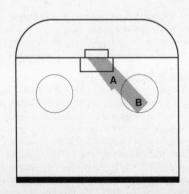

CURTIS JOSEPH

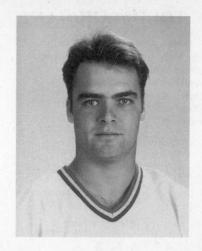

Yrs. of NHL service: 6
Born: Keswick, Ont.; Apr. 29, 1967
Position: goaltender
Height: 5-10
Weight: 182
Uniform no.: 31
Catches: left

Career statistics:

GP	MIN	GA	SO	GAA	A	PIM
314	17923	921	5	3.08	17	24

1992-93 statistics:

GP	MIN	GAA	W	L	T	SO	GA	S	SAPCT	PIM
68	3890	3.02	29	28	9	1	196	2202	.911	8

1993-94 statistics:

GP	MIN	GAA	W	L	T	SO	GA	S	SAPCT	PIM
71	4127	3.10	36	23	0	1	213	2382	.911	4

1994-95 statistics:

GP	MIN	GAA	W	L	T	SO	GA	S	SAPCT	PIM
36	1914	2.79	20	10	1	1	89	904	.902	0

1995-96 statistics:

GP	MIN	GAA	W	L	T	SO	GA	S	SAPCT	PIM
34	1936	3.44	15	16	2	0	111	971	.886	4

LAST SEASON

Acquired from St. Louis with Michael Grier for two first-round draft picks, Aug. 4, 1995. Missed 43 games in contract dispute. Missed three games with knee injury. Played 15 games with Las Vegas (IHL), compiling a 12-2-1 record with a 1.99 GAA.

THE PHYSICAL GAME

Nothing Joseph does is by the book. He always looks unorthodox and off-balance, but he is one of those hybrid goalies — like Ed Belfour and Felix Potvin — whose success can't be argued with.

Joseph positions himself well, angling out to challenge the shooter, and is one of the best goalies against the breakaway in the NHL. He has stopped all four penalty shot attempts he has faced in the past five seasons. Joseph goes to his knees quickly, but bounces back to his skates fast for the rebound. He tends to keep rebounds in front of him. His glove hand is outstanding.

A strong, if bizarre, stickhandler, he has to move his hands on the stick, putting the butt-end into his catching glove and lowering his blocker. His favourite move is a weird backhand whip off the boards. He is a good skater who moves out of his cage confidently to handle the puck. He needs to improve his lateral movement. He also uses his stick to harass anyone who dares to camp on his doorstep. He's not Billy Smith, but he's getting more aggressive with his whacks.

THE MENTAL GAME

Joseph can handle a lot of ice time — he thrives on it, actually — and seeing a lot of pucks doesn't faze him.

Good thing, since he will have to cope with a rain of rubber with Edmonton. Missing half the season hurt him a bit, although he stepped in and won his first three starts.

THE INTANGIBLES

Joseph's fate was sealed when he feuded with Mike Keenan in St. Louis in 1994-95 and it was no surprise to see him in a new city last season (two, if you count his Las Vegas stint). He is not among the top five or six NHL goalies (despite his selection to Team Canada for the World Cup) and will have a tough year in Edmonton.

TODD MARCHANT

Yrs. of NHL service: 2
Born: Buffalo, N.Y.; Aug. 12, 1973
Position: centre
Height: 6-0
Weight: 180
Uniform no.: 26
Shoots: left

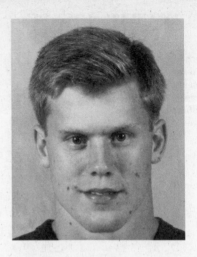

Career statistics:

GP	G	A	TP	PIM
130	32	34	66	100

1993-94 statistics:

GP	G	A	TP	+/-	PIM	PP	SH	GW	GT	S	PCT
4	0	1	1	-2	2	0	0	0	0	6	0.0

1994-95 statistics:

GP	G	A	TP	+/-	PIM	PP	SH	GW	GT	S	PCT
45	13	14	27	-3	32	3	2	2	0	95	13.7

1995-96 statistics:

GP	G	A	TP	+/-	PIM	PP	SH	GW	GT	S	PCT
81	19	19	38	-19	66	2	3	2	1	221	8.6

LAST SEASON

Led team in shorthanded goals. Second on team in shots.

THE FINESSE GAME

Marchant is a strong one-on-one player with zippy outside speed. His quick hand skills keep pace with his feet, and he is particularly adept at tempting the defender with the puck then dragging it through the victim's legs. He then continues to the net for his scoring chances, and he is a strong finisher. Marchant is a product of the U.S. national program, which despite producing lousy results at the Olympics has been highly successful as a breeding ground for high-flying NHL stars.

Marchant is opportunistic, and with his pace reminds scouts of a young Theo Fleury. However, he has a long way to go to match Fleury's scoring touch. He didn't make the big leap last season, and he will never be a 50-goal, 100-point scorer like Fleury.

Marchant is smart, sees the ice well and is a solid playmaker as well as shooter. He is no puck hog. He is an excellent penalty killer and a shorthanded threat because of his speed.

THE PHYSICAL GAME

Marchant is average size but his grit makes him look bigger. He sacrifices his body, but, as with scrappy Jeremy Roenick, you wonder how long his body will last under the stress he puts it through. He is well conditioned and can handle a lot of ice time. The mental toughness is there, too. He will take a hit to make a play, but has to get smarter about picking his spots in order to survive. Edmonton has turned into a very mobile team and Marchant's lack of size might not be as much of a detriment as it could be on other teams.

THE INTANGIBLES

Marchant has to keep his legs moving to be effective. He stopped doing that for a time last season, and when he did, coach Ron Low benched him for the only game Marchant missed last season. Marchant had the guts to face up to the coach and ask why, instead of sulking. After their chat, he scored eight points in the next five games, a positive sign.

The problem for Marchant is finding a role on the Oilers. He spent most of last season as a third-line checking centre, but he doesn't have the physical ability to match up with the league's better power centres.

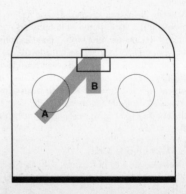

BRYAN MARCHMENT

Yrs. of NHL service: 6

Born: Toronto, Ont.; May 1, 1969

Position: left defense

Height: 6-1

Weight: 205

Uniform no.: 24

Shoots: left

Career statistics:

GP	G	A	TP	PIM
346	20	60	80	1154

1992-93 statistics:

GP	G	A	TP	+/-	PIM	PP	SH	GW	GT	S	PCT
78	5	15	20	+15	313	1	0	1	0	75	6.7

1993-94 statistics:

GP	G	A	TP	+/-	PIM	PP	SH	GW	GT	S	PCT
55	4	11	15	-14	166	0	1	1	0	92	4.3

1994-95 statistics:

GP	G	A	TP	+/-	PIM	PP	SH	GW	GT	S	PCT
40	1	5	6	-11	184	0	0	0	0	57	1.8

1995-96 statistics:

GP	G	A	TP	+/-	PIM	PP	SH	GW	GT	S	PCT
78	3	15	18	-7	202	0	0	0	0	96	3.1

LAST SEASON

Led team in penalty minutes for second consecutive season.

THE FINESSE GAME

Because of Marchment's reputation as a ferocious hitter, his skills are often overlooked, but they are impressive for a big man.

He loves to play, and he loves to get involved from the very first shift. He's never happier than when there's some blood on his jersey, even if it's his own.

Marchment has started making better decisions with and without the puck. He is more aware of when it's appropriate to pinch and when to back off, although he is still overeager. He lacks the skating ability to cover up for some of his mental errors, though he is competent enough to join in on rushes.

Marchment has an underrated shot and can drill a one-timer or snap a quick shot on net. He is not much of a passer, since he doesn't sense when to feather or fire a puck to a receiver.

THE PHYSICAL GAME

One scout describes Marchment as "the ultimate legbreaker." Marchment puts the big hurt on big names. He is a throwback to the days of the destructive open-ice hitters. This requires great strength along with good lateral mobility, or else the checker can be left spinning around at centre ice and watching the back of the puck carrier tearing up the ice on a breakaway. Marchment has become less of a headhunter and picks his spots better. The Oilers want him to be aggressive, but also want him on the ice.

Marchment will make mistakes, but they are usu-ally errors of aggression. Where he won't make mistakes is in his down low coverage. He makes the transition game for the opposition a little slower when he's on the ice.

In keeping with the old-fashioned theme, Marchment is a good fighter. He also finishes every check, blocks shots and uses his upper body well. In one-on-one battles, however, he lacks drive from his legs, and he is not a balanced skater.

THE INTANGIBLES

Marchment's improved approach to conditioning paid off big time last season, and he will be even better this season. The Oilers have told him they want him to handle 27-30 minutes of ice time a game as one half of the team's top defense pair, and Marchment is eager for the challenge. Coaches love him because he constantly works hard at trying to improve his game and is a good team man. Having Marchment and possibly Jiri Slegr as a top defense pair is not a bad start for any team.

BORIS MIRONOV

Yrs. of NHL service: 3
Born: Moscow, Russia; March 21, 1972
Position: defense
Height: 6-3
Weight: 220
Uniform no.: 2
Shoots: right

Career statistics:

GP	G	A	TP	PIM
186	16	55	71	251

1993-94 statistics:

GP	G	A	TP	+/-	PIM	PP	SH	GW	GT	S	PCT
79	7	24	31	-33	110	5	0	0	1	145	4.8

1994-95 statistics:

GP	G	A	TP	+/-	PIM	PP	SH	GW	GT	S	PCT
29	1	7	8	-9	40	0	0	0	0	48	2.1

1995-96 statistics:

GP	G	A	TP	+/-	PIM	PP	SH	GW	GT	S	PCT
78	8	24	32	-23	101	7	0	1	0	158	5.1

LAST SEASON

Led team defensemen in scoring. Worst plus-minus among team defensemen.

THE FINESSE GAME

Mironov is basically a stay-at-home defenseman, but he has the talent to get involved offensively when he wants to. He has a huge slap shot and is a good puckhandler as well, so he can start a rush out of his own zone and finish things up at the other end.

He uses his size well to protect the puck, but getting it away from an attacker is another matter. Mironov tends to give up on his checks, and he doesn't always read plays coming at him well, so he gets beaten wide by lesser skaters. He doesn't see much time on the penalty-killing unit because of his defensive deficiencies.

Mironov plays well on the point on the power play, getting his heavy low shot through or working a pass in deep. He seldom ventures in closer than the tops of the circles.

THE PHYSICAL GAME

Mironov is big and mobile. He isn't a thumper, but he's strong and he eliminates people. He has been compared to Viacheslav Fetisov, and although he will probably never be a checker who puts victims into the mezzanine, we would like to see him play more to his size. So would his coaches.

THE INTANGIBLES

After being benched for his indifferent play, Mironov shrugged it off and said he wasn't upset. Wrong answer. A player of Mironov's skills should be very upset. He is a world-class talent who was the defense partner of Sandis Ozolinsh for the Soviet Junior National team a few seasons ago, but there are serious doubts about his commitment to the game, on and off the ice. He could very well be on the block.

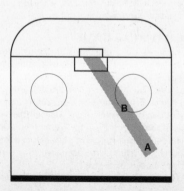

JEFF NORTON

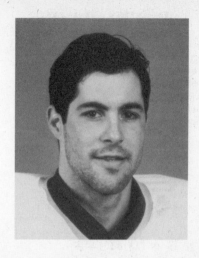

Yrs. of NHL service: 8
Born: Acton, Mass.; Nov. 25, 1965
Position: right defense
Height: 6-2
Weight: 195
Uniform no.: 6
Shoots: left

Career statistics:

GP	G	A	TP	PIM
460	40	249	289	382

1992-93 statistics:

GP	G	A	TP	+/-	PIM	PP	SH	GW	GT	S	PCT
66	12	38	50	-3	45	5	0	0	0	127	9.4

1993-94 statistics:

GP	G	A	TP	+/-	PIM	PP	SH	GW	GT	S	PCT
64	7	33	40	+16	36	1	0	0	0	92	7.6

1994-95 statistics:

GP	G	A	TP	+/-	PIM	PP	SH	GW	GT	S	PCT
48	3	27	30	+22	72	0	0	1	0	48	6.3

1995-96 statistics:

GP	G	A	TP	+/-	PIM	PP	SH	GW	GT	S	PCT
66	8	23	31	+9	42	1	0	2	0	85	9.4

LAST SEASON

Acquired from St. Louis with Donald Dufresne for Igor Kravchuk and Ken Sutton, Jan. 4, 1996. Led team in plus-minus. Missed 16 games with charley horse and season-ending knee surgery.

THE FINESSE GAME

An offensive defenseman, Norton has deep edges and seems to make his turns and cuts with his body set at a 45-degree angle to the ice. His skating ability allows him to cover up for some of his more erratic defensive play. Norton gets too excited about joining the attack and forgets gap control or makes ill-timed pinches. Many times, he is able to gallop back into position, but he still makes a risky defensive proposition. His knee injury may affect his skating, which is his chief asset.

His hockey sense is good, especially offensively, but Norton has never been able to combine his skating with the kind of scoring impact he should. He doesn't have a great shot. He will generate a play with his skating and puckhandling and get the puck into the attacking zone, but he never seems to have the finishing touch, either with a shot or the good pass down low.

THE PHYSICAL GAME

Norton is not strong in his own end of the ice. On many nights, he will drift up as if he is ready to leave the zone prematurely and leave his teammates scrambling behind. His mental toughness is a question mark, and his focus and concentration waver.

THE INTANGIBLES

Norton was near tears after his trade from St. Louis, but he soldiered on and scored 20 points in 30 games for the Oilers before his knee injury. Norton is actually in an ideal slot in Edmonton as a number three or four defenseman who will see significant power play time. If he comes back healthy and confident, he could rebound with a 50-point season.

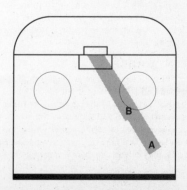

DAVID OLIVER

Yrs. of NHL service: 2
Born: Sechelt, B.C.; April 17, 1971
Position: right wing
Height: 6-0
Weight: 190
Uniform no.: 20
Shoots: right

Career statistics:

GP	G	A	TP	PIM
132	36	33	69	54

1994-95 statistics:

GP	G	A	TP	+/-	PIM	PP	SH	GW	GT	S	PCT
44	16	14	30	-11	20	10	0	0	1	79	20.3

1995-96 statistics:

GP	G	A	TP	+/-	PIM	PP	SH	GW	GT	S	PCT
80	20	19	39	-22	34	14	0	0	0	131	15.3

LAST SEASON

Second NHL season. Led team in power play goals for second consecutive season. Fifth on team in points.

THE FINESSE GAME

Oliver is one-dimensional. He's a sniper, pure and simple, and exceptionally good at what he does. Goal scoring can't be taught, and teams will often live with other deficiencies if a guy can bury the puck. Oliver has a lightning release and is close to unstoppable on the power play, where he was a major force for the Oilers. Of his 36 goals in his first two NHL seasons, 24 have come with a manpower advantage.

Oliver plays a very mature game offensively. He's strong on the puck, but is decidedly more shooter than playmaker. He lacks skating speed.

He has problems in his own zone. The pace is so much faster in the NHL than in college that Oliver struggled defensively, losing his man. He is too focused on the puck.

THE PHYSICAL GAME

Oliver reminds scouts of Joey Mullen. He has a wiry strength and gets involved physically when he has to, but wisely uses his skating ability to get himself in the open. He has poise in traffic and will take a hit to make a play, although he wore down in the second half last season (which was technically his first full NHL year, since his rookie season was shortened by the lockout).

THE INTANGIBLES

Oliver fell from the first line to the fourth during the season, and on the heels of his lauded rookie campaign, that was a hard fall. He needs to come into camp in top condition and show a willingness to play the defensive game to regain a spot on the top two lines, and as a power play specialist. Even Mike Bossy learned to play defense, so there is hope for Oliver.

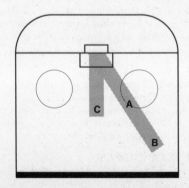

LUKE RICHARDSON

Yrs. of NHL service: 9
Born: Ottawa, Ont.; Mar. 26, 1969
Position: left defense
Height: 6-4
Weight: 215
Uniform no.: 22
Shoots: left

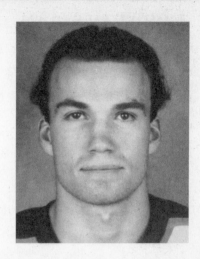

Career statistics:

GP	G	A	TP	PIM
632	23	90	113	1095

1992-93 statistics:

GP	G	A	TP	+/-	PIM	PP	SH	GW	GT	S	PCT
82	3	10	13	-18	142	0	2	0	0	78	3.8

1993-94 statistics:

GP	G	A	TP	+/-	PIM	PP	SH	GW	GT	S	PCT
69	2	6	8	-13	131	0	0	0	0	92	2.2

1994-95 statistics:

GP	G	A	TP	+/-	PIM	PP	SH	GW	GT	S	PCT
46	3	10	13	-6	40	1	1	1	0	51	5.9

1995-96 statistics:

GP	G	A	TP	+/-	PIM	PP	SH	GW	GT	S	PCT
82	2	9	11	-27	108	0	0	0	0	61	3.3

THE INTANGIBLES

Hockey sense is slow in coming to Richardson. He has good size and strength, but his lack of effectiveness on special teams limits his usefulness. He needs to play with a mobile offense-minded partner (such as Jeff Norton) to stay as a number three or four defenseman.

LAST SEASON

One of only two Oilers to appear in all 82 games.

THE FINESSE GAME

Richardson can sometimes play solid defense, but he is more often indecisive. He makes poor reads, and at this stage of his career, that skill is not likely to improve much.

He is a good skater with lateral mobility and balance, but not much speed. He can't carry the puck and doesn't jump up into the rush well. He seldom uses his point shot, which is merely adequate.

Defensively, Richardson doesn't know when to stay in front of his net and when to challenge in the corners. It's now his ninth year in the league and the necessary improvement hasn't shown. He always seems to be trying hard, but on replays of an opposing team's goal, he is often seen skating in with a late hit.

THE PHYSICAL GAME

Richardson is the kind of player you hate to play against but love to have on your side. He hits to hurt and is an imposing presence on the ice. He scares people. Richardson separates the puck carrier from the puck down low, which is especially important on a fast transition team like Edmonton's.

He will take that too far, though, and start running around getting caught out of position. He needs to improve his patience and reads. When he checks, he separates the puck carrier from the puck and doesn't let the man get back into the play. When he is on the ice, his teammates play a bit bigger and braver. Richardson plays hurt, and took few bad penalties last season.

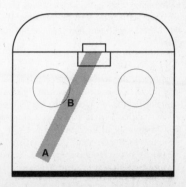

MIROSLAV SATAN

Yrs. of NHL service: 1
Born: Topolcany, Czech.; Oct. 22, 1974
Position: left wing
Height: 6-1
Weight: 180
Uniform no.: 32
Shoots: left

Career statistics:

GP	G	A	TP	PIM
62	18	17	35	22

1995-96 statistics:

GP	G	A	TP	+/-	PIM	PP	SH	GW	GT	S	PCT
62	18	17	35	0	22	6	0	4	0	113	15.9

LAST SEASON

First NHL season. Tied for lead among NHL rookies and second on team in game-winning goals. Second among NHL rookies and third on team in shooting percentage. Tied for ninth among NHL rookies in points. Tied for fourth among rookies in power play goals. Had longest point-scoring streak of season by an NHL rookie (11 games). Missed four games with separated shoulder.

THE FINESSE GAME

Satan's speed allowed him to leapfrog over several other prospects in training camp and he fit in nicely with a fairly quick Edmonton team last season. Satan has breakaway speed, not in Mike Gartner's class, certainly, but good enough to allow him to pull away from many defenders.

Satan isn't shy about shooting. He keeps his head up and looks for his shooting holes, and is accurate with a wrist and snap shot. Satan is also unselfish and sees his passing options.

Since Satan had a brief taste of pro hockey (in the IHL) in 1994-95, he came to Edmonton with a fairly well-developed all-around game. He has good hockey sense.

THE PHYSICAL GAME

Satan is average size but has gradually added about 10 pounds of muscle over the past few seasons. He is a fairly solid checker and plays a conscientious checking game.

THE INTANGIBLES

Satan was one of the few pleasant surprises for the Oilers last season, and while he occasionally saw time on the top line with Doug Weight, he isn't a top-line winger and may have trouble finding a slot on the team this season (unless Weight doesn't re-sign with the Oilers, in which case some personnel shuffling will take place). If he gets ample ice time, Satan is a two-way forward who may provide 20 goals.

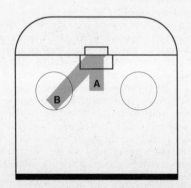

JIRI SLEGR

Yrs. of NHL service: 4

Born: Jihlava, Czechoslovakia; May 30, 1971

Position: left defense

Height: 6-1

Weight: 205

Uniform no.: 28

Shoots: left

Career statistics:

GP	G	A	TP	PIM
207	15	78	93	315

1992-93 statistics:

GP	G	A	TP	+/-	PIM	PP	SH	GW	GT	S	PCT
41	4	22	26	+16	109	2	0	0	0	89	4.5

1993-94 statistics:

GP	G	A	TP	+/-	PIM	PP	SH	GW	GT	S	PCT
78	5	33	38	0	86	1	0	0	0	160	3.1

1994-95 statistics:

GP	G	A	TP	+/-	PIM	PP	SH	GW	GT	S	PCT
31	2	10	12	-5	46	1	0	1	0	69	2.9

1995-96 statistics:

GP	G	A	TP	+/-	PIM	PP	SH	GW	GT	S	PCT
57	4	13	17	-1	74	0	1	1	0	91	4.4

his fifth NHL season and if there's a year to bust out, this could be it. He won't be in the elite class of scoring defensemen, but there's no reason why he can't pump his production up to 50 points.

LAST SEASON

Missed 19 games with knee injury. Played four games with Cape Breton (AHL), scoring 1-2 — 3.

THE FINESSE GAME

Slegr is a one-dimensional defenseman, with his outstanding skills applied almost exclusively to the offensive part of his game. He is a power play specialist.

An excellent skater, he is fluid and mobile, with good balance. His forte is puck control, and he rushes the puck well. From the offensive half of the ice in, Slegr looks fine. It's the other half of the ice where he is still a student of the game. He does not read defensive plays well and needs a great deal of improvement in handling the rush until he can emerge as an everyday player.

Slegr especially has trouble handling a strong forecheck. He doesn't move the puck quickly enough under pressure. On offense, he doesn't like to play dump-and-chase and will hold onto the puck too long or make bad plays at the blueline.

THE PHYSICAL GAME

Slegr is very strong, and when so inclined, he can tie up opponents in front of the net. He isn't big enough to bulldoze people out of the slot, so he usually resorts to his finesse skills, trying to pick off passes or playing the attacker's stick. He tends to carry his stick high. He doesn't like to get hit.

THE INTANGIBLES

Slegr's offensive skills keep everyone waiting for the big breakout season. His knee injury early last season precluded that from happening, but Slegr is entering

RYAN SMYTH

Yrs. of NHL service: 1
Born: Banff, Alta.; Feb. 21, 1976
Position: left wing
Height: 6-1
Weight: 195
Uniform no.: 94
Shoots: left

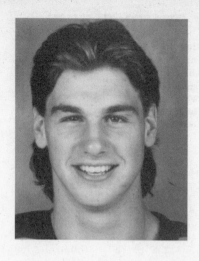

Career statistics:

GP	G	A	TP	PIM
51	2	9	11	28

1994-95 statistics:

GP	G	A	TP	+/-	PIM	PP	SH	GW	GT	S	PCT
3	0	0	0	-1	0	0	0	0	0	2	0.0

1995-96 statistics:

GP	G	A	TP	+/-	PIM	PP	SH	GW	GT	S	PCT
48	2	9	11	-10	28	1	0	0	0	65	3.1

LAST SEASON

First NHL season. Played nine games with Cape Breton, scoring 6-5 — 11.

THE FINESSE GAME

Players with size who can also score goals are a valuable commodity. Smyth has shown an ability to produce at the junior and minor-league levels, and now may be ready to take the next step.

Smyth often plays with the kind of reckless spirit that Jeremy Roenick possesses. He is a good skater who forces the play and creates scoring chances off the turnover. Smyth can finish as well as set up plays. His shot has to be a little quicker to be more dangerous at this level, but he is not afraid to pull the trigger.

Smyth saw some second-unit power play time last season. He is a capable special teams' player.

THE PHYSICAL GAME

Smyth isn't built like a power forward, but he sure tries to play like one. He is a pesky net-crasher and can be an irritating presence. He needs to develop more confidence to do this on a nightly basis in the NHL.

THE INTANGIBLES

Smyth probably wasn't ready for prime time last season, but experience was one of his weaknesses, so the half-season spent at the NHL level will give him a head start going into this year. He could develop into a second-line winger.

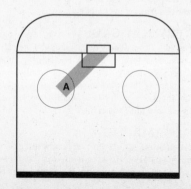

SCOTT THORNTON

Yrs. of NHL service: 4
Born: London, Ont.; Jan. 9, 1971
Position: left wing
Height: 6-3
Weight: 210
Uniform no.: 17
Shoots: left

Career statistics:

GP	G	A	TP	PIM
242	24	33	57	415

1992-93 statistics:

GP	G	A	TP	+/-	PIM	PP	SH	GW	GT	S	PCT
9	0	1	1	-4	0	0	0	0	0	7	0.0

1993-94 statistics:

GP	G	A	TP	+/-	PIM	PP	SH	GW	GT	S	PCT
61	4	7	11	-15	104	0	0	0	0	65	6.2

1994-95 statistics:

GP	G	A	TP	+/-	PIM	PP	SH	GW	GT	S	PCT
47	10	12	22	-4	89	0	1	1	0	69	14.5

1995-96 statistics:

GP	G	A	TP	+/-	PIM	PP	SH	GW	GT	S	PCT
77	9	9	18	-25	149	0	2	3	0	95	9.5

LAST SEASON

Tied for second on team in shorthanded goals. Tied for third on team in game-winning goals. Missed three games with viral infection.

THE FINESSE GAME

Thornton's best asset is his face-off ability. He is outstanding on draws, especially in the defensive zone, and matches up against just about any centre in the league when it comes to winning puck battles. If Thornton doesn't win a draw outright, he will use his muscle to tie up the opponent and work the puck to a teammate.

He uses his toughness to get rid of a defender, then has good hands when he works in tight to get his scoring chances. Thornton is by no means a sniper, and even though he has concentrated more on the defensive aspects of the game, he is able to convert a scoring chance when the opportunity presents itself. He was a scorer at the junior level, and knows what to do with the puck around the cage, although he doesn't have an NHL release.

Thornton is a good skater, not overly fast but no plodder. He is strong and balanced on his feet and hard to knock off the puck. He is alert positionally. If one of his defensemen goes in deep on the attack, Thornton will be the forward back covering for him.

THE PHYSICAL GAME

Thornton is a big, solid, defensive centre, a young Joel Otto but with better mobility. Seriously tough without being chippy or taking bad penalties, he can play against just about any big number one centre in the league.

THE INTANGIBLES

The Oilers think highly of Thornton, whose 1995-96 season can't be fairly judged because of a persistent viral infection that weakened him and caused a major weight loss. As a result, he spent most of the year on the fourth line.

Thornton will never be a major point producer, but he will fill a steady checking role for the team in many seasons to come. Expect a lot of trade rumours surrounding him every playoff year if Edmonton isn't in contention, because he's the kind of reliable, defensive forward any team could use for a serious Cup run. Because Thornton never fulfilled his offensive promise as a high draft pick (third overall in 1989 by Toronto), he may be viewed as a failure, but he delivers in other areas.

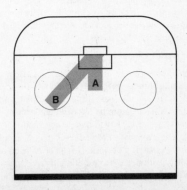

DOUG WEIGHT

Yrs. of NHL service: 5
Born: Warren, Mich.; Jan. 21, 1971
Position: centre
Height: 5-11
Weight: 195
Uniform no.: 39
Shoots: left

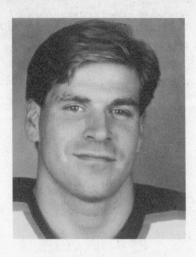

Career statistics:

GP	G	A	TP	PIM
345	81	206	296	299

1992-93 statistics:

GP	G	A	TP	+/-	PIM	PP	SH	GW	GT	S	PCT
78	17	31	48	+2	65	3	0	1	0	125	13.6

1993-94 statistics:

GP	G	A	TP	+/-	PIM	PP	SH	GW	GT	S	PCT
84	24	50	74	-22	47	4	1	1	0	188	12.8

1994-95 statistics:

GP	G	A	TP	+/-	PIM	PP	SH	GW	GT	S	PCT
48	7	33	40	-17	69	1	0	1	0	104	6.7

1995-96 statistics:

GP	G	A	TP	+/-	PIM	PP	SH	GW	GT	S	PCT
82	25	70	104	-19	95	9	0	2	1	204	12.3

LAST SEASON

Led team in assists and points, both for third consecutive season. Career high in points. Third on team in goals, power play goals and shots. One of three Oilers to appear in all 82 games.

THE FINESSE GAME

Playmaking is Weight's strong suit. He has good vision and passes well to either side. His hands are good. When he utilizes his shot, he has quick and accurate wrist and snap shots. He handles the puck well in traffic, is strong on the puck and creates a lot of scoring chances. Weight is an outstanding one-on-one player.

Weight won't win many foot races, but he keeps his legs pumping and he often surprises people on the rush who think they had him contained, only to see him push his way past. He frequently draws penalties. He has decent quickness, good balance and a fair change of direction.

Weight has improved his defensive play slightly. He is an offensive Doug Risebrough. A late bloomer, he has succeeded on a poor team in the role of a number one centre.

THE PHYSICAL GAME

Weight is inconsistent in his physical play. He shows flashes of grittiness, but doesn't bring it to the ice every night. He is built like a little fire hydrant, and on the night when he's on, he hits with enthusiasm, finishing every check. He will initiate and annoy.

He's also a bit of a trash talker, yapping and playing with a great deal of spirit. He can be counted on to provide a spark to the darkest of nights.

Weight has worked on his strength and condition-ing and can handle a lot of ice time. He is very strong on his skates and hard to knock off the puck.

THE INTANGIBLES

Weight was a Group 2 free agent after last season, and there may be a team who will sign him to an offer sheet and dare the parsimonious Oilers to match it. Weight would make an ideal number two centre on a better team. His 100 points last season was no fluke. He is going to get even better, because he has developed confidence in his game.

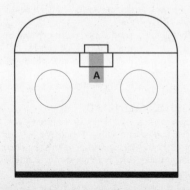

FLORIDA PANTHERS

Players' Statistics 1995-96

POS.	NO.	PLAYER	GP	G	A	PTS	+/-	PIM	PP	SH	GW	GT	S	PCT
R	27	SCOTT MELLANBY	79	32	38	70	4	160	19		3	1	225	14.2
C	44	ROB NIEDERMAYER	82	26	35	61	1	107	11		6		155	16.8
R	26	RAY SHEPPARD	70	37	23	60	-19	16	14		7		231	16.0
D	24	ROBERT SVEHLA	81	8	49	57	-3	94	7				146	5.5
L	29	JOHAN GARPENLOV	82	23	28	51	-10	36	8		7	1	130	17.7
C	14	STU BARNES	72	19	25	44	-12	46	8		5	2	158	12.0
R	28	MARTIN STRAKA	77	13	30	43	-19	41	6		1		98	13.3
R	12	JODY HULL	78	20	17	37	5	25	2		3	1	120	16.7
R	21	TOM FITZGERALD	82	13	21	34	-3	75	1	6	2		141	9.2
L	11	BILL LINDSAY	73	12	22	34	13	57		3	2		118	10.2
D	6	JASON WOOLLEY	52	6	28	34	-9	32	3				98	6.1
D	5	GORD MURPHY	70	8	22	30	5	30	4				125	6.4
L	9	*RADEK DVORAK	77	13	14	27	5	20			4		126	10.3
C	20	BRIAN SKRUDLAND	79	7	20	27	6	129		1	1		90	7.8
L	10	DAVE LOWRY	63	10	14	24	-2	36			1		83	12.0
L	18	MIKE HOUGH	64	7	16	23	4	37		1	1		66	10.6
D	55	*ED JOVANOVSKI	70	10	11	21	-3	137	2		2		116	8.6
D	2	TERRY CARKNER	73	3	10	13	10	80	1				42	7.1
D	8	MAGNUS SVENSSON	27	2	9	11	-1	21	2		1		58	3.4
D	25	GEOFF SMITH	31	3	7	10	-4	20	2				34	8.8
D	3	PAUL LAUS	78	3	6	9	-2	236					45	6.7
L	16	GILBERT DIONNE	7	1	3	4	0						12	8.3
L	15	*BRETT HARKINS	8		3	3	-2	6					4	
D	23	*RHETT WARRENER	28		3	3	4	46					19	
R	19	BRAD SMYTH	7	1	1	2	-3	4	1				12	8.3
R	51	*DAVID NEMIROVSKY	9		2	2	-1	2					6	
G	34	J. VANBIESBROUCK	57		2	2	0	10						
C	40	*STEVE WASHBURN	1		1	1	1						1	
R	22	BOB KUDELSKI	13		1	1	1						23	
C	7	MIKE CASSELMAN	3				-1						2	
G	30	MARK FITZPATRICK	34				0	12						

GP = games played; G = goals; A = assists; PTS = points; +/- = goals-for minus goals-against while player is on ice; PIM = penalties in minutes; PP = power play goals; SH = shorthanded goals; GW = game-winning goals; GT = game-tying goals; S = no. of shots; PCT = percentage of goals to shots; * = rookie

STU BARNES

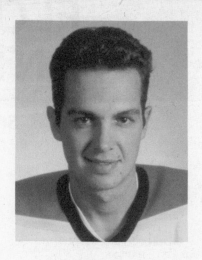

Yrs. of NHL service: 5
Born: Edmonton, Alta.; Dec. 25, 1970
Position: centre
Height: 5-11
Weight: 175
Uniform no.: 14
Shoots: right

Career statistics:

GP	G	A	TP	PIM
274	72	87	159	128

1992-93 statistics:

GP	G	A	TP	+/-	PIM	PP	SH	GW	GT	S	PCT
38	12	10	22	-3	10	3	0	3	0	73	16.4

1993-94 statistics:

GP	G	A	TP	+/-	PIM	PP	SH	GW	GT	S	PCT
77	23	24	47	+4	38	8	1	3	0	172	13.4

1994-95 statistics:

GP	G	A	TP	+/-	PIM	PP	SH	GW	GT	S	PCT
41	10	19	29	+7	8	1	0	2	0	93	10.8

1995-96 statistics:

GP	G	A	TP	+/-	PIM	PP	SH	GW	GT	S	PCT
72	19	25	44	-12	46	8	0	5	2	158	12.0

LAST SEASON

Missed 10 games with sprained knee.

THE FINESSE GAME

Seeing the enthusiasm with which Barnes killed penalties, it is hard to believe he had never been asked to perform in that role before coming to Florida. He purses the puck intelligently and finishes his checks. Barnes employs these traits at even strength, too, reading the play coming out of the zone and using his anticipation to pick off passes.

Barnes has sharply honed puck skills and offensive instincts, which he puts to especially effective use on the power play. He has good quickness and can control the puck in traffic. He uses a slap shot or a wrist shot in tight. He was the Panthers' most consistent forward in the playoffs.

Barnes has a good work ethic, and his effort overcomes his deficiency in size. He's clever and plays a smart small man's game.

THE PHYSICAL GAME

Barnes is not big but he gets in the way. He brings a little bit of grit to the lineup, but what really stands out is his intensity and spirit. He can energize his team with one gutsy shift. Barnes always keeps his feet moving and draws penalties.

THE INTANGIBLES

Barnes is the number one centre on the team by default, and he makes the most of his opportunity. He isn't the biggest, or the most skilled player on the Panthers, but on most nights he is one of the most effective. His top end is probably 25-30 goals.

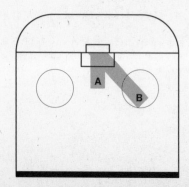

TOM FITZGERALD

Yrs. of NHL service: 8
Born: Melrose, Mass.; Aug. 28, 1968
Position: right wing/centre
Height: 6-1
Weight: 191
Uniform no.: 21
Shoots: right

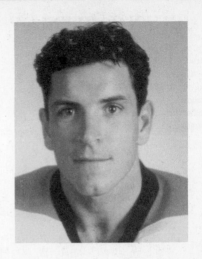

Career statistics:

GP	G	A	TP	PIM
418	59	92	151	260

1992-93 statistics:

GP	G	A	TP	+/-	PIM	PP	SH	GW	GT	S	PCT
77	9	18	27	-2	34	0	3	1	0	83	10.8

1993-94 statistics:

GP	G	A	TP	+/-	PIM	PP	SH	GW	GT	S	PCT
83	18	14	32	-3	54	0	3	1	0	144	12.5

1994-95 statistics:

GP	G	A	TP	+/-	PIM	PP	SH	GW	GT	S	PCT
48	3	13	16	-3	31	0	0	0	0	78	3.8

1995-96 statistics:

GP	G	A	TP	+/-	PIM	PP	SH	GW	GT	S	PCT
82	13	21	34	-3	75	1	6	2	0	141	9.2

recognition. Fitzgerald will contribute 10-15 goals in a checking role, but lacks the finishing touch to do much more.

LAST SEASON

Led team and tied for second in the NHL in short-handed goals. Career highs in assists and points. One of three Panthers to appear in all 82 games.

THE FINESSE GAME

Fitzgerald is a good penalty killer but has elevated his game another step by becoming a reliable crunch-time player (two of his four playoff goals were game winners).

He is very quick and uses his outside speed to take the puck to the net. He is also less shy about using his shot, perhaps because he is working to get himself into better shooting situations, but he doesn't have the quickest release and the goalie can usually adjust in time despite Fitzgerald's speed.

Fitzgerald played both centre and right wing last season, but the constant shifting doesn't faze him. There is a logjam at centre in Florida, so his versatility helps get him ice time.

THE PHYSICAL GAME

Fitzgerald is gritty and strong. He has fairly good size and uses it along the boards and in front of the net, and he's a pesky checker who gets people teed off, though his own discipline keeps him from taking many cheap penalties. He gives his team some bang and pop and finishes his checks. Although he isn't huge, he is among the best open-ice hitters in the league.

THE INTANGIBLES

Fitzgerald is one of Florida's most consistent forwards. He is developing into a top-notch checking forward who probably deserves some Selke Trophy

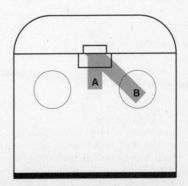

JOHAN GARPENLOV

Yrs. of NHL service: 6
Born: Stockholm, Sweden; Mar. 21, 1968
Position: left wing
Height: 5-11
Weight: 183
Uniform no.: 29
Shoots: left

Career statistics:

GP	G	A	TP	PIM
380	91	146	237	148

1992-93 statistics:

GP	G	A	TP	+/-	PIM	PP	SH	GW	GT	S	PCT
79	22	44	66	-26	56	14	0	1	0	171	12.9

1993-94 statistics:

GP	G	A	TP	+/-	PIM	PP	SH	GW	GT	S	PCT
80	18	35	53	+9	28	7	0	3	0	125	14.4

1994-95 statistics:

GP	G	A	TP	+/-	PIM	PP	SH	GW	GT	S	PCT
40	4	10	14	+1	2	0	0	0	0	44	9.1

1995-96 statistics:

GP	G	A	TP	+/-	PIM	PP	SH	GW	GT	S	PCT
82	23	28	51	-10	36	8	0	7	1	130	17.7

LAST SEASON

Led team in shooting percentage. Tied for team lead in game-winning goals. Fifth on team in points. Career high in goals. One of three Panthers to appear in all 82 games.

THE FINESSE GAME

A strong skater with good balance, Garpenlov will carry the puck through checks. He has a hard wrist shot from the off-wing and shoots well in stride, but he doesn't shoot often enough. His quickness gets him into high-quality scoring areas, but he then looks to make a pass.

Garpenlov is a better playmaker than finisher. A solid forechecker, he will create turnovers and then look to do something intelligent with the puck.

The story is different on the power play, perhaps because the open ice gives him more time and confidence. He likes to work low and use his one-timer from the left circle. If he were as eager to shoot in five-on-five situations, he could elevate his game another level.

THE PHYSICAL GAME

Garpenlov is not physical. His forechecking pressure comes not from physical contact, but from his skating ability, which gets him in on top of a player to force a pass he can intercept.

THE INTANGIBLES

Garpenlov remains shot-shy, and we doubt he'll ever net more than 25 goals in a season unless he gets a little more selfish. He can help the Panthers if teamed with a sniper. Because he is not an assertive forward and doesn't have elite skills, there are too many nights when you barely notice Garpenlov in the lineup . . . and that was the case in the playoffs.

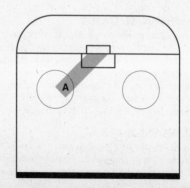

JODY HULL

Yrs. of NHL service: 8
Born: Cambridge, Ont.; Feb. 2, 1969
Position: right wing
Height: 6-2
Weight: 195
Uniform no.: 12
Shoots: right

Career statistics:

GP	G	A	TP	PIM
364	74	87	161	90

1992-93 statistics:

GP	G	A	TP	+/-	PIM	PP	SH	GW	GT	S	PCT
69	13	21	34	-24	14	5	1	0	1	134	9.7

1993-94 statistics:

GP	G	A	TP	+/-	PIM	PP	SH	GW	GT	S	PCT
69	13	13	26	+6	8	0	1	5	1	100	13.0

1994-95 statistics:

GP	G	A	TP	+/-	PIM	PP	SH	GW	GT	S	PCT
46	11	8	19	-1	8	0	0	4	0	63	17.5

1995-96 statistics:

GP	G	A	TP	+/-	PIM	PP	SH	GW	GT	S	PCT
78	20	17	37	+5	25	2	0	3	1	120	16.7

He could probably last for another dozen NHL seasons doing what he does without any particular distinction, since he doesn't hurt a team.

LAST SEASON

Career high in goals and points. Missed four games with fractured rib.

THE FINESSE GAME

Hull has some fine natural skills. His powerful skating stride is almost syrupy smooth. He has some range and can skate with people, slowing them down and picking off passes.

His snap shot is heavy and effective, though his release isn't the fastest. There are times when it seems you can hear him thinking. He will cut into the middle at the blueline, then outguess himself on the proper play. Even if he has skating room and could take the puck closer to the net, he does not penetrate, drive the defense and pull the goalie out to him.

Hull kills penalties well and will play positionally in a checking role. He has been given a lot more responsibility with Florida and has responded.

THE PHYSICAL GAME

Hull is a polite player. He has no mean streak to speak of. He can be goaded into an occasional slash, just to prove there is a pulse, but his lack of an aggressive game is what usually keeps him on the bubble.

THE INTANGIBLES

Hull has a lot of ability he appears not to use. He does not show much expression on the ice and tends to fade into the background. Hull was a little more involved last season but still played a lot of quiet games, especially in the playoffs. He does more defensive than offensive things, but there are too many others of his ilk to make him anything more than a marginal player.

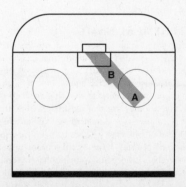

ED JOVANOVSKI

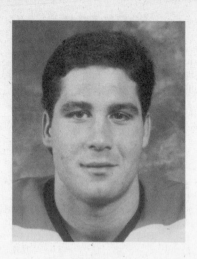

Yrs. of NHL service: 1
Born: Windsor, Ont.; June 26, 1976
Position: left defense
Height: 6-2
Weight: 205
Uniform no.: 55
Shoots: left

Career statistics:

GP	G	A	TP	PIM
62	15	35	50	221

1995-96 statistics:

GP	G	A	TP	+/-	PIM	PP	SH	GW	GT	S	PCT
70	10	11	21	-3	137	2	0	2	0	116	8.6

LAST SEASON

First NHL season. Finalist for 1996 Calder Trophy. Named to NHL All-Rookie team. Third among NHL rookie defensemen in scoring. Missed 11 games with fractured finger.

THE FINESSE GAME

As well as Jovanovski played last season, there is still a tremendous upside because his talent is so raw. Jovanovski started playing hockey later than most NHLers, and his skating, which has improved dramatically, may still be improved a notch. He already streaks through the neutral zone like a freight train. He sure isn't pretty, but he's powerful.

He is strong on his feet with a powerful, quick stride. He has more quickness than most big men, perhaps because of early soccer training, and he can use his feet to move the puck if his stick is tied up. His powerful hitting is made more wicked by the fact that he gets so much speed and leg drive. Jovanovski can make plays, too. He gets a little time because his speed forces the opposition to back off, and he has a nice passing touch.

Jovanovski can also score. He has an excellent point shot and good vision of the ice for passing. He may develop along Scott Stevens/Ray Bourque lines and become a defenseman who can dominate in all zones.

THE PHYSICAL GAME

If he isn't yet the best open-ice hitter in the NHL — and many scouts and GMs affirm that he is — then Jovanovski will be wearing that mantle soon. He hits to hurt. Because of his size and agility, he is able to catch people right where he wants them. They aren't dirty hits, but they are real old-time hockey throwbacks administered by a modern-sized defenseman.

Instead of worrying whether he is up for a game, coaches will probably have to curb some of his natural aggressiveness to keep him from headhunting and taking bad penalties. Jovanovski couldn't fight much of last season because of his hand injury. Expect that to change.

THE INTANGIBLES

Jovanovski will have to deal with not only his own expected sophomore slump, but that of the team's after being swept in the Stanley Cup finals in the Panthers' first playoff appearance. Jovanovski showed remarkable poise and has a very relaxed attitude, but expectations will be sky-high for him and if the team gets off to a slow start he is bound to be one of the scapegoats.

Even if Jovanovski sags a bit this season, he is the genuine article. Still only 20, he is starting to build a reputation as a potential Norris Trophy winner.

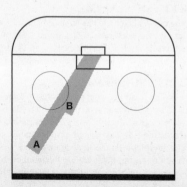

PAUL LAUS

Yrs. of NHL service: 3
Born: Beamsville, Ont.; Sept. 26, 1970
Position: right defense
Height: 6-1
Weight: 215
Uniform no.: 3
Shoots: right

Career statistics:

GP	G	A	TP	PIM
154	5	13	18	483

1993-94 statistics:

GP	G	A	TP	+/-	PIM	PP	SH	GW	GT	S	PCT
39	2	0	2	+9	109	0	0	1		9	15	13.3

1994-95 statistics:

GP	G	A	TP	+/-	PIM	PP	SH	GW	GT	S	PCT
37	0	7	7	+12	138	0	0	0	0	18	0.0

1995-96 statistics:

GP	G	A	TP	+/-	PIM	PP	SH	GW	GT	S	PCT
78	3	6	9	-2	236	0	0	0	0	45	6.7

LAST SEASON

Led team in penalty minutes for second consecutive season.

THE FINESSE GAME

People don't like to play against a club that has Laus on it. He is a legitimate tough guy, but one who has worked at the other aspects of his game to become a more useful player.

Laus has borderline NHL skating speed. He is powerful and well-balanced for battles along the boards and in the corners. He seems to know his limitations and doesn't try to overextend himself. He needs to be paired with a mobile partner, since he doesn't cover a lot of ice.

Laus uses his size and strength effectively at all times. He has to control both his temper and his playing style. His success in the NHL will come from him playing his position and not running around headhunting.

Laus doesn't have much offensive instinct, but gets a little room to take shots from the point because no one wants to come near him.

THE PHYSICAL GAME

Laus hits. Anyone. At any opportunity. Since his skating isn't great, he can't catch people in open ice, but he's murder along the boards, in the corners and in front of the net. He hits to hurt. He's big, but not scary-sized like a lot of today's NHL defensemen. He is, however, powerful and mean, and he stands up for his teammates.

THE INTANGIBLES

Laus has worked hard to become more than a mere goon, and the work has paid off. He is a perfectly serviceable fifth or sixth defenseman who has made him-self a valuable member of the team. He makes his teammates braver, and if his skills keep improving as they have been over the past two seasons, that will keep him on the ice. Florida rolls over its defense pairs, so Laus gets a lot of ice instead of sitting on the bench and waiting for the odd shift.

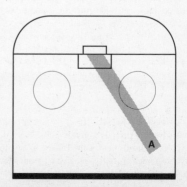

BILL LINDSAY

Yrs. of NHL service: 4
Born: Big Fork, Mont.; May 17, 1971
Position: left wing
Height: 5-11
Weight: 190
Uniform no.: 11
Shoots: left

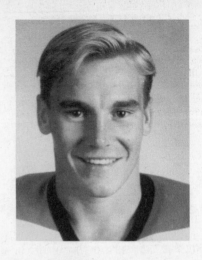

Career statistics:

GP	G	A	TP	PIM
272	34	50	84	230

1992-93 statistics:

GP	G	A	TP	+/-	PIM	PP	SH	GW	GT	S	PCT
44	4	9	13	0	16	0	0	0	0	58	6.9

1993-94 statistics:

GP	G	A	TP	+/-	PIM	PP	SH	GW	GT	S	PCT
84	6	6	12	-2	97	0	0	0	0	90	6.7

1994-95 statistics:

GP	G	A	TP	+/-	PIM	PP	SH	GW	GT	S	PCT
48	10	9	19	+1	46	0	1	0	0	63	15.9

1995-96 statistics:

GP	G	A	TP	+/-	PIM	PP	SH	GW	GT	S	PCT
73	12	22	34	+13	57	0	3	2	0	118	10.2

LAST SEASON

Led team in plus-minus. Second on team in short-handed goals. Career highs in goals, assists and points. Missed seven games with lacerated hand. Missed two games with hip flexor.

THE FINESSE GAME

Lindsay continues to add more offensive touches to a predominantly defensive game. He may be well-remembered from last season as the player who drove wide around Ray Bourque to score a key goal in the Panthers' playoff series win over Boston. Lindsay has a big shot, but an average release. His first instinct is to try to beat the goalie between the pads. He has a long reach and scores many of his goals from his work in front of the net. He has decent hands, but it's his second and third effort that make the difference.

Lindsay is a support player who, teamed with more offensive linemates, acts as a safety valve. He is not very creative, but he will follow the play to the net.

His skating speed and agility are average, but he is balanced and strong on his skates. He has good size, which he uses in a checking role. He sometimes gets a bit lazy and doesn't keep his feet moving. When he doesn't take that extra step, he will take a bad hooking or tripping penalty. There is no subtlety to Lindsay's forechecking. He skates in a straight line with limited agility.

THE PHYSICAL GAME

Lindsay uses his body effectively but doesn't thrash people. He is sturdy and sometimes gets it into his head to stir things up, to try and give his team a bit of a spark. He plays much bigger than his size.

THE INTANGIBLES

Lindsay's skill level makes him a borderline third-line winger, but since Florida rolls over four lines under coach Doug MacLean, he gets his fair share of ice time. Scoring 20 goals would be a real stretch for him, but he has improved slightly in each of the past two years.

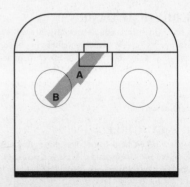

DAVE LOWRY

Yrs. of NHL service: 11
Born: Sudbury, Ont.; Feb. 14, 1965
Position: left wing
Height: 6-1
Weight: 200
Uniform no.: 10
Shoots: left

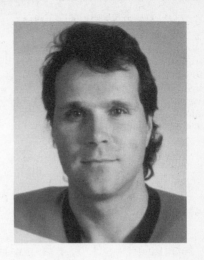

Career statistics:

GP	G	A	TP	PIM
664	107	118	225	914

1992-93 statistics:

GP	G	A	TP	+/-	PIM	PP	SH	GW	GT	S	PCT
58	5	8	13	-18	101	0	0	0		0	59	8.5

1993-94 statistics:

GP	G	A	TP	+/-	PIM	PP	SH	GW	GT	S	PCT
80	15	22	37	-4	64	3	0	3	1	122	12.3

1994-95 statistics:

GP	G	A	TP	+/-	PIM	PP	SH	GW	GT	S	PCT
45	10	10	20	-3	25	2	0	3	0	70	14.3

1995-96 statistics:

GP	G	A	TP	+/-	PIM	PP	SH	GW	GT	S	PCT
63	10	14	24	-2	36	0	0	1	0	83	12.0

LAST SEASON

Missed 18 games with sprained knee.

THE FINESSE GAME

Skating stands out among Lowry's skills. He is fast and powerful, though he lacks subtlety. All Lowry knows is straight ahead, whether it's to smack into an opponent or to crash the net for a scoring chance. He does little in the way of shooting from anywhere other than dead in front of the net.

Not a creative playmaker, Lowry is most content in the role of an up-and-down winger. He gradually worked his way up to the first power play unit in the playoff last season and showed an opportunistic scoring touch. Lowry pays the price in front of the net setting screens and scrapping for rebounds.

He is primarily a strong forechecker and defensive forward, but Lowry won't limit himself and will adapt to whatever role is given him.

THE PHYSICAL GAME

Lowry has decent size, and when he combines it with his speed he becomes an effective hitter. He will harry the puck carrier on a forechecking mission and will use his stick and body to slow down a skater. He is very gritty and his effort is non-stop.

THE INTANGIBLES

Every so often, the playoffs produce an unlikely hero, and Lowry was last year's John Druce. He scored as many goals in 22 playoff games as in 63 regular-season games. Ideally, he is a third-line role player who gives his team 15 to 20 goals a season, and we don't expect last spring to change that.

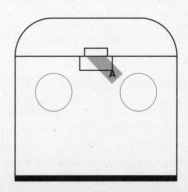

SCOTT MELLANBY

Yrs. of NHL service: 10
Born: Montreal, Que.; June 11, 1966
Position: right wing
Height: 6-1
Weight: 205
Uniform no.: 27
Shoots: right

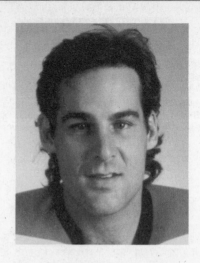

Career statistics:

GP	G	A	TP	PIM
711	196	238	434	1437

1992-93 statistics:

GP	G	A	TP	+/-	PIM	PP	SH	GW	GT	S	PCT
69	15	17	32	-4	147	6	0	3	1	114	13.2

1993-94 statistics:

GP	G	A	TP	+/-	PIM	PP	SH	GW	GT	S	PCT
80	30	30	60	0	149	17	0	4	1	204	14.7

1994-95 statistics:

GP	G	A	TP	+/-	PIM	PP	SH	GW	GT	S	PCT
48	13	12	25	-16	90	4	0	5	0	130	10.0

1995-96 statistics:

GP	G	A	TP	+/-	PIM	PP	SH	GW	GT	S	PCT
79	32	38	70	+4	160	19	0	3	1	225	14.2

LAST SEASON

Led team in points with career high. Led team and tied for fifth in NHL in power play goals. Second on team in goals and assists. Missed three games with fractured finger.

THE FINESSE GAME

Not having a great deal of speed or agility, Mellanby generates most of his effectiveness in tight spaces where he can use his size. He is good on the power play, working down low for screens and tips. He doesn't have many moves, but he can capitalize on a loose puck. Goals don't come naturally to him, but he is determined and pays the price in front of the net.

Mellanby's big jump in goals last season was due in part to working with centre Stu Barnes, and in part to developing a quicker release on his shot. He became a key man on the first power play unit, scoring well from the slot area.

He has become very responsible defensively and can kill penalties, though he is never a shorthanded threat. He lacks the speed and scoring instincts to convert turnovers into dangerous chances.

THE PHYSICAL GAME

Mellanby forechecks aggressively, using his body well to hit and force mistakes in the attacking zone. He participates in one-on-one battles in tight areas and tries to win his share. He is also willing to mix it up and takes penalties for aggression.

THE INTANGIBLES

Mellanby is the man responsible for "Ratmania" in Miami, but we won't hold that against him. His suc-

cess is based on his work ethic. Any let up and the letdown will come in the scoring department. Because of the heightened expectations for Mellanby this season, we doubt his production will be as dazzling as it was last year.

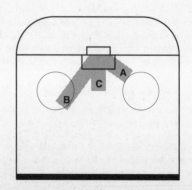

GORD MURPHY

Yrs. of NHL service: 8
Born: Willowdale, Ont.; Mar. 23, 1967
Position: right defense
Height: 6-2
Weight: 195
Uniform no.: 5
Shoots: right

Career statistics:

GP	G	A	TP	PIM
552	67	182	249	492

1992-93 statistics:

GP	G	A	TP	+/-	PIM	PP	SH	GW	GT	S	PCT
49	5	12	17	-13	62	3	0	2	0	68	7.4

1993-94 statistics:

GP	G	A	TP	+/-	PIM	PP	SH	GW	GT	S	PCT
84	14	29	43	-11	71	9	0	2	3	172	8.1

1994-95 statistics:

GP	G	A	TP	+/-	PIM	PP	SH	GW	GT	S	PCT
46	6	16	22	-14	24	5	0	0	0	94	6.4

1995-96 statistics:

GP	G	A	TP	+/-	PIM	PP	SH	GW	GT	S	PCT
70	8	22	30	+5	30	4	0	0	0	125	6.4

LAST SEASON

Missed nine games with ankle injury. Missed three games with fractured toe.

THE FINESSE GAME

The development of rookie Robert Svehla took much of the offensive responsibility away from Murphy, who has concentrated on becoming a better defensive player. Murphy uses his finesse skills in a two-way role. He is a strong and agile skater, and he executes tight turns and accelerates in a stride or two. He moves the puck well and then joins the play eagerly.

He also carries the puck well, although he gets into trouble when he overhandles in his own zone. He usually makes a safe pass, holding on until he is just about decked and then making a nice play. Murphy plays the point on the power play, and uses a pull and drag shot, rather than a big slap shot, giving him a very quick release.

Murphy plays a smart positional game and makes intelligent defensive reads.

THE PHYSICAL GAME

Murphy uses his finesse skills to defend. His long reach makes him an effective poke-checker, and he would rather wrap his arms around an attacker than move him out of the crease with a solid hit. He's more of a pusher than a hitter. He is responsible defensively and is used to kill penalties. He logs a lot of ice time and holds up well under the grind.

THE INTANGIBLES

Murphy is not, and will never be, a tough customer, but he has improved his positional play and can step up and provide some offensive spark. He is best with a physical, stay-at-home partner, but he can also be paired with a mobile defenseman and stay back for the defensive work himself.

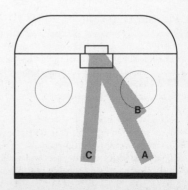

ROB NIEDERMAYER

Yrs. of NHL service: 3
Born: Cassiar, B.C.; Dec. 28, 1974
Position: centre
Height: 6-2
Weight: 200
Uniform no.: 44
Shoots: left

Career statistics:

GP	G	A	TP	PIM
195	39	58	97	194

1993-94 statistics:

GP	G	A	TP	+/-	PIM	PP	SH	GW	GT	S	PCT
65	9	17	26	-11	51	3	0	2	0	67	13.4

1994-95 statistics:

GP	G	A	TP	+/-	PIM	PP	SH	GW	GT	S	PCT
48	4	6	10	-13	36	1	0	0	0	58	6.9

1995-96 statistics:

GP	G	A	TP	+/-	PIM	PP	SH	GW	GT	S	PCT
82	26	35	61	+1	107	11	0	6	0	155	16.8

among the league's elite centres, although he has elite speed.

LAST SEASON

Second on team in points. Third on team in goals, assists and power play goals. One of three Panthers to appear in all 82 games.

THE FINESSE GAME

Niedermayer is slowly growing into the role of a number one centre in Florida, but may have another season or two to go before he really hits his stride. Niedermayer is an excellent skater. He is big and strong and he has the speed to stay with some of the league's best power centres. He drives to the net and is learning to play that way on a nightly basis.

Niedermayer is a strong passer and an unselfish player, probably too unselfish. He controls the puck well at tempo and can beat a defender one-on-one. He has started to finish better and play with much more authority.

Because of his inconsistency, Niedermayer was often used on the fourth line, but Florida rolls over its lines and he saw a lot of ice time. Niedermayer was a mainstay on Florida's power play. One of his flaws is a slight hesitation in his shot release.

THE PHYSICAL GAME

Although not overly physical, Niedermayer has good size and is still growing. He has a bit of a temper, but he is an intelligent player and doesn't hurt his team by taking bad penalties. His attitude is outstanding. He is a coachable kid and good team man. He works hard along the boards and in the corners.

THE INTANGIBLES

Niedermayer started to fulfill his promise last season, and should provide a consistent 25-30 goals. He needs to develop a more well-rounded game, which should come with experience. He probably will never be

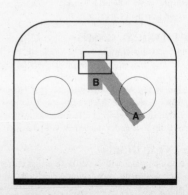

RAY SHEPPARD

Yrs. of NHL service: 9
Born: Pembroke, Ont.; May 27, 1966
Position: right wing
Height: 6-1
Weight: 195
Uniform no.: 26
Shoots: right

Career statistics:

GP	G	A	TP	PIM
557	275	207	482	165

1992-93 statistics:

GP	G	A	TP	+/-	PIM	PP	SH	GW	GT	S	PCT
70	32	34	66	+7	29	10	0	1	0	183	17.5

1993-94 statistics:

GP	G	A	TP	+/-	PIM	PP	SH	GW	GT	S	PCT
82	52	41	93	+13	26	19	0	5	0	260	20.0

1994-95 statistics:

GP	G	A	TP	+/-	PIM	PP	SH	GW	GT	S	PCT
43	30	10	40	+11	17	11	0	5	1	125	24.0

1995-96 statistics:

GP	G	A	TP	+/-	PIM	PP	SH	GW	GT	S	PCT
70	37	23	60	-19	16	14	0	7	0	231	16.0

LAST SEASON

Acquired by San Jose from Detroit for Igor Larionov, Oct. 24, 1995. Acquired from San Jose for two draft picks, Mar. 16, 1996. Led team in goals and shots. Tied for team lead in game-winning goals. Third on team in points. Missed nine games with shoulder separation.

THE FINESSE GAME

Sheppard has great hands, but is a liability everywhere else on the ice except for a 10-foot radius around the net. He is not a great skater. He looks excruciatingly slow, but this is deceptive because he is almost always in a good scoring position. He doesn't turn quickly and doesn't have great balance, but he can curl out of the right circle on his backhand and get off a wrist or snap shot. He is also strong enough to ward off a defender with one hand and shovel a pass or push a shot towards the net with his other hand. He must play with a centre who will get him the puck.

There are times when Sheppard looks like a puck magnet. He is always eager to move to the puck and has good hockey sense and vision. Although he is a winger, he has a centre's view of the ice. He is also not selfish; he loves to shoot but will dish off if he spies a teammate with a better percentage shot. He has good hands with a quick release and doesn't waste time with a big backswing. He prefers efficiency and accuracy.

Sheppard is usually the last player back when play breaks back out of the offensive zone.

THE PHYSICAL GAME

Sheppard does not play a big game. He's an average-sized forward who plays below his size. He won't work along the boards but will go to the front of the net, so he has to play with one grinder to get him the puck and one quick forward to serve as the safety valve defensively. Sheppard has improved his lower body strength.

THE INTANGIBLES

We predicted Sheppard would net 40 goals last season, and also said it would be the last time he reached that level, and we will stick by that assessment. Playing for three teams last season was one indication. Sheppard has a problem playing in pressure situations, and had to be benched again in the playoffs as he was in 1995 by Detroit (to his credit, he did have eight playoff goals for the Panthers, but only one in the last eight games).

BRIAN SKRUDLAND

Yrs. of NHL service: 11
Born: Peace River, Alta.; July 31, 1963
Position: centre
Height: 6-0
Weight: 195
Uniform no.: 20
Shoots: left

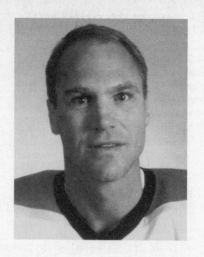

Career statistics:

GP	G	A	TP	PIM
696	107	197	304	955

1992-93 statistics:

GP	G	A	TP	+/-	PIM	PP	SH	GW	GT	S	PCT
39	7	7	14	+4	65	0	2	1	0	51	13.7

1993-94 statistics:

GP	G	A	TP	+/-	PIM	PP	SH	GW	GT	S	PCT
79	15	25	40	+13	136	0	2	1	0	110	13.6

1994-95 statistics:

GP	G	A	TP	+/-	PIM	PP	SH	GW	GT	S	PCT
47	5	9	14	0	88	1	0	0	0	44	11.4

1995-96 statistics:

GP	G	A	TP	+/-	PIM	PP	SH	GW	GT	S	PCT
79	7	20	27	+6	129	0	1	1	0	90	7.8

LAST SEASON

Three games missed were coaches' decision.

THE FINESSE GAME

Skrudland is among the top face-off men in the league, and that, along with his strong skating and tenacious forechecking, helps make him a reliable defensive forward.

His primary job is to keep the other team's top lines off the scoreboard, and he will get his scoring chances from forcing turnovers. He has a good short game and will look to make a creative play with the puck once he gains control. Skrudland has become less of an offensive threat in the past two seasons, settling more into a strictly defensive mode.

He is an outstanding penalty killer. He forechecks aggressively and attacks the points.

THE PHYSICAL GAME

Skrudland is tough to knock off balance. He has a wide skating stance, which also gives him a strong power base for checking. He seldom fails to get a piece of his opponent. He has a compact build and makes his presence felt.

If anything, Skrudland takes too much emotion into a game and will take a bad penalty at what always seems to be the worst time. It's a small price to pay for someone who never takes a night off unless forced to do so.

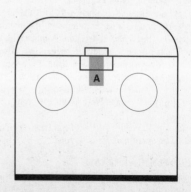

THE INTANGIBLES

Skrudland was a major reason why the Panthers reached the finals last season. His contributions are the kind that don't show up on the scoresheet.

MARTIN STRAKA

Yrs. of NHL service: 4
Born: Plzen, Czechoslovakia; Sept. 3, 1972
Position: centre
Height: 5-10
Weight: 178
Uniform no.: 28
Shoots: left

Career statistics:

GP	G	A	TP	PIM
240	51	90	141	110

1992-93 statistics:

GP	G	A	TP	+/-	PIM	PP	SH	GW	GT	S	PCT
42	3	13	16	+2	29	0	0	1	0	28	10.7

1993-94 statistics:

GP	G	A	TP	+/-	PIM	PP	SH	GW	GT	S	PCT
84	30	34	64	+24	24	2	0	6	1	130	23.1

1994-95 statistics:

GP	G	A	TP	+/-	PIM	PP	SH	GW	GT	S	PCT
37	5	13	18	-1	16	0	0	0	0	49	10.2

1995-96 statistics:

GP	G	A	TP	+/-	PIM	PP	SH	GW	GT	S	PCT
77	13	30	43	-19	41	6	0	1	0	98	13.3

LAST SEASON

Acquired by Florida from Islanders on waivers, Mar. 16, 1996. Acquired by Islanders with Bryan Berard and Don Beaupre from Ottawa for Damian Rhodes and Wade Redden, Jan. 23, 1996. Missed two games with bruised buttocks.

THE FINESSE GAME

Straka is always highly productive for a week or two, then vanishes. His game is a major tease, because when he's on he can do a lot of things. He is a water bug with imagination. He makes clever passes that always land on the tape and give the recipient time to do something with the puck. He's more of a playmaker than a shooter and will have to learn to go to the net more to make his game less predictable. He draws people to him and creates open ice for his linemates.

Straka doesn't have the outside speed to burn defenders, but creates space for himself with his wheeling in tight spaces. He has good balance and is tough to knock off his feet even though he's not big.

Not a great defensive player, Straka is effective in five-on-five situations. He is an offensive threat every time he steps on the ice, but he doesn't bring much else to the ice when he's in one of his funks.

THE PHYSICAL GAME

Straka has shown little inclination for the typical North American style of play. He is small and avoids corners and walls, and will have to be teamed with more physical linemates to give him some room. He has to learn to protect the puck better with his body and buy some time.

THE INTANGIBLES

Whether he plays on a bad team (Ottawa) or a good one (Florida), Straka is frustratingly inconsistent. He's worn four jerseys in the past two seasons, and it may not be long before the Panthers throw up their paws and move him, since they benched him repeatedly in the playoffs.

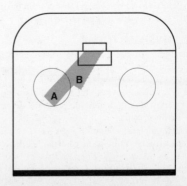

ROBERT SVEHLA

Yrs. of NHL service: 1
Born: Martin, Czech Republic; Jan. 2, 1969
Position: right defense
Height: 6-1
Weight: 190
Uniform no.: 24
Shoots: right

Career statistics:

GP	G	A	TP	PIM
86	9	50	59	94

1994-95 statistics:

GP	G	A	TP	+/-	PIM	PP	SH	GW	GT	S	PCT
5	1	1	2	+3	0	1	0	0	0	6	16.7

1995-96 statistics:

GP	G	A	TP	+/-	PIM	PP	SH	GW	GT	S	PCT
81	8	49	57	-3	94	7	0	0	0	146	5.5

LAST SEASON

Led team in assists. Led team defensemen and fourth on team in points.

THE FINESSE GAME

Svehla reminds one hockey expert of Denis Potvin. We might be quick to dismiss that kind of grand statement, except that the expert in question happens to be Potvin himself.

Svehla may not be destined for the Hall of Fame, but someone in Calgary (who has probably already been fired) has to be kicking himself for giving up Svehla for a couple of draft picks two years ago. He is going to be an impact defenseman for a long time.

Svehla is among the best in the league at the lost art of the sweep-check. If he does lose control of the puck, and an attacker has a step or two on him on a breakaway, Svehla has the poise to dive and use his stick to knock the puck away without touching the man's skates.

Svehla is a terrific skater. No one, not even Jaromir Jagr, can beat Svehla wide, because he skates well backwards and laterally. He plays a quick transition. He is among the best NHL defensemen one-on-one in open ice.

Svehla works on the first power play and penalty-killing units. He uses a long wrist shot from the point to make sure the puck will get through on net.

THE PHYSICAL GAME

Svehla does not avoid contact. He is not as aggressive as Potvin was, but he gets into the thick of things by battling along the wall and in the corners for the puck. He is not a huge checker, but he pins his man and doesn't allow him back into the play. His defensive reads are impeccable.

Svehla is in peak condition and needs little recovery time between shifts, so he can handle a lot of ice time.

THE INTANGIBLES

A few Panthers can be expected to sag this season after their great run to the finals last year, but we don't think Svehla will be one of them. He is consistent, and he only gets better under pressure. He should be among the top 10 defensemen in scoring for the next few years, and is potential Norris Trophy material.

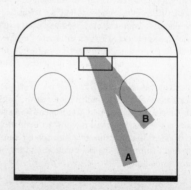

JOHN VANBIESBROUCK

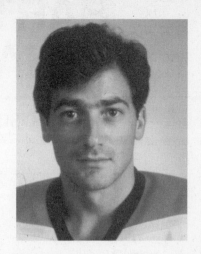

Yrs. of NHL service: 12
Born: Detroit, Mich.; Sept. 4, 1963
Position: goaltender
Height: 5-9
Weight: 175
Uniform no.: 34
Catches: left

Career statistics:

GP	MIN	GA	SO	GAA	A	PIM
600	34085	1831	23	3.22	28	266

1992-93 statistics:

GP	MIN	GAA	W	L	T	SO	GA	S	SAPCT	PIM
48	2757	3.31	20	18	7	4	152	1525	.900	18

1993-94 statistics:

GP	MIN	GAA	W	L	T	SO	GA	S	SAPCT	PIM
57	3440	2.53	21	25	11	1	145	1912	.924	38

1994-95 statistics:

GP	MIN	GAA	W	L	T	SO	GA	S	SAPCT	PIM
37	2087	2.47	14	15	4	4	86	1000	.914	6

1995-96 statistics:

GP	MIN	GAA	W	L	T	SO	GA	S	SAPCT	PIM
57	3178	2.68	26	20	7	2	142	1473	.904	10

LAST SEASON

Seventh season with 20 or more wins. Third among active goalies in career shutouts.

THE PHYSICAL GAME

There are few goalies who play a better positional game than Vanbiesbrouck. He blends a strong technical game with good reflexes, anticipation and confidence. He isn't very big, so he plays his angles and squares himself to the shooter to take away as much of the net as possible. He makes himself look like a much bigger goalie. He is very aggressive, forcing the shooter to make the first move. Vanbiesbrouck doesn't beat himself often.

He plays a butterfly-style that takes away a lot of low shots, and has a quick glove hand, so most shooters try to go high stick-side on him, but that's a hard corner to pick. Vanbiesbrouck is a good skater with fine lateral motion.

Vanbiesbrouck is very active with his stick, using it to poke-check, guide rebounds, break up passes or whack at any ankles camping out too close to his crease. He won't surrender a centimetre of his ice. Vanbiesbrouck is also confident out of his net with the puck, sometimes overly so.

THE MENTAL GAME

Vanbiesbrouck is unapproachable on game day, because his intensity and concentration is an all-day process. He is highly competitive, which was never more dramatically illustrated than by Vanbiesbrouck's superb effort in a losing cause in game four of the Stanley Cup finals against Colorado, which went three overtimes. Even though his team had almost no chance of coming back from the 0-3 deficit in the series, Vanbiesbrouck made one brilliant save after another until long into the next morning, and deserved a far better fate than the 1-0 loss.

THE INTANGIBLES

Vanbiesbrouck is a better goalie at age 33 than he was at any other time in his career. Part of the credit belongs to goalie coach Bill Smith, who has refined the technical aspects of Vanbiesbrouck's game.

HARTFORD WHALERS

Players' Statistics 1995-96

POS.	NO.	PLAYER	GP	G	A	PTS	+/-	PIM	PP	SH	GW	GT	S	PCT
L	94	BRENDAN SHANAHAN	74	44	34	78	2	125	17	2	6		280	15.7
L	8	GEOFF SANDERSON	81	34	31	65	0	40	6		7		314	10.8
C	21	ANDREW CASSELS	81	20	43	63	8	39	6		1	2	135	14.8
R	16	NELSON EMERSON	81	29	29	58	-7	78	12	2	5		247	11.7
D	27	JEFF BROWN	76	8	47	55	8	56	5				177	4.5
C	13	ANDREI NIKOLISHIN	61	14	37	51	-2	34	4	1	3		83	16.9
R	18	ROBERT KRON	77	22	28	50	-1	6	8	1	3		203	10.8
L	28	PAUL RANHEIM	73	10	20	30	-2	14		1	1		126	7.9
C	92	*JEFF O'NEILL	65	8	19	27	-3	40	1		1		65	12.3
D	20	GLEN WESLEY	68	8	16	24	-9	88	6		1		129	6.2
R	12	STEVEN RICE	59	10	12	22	-4	47	1		2		108	9.3
D	6	ADAM BURT	78	4	9	13	-4	121			1		90	4.4
D	36	GLEN FEATHERSTONE	68	2	10	12	10	138			1		62	3.2
R	11	KEVIN DINEEN	46	2	9	11	-1	117					66	3.0
D	4	GERALD DIDUCK	79	1	9	10	7	88					93	1.1
L	24	*SAMI KAPANEN	35	5	4	9	0	6					46	10.9
D	10	BRAD McCRIMMON	58	3	6	9	15	62		1			39	7.7
C	22	MARK JANSSENS	81	2	7	9	-13	155					63	3.2
L	15	*SCOTT DANIELS	53	3	4	7	-4	254					43	7.0
R	39	KELLY CHASE	55	2	4	6	-4	220			1		19	10.5
G	1	SEAN BURKE	66		6	6	0	16					1	
C	32	*STEVE MARTINS	23	1	3	4	-3	8					27	3.7
D	7	BRIAN GLYNN	54		4	4	-15	44					46	
L	14	KEVIN SMYTH	21	2	1	3	-5	8	1				27	7.4
C	33	JIMMY CARSON	11	1		1	1						9	11.1
D	5	ALEXANDER GODYNYUK	3				-1	2					1	
D	25	*JASON McBAIN	3				-1							
D	23	*MAREK MALIK	7				-3	4					2	
G	29	*JASON MUZZATTI	22				0	33						

GP = games played; G = goals; A = assists; PTS = points; +/- = goals-for minus goals-against while player is on ice; PIM = penalties in minutes; PP = power play goals; SH = shorthanded goals; GW = game-winning goals; GT = game-tying goals; S = no. of shots; PCT = percentage of goals to shots; * = rookie

JEFF BROWN

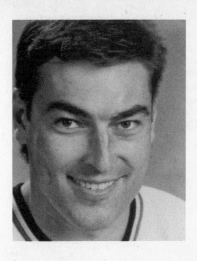

Yrs. of NHL service: 10
Born: Ottawa, Ont.; Apr. 30, 1966
Position: right defense
Height: 6-1
Weight: 204
Uniform no.: 27
Shoots: right

Career statistics:

GP	G	A	TP	PIM
686	153	405	555	466

1992-93 statistics:

GP	G	A	TP	+/-	PIM	PP	SH	GW	GT	S	PCT
71	25	53	78	-6	58	12	2	3	0	220	11.4

1993-94 statistics:

GP	G	A	TP	+/-	PIM	PP	SH	GW	GT	S	PCT
74	14	52	66	-11	56	7	0	3	1	237	5.9

1994-95 statistics:

GP	G	A	TP	+/-	PIM	PP	SH	GW	GT	S	PCT
33	8	23	31	-2	16	3	0	0	0	111	7.2

1995-96 statistics:

GP	G	A	TP	+/-	PIM	PP	SH	GW	GT	S	PCT
76	8	47	55	+8	56	5	0	0	0	177	4.5

LAST SEASON

Acquired from Vancouver with third-round draft pick for Jim Dowd, Frantisek Kucera and second-round draft pick, Dec. 19, 1995. Led team defensemen in scoring. Led team in assists.

THE FINESSE GAME

Brown is a natural quarterback on the power play. He moves to the left side on the point and likes to glide to the top of the circle to step into a one-timer.

Brown's game stems from his skating ability, and he fit in well with Hartford, which had a fast team last season. He has impressive lateral movement and can handle the puck at tempo. He's a very good playmaker for a defenseman, ready to unleash his strong point shot or fake the slap and pass, or headman the pass off a break out of the defensive zone. He sees the ice well and slips perfect passes ahead to speedy wingers like Geoff Sanderson.

Defensively, Brown's game needs improvement. He has too much hockey sense and too much skill not to be a better player. He was one of the few "plus" players on the Whalers last season, which indicates an improvement in that area.

THE PHYSICAL GAME

Brown is an offensive defenseman, but that doesn't mean he should be fishing for the puck in front of the net when he could be dropping someone onto the seat of his pants. He will be one of the veterans on the Whalers now that Brad McCrimmon has left.

Brown doesn't finish his checks consistently, and he lacks the mean streak needed to be a more dominating player.

THE INTANGIBLES

Brown is not an elite class defenseman, but when he elevates his game he is a B version of Ray Bourque. His work ethic was questioned in Vancouver, but his effort in Hartford was satisfactory. It's going to be another long season (and maybe the last one) in Hartford, which will prove very draining, but as one of the team's top offensive defensemen, Brown will get a lot of ice time and should be in the 55-60 point range. Brown scored 38 points in his 48 games with the Whalers in 1995-96.

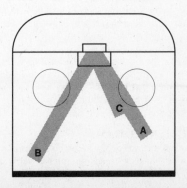

SEAN BURKE

Yrs. of NHL service: 7
Born: Windsor, Ont.; Jan. 29, 1967
Position: goaltender
Height: 6-4
Weight: 210
Uniform no.: 1
Catches: left

Career statistics:

GP	MIN	GA	SO	GAA	A	PIM
367	20556	1171	10	3.42	13	181

1992-93 statistics:

GP	MIN	GAA	W	L	T	SO	GA	S	SAPCT	PIM
50	2656	4.16	16	27	3	0	184	1485	.876	25

1993-94 statistics:

GP	MIN	GAA	W	L	T	SO	GA	S	SAPCT	PIM
47	2750	2.99	17	24	5	2	137	1458	.906	16

1994-95 statistics:

GP	MIN	GAA	W	L	T	SO	GA	S	SAPCT	PIM
42	2418	2.68	17	19	4	0	108	1233	.912	8

1995-96 statistics:

GP	MIN	GAA	W	L	T	SO	GA	S	SAPCT	PIM
66	3669	3.11	28	28	6	4	190	2034	.907	16

LAST SEASON

Led NHL goalies in assists. Missed six games with back spasms.

THE PHYSICAL GAME

Burke was the team's MVP last season. He is consistent, seldom beating himself, and will steal games the Whalers have no right winning. Burke challenges the shooter well and comes out to the top of his crease, instead of sitting back, an old habit he appears to have shed.

How well does Burke handle the puck? He outscored seven other Whalers last season. He is confident and active on the dump-ins, and with the type of neutral-zone defense Hartford plays, his work out of the net is crucial. He gives his defensemen a chance to handle the puck more easily and break out of the zone with less effort.

Burke fills up the net and is very quick for a netminder of his size. He may be one of the best big goalies in the league on shots in tight because of his superior reflexes. He has improved his angle play and control of rebounds, though the latter is one area where he could still improve.

Burke has a quick glove hand, but he will often drop it and give the shooter the top corner over his left shoulder. He also holds his blocker hand too low on his stick, which makes him lean over too far and throws him off balance.

THE MENTAL GAME

Burke has the respect of his teammates and coaches, and has a big-game mentality. Too bad the Whalers are involved in so few big games.

THE INTANGIBLES

The only concern for Burke is his recurring back injuries, which are common for a big goalie. Burke may be on the trading block as the Whalers look to dump salaries. It would be interesting to see him play again for a team whose games count. Burke is the new version of Bill Ranford, who played well all those seasons in obscurity in Edmonton. You wonder how good the guy really is.

ADAM BURT

Yrs. of NHL service: 7
Born: Detroit, Mich.; Jan. 15, 1969
Position: left defense
Height: 6-0
Weight: 195
Uniform no.: 6
Shoots: left

Career statistics:

GP	G	A	TP	PIM
428	33	81	114	644

1992-93 statistics:

GP	G	A	TP	+/-	PIM	PP	SH	GW	GT	S	PCT
65	6	14	20	-11	116	0	0	0	0	81	7.4

1993-94 statistics:

GP	G	A	TP	+/-	PIM	PP	SH	GW	GT	S	PCT
63	1	17	18	-4	75	0	0	0	0	91	1.1

1994-95 statistics:

GP	G	A	TP	+/-	PIM	PP	SH	GW	GT	S	PCT
46	7	11	18	0	65	3	0	1	0	73	9.6

1995-96 statistics:

GP	G	A	TP	+/-	PIM	PP	SH	GW	GT	S	PCT
78	4	9	13	-4	121	0	0	1	0	90	4.4

LAST SEASON

Missed three games with shoulder injury.

THE FINESSE GAME

Burt is reliable night in and night out, although he hit a little slump last season when he came back from his shoulder injury. He plays a strong physical game, and brings the puck out of the zone with authority, if not great speed.

Burt gets involved in the attack, but not to an overwhelming extent. He gets some time on the second power play unit, but is not a top-flight point man. Once in a great while Burt will surprise everyone and sneak into the circle for a shot, but this is rare.

An excellent one-on-one defender on a transition defense, Burt will strip the puck from a player using a poke-check and stand up to skaters at the blueline.

Burt has evolved into a pretty smart defenseman. He makes much better decisions with the puck and has limited his mental mistakes. He moves the puck smartly without creating opportunities for the opposing team — once one of his greatest weaknesses — and has cut down on his turnovers.

THE PHYSICAL GAME

Big but not strong, Burt works hard off the ice to gain more upper body and leg strength. He does not consistently control his man along the wall, nor does he drive people off the puck as well as a player of his size should. He is aware that his team needs him to establish a more physical presence, and he combines a willingness to hit with the desire to build himself up so he can be a legitimate thrasher. A more uptempo physical game will give him more room to move and more time to make better plays — an asset, since his hand and foot speed is only average.

Fighting does not come naturally to Burt, but he will do it and hold his own in order to make a point or aid a teammate.

THE INTANGIBLES

Burt is a coach's favourite, since no one ever has to worry about whether or not he will show up every night. He is never going to accumulate showy point totals — 20 points in a season should be his max — but he will be a steady defenseman who can contribute in all zones. His attitude is upbeat and he is quick to learn and improve. If the Whalers try to break in a young defenseman or two this season, Burt will help them out.

ANDREW CASSELS

Yrs. of NHL service: 6
Born: Bramalea, Ont.; July 23, 1969
Position: centre
Height: 6-0
Weight: 192
Uniform no.: 21
Shoots: left

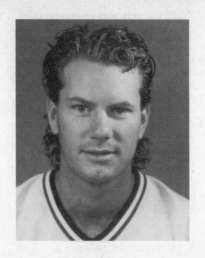

Career statistics:

GP	G	A	TP	PIM
417	83	228	311	196

1992-93 statistics:

GP	G	A	TP	+/-	PIM	PP	SH	GW	GT	S	PCT
84	21	64	85	-11	62	8	3	6	2	235	16.6

1993-94 statistics:

GP	G	A	TP	+/-	PIM	PP	SH	GW	GT	S	PCT
79	16	42	58	-21	37	8	1	3	0	126	12.7

1994-95 statistics:

GP	G	A	TP	+/-	PIM	PP	SH	GW	GT	S	PCT
46	7	30	37	-3	18	1	0	1	0	74	9.5

1995-96 statistics:

GP	G	A	TP	+/-	PIM	PP	SH	GW	GT	S	PCT
81	20	43	63	+8	39	6	0	1	2	135	14.8

LAST SEASON

Second on team in assists. Third on team in points and plus-minus.

THE FINESSE GAME

The first word most people associate with Cassels is smart. He is a very intelligent player with terrific hockey instincts, who knows when to recognize passing situations, when to move the puck and who to move it to. He has a good backhand pass in traffic and is almost as good on his backhand as his forehand. He is a creative passer who is aware of his teammates.

Cassels just hates to shoot. He won't do it much, and though he has spent a great deal of practice time at it, his release is just not NHL calibre. He has quick hands, though, and can swipe a shot off a bouncing puck in mid-air. He doesn't always fight through checks to get the kind of shots he should.

A mainstay on both specialty teams, Cassels has improved on draws. He backchecks and blocks shots. Cassels has good speed but lacks one-step quickness. He has improved his puckhandling at a high tempo.

THE PHYSICAL GAME

To complement his brains, Cassels needs brawn. He is facing a lot of defensive pressure now and has to force his way through strong forechecks and traffic around the net. He tends to get run down late in the season or during a tough stretch in the schedule, and when he gets fatigued, he is not nearly as effective.

THE INTANGIBLES

Cassels received a new three-year, U.S.$3-million contract after last season. Cassels is a number two centre who is sometimes forced into the number one role. He's smart, but his skill level isn't high. He will get 60-65 points because there is no one else.

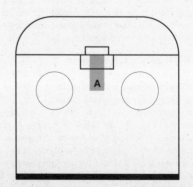

NELSON EMERSON

Yrs. of NHL service: 5
Born: Hamilton, Ont.; Aug. 17, 1967
Position: centre/left wing
Height: 5-11
Weight: 175
Uniform no.: 16
Shoots: right

Career statistics:

GP	G	A	TP	PIM
377	121	183	304	314

1992-93 statistics:

GP	G	A	TP	+/-	PIM	PP	SH	GW	GT	S	PCT
82	22	51	73	+2	62	5	2	4	0	196	11.2

1993-94 statistics:

GP	G	A	TP	+/-	PIM	PP	SH	GW	GT	S	PCT
83	33	41	74	-38	80	4	5	6	1	282	11.7

1994-95 statistics:

GP	G	A	TP	+/-	PIM	PP	SH	GW	GT	S	PCT
48	14	23	37	-12	26	4	1	1	0	122	11.5

1995-96 statistics:

GP	G	A	TP	+/-	PIM	PP	SH	GW	GT	S	PCT
81	29	29	58	-7	78	12	2	5	0	247	11.7

LAST SEASON

Acquired from Winnipeg for Darren Turcotte, Oct. 6, 1995. Missed one game with concussion. Tied for team lead in shorthanded goals. Second on team in power play goals. Third on team in goals, shots and game-winning goals. Fourth on team in points.

THE FINESSE GAME

Emerson was reunited with former St. Louis team-mate Brendan Shanahan in Hartford, and the result was harmonious. Emerson can finish, but also brings a centre's playmaking ability to the wing.

On the power play, Emerson can either play the point or work down low. He has an excellent point shot, keeping it low, on target and tippable. He is intelligent with the puck and doesn't always fire from the point, but works it to the middle of the blueline and uses screens well. When he carries in one-on-one against a defender, especially on a shorthanded rush, he always manages to use the defenseman to screen the goalie.

Emerson works well down low at even strength. He is mature and creative, with a terrific short game. He has quick hands for passing or snapping off a shot. He likes to work from behind the net, tempting the defense to chase him behind the cage. Speed and puck control are the essence of his game.

He has nice quickness and balance, and he darts in and out of traffic in front of the net. He's too small to do any physical damage, which is why playing with Shanahan gives him an edge. Shanahan opens up a lot of space. Emerson can use his speed to drive wide on a defenseman, who will think he has Emerson angled off, only to watch him blast past.

THE PHYSICAL GAME

Emerson has good skating balance, and that will give him a little edge to knock a bigger player off-stride once in a while. He will work hard defensively but has to play a smart, small man's game to avoid getting pasted. He plays bigger than his size, but isn't really feisty.

THE INTANGIBLES

Emerson's point total was disappointing last season, given his ice time, although Shanahan's slow start might have been a factor. Emerson should be in the 70-point range, although if the Whalers move Shanahan next season as expected, he might not fare as well.

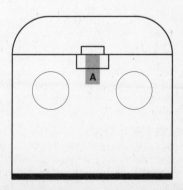

MARK JANSSENS

Yrs. of NHL service: 8
Born: Surrey, B.C.; May 19, 1968
Position: centre
Height: 6-3
Weight: 216
Uniform no.: 22
Shoots: left

Career statistics:

GP	G	A	TP	PIM
447	32	54	76	420

1992-93 statistics:

GP	G	A	TP	+/-	PIM	PP	SH	GW	GT	S	PCT
76	12	17	29	-15	237	0	0	1	0	63	19.0

1993-94 statistics:

GP	G	A	TP	+/-	PIM	PP	SH	GW	GT	S	PCT
84	2	10	12	-13	137	0	0	0	0	52	3.8

1994-95 statistics:

GP	G	A	TP	+/-	PIM	PP	SH	GW	GT	S	PCT
46	2	5	7	-8	93	0	0	0	0	33	6.1

1995-96 statistics:

GP	G	A	TP	+/-	PIM	PP	SH	GW	GT	S	PCT
81	2	7	9	-13	155	0	0	0	0	63	3.2

Janssens was a restricted free agent at the end of last season and the Whalers won't pay much to keep him. He is strictly a defensive forward.

LAST SEASON

Missed one game with fractured orbital bone.

THE FINESSE GAME

Janssens does a lot of little things well and he is the prototypical team player. He is very slow afoot — the major reason why he spent a great deal of time in the minors in the early part of his career — but compensates for his flawed skating with smarts and hustle. He seldom looks out of place on the ice because he's so solid positionally.

Janssens is excellent on face-offs and takes the key defensive draws. He is part of the number one penalty killing unit and is a tenacious hitter and forechecker. He never loses his zeal for the game, even on nights when he gets only a handful of shifts.

THE PHYSICAL GAME

Janssens will fight if he has to, and his courage in these situations is remarkable given the fact that he suffered a fractured skull and cerebral concussion during a fight in the IHL in 1988-89. His size is a big asset, especially in tight. While he can flounder in open ice because of his sluggish foot speed, he is at his best in the slot or in the corners because of his strength and balance. He has the ability to sway momentum in a game with his physical play. Janssens always finishes his checks and will rub his glove in an opponent's face.

THE INTANGIBLES

Janssens is a talkative, upbeat player on the bench and in the room and is very popular with his teammates, who know that he fights for the team and not himself.

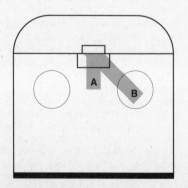

SAMI KAPANEN

Yrs. of NHL service: 1
Born: Vantaa, Finland; June 14, 1973
Position: left wing
Height: 5-10
Weight: 169
Uniform no.: 24
Shoots: left

Career statistics:

GP	G	A	TP	PIM
35	5	4	9	6

1995-96 statistics:

GP	G	A	TP	+/-	PIM	PP	SH	GW	GT	S	PCT
35	5	4	9	0	6	0	0	0	0	46	10.9

LAST SEASON

First NHL season. Played in 28 games with Springfield (AHL), scoring 14-17 — 31.

THE FINESSE GAME

Kapanen is a small, skilled forward who is always in motion. He handles the puck well while in motion, although like a lot of European forwards, he tends to hold onto the puck too long. He will shoot on the fly, however, and has an NHL shot when he does release it. He has a fine wrist shot.

Kapanen is still learning the North American game, and he suffered an injury in training camp that got him off to a late start. He will have to learn to survive in a small man's game, but he lacks the kind of quickness that may allow him to do so.

Kapanen can work on the second power play unit and, being very young, he may have a few more levels to his game.

THE PHYSICAL GAME

Kapanen's size will always be a detriment, because he is very lean without much muscle mass. He wants to play a spunkier game, but he is going to have to avoid the trouble spots to survive.

THE INTANGIBLES

Whalers fans didn't have much to cheer about last season, but Kapanen provided some entertainment with his skill and speed. His major problem is a lack of team size. If the Finn had some bigger forwards to play with, he would have a better chance at getting some ice time, but the Whalers were a pretty soft bunch at the end of last season. Kapanen's ice time may be compromised because of that because he is not an elite player.

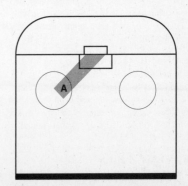

ROBERT KRON

Yrs. of NHL service: 6
Born: Brno, Czechoslovakia; Feb. 27, 1967
Position: left wing
Height: 5-10
Weight: 180
Uniform no.: 18
Shoots: left

Career statistics:

GP	G	A	TP	PIM
348	84	97	181	65

1992-93 statistics:

GP	G	A	TP	+/-	PIM	PP	SH	GW	GT	S	PCT
45	14	13	27	+5	18	4	2	2	1	97	14.4

1993-94 statistics:

GP	G	A	TP	+/-	PIM	PP	SH	GW	GT	S	PCT
77	24	26	50	0	8	2	1	3	0	194	12.4

1994-95 statistics:

GP	G	A	TP	+/-	PIM	PP	SH	GW	GT	S	PCT
37	10	8	18	-3	10	3	1	1	0	88	11.4

1995-96 statistics:

GP	G	A	TP	+/-	PIM	PP	SH	GW	GT	S	PCT
77	22	28	50	-1	6	8	1	3	0	203	10.8

LAST SEASON

Third on team in power play goals.

THE FINESSE GAME

Kron has good speed and can control the puck at high tempo, which gives him the ability to intimidate and drive opposing defensemen back off the blueline.

One of the best things to happen to his career was the reinstatement of four-on-four play in the case of coincidental minor penalties. Kron thrives on the extra open ice. There are many game situations where four-on-four comes into play, and with the Whalers' team speed, Kron was a key player in those spots

Kron is aware in all three zones. He can kill penalties and work on the power play as well. Defensively reliable, he can be used on the ice at any time in the game. He is a very creative player, more of a playmaker than a shooter, but he needs to shoot more because of his good hands. He tries to be too fine with his shot and misses the net frequently when he is in a prime scoring area. He likes to use a snap shot more than a slapper and will get a quick release away from 15 to 20 feet out.

THE PHYSICAL GAME

Kron is very fit but he is a small player and doesn't play a physical style. He's not afraid and doesn't bail out of tough situations. He will need to be shored up by big forwards, but linemates with hands, since Kron will create good scoring chances that shouldn't go to waste.

THE INTANGIBLES

Kron wavered between the second and third lines last season, but doesn't figure prominently in Hartford's plans and could be dealt. His skills should net him more than 20 goals a season, but that looks to be the limit he's set for himself.

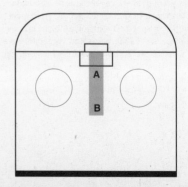

MAREK MALIK

Yrs. of NHL service: 1
Born: Ostrava, Czechoslovkia; June 24, 1975
Position: defense
Height: 6-5
Weight: 190
Uniform no.: 23
Shoots: left

Career statistics:

GP	G	A	TP	PIM
8	0	1	1	4

1994-95 statistics:

GP	G	A	TP	+/-	PIM	PP	SH	GW	GT	S	PCT
1	0	1	1	+1	0	0	0	0	0	0	0.0

1995-96 statistics:

GP	G	A	TP	+/-	PIM	PP	SH	GW	GT	S	PCT
7	0	0	0	-3	4	0	0	0	0	2	0.0

LAST SEASON

Will be entering first full NHL season. Played 68 games with Springfield (AHL), second among defensemen in scoring with 8-14 — 22 and 135 PIM.

THE FINESSE GAME

Malik has very good potential because of his high skill level in all areas. He is an excellent skater for his size. He uses his range mostly as a defensive tool, and isn't much involved in the attack.

Malik is poised with the puck. He is a good passer and playmaker and moves the puck out of his own end quickly. He won't try to do too much himself but will use his teammates well. He's big, but does a lot of the little things, which makes him a solid defensive player. He limits his offensive contributions to a shot from the point, but he may develop better skill as a playmaking assist man.

THE PHYSICAL GAME

Tall but weedy, Malik needs to fill out more to be able to handle some of the NHL's big boys. Like Kjell Samuelsson, he takes up a lot of space with his arms and stick, and is more of an octopus-type defenseman than a solid hitter. He is strong in front of his net. He has some aggressiveness in him but needs to find a consistency level. Malik was one of the best young defensemen in the AHL last season.

THE INTANGIBLES

Malik should be ready physically to win a job this season, but he has to mature in other ways. Once he is ready to approach his job as a professional, he will be a steady NHL defenseman.

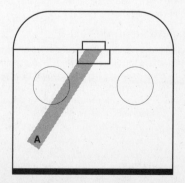

ANDREI NIKOLISHIN

Yrs. of NHL service: 2
Born: Vorkuta, USSR; March 25, 1973
Position: left wing/centre
Height: 5-11
Weight: 180
Uniform no.: 13
Shoots: left

Career statistics:

GP	G	A	TP	PIM
100	22	47	69	44

1994-95 statistics:

GP	G	A	TP	+/-	PIM	PP	SH	GW	GT	S	PCT
39	8	10	18	+7	10	1	1	0	0	57	14.0

1995-96 statistics:

GP	G	A	TP	+/-	PIM	PP	SH	GW	GT	S	PCT
61	14	37	51	-2	34	4	1	3	0	83	16.9

LAST SEASON

Led team in shooting percentage. Second on team in assists. Missed 20 games with back injury. Missed one game with ankle injury.

THE FINESSE GAME

Nikolishin is a strong skater with a powerful stride. He makes some of the tightest turns in the league. His great talent is puckhandling, but like many Europeans he tends to hold onto the puck too long and leaves himself open for hits.

Nikolishin sees the ice well and is a gifted play-maker. He needs to shoot more so that his game will be less predictable. He saw a lot of ice time with Brendan Shanahan, and needs to play with a power winger who can finish off passes and stand up for him a bit. He is eager to learn the game. Nikolishin saw time on the second power play unit and killed some penalties. He is defensively aware, backchecks and blocks shots.

THE PHYSICAL GAME

Nikolishin is extremely strong on his skates and likes to work in the corners for the puck. He is tough to knock off balance and has a low centre of gravity. He has adapted smoothly to the more physical style of play in the NHL, and while he isn't very big, he will plow into heavy going for the puck.

THE INTANGIBLES

Nikolishin lost valuable playing time due to injuries, and still has a lot of upside. He was a captain of Moscow Dynamo at age 21, and it wouldn't be a surprise to see him wearing a letter someday for an NHL team. Nikolishin is very popular with his teammates, both for his personality and his work habits.

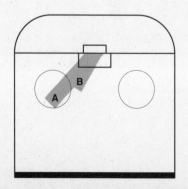

JEFF O'NEILL

Yrs. of NHL service: 1
Born: Richmond Hill, Ont.; Feb. 23, 1976
Position: centre
Height: 6-0
Weight: 176
Uniform no.: 92
Shoots: right

Career statistics:

GP	G	A	TP	PIM
65	8	19	27	40

1995-96 statistics:

GP	G	A	TP	+/-	PIM	PP	SH	GW	GT	S	PCT
65	8	19	27	-3	40	1	0	1	0	65	12.3

LAST SEASON

First NHL season. Missed four games with shoulder injury. Missed eight games with foot injury.

THE FINESSE GAME

O'Neill is a youngster who has already shown signs of a solid two-way game. Offensively, he is an excellent skater with balance, speed, acceleration and quickness. Of all his skills, skating is the only one where he ranks in the elite class.

To be a Pat LaFontaine — to whom O'Neill has often been compared — a player needs other tools, and O'Neill's skills are not good enough to place him among the top centres. He has a good sense of timing and is patient with his passes. He doesn't have a big-time release, but he has a decent one-timer.

O'Neill likes to carry the puck down the left wing boards to protect the puck, and with his speed he is able to blow by defensemen wide. He does not follow this move up by driving to the net. Defensively, O'Neill has to remind himself not to leave the zone before the puck does. He is often too anxious to get the counterattack going before his team has control.

THE PHYSICAL GAME

O'Neill has to demonstrate a better nose for the net, like his idol, Jeremy Roenick. He has a good work ethic, and if he plays a little grittier he would step up his game.

THE INTANGIBLES

O'Neill played with talented veterans in Brendan Shanahan and Nelson Emerson in his rookie year, and that helped the transition from junior to the NHL, but he is not a true number one centre. Hartford really doesn't have one. O'Neill will never be a 90-100 point scorer because of the minor flaws in his game that keep him from being top-drawer.

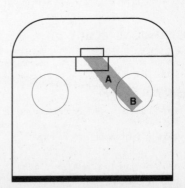

PAUL RANHEIM

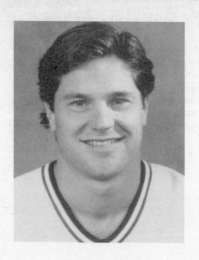

Yrs. of NHL service: 7
Born: St. Louis, Mo.; Jan. 25, 1966
Position: left wing
Height: 6-0
Weight: 195
Uniform no.: 28
Shoots: right

Career statistics:

GP	G	A	TP	PIM
489	110	137	247	131

1992-93 statistics:

GP	G	A	TP	+/-	PIM	PP	SH	GW	GT	S	PCT
83	21	22	43	-4	26	3	4	1	0	179	11.7

1993-94 statistics:

GP	G	A	TP	+/-	PIM	PP	SH	GW	GT	S	PCT
82	10	17	27	-18	22	0	2	2	0	131	7.6

1994-95 statistics:

GP	G	A	TP	+/-	PIM	PP	SH	GW	GT	S	PCT
47	6	14	20	-3	10	0	0	1	0	73	8.2

1995-96 statistics:

GP	G	A	TP	+/-	PIM	PP	SH	GW	GT	S	PCT
73	10	20	30	-2	14	0	1	1	0	126	7.9

LAST SEASON

Missed games with finger injury.

THE FINESSE GAME

Ranheim is a right-handed shot who plays the left wing, meaning he takes most of his passes on the backhand and needs more time to handle the pass. He is an excellent skater, one of the fastest in the NHL, and gets a huge number of chances just off his speed. His chief flaw is his utter lack of creativity with his shot. He is also astoundingly inaccurate, which may be a result of looking too much at the puck and not enough at his target. Ranheim's speed is all straight ahead. He has little agility.

He merits little power play time. Ranheim is a strong penalty killer, using his breakaway speed to create shorthanded chances.

Defensively, Ranheim is top drawer. He has worked hard to improve in this area after coming out of the college ranks (University of Wisconsin) as a scorer.

THE PHYSICAL GAME

Ranheim plays a solid physical game, though with his leg drive and power he could deliver more impressive hits. He does not initiate hits as well as he should.

THE INTANGIBLES

Don't expect any new spots on this leopard. He is a role player with a top potential of 20 goals a season, but is more likely to supply only half that total.

GEOFF SANDERSON

Yrs. of NHL service: 5
Born: Hay River, N.W.T.; Feb. 1, 1972
Position: left wing
Height: 6-0
Weight: 185
Uniform no.: 8
Shoots: left

Career statistics:

GP	G	A	TP	PIM
357	153	132	285	152

1992-93 statistics:

GP	G	A	TP	+/-	PIM	PP	SH	GW	GT	S	PCT
82	46	43	89	-21	28	21	2	4	0	271	17.0

1993-94 statistics:

GP	G	A	TP	+/-	PIM	PP	SH	GW	GT	S	PCT
82	41	26	67	-13	42	15	1	6	2	266	15.4

1994-95 statistics:

GP	G	A	TP	+/-	PIM	PP	SH	GW	GT	S	PCT
46	18	14	32	-10	24	4	0	4	0	170	10.6

1995-96 statistics:

GP	G	A	TP	+/-	PIM	PP	SH	GW	GT	S	PCT
81	34	31	65	0	40	6	0	7	0	314	10.8

LAST SEASON

Led team in game-winning goals and shots for third consecutive season. Second on team in goals and assists.

THE FINESSE GAME

Sanderson still doesn't make the best use of his speed, which prevents him from becoming the southpaw version of Mike Gartner. His skating speed gives him a tremendous edge over the majority of NHL players, but it's not as big a weapon as it should be.

In the second half of the season, there were probably few players who had as many shots on net as Sanderson, who may have had 10 or 11 on some nights. When he plays that way, he is far more dangerous. He can drive wide on a defenseman, or open up space by forcing the defense to play back off him.

He has an excellent release and a superb one-timer on the power play, where he likes to score on his off-wing in the deep right slot. Sanderson has become a better all-around player. He is more intelligent in his own end and his checking is more consistent. He can also kill penalties. His speed makes him a shorthanded threat.

THE PHYSICAL GAME

Sanderson has to learn and desire to fight his way through checkers. He is wiry but gets outmuscled, and although his speed keeps him clear of a lot of traffic, he has to battle when the room isn't there. Sanderson would benefit if the team added a little muscle up front.

THE INTANGIBLES

Sanderson has the speed and the trigger to be a 50-goal scorer. The step to that elite class will take some help from his teammates, but a lot more has to come from Sanderson's mental toughness and commitment. The question is whether he wants to work harder to become an elite player, or if he is content being a very good one. He is a more complete player now that his work ethic has improved.

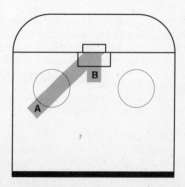

BRENDAN SHANAHAN

Yrs. of NHL service: 9
Born: Mimico, Ont.; Jan. 23, 1969
Position: left wing
Height: 6-3
Weight: 215
Uniform no.: 94
Shoots: right

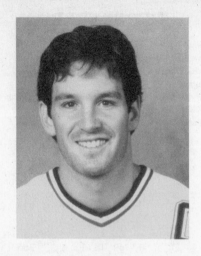

Career statistics:

GP	G	A	TP	PIM
632	288	310	598	1341

1992-93 statistics:

GP	G	A	TP	+/-	PIM	PP	SH	GW	GT	S	PCT
71	51	43	94	+10	174	18	0	8	8	232	22.0

1993-94 statistics:

GP	G	A	TP	+/-	PIM	PP	SH	GW	GT	S	PCT
81	52	50	102	-9	211	15	7	8	1	397	13.1

1994-95 statistics:

GP	G	A	TP	+/-	PIM	PP	SH	GW	GT	S	PCT
45	20	21	41	+7	136	6	2	6	0	153	13.1

1995-96 statistics:

GP	G	A	TP	+/-	PIM	PP	SH	GW	GT	S	PCT
74	44	34	78	+2	125	17	2	6	0	280	15.7

LAST SEASON

Led team in goals, points and power play goals. Tied for team lead in shorthanded goals. Second on team in game-winning goals, shots and shooting percentage. Missed eight games with wrist injury.

THE FINESSE GAME

Shanahan had a miserable start last season, with only nine goals in the Whalers' first 30 games, thanks to a damaged wrist ligament. He closed with 35 goals in the last 52 games.

Shanahan is a wonderful package of grit, skills and smarts. He will battle in front of the net for a puck, but he is also savvy enough to avoid an unnecessary thrashing. On the power play, he is one of the best in the league at staying just off the crease, waiting for a shot to come from the point, then timing his entry to the front of the net for the moving screen, the tip or the rebound. He can get a lot on his shot even when the puck is near his feet, because of a short backswing and strong wrists.

He has wonderfully soft hands for nifty goal-mouth passes, and he has a hard, accurate snap and slap shot with a quick release. He will take some face-offs, especially in the offensive zone, and succeeds by tying up the opposing centre and using his feet to control the puck. Even though he plays on the "off" wing, his backhand is good enough to take passes and create some offense. Shanahan can fill in at centre (his position in junior) in a pinch.

One of Shanahan's few flaws is his skating. He lacks quickness but does have great strength and balance. He is more apt to use all of the ice instead of just skating up and down his wing.

THE PHYSICAL GAME

The dilemma for rival teams: if you play Shanahan aggressively, it brings out the best in him. If you lay off and give him room, he will kill you with his skills. Shanahan spent his formative NHL years establishing his reputation by dropping his gloves with anybody who challenged him, but he has gotten smarter without losing his tough edge. He will still lose it once in awhile, which only makes rivals a little more wary.

He will take or make a hit to create a play. He is willing to eat glass to make a pass, but would rather strike the first blow.

THE INTANGIBLES

Shanahan was asking out of Hartford after last season, looking to play for a contender, and the Whalers were expected to comply with his request.

Shanahan can't help but improve a contending team. He is among the top power forwards in the NHL, and should return to the 100-point mark this season if he does land on a strong team. He is a leader, a gamer.

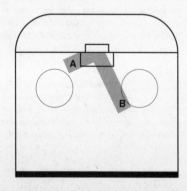

GLEN WESLEY

Yrs. of NHL service: 9
Born: Red Deer, Alta.; Oct. 2, 1968
Position: defense
Height: 6-1
Weight: 195
Uniform no.: 20
Shoots: left

Career statistics:

GP	G	A	TP	PIM
653	87	260	347	559

1992-93 statistics:

GP	G	A	TP	+/-	PIM	PP	SH	GW	GT	S	PCT
64	8	25	33	-2	47	4	1	0	0	183	4.4

1993-94 statistics:

GP	G	A	TP	+/-	PIM	PP	SH	GW	GT	S	PCT
81	14	44	58	+1	64	6	1	1	1	265	5.3

1994-95 statistics:

GP	G	A	TP	+/-	PIM	PP	SH	GW	GT	S	PCT
48	2	14	16	-6	50	1	0	1	0	125	1.6

1995-96 statistics:

GP	G	A	TP	+/-	PIM	PP	SH	GW	GT	S	PCT
68	8	16	24	-9	88	6	0	1	0	129	6.2

LAST SEASON

Missed nine games with groin injuries. Missed one game with shin injury. Missed four games with knee injury.

THE FINESSE GAME

Wesley simply isn't an offensive force, although he keeps being shoehorned into that role. He is at best a number two defenseman, and is ideally suited as a three or four, but since the Whalers paid a huge price to get him, they'll keep trying to get their money's worth.

Wesley is solid, but not elite class. He is very good with the puck. He works well on the power play because he knows when to jump into the holes. He has good but not great offensive instincts, gauging when to pinch, when to rush, when to pass the puck and when to back off. He is a good skater who is not afraid to veer into the play deep; he seldom gets trapped there. He has a good slap shot from the point and snap shot from the circle.

You could count on two hands the number of times Wesley has been beaten one-on-one throughout his career, and there are very few defensemen you can say that about. He makes defensive plays with confidence and is poised even when outnumbered in the rush. He has to keep his feet moving.

THE PHYSICAL GAME

Wesley is not a bone-crunching defenseman, but neither was Jacques Laperriere, and he's in the Hall of Fame. We're not suggesting that Wesley is in that class, but just that you don't have to shatter glass to be a solid checker, which he is. He's not a mean hitter, but he will execute a take-out check and not let his man get back into the play.

He is also sly about running interference for his defense partner, allowing him time to move the puck and giving him confidence that he won't get hammered by a forechecker.

THE INTANGIBLES

Wesley's season was compromised by his groin and knee injuries, since so much of his game is based in his fine skating. He is, at best, a 40-50 point scorer.

LOS ANGELES KINGS

Players' Statistics 1995-96

POS	NO.	PLAYER	GP	G	A	PTS	+/-	PIM	PP	SH	GW	GT	S	PCT
L	8	DIMITRI KHRISTICH	76	27	37	64	0	44	12		3		204	13.2
C	20	RAY FERRARO	76	29	31	60	0	92	9		4		178	16.3
R	43	*VITALI YACHMENEV	80	19	34	53	-3	16	6	1	2		133	14.3
C	44	YANIC PERREAULT	78	25	24	49	-11	16	8	3	7		175	14.3
C	12	KEVIN TODD	74	16	27	43	6	38		2	4		132	12.1
L	25	KEVIN STEVENS	61	13	23	36	-10	71	6		1		170	7.6
L	21	TONY GRANATO	49	17	18	35	-5	46	5		1	2	156	10.9
L	28	ERIC LACROIX	72	16	16	32	-11	110	3		1		107	15.0
L	23	*CRAIG JOHNSON	60	13	11	24	-8	36	4				97	13.4
D	26	PHILIPPE BOUCHER	53	7	16	23	-26	31	5		1	1	145	4.8
C	13	ROBERT LANG	68	6	16	22	-15	10		2		1	71	8.5
D	15	JAROSLAV MODRY	73	4	17	21	-21	44	1		1		106	3.8
D	27	JOHN SLANEY	38	6	14	20	7	14	3	1			75	8.0
C	22	IAN LAPERRIERE	71	6	11	17	-11	155	1		1	1	70	8.6
C	14	GARY SHUCHUK	33	4	10	14	3	12					22	18.2
L	9	VLADIMIR TSYPLAKOV	23	5	5	10	1	4					40	12.5
D	77	ROB COWIE	46	5	5	10	-16	32	2			1	86	5.8
D	2	DOUG ZMOLEK	58	2	5	7	-5	87					36	5.6
D	6	*SEAN O'DONNELL	71	2	5	7	3	127					65	3.1
D	5	*AKI BERG	51		7	7	-13	29					56	
C	24	NATHAN LAFAYETTE	17	2	4	6	-4	8	1				28	7.1
D	3	DENIS TSYGUROV	18	1	5	6	0	22	1				21	4.8
C	37	PATRICE TARDIF	38	4	1	5	-11	49	1		1		50	8.0
L	40	*BARRY POTOMSKI	33	3	2	5	-7	104	1				23	13.0
D	29	STEVEN FINN	66	3	2	5	-12	126					54	5.6
D	3	*JAN VOPAT	11	1	4	5	3	4					13	7.7
D	11	MATTIAS NORSTROM	36	2	2	4	-3	40					34	5.9
D	4	ROB BLAKE	6	1	2	3	0	8					13	7.7
C	20	*STEVE LAROUCHE	8	1	2	3	0	4	1				14	7.1
R	7	*KEVIN BROWN	7	1		1	-2	4					9	11.1
R	55	TROY CROWDER	15	1		1	-3	42					11	9.1
D	35	ARTO BLOMSTEN	2		1	1	1						1	
L	34	*MATT JOHNSON	1				0	5					1	
D	45	*RUSLAN BATYRSHIN	2				0	6						
L	42	*DAN BYLSMA	4				0						6	
G	1	*JAMIE STORR	5				0							
G	32	KELLY HRUDEY	36				0	4						
G	31	*BYRON DAFOE	47				0	6						

GP = games played; G = goals; A = assists; PTS = points; +/- = goals-for minus goals-against while player is on ice; PIM = penalties in minutes; PP = power play goals; SH = shorthanded goals; GW = game-winning goals; GT = game-tying goals; S = no. of shots; PCT = percentage of goals to shots; * = rookie

AKI-PETTERI BERG

Yrs. of NHL service: 1
Born: Turku, Finland; July 28, 1977
Position: left defense
Height: 6-3
Weight: 200
Uniform no.: 5
Shoots: left

Career statistics:

GP	G	A	TP	PIM
51	0	7	7	29

1995-96 statistics:

GP	G	A	TP	+/-	PIM	PP	SH	GW	GT	S	PCT
51	0	7	7	-13	29	0	0	0	0	56	0.0

LAST SEASON

First NHL season. Missed four games with shoulder injury. Played 20 games with Phoenix (IHL), scoring 0-3 — 3.

THE FINESSE GAME

It's tough to judge anyone off the terrible season the Kings suffered through last season, let alone a European rookie defenseman in his first season in North America. Berg joined the Kings as a highly touted 19-year-old, but by March he was demoted to the minors for not playing with confidence. Who could, with this bunch?

But if anyone can make an NHL defenseman out of Berg, it's his Hall of Fame coach, Larry Robinson. Berg is a pleasing combination of offensive and defensive skills. His skating is top-notch. He has a powerful stride with great mobility and balance. And he gets terrific drive from perfect leg extension and deep knee bends.

He sees the ice well and has excellent passing skills. He can also rush with the puck, but he prefers to make a pass and then join the play. He quarterbacked the Kings' second power play unit.

While his offensive skills grab the attention, the young Finn is also conscientious defensively. He is a solid prospect as a two-way defenseman.

THE PHYSICAL GAME

Berg loves to hit. He's big and strong, and has the mobility to lay down some serious open-ice checks. His punishing checks have had some scouts comparing him to Scott Stevens. Berg wasn't as assertive as we expected last season, but given time, he should start playing his game.

THE INTANGIBLES

Some onlookers believed Berg was the best player available in the 1995 draft. He has a lot of learning to do, and in 20-20 hindsight, he would have been better off in the minors learning the pro game than stuck in the mire at the not-so-Great Western Forum. This season figures to be a struggle as well, but Berg could get a big personal boost if he has a good World Cup.

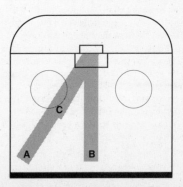

ROB BLAKE

Yrs. of NHL service: 6
Born: Simcoe, Ont.; Dec. 10, 1969
Position: right defense
Height: 6-3
Weight: 215
Uniform no.: 4
Shoots: right

Career statistics:

GP	G	A	TP	PIM
326	60	147	207	566

1992-93 statistics:

GP	G	A	TP	+/-	PIM	PP	SH	GW	GT	S	PCT
76	16	43	59	+18	152	10	0	4	1	243	6.6

1993-94 statistics:

GP	G	A	TP	+/-	PIM	PP	SH	GW	GT	S	PCT
84	20	48	68	-7	137	7	0	6	0	304	6.6

1994-95 statistics:

GP	G	A	TP	+/-	PIM	PP	SH	GW	GT	S	PCT
24	4	7	11	-16	38	4	0	1	0	76	5.3

1995-96 statistics:

GP	G	A	TP	+/-	PIM	PP	SH	GW	GT	S	PCT
6	1	2	3	0	8	0	0	0	0	13	7.7

LAST SEASON

Missed 76 games with knee injury and reconstructive knee surgery.

THE FINESSE GAME

Just how many seasons will it take before we can see the real Blake again? Serious injuries have cost him the last two seasons, and severely inhibited the progress of a once-promising defenseman.

We'll use the past tense in the following analysis, since we're not sure how much of Blake's game will be intact when he does return.

Most scouts agreed that Blake had the potential to be a West Coast Scott Stevens, a defenseman who was solid in his own zone and a serious open-ice hitter, with finesse skills that made an impact in any zone of the ice.

Before his injuries, Blake was a powerful skater, quick and agile, with good balance. He would step up and challenge at the blueline. He had great anticipation and was quite bold, forcing turnovers at the blueline with his body positioning and quick stickwork.

Blake could work the point on the power play, but lacked the vision to be as creative as he could be. He had a good, low shot and was able to rifle it off the pass. He had quality hand skills and was not afraid to skip in deep to try to make something happen low. He had become more confident about attempting to force the play deep in the offensive zone, and had good enough passing skills to use a backhand pass across the goalmouth.

THE PHYSICAL GAME

When healthy, Blake is among the hardest hitters in the league. He has a nasty streak and will bring up his gloves and stick them into the face of an opponent when he thinks the referee isn't watching. He can dominate with his physical play; when he does he opens up a lot of ice for himself and his teammates.

THE INTANGIBLES

Blake's health makes him a huge, huge question mark. Even if he is effective, it probably won't be until around the All-Star break that he starts playing with any confidence.

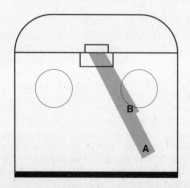

PHILIPPE BOUCHER

Yrs. of NHL service: 3
Born: St. Apollinaire, Que.; March 24, 1973
Position: right defense
Height: 6-2
Weight: 189
Uniform no.: 26
Shoots: right

Career statistics:

GP	G	A	TP	PIM
124	15	32	47	78

1992-93 statistics:

GP	G	A	TP	+/-	PIM	PP	SH	GW	GT	S	PCT
18	0	4	4	+1	14	0	0	0	0	8	0.0

1993-94 statistics:

GP	G	A	TP	+/-	PIM	PP	SH	GW	GT	S	PCT
38	6	8	14	-1	29	4	0	1	0	67	9.0

1994-95 statistics:

GP	G	A	TP	+/-	PIM	PP	SH	GW	GT	S	PCT
15	2	4	6	+3	4	0	0	0	0	30	6.7

1995-96 statistics:

GP	G	A	TP	+/-	PIM	PP	SH	GW	GT	S	PCT
53	7	16	23	-26	31	5	0	1	1	145	4.8

fault, Boucher is one of the team's top four defensemen, and he actually seemed to get better as he was given more responsibility, until the wrist injury flared up again. Boucher will probably get a lot of ice time this season and if he isn't achy he is capable of 40-50 points.

LAST SEASON

Led team defense in scoring. Worst plus-minus on team. Missed 19 games with wrist injury. Played 10 games with Phoenix (IHL), scoring 4-3 — 7.

THE FINESSE GAME

Boucher has a booming slap shot that draws most of the attention, but he also has more subtle finesse skills, such as deft puckhandling. He sees the ice and moves the puck well. He has slow feet, though, and it takes him a few strides to get up to speed. Attackers can get a step on him, but once Boucher is in flight he is fairly agile and can skate well with the puck.

Boucher likes to jump up into the play, and was one of L.A.'s best offensive defensemen last season when he was healthy. His wrist problems affected his shot, which is very heavy. A healthy Boucher will be more of a factor on the power play.

Boucher is a risk defensively. He is often too anxious to get into the attack and will leave a partner exposed when he forces a play in the neutral zone and turns over the puck. He is a one-way defenseman.

THE PHYSICAL GAME

Boucher is a fair size but doesn't play to it. He needs to develop more upper-body strength to become an assertive checker. He doesn't have the temperament to be a mean hitter, but he has the leg drive to be more effective with his take-outs. He doesn't cover well, doesn't close quickly and doesn't have impact.

THE INTANGIBLES

Boucher underwent off-season surgery for a second time this summer to correct a wrist problem. By de-

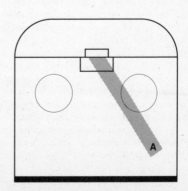

RAY FERRARO

Yrs. of NHL service: 12
Born: Trail, B.C.; Aug. 23, 1964
Position: centre
Height: 5-10
Weight: 185
Uniform no.: 20
Shoots: left

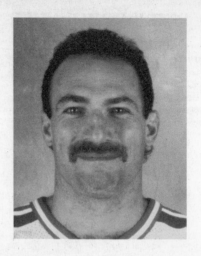

Career statistics:

GP	G	A	TP	PIM
834	302	343	649	822

1992-93 statistics:

GP	G	A	TP	+/-	PIM	PP	SH	GW	GT	S	PCT
46	14	13	27	0	40	3	0	1	0	72	19.4

1993-94 statistics:

GP	G	A	TP	+/-	PIM	PP	SH	GW	GT	S	PCT
82	21	32	53	+1	83	5	0	3	3	136	15.4

1994-95 statistics:

GP	G	A	TP	+/-	PIM	PP	SH	GW	GT	S	PCT
47	22	21	43	+1	30	2	0	1	2	94	23.4

1995-96 statistics:

GP	G	A	TP	+/-	PIM	PP	SH	GW	GT	S	PCT
76	29	31	60	0	92	9	0	4	0	178	16.3

LAST SEASON

Acquired from Rangers with Mattias Norstrom, Ian Laperriere, Nathan LaFayette and a fourth-round draft pick for Jari Kurri, Shane Churla and Marty McSorley, Mar. 14, 1996. Led Kings in goals and shooting percentage. Second on team in points and power play goals. Tied for team lead in game-winning goals. Third on team in assists. Missed two games with injury.

THE FINESSE GAME

Ferraro excels at the short game. From the bottoms of the circles in, he uses his quickness and hand skills to work little give-and-go plays through traffic.

A streaky player, when he is in the groove he plays with great concentration and hunger around the net. He is alert to not only his first, but also his second and third options, and he makes a rapid play selection. His best shot is his wrist shot from just off to the side of the net, which is where he likes to work on the power play. He has good coordination and timing for deflections. When his confidence is down, however, Ferraro gets into serious funks.

Ferraro's skating won't win medals. He has a choppy stride and lacks rink-long speed, but he shakes loose in a few quick steps and maintains his balance well. Handling the puck does not slow him down.

Defensively, Ferraro has improved tremendously and is no longer a liability. In fact, he's a pretty decent two-way centre, though the scales still tip in favour of his offensive ability. He has particularly improved in his defensive work down low. He's good on face-offs.

THE PHYSICAL GAME

Ferraro is on the small side but is deceptively strong. Many players aren't willing to wade into the areas where they will get crunched, and Ferraro will try to avoid those situations when he can. But if it's the right play, he will take the abuse and whack a few ankles himself.

THE INTANGIBLES

Ferraro was devastated by the trade from New York to L.A., and became a free agent after the season. He's not a guy who can carry a team but he has sufficient skills to play in the right spot on a number two line and help a team's power play.

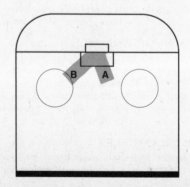

STEPHANE FISET

Yrs. of NHL service: 6
Born: Montreal, Que. June 17, 1970
Position: goaltender
Height: 6-1
Weight: 195
Uniform no.: 35
Catches: left

Career statistics:

GP	MIN	GA	SO	GAA	A	PIM
188	10384	575	6	3.32	9	20

1992-93 statistics:

GP	MIN	GAA	W	L	T	SO	GA	S	SAPCT	PIM
37	1939	3.40	18	9	4	0	110	945	.884	2

1993-94 statistics:

GP	MIN	GAA	W	L	T	SO	GA	S	SAPCT	PIM
50	2798	3.39	20	25	4	2	158	1434	.890	8

1994-95 statistics:

GP	MIN	GAA	W	L	T	SO	GA	S	SAPCT	PIM
32	1879	2.78	17	10	3	2	87	968	.910	8

1995-96 statistics:

GP	MIN	GAA	W	L	T	SO	GA	S	SAPCT	PIM
37	2107	2.93	22	6	7	1	103	1012	.898	2

cinch either, since the Kings will be breaking in Jamie Storr. Fiset will have his hands full behind what promises to be a terrible Kings team.

LAST SEASON
Acquired from Colorado for Eric Lacroix.

THE PHYSICAL GAME
Fiset plays a butterfly style and looks an awful lot like his former teammate, Ron Hextall, in the way he faces shooters. When he's on his game, Fiset appears enormous in the net.

With his very quick hands and feet, Fiset dares shooters to go for the upper corners, then snaps out a glove hand, which he normally carries a bit low. In close, he is especially good because of his reflexes.

Fiset's major weaknesses lie in his use of the stick and control of his rebounds, and the two are connected. Many NHL goalies are aggressive in using their sticks to break up plays around the net, and Fiset needs to learn this skill. He handles the puck well on hard-arounds and moves the puck well.

He has improved in angle play and lets in fewer soft goals. Fiset is starting to rely less on his reflexes and is becoming more of a student of the game.

THE MENTAL GAME
Fiset has become a better battler, but still suffers lapses of concentration. He doesn't control the puck and play with the kind of command that very successful goalies, such as his former teammate Patrick Roy, demonstrate when they are on form. He is maturing, and doesn't get rattled so easily anymore.

THE INTANGIBLES
Fiset saw very little playing time after the Avalanche acquired Roy in December, starting 16 of the last 54 games. His role as a number one goalie in L.A. isn't a

CRAIG JOHNSON

Yrs. of NHL service: 1
Born: St. Paul, MN; Mar. 18, 1972
Position: left wing/centre
Height: 6-2
Weight: 197
Uniform no.: 23
Shoots: left

Career statistics:

GP	G	A	TP	PIM
75	16	14	30	42

1994-95 statistics:

GP	G	A	TP	+/-	PIM	PP	SH	GW	GT	S	PCT
15	3	3	6	+4	6	0	0	0	0	19	15.8

1995-96 statistics:

GP	G	A	TP	+/-	PIM	PP	SH	GW	GT	S	PCT
60	13	11	24	-8	36	4	0	0	0	97	13.4

LAST SEASON

Acquired from St. Louis with Patrice Tardif, Roman Vopat, a first-round draft pick and a fourth-round draft pick for Wayne Gretzky, Feb. 27, 1996. Missed three games with shoulder injury. Played five games with Worcester (AHL), scoring 3-0 — 3.

THE FINESSE GAME

Johnson is a quick skater who uses his speed to gain a jump in the neutral zone and will forecheck or take a pass in full stride and drive to the net. He doesn't have great hands, so he needs to get the pass late as he's whizzing in to force the defense back.

Although Johnson has played some centre, he looks better suited as a left-winger. He is not a natural scorer and has to work hard for anything he gets. Johnson isn't quite good enough to be a second-line winger (he's behind Dimitri Khristich and Kevin Stevens on the depth chart), so the Kings' problem will be where to spot him.

Johnson is fairly alert defensively and brings a level of energy to his shifts that will be appreciated. He is a poor man's Paul Ranheim.

THE PHYSICAL GAME

Coming out of the U.S. college system generally requires a period of adjustment to the physical style of the NHL, and Johnson doesn't have much of a taste for body work. He is a good size but plays smaller, and if he can gain a little strength and a little assertiveness, his game will improve.

THE INTANGIBLES

Johnson impressed in his brief stint with the Kings, scoring nine points in 11 games before being sidelined with a shoulder ailment. Of all the young and the hopeless expected to attend L.A. training camp this fall, Johnson is one of the few who may add some life, and perhaps 40 points. He was an older rookie last season and doesn't have a great deal of upside.

DIMITRI KHRISTICH

Yrs. of NHL service: 6
Born: Kiev, Ukraine; July 23, 1969
Position: left wing
Height: 6-2
Weight: 195
Uniform no.: 8
Shoots: right

Career statistics:

GP	G	A	TP	PIM
391	148	166	314	162

1992-93 statistics:

GP	G	A	TP	+/-	PIM	PP	SH	GW	GT	S	PCT
64	31	36	67	+29	28	9	1	1	1	127	24.4

1993-94 statistics:

GP	G	A	TP	+/-	PIM	PP	SH	GW	GT	S	PCT
83	29	29	58	-2	73	10	0	4	1	195	14.9

1994-95 statistics:

GP	G	A	TP	+/-	PIM	PP	SH	GW	GT	S	PCT
48	12	14	26	0	41	8	0	2	2	92	13.0

1995-96 statistics:

GP	G	A	TP	+/-	PIM	PP	SH	GW	GT	S	PCT
76	27	37	64	0	44	12	0	3	0	204	13.2

LAST SEASON

Led team in assists, points, power play goals and shots. Second on team in goals.

THE FINESSE GAME

Khristich is a key component on the power play, because while the point men work the puck back and forth looking for an opening, he is ready and waiting down low, just off to the goalie's right, with his forehand open and ready for the pass. When the puck reaches his blade, he slams the shot in one quick motion. If the penalty killers are drawn to him, then it opens ice for another forward. Either way, Khristich gets the job done.

He has good hand-eye coordination for deflections and can even take draws. He is not an especially fast skater, but he has a long, strong stride and very good balance. His hockey sense is excellent, and he is responsible defensively as well.

One weakness is his tendency to put himself in a position where he gets hit, and hurt. Part of that stems from holding onto the puck to make a perfect play.

THE PHYSICAL GAME

Khristich is a very sturdy skater but lacks physical presence. He will go into the trenches and is tough to knock off the puck. He protects the puck well.

THE INTANGIBLES

Until and unless the Kings upgrade their personnel, Khristich ranks as their best forward. He doesn't have much talent to work with, and he's not a great one-on-one player. A 30-goal season would be amazing under such circumstances.

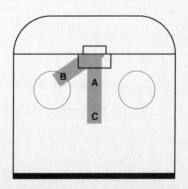

ROBERT LANG

Yrs. of NHL service: 3
Born: Teplice, Czech.; Dec. 19, 1970
Position: centre
Height: 6-2
Weight: 189
Uniform no.: 13
Shoots: right

Career statistics:

GP	G	A	TP	PIM
147	19	39	58	26

1992-93 statistics:

GP	G	A	TP	+/-	PIM	PP	SH	GW	GT	S	PCT
11	0	5	5	-3	2	0	0	0	0	3	0.0

1993-94 statistics:

GP	G	A	TP	+/-	PIM	PP	SH	GW	GT	S	PCT
32	9	10	19	+7	10	0	0	0	0	41	22.0

1994-95 statistics:

GP	G	A	TP	+/-	PIM	PP	SH	GW	GT	S	PCT
36	4	8	12	-7	4	0	0	0	0	38	10.5

1995-96 statistics:

GP	G	A	TP	+/-	PIM	PP	SH	GW	GT	S	PCT
68	6	16	22	-15	10	0	2	0	1	71	8.5

LAST SEASON

Career high in goals, assists and points. Missed seven games with back injury.

THE FINESSE GAME

Coaches have a love-hate relationship with players like Lang. He has so much talent he is able to turn a game around with several moves. But he is inconsistent and has nights where he is invisible.

Lang has excellent skating ability with quickness and balance. He has great hockey sense to go along with his skills and the potential to develop into a crafty playmaker. He is an adept backhand passer, so players on both sides of him have to be prepared for feeds. He is patient with the puck, often holding on too long; he will always opt for a pass instead of a shot. He draws defenders to him to open up ice, but he will not take a hit to make a play around the net. He will sometimes dish off early if he thinks he's going to get hit.

Lang covers a lot of ice with his long, strong stride and is conscientious about getting back into position for backchecking, though he doesn't do much more than look to intercept passes.

THE PHYSICAL GAME

Lang has to show more of a willingness to use his body. He will never trounce anyone, but he has to be willing to fight for the puck and battle through checks. His intensity level is still not consistent enough for the NHL.

THE INTANGIBLES

Lang is fortunate there isn't much depth in L.A., or he would be out of a job. The Czech plays like he is still in international competition, and hasn't adjusted to the smaller ice surface. We're not sure he will. He has such good skills that he is a terrible tease.

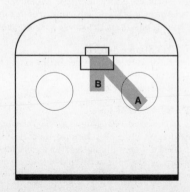

IAN LAPERRIERE

Yrs. of NHL service: 2
Born: Montreal, Que.; Jan. 19, 1974
Position: centre
Height: 6-1
Weight: 195
Uniform no.: 22
Shoots: right

Career statistics:

GP	G	A	TP	PIM
109	19	25	44	240

1993-94 statistics:

GP	G	A	TP	+/-	PIM	PP	SH	GW	GT	S	PCT
1	0	0	0	0	0	0	0	0	0	1	0.0

1994-95 statistics:

GP	G	A	TP	+/-	PIM	PP	SH	GW	GT	S	PCT
37	13	14	27	+12	85	1	0	1	0	53	24.5

1995-96 statistics:

GP	G	A	TP	+/-	PIM	PP	SH	GW	GT	S	PCT
71	6	11	17	-11	155	1	0	1	1	70	8.6

LAST SEASON

Acquired from N.Y. Rangers from St. Louis for Stephane Matteau, Dec. 28, 1995. Acquired from Rangers with Ray Ferraro, Mattias Norstrom, Nathan LaFayette and a fourth-round draft pick for Jari Kurri, Shane Churla and Marty McSorley, Mar. 14, 1996. Led team in penalty minutes. Second NHL season. Missed two games with shoulder injury. Played three games with Worcester (AHL), scoring 2-1 — 3.

THE FINESSE GAME

The knock on Laperriere earlier in his career was his skating ability, but he has improved tremendously in that department. Although he'll never be a speed demon, Laperriere doesn't look out of place at the NHL level. He will always try to take the extra stride when he is backchecking so he can make a clean check, instead of taking the easy way out and committing a lazy hooking foul. Laperriere wins his share of races for the loose puck.

Laperriere grew up watching Guy Carbonneau in Montreal, and he studied well. Laperriere knows how to win a draw between his feet. He uses his stick and his body to make sure the opposing centre doesn't get the puck. He gets his right (bottom) hand way down on the stick and tries to win draws on his backhand. He gets very low to the ice on draws.

Laperriere is ever willing to use the backhand, either for shots or to get the puck deep. He is very reliable defensively and shows signs of becoming a two-way centre.

THE PHYSICAL GAME

Laperriere is an obnoxious player in the Bob Bassen mold. He really battles for the puck. Though smallish, he has absolutely no fear of playing in the "circle" that extends from the lower inside of the face-off circles to behind the net. He will pay any price. He finishes every check and gives the extra effort. But he will have to learn to apportion his resources better over the course of a full 82-game season, or he will be worn out before the playoffs.

THE INTANGIBLES

A late-round surprise, Laperriere adds true grit to the lineup despite his small size, which is his major weakness. His nightly effort puts a lot of bigger guys to shame. He lost any bad habits the hard way by playing for a hard-nosed coach (Mike Keenan) early in his career. He is best suited as a number two centre who may produce 50-60 points. Changing teams twice last year did nothing to help his confidence, but he could be a surprise in Los Angeles, where he should merit a lot of ice time.

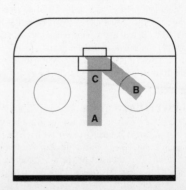

MATTIAS NORSTROM

Yrs. of NHL service: 1
Born: Mora, Sweden; Jan. 2, 1972
Position: defense
Height: 6-1
Weight: 200
Uniform no.: 11
Shoots: left

Career statistics

GP	G	A	TP	PIM
54	2	6	8	48

1993-94 statistics:

GP	G	A	TP	+/-	PIM	PP	SH	GW	GT	S	PCT
9	0	1	1	0	6	0	0	0	0	3	0.0

1994-95 statistics:

GP	G	A	TP	+/-	PIM	PP	SH	GW	GT	S	PCT
9	0	3	3	+2	2	0	0	0	0	4	0

1995-96 statistics:

GP	G	A	TP	+/-	PIM	PP	SH	GW	GT	S	PCT
36	2	2	4	-3	40	0	0	0	0	34	5.9

LAST SEASON

Acquired from N.Y. Rangers with Ray Ferraro, Ian Laperriere, Nathan LaFayette and a fourth-round draft pick for Jari Kurri, Shane Churla and Marty McSorley, Mar. 14, 1996. Missed seven games with shoulder separation.

THE FINESSE GAME

The Kings consider Norstrom the key player in the deal they made to get rid of three aging forwards (two of whom were FOG, or Friends of Gretzky, and destined to leave town once Wayne did). Norstrom is an above-average skater who is still working on his pivots and turns. He does have straight-ahead speed, to a degree, thanks to a long stride. Along the boards, he delivers strong hits.

His foot skills outdistance his hand skills, however. Norstrom can make a decent pass, but mostly he'll keep things simple with the puck — smack it around the boards if he gets into trouble, rather than try to make a play.

For so large a player, Norstrom uses a surprisingly short stick that cuts down on his reach defensively and limits some of his offensive options. But he feels his responsibility is to break down the play, rather than create it. He will pinch down the boards occasionally, but only to drive the puck deeper, not to grab the puck and make a play. And he won't jump into the play on offense until he has more confidence with his puck skills.

THE PHYSICAL GAME

The things that stand out about Norstrom are his willingness to do what it takes to help his team and his willingness to hit. He is solidly built and likes to throw big, loud hits. If he doesn't hit, he's not going to be around long, because his talent is not going to carry

him and his hockey sense needs a lot of improvement.

He knows what he's good at. Norstrom has tremendously powerful legs and is strong on his skates. He has confidence in his power game and has developed a great enthusiasm for physical play.

THE INTANGIBLES

Norstrom is a hard-working athlete who loves to practice, a player acquired more for his character than for his abilities, which are limited. He will be a defensive-style defenseman who will give his coach what's asked for, but won't try to do things that will put the puck, or the team, in trouble. Norstrom could easily move up on the Kings' defensive depth chart. Expect him to be a special project of Larry Robinson.

SEAN O'DONNELL

Yrs. of NHL service: 1
Born: Ottawa, Ont.; Oct. 13, 1971
Position: left defense
Height: 6-2
Weight: 224
Uniform no.: 6
Shoots: left

Career statistics:

GP	G	A	TP	PIM
86	2	7	9	176

1994-95 statistics:

GP	G	A	TP	+/-	PIM	PP	SH	GW	GT	S	PCT
15	0	2	2	-2	49	0	0	0	0	12	0.0

1995-96 statistics:

GP	G	A	TP	+/-	PIM	PP	SH	GW	GT	S	PCT
71	2	5	7	+3	127	0	0	0	0	65	3.1

LAST SEASON

First NHL season. Second on team in plus-minus. Second on team in penalty minutes.

THE FINESSE GAME

O'Donnell has worked very hard to rise above being a one-dimensional player, but his skating may hold him back. He is not very good laterally, and that results in his being beaten wide. He tries to line up someone and misses, because he doesn't have the quickness to get there.

It's especially tough for him playing as a defenseman on a team that rarely scores. He has some offensive upside because he is alert and tries so hard, and that could compensate for his hand skills which are average at best.

O'Donnell has to improve his defensive reads. He has become a fairly good shot-blocker.

THE PHYSICAL GAME

O'Donnell is fearless. He is a legitimate tough guy who will fight anybody. He hits anybody. He will use his stick. He's a nasty customer.

THE INTANGIBLES

O'Donnell has paid his dues in the minors, and there are a lot of rough edges to his game. He has a good distance to go yet, but under the tutelage of Larry Robinson in L.A., he could learn to supplement his game and develop along the lines of Paul Laus, who was once considered a pure goon but is now a serviceable tough defenseman. O'Donnell is a project.

ED OLCZYK

Yrs. of NHL service: 12
Born: Chicago, Ill.; Aug. 16, 1966
Position: centre
Height: 6-1
Weight: 205
Uniform no.: 16
Shoots: left

Career statistics:

GP	G	A	TP	PIM
802	294	394	688	747

1992-93 statistics:

GP	G	A	TP	+/-	PIM	PP	SH	GW	GT	S	PCT
71	21	28	49	-2	52	2	0	1	1	190	11.1

1993-94 statistics:

GP	G	A	TP	+/-	PIM	PP	SH	GW	GT	S	PCT
37	3	8	11	-1	28	0	0	1	0	40	7.5

1994-95 statistics:

GP	G	A	TP	+/-	PIM	PP	SH	GW	GT	S	PCT
33	4	9	13	-1	12	2	0	0	0	56	7.1

1995-96 statistics:

GP	G	A	TP	+/-	PIM	PP	SH	GW	GT	S	PCT
51	27	22	49	0	65	16	0	1	0	147	18.4

LAST SEASON

Second on Jets in goals and power play goals. Missed 16 games with a knee injury. Signed as a free agent with L.A., July 8, 1996.

THE FINESSE GAME

When Olcyzk gets the playing time, he scores. It's as simple, and as complicated, as that. Olczyk has had a difficult time getting ice with certain teams, but with a full-time role in Winnipeg last season, Olczyk was productive.

Olcyzk doesn't have great speed, but he is deceptive, and works hard to get open. He loves to shoot but is also unselfish. He can play all three forward positions, and brings a centre's playmaking sense to the wing. He is most effective from the left side, from the top of the circle in. Olczyk has a long reach with a fair backhand shot.

Olczyk is at his best on the power play. He likes the extra open ice and is creative.

THE PHYSICAL GAME

The reason Olczyk falls out of favour with so many coaches is that he is a big guy who doesn't play big. He will fight for the puck, but isn't as determined in his play away from the puck. He will take a hit to make a play, but doesn't initiate and isn't strong along the wall.

THE INTANGIBLES

Olczyk was a free agent last season and if he ends up in the right spot, he could be a 60-point producer. He doesn't have a lot of hockey miles on him and is a "young 29."

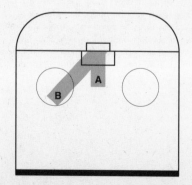

YANIC PERREAULT

Yrs. of NHL service: 2
Born: Sherbrooke, Que.; Apr. 4, 1971
Position: centre
Height: 5-11
Weight: 182
Uniform no.: 44
Shoots: left

Career statistics:

GP	G	A	TP	PIM
117	30	32	62	36

1993-94 statistics:

GP	G	A	TP	+/-	PIM	PP	SH	GW	GT	S	PCT
13	3	3	6	+1	0	2	0	0	0	24	12.5

1994-95 statistics:

GP	G	A	TP	+/-	PIM	PP	SH	GW	GT	S	PCT
26	2	5	7	+3	20	0	0	1	0	43	4.7

1995-96 statistics:

GP	G	A	TP	+/-	PIM	PP	SH	GW	GT	S	PCT
78	25	24	49	-11	16	8	3	7	0	175	14.3

LAST SEASON

Led team in game-winning goals and shorthanded goals. Second on team in goals. Fourth on team in points.

THE FINESSE GAME

Perreault has been a success at the junior and minor-league levels, but his speed is marginal NHL level. He tries to compensate with his intelligence, and at least on the Kings' roster, it was sufficient to help him win a full-time role. Perreault is nifty and shifty, and has all of the gears except top speed.

He has very good hands and always has his head up, looking at the goal for openings. While he doesn't have open-ice speed, he has short bursts of quickness that he uses to good effect in the attacking zone to elude checkers. He waits for the goalie to commit.

Tricky and solid on his feet, Perreault works the power play well on the half boards on the second unit.

THE PHYSICAL GAME

Perreault lacks the size to do the work in traffic areas and lacks the speed to be a strictly open-ice player. He is an in-betweener, and if forced to play hard in all zones the flaws in his game are apparent.

THE INTANGIBLES

What separates Perreault from other minor-league stars who can't quite make the jump is his desire. He wants the NHL badly, and he's in the ideal spot to keep a job. Perreault played very well in the World Championships, which may have helped erase some of his nightmarish memories of the Kings' season and given him a shot of confidence.

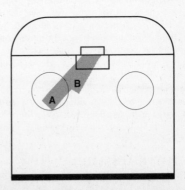

KEVIN STEVENS

Yrs. of NHL service: 8
Born: Brockton, Mass.; Apr. 15, 1965
Position: left wing
Height: 6-3
Weight: 217
Uniform no.: 25
Shoots: left

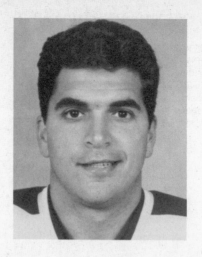

Career statistics:

GP	G	A	TP	PIM
518	264	299	563	1039

1992-93 statistics:

GP	G	A	TP	+/-	PIM	PP	SH	GW	GT	S	PCT
72	55	56	111	+17	177	26	9	5	1	325	16.9

1993-94 statistics:

GP	G	A	TP	+/-	PIM	PP	SH	GW	GT	S	PCT
83	41	47	88	-24	155	21	0	4	0	284	14.4

1994-95 statistics:

GP	G	A	TP	+/-	PIM	PP	SH	GW	GT	S	PCT
27	15	12	27	0	51	6	0	4	0	80	18.8

1995-96 statistics:

GP	G	A	TP	+/-	PIM	PP	SH	GW	GT	S	PCT
61	13	23	36	-10	71	6	0	1	0	170	7.6

LAST SEASON

Acquired from Pittsburgh with Shawn McEachern by Boston for Bryan Smolinski and Glen Murray, Aug. 2, 1995. Acquired from Boston for Rick Tocchet, Jan. 25, 1996. Missed 17 games with fractured fibula.

THE FINESSE GAME

Despite being an injury magnet, Stevens can still be an effective NHL player. He just won't ever be back in the elite class of left wingers without an elite centre to play with.

Stevens has the size and strength to battle for and win position in front of the net. He has an astonishingly quick release on his shot. His objective is to get rid of the puck as fast as he can, even if he doesn't know where it's going, and he always follows up on his shot for a rebound.

Stevens simply drops anchor in the slot on the power play. His huge frame blocks the goalie's view and he has good hand-eye coordination for tips and deflections. Those moves aren't instinctive, but came from hours of practice. He also has a devastating one-timer. He does not have to be overly clever with the puck, since he can overpower goalies with his shot. Stevens is a power play specialist. His work on the give-and-go is pure instinct.

His play at even strength is not as strong. He is an average skater at best, and he often seems overanxious to get started on the attacking rush to keep up with his fleeter linemates. His reach and range make him appear faster than he is.

THE PHYSICAL GAME

Stevens has to initiate. He doesn't react well to being knocked down. (It's surprising, given his size and strength, that he all too often is.) He isn't one of the meanest guys around, although he can throw 'em (punches and devastating hits both). He needs to be more consistent with his physical play, and look as hungry as he did when he was breaking in.

THE INTANGIBLES

Two dreadful things have happened to Stevens in his career: Losing Mario Lemieux as his centre, and the 1993 playoff injury in which he broke numerous facial bones. Playing in Boston, his hometown, was a nightmare because he never clicked with Adam Oates, one of the game's great centres. Oates's right wingers have always been more successful than his left wingers.

Things didn't get much better in L.A., a team weak up the middle, and Stevens suffered a fractured fibula after only a month with the Kings. It's not likely to get any better for him. He will never be a 50-goal scorer again. His top end is likely 35 goals, but only if L.A. can acquire a decent pivotman. He is in the second year of a big contract (U.S.$15-million) and has a lot to live up to.

One odd note: Stevens was drafted by L.A. in the fifth round of the 1983 draft, but never played a game in the Kings' system until last season.

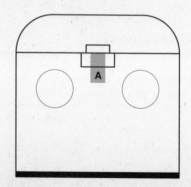

VITALI YACHMENEV

Yrs. of NHL service: 1
Born: Chelyabinsk, USSR; Jan. 8, 1975
Position: right wing
Height: 5-9
Weight: 180
Uniform no.: 43
Shoots: left

Career statistics:

GP	G	A	TP	PIM
80	19	34	53	16

1995-96 statistics:

GP	G	A	TP	+/-	PIM	PP	SH	GW	GT	S	PCT
80	19	34	53	-3	16	6	1	2	0	133	14.3

LAST SEASON

First NHL season. Second among NHL rookies and on team in assists. Tied for second among NHL rookies and third on team in points. Tied for fourth among rookies in power play goals. Fifth among rookies in shots. One of only four rookies to score a hat trick.

THE FINESSE GAME

Playing two seasons of major junior and experiencing a taste of the IHL playoffs prepared Yachmenev well for his first NHL season, but even so he progressed ahead of schedule to be one of the few pleasant surprises for the woeful Kings last season.

Yachmenev's shot gained him early entry to the NHL. He has a sniper's touch, and has to learn to shoot more because that is his prime skill. Yachmenev has a tendency to hang onto the puck too long, a holdover from his Soviet training and his junior career when he could control the puck better, but the NHL pace is too quick for that.

He is an intelligent player with good hockey sense, and was used on the point by the Kings on the power play when they simply ran out of anyone else to use, although he will be more effective when used down low. He can kill penalties, where his anticipation is key.

THE PHYSICAL GAME

Yachmenev isn't very big but he is strong on his skates and solidly built. He is willing to go through traffic and scraps along the boards for the puck, and he protects it well with his body. Yachmenev showed some signs of wear and tear, and will need to work on his upper-body strength.

THE INTANGIBLES

A rookie-of-the-year candidate in the first half, Yachmenev had a slow second half, with only five goals over the last 41 games. That's not unusual for a player in his first year of pro, given the grind of the season. His game was also affected by Wayne Gretzky's departure, since Yachmenev frequently played on Gretzky's line early in the season in L.A.

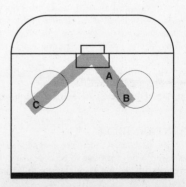

DOUG ZMOLEK

Yrs. of NHL service: 4
Born: Rochester, Minn.; Nov, 3, 1970
Position: left defense
Height: 6-2
Weight: 220
Uniform no.: 2
Shoots: left

Career statistics:

GP	G	A	TP	PIM
259	8	24	32	516

1992-93 statistics:

GP	G	A	TP	+/-	PIM	PP	SH	GW	GT	S	PCT
84	5	10	15	-50	229	2	0	0	0	94	5.3

1993-94 statistics:

GP	G	A	TP	+/-	PIM	PP	SH	GW	GT	S	PCT
75	1	4	5	-8	133	0	0	0	0	32	3.1

1994-95 statistics:

GP	G	A	TP	+/-	PIM	PP	SH	GW	GT	S	PCT
42	0	5	5	-6	67	0	0	0	0	28	0.0

1995-96 statistics:

GP	G	A	TP	+/-	PIM	PP	SH	GW	GT	S	PCT
58	2	5	7	-5	87	0	0	0	0	36	5.6

already solid, conservative defensive style, and makes him a more valuable rearguard. His point totals will be negligible, but he is seriously tough.

LAST SEASON

Acquired from Dallas with Shane Churla for Darryl Sydor and a fifth-round draft pick, Feb. 17, 1996.

THE FINESSE GAME

Zmolek is a reliable, stay-at-home defenseman, whose value to a team is underestimated.

A fine skater with a strong stride, Zmolek has good balance and agility and moves well laterally. His skating helps him angle attackers to the boards. He is a little awkward in his turning and can be victimized.

He has some nice offensive instincts. He moves the puck out of the zone well with quick, accurate passes, and he has soft hands for touch passes in tighter quarters. His understanding of the game is growing.

Zmolek is an excellent penalty killer. He is intelligent and alert.

THE PHYSICAL GAME

Zmolek developed in college (University of Minnesota) where the physical element of the game is not as important, but he took a great step forward last season by incorporating more physical play in his game. He was defensively consistent, and he had some major battles with NHL heavyweights like Marty McSorley. He proved that not only is he a feisty player, but he can also be effective with his body work.

THE INTANGIBLES

Zmolek has established a more physical presence, and seems eager to pay the price to become that kind of defenseman. It's an important element to add to his

MONTREAL CANADIENS

Players' Statistics 1995-96

POS.	NO.	PLAYER	GP	G	A	PTS	+/-	PIM	PP	SH	GW	GT	S	PCT
C	77	PIERRE TURGEON	80	38	58	96	19	44	17	1	6		297	12.8
C	25	VINCENT DAMPHOUSSE	80	38	56	94	5	158	11	4	3		254	15.0
R	8	MARK RECCHI	82	28	50	78	20	69	11	2	6		191	14.7
L	26	MARTIN RUCINSKY	78	29	46	75	18	68	9	2	4		181	16.0
R	51	ANDREI KOVALENKO	77	28	28	56	20	49	6		6	1	131	21.4
L	11	*SAKU KOIVU	82	20	25	45	-7	40	8	3	2	1	136	14.7
R	18	*VALERI BURE	77	22	20	42	10	28	5		1	2	143	15.4
D	43	PATRICE BRISEBOIS	69	9	27	36	10	65	3		1		127	7.1
L	49	BRIAN SAVAGE	75	25	8	33	-8	28	4		4		150	16.7
D	38	VLADIMIR MALAKHOV	61	5	23	28	7	79	2				122	4.1
R	30	TURNER STEVENSON	80	9	16	25	-2	167			2		101	8.9
D	24	LYLE ODELEIN	79	3	14	17	8	230		1			74	4.1
D	5	STEPHANE QUINTAL	68	2	14	16	-4	117		1	1	1	104	1.9
L	22	BENOIT BRUNET	26	7	8	15	-4	17	3	1	4		48	14.6
D	34	PETER POPOVIC	76	2	12	14	21	69					59	3.4
R	6	OLEG PETROV	36	4	7	11	-9	23			2		44	9.1
C	28	MARC BUREAU	65	3	7	10	-3	46			1		43	7.0
R	57	*CHRIS MURRAY	48	3	4	7	5	163			1		32	9.4
D	27	*DAVID WILKIE	24	1	5	6	-10	10	1				39	2.6
D	52	*CRAIG RIVET	19	1	4	5	4	54					9	11.1
D	23	*MARKO KIPRUSOFF	24		4	4	-3	8					36	
L	35	DONALD BRASHEAR	67		4	4	-10	223					25	
D	3	ROBERT DIRK	47	1	2	3	8	48					20	5.0
C	56	*SCOTT FRASER	14	2		2	-1	4					9	22.2
D	53	*RORY FITZPATRICK	42		2	2	-7	18					31	
D	48	*FRANCOIS GROLEAU	2	1	1	2	2	2					1	
G	39	PAT JABLONSKI	24	1	1	0	2							
C	17	MARK LAMB	1			0								
G	37	*JOSE THEODORE	1			0								
G	31	*PATRICK LABRECQUE	2			0	2							
C	42	*DARCY TUCKER	3			-1							1	
C	71	*SEBASTIEN BORDELEAU	4			-1								
C	20	*CRAIG CONROY	7			-4	2						1	
G	41	JOCELYN THIBAULT	50			0	2							

GP = games played; G = goals; A = assists; PTS = points; +/- = goals-for minus goals-against while player is on ice; PIM = penalties in minutes; PP = power play goals; SH = shorthanded goals; GW = game-winning goals; GT = game-tying goals; S = no. of shots; PCT = percentage of goals to shots; * = rookie

PATRICE BRISEBOIS

Yrs. of NHL service: 5
Born: Montreal, Que.; Jan. 27, 1971
Position: right defense
Height: 6-1
Weight: 188
Uniform no.: 43
Shoots: right

Career statistics:

GP	G	A	TP	PIM
263	27	87	114	228

1992-93 statistics:

GP	G	A	TP	+/-	PIM	PP	SH	GW	GT	S	PCT
70	10	21	31	+6	79	4	0	2	0	123	8.1

1993-94 statistics:

GP	G	A	TP	+/-	PIM	PP	SH	GW	GT	S	PCT
53	2	21	23	+5	63	1	0	0	0	71	2.8

1994-95 statistics:

GP	G	A	TP	+/-	PIM	PP	SH	GW	GT	S	PCT
35	4	8	12	-2	26	0	0	2	0	67	6.0

1995-96 statistics:

GP	G	A	TP	+/-	PIM	PP	SH	GW	GT	S	PCT
69	9	27	36	+10	65	3	0	1	0	127	7.1

LAST SEASON

Led team defensemen in scoring. Missed 13 games with back injuries.

THE FINESSE GAME

Brisebois has some nice skills, but doesn't have the hockey sense to put them in a complete package to be an elite level defenseman. He has a decent first step to the puck. He has a good stride with some quickness, although he won't rush end-to-end. He carries the puck with authority, but will usually take one or two strides and look for a pass, or else make the safe dump out of the zone. He steps up in the neutral zone to slow an opponent's rush.

Brisebois plays the point well enough to be on the first power play unit, but he doesn't have the rink vision that marks truly successful point men. Brisebois has a great point shot, with a sharp release, and he keeps it low and on target. He doesn't often venture to the circles on offense, but when he does he has the passing skills and the shot to make something happen.

Brisebois improved on his positional play but often starts running around as if he is looking for someone to belt. He winds up hitting no one, while his partner is left outnumbered in the front of the net. He is a good outlet passer but will sometimes get flustered and throw the puck away.

THE PHYSICAL GAME

Brisebois does not take the body much and will play the puck instead of the man. He'll have to work on his conditioning since he does not appear to be a very strong player — at least, he doesn't use his body well. He's tough only when he has a stick in his hands. His back problems during the past two seasons have made him even less of a factor.

THE INTANGIBLES

The Canadiens had high hopes for Brisebois, but even allowing for his physical ailments, we don't think we'll see much more out of him than has already been shown. David Wilkie should be eating up his ice time by the second half, and Brisebois will be a number four or even number five defenseman.

BENOIT BRUNET

Yrs. of NHL service: 4
Born: Pointe-Claire, Que.; Aug. 24, 1968
Position: left wing
Height: 5-11
Weight: 195
Uniform no.: 22
Shoots: left

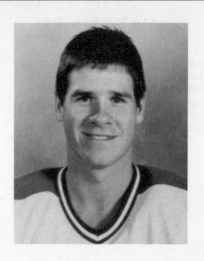

Career statistics:

GP	G	A	TP	PIM
226	39	71	110	86

1992-93 statistics:

GP	G	A	TP	+/-	PIM	PP	SH	GW	GT	S	PCT
47	10	15	25	+13	19	0	0	1	1	71	14.1

1993-94 statistics:

GP	G	A	TP	+/-	PIM	PP	SH	GW	GT	S	PCT
71	10	20	30	+14	20	0	3	1	0	92	10.9

1994-95 statistics:

GP	G	A	TP	+/-	PIM	PP	SH	GW	GT	S	PCT
45	7	18	25	+7	16	1	1	2	1	80	8.8

1995-96 statistics:

GP	G	A	TP	+/-	PIM	PP	SH	GW	GT	S	PCT
26	7	8	15	-4	17	3	1	4	0	48	14.6

LAST SEASON

Missed 56 games with back surgery and wrist injury.

THE FINESSE GAME

Brunet is one of the most anonymous Montreal forwards because of his quiet, efficient role as a checking winger on the third line. Developing into a top penalty killer, he is strong on his skates and forechecks tenaciously.

When Brunet does choose to do anything offensively, he cuts to the net and uses a confident, strong touch in deep. He is always hustling back on defense, though, and seldom makes any high-risk plays deep in his own zone. He takes few chances, and seems to come up with big points.

Brunet's hands aren't great, or he would be able to create more scoring off his forecheck.

THE PHYSICAL GAME

Brunet isn't very big and is overmatched when he plays against many of the league's top lines. His strength is his positional play. He takes fewer steps than other players to accomplish the same chore. He's not a big hitter, but he will tie up an opponent's stick and play smothering defense.

THE INTANGIBLES

Brunet has a strong work ethic and comes to play every night. He is like a good referee. On his best nights, you seldom notice him. Brunet had a benign tumor removed from his spine last season, and showed courage in coming back in time for the playoffs, but this season he could slip to a fourth-line role.

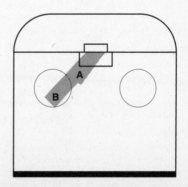

VALERI BURE

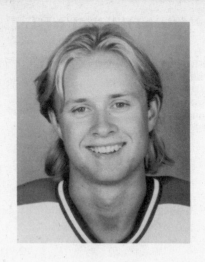

Yrs. of NHL service: 1
Born: Moscow, Russia; June 13, 1974
Position: right wing
Height: 5-10
Weight: 165
Uniform no.: 18
Shoots: right

Career statistics:

GP	G	A	TP	PIM
101	25	21	46	34

1994-95 statistics:

GP	G	A	TP	+/-	PIM	PP	SH	GW	GT	S	PCT
24	3	1	4	-1	6	0	0	1	0	39	7.7

1995-96 statistics:

GP	G	A	TP	+/-	PIM	PP	SH	GW	GT	S	PCT
77	22	20	42	+10	28	5	0	1	2	143	15.4

LAST SEASON

First NHL season. Tied for fifth among NHL rookies in scoring. Third among rookies in goals and shots. Fourth among rookies in shooting percentage.

THE FINESSE GAME

Valeri Bure isn't as fast as his famous older brother, Pavel, but he has his own distinct qualities. He has a great sense of anticipation and wants the puck every time he's on the ice. And he can make things happen, though he sometimes tries to force the action rather than let the game flow as naturally as it should. He will get carried away in his pursuit of the puck and get caught out of position, whereas if he just showed patience the puck would come to him.

Bure works well down low on the power play, but will also switch off and drop back to the point. He is gaining confidence in his shot and his scoring ability.

Bure has great hands to go along with his speed and seems to get a shot on goal or a scoring chance on every shift. He is smart and creative, and can make plays as well as finish. He played his best hockey last season while on a line with Vincent Damphousse and Martin Rucinsky.

THE PHYSICAL GAME

Bure is strong for his size, but isn't battle-tough yet. He can be intimidated, and if he wants to play on the top two lines he'll need to be a little grittier.

THE INTANGIBLES

Bure's development is very encouraging to the Canadiens. Unfortunately for Bure, most of the Canadiens' skill players are small, like him. If Bure had a power forward as a linemate, he would get a little more room, but he'll have to make his own space until then.

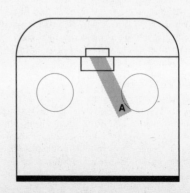

VINCENT DAMPHOUSSE

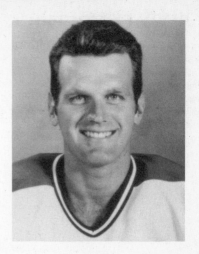

Yrs. of NHL service: 10
Born: Montreal, Que.; Dec. 17, 1967
Position: left wing
Height: 6-1
Weight: 200
Uniform no.: 25
Shoots: left

Career statistics:

GP	G	A	TP	PIM
770	283	457	740	688

1992-93 statistics:

GP	G	A	TP	+/-	PIM	PP	SH	GW	GT	S	PCT
84	39	58	97	+5	98	9	3	8	1	287	13.6

1993-94 statistics:

GP	G	A	TP	+/-	PIM	PP	SH	GW	GT	S	PCT
84	40	51	91	0	75	13	0	10	1	274	14.6

1994-95 statistics:

GP	G	A	TP	+/-	PIM	PP	SH	GW	GT	S	PCT
48	10	30	40	+15	42	4	0	4	0	123	8.1

1995-96 statistics:

GP	G	A	TP	+/-	PIM	PP	SH	GW	GT	S	PCT
80	38	56	94	+5	158	11	4	3	0	254	15.0

LAST SEASON

Tied for team lead in goals. Led team in shorthanded goals. Second on team in assists and points. Tied for second on team in power play goals. Served one-game suspension for second stick-related game misconduct, ending his consecutive games-played streak at 399. Has missed only eight games in 10 NHL seasons.

THE FINESSE GAME

Cool in tight, Damphousse has a marvellous backhand shot that he can roof, and he will create opportunites low by shaking and faking checkers with his skating. He likes to set up from behind the net to make plays. Goalies have to always be on the alert when he's on the attack, because he is unafraid to take shots from absurd angles just to get a shot on net and get the goalie and defense scrambling. It's an effective tactic.

Damphousse, who can also play centre, shows poise with the puck. Although he is primarily a finisher, he will also dish off to a teammate if that is a better option. He's a superb player in four-on-four situations. He has sharp offensive instincts, and is good in traffic.

Damphousse won't leave any vapour trails with his skating in open ice, but he is quick around the net, especially with the puck. He has exceptional balance to hop through sticks and checks. In open ice, he will use his weight to shift and change direction, making it appear as if he's going faster than he is — and he can juke without losing the puck while looking for his passing and shooting options.

THE PHYSICAL GAME

Damphousse will use his body to protect the puck, but he is not much of a grinder and loses most of his one-on-one battles. He has to be supported with physical linemates who will get him the puck. He will expend a great deal of energy in the attacking zone, but little in his own end of the ice, although he is more diligent about this in crunch times (like the playoffs).

He is a well-conditioned athlete who can handle long shifts and lots of ice time. He is not shy about using his stick, as his list of stick fouls and New Jersey defenseman Shawn Chambers' fractured hand will attest.

THE INTANGIBLES

Damphousse has emerged as the team's true leader and should have been given the captaincy last season instead of Pierre Turgeon after Mike Keane was traded. We predicted last year that he would hit the 100-point mark and he just missed. Montreal will be a slightly deeper team this season, and he should flirt with 100 again. Note that if Damphousse has a slow first half, he has a tendency to pick things up in the second half.

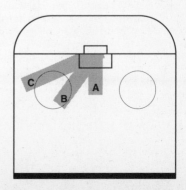

RORY FITZPATRICK

Yrs. of NHL service: 1
Born: Rochester, NY; Jan. 11, 1975
Position: right defense
Height: 6-1
Weight: 195
Uniform no.: 53
Shoots: right

Career statistics:

GP	G	A	TP	PIM
42	0	2	2	18

1995-96 statistics:

GP	G	A	TP	+/-	PIM	PP	SH	GW	GT	S	PCT
42	0	2	2	-7	18	0	0	0	0	31	0.0

LAST SEASON

First NHL season. Played 18 games with Fredericton (AHL), scoring 4-6 — 10.

THE FINESSE GAME

Fitzpatrick has the ability to play right or left defense, which is a considerable skill for a young defenseman and underscores his knowledge of the game.

Fitzpatrick's other assets lie in his skill and his willingness to use his talent defensively. He is strong in the corners and along the boards. He moves the puck well, but is more interested in clearing his zone than in getting involved at the other end of the ice.

Fitzpatrick was a captain in junior and will develop a commanding presence on the ice in the NHL in time. He communicates well with his partner and goalie. His defensive reads are well advanced for a player of his experience.

THE PHYSICAL GAME

Fitzpatrick is strong for his age and getting stronger. Think of him as a potential Rod Langway. Fitzpatrick isn't a pugilist, but he is rock-solid and won't be intimidated. He gets in people's faces without getting into scraps. He plays a tough and honest game.

THE INTANGIBLES

The Canadiens didn't hesitate to pair Fitzpatrick and fellow rookie David Wilkie (both American, by the way) during the playoffs, and this could be the partnership of the future for Montreal. Wilkie's offensive play nicely complements Fitzpatrick's sturdy, stay-at-home style. They will make mistakes together, but they will learn from them, and get better.

SAKU KOIVU

Yrs. of NHL service: 1
Born: Turku, Finland; Nov. 23, 1974
Position: centre
Height: 5-9
Weight: 165
Uniform no.: 11
Shoots: left

Career statistics:

GP	G	A	TP	PIM
82	20	25	45	40

1995-96 statistics:

GP	G	A	TP	+/-	PIM	PP	SH	GW	GT	S	PCT
82	20	25	45	-7	40	8	3	2	1	136	14.7

LAST SEASON

First NHL season. Fourth among NHL rookies in goals, assists and points. Tied for NHL rookie lead in power play goals. Led rookies and second in team in shorthanded goals. Fourth among rookies in shots. Fifth among rookies in shooting percentage. One of only three rookies to appear in all 82 games.

THE FINESSE GAME

Koivu brings brilliance and excitement to every shift. Considered one of the world's best playmakers, he makes things happen with his speed and intimidates by driving the defense back, then using the room to create scoring chances.

Koivu has great hands and can handle the puck at a fast pace. He stickhandles through traffic and reads plays well. He is intelligent and involved.

He has a variety of shots. Like many Europeans, he has an effective backhand for shooting or passing. He also has a strong wrist shot and is deadly accurate.

THE PHYSICAL GAME

It was remarkable for Koivu to step into the pros straight from Europe and not miss a game. He gets a lot of ice time and did slow down slightly in the second half (only six goals in the last 39 games), showing understandable signs of wear.

The lone knock on Koivu is his lack of size. He gets involved in a scrappy way, but gets shoved around. He won't be intimidated, though. He will use his stick to level the playing field a bit. He acquitted himself well in his first taste of the playoffs.

THE INTANGIBLES

Koivu played well in adapting to his first year in North America. His skill level is very high and if the Canadiens add a little size up front, he will get a little more room. We don't expect a sophomore slump because of his work ethic.

ANDREI KOVALENKO

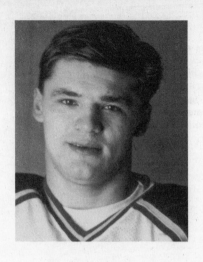

Yrs. of NHL service: 4
Born: Balakovo, Russia; June 7, 1970
Position: right wing
Height: 5-10
Weight: 200
Uniform no.: 51
Shoots: left

Career statistics:

GP	G	A	TP	PIM
261	85	96	181	183

1992-93 statistics:

GP	G	A	TP	+/-	PIM	PP	SH	GW	GT	S	PCT
81	27	41	68	+13	57	8	1	4	0	153	17.6

1993-94 statistics:

GP	G	A	TP	+/-	PIM	PP	SH	GW	GT	S	PCT
58	16	17	33	-5	46	5	0	4	0	92	17.4

1994-95 statistics:

GP	G	A	TP	+/-	PIM	PP	SH	GW	GT	S	PCT
45	14	10	24	-4	31	1	0	3	0	63	22.2

1995-96 statistics:

GP	G	A	TP	+/-	PIM	PP	SH	GW	GT	S	PCT
77	28	28	56	+20	49	6	0	6	1	131	21.4

LAST SEASON

Acquired from Colorado with Jocelyn Thibault and Martin Rucinsky for Patrick Roy and Mike Keane, Dec. 6, 1995. Led team in shooting percentage. Tied for team lead in game-winning goals. Tied for second on team in plus-minus.

THE FINESSE GAME

Kovalenko has the skills associated with many Russian forwards, but he also has a brisk, sometimes abrasive style.

Kovalenko will bustle right into traffic and make things happen around the net. He is an intelligent player who doesn't panic with the puck and is a natural on the power play. He doesn't hang onto the puck long but likes to make short give-and-go plays in the offensive zone. Kovalenko always keeps his wheels in motion. He is a very accurate shooter with a quick release on his wrist shot.

Defensive work is his downfall. He needs to be more conscientious of his checking role.

THE PHYSICAL GAME

Kovalenko's nickname in Russia was "the Little Tank," because of his chunky build. Although he was inconsistent in his physical play last season, perhaps due to the shock of being traded, Kovalenko can be tough around the net and in the offensive corners. He will take some punishment in front of the net on the power play, and gets a lot of goals off the rebounds.

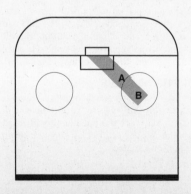

THE INTANGIBLES

Kovalenko had an inconsistent year and a very quiet playoffs and might be on the move again.

VLADIMIR MALAKHOV

Yrs. of NHL service: 4
Born: Sverdlovsk, Russia; Aug. 30, 1968
Position: right defense
Height: 6-3
Weight: 225
Uniform no.: 38
Shoots: left

Career statistics:

GP	G	A	TP	PIM
241	33	125	158	264

1992-93 statistics:

GP	G	A	TP	+/-	PIM	PP	SH	GW	GT	S	PCT
64	14	38	52	+14	59	7	0	0	0	178	7.9

1993-94 statistics:

GP	G	A	TP	+/-	PIM	PP	SH	GW	GT	S	PCT
76	10	47	57	+29	80	4	0	2	0	235	4.3

1994-95 statistics:

GP	G	A	TP	+/-	PIM	PP	SH	GW	GT	S	PCT
40	4	17	21	-3	46	1	0	0	0	91	4.4

1995-96 statistics:

GP	G	A	TP	+/-	PIM	PP	SH	GW	GT	S	PCT
61	5	23	28	+7	79	2	0	0	0	122	4.1

LAST SEASON

Missed 21 games with torn knee ligaments.

THE FINESSE GAME

Malakhov has elite pro skills and an amateur attitude.
We don't mean to insult hard-working amateurs,
we're just trying to make a point.

Malakhov has an absolute bullet shot, which he
rifles off the one-timer or on the fly. He has outstanding offensive instincts for both shooting and
playmaking. He moves the puck and jumps into the
play, but lacks vision, lateral movement and confidence.

Malakhov is so talented he never looks like he's
trying hard. Most nights he's not. He has learned on
the job, and as he doesn't speak English well, he struggled through some of the learning process. He seems
discouraged at times when things aren't going
smoothly. If he tries a few plays early in a game that
don't work, you might as well put him on the bench
the rest of the night.

Malakhov is strong defensively and can be used
on both special teams. He is a mobile skater, with
good agility and balance. He has huge strides, which
he developed playing bandy — a Russian game similar to hockey, but played on an ice surface the size of a
soccer field.

THE PHYSICAL GAME

Malakhov relies on his positioning and anticipation
for his defensive plays more than his hitting. He could
be a major physical force because of his size and
strength, but injuries may have made him leery of getting hurt, and he really doesn't have the taste for the
physical game.

THE INTANGIBLES

Malakhov seems to save his best hockey for when a
marquee player, such as Mario Lemieux, is on the opposing team. He doesn't get as pumped up the rest of
the year. Malakhov is his own worst enemy, because
he keeps to himself and won't allow the coaches or his
teammates to help him. He has awesome talent, but
we wouldn't want him on our team for an 82-game
schedule.

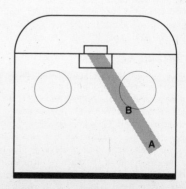

LYLE ODELEIN

Yrs. of NHL service: 6
Born: Quill Lake, Sask.; July 21, 1968
Position: right defense
Height: 5-10
Weight: 205
Uniform no.: 24
Shoots: left

Career statistics:

GP	G	A	TP	PIM
420	20	75	95	1367

1992-93 statistics:

GP	G	A	TP	+/-	PIM	PP	SH	GW	GT	S	PCT
83	2	14	16	+35	205	0	0	0	0	79	2.5

1993-94 statistics:

GP	G	A	TP	+/-	PIM	PP	SH	GW	GT	S	PCT
79	11	29	40	+8	276	6	0	2	0	116	9.5

1994-95 statistics:

GP	G	A	TP	+/-	PIM	PP	SH	GW	GT	S	PCT
48	3	7	10	-13	152	0	0	0	0	74	4.1

1995-96 statistics:

GP	G	A	TP	+/-	PIM	PP	SH	GW	GT	S	PCT
79	3	14	17	+8	230	0	1	0	0	74	4.1

LAST SEASON

Led team in penalty minutes for fourth consecutive season. Served two-game suspension.

THE FINESSE GAME

Odelein deserves great credit for having molded himself into more than an overachieving goon. He is Montreal's most reliable defenseman, a physical presence despite being smaller than most NHL defensemen — and smaller than many NHL forwards.

Defense is his forte. Odelein is very calm with the puck. He can hold on until a player is on top of him and then carry the puck or find an open man. His skating is average at best, but he keeps himself out of trouble by playing a conservative game and not getting caught out of position. An attacker who comes into Odelein's piece of the ice will have to pay the price by getting through him.

Odelein's finesse skills are modest at best, but he has developed sufficient confidence to get involved in the attack if needed. He prefers to limit his contribution to shots from the point. He needs to be paired with a puck-carrying partner.

THE PHYSICAL GAME

Odelein is a banger, a limited player who knows what those limits are, stays within them and plays effectively as a result. He's rugged and doesn't take chances. He takes the man at all times in front of the net and he plays tough. Heavy but not tall, he gives the impression of being a much bigger man. He will fight, but not very well. He is forced to engage in fisticuffs as the biggest, toughest Canadien — often the only big, tough Canadien.

Odelein also snaps in a minor way now and again. He earned his suspension by firing the puck into the Buffalo Sabres' bench.

THE INTANGIBLES

Reliable and physical, Odelein is a solid defenseman who continues to improve season by season. He would be more effective if the team could add some toughness up front so that he doesn't have to do it all. He is one of the team's true leaders, along with Vincent Damphousse.

STEPHANE QUINTAL

Yrs. of NHL service: 8
Born: Boucherville, Que.; Oct. 22, 1968
Position: right defense
Height: 6-3
Weight: 215
Uniform no.: 5
Shoots: right

Career statistics:

GP	G	A	TP	PIM
651	25	84	109	663

1992-93 statistics:

GP	G	A	TP	+/-	PIM	PP	SH	GW	GT	S	PCT
75	1	10	11	-6	100	0	1	0	0	81	1.2

1993-94 statistics:

GP	G	A	TP	+/-	PIM	PP	SH	GW	GT	S	PCT
81	8	18	26	-25	119	1	1	1	0	154	5.2

1994-95 statistics:

GP	G	A	TP	+/-	PIM	PP	SH	GW	GT	S	PCT
43	6	17	23	0	78	3	0	2	0	107	5.6

1995-96 statistics:

GP	G	A	TP	+/-	PIM	PP	SH	GW	GT	S	PCT
68	2	14	16	-4	117	0	1	1	1	104	1.9

and he handled the responsibility professionally. A more limited role is in his future as the Canadiens will break at least two young defensemen into the lineup.

LAST SEASON

Missed 14 games with arthroscopic knee surgery.

THE FINESSE GAME

Quintal's game is limited by his lumbering skating. He has some nice touches, like a decent point shot and a good head and hands for passing, but his best moves have to be executed at a virtual standstill. He needs to be paired with a quick skater or his shifts will be spent solely in the defensive zone.

Fortunately, Quintal is as aware of his flaws. He plays a smart positional game and doesn't get involved in low-percentage plays in the offensive zone. He won't step up in the neutral zone to risk an interception, but will fall back into a defensive mode. He takes up a lot of ice with his body and stick, and when he doesn't overcommit, he reduces the space available to a puck carrier.

While he can exist as an NHL regular in the five-on-five mode, Quintal is a risky proposition for any specialty teams play.

Quintal does not like to carry the puck, and under pressure in the right corner he will simply slam it out along the left corner boards behind the net.

THE PHYSICAL GAME

Quintal is slow but very strong on his skates. He thrives on contact and works hard along the boards and in front of the net. He hits hard without taking penalties and is a tough and willing fighter.

THE INTANGIBLES

Quintal is ideally a number five or six defenseman, but injuries forced him into the top four in Montreal

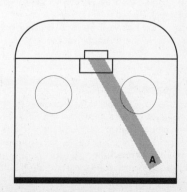

MARK RECCHI

Yrs. of NHL service: 7
Born: Kamloops, B.C.; Feb. 1, 1968
Position: right wing
Height: 5-9
Weight: 185
Uniform no.: 8
Shoots: left

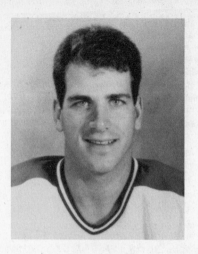

Career statistics:

GP	G	A	TP	PIM
546	251	384	635	426

1992-93 statistics:

GP	G	A	TP	+/-	PIM	PP	SH	GW	GT	S	PCT
84	53	70	123	+1	95	15	4	6	0	274	19.3

1993-94 statistics:

GP	G	A	TP	+/-	PIM	PP	SH	GW	GT	S	PCT
84	40	67	107	-2	46	11	0	5	0	217	18.4

1994-95 statistics:

GP	G	A	TP	+/-	PIM	PP	SH	GW	GT	S	PCT
49	16	32	48	-9	28	9	0	3	0	121	13.2

1995-96 statistics:

GP	G	A	TP	+/-	PIM	PP	SH	GW	GT	S	PCT
82	28	50	78	+20	69	11	2	6	0	191	14.7

LAST SEASON

Tied for team lead in power play goals. Tied for second on team in power play goals and plus-minus. Third on team in assists and points. One of only two Canadiens to appear in all 82 games. Second-longest consecutive games played streak among active players.

THE FINESSE GAME

Recchi is a small package with a lot of firepower. He is one of the top small players in the game, and certainly one of the most productive. Recchi is feisty and a relentless worker in the offensive zone. He busts into open ice, finding the holes almost before they open. He excels at the give-and-go, and is versatile enough to play wing or centre, though he is better on the wing.

Recchi has a dangerous shot from the off-wing. While he is not as dynamic as Maurice Richard, he likes to use the Richard cut-back while rifling a wrist shot back across. It's heavy, it's on net and it requires no backswing. He will follow his shot to the net for a rebound. He can make a play as well. He has excellent hands, vision and anticipation for any scoring opportunity.

Recchi has worked hard to improve his defense and judging by his plus-minus, he's doing a better job. He kills penalties well because he hounds the point men aggressively and knocks the puck out of the zone. Then he heads off on a breakaway or forces the defender to pull him down.

He isn't a pretty skater but he always keeps his feet moving. While other players are coasting, Recchi's blades are in motion, and he draws penalties.

He is ready to spring into any play. He resembles a puck magnet because he is always going where the puck is.

THE PHYSICAL GAME

Recchi gets chopped at because he doesn't hang around the perimeter. He accepts the punishment to get the job done. He is a solid player with a low centre of gravity, and is tough to knock off the puck. He is remarkably durable for the style of game he plays.

THE INTANGIBLES

Montreal was shopping for a big forward during the off-season and Recchi is the bait, coming off one of his worst seasons. He can be a 100-point scorer again, but we think he needs to get out of Montreal to do it.

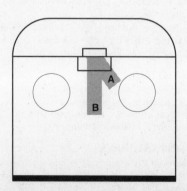

MARTIN RUCINSKY

Yrs. of NHL service: 4
Born: Most, Czechoslovkia; March 11, 1971
Position: left wing
Height: 6-0
Weight: 190
Uniform no.: 26
Shoots: left

Career statistics:

GP	G	A	TP	PIM
241	60	106	166	193

1992-93 statistics:

GP	G	A	TP	+/-	PIM	PP	SH	GW	GT	S	PCT
77	18	30	48	+16	51	4	0	1	3	133	13.5

1993-94 statistics:

GP	G	A	TP	+/-	PIM	PP	SH	GW	GT	S	PCT
60	9	23	32	+4	58	4	0	1	0	96	9.4

1994-95 statistics:

GP	G	A	TP	+/-	PIM	PP	SH	GW	GT	S	PCT
20	3	6	9	+5	14	0	0	0	0	32	9.4

1995-96 statistics:

GP	G	A	TP	+/-	PIM	PP	SH	GW	GT	S	PCT
78	29	46	75	+18	68	9	2	4	0	18	16.0

LAST SEASON

Acquired from Colorado with Jocelyn Thibault and Andrei Kovalenko for Patrick Roy and Mike Keane, Dec. 6, 1995. Missed two games with knee injury.

THE FINESSE GAME

Rucinsky had a hard time getting ice time on a deep Colorado team, but he was a happy camper playing alongside Vincent Damphousse after the trade to Montreal. Rucinsky scored at a better than a point-per-game pace (25-35 — 60 in 56 games) with the Habs. A knee injury derailed him late in the season and prevented him from appearing in the playoffs.

Rucinsky is very quick with hand skills to match at high tempo. He is most dangerous off the rush, where he can use his speed to intimidate the defense and then use the room they give him to fire his shot.

Rucinsky's flaw is that he is not overly patient. He has nice little moves, and can beat people one-on-one. He loves to shoot, though, and that is often a problem with European players.

THE PHYSICAL GAME

Rucinsky is wiry, but isn't a big banger. His physical effectiveness will depend on his recovery from surgery. Confidence will allow him to continue to play in traffic and take hits to protect the puck.

THE INTANGIBLES

Rucinsky has the potential to become a game-breaking scorer. He could enjoy a big breakthrough year in Montreal, since he figures to play on the top line with Damphousse.

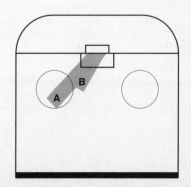

BRIAN SAVAGE

Yrs. of NHL service: 2
Born: Sudbury, Ontario; Feb. 24, 1971
Position: centre
Height: 6-2
Weight: 195
Uniform no.: 49
Shoots: left

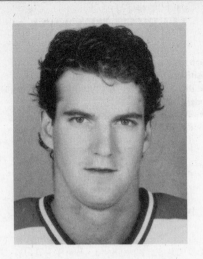

Career statistics:

GP	G	A	TP	PIM
115	38	15	53	55

1993-94 statistics:

GP	G	A	TP	+/-	PIM	PP	SH	GW	GT	S	PCT
3	1	0	1	0	0	0	0	0	0	3	33.3

1994-95 statistics:

GP	G	A	TP	+/-	PIM	PP	SH	GW	GT	S	PCT
37	12	7	19	+5	27	0	0	0	0	64	18.8

1995-96 statistics:

GP	G	A	TP	+/-	PIM	PP	SH	GW	GT	S	PCT
75	25	8	33	-8	28	4	0	4	0	150	16.7

LAST SEASON

Missed six games with hip pointer. Missed one game with flu.

THE FINESSE GAME

Savage's goal-to-assist ratio gives a good indication of what his biggest asset is. He is a finisher. Period. Although Savage broke into the league as something of a playmaker, he has real tunnel vision with the puck and all he sees is net. Fortunately, he has a quick release and is accurate with his shot. He feasts from the hash marks in.

Savage is a streaky scorer, though, and he doesn't bring much to the game when he isn't scoring. A young player, he lets the slumps slow him down instead of working harder through the dry spells. Then it becomes a vicious circle where it's hard for him to get ice time to break out of it.

Savage has quick hands for picking up the puck and for working on face-offs. He is a good skater.

THE PHYSICAL GAME

Savage doesn't use his body well yet, but playing with tough linemate Turner Stevenson gives him a bit of heart and inspiration. Savage is strong on his skates and has decent size. He may not initiate, but he won't be intimidated.

THE INTANGIBLES

We predicted 25 goals for Savage last year, and that appears to be his limit. Montreal has moved him to left wing and he seems better suited to that position than centre.

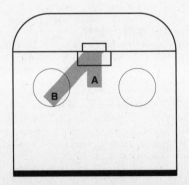

TURNER STEVENSON

Yrs. of NHL service: 2
Born: Prince George, B.C.; May 18, 1972
Position: right wing
Height: 6-3
Weight: 215
Uniform no.: 30
Shoots: right

Career statistics:

GP	G	A	TP	PIM
124	15	17	32	255

1992-93 statistics:

GP	G	A	TP	+/-	PIM	PP	SH	GW	GT	S	PCT
1	0	0	0	-1	0	0	0	0	0	0	0.0

1993-94 statistics:

GP	G	A	TP	+/-	PIM	PP	SH	GW	GT	S	PCT
2	0	0	0	-2	2	0	0	0	0	0	0.0

1994-95 statistics:

GP	G	A	TP	+/-	PIM	PP	SH	GW	GT	S	PCT
41	6	1	7	0	86	0	0	1	0	35	17.1

1995-96 statistics:

GP	G	A	TP	+/-	PIM	PP	SH	GW	GT	S	PCT
80	9	16	25	-2	167	0	0	2	0	101	8.9

LAST SEASON
Second NHL season.

THE FINESSE GAME
A big, strong two-way winger, Stevenson is the type of forward desperately needed by Montreal, but he has to improve his shot to be a more consistent finisher.

A good skater for a player of his size, he has a good long stride and is balanced and agile.

Stevenson has a variety of shots and uses all of them with power and accuracy. He will follow the puck to the net and not give up on shots. He is also a decent passer and possesses some vision and creativity. His release has improved but could get even better. Stevenson plays a short power game.

THE PHYSICAL GAME
Stevenson has an impressive mean streak. The problem for the coaching staff will be lighting a fire under him on a regular basis, because he doesn't bring the same intensity to the ice every night. He seems to have no idea what kind of physical presence he can add to the team.

THE INTANGIBLES
Stevenson has been slow to develop, like many big forwards, but Montreal believes he will be worth the wait, and he has the potential to move up into the 20-goal range next season while improving his overall game.

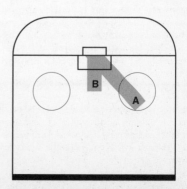

JOCELYN THIBAULT

Yrs. of NHL service: 3
Born: Montreal, Que.; Jan. 12, 1975
Position: goaltender
Height: 5-11
Weight: 170
Uniform no.: 41
Catches: left

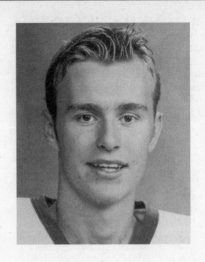

Career statistics:

GP	MIN	GA	SO	GAA	A	PIM
97	5294	256	4	2.90	0	4

1993-94 statistics:

GP	MIN	GAA	W	L	T	SO	GA	S	SAPCT	PIM
29	1504	3.31	8	13	3	0	83	768	.892	2

1994-95 statistics:

GP	MIN	GAA	W	L	T	SO	GA	S	SAPCT	PIM
18	898	2.34	12	2	2	1	35	423	.917	0

1995-96 statistics:

GP	MIN	GAA	W	L	T	SO	GA	S	SAPCT	PIM
50	2892	2.86	26	17	5	3	138	1480	.907	2

LAST SEASON

Acquired from Colorado with Martin Rucinsky and Andrei Kovalenko for Patrick Roy and Mike Keane, Dec. 6, 1995. Missed two games with thumb injury.

THE PHYSICAL GAME

Thibault is a small goalie whose technique makes him look even tinier. He is a butterfly-style goalie, but when he goes to his knees, he doesn't keep his torso upright (as Roy does so splendidly), and that costs Thibault a big chunk of net.

He is terrible with his rebounds. He doesn't direct them, and they bounce right out into no man's land where he can't reach the pucks to clear them and the attackers are swooping in. Thibault's puckhandling is average on his best nights.

Thibault plays deep in his net and that means he has to rely on his reflexes — which, happily for the Habs, happen to be excellent. Thibault has a good glove hand, quick feet, and is a good skater with lateral mobility.

THE MENTAL GAME

Thibault wants to be a Roy clone. He embraced the trade to Montreal, despite the high stress of being a French-Canadian hockey player in that city. Thibault is very competitive and performs well in pressure situations, but whether he can do it over the long haul is a huge question mark.

THE INTANGIBLES

Thibault is very inexperienced to be handed the number one role for the Canadiens, and his game is imperfect. Losing goalie coach Francois Allaire isn't going to help. Thibault will struggle until his fundamentals improve.

PIERRE TURGEON

Yrs. of NHL service: 9
Born: Rouyn, Que.; Aug. 28, 1969
Position: centre
Height: 6-1
Weight: 195
Uniform no.: 77
Shoots: left

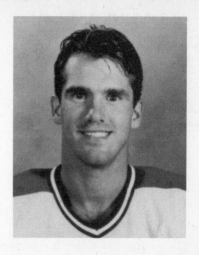

Career statistics:

GP	G	A	TP	PIM
672	318	461	779	237

1992-93 statistics:

GP	G	A	TP	+/-	PIM	PP	SH	GW	GT	S	PCT
83	58	74	132	-1	26	24	0	10	2	301	19.3

1993-94 statistics:

GP	G	A	TP	+/-	PIM	PP	SH	GW	GT	S	PCT
69	38	56	94	+14	18	10	4	6	0	254	15.0

1994-95 statistics:

GP	G	A	TP	+/-	PIM	PP	SH	GW	GT	S	PCT
49	24	23	47	0	14	5	2	4	0	160	15.0

1995-96 statistics:

GP	G	A	TP	+/-	PIM	PP	SH	GW	GT	S	PCT
80	38	58	96	+19	44	17	1	6	0	297	12.8

LAST SEASON

Tied for team lead in goals and game-winning goals. Led team in assists, points, power play goals and shots. Missed two games with shoulder injury.

THE FINESSE GAME

Turgeon's skills are amazing. He never seems to be looking at the puck, yet he is always in perfect control of it. He has a style unlike just about anyone else in the NHL. He's not a fast skater, but he can deke a defender or make a sneaky surprise pass. He is tough to defend against, because if you aren't aware of where he is on the ice and don't deny him the pass, he can kill a team with several moves.

Turgeon can slow or speed up the tempo of a game. He lacks the breakout speed of a Pat LaFontaine, but because he is slippery and can change speeds so smoothly, he's deceptive. His control with the puck down low is remarkable. He protects the puck well with the body.

While best known for his playmaking, Turgeon has an excellent shot. He will curl out from behind the net with a wrist shot, shoot off the fly from the right wing (his preferred side of the ice) or stand just off to the side of the net on a power play and reach for a tip or redirection of a point shot. He doesn't have a bazooka shot, but he uses quick, accurate wrist and snap shots. He has to create odd-man rushes. This is when he is at his finest.

THE PHYSICAL GAME

Turgeon has to decide if he wants to be a good statistical player or a winner, and to be the latter he will have to add a more physical element to his game. He is strong, but clearly does not like the contact part of the game, and he can be taken out of a game by a team that hounds him. Turgeon must play through it. When the Canadiens played Vincent Damphousse at centre last season, that relieved some of the checking pressure from Turgeon.

THE INTANGIBLES

Despite Turgeon's lack of leadership credentials, he was given the captain's "C" after Mike Keane was traded to Colorado. It is probably wishful thinking on the part of Montreal's management, which hopes Turgeon will grow into the role. It won't be a snug fit, since he doesn't have the right personality for the job, and he will really feel the pressure this season.

Turgeon isn't Wayne Gretzky or Doug Gilmour. He isn't a leader. He will create a considerable amount of brilliance, but never take his game to the next level, and he won't bring the team along with him. Turgeon may have another fine regular season, but he was microscopic in last year's playoffs.

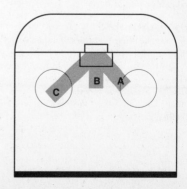

DAVID WILKIE

Yrs. of NHL service: 1
Born: Ellensburgh, WA; May 30, 1974
Position: right defense
Height: 6-2
Weight: 210
Uniform no.: 27
Shoots: right

Career statistics:

GP	G	A	TP	PIM
25	1	5	6	10

1994-95 statistics:

GP	G	A	TP	+/-	PIM	PP	SH	GW	GT	S	PCT
1	0	0	0	0	0	0	0	0	0	0	0.0

1995-96 statistics:

GP	G	A	TP	+/-	PIM	PP	SH	GW	GT	S	PCT
24	1	5	6	-10	10	1	0	0	0	39	2.6

LAST SEASON

First NHL season. Played 23 games with Fredericton (AHL), scoring 5-12 — 17.

THE FINESSE GAME

Wilkie is a good skater on the straight, but needs to improve his lateral mobility to be more effective defensively. Wilkie is an offense-oriented defenseman at this stage, but he is intelligent and is less of a defensive liability than some of the more experienced Montreal defensemen.

Wilkie has a terrific point shot and refined offensive instincts, a result of having started his hockey career as a forward. Wilkie loves to rush with the puck, and can go end-to-end. His passes are crisp and he doesn't throw the puck away under pressure.

Wilkie was hit by some injuries early in his career, which is why the Canadiens have brought him along slowly. After spending the last year and a half in the minors, he appears ready to step up.

THE PHYSICAL GAME

Wilkie is a big skater who tends to play a little smaller than he should. He's not very aggressive, but he doesn't get knocked off the puck. He will have to use his body more because he's just too darn big to tiptoe around in his own end.

THE INTANGIBLES

Wilkie has good offensive upside and should step in to help the Canadiens run their first-unit power play before long. Montreal assistant coach Jacques Laperriere has a knack for developing smart defensemen (two of the best, Eric Desjardins and Mathieu Schneider, play for other teams, however), and Wilkie will be his project this season.

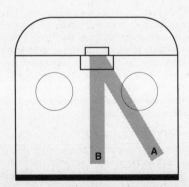

NEW JERSEY DEVILS

Players' Statistics 1995-96

POS.	NO.	PLAYER	GP	G	A	PTS	+/-	PIM	PP	SH	GW	GT	S	PCT
D	6	PHIL HOUSLEY	81	17	51	68	-6	30	6		1		205	8.3
L	32	STEVE THOMAS	81	26	35	61	-2	98	6		6	1	192	13.5
L	23	DAVE ANDREYCHUK	76	28	29	57	-9	64	14	2	3	1	241	11.6
R	12	BILL GUERIN	80	23	30	53	7	116	8		6	1	216	10.6
R	15	JOHN MACLEAN	76	20	28	48	3	91	3	3	3		237	8.4
C	17	*PETR SYKORA	63	18	24	42	7	32	8		3		128	14.1
D	27	SCOTT NIEDERMAYER	79	8	25	33	5	46	6				179	4.5
R	44	STEPHANE RICHER	73	20	12	32	-8	30	3	4	3		192	10.4
L	16	BOBBY HOLIK	63	13	17	30	9	58	1		1	1	157	8.3
D	4	SCOTT STEVENS	82	5	23	28	7	100	2	1	1		174	2.9
L	14	BRIAN ROLSTON	58	13	11	24	9	8	3	1	4	1	139	9.4
C	9	NEAL BROTEN	55	7	16	23	-3	14	1	1	1		73	9.6
D	29	SHAWN CHAMBERS	64	2	21	23	1	18	2		1		112	1.8
R	21	RANDY MCKAY	76	11	10	21	7	145	3		3	1	97	11.3
L	25	VALERI ZELEPUKIN	61	6	9	15	-10	107	3		1	1	86	7.0
L	8	MIKE PELUSO	57	3	8	11	4	146					41	7.3
L	19	BOB CARPENTER	52	5	5	10	-10	14		1			63	7.9
C	24	*STEVE SULLIVAN	16	5	4	9	3	8	2		1		23	21.7
C	18	SERGEI BRYLIN	50	4	5	9	-2	26			1		51	7.8
D	3	KEN DANEYKO	80	2	4	6	-10	115					67	3.0
L	33	REID SIMPSON	23	1	5	6	2	79					8	12.5
D	28	KEVIN DEAN	41		6	6	4	28					29	
C	10	*DENIS PEDERSON	10	3	1	4	-1		1		2		6	50.0
R	20	SCOTT PELLERIN	6	2	1	3	1						9	22.2
D	5	RICARD PERSSON	12	2	1	3	5	8	1				41	4.9
D	26	JASON SMITH	64	2	1	3	5	86					52	3.8
G	30	MARTIN BRODEUR	77		1	1	0	6					1	
R	24	*PATRIK ELIAS	1				-1						2	
G	35	*COREY SCHWAB	10				0	31						

GP = games played; G = goals; A = assists; PTS = points; +/- = goals-for minus goals-against while player is on ice; PIM = penalties in minutes; PP = power play goals; SH = shorthanded goals; GW = game-winning goals; GT = game-tying goals; S = no. of shots; PCT = percentage of goals to shots; * = rookie

DAVE ANDREYCHUK

Yrs. of NHL service: 14
Born: Hamilton, Ont.; Sept. 29, 1963
Position: left wing
Height: 6-3
Weight: 220
Uniform no.: 23
Shoots: right

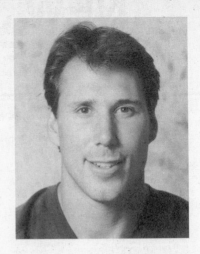

Career statistics:

GP	G	A	TP	PIM
1017	476	526	1002	768

1992-93 statistics:

GP	G	A	TP	+/-	PIM	PP	SH	GW	GT	S	PCT
83	54	45	99	+4	56	32	0	4	1	310	17.4

1993-94 statistics:

GP	G	A	TP	+/-	PIM	PP	SH	GW	GT	S	PCT
83	53	45	98	+22	98	21	5	8	0	333	15.9

1994-95 statistics:

GP	G	A	TP	+/-	PIM	PP	SH	GW	GT	S	PCT
48	22	16	38	-7	34	8	0	2	2	168	13.1

1995-96 statistics:

GP	G	A	TP	+/-	PIM	PP	SH	GW	GT	S	PCT
76	28	29	57	-9	64	14	2	3	1	241	11.6

LAST SEASON

Acquired from Toronto for selection of draft picks on Mar. 13, 1996. Played in 1,000th NHL game and scored 1,000th NHL point. Led team in goals, power play goals and shots. Third on team in points. Fewest points (not counting lockout season) since 1988-89. Missed two games with thumb surgery. Missed five games with shoulder injury.

THE FINESSE GAME

Andreychuk just can't get enough of the game, but defenders have certainly had their fill of him. The big winger uses a very stiff shaft on his long stick, allowing him to lean on it hard in front of the net. He tries to keep his blade on the ice for deflections, and by pushing his 220 pounds on the stick, he makes it almost impossible for a defender to lift it off the ice.

Andreychuk has slow feet but a cherry-picker reach, which he uses with strength and intelligence. He is a lumbering skater, but since he works in tight areas, he only needs a big stride or two to plant himself where he wants. He has marvellous hand skills in traffic and can use his stick to artfully pick pucks out of mid-air, slap at rebounds, or for wraparounds. He has quick and accurate wrist and snap shots. Andreychuk's hands are so quick that he will sometimes step in for offensive-zone draws.

From the hash marks in, Andreychuk is one of the most dangerous snipers in the league. On the other four-fifths of the ice, he is a liability. He doesn't finish his checks and he doesn't skate well. He understands the game well enough to position himself, but won't battle anywhere other than right in front of the net.

Increasingly, Andreychuk is becoming a power play specialist. He needs to play with people who can get him the puck and with people who can skate, to cover up for his skating deficiencies. He gets into occasional slumps when he overhandles the puck and last season was affected by his thumb injury. He is at his peak when he works the give-and-go and keeps his legs moving.

THE PHYSICAL GAME

If you're looking for someone to protect his smaller teammates, or to inspire a team with his hitting, then Andreychuk is not the man for you. Andreychuk is a giant shock absorber, soaking up hits without retaliating. He has a long fuse and will seldom take a bad penalty, especially when his team is on the power play.

He's tough in his own way, in front of the opponent's net, at least. He is nearly impossible to budge, and with his long arms can control pucks. He isn't dominating, but he is physically prominent within five feet of the crease. He pays the price to score goals and knows how to use his talent.

THE INTANGIBLES

New Jersey's acquisition of this one-way forward was surprising, given coach Jacques Lemaire's defense-first philosophy. But the Devils were desperately hurting for offense last year. Finding a centre who will work well with Andreychuk will be crucial if he is to produce under the team's restrictive system.

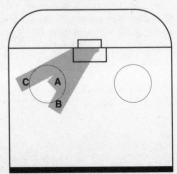

MARTIN BRODEUR

Yrs. of NHL service: 3
Born: Montreal, Que.; May 6, 1972
Position: goaltender
Height: 6-1
Weight: 205
Uniform no.: 30
Catches: left

Career statistics:

GP	MIN	GA	SO	GAA	A	PIM
82	9421	377	12	2.40	3	10

1993-94 statistics:

GP	MIN	GAA	W	L	T	SO	GA	S	SAPCT	PIM
47	2625	2.40	27	11	8	3	105	1238	.915	2

1994-95 statistics:

GP	MIN	GAA	W	L	T	SO	GA	S	SAPCT	PIM
40	2184	2.45	19	11	6	3	89	908	.902	2

1995-96 statistics:

GP	MIN	GAA	W	L	T	SO	GA	S	SAPCT	PIM
77	4434	2.34	34	30	12	6	173	1954	.911	6

LAST SEASON

Set NHL record in minutes played (4,434). Fifth in NHL in goals-against average. Tied for third in NHL in wins. Second in NHL with career high in shutouts. Appeared in 52 consecutive games and started 44 straight.

THE PHYSICAL GAME

Brodeur has developed from a strictly stand-up goalie to a hybrid, and he is smart enough to adapt his style to the team or the shooter he is playing against. Brodeur makes the most of his generous size. He stands so upright in the net and squares himself so well to the shooter that he looks enormous. He has become one of the game's best at using his stick around the net. He breaks up passes and will make a quick jab to knock the puck off an opponent's stick. Brodeur helps his team out immensely with this skill.

Opponents want to get Brodeur's feet moving — wraparound plays, rebounds, anything involving his skates exposes his weaknesses. Yet because of his puck control, Brodeur prevents a lot of scrambles and minimizes his flaws. When he falls into bad streaks, it is usually because of his footwork. Brodeur went through a slump of getting beat by angle shots from the circle because he was taking too large a stride laterally, but he worked to correct the error in technique.

Brodeur has improved his play out of the net but has to guard against cockiness. He has visions of becoming the next goalie to score a goal (he was disappointed when Chris Osgood beat him to it last season), and will get carried away in his shots through the middle of the ice.

Brodeur's physique is an advantage against crease-crashers. He also guards against poachers with the occasional ankle whack or jab to the back.

THE MENTAL GAME

Bad games and bad goals don't rattle Brodeur for long. While he has a tendency to show his frustration on-ice, he also bounces back quickly with strong ef-forts. He concentrates and doesn't lose his intensity throughout a game. Teammates love playing in front of him because of the confidence he exudes — even through the layers of padding and the mask. When Brodeur is on, his glove saves are snappy and he bounces on his feet with flair.

No one intimidates Brodeur — with the possible exception of Mario Lemieux — and he thrives on pressure situations. But the toll of playing so many nights (especially after the Devils traded his backup and friend Chris Terreri) and getting so few goals in support (only Ottawa scored fewer goals than the Devils, who averaged a puny 2.6 goals per game) drained him physically and mentally. The fact that he stayed as sharp as he did for as long as he did was a tribute to his skill and mental toughness.

THE INTANGIBLES

Brodeur missed part of training camp in 1995 while renegotiating a new contract. He is worth every cent of the three-year, U.S.$5.2 million the Devils were so reluctant to give him. Following his impressive rookie season in 1993-94, Brodeur never went into the predictable goalie fade that so many young netminders experience, but he will need a dependable backup and some goals from his teammates this season, or his performance may finally suffer. Although he was ignored in the NHL awards balloting, Brodeur is probably the second-best goalie in the NHL right now, bowing only to his idol, Patrick Roy.

NEAL BROTEN

Yrs. of NHL service: 15
Born: Roseau, Minn.; Nov. 29, 1959
Position: centre
Height: 5-9
Weight: 175
Uniform no.: 9
Shoots: left

Career statistics:

GP	G	A	TP	PIM
1057	281	622	903	557

1992-93 statistics:

GP	G	A	TP	+/-	PIM	PP	SH	GW	GT	S	PCT
82	12	21	33	+7	22	0	3	3	0	123	9.8

1993-94 statistics:

GP	G	A	TP	+/-	PIM	PP	SH	GW	GT	S	PCT
79	17	35	52	+10	62	2	1	0	0	153	11.1

1994-95 statistics:

GP	G	A	TP	+/-	PIM	PP	SH	GW	GT	S	PCT
47	8	24	32	+1	24	2	0	3	0	72	11.1

1995-96 statistics:

GP	G	A	TP	+/-	PIM	PP	SH	GW	GT	S	PCT
55	7	16	23	-3	14	1	1	1	0	73	9.6

LAST SEASON

Fewest points scored in career. Missed 20 games with sprained left ankle. Missed one game for disciplinary reasons.

THE FINESSE GAME

With the retirement of Detroit's Mike Ramsey, Broten is the last player from the 1980 U.S. Olympic squad to play in the NHL. He might have one good season left in him before joining his gold medal teammates on the golf course, but it won't be a "good" season unless the Devils do the humane thing and trade Broten back to the Stars organization, where he would like to finish his career.

Broten is one of the game's quiet, intelligent leaders. He no longer has the goods to be bona fide number one or number two centre, but he can certainly play a checking role and also be used to kill penalties and work on the power play. He is very creative in a small amount of space.

Broten is able to play with almost any linemates because of his vision, but it helps to have him paired with at least one young winger with some jump (one of his most effective partners last season was Brian Rolston). Broten is not a speedy skater anymore, but his good hands and quick thinking create passes that put teammates in the open and compensate for his own lack of quickness. Broten also sees the ice surface like a chessboard, backchecks diligently and doesn't gamble, so he is seldom caught scrambling to get back into the play defensively. That makes him an ideal linemate for a younger player who is learning the game.

Broten isn't great on draws, but wins his share and seldom gets beaten outright because he will stick with his opposite number.

THE PHYSICAL GAME

Broten has never been a physical presence, but he will lean on an opponent to slow his progress. Broten keeps his stick down, plays it clean, and while he can be overmatched physically he won't often be outsmarted. His work ethic is unquestioned.

THE INTANGIBLES

Broten has had the best and worst moments of his career in his brief stay in New Jersey. He scored the Stanley Cup-winning goal in 1995, but last season touched off fireworks when he refused to report for a practice called by coach Jacques Lemaire and the veteran center was publicly embarrassed by being benched for the first game after the All-Star break. A severe ankle injury a few weeks later effectively ended his season. Broten should be allowed to finish his career on a prouder note. He can still be a very useful defensive centre.

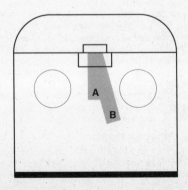

SHAWN CHAMBERS

Yrs. of NHL service: 8
Born: Royal Oaks, Mich.; Oct. 11, 1966
Position: left defense
Height: 6-2
Weight: 200
Uniform no.: 29
Shoots: left

Career statistics:

GP	G	A	TP	PIM
430	42	137	179	297

1992-93 statistics:

GP	G	A	TP	+/-	PIM	PP	SH	GW	GT	S	PCT
55	10	29	39	-21	36	5	0	1	0	152	6.6

1993-94 statistics:

GP	G	A	TP	+/-	PIM	PP	SH	GW	GT	S	PCT
66	11	23	34	-6	23	6	1	1	0	142	7.7

1994-95 statistics:

GP	G	A	TP	+/-	PIM	PP	SH	GW	GT	S	PCT
45	4	17	21	+2	12	2	0	0	0	67	6.0

1995-96 statistics:

GP	G	A	TP	+/-	PIM	PP	SH	GW	GT	S	PCT
64	2	21	23	+1	18	2	0	1	0	112	1.8

LAST SEASON

Missed 13 games with fractured hand. Missed one game with charley horse. Missed four games with shoulder injuries.

THE FINESSE GAME

Chambers quietly developed into the Devils' most underrated defenseman last season. As Scott Stevens's usual partner, Chambers helped shoulder the load against opponents' top lines and did a creditable job. Much of Chambers's success is his ability to understand his limitations and play within them. The ill-advised gambles that plagued his early career are now a rarity.

Working on the Devils' first power play unit, he has an awkward-looking shot, but he manages to get it away quickly, low and on net. He has the poise and the hand skills to be able to fake out a checker with a faux slapper, move to the top of the circle and drill it. Chambers has a nice touch for keeping the puck in along the blueline.

His smarts put him a cut above the rest. Although his finesse skills may be average, he has great anticipation. He understands the game well and knows where the puck is going before the play is made. He does the little things well — little wrist shots, little dump-ins, nothing that shouts out.

Chambers prefers to move the puck out of the zone with a quick pass rather than lug it. His skating isn't dazzling, but he's got some wheels and is more efficient than his style indicates.

THE PHYSICAL GAME

A big defenseman, Chambers was not much of a hitter until he joined the Devils, where the sacrifice was demanded. Confidence in his knee (he underwent arthroscopic surgery in 1993-94) showed with his willingness to play the body. Although he won't put people into the third row of the stands, he will hit often enough and hard enough so that later in a game the puck carrier will move the puck a little faster and maybe get hurried into a mistake. He had a couple of memorable collisions with Eric Lindros during the past two seasons, and while Chambers occasionally emerged a little worse for the wear, he deserves credit for not bailing out. Many do.

He plays with a lot of enthusiasm and is a workhorse. He thrives on ice time and seems to have fun playing the game.

THE INTANGIBLES

The Devils lost Chambers just when they needed him most, during their late-season stretch drive. In the 13 games he missed with a hand fractured by a Vincent Damphousse slash, the Devils went 5-7-1 and ended up missing the playoffs.

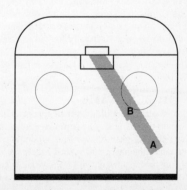

KEN DANEYKO

Yrs. of NHL service: 12
Born: Windsor, Ont.; Apr. 17, 1964
Position: right defense
Height: 6-0
Weight: 210
Uniform no.: 3
Shoots: left

Career statistics:

GP	G	A	TP	PIM
796	30	102	132	2048

1992-93 statistics:

GP	G	A	TP	+/-	PIM	PP	SH	GW	GT	S	PCT
84	2	11	13	+4	236	0	0	0	0	71	2.8

1993-94 statistics:

GP	G	A	TP	+/-	PIM	PP	SH	GW	GT	S	PCT
78	1	9	10	+27	176	0	0	1	0	60	1.7

1994-95 statistics:

GP	G	A	TP	+/-	PIM	PP	SH	GW	GT	S	PCT
25	1	2	3	+4	54	0	0	0	0	19	3.7

1995-96 statistics:

GP	G	A	TP	+/-	PIM	PP	SH	GW	GT	S	PCT
80	2	4	6	-10	115	0	0	0	0	67	3.0

LAST SEASON

Missed two games with flu. Tied for worst plus-minus on team. First Devil to record more than 2,000 PIM.

THE FINESSE GAME

Break down Daneyko's game — average skater, average passer, below-average shooter — and he looks like someone who would have trouble getting ice time. The edge is Daneyko's competitive drive. He will do anything to win a hockey game. Add to that Daneyko's strength and sound hockey sense, and the result is a powerful defensive defenseman who has been coveted by other teams for many years.

Despite his lack of footwork, Daneyko has evolved into one of the team's top penalty killers. He is a good shot-blocker, though he could still use some improvement. When he goes down and fails to block a shot, he does little more than screen his goalie with his burly body.

A Daneyko rush is a rare thing. He's smart enough to recognize his limitations and he seldom joins the play or gets involved deep in the attacking zone. His offensive involvement is usually limited to a smart, safe breakout pass.

Although not a fast skater, Daneyko is fairly agile for his size in tight quarters.

THE PHYSICAL GAME

Daneyko is very powerful, with great upper and lower body strength. His legs give him drive when he's moving opposing forwards out from around the net. He is a punishing hitter, and when he makes a take-out, the opponent stays out of the play. He is smart enough not to get beaten by superior skaters and will force an attacker to the perimeter. He has cut down on his bad penalties; emotions still sometimes get the better of him, but he will usually get his two or five minutes' worth.

Daneyko is a formidable fighter, a player few are willing to tangle with, and he has to prove himself less frequently these days. If somebody wants a scrap, though, he's willing and extremely able, and he stands up for his teammates. It helps that players such as Randy McKay and Reid Simpson are on hand, and Daneyko can spend more time on the ice than in the box.

THE INTANGIBLES

Daneyko can last a few more seasons as a consistent, durable defensive defenseman. His leadership on and off the ice has become even more evident. He will speak up in the dressing room to quell teammates' arguments, and a coach never has to worry about Daneyko being "up" for a game. Off nights are rare, because he knows his limitations and plays well within the boundaries. Daneyko truly takes the game of hockey to heart.

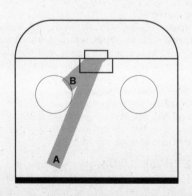

BILL GUERIN

Yrs. of NHL service: 4
Born: Wilbraham, Mass.; Nov. 9, 1970
Position: right wing
Height: 6-2
Weight: 200
Uniform no.: 12
Shoots: right

Career statistics:

GP	G	A	TP	PIM
279	74	83	157	361

1992-93 statistics:

GP	G	A	TP	+/-	PIM	PP	SH	GW	GT	S	PCT
65	14	20	34	+14	63	0	0	2	0	123	11.4

1993-94 statistics:

GP	G	A	TP	+/-	PIM	PP	SH	GW	GT	S	PCT
81	25	19	44	+14	101	2	0	3	0	195	12.8

1994-95 statistics:

GP	G	A	TP	+/-	PIM	PP	SH	GW	GT	S	PCT
48	12	13	25	+6	72	4	0	3	0	96	12.5

1995-96 statistics:

GP	G	A	TP	+/-	PIM	PP	SH	GW	GT	S	PCT
80	23	30	53	+7	116	8	0	6	1	216	10.6

LAST SEASON

Tied for team lead in game-winning goals. Third on team in goals, assists, shots and tied for third in plus-minus. Tied for second on team in plus-minus. Missed two games with flu.

THE FINESSE GAME

Power forwards take a long time to develop, but Guerin has taken longer than most. Half the battle is confidence, which Guerin is gaining bit by bit. The other half is intelligence. Guerin has a terrifying slap shot, a wicked screamer that he unleashes off the wing in full flight. But like a young pitcher who lives off his fastball, he must master the change-up. There are times when a snap or wrist shot is the better choice, especially when he is set up for a one-timer. What he must do is keep driving to the net instead of curling around and looking to make a pass. His speed is a potent weapon.

Combined with Guerin's powerful skating, his shot becomes even more of a potent weapon. He puts on a strong burst of speed and has good balance and agility. He is an excellent passer who leads the man well on a breakout.

Hockey sense and creativity are lagging a tad behind his other attributes, but Guerin is a smart and conscientious player, and those qualities should develop. He is aware defensively and has worked hard at learning that part of the game, although he will still lose his checking assignments and start running around in the defensive zone. Two of Guerin's game-winning goals were scored in overtime last season, which indicates a willingness to keep playing hard no matter what the clock says.

THE PHYSICAL GAME

The more physical the game is, the more Guerin gets involved. He is big, strong and tough in every sense of the word, and frankly, he is useless when he plays the game on the perimeter. He can play it clean or mean, with big body checks or the drop of a glove. He will move to the puck carrier and battle for control until he gets it, and he's hard to knock off his skates.

In front of the net, Guerin is at his best. He works to establish position and has the hand skills to make something happen with the puck when it gets to his stick.

THE INTANGIBLES

This could be the last season the Devils — and we here at *HSR* — wait for the big breakout season from Guerin. One key may be his performance in the World Cup. If Guerin has a strong tournament for Team USA, he could come up with that 30-goal season we keep predicting. If not, he'll be in another jersey before the playoffs because coach Jacques Lemaire's patience is just about at an end.

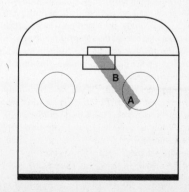

BOBBY HOLIK

Yrs. of NHL service: 6
Born: Jihlava, Czech.; Jan. 1, 1971
Position: centre
Height: 6-3
Weight: 220
Uniform no.: 16
Shoots: right

Career statistics:

GP	G	A	TP	PIM
396	98	112	210	381

1992-93 statistics:

GP	G	A	TP	+/-	PIM	PP	SH	GW	GT	S	PCT
61	20	19	39	-6	76	7	0	4	0	180	11.1

1993-94 statistics:

GP	G	A	TP	+/-	PIM	PP	SH	GW	GT	S	PCT
70	13	20	33	+28	72	2	0	3	0	130	10.0

1994-95 statistics:

GP	G	A	TP	+/-	PIM	PP	SH	GW	GT	S	PCT
48	10	10	20	+9	18	0	0	2	0	84	11.9

1995-96 statistics:

GP	G	A	TP	+/-	PIM	PP	SH	GW	GT	S	PCT
63	13	17	30	+9	58	1	0	1	1	157	8.3

LAST SEASON

Missed 13 games with fractured index finger. Missed six games with sprained ankle. Tied for team lead in plus-minus.

THE FINESSE GAME

The Crash Line fell to earth last season. Holik and linemates Randy McKay and Mike Peluso were injured for long stretches at different times, and the chemistry that helped make them the best fourth line in hockey in the team's Stanley Cup season was never recaptured.

Holik is a far more effective player with his two usual mates. Put him with anyone else on the team and his power and usefulness are diminished. While he is a strong skater with some passing skills and a hard, if often inaccurate, shot, he suffers from severe tunnel vision.

Holik has a terrific shot, a bullet drive that he gets away quickly from a rush down the left side. He also has the great hands to work in tight, in traffic and off the backhand. On the backhand (at which Europeans are so much more adept than North Americans), Holik uses his great bulk to obscure the vision of his defenders, protecting the puck and masking his intentions. He has a fair wrist shot.

Playing centre (Holik played the position almost exclusively last season after spins on the wing the previous few years) gets Holik more consistently involved. While he lacks the creativity to be a truly effective centre, he brings other assets to the table. He crashes the net and is a scary forechecker.

Although he's a powerful skater with good balance, Holik lacks jump and agility. Once he starts churning, he can get up a good head of steam, but he can be caught out of position. He has become more responsible defensively.

THE PHYSICAL GAME

Holik is just plain big, and his linemates have helped light a fire in him that brings out his best on a nightly basis. Never given much credit for being an intelligent player, he has adapted to the defensive style of the Devils and is reliable to the point that Jacques Lemaire is never afraid to throw his fourth line out on the ice in most situations.

Holik is a serious hitter and applies his bone-jarring body checks at the appropriate times. He takes few bad penalties.

THE INTANGIBLES

Holik remains a consistent forward who will never wander much above the 40-point mark. He has become a more confident player and team leader. He suffered one of the stranger injuries of last season, spraining his ankle while playing Ping-Pong.

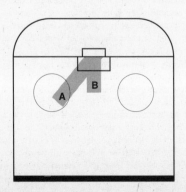

JOHN MACLEAN

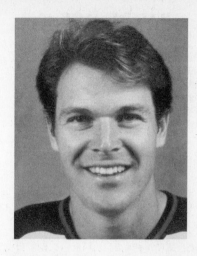

Yrs. of NHL service: 12
Born: Oshawa, Ont.; Nov. 20, 1964
Position: right wing
Height: 6-0
Weight: 200
Uniform no.: 15
Shoots: right

Career statistics
GP	G	A	TP	PIM
782	298	309	607	1073

1992-93 statistics:
GP	G	A	TP	+/-	PIM	PP	SH	GW	GT	S	PCT
80	24	24	48	-6	102	7	1	3	0	195	12.3

1993-94 statistics:
GP	G	A	TP	+/-	PIM	PP	SH	GW	GT	S	PCT
80	37	33	70	+30	95	8	0	4	0	277	13.4

1994-95 statistics:
GP	G	A	TP	+/-	PIM	PP	SH	GW	GT	S	PCT
46	17	12	29	+13	32	2	1	0	0	139	12.2

1995-96 statistics:
GP	G	A	TP	+/-	PIM	PP	SH	GW	GT	S	PCT
76	20	28	48	+3	91	3	3	3	0	237	8.4

LAST SEASON
Second on team in shots and shorthanded goals. Fifth on team in points. Missed six games with arthroscopic knee surgery.

THE FINESSE GAME
There is no such thing as an impossible angle for MacLean. He will shoot anytime, from anywhere on the ice, and will usually put the puck on net or out into traffic in front of the crease where there is always a chance the puck will hit someone or something and go skittering into the net. So what if all of his scoring chances are no longer the brilliant highlight shots that characterized his pre-surgery (1991) career? His pure goal-scoring instincts still make MacLean a threat.

But last season he was less of a threat than usual, even joking about becoming a Selke Trophy candidate. MacLean was given duty as one of the two forwards on the top penalty-killing unit and played a predominantly checking role (and what Devil doesn't?). MacLean lacks the speed to be an effective shadow against the league's faster forwards, but he is an intelligent player positionally and harasses puck carriers into clumsy passes with his forechecking. He pressures the points when killing penalties.

Slow in open ice but strong along the boards and in the corners, he chugs and churns, and by keeping his feet in motion he draws restraining fouls. Somehow, MacLean gets to where he has to go, but his wheels are average on a good night.

THE PHYSICAL GAME
MacLean uses a wide-based skating stance and is tough to budge from the front of the net. He will take a lot of abuse to get the job done in traffic, and will not be intimidated. He has cut down on his retaliatory penalties. He is extremely competitive.

Last season's surgery took place on the same knee that was reconstructed in 1991, but was supposedly unrelated to the original injury. Wear and tear is catching up with him, however.

THE INTANGIBLES
MacLean's big-number days are over as he has become more of a two-way forward, but he can still kick in 25 goals a season and is a strong presence in the dressing room. His recovery from knee surgery is an inspiration to younger teammates such as Jason Smith, who made a similar recovery last season.

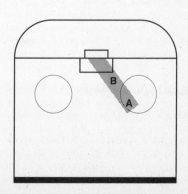

RANDY MCKAY

Yrs. of NHL service: 7
Born: Montreal, Que.; Jan. 25, 1967
Position: right wing
Height: 6-1
Weight: 205
Uniform no.: 21
Shoots: right

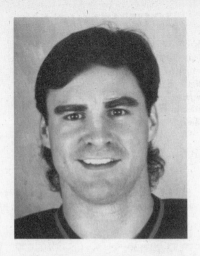

Career statistics:

GP	G	A	TP	PIM
423	60	72	132	1119

1992-93 statistics:

GP	G	A	TP	+/-	PIM	PP	SH	GW	GT	S	PCT
73	11	11	22	0	206	1	0	2	0	94	11.7

1993-94 statistics:

GP	G	A	TP	+/-	PIM	PP	SH	GW	GT	S	PCT
78	12	15	27	+24	244	0	0	1	1	77	15.6

1994-95 statistics:

GP	G	A	TP	+/-	PIM	PP	SH	GW	GT	S	PCT
33	5	7	12	+10	44	0	0	0	0	44	11.4

1995-96 statistics:

GP	G	A	TP	+/-	PIM	PP	SH	GW	GT	S	PCT
76	11	10	21	+7	145	3	0	3	1	97	11.3

LAST SEASON

Missed one game with flu. Missed five games with concussion. Tied for third on team in plus-minus.

THE FINESSE GAME

As part of the popular and hugely effective Crash Line, (with Mike Peluso and Bobby Holik), McKay helped wake up the Devils on some of their doleful regular-season nights. McKay never cruises through a game. His reputation earns him extra ice and extra time, and he makes use of both. He has worked hard to improve his shooting and passing skills. But injuries to McKay, Holik and Peluso prevented the line from working the same kind of magic it did in the Devils' Stanley Cup season.

McKay is one of those rare tough guys who has enough skills to make himself a useful player in other areas, including the power play. He has the ability to beat a defender one-on-one by setting his skates wide, dangling the puck, then drawing it through the defenseman's legs and blowing past him for a shot.

McKay is also alert enough to find a linemate with a pass. He doesn't have great hockey vision, but he doesn't keep his eyes glued to the puck, either. Still, most of his points come from driving to the net.

THE PHYSICAL GAME

McKay is an absolutely ferocious fighter. He is a legitimate heavyweight who is among the first to step in to protect a teammate, yet he won't initiate with cheap nonsense. He does everything with intensity, whether it's a body check or bulling his way to the front of the net. He is astoundingly strong on his skates, tough to knock down and nearly impossible to knock out (al-

though linemate Peluso did so with an accidental skate to the face that resulted in a broken nose and concussion for McKay in midseason).

THE INTANGIBLES

McKay makes everyone around him braver. He will leap to the defense of a teammate, yet he seldom gets involved in histrionics. He picks his spots and doesn't hurt his team by being selfish. Throw in 10-15 goals and he is invaluable. Coaches never have to worry about McKay being up for a game.

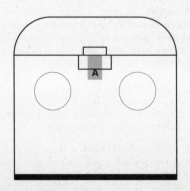

SCOTT NIEDERMAYER

Yrs. of NHL service: 4
Born: Edmonton, Alta.; Aug. 31, 1973
Position: right defense
Height: 6-0
Weight: 200
Uniform no.: 27
Shoots: left

Career statistics:

GP	G	A	TP	PIM
292	33	106	139	155

1992-93 statistics:

GP	G	A	TP	+/-	PIM	PP	SH	GW	GT	S	PCT
80	11	29	40	+8	47	5	0	0	1	131	8.4

1993-94 statistics:

GP	G	A	TP	+/-	PIM	PP	SH	GW	GT	S	PCT
81	10	36	46	+34	42	5	0	2	1	135	7.4

1994-95 statistics:

GP	G	A	TP	+/-	PIM	PP	SH	GW	GT	S	PCT
48	4	15	19	+19	18	4	0	0	0	52	7.7

1995-96 statistics:

GP	G	A	TP	+/-	PIM	PP	SH	GW	GT	S	PCT
79	8	25	33	+5	46	6	0	0	0	179	4.5

LAST SEASON

Second among team defensemen in scoring. Missed three games with knee injury.

THE FINESSE GAME

Coach Jacques Lemaire has been blamed for cementing Niedermayer to the blueline and restricting his offensive instincts, and there is some truth to that. The joke was that when Niedermayer took his first career penalty shot last season, he failed because he was worried about getting back defensively. Niedermayer did not step forward from his outstanding 1995 playoffs to become the kind of force that many of us have been anticipating. Much of last season, Niedermayer took a step back.

Niedermayer has often been compared to Paul Coffey because of his phenomenal skating, but the comparison is not really apt. Niedermayer will never be the offensive force that Coffey is, but he is a better defensive player than Coffey is, or ever was.

Niedermayer carries the puck well on the rush, but is still learning to create offensive chances by using his speed in the attacking zone. Niedermayer played some of his best hockey last season after Phil Housley joined the team. Housley has the confidence to leap into the attack that Niedermayer lacks, and the association, although brief, helped Niedermayer's game.

The 23-year-old is an exceptional skater, one of the best-skating defensemen in the NHL. Niedermayer has it all: speed, balance, agility, mobility, lateral movement and strength. He has unbelievable edge for turns and eluding pursuers. Even when he makes a commitment mistake in the offensive zone, he can get back so quickly his defense partner is seldom outnumbered.

THE PHYSICAL GAME

An underrated body checker because of the focus on the glitzier parts of his game, Niedermayer has continued to improve his strength and is a willing, if not vicious, hitter. His skating ability helps him tremendously, giving more impetus to his open-ice checks. He will sacrifice his body to block shots.

THE INTANGIBLES

After a training camp holdout, Niedermayer (a Group Two free agent) saw his salary jump from U.S.$250,000 to just over $2 million last season. Rumours about potential trades continue to rustle around Niedermayer, who has let it be known he would not be crushed to leave the Devils.

On a less defensive-minded team, Niedermayer would probably net 70 points, but whether he likes it or not, his tutelage under Lemaire will end up making him a more superior all-around defenseman than if he had just been allowed to roam at will in his first few NHL seasons. The question is how long will the Devils wait before turning him loose, on the ice or off?

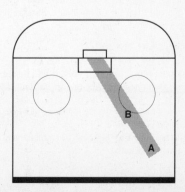

DENIS PEDERSON

Yrs. of NHL service: 0
Born: Prince Albert, Sask.; Sept. 10, 1975
Position: centre
Height: 6-2
Weight: 190
Uniform no.: 10
Shoots: right

Career statistics:

GP	G	A	TP	PIM
10	3	1	4	0

1995-96 statistics:

GP	G	A	TP	+/-	PIM	PP	SH	GW	GT	S	PCT
10	3	1	4	-1	0	1	0	2	0	6	50.0

LAST SEASON

Will be entering first NHL season. Fourth in scoring for Albany (AHL), with 28-43 — 71 in 68 games.

THE FINESSE GAME

Pederson is a very intelligent hockey player who has the potential to develop into a solid two-way centre. His skills aren't elite level, but he makes the most of all of his abilities with his hockey sense.

Pederson has been groomed as a defensive forward by the Devils, but try as they might, they can't wring the offensive production out of his game. Pederson scored 98 points in junior with Prince Albert in 1993-94, so he knows his way around the net.

Pederson can work on the power play, where he uses his size down low and crashes the net. He works well in traffic, and has nice hands for picking the puck out of a tangle of skates and sticks. Pederson is a puck magnet because he gives a second and third effort and the puck always seems to end up on his stick. He has a decent array of shots, including a backhand, but will get most of his goals from thrashing around the crease.

THE PHYSICAL GAME

Pederson is strong and competes hard for the puck. He has a little mean streak in him, enough to keep his opponents on their toes, and he will come unglued once in awhile. But for the most part he is disciplined and does not take lazy penalties.

THE INTANGIBLES

Pederson is very close to an NHL job and if he does not start the season in New Jersey, it will be because the team hasn't decided what to do with Neal Broten, because it's Broten's slot that Pederson should inherit. If he gets a full-time role, we would expect Pederson to score 20 goals while serving a largely defensive role. He is a character guy who is a quiet leader and his work ethic is sound.

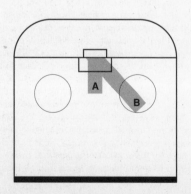

STEPHANE RICHER

Yrs. of NHL service: 11
Born: Ripon, Que.; June 7, 1966
Position: right wing
Height: 6-2
Weight: 215
Uniform no.: 44
Shoots: right

Career statistics:

GP	G	A	TP	PIM
763	344	302	646	487

1992-93 statistics:

GP	G	A	TP	+/-	PIM	PP	SH	GW	GT	S	PCT
78	38	35	73	-1	44	7	1	7	1	286	13.3

1993-94 statistics:

GP	G	A	TP	+/-	PIM	PP	SH	GW	GT	S	PCT
80	36	36	72	+31	16	7	3	9	3	217	16.6

1994-95 statistics:

GP	G	A	TP	+/-	PIM	PP	SH	GW	GT	S	PCT
45	23	16	39	+8	10	1	2	5	1	133	17.3

1995-96 statistics:

GP	G	A	TP	+/-	PIM	PP	SH	GW	GT	S	PCT
73	20	12	32	-8	30	3	4	3	0	192	10.4

LAST SEASON

Led team in shorthanded goals. Missed seven games with wrist injury. Missed one game with flu. Lowest point production of career.

THE FINESSE GAME

We said in last year's *HSR* that Richer's days as a 50-goal scorer were well behind him. We had no idea his days as a 20-goal scorer were in jeopardy.

The ever-enigmatic Richer was at his most puzzling last season. His size, speed and shot still seemed to be in attendance, but he was never the dangerous game-breaker that he had been the past four seasons with the Devils. Richer seemed to be content to be a defensive specialist, which hints at a loss of mental toughness instead of a deterioration of physical skills.

Richer gets great drive from his legs. He has powerful acceleration and true rink-length speed. He can intimidate with his rush, opening up the ice for himself and his linemates. He can also be crafty, slipping in and out of the open ice. He has very good vision offensively and keen hockey sense. Richer possesses a true goal-scorer's slap shot, a wicked blur that he will fire from the tops of the circles.

A player with Richer's abilities should be more successful on the power play, but he has not hit double figures in five seasons and saw only limited power play time again last season. It is coach Jacques Lemaire's contention that Richer does not bear down as hard during manpower advantages. He has become a fine penalty killer, but that should enhance his value as a hockey player, and not be the sum total of it. Richer is probably a better all-around player now than at any other point in his career, but is that worth the sacrifice of 20 goals a season?

Because Richer is so strong on his stick and has a long reach, he can strip an opponent of the puck when his body isn't even close, and the puck carrier is always surprised.

THE PHYSICAL GAME

Richer is much better in open ice than in traffic. Although he has the size, strength and balance for trench warfare, he doesn't always show the inclination. He will go to the net with the puck, though, and has a wonderful long reach that allows him to be checked and still whip off a strong shot on net. When Richer is determined, it is just about impossible to peel him off the puck. He is slow to rile and seldom takes bad penalties.

THE INTANGIBLES

The Stanley Cup champion Devils missed the playoffs last season, and Richer was singled out as one of the major reasons why the team failed to get a chance to defend its title. As the team broke up at the end of the season, Richer was sure he would be with a new team come October. We are, too. With a less defensive-minded team, he might hit 30 again.

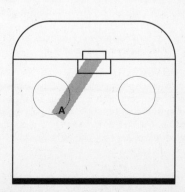

BRIAN ROLSTON

Yrs. of NHL service: 2
Born: Flint, Mich.; Feb. 21, 1973
Position: centre/left wing
Height: 6-2
Weight: 185
Uniform no.: 14
Shoots: left

Career statistics:

GP	G	A	TP	PIM
98	20	22	42	25

1994-95 statistics:

GP	G	A	TP	+/-	PIM	PP	SH	GW	GT	S	PCT
40	7	11	18	+5	17	2	0	3	0	92	7.6

1995-96 statistics:

GP	G	A	TP	+/-	PIM	PP	SH	GW	GT	S	PCT
58	13	11	24	+9	8	3	1	4	1	139	9.4

LAST SEASON

Tied for team lead in plus-minus. Third on team in game-winning goals. Missed 11 games with fractured foot.

THE FINESSE GAME

Rolston's game is speed. He is a fast, powerful skater who drives to the net and loves to shoot. He passes well forehand and backhand, and reads breakout plays by leading his man smartly. He's better as a shooter, though. He has a cannon from the top of the circles in with a quick release. He tends to hurry his shots, even when he has time to wait, but that may improve as he becomes more comfortable and relaxed. His anticipation is excellent, and so is his attitude. No one has to worry about Rolston being up for a game.

Rolston has a history of clutch moments. He scored the NCAA championship goal for Lake Superior State as a freshman, and was one of the top U.S. performers at the 1994 Olympics and at the 1996 World Championships. Seven of his 20 career NHL goals have been game-winners.

As is usual with young players, Rolston needs schooling on the defensive responsibilities of a centre (he has one of the best to learn from in coach Jacques Lemaire, but Lemaire appears to have little trust in Rolston's overall game). He is a diligent penalty killer.

Rolston should earn more power play time. He is smart with the puck with the extra man.

THE PHYSICAL GAME

Rolston will take a hit to make a play, and he has taken the next step to start initiating to fight for pucks. His lack of toughness and tenacity were a concern, but he has indicated he can't be kicked around. Rolston is no tough guy, but he has good size and balance.

THE INTANGIBLES

Rolston played the best hockey of his career when he helped Team USA win the bronze at the 1996 World Hockey Championships. Rolston played centre and was given a great deal of ice time and responsibility, and he was a different player than the lost sophomore in the Devils' dressing room.

Rolston has a big upside and it could come as early as this season. Adding Robbie Ftorek as an assistant coach will be a huge boon to Rolston's shaky confidence. If the Devils play him at centre, they will get a much better player than the erratic left wing they watched last season. Rolston could be a 30-goal scorer if utilized well this season. We target him as one of the potential surprises of 1996-97.

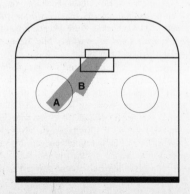

JASON SMITH

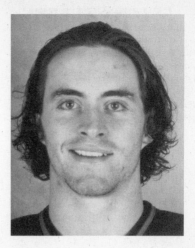

Yrs. of NHL service: 3
Born: Calgary, Alta.; Nov. 2, 1973
Position: right defense
Height: 6-3
Weight: 205
Uniform no.: 26
Shoots: right

Career statistics:

GP	G	A	TP	PIM
107	2	1	3	129

1993-94 statistics:

GP	G	A	TP	+/-	PIM	PP	SH	GW	GT	S	PCT
41	0	5	5	+7	43	0	0	0	0	47	0.0

1994-95 statistics:

GP	G	A	TP	+/-	PIM	PP	SH	GW	GT	S	PCT
2	0	0	0	-3	0	0	0	0	0	5	0.0

1995-96 statistics:

GP	G	A	TP	+/-	PIM	PP	SH	GW	GT	S	PCT
64	2	1	3	+5	86	0	0	0	0	52	3.8

LAST SEASON

Missed 15 games with bruised hand.

THE FINESSE GAME

Smith won't make anyone forget Brian Leetch. After all, the only full-time member of the Devils he edged on the scoresheet was goalie Martin Brodeur. His first career NHL goal was scored into an empty net, and that is about the extent of his scoring prowess. He has a fairly heavy shot, but it has little movement on it. Smith is not very creative offensively and doesn't gamble.

Smith has a very low-key personality and will never be the kind of defenseman who can control a game. Knee surgery has affected his skating somewhat, but he has better than average speed and fair mobility. He can be erratic in his defensive reads, but was showing improvement late in the season and that weakness may become less of a liability.

Smith did little penalty killing last season, probably due to his lack of foot speed, and in order to move up on the depth chart will need to be able to contribute in this area. He is very strong on his skates.

Smith works well paired with an offensive defenseman (his partner in the last quarter of the season was Phil Housley), since Smith does the stay-at-home job and allows his partner some freedom.

THE PHYSICAL GAME

Smith made a speedy recovery from reconstructive knee surgery, but at the start of last season was hesitant to make hits because he was afraid of testing the knee. Just a few weeks into the season, he gained confidence, and diligent daily maintenance prevented the knee from being a problem, mentally or physically.

Smith is a solid hitter with a latent mean streak, and his take-outs are effective along the boards and in front of the net. He is not as good in open ice because his mobility is not exceptional. He has a fairly long fuse but is a capable fighter once he gets the hair out of his eyes (Smith tends to let it get a little long).

THE INTANGIBLES

This will be the year that determines which direction Smith's career will go. He ended the season as the number five defenseman, but he could move into the top four. He is the heir apparent to Ken Daneyko's defensive defenseman role but it remains to be seen if he can be that same kind of reliable, crunch-time player.

SCOTT STEVENS

Yrs. of NHL service: 14
Born: Kitchener, Ont.; Apr. 1, 1964
Position: left defense
Height: 6-2
Weight: 215
Uniform no.: 4
Shoots: left

Career statistics:

GP	G	A	TP	PIM
1041	157	565	722	2290

1992-93 statistics:

GP	G	A	TP	+/-	PIM	PP	SH	GW	GT	S	PCT
81	12	45	57	+14	120	8	0	1	0	146	8.2

1993-94 statistics:

GP	G	A	TP	+/-	PIM	PP	SH	GW	GT	S	PCT
83	18	60	78	+53	112	5	1	4	0	215	8.4

1994-95 statistics:

GP	G	A	TP	+/-	PIM	PP	SH	GW	GT	S	PCT
48	2	20	22	+4	56	1	0	1	0	111	1.8

1995-96 statistics:

GP	G	A	TP	+/-	PIM	PP	SH	GW	GT	S	PCT
82	5	23	28	+7	100	2	1	1	0	174	2.9

LAST SEASON

Only Devil to appear in all 82 games. Tied for third on team in plus-minus. Led team defensemen in plus-minus.

THE FINESSE GAME

Throughout most of his career, Stevens has been a hybrid defenseman who contributes offensively as well as producing in his own end. Perhaps because of the Devils' emphasis on defense-first, Stevens's game has become ever more tilted towards the defensive aspect of the game in the past two seasons.

Stevens has a nice pair of hands for work in close to the net. He usually stays out at the point, and does a good job by taking something off his drive instead of spraying wild, untippable slap shots, but his release is a little slow.

A very good skater, secure and strong, he is capable both forwards and backwards and has good lateral mobility. He has to battle a tendency to overhandle the puck in the defensive zone.

Stevens has a tremendous work ethic that more than makes up for some of his shortcomings (and most of those are sins of commission rather than omission). He is a bear on penalty killing because he just won't quit, but sometimes he is unable to make a simple bank off the boards to clear the puck and keeps his team pinned in. Stevens is a fearless shot blocker.

THE PHYSICAL GAME

The most punishing open-ice hitter in the NHL, Stevens has the skating ability to line up the puck-carrier, and the size and strength to explode on impact. He simply shovels most opponents out from in front of the net and crunches them along the boards. Stevens is one of the few NHL defensemen willing and able to tackle Eric Lindros head-on. Most of Stevens's best games occur against the Flyers because he thrives on the challenge.

Stevens fights well when provoked and other teams make a point of trying to lure him into bad penalties. He has matured and is now able to keep a tighter lid on his temper.

THE INTANGIBLES

Stevens's hefty contract could be his ticket out of New Jersey this season. It would be a gamble, because the Devils are happy with his play and his leadership, but they might want to move him while he still has high trade value and two years remaining on a contract that pays him over U.S.$4 million annually. He is a proud warrior who never fails to show up at the rink ready to play, and the younger defensemen on the club can learn from playing with him.

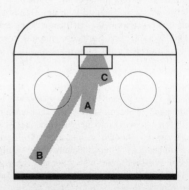

PETR SYKORA

Yrs. of NHL service: 1
Born: Plzen, Czech.; Nov. 19, 1976
Position: centre
Height: 5-11
Weight: 183
Uniform no.: 17
Shoots: left

Career statistics:

GP	G	A	TP	PIM
63	18	24	42	32

1995-96 statistics:

GP	G	A	TP	+/-	PIM	PP	SH	GW	GT	S	PCT
63	18	24	42	+7	32	8	0	3	0	128	14.1

LAST SEASON

First NHL season. Named to NHL All-Rookie team. Tied for sixth among NHL rookies in points. Fifth among rookies in assists. Tied for rookie lead in power play goals. Led team in shooting percentage. Tied for second on team in power play goals. Missed two games with back injury.

THE FINESSE GAME

There are only a few things Sykora doesn't do well technically, but what really sets him apart from other 19-year-old rookies is his intelligence. Playing against men as a 17-year-old in the IHL in 1994-95 obviously spurred Sykora's development, and taught him how to survive as a smaller player in the mean NHL.

Sykora is a fine skater. He has a fluid stride and accelerates in a few steps. He is quick on a straight-away, with or without the puck, and is also agile in his turns. He picks his way through traffic well, and would rather try to outfox a defender and take the shortest path to the net than try to drive wide.

Sykora has excellent hands in tight, for passing or shooting. He defies the usual European stereotype of the reluctant shooter because he's a goal scorer, but he does tend to pass up a low-percentage shot to work for a better one. His wrist shot is excellent but he also has an adequate snap and slap shot.

He sees the ice well and is a heads-up passer with a great touch. He needs to improve on his face-offs.

THE PHYSICAL GAME

Sykora won't be intimidated. He'll battle for the puck behind or in front of the net but he is simply not a big or mean player. He is strong for his size and his skating provides him with good balance. His work ethic is strong.

THE INTANGIBLES

The Devils didn't think Sykora would be in the team's plans last season, but Sykora thought differently; after a brief stint in the minors he joined the club for good in late October. Sykora wore down physically and mentally late in the season, finding his first taste of the extensive NHL schedule difficult to handle. He should be more consistent this season.

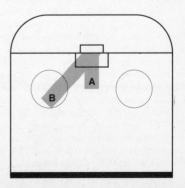

STEVE THOMAS

Yrs. of NHL service: 12
Born: Stockport, England; July 15, 1963
Position: left wing
Height: 5-11
Weight: 185
Uniform no.: 32
Shoots: left

Career statistics:

GP	G	A	TP	PIM
748	295	343	638	986

1992-93 statistics:

GP	G	A	TP	+/-	PIM	PP	SH	GW	GT	S	PCT
79	37	50	87	+3	111	12	0	7	0	264	14.0

1993-94 statistics:

GP	G	A	TP	+/-	PIM	PP	SH	GW	GT	S	PCT
78	42	33	75	-9	139	17	0	5	2	249	16.9

1994-95 statistics:

GP	G	A	TP	+/-	PIM	PP	SH	GW	GT	S	PCT
47	11	15	26	-14	60	3	0	2	0	133	8.3

1995-96 statistics:

GP	G	A	TP	+/-	PIM	PP	SH	GW	GT	S	PCT
81	26	35	61	-2	98	6	0	6	1	192	13.5

LAST SEASON

Acquired from the Islanders for Claude Lemieux, October 3, 1995. Tied for team lead in game-winning goals. One of two NHL players (with Paul Kariya) to score three overtime goals. Second on team in goals, assists, points and shooting percentage. Missed one game with head injury.

THE FINESSE GAME

Thomas wasn't quite the powerful offensive force the Devils had hoped for in return for trading away their nettlesome 1995 Conn Smythe Trophy winner. Not all of this was Thomas's fault. He did miss most of training camp as a Group 2 free agent, but when he was ready to get back in gear the Devils played him nearly the entire season on the "wrong" (left) side. While he is a left-handed shooter, Thomas has always been a more effective player on the right wing.

Thomas has a great shot and he loves to fire away. He will look to shoot first instead of pass, sometimes to his detriment, but subtlety is not his forte. His game is speed and power.

He has a strong wrist shot and an excellent one-timer. He likes to win the battle for the puck in deep, feed his centre, then head for the right circle for the return pass. Playing the left side he was not as effective. Thomas has a very short backswing, which allows him to get his shots away quickly.

Thomas is a wildly intense player. His speed is straight ahead, without much deking or trying to put a move on a defender. He works along the boards and in the corners, willing to do the dirty work. He works hard and has the knack for scoring big goals.

THE PHYSICAL GAME

Thomas is hard-nosed and finishes his checks. He is a very good forechecker because he comes at the puck carrier like a human train. He is not big, but he is wide, and tough. He is great along the boards and among the best in the league (with Kirk Muller and Peter Zezel) at keeping the puck alive by using his feet. He is a feisty and fierce competitor and will throw the odd punch. On the occasions when he drops his gloves, Thomas can hold his own.

THE INTANGIBLES

Thomas, who tends to be a streaky scorer, shouldered the brunt of what was a disappointing season for the Devils. While he worked well with rookie Petr Sykora and right wing Bill Guerin on the team's top line last year, it would help Thomas to be moved back to the right side.

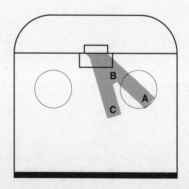

NEW YORK ISLANDERS

Players' Statistics 1995-96

POS	NO	PLAYER	GP	G	A	PTS	+/-	PIM	PP	SH	GW	GT	S	PCT
R	16	ZIGMUND PALFFY	81	43	44	87	-17	56	17	1	6		257	16.7
C	39	TRAVIS GREEN	69	24	45	69	-21	42	14	1	2	1	186	12.9
L	18	MARTY MCINNIS	74	12	34	46	-11	39	2		1		167	7.2
R	44	*TODD BERTUZZI	76	18	21	39	-14	83	4		2		127	14.2
C	28	ALEXANDER SEMAK	69	20	14	34	-4	68	6		2	1	128	15.6
L	27	DEREK KING	61	12	20	32	-10	23	5	1		1	154	7.8
D	3	KENNY JONSSON	66	4	26	30	7	32	3		1		130	3.1
L	32	*NIKLAS ANDERSSON	48	14	12	26	-3	12	3	2	1		89	15.7
D	4	*BRYAN MCCABE	82	7	16	23	-24	156	3		1		130	5.4
R	26	PATRICK FLATLEY	56	8	9	17	-24	21					89	9.0
C	17	*DARBY HENDRICKSON	62	7	10	17	-8	80			1		73	9.6
D	7	SCOTT LACHANCE	55	3	10	13	-19	54	1				81	3.7
D	6	CHRIS LUONGO	74	3	7	10	-23	55	1				46	6.5
L	25	PAT CONACHER	55	6	3	9	-13	18		1	2		45	13.3
D	24	BRENT SEVERYN	65	1	8	9	3	180					40	2.5
R	21	*DAN PLANTE	73	5	3	8	-22	50		2			103	4.9
D	11	DARIUS KASPARAITIS	46	1	7	8	-12	93					34	2.9
L	34	*ANDREY VASILYEV	10	2	5	7	4	2			1		12	16.7
D	37	DENNIS VASKE	19	1	6	7	-13	21	1		1		19	5.3
D	2	BOB BEERS	13		5	5	-2	10					9	
C	14	*DEREK ARMSTRONG	19	1	3	4	-6	14					23	4.3
D	33	*MILAN TICHY	8		4	4	3	8					6	
R	15	BRAD DALGARNO	18	1	2	3	-2	14					11	9.1
R	75	BRETT LINDROS	18	1	2	3	-6	47					10	10.0
D	47	RICHARD PILON	27		3	3	-9	72					7	
C	38	*ANDREAS JOHANSSON	3	1	1	2	2						6	16.7
R	12	MICK VUKOTA	33	1	1	2	-3	106					11	9.1
C	10	*CRAIG DARBY	10		2	2	-1						1	
D	34	*JASON HERTER	1		1	1	1						1	
C	43	*CHRIS TAYLOR	11		1	1	1	2					4	
C	36	MICAH AIVAZOFF	12		1	1	-6	6					8	
L	34	*JARRETT DEULING	14		1	1	-1	11					11	
G	1	*ERIC FICHAUD	24		1	1	0							
D	36	*JASON STRUDWICK	1				0	7						
L	32	GRIGORI PANTELEEV	4				-3						1	
D	34	*JASON WIDMER	4				0	7					1	
C	43	MICHAEL MACWILLIAM	6				-1	14					4	
L	33	*KEN BELANGER	7				-2	27						
D	36	BOB HALKIDIS	8				-4	37					2	
G	35	*TOMMY SALO	10				0							
G	29	JAMIE MCLENNAN	13				0	2						
G	30	TOMMY SODERSTROM	51				0	7						

GP = games played; G = goals; A = assists; PTS = points; +/- = goals-for minus goals-against while player is on ice; PIM = penalties in minutes; PP = power play goals; SH = shorthanded goals; GW = game-winning goals; GT = game-tying goals; S = no. of shots; PCT = percentage of goals to shots; * = rookie

NIKLAS ANDERSSON

Yrs. of NHL service: 1
Born: Kungalv, Sweden; May 20, 1971
Position: left wing
Height: 5-9
Weight: 175
Uniform no.: 32
Shoots: left

Career statistics:

GP	G	A	TP	PIM
51	14	13	27	14

1995-96 statistics:

GP	G	A	TP	+/-	PIM	PP	SH	GW	GT	S	PCT
48	14	12	26	-3	12	3	2	1	0	89	15.7

LAST SEASON

First NHL season. Led team in shorthanded goals. One of only four rookies to score a hat trick. Played 30 games with Utah (IHL), scoring 13-22 — 35.

THE FINESSE GAME

If you threw Mats Sundin in the dryer for an hour on a "hot" setting, Andersson would tumble out.

Andersson is small and quick, with good offensive instincts. His unexpected scoring outburst was one of the few good things to happen to the Islanders last season, along with the announcement that they were abandoning their fisherman logo.

Andersson has always been noted for his fine passing skills. He creates with his speed, then dishes off on the forehand or backhand with accuracy. Andersson is less reluctant about shooting, and has a quick release on his wrist shot. His speed and anticipation make him a good penalty killer.

THE PHYSICAL GAME

Andersson isn't thickly built, as a lot of successful small NHL players are, and he really has to keep his feet moving to steer clear of trouble. He can handle the puck in traffic.

THE INTANGIBLES

You would have needed binoculars to find Andersson on the Islanders' depth chart at training camp last season, but a rash of injuries prompted his December call-up from Utah and Andersson took off. He has earned a shot in training this year, but his lack of size is a major drawback. There is the question of whether he can survive the rigors of a full NHL schedule.

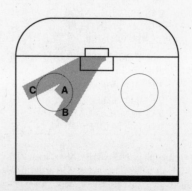

BRYAN BERARD

Yrs. of NHL service: 0
Born: Woonsocket, R.I.; March 5, 1977
Position: left defense
Height: 6-1
Weight: 190
Uniform no.: n.a.
Shoots: left

Career junior statistics:

GP	G	A	TP	PIM
114	51	112	163	213

1994-95 statistics:

GP	G	A	TP	PIM
58	20	54	74	97

1995-96 statistics:

GP	G	A	TP	PIM
56	31	58	89	116

LAST SEASON

Rights acquired from Ottawa in three-way trade with Toronto involving Kirk Muller, Jan. 23, 1996. Named CHL's Top Defenseman. Third on team in scoring for Detroit (OHL).

THE FINESSE GAME

Berard is a sleek, swift attacking defenseman, a joy to watch because of his speedy yet effortless skating style. He loves to rush with the puck, but like New Jersey's Scott Niedermayer he is so quick to recover from any counterattack that he's usually back in a defensive posture in no time. He is seldom caught out of position.

Berard carries the puck with confidence and does not panic under pressure. His show is low and accurate. He is also a fine passer. With his combination of skills and intelligence he can control the tempo of a game.

Berard is an excellent two-way defenseman. He does not neglect his duties in his own zone. He takes pride in his complete game.

THE PHYSICAL GAME

While not overly physical, Berard has shown a willingness to use his body to slow people down. He is also very good using his stick to poke-check or break up passes, and opponents would be wise not to make cross-ice passes high in the attacking zone or he will easily step up and pick them off. He tends to run around and try to do too much sometimes, but coaches prefer sins of commission to sins of omission.

THE INTANGIBLES

Berard is playing hardball with the Islanders over his contract (there is a rookie salary cap of U.S.$850,000, but bonuses and incentives could total over $2 million). Berard is eager to play in the NHL, and if they can come to terms he will get plenty of playing time with a team that is in desperate need of defensive and scoring help. Berard could provide both. It's been a long time since the Islanders have had a legitimate offensive defenseman (since Denis Potvin's era). Berard, along with Kenny Jonsson and Bryan McCabe, should provide a solid nucleus.

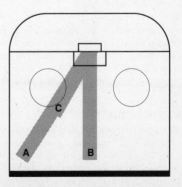

TODD BERTUZZI

Yrs. of NHL service: 1
Born: Sudbury, Ont.; Feb. 2, 1975
Position: centre
Height: 6-3
Weight: 227
Uniform no.: 44
Shoots: left

Career statistics:

GP	G	A	TP	PIM
76	18	21	39	83

1995-96 statistics:

GP	G	A	TP	+/-	PIM	PP	SH	GW	GT	S	PCT
76	18	21	39	-14	83	4	0	2	0	127	14.2

LAST SEASON

First NHL season. Fourth on team in points. Tied for seventh among NHL rookies in points. Tied for sixth among NHL rookies in goals. Missed three games with suspension for abuse of official. Missed two games with corneal abrasion. Missed one game with concussion.

THE FINESSE GAME

Bertuzzi is quick for his size and mobile, and he's got a good, soft pair of hands to complement his skating. Bertuzzi adapted throughout the season to getting his shot away more quickly, and proved to be an accurate shooter.

He is effective in the slot area, but he is also creative with the puck and can make some plays. He can find people down low and make things happen on the power play. With the puck, he is powerful and hard to stop, but he needs to improve his game without the puck.

Defensively, Bertuzzi needs work as a lot of young players just out of junior do, but he won't hurt his team. Bertuzzi did not have a strong second half, which is not a good sign, but the Islanders were so dismal we can cut him some slack in this area and see how he responds at the beginning of next year.

THE PHYSICAL GAME

Bertuzzi is a solid physical specimen who shows flashes of aggression and an occasional mean streak, but he really has to be pushed and aggravated to reach a boiling point. It doesn't come naturally to him. He won't run through people or challenge them consistently, and as a result won't establish a physical presence until he does.

THE INTANGIBLES

The Islanders envision Bertuzzi developing along John Leclair lines, but it took Leclair four seasons (and a couple of pretty good linemates in Philadelphia) before he reached his potential, and

Bertuzzi has some maturing to do. He could grow and turn into a leader, or he could become a frustrating enigma. The key to Bertuzzi's game now is his first few shifts of the first period. If he accomplishes something, he will have a strong game.

The Islanders can be expected to cut loose some of their older players, and it will be interesting to watch the team dynamics as the core of the next generation solidifies. Will Bertuzzi be a leader, or be on the fringe?

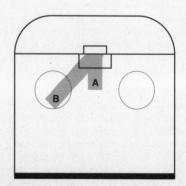

ERIC FICHAUD

Yrs. of NHL service: 1
Born: Montreal, Que.; Nov. 4, 1975
Position: goaltender
Height: 5-11
Weight: 165
Uniform no.: 1
Catches: left

Career statistics:

GP	MIN	GA	SO	GAA	A	PIM
24	1234	68	1	3.31	1	0

1995-96 statistics:

GP	MIN	GAA	W	L	T	SO	GA	S	SAPCT	PIM
24	1234	3.31	7	12	2	1	68	659	.897	0

LAST SEASON

First NHL season. Appeared in 34 games with Worcester (AHL), compiling a 13-15-6 record with a 2.93 goals-against average.

THE PHYSICAL GAME

Busy, busy, busy. A smallish goalie, Fichaud looks even smaller because he plays in a crouch in the stereotypical Patrick Roy butterfly style (just how many Roy wannabes are there, anyway?) and tends to stay deep in his nets.

Fichaud will live and die by his reflexes until he learns better technique. He is very similar to Felix Potvin (Fichaud was drafted by Toronto) in that he stays deep in his crease and scrambles rather than playing a poised angles game.

Fichaud needs to be stronger on his stick to break up plays around the net. He will be playing behind a young defense this season, and it will help if he learns to control his rebounds better (something Potvin does very well).

THE MENTAL GAME

Fichaud is outgoing and projects a breezy confidence that doesn't go unnoticed by his teammates. His confidence will grow as he becomes more acclimated to the NHL.

THE INTANGIBLES

Fichaud was probably promoted too soon, but given the truly awful level of goaltending with the club, the Islanders didn't have much choice. The Islanders' priority should be to acquire an elite goaltending coach for Fichaud to work with, because he has a lot of work to do. It's sink or swim.

TRAVIS GREEN

Yrs. of NHL service: 4
Born: Castlegar, B.C.; Dec. 20, 1970
Position: centre
Height: 6-1
Weight: 193
Uniform no.: 39
Shoots: right

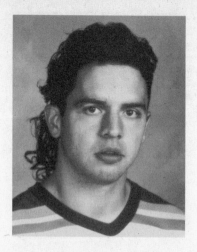

Career statistics:

GP	G	A	TP	PIM
255	54	92	146	154

1992-93 statistics:

GP	G	A	TP	+/-	PIM	PP	SH	GW	GT	S	PCT
61	7	18	25	+4	43	1	0	0	0	115	6.1

1993-94 statistics:

GP	G	A	TP	+/-	PIM	PP	SH	GW	GT	S	PCT
83	18	22	40	+16	44	1	0	2	0	164	11.0

1994-95 statistics:

GP	G	A	TP	+/-	PIM	PP	SH	GW	GT	S	PCT
42	5	7	12	-10	25	0	0	0	0	59	8.5

1995-96 statistics:

GP	G	A	TP	+/-	PIM	PP	SH	GW	GT	S	PCT
69	24	45	69	-21	42	14	1	2	1	186	12.9

LAST SEASON

Led team in assists with career high. Second on team in goals with career high. Second on team in points and power play goals. Tied for second on team in game-winning goals. Missed nine games with sprained knee. Missed four games with groin injury.

THE FINESSE GAME

Green deserves a lot of credit for reinventing himself as a hockey player. Considered a pure scorer at the minor league and junior levels, Green was taken in hand by Islanders minor-league coach Butch Goring — whose defensive play was a key factor in all four of the team's Stanley Cups — and he added a completely new dimension to Green's game. The result is one of the league's more underrated defensive forwards, one who can also produce timely goals.

Green is on the ice in the waning seconds of the period or the game to protect a lead. He has worked hard to improve his skating and has better balance and agility, with some quickness, although he lacks straight-ahead speed.

He controls the puck well. He plays more of a finesse game than a power game, and he has to learn to charge the net with more authority. He is an unselfish player and passes equally well to either side. He sees the ice well, but he has a very heavy shot. Green's release needs to be quicker, which is why he'll never be the scorer at the NHL level that he was in the minors.

Green is the Islanders' top man on draws. He uses his body to tie up an opponent and allow his linemates to skate in for the puck. Because of the Islanders' in-juries, Green was often asked to step in as a number one centre, and he performed at a surprisingly high level, but he will be a superb number three centre — maybe even a number two — when the team gets deeper.

THE PHYSICAL GAME

Green has learned to be involved in the play. He's not a huge guy, but he will use his body to get in the way. He is not by nature an intense competitor, but Green wants to be on the ice and has learned to pay the price to be there.

THE INTANGIBLES

Sometimes we nearly dislocate our shoulder patting ourselves on the back. In last year's *HSR* we said of Green, "He could score 20 to 25 goals as a two-way forward." We'll add the word "consistently" to that statement, because Green is clearly capable of a repeat performance. Because of his size, age and skill level, Green is one of the first players rival GMs ask for when they talk trade with Mike Milbury. Don't expect Green to be heading anywhere soon, although as a Group 2 free agent he will be looking for a big boost from last season's U.S.$400,000 salary, and some team may sign him to an offer sheet.

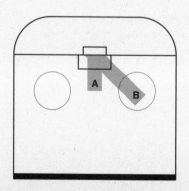

DARBY HENDRICKSON

Yrs. of NHL service: 1
Born: Richfield, Minn.; Aug. 28, 1972
Position: centre/left wing
Height: 6-0
Weight: 185
Uniform no.: 17
Shoots: right

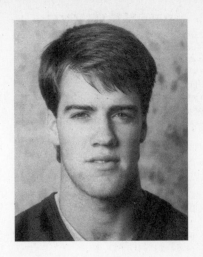

Career statistics:

GP	G	A	TP	PIM
70	7	11	18	84

1994-95 statistics:

GP	G	A	TP	+/-	PIM	PP	SH	GW	GT	S	PCT
8	0	1	1	0	4	0	0	0	0	4	0.0

1995-96 statistics:

GP	G	A	TP	+/-	PIM	PP	SH	GW	GT	S	PCT
62	7	10	17	-8	80	0	0	1	0	73	9.6

LAST SEASON

Acquired from Toronto with Kenny Jonsson, Sean Haggerty and a number one draft pick for Wendel Clark, Mathieu Schneider and D.J. Smith, Mar. 13, 1996. Served three-game suspension. Missed one game with flu.

THE FINESSE GAME

Hendrickson is an in-between forward, since he isn't big enough to play an effective power game, but his skills aren't elite enough for him to be considered a pure finesse playmaker.

Hendrickson is a two-way forward with better-than-average skills for a checking role. He is a good, quick skater in small areas. He is clever with the puck and will look to make a pass rather than shoot.

Hendrickson is defensively alert, and with increased ice time could develop into a more confident all-around player.

THE PHYSICAL GAME

Hendrickson has a feisty side to him, and isn't afraid to get involved with some of the league's name players (like Chris Chelios) if not the heavyweights.

THE INTANGIBLES

Hendrickson is best suited as a third-line centre or winger, but the Islanders are thin up the middle and if he has a good camp, he could move up into a number two role. He was a star scorer as a Minnesota schoolboy, but hasn't been able to display the same touch at the NHL level.

BRENT HUGHES

Yrs. of NHL service: 7
Born: New Westminster, B.C.; Apr. 5, 1966
Position: left wing
Height: 5-11
Weight: 194
Uniform no.: 17
Shoots: left

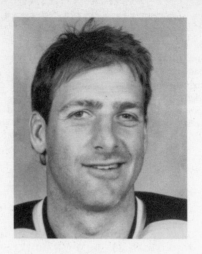

Career statistics:

GP	G	A	TP	PIM
306	34	36	70	774

1992-93 statistics:

GP	G	A	TP	+/-	PIM	PP	SH	GW	GT	S	PCT
62	5	4	9	-4	191	0	0	0	0	54	9.3

1993-94 statistics:

GP	G	A	TP	+/-	PIM	PP	SH	GW	GT	S	PCT
77	13	11	24	+10	143	1	0	1	0	100	13.0

1994-95 statistics:

GP	G	A	TP	+/-	PIM	PP	SH	GW	GT	S	PCT
44	6	6	12	+6	139	0	0	0	0	75	8.0

1995-96 statistics:

GP	G	A	TP	+/-	PIM	PP	SH	GW	GT	S	PCT
76	5	10	15	-9	148	0	0	0	0	56	8.9

LAST SEASON

Acquired by Buffalo in waiver draft, Oct. 7, 1995. Signed as a free agent by Islanders, July 25, 1996.

THE FINESSE GAME

Hughes always seems to be on the bubble or on waivers at the start of a season — as he was last season, when Buffalo nabbed him — but is a regular in the lineup once the playoffs roll around (if there had been a playoffs for the Sabres). Opponents have an even harder time ridding themselves of this pesky forward.

Hughes is infused with a work ethic, but his skills are moderate. He has some quickness, but is not very agile. He is a strong skater.

Most of his goals come from close range and just plain cussedness around the net. He can kill penalties because of his pesky forechecking.

THE PHYSICAL GAME

Hughes crease-crashes and takes advantage of the increasingly relaxed rules in that area. Goalies hate him. He is unafraid to take on the biggest, meanest guy on the other team, even though he seldom wins a fight. If that's the price for playing in the NHL, Hughes will willingly pay it.

THE INTANGIBLES

No doubt Hughes will be on the bubble again this fall. No doubt by the end of the season he will have worked his way into a regular's role. He seldom fails to add some intensity when he's on the ice.

KENNY JONSSON

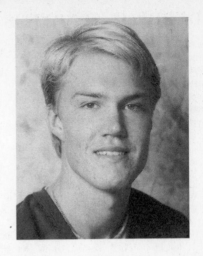

Yrs. of NHL service: 2
Born: Angelholm, Sweden; Oct. 6, 1974
Position: left defense
Height: 6-3
Weight: 195
Uniform no.: 3
Shoots: left

Career statistics:

GP	G	A	TP	PIM
105	6	33	39	48

1994-95 statistics:

GP	G	A	TP	+/-	PIM	PP	SH	GW	GT	S	PCT
39	2	7	9	-8	16	0	0	1	0	50	4.0

1995-96 statistics:

GP	G	A	TP	+/-	PIM	PP	SH	GW	GT	S	PCT
66	4	26	30	+7	32	3	0	1	0	130	3.1

LAST SEASON

Acquired from Toronto with Darby Hendrickson, Sean Haggerty and a first-round draft pick in 1997 for Wendel Clark, Mathieu Schneider and D.J. Smith, Mar. 13, 1996. Missed 17 games with shoulder separation.

THE FINESSE GAME

Excuse us, but just how did Islanders' GM Mike Milbury make it across the border after committing this act of larceny? Jonsson, in only his second NHL season, has yet to hit the top level of his game, and is not going to be doing it for the Toronto team that drafted him, despite the fact that he was the Leafs' best defenseman last season.

Jonsson reads the ice and passes the puck very well. He can be used in almost every game situation. He kills penalties, works the point on the power play, plays four-on-four, and can be used in the late stages of a period or a game to protect a lead. He's coachable, and isn't satisfied with being an NHL player. He wants to be a good one.

Jonsson is a talented skater but part of his adjustment will be learning to protect himself by using the net in his own zone. He tends to leave himself open after passes and gets nailed.

THE PHYSICAL GAME

Jonsson needs to get stronger, and it appears he is still filling out with some muscle. He is big and mobile, but doesn't have a very aggressive side and will need to be more assertive.

THE INTANGIBLES

Jonsson may have been intimidated by playing in Toronto because of all the Leaf veterans, but with a younger team like the Islanders he will become part of a core group of leaders. Jonsson will be a top two defenseman for years to come for the Islanders.

DARIUS KASPARAITIS

Yrs. of NHL service: 4
Born: Elektrenai, Lithuania; Oct. 16, 1972
Position: right defense
Height: 5-11
Weight: 195
Uniform no.: 11
Shoots: left

Career statistics:

GP	G	A	TP	PIM
214	6	35	41	423

1992-93 statistics:

GP	G	A	TP	+/-	PIM	PP	SH	GW	GT	S	PCT
79	4	17	21	+15	166	0	0	0	0	92	4.3

1993-94 statistics:

GP	G	A	TP	+/-	PIM	PP	SH	GW	GT	S	PCT
76	1	10	11	-6	142	0	0	0	0	81	1.2

1994-95 statistics:

GP	G	A	TP	+/-	PIM	PP	SH	GW	GT	S	PCT
13	0	1	1	-11	22	0	0	0	0	8	0.0

1995-96 statistics:

GP	G	A	TP	+/-	PIM	PP	SH	GW	GT	S	PCT
46	1	7	8	-12	93	0	0	0	0	34	2.9

LAST SEASON

Missed 15 games with knee surgery. Missed 16 games with severed tendons in hand. Missed two games with flu. Missed two games with groin injury.

THE FINESSE GAME

Kasparaitis is a strong, powerful skater who can accelerate in all directions. You can run, but you can't hide from this defenseman, who accepts all challenges. He is aggressive in the neutral zone, sometimes overly so, stepping up to break up a team's attack. Kasparaitis missed the first 15 games of the season recuperating from knee surgery from the previous season, but seemed confident in his skating.

He concentrates mainly on his defensive role, but Kasparaitis has the skills to get more involved in the offense. He will make a sharp outlet pass and then follow up into the play. He also has good offensive instincts, moves the puck well and, if he plays on his off side, will open up his forehand for the one-timer.

Kasparaitis has infectious enthusiasm that is an inspiration to the rest of his team. There is a purpose to whatever he does, and he's highly competitive.

THE PHYSICAL GAME

Kasparaitis is well on his way to succeeding Ulf Samuelsson as the player most NHLers would like to see run over by a bus. It's always borderline interference with Kasparaitis, who uses his stick liberally, waiting three or four seconds after a victim has gotten rid of the puck to apply the lumber. Cross-check, butt-end, high stick — through the course of a season Kasparaitis will illustrate all of the stick infractions.

His timing isn't always the best, and he has to think about the good of the team rather than indulging his own vendettas.

But Kasparaitis is legitimately tough. It doesn't matter whose name is on back of the jersey — Lemieux, Tocchet, McKay, Messier — he will goad the stars and the heavyweights equally. He yaps, too, and is as irritating as a car alarm at 3 a.m.

THE INTANGIBLES

Kasparaitis started off the season on the wrong skate — injured, and playing for a new coach who was prepared to dislike him. But Kasparaitis proved reliable, and he will add some veteran grit to a mix that includes youngsters Kenny Jonsson, Bryan Berard and Bryan McCabe.

DEREK KING

Yrs. of NHL service: 9
Born: Hamilton, Ont.; Feb. 11, 1967
Position: left wing
Height: 6-1
Weight: 200
Uniform no.: 27
Shoots: left

Career statistics:

GP	G	A	TP	PIM
568	188	258	446	324

1992-93 statistics:

GP	G	A	TP	+/-	PIM	PP	SH	GW	GT	S	PCT
77	38	38	76	-3	47	21	0	7	0	201	18.9

1993-94 statistics:

GP	G	A	TP	+/-	PIM	PP	SH	GW	GT	S	PCT
78	30	40	70	+18	59	10	0	7	1	171	17.5

1994-95 statistics:

GP	G	A	TP	+/-	PIM	PP	SH	GW	GT	S	PCT
43	10	16	26	-5	41	7	0	0	0	118	8.5

1995-96 statistics:

GP	G	A	TP	+/-	PIM	PP	SH	GW	GT	S	PCT
61	12	20	32	-10	23	5	1	0	1	154	7.8

LAST SEASON

Missed one game with foot injury. Missed 19 games with broken jaw and concussion.

THE FINESSE GAME

There is only one thing King does well, and that is score goals. He is at his best from the face-off dot of the left circle to the front of the net. He has great concentration through traffic and soft, soft hands for cradling passes and then snapping off the shot the instant the puck hits his blade. King has to play with someone who will get him the puck, and since the Islanders traded Pierre Turgeon two seasons ago, his goal production has dwindled accordingly.

Among the best in the league on the power play, King has good anticipation and reads the offensive plays well. He is not a great skater but has improved his defensive awareness. Last season, King scored his first career shorthanded goal.

THE PHYSICAL GAME

King is a solid and durable player who takes a pounding in front of the net. He doesn't use his body well in other areas of the ice, though, which is one of the reasons for his defensive problems. His serious concussion, the result of an open-ice hit, may make him even more reluctant to pay a physical price.

THE INTANGIBLES

Even before suffering his season-ending injury in March, King was suffering through a nightmare season. He had only eight goals by the midpoint of the season. King is a Group 2 free agent, but has little bargaining power, since his days as a 40-goal scorer appear to be behind him, and he does not bring much else to the ice. The Islanders would love to move him, but will have a hard time finding any takers.

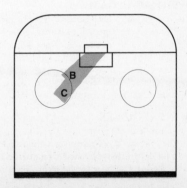

SCOTT LACHANCE

Yrs. of NHL service: 4
Born: Charlottesville, Va.; Oct. 22, 1972
Position: left defense
Height: 6-1
Weight: 197
Uniform no.: 7
Shoots: left

Career statistics:

GP	G	A	TP	PIM
247	20	49	69	226

1992-93 statistics:

GP	G	A	TP	+/-	PIM	PP	SH	GW	GT	S	PCT
75	7	17	24	-1	67	0	1	2	0	62	11.3

1993-94 statistics:

GP	G	A	TP	+/-	PIM	PP	SH	GW	GT	S	PCT
74	3	11	14	-5	70	0	0	1	0	59	5.1

1994-95 statistics:

GP	G	A	TP	+/-	PIM	PP	SH	GW	GT	S	PCT
26	6	7	13	+2	26	3	0	0	0	56	10.7

1995-96 statistics:

GP	G	A	TP	+/-	PIM	PP	SH	GW	GT	S	PCT
55	3	10	13	-19	54	1	0	0	0	81	3.7

LAST SEASON

Missed 27 games with groin injury.

THE FINESSE GAME

Lachance has good hockey sense. He is very clever with the puck, moving it smartly and he remains poised under pressure. He will never have truly impressive offensive numbers, because his skating isn't good enough to propel him into the elite class, but he can complement another defenseman who does have good offensive instincts. Lachance is smart enough not to take too many chances.

Lachances's development has been slowed by injuries during the past two seasons. He will be stepping into a new role as an elder statesman this season, and it will be interesting to see how he handles the role.

Lachance is not an exceptional skater. He has to work on his quickness (his feet look a little heavy at times), but he is balanced and strong on his skates.

THE PHYSICAL GAME

This is the area where Lachance has to apply himself most. Though not a very big blueliner, he is built solidly enough to be an effective if not devastating checker, but there are nights when he just lets his attacker skate through without paying the price. Lachance kills penalties well and blocks shots. His mental toughness has to improve.

THE INTANGIBLES

Lachance can score 30 points a season if he can stay intact. The Islanders don't have a very strong team up front, so the defense may be relied upon to generate a lot of the scoring. Lachance should do his share.

BRYAN MCCABE

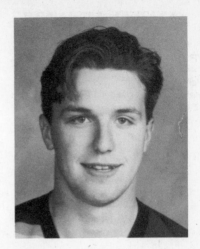

Yrs. of NHL service: 1
Born: St. Catharines, Ont.; June 8, 1975
Position: defense
Height: 6-2
Weight: 205
Uniform no.: 4
Shoots: left

Career statistics:

GP	G	A	TP	PIM
82	7	16	23	156

1995-96 statistics:

GP	G	A	TP	+/-	PIM	PP	SH	GW	GT	S	PCT
82	7	16	23	-24	156	3	0	1	0	130	5.4

LAST SEASON

First NHL season. Only Islander, and one of only three NHL rookies, to appear in all 82 games. Second among team defensemen and second among rookie defensemen in scoring. Second on team in penalty minutes.

THE FINESSE GAME

McCabe's offensive game was supposed to be ahead of his defensive aspects, but he sat back and studied the game a bit in his rookie season. He is still hesitant in his own zone when reading the rush and will get caught, but he is willing to work to improve.

McCabe has tremendous offensive instincts. He knows when to jump up into the attacking zone. He has a heavy, major-league slap shot. McCabe moves the puck well and it won't be long before he is running the team's power play.

McCabe's skating style is unorthodox. It's not fluid, and there appears to be a hitch in his stride. When he has the puck or is jumping into the play, he has decent speed, but his lack of mobility defensively is one of his few flaws.

McCabe loves to play and loves to compete. Last season was a maturing year and he will need more time to become a complete defenseman, but he took a big first step in the right direction in 1995-96.

THE PHYSICAL GAME

McCabe is not afraid to drop his gloves, and can handle himself in a bout. He is a sturdy body checker, and if his skating improves he will become a more efficient hitter. He is big and strong and shows leadership.

THE INTANGIBLES

We gave McCabe a shot to make the Islanders team last year, but his performance exceeded even some of the more optimistic expectations. Given the carnage around him on the Islander blueline, he proceeded cautiously but improved throughout the season. A potential blueline corps that includes McCabe, Darius Kasparaitis, Kenny Jonsson, Scott Lachance and rookie Bryan Berard should give long-suffering Islander fans a reason to live. Expect McCabe to add more offense to his game once he has a stronger supporting cast.

This is a lot to saddle a young man with, but McCabe has a wonderful attitude and is a possible future team captain.

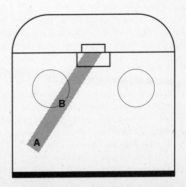

MARTY MCINNIS

Yrs. of NHL service: 4
Born: Hingham, Mass.; June 2, 1970
Position: left wing
Height: 6-0
Weight: 185
Uniform no.: 18
Shoots: right

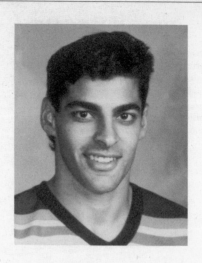

Career statistics:

GP	G	A	TP	PIM
267	59	97	156	95

1992-93 statistics:

GP	G	A	TP	+/-	PIM	PP	SH	GW	GT	S	PCT
56	10	20	30	+7	24	0	1	0	0	60	16.7

1993-94 statistics:

GP	G	A	TP	+/-	PIM	PP	SH	GW	GT	S	PCT
81	25	31	56	+31	24	3	5	3	1	136	18.4

1994-95 statistics:

GP	G	A	TP	+/-	PIM	PP	SH	GW	GT	S	PCT
41	9	7	16	-1	8	0	0	1	0	68	13.2

1995-96 statistics:

GP	G	A	TP	+/-	PIM	PP	SH	GW	GT	S	PCT
74	12	34	46	-11	39	2	0	1	0	167	7.2

LAST SEASON

Third on team in assists and points. Career high in assists. Missed seven games with rib injuries.

THE FINESSE GAME

McInnis does a lot of the little things well. He plays positionally, is smart and reliable defensively, and turns his checking work into scoring opportunities with quick passes and his work down low.

He isn't fast, but he is deceptive with a quick first few strides to the puck. He seems to be more aware of where the puck is than his opponents, so while they're looking for the puck, he's already heading towards it.

McInnis is a good penalty killer because of his tenacity and anticipation. He reads plays well on offense and defense. Playing the off-wing opens up his shot for a quick release. He is always a shorthanded threat.

THE PHYSICAL GAME

McInnis is not very big, but he is sturdy and will use his body to bump and scrap for the puck. He always tries to get in the way, but he loses a lot of battles in tight to larger forwards because he is not that strong.

THE INTANGIBLES

After a mediocre 1994-95, McInnis was off to another slow start last season and was benched one game, but he eventually came around. There should be even more in the tank than McInnis tapped last year. He is a suitable third-line checking winger with enough talent for 15-20 goals a season.

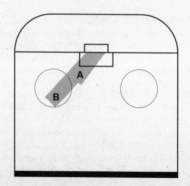

ZIGMUND PALFFY

Yrs. of NHL service: 2
Born: Skalica, Czechoslovakia; May 5, 1972
Position: left wing
Height: 5-10
Weight: 169
Uniform no.: 16
Shoots: left

Career statistics:

GP	G	A	TP	PIM
119	53	51	104	62

1993-94 statistics:

GP	G	A	TP	+/-	PIM	PP	SH	GW	GT	S	PCT
5	0	0	0	-6	0	0	0	0	0	5	0.0

1994-95 statistics:

GP	G	A	TP	+/-	PIM	PP	SH	GW	GT	S	PCT
33	10	7	17	+3	6	1	0	1	0	75	13.3

1995-96 statistics:

GP	G	A	TP	+/-	PIM	PP	SH	GW	GT	S	PCT
81	43	44	87	-17	56	17	1	6	0	257	16.7

LAST SEASON

Led team in goals, points, power play goals, game-winning goals and shots in second NHL season. Tied for eighth in league in power play goals. Missed one game with concussion.

THE FINESSE GAME

Palffy has deceptive quickness. He is an elusive skater with a quick first step and is very shifty, and he can handle the puck while he's dancing across the ice. He won't burn around people, but when there's an opening he can get to it in a hurry. His effort was far more consistent last season than in previous years when he flirted with making the NHL as a regular. He has started to grasp the NHL game and North American culture.

One thing Palffy can do exceptionally well is run a power play. He has elite hockey instincts — and that's what sets him apart.

Palffy has excellent hands for passing or shooting. Earlier in his career, he would look to make a play before shooting, but he has become a bona fide sniper.

THE PHYSICAL GAME

Palffy is decidedly on the small side. He can't afford to get into any battles in tight areas where he'll get crunched. He can jump in and out of holes and pick his spots, and he often plays with great spirit. Palffy never puts himself in a position to get bowled over, but he has become less of a perimeter player and is more willing to take the direct route to the net, which has paid off in more quality scoring chances. He's not really a soft player, but he won't go into the corner if he's going to get crunched. Palffy will battle for loose pucks around the net.

THE INTANGIBLES

Last year's *HSR* said that if Palffy could sustain the level of play he had shown late in the 1994-95 season, he would be a 40-goal scorer. Done and done. But as *HSR* went to press, Palffy was seeking a new contract that would put him in a league with Peter Forsberg and Paul Kariya, and Palffy is not in that league. Yet.

We're pretty sure Palffy isn't a one-season wonder. We're pretty sure he could score 40 goals again. We're very sure we wouldn't pay him $2 million until he does, which puts the Islanders in a tough spot, since he is threatening to play in Europe this season if he doesn't get the dough. We're very sure we are happy this is Mike Milbury's call, and not ours.

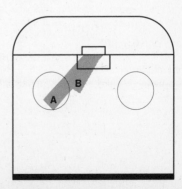

259

DAN PLANTE

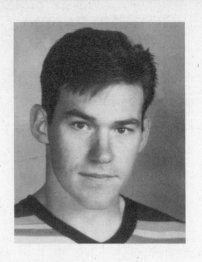

Yrs. of NHL service: 1
Born: St. Louis, Mo.; Oct. 5, 1971
Position: right wing
Height: 5-11
Weight: 198
Uniform no.: 21
Shoots: right

Career statistics:

GP	G	A	TP	PIM
85	5	4	9	54

1993-94 statistics:

GP	G	A	TP	+/-	PIM	PP	SH	GW	GT	S	PCT
12	0	1	1	-2	4	0	0	0	0	9	0.0

1994-95 statistics:

GP	G	A	TP	+/-	PIM	PP	SH	GW	GT	S	PCT

Did Not Play in NHL

1995-96 statistics:

GP	G	A	TP	+/-	PIM	PP	SH	GW	GT	S	PCT
73	5	3	8	-22	50	0	2	0	0	103	4.9

LAST SEASON

First NHL season. Tied for team lead in shorthanded goals. Missed five games with bruised knee. Missed one game with bruised shoulder.

THE FINESSE GAME

Plante's first NHL goal was scored shorthanded, which sums up his style. Plante plays defense first, and does so intelligently. He is a non-stop skater whose first duty is his checking role.

Plante worked hard to get back to the NHL after undergoing reconstructive knee surgery in 1994-95 (he played only two minor-league games that season). He knows the value of an NHL job, and mucks and grinds and does what he has to do to earn his paycheck.

Plante's offensive skills are negligible, although he was a decent scorer at the collegiate level.

THE PHYSICAL GAME

Plante is not a fighter, but he is a banger. He skates hard and battles for the puck. He is a sparkplug and is willing to sacrifice his body. Plante is very balanced and tough to knock off his feet. His work ethic is unquestioned.

THE INTANGIBLES

Plante raises the energy level of a game. He can function on a third or fourth line, kill penalties, distract some opponents and pick up a few (but not many) points.

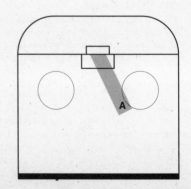

DENNIS VASKE

Yrs. of NHL service: 5
Born: Rockford, Ill.; Oct. 11, 1967
Position: left defense
Height: 6-2
Weight: 210
Uniform no.: 37
Shoots: left

Career statistics:

GP	G	A	TP	PIM
196	5	34	39	223

1992-93 statistics:

GP	G	A	TP	+/-	PIM	PP	SH	GW	GT	S	PCT
27	1	5	6	+9	32	0	0	0	0	15	6.7

1993-94 statistics:

GP	G	A	TP	+/-	PIM	PP	SH	GW	GT	S	PCT
65	2	11	13	+21	76	0	0	0	0	71	2.8

1994-95 statistics:

GP	G	A	TP	+/-	PIM	PP	SH	GW	GT	S	PCT
41	1	11	12	+3	53	0	0	0	0	48	2.1

1995-96 statistics:

GP	G	A	TP	+/-	PIM	PP	SH	GW	GT	S	PCT
19	1	6	7	-13	21	1	0	1	0	19	5.3

jury. His concussion symptoms lasted until February and he resumed skating in March, although he did not return to the lineup.

LAST SEASON

Missed 63 games with concussion and facial laceration.

THE FINESSE GAME

The Islanders have already lost one young player, Brett Lindros, to premature retirement due to a severe concussion. Vaske's season ended in November due to a similar injury when he was hit from behind by Los Angeles' Eric Lacroix. Vaske's future is in question.

Vaske has made progress over the past few seasons and is establishing himself as a steady, stay-at-home defenseman.

He has what is a common flaw among young defensemen: he occasionally gets mesmerized and starts playing the puck instead of the body. Overall, however, he plays a sound positional game and forces attackers to try to get through him.

Although strong on his skates, Vaske doesn't have great speed or quickness, so when he stands his ground and forces the play to come to him he is the most effective.

THE PHYSICAL GAME

Vaske is a solid hitter. Because he doesn't skate well and lacks the first few steps to drive into an opponent, he doesn't bowl people over, but he is incredibly strong in the tough, close, one-on-one battles. He likes the physical play, too, but doesn't fight much.

THE INTANGIBLES

Vaske reminds a lot of Islander old-timers of defenseman Dave "Bam Bam" Langevin. Vaske's physical play will certainly depend on his return from his in-

NEW YORK RANGERS

Players' Statistics 1995-96

POS.	NO.	PLAYER	GP	G	A	PTS	+/-	PIM	PP	SH	GW	GT	S	PCT
C	11	MARK MESSIER	74	47	52	99	29	122	14	1	5	1	241	19.5
D	2	BRIAN LEETCH	82	15	70	85	12	30	7		3		276	5.4
R	16	PAT VERBEEK	69	41	41	82	29	129	17		6	2	252	16.3
L	20	LUC ROBITAILLE	77	23	46	69	13	80	11		4	2	223	10.3
R	27	ALEXEI KOVALEV	81	24	34	58	5	98	8	1	7		206	11.7
L	9	ADAM GRAVES	82	22	36	58	18	100	9	1	2		266	8.3
L	17	JARI KURRI	71	18	27	45	-16	39	5	1		2	158	11.4
D	33	BRUCE DRIVER	66	3	34	37	2	42	3			1	140	2.1
D	55	MARTY MCSORLEY	68	10	23	33	-20	169	1	1	1		130	7.7
C	13	SERGEI NEMCHINOV	78	17	15	32	9	38			2		118	14.4
L	32	SERGIO MOMESSO	73	11	12	23	-13	142	6		1	2	126	8.7
L	24	*NIKLAS SUNDSTROM	82	9	12	21	2	14	1	1	2		90	10.0
D	5	ULF SAMUELSSON	74	1	18	19	9	122					66	1.5
D	25	A. KARPOVTSEV	40	2	16	18	12	26	1		1		71	2.8
D	6	DOUG LIDSTER	59	5	9	14	11	50					73	6.8
D	23	JEFF BEUKEBOOM	82	3	11	14	19	220			1	1	65	4.6
L	15	*DARREN LANGDON	64	7	4	11	2	175			1	1	29	24.1
R	22	SHANE CHURLA	55	4	6	10	-8	231					32	12.5
D	4	KEVIN LOWE	53	1	5	6	20	76					30	3.3
L	18	BILL BERG	41	3	2	5	-6	41		1			60	5.0
C	12	KEN GERNANDER	10	2	3	5	-3	4	2				10	20.0
L	37	DAN LACROIX	25	2	2	4	-1	30					14	14.3
R	14	*CHRIS FERRARO	2	1		1	-3		1				4	25.0
D	29	*BARRY RICHTER	4		1	1	2						3	
C	21	*PETER FERRARO	5		1	1	-5						6	
G	35	MIKE RICHTER	41		1	1	0	4						
G	30	GLENN HEALY	44		1	1	0	8						
G	34	*JAMIE RAM	1				0							

GP = games played; G = goals; A = assists; PTS = points; +/- = goals-for minus goals-against while player is on ice; PIM = penalties in minutes; PP = power play goals; SH = shorthanded goals; GW = game-winning goals; GT = game-tying goals; S = no. of shots; PCT = percentage of goals to shots; * = rookie

JEFF BEUKEBOOM

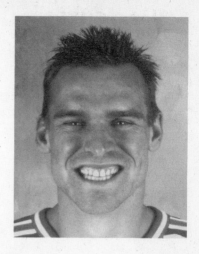

Yrs. of NHL service: 10
Born: Ajax, Ont.; Mar. 28, 1965
Position: right defense
Height: 6-5
Weight: 230
Uniform no.: 23
Shoots: right

Career statistics:

GP	G	A	TP	PIM
616	27	106	133	1468

1992-93 statistics:

GP	G	A	TP	+/-	PIM	PP	SH	GW	GT	S	PCT
82	2	17	19	+9	153	0	0	0	0	54	3.7

1993-94 statistics:

GP	G	A	TP	+/-	PIM	PP	SH	GW	GT	S	PCT
68	8	8	16	+18	170	1	0	0	0	58	13.8

1994-95 statistics:

GP	G	A	TP	+/-	PIM	PP	SH	GW	GT	S	PCT
44	1	3	4	+3	70	0	0	0	0	29	3.4

1995-96 statistics:

GP	G	A	TP	+/-	PIM	PP	SH	GW	GT	S	PCT
82	3	11	14	+19	220	0	0	1	1	65	4.6

LAST SEASON

One of four Rangers to appear in all 82 games. Second on team in penalty minutes.

THE FINESSE GAME

Beukeboom is not an agile skater, but he takes up a lot of room on the ice, especially when he uses his long reach. He has a quick stick. On penalty-killing shifts, he is able to get the stick down on the left or right side of his body into the passing lanes. He will also use his stick to reach around a puck carrier and knock the puck loose, or for a sweep-check at the blueline.

Beukeboom needs a mobile partner so he can play a simple defensive game. He is most effective when he angles the attacker to the corners, then uses his superior size and strength to eliminate the player physically. Attackers think they can burn Beukeboom to the outside because of his lumbering style, but they find themselves running out of real estate fast. But Beukeboom can get burned himself on ill-timed pinches, which happened at some key moments in last year's playoffs.

Beukeboom moves the puck fairly well. He certainly has no fear of anyone bearing down on him, but he needs support because he can't carry the puck out himself.

THE PHYSICAL GAME

Beukeboom almost swaggers about his size, as though he dares you to come hit him. He makes you worry about him; he's not going to worry about you. He commands room. He takes his time getting to the puck because not many people want to throw themselves at him. He focusses on the man first, the puck second at all times.

He is most effective crunching along the boards, and he clears the front of his net efficiently. The bigger the game, the more thunderous his hits. Beukeboom blocks shots fearlessly and often limps to the bench, only to return on his next shift.

THE INTANGIBLES

Beukeboom is well aware of his limitations on the ice, but that won't stop him from seeking big bucks through free agency. If the ticket is too steep, the Rangers won't pay it, and then we'll learn how much Brian Leetch has meant to Beukeboom's career. He will always need to be paired to a mobile defenseman, because he lacks range and puck-carrying ability.

SHANE CHURLA

Yrs. of NHL service: 8
Born: Fernie, B.C.; June 24, 1965
Position: right wing
Height: 6-1
Weight: 200
Uniform no.: 22
Shoots: right

Career statistics:

GP	G	A	TP	PIM
443	26	44	70	2193

1992-93 statistics:

GP	G	A	TP	+/-	PIM	PP	SH	GW	GT	S	PCT
73	5	16	21	-8	286	1	0	1	0	61	8.2

1993-94 statistics:

GP	G	A	TP	+/-	PIM	PP	SH	GW	GT	S	PCT
69	6	7	13	-8	333	3	0	0	1	62	9.7

1994-95 statistics:

GP	G	A	TP	+/-	PIM	PP	SH	GW	GT	S	PCT
27	1	3	4	0	186	0	0	1	0	22	4.5

1995-96 statistics:

GP	G	A	TP	+/-	PIM	PP	SH	GW	GT	S	PCT
55	4	6	10	-8	231	0	0	0	0	32	12.5

LAST SEASON

Acquired from Los Angeles with Marty McSorley and Jari Kurri for Ray Ferraro, Mattias Norstrom, Ian Laperriere, Nathan LaFayette and a 1997 fourth-round draft choice. Led team in PIM for sixth consecutive season. Missed five games with separated shoulder. Served a three-game suspension. Missed seven games with fractured ankle.

THE FINESSE GAME

Churla is among the new breed of physical role players. He brings more to his game than his fists. He can be effective with his checking and play without being a heavyweight fighter, and he has made himself more valuable. He doesn't have sharp scoring instincts but will go to the net and get his goals by thrashing around for loose pucks.

Like a lot of players of his ilk, Churla gets a little too carried away by overhandling the puck. By keeping his game simple, he will be more effective.

Churla gains more confidence with increased ice time, and could play a steady third-line role as a checker, although the Rangers had him relegated to the fourth line many nights. He will continue to try to stretch his game and his offensive numbers will improve, but not by a great deal.

THE PHYSICAL GAME

Churla hits hard and loves it. He's a tenacious checker and isn't afraid of anyone. He moves to the front of the net with authority and power, and stays there. He can still use his dukes when he has to, but he has already earned a fair amount of respect around the league. Churla can change the emotional tide of a game with his adrenaline. Because of his reputation, however, good clean checks sometimes result in penalties.

THE INTANGIBLES

Churla is among the best in the league at what he does. He will protect his teammates or help protect a lead. He plays with a lot of fire. Churla didn't get too much ice time in the playoffs because of the Rangers' tendency to overplay their key personnel, but he was frequently one of their most effective players when he did get off the bench.

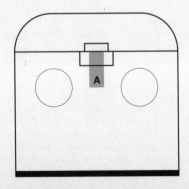

BRUCE DRIVER

Yrs. of NHL service: 12
Born: Toronto, Ont.; Apr. 29, 1962
Position: left defense
Height: 6-0
Weight: 185
Uniform no.: 33
Shoots: left

Career statistics:

GP	G	A	TP	PIM
768	29	350	436	576

1992-93 statistics:

GP	G	A	TP	+/-	PIM	PP	SH	GW	GT	S	PCT
83	14	40	54	-10	66	6	0	0	0	177	7.9

1993-94 statistics:

GP	G	A	TP	+/-	PIM	PP	SH	GW	GT	S	PCT
66	8	24	32	+29	63	3	1	0	1	109	7.3

1994-95 statistics:

GP	G	A	TP	+/-	PIM	PP	SH	GW	GT	S	PCT
41	4	12	16	-1	18	1	0	1	0	62	6.5

1995-96 statistics:

GP	G	A	TP	+/-	PIM	PP	SH	GW	GT	S	PCT
66	3	34	37	+2	42	3	0	0	1	140	2.1

LAST SEASON

Signed as free agent. Missed 13 games recovering from off-season shoulder surgery. Missed three games with flu. Second among team defensemen in scoring.

THE FINESSE GAME

Driver's game is based in his feet and in his helmet. He's a fluid skater, with secure strides and quick acceleration. He is hardly greased lightning, but he can get the jump on faster skaters with his mobility, and he's very good moving laterally and backwards.

Driver sees the ice well offensively and defensively and can kill penalties or work on the power play. He has a nice wrist shot, which he uses when he cheats into the right circle, but his point shot is a waste. Despite his skills, he is not really an effective man at the point, but because he is paired with the gambling Brian Leetch on the power play, Driver does not often venture in deep.

He has top-notch hand skills for passing, receiving a pass or carrying the puck, and he is an above-average playmaker.

THE PHYSICAL GAME

Driver does not play a hitting game. He lacks the size, strength and temperament for it. He plays defense by body position and containment, trying to occupy as much good ice space as possible by his positioning against the rush, and then using his poke-check to try to knock the puck free. With his good finesse kills, he can easily mount a countering rush.

He fails in the one-on-one battles in the trenches, simply outmuscled along the boards and in front of the net. With the NHL trend towards power forwards like Eric Lindros and Trevor Linden, this makes the weak link in Driver's game more of a detriment, since he does not have the high-scoring numbers to offset it.

THE INTANGIBLES

Driver would have been happy to finish his career with New Jersey, but the Devils wouldn't give him a no-trade clause in his contract, so the veteran defenseman hopped across the river to the Rangers, who did. Driver was supposed to take up some of the power play slack left from the trade of Sergei Zubov, but even in his prime Driver was never that kind of point man and he was often booed at the Garden. He got off to a slow start due to his shoulder surgery, and is on his best days a number four defenseman now.

ADAM GRAVES

Yrs. of NHL service: 8
Born: Toronto, Ont.; Apr. 12, 1968
Position: left wing
Height: 6-0
Weight: 210
Uniform no.: 9
Shoots: left

Career statistics:

GP	G	A	TP	PIM
594	176	176	352	1207

1992-93 statistics:

GP	G	A	TP	+/-	PIM	PP	SH	GW	GT	S	PCT
84	36	29	65	-4	148	12	1	6	1	275	13.1

1993-94 statistics:

GP	G	A	TP	+/-	PIM	PP	SH	GW	GT	S	PCT
84	52	27	79	+27	127	20	4	4	1	291	17.9

1994-95 statistics:

GP	G	A	TP	+/-	PIM	PP	SH	GW	GT	S	PCT
47	17	14	31	+9	51	9	0	3	0	185	9.2

1995-96 statistics:

GP	G	A	TP	+/-	PIM	PP	SH	GW	GT	S	PCT
82	22	36	58	+18	100	9	1	2	0	266	8.3

LAST SEASON

Tied for fifth on team in points. One of four Rangers to appear in all 82 games.

THE FINESSE GAME

Graves is a short-game player who scores a whopping percentage of his goals off deflections, rebounds and slam-dunks. A shot from the top of the circle is a long-distance effort for him. He favours the wrist shot, and his slap shot barely exists, so seldom does he use it. He is much better when working on instinct, because when he has time to make plays, he will out-think himself. Graves is far from a natural scorer, which makes his 52-goal season in 1993-94 look more and more like a misprint.

Although a somewhat awkward skater, his balance and strength are good and he can get a few quick steps on a rival, although he isn't very fast in open ice. He is smart with the puck. He protects it with his body and is strong enough to fend off a checker with one arm and shovel the puck to a linemate with the other.

Graves is an ex-centre who can step in on draws. He is an intelligent penalty killer.

THE PHYSICAL GAME

Back surgery two summers ago still obviously affects Graves, who has to be physical to be effective. Graves tries to play Eric Lindros-size. He grinds and plays against other teams' top defensemen without fear. He blocks shots and is a force on the ice. Other teams are always aware when Graves is around, because he doesn't play a quiet game. He finishes every check.

He stands up for his teammates and fights when necessary. He's so valuable to his team that the Rangers hate to see him in the box, and he's gotten much better at controlling his temper and not getting goaded into bad trade-off penalties. A tenacious forechecker, he plows into the corners and plunges into his work along the boards with intelligence, but no fear. He is one of the best goalie-screeners in the league.

THE INTANGIBLES

We thought Graves would have a bigger rebound season last year than he did, and we have to estimate that 60-70 points is his top end now. A back problem, supposedly unrelated to his surgery, affected him in the playoffs, which marks him as a bit risky health-wise.

Graves is a natural leader, and on those nights when the rest of his teammates fail to show up, he does. On nights when the points aren't coming, he never hurts his club but contributes in other ways. He is absurdly modest. Off the ice, Graves is one of the genuine good guys. On the ice, he can be one of the meanest. He simply wants to win.

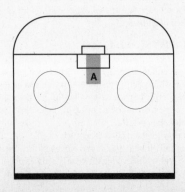

WAYNE GRETZKY

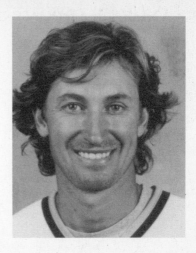

Yrs. of NHL service: 17
Born: Brantford, Ont.; Jan. 26, 1961
Position: centre
Height: 6-0
Weight: 180
Uniform no.: 99
Shoots: left

Career statistics:

GP	G	A	TP	PIM
1253	837	1771	2608	507

1992-93 statistics:

GP	G	A	TP	+/-	PIM	PP	SH	GW	GT	S	PCT
45	16	49	65	+6	6	0	2	1	0	141	11.3

1993-94 statistics:

GP	G	A	TP	+/-	PIM	PP	SH	GW	GT	S	PCT
81	38	92	130	-25	20	14	4	0	1	233	16.3

1994-95 statistics:

GP	G	A	TP	+/-	PIM	PP	SH	GW	GT	S	PCT
48	11	37	48	-20	6	3	0	1	0	142	7.7

1995-96 statistics:

GP	G	A	TP	+/-	PIM	PP	SH	GW	GT	S	PCT
80	23	79	102	-13	34	6	1	3	1	195	11.8

LAST SEASON

Acquired by St. Louis for Craig Johnson, Patrice Tardif, Roman Vopat, a first-round draft pick and a fifth-round draft pick, Feb. 27, 1996. Signed as a free agent with Rangers, July 20, 1996. Tied for fifth in NHL in assists. Recorded NHL record 15th 100-point season.

THE FINESSE GAME

Gretzky may have had his last "great" season, but despite the slight decline in his game, he remains one of the most exceptional players the sport has ever known. Gretzky has become a better all-around forward in recent years.

Gretzky is more eager to shoot than in the past, when he was known primarily as a passer. Playmaking is still his forte, but defenders can no longer just look to shut off his passing lanes, because Gretzky will rifle one of his deceptive shots if they play off him. He doesn't overpower goalies, but he masks his shot well and gets it off quickly.

Gretzky has lost half a step in his skating, but he has such great anticipation it is barely noticeable. He was never a breakaway player, but the sight of him getting crunched by the likes of Tim Taylor in the playoffs was cringe-worthy. As ever, he is patient, patient, patient with the puck, waiting until the last split-second to dish off.

THE PHYSICAL GAME

Anyone seeing Gretzky in civilian clothes for the first time is shocked at how slightly built the Great One is. His image and aura are so imposing that you expect him to be built more along the lines of Mario Lemieux, or the Statue of Liberty, but he remains whippet-lean — and that makes his career all the more remarkable. He has back problems and suffered a concussion last season when he was hammered by Edmonton's Kelly Buchberger.

THE INTANGIBLES

The Home Shopping Network conducts more tasteful sales than Gretzky and his agent, Mike Barnett, held during the off-season. Still, Barnett landed number 99 in the nearly identical spot. Gretzky took a pay cut to sign a two-year, U.S.$8-million contract with the Rangers where he is reunited with a bunch of Oilers from the early 1980s. In New York, Gretzky can play as a second-line centre behind Mark Messier, run the power play, and his kids can get immediate seating at Planet Hollywood. Gretzky will find the travel easier, but the physical play much tougher in the Eastern Conference.

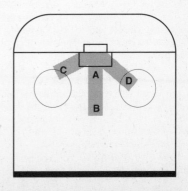

ALEXANDER KARPOVTSEV

Yrs. of NHL service: 3
Born: Moscow, Russia; Feb. 25, 1974
Position: left defense
Height: 6-1
Weight: 210
Uniform no.: 25
Shoots: left

Career statistics:

GP	G	A	TP	PIM
154	9	39	48	114

1993-94 statistics:

GP	G	A	TP	+/-	PIM	PP	SH	GW	GT	S	PCT
67	3	15	18	+12	58	1	0	1	0	78	3.8

1994-95 statistics:

GP	G	A	TP	+/-	PIM	PP	SH	GW	GT	S	PCT
47	4	8	12	-4	30	1	0	1	0	82	4.9

1995-96 statistics:

GP	G	A	TP	+/-	PIM	PP	SH	GW	GT	S	PCT
40	2	16	18	+12	26	1	0	1	0	71	2.8

LAST SEASON

Missed one game with elbow injury. Mised two games with finger injury. Missed 10 games with recurring back spasms.

THE FINESSE GAME

Karpovtsev is a strong skater with some quickness and agility. He turns nicely in both directions.

He has decent puck-carrying skills but has no interest whatsoever in doing anything beyond getting to the redline and dumping the puck into the corner or making a short outlet pass. He does, at times, show a good instinct for seeing a better passing option than the obvious in the attacking zone. He has an effective shot from the point, low, reasonably accurate and very hard.

Karpovtsev is a bang-it-off-the-boards guy from behind his own net, and looked quicker on his feet last season.

THE PHYSICAL GAME

Karpovtsev is an extremely strong skater who is not shy about using that strength in front of the net or in the corners. He does not hesitate to get involved if things turn nasty, and while hardly a polished fighter, he is a willing one. He likes the big hit, but doesn't mind the smaller ones. His back problems limited his physical play last season.

He is a crease-clearer and shot-blocker who is far more comfortable and poised in front of his net than when he chases to the corners or sideboards to challenge the puck. Once he gets away from the slot, with or without the puck, he loses either confidence or focus or both, which can lead to unforced errors or turnovers that result in scoring chances.

Still, he is an effective weapon against a power forward. He can tie up the guy in front, lean on him, hit and skate with a Cam Neely or Eric Lindros.

THE INTANGIBLES

The Rangers expect to lose Jeff Beukeboom to free agency, and Kevin Lowe doesn't figure in the club's top six, which means younger defensemen like Karpovtsev may finally get to show their stuff. Karpovtsev is a potential number four defenseman, a stay-at-home type who will work best alongside a more mobile partner.

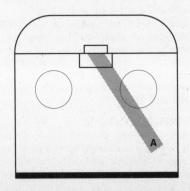

ALEXEI KOVALEV

Yrs. of NHL service: 4
Born: Togliatti, Russia; Feb. 24, 1973
Position: right wing/centre
Height: 6-0
Weight: 210
Uniform no.: 27
Shoots: left

Career statistics:

GP	G	A	TP	PIM
270	80	98	180	361

1992-93 statistics:

GP	G	A	TP	+/-	PIM	PP	SH	GW	GT	S	PCT
65	20	18	38	-10	79	3	0	3	1	134	14.9

1993-94 statistics:

GP	G	A	TP	+/-	PIM	PP	SH	GW	GT	S	PCT
76	23	33	56	+18	154	7	0	3	0	184	12.5

1994-95 statistics:

GP	G	A	TP	+/-	PIM	PP	SH	GW	GT	S	PCT
48	13	15	28	-6	30	1	1	1	0	103	12.6

1995-96 statistics:

GP	G	A	TP	+/-	PIM	PP	SH	GW	GT	S	PCT
81	24	34	58	+5	98	8	1	7	0	206	11.7

LAST SEASON

Led team in game-winning goals. Third on team in goals. Missed one game with flu.

THE FINESSE GAME

You don't often see hands as quick as Kovalev's on a player of his size. He has the dexterity, puck control skills, strength, balance and speed to beat the first forechecker coming out of the zone or the first line of defense once he crosses the attacking blueline. He gets into trouble, though, when it comes down to what should be done after those men are beaten. Kovalev's decision-making procress oftens seems to be a beat off. He will be looking to pass, then decide it's best to shoot — but by then, he is in too deep or is at a bad angle for the shot.

There are too many occasions when the slithery moves don't do enough offensive damage. Sometimes he overhandles, then turns the puck over. Other times, too many times, he fails to get the puck deep. He hates to surrender the puck even when dump-and-chase is the smartest option, and as a result he causes turnovers at the blueline.

He is one of the few players in the NHL agile and balanced enough to duck under a check at the sideboards and maintain possession of the puck. Exceptional hands allow him to make remarkable moves, but he doesn't always finish them off well.

THE PHYSICAL GAME

Kovalev is sneaky dirty. He will run goalies and try to make it look as if he was pushed in by a defender. He's so strong and balanced on his skates that when he goes down odds are it's a dive. Kovalev has a well-deserved reputation among NHL referees as a whiner who feigns injuries, which is probably another reason he merits little respect among his NHL peers. The chippier the game, the happier Kovalev is; he'll bring his stick up and wade into the fray.

Kovalev has very good size and is a willing hitter. He likes to make highlight reel hits that splatter people. Because he is such a strong hitter, he is very hard to knock down, unless he's leaning. Kovalev makes extensive use of his edges, because he combines balance and a long reach to keep the puck well away from his body, and from a defender's. But there are moments when he seems at a 45-degree angle and then he can be nudged over.

He thrives on extra ice time and has to be dragged off the ice to make a line change.

THE INTANGIBLES

The Rangers have finally had enough of Kovalev's inconsistency and immaturity, and if the right trade comes along, he will take his showy skills elsewhere. There is a chance the Russian will blossom in the right situation, as Petr Nedved did after the Rangers traded him to Pittsburgh last season, but four years of waiting is apparently enough for Kovalev's biggest booster, GM Neil Smith, who drafted him in 1991.

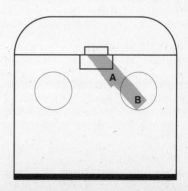

JARI KURRI

Yrs. of NHL service: 15
Born: Helsinki, Finland; May 18, 1960
Position: right wing
Height: 6-1
Weight: 195
Uniform no.: 17
Shoots: right

Career statistics:

GP	G	A	TP	PIM
1099	583	758	1341	521

1992-93 statistics:

GP	G	A	TP	+/-	PIM	PP	SH	GW	GT	S	PCT
82	27	60	87	+19	38	12	2	3	0	210	12.9

1993-94 statistics:

GP	G	A	TP	+/-	PIM	PP	SH	GW	GT	S	PCT
81	31	46	77	-24	48	14	4	3	1	198	15.7

1994-95 statistics:

GP	G	A	TP	+/-	PIM	PP	SH	GW	GT	S	PCT
38	10	19	29	-17	24	2	0	0	1	84	11.9

1995-96 statistics:

GP	G	A	TP	+/-	PIM	PP	SH	GW	GT	S	PCT
71	18	27	45	-16	39	5	1	0	2	158	11.4

LAST SEASON

Acquired from Los Angeles with Marty McSorley and Shane Churla for Ray Ferraro, Mattias Norstrom, Ian Laperriere, Nathan LaFayette and a fourth-round draft pick in 1997, Mar. 14, 1996. Missed 13 games with thumb injury.

THE FINESSE GAME

Kurri has gone from one of the game's top snipers to a strictly defensive forward. His one-timers no longer terrorize goalies and he has lost a half-step on the outside move that used to burn defenders. Goals are now a bonus instead of his hallmark.

Kurri's quickness and anticipation make him a great shorthanded threat when killing penalties. Even so, he is more likely to make a conservative play or pass than try to take the puck to the net himself.

Kurri's knowledge of the game and the way shooters think help him as a checking forward. He has also become quite adept at face-offs, and uses his feet to help control the puck. His skills are still intact enough that he can be useful on a second power-play unit.

THE PHYSICAL GAME

Kurri will get involved for a battle for a loose puck and protects the puck well along the wall. The trade to the Rangers, where he was reunited with several creaky ex-Oilers, rekindled a spark of Kurri's old competitive nature, and he was a more determined player than he had been during his last two seasons with the Kings.

THE INTANGIBLES

Kurri became a free agent at the end of the season and may play only one more year in the NHL. He can still be a useful defensive forward, but unless the right situation develops, Kurri may play in Europe.

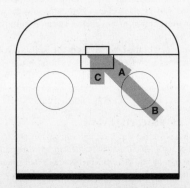

BRIAN LEETCH

Yrs. of NHL service: 8
Born: Corpus Christi, Tex.; Mar. 3, 1968
Position: left defense
Height: 5-11
Weight: 190
Uniform no.: 2
Shoots: left

Career statistics:

GP	G	A	TP	PIM
567	137	445	572	285

1992-93 statistics:

GP	G	A	TP	+/-	PIM	PP	SH	GW	GT	S	PCT
36	6	30	36	+2	26	2	1	1	0	150	4.0

1993-94 statistics:

GP	G	A	TP	+/-	PIM	PP	SH	GW	GT	S	PCT
84	23	56	79	+28	67	17	1	4	0	328	7.0

1994-95 statistics:

GP	G	A	TP	+/-	PIM	PP	SH	GW	GT	S	PCT
48	9	32	41	0	18	3	0	2	0	182	4.9

1995-96 statistics:

GP	G	A	TP	+/-	PIM	PP	SH	GW	GT	S	PCT
82	15	70	85	+12	30	7	0	3	0	276	5.4

LAST SEASON

Finalist for 1996 Norris Trophy. Led NHL defensemen in assists and points. Led team in assists and shots. Second on team in points. Seventh in NHL in assists. One of four Rangers to appear in all 82 games. Has consecutive games-played streak of 216.

THE FINESSE GAME

Such quick hands, feet and thoughts. Leetch is a premier passer who sees the ice clearly, identifies the optimum passing option on the move and hits his target with a forehand or backhand pass. He is terrific at picking passes out of the air and keeping attempted clearing passes from getting by him at the point.

Leetch has a fine first step that sends him towards top speed almost instantly. He can be posted at the point, then see an opportunity to jump into the play down low and bolt into action.

His anticipation is superb. He knows what he's going to do with the puck before he has it. He seems to be thinking about five seconds ahead of everyone else on the ice. He instantly starts a transition from defense to offense, and always seems to make the correct decision to pass or skate with the puck.

Leetch has a remarkable knack for getting his point shot through traffic and to the net. He even uses his eyes to fake. He is adept as looking and/or moving in one direction, then passing the opposite way.

Leetch smartly jumps into holes to make the most of a odd-man rush, and he is more than quick enough to hop back on defense if the puck turns the other way. He has astounding lateral movement, the best in the league among defensemen, leaving forwards completely out of room when it looked like there was open ice to get by him. He uses this as a weapon on offense to open up space for his teammates.

Leetch has a range of shots. He'll use a slap shot from the point — usually through a screen because it won't overpower any NHL goalie — but he'll also use a wrist shot from the circle. He also is gifted with the one-on-one moves that help him wriggle in front for 10-footers on the forehand or backhand.

THE PHYSICAL GAME

Not a punishing hitter, Leetch does initiate contact and doesn't hesitate to make plays in the face of being hit. He is more dependable in front of his net than he once was, and much more responsible in his defensive zone. He simply does not have the strength to man-handle people, but he gets involved. Because taking the body is not his first option, he does more stickhandling than he should. Still, he competes on the puck and has significantly improved on defense. He has developed into a first-rate penalty killer.

Leetch cuts off the ice, gives the skater nowhere to go, strips the puck or steals a pass, then starts the transition game. He'll then follow the rush and may finish off the play with a goal.

THE INTANGIBLES

After a healthy regular season, Leetch was plagued by foot and shoulder problems in the playoffs and was at about 75 per cent effectiveness, or less. His skating was most obviously affected.

Leetch will continue to be an elite scoring defenseman for the next few years, but he needs to be paired with a more physical type. If the Rangers don't sign his partner of five seasons, free agent Jeff Beukeboom, then Leetch will have to do some adjusting this season.

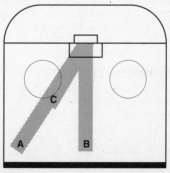

MARTY MCSORLEY

Yrs. of NHL service: 13
Born: Hamilton, Ont.; May 18, 1963
Position: right defense
Height: 6-1
Weight: 235
Uniform no.: 55
Shoots: right

Career statistics:

GP	G	A	TP	PIM
775	98	223	321	2894

1992-93 statistics:

GP	G	A	TP	+/-	PIM	PP	SH	GW	GT	S	PCT
81	15	26	41	+1	401	3	3	0	0	197	7.6

1993-94 statistics:

GP	G	A	TP	+/-	PIM	PP	SH	GW	GT	S	PCT
65	7	24	31	-12	194	1	0	1	1	160	4.4

1994-95 statistics:

GP	G	A	TP	+/-	PIM	PP	SH	GW	GT	S	PCT
41	3	18	21	-14	83	1	0	0	1	75	4.0

1995-96 statistics:

GP	G	A	TP	+/-	PIM	PP	SH	GW	GT	S	PCT
68	10	23	33	-20	169	1	1	1	0	130	7.7

LAST SEASON

Acquired from Los Angeles with Shane Churla and Jari Kurri for Ray Ferraro, Ian Laperriere, Nathan LaFayette, Mattias Norstrom and a fourth-round draft pick, Mar. 14, 1996. Missed 11 games with hip injury. Missed five games with groin injury.

THE FINESSE GAME

One of the first things you notice about McSorley is his feet. His skates are big and heavy (he has custom-made skates that are more cumbersome than the average player's). Add to that his sluggish skating and you get a player whose rushes can be timed with a calendar. His injuries last season made him even slower. It was painful to watch.

McSorley works hard and plays a pretty smart game. He has been used almost exclusively on the backline over the past three seasons, although he can go up front on the power play at times.

McSorley's finesse skills are average at best. He does not have good vision of the ice for creative playmaking. Unfortunately, every so often he tries to make the fancy play instead of the safe shot, and he gets burned because he can't recover quickly defensively. He has to be paired with a mobile defense partner.

THE PHYSICAL GAME

McSorley works hard at his conditioning, but couldn't overcome his injuries last season. He has a lot of hockey miles on him.

He also ranks among the best fighters in the league. He does annoying things after the whistle — well after the whistle — such as shooting the puck at the goalie on an offside call or giving an attacker a shove after a save.

THE INTANGIBLES

In order for the Rangers to get Kurri and Churla from the Kings, they were forced to take McSorley. He was damaged goods, but if he can play at all this season, he will, because ex-Oiler teammate Mark Messier wants McSorley's intensity in the lineup.

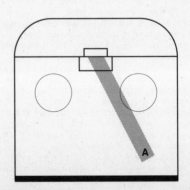

MARK MESSIER

Yrs. of NHL service: 17
Born: Edmonton, Alta.; Jan. 18, 1961
Position: centre
Height: 6-1
Weight: 210
Uniform no.: 11
Shoots: left

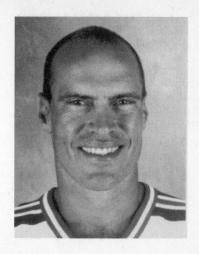

Career statistics:

GP	G	A	TP	PIM
1201	539	929	1468	1508

1992-93 statistics:

GP	G	A	TP	+/-	PIM	PP	SH	GW	GT	S	PCT
75	25	66	91	-6	72	7	2	2	0	215	11.6

1993-94 statistics:

GP	G	A	TP	+/-	PIM	PP	SH	GW	GT	S	PCT
76	26	58	84	+25	76	6	2	5	0	216	12.0

1994-95 statistics:

GP	G	A	TP	+/-	PIM	PP	SH	GW	GT	S	PCT
46	14	39	53	+8	40	3	3	2	0	126	11.1

1995-96 statistics:

GP	G	A	TP	+/-	PIM	PP	SH	GW	GT	S	PCT
74	47	52	99	+29	122	14	1	5	1	241	19.5

LAST SEASON

Finalist for 1996 Hart Trophy. Led team in goals, assists and shooting percentage. Tied for ninth in NHL in goals. Tied for team lead in plus-minus. Scored 500th NHL goal. Moved into fifth place on NHL's all-time scoring list. Missed two games with bruised shoulder. Missed four games with rib injury.

THE FINESSE GAME

Messier loves the wrist shot off the back foot from the right-wing circle, which is where he always seems to gravitate. He makes more use of the backhand, for passing and shooting, than any other North American player in the league. Messier will weave to the right-wing circle, fake a centring pass, get the goalie to cheat away from the post, then flip a backhand under the crossbar. He shoots from almost anywhere and is unpredictable in his shot selection. Sometimes he will not bother with the pretty play, but just throw it to the net through a screen to make things happen.

Messier is smart when he is being shadowed. In the offensive zone he will go into an area where there is another defensive player, drawing his checker with him. That puts two defenders in a small zone and opens up ice for his teammates.

Messier will use his speed — he has a long, strong stride — to drive the defenders back, then stop and quickly check his options, making the most of the time and space he has earned. Messier is unlikely to try many one-on-one moves, but he makes the utmost use of his teammates.

Messier still has tremendous acceleration and a powerful burst of straightaway speed, which is tailor-made for killing penalties and scoring shorthanded goals. He is strong on his skates, changes directions, pivots, bursts into open ice and does it all with or without the puck.

With the arrival of Jari Kurri and the emergence of rookie Niklas Sundstrom, Messier saw less time on defensive-zone draws last season.

THE PHYSICAL GAME

Anyone who doesn't believe there is a double standard for stars in the NHL only has to view the swath of destruction Messier carves through the league without fear of retribution. Hits that would earn a lesser player a game misconduct and suspensions are ignored, even when the victim has to be carried off the ice. Messier is downright mean. His stick and elbows are carried high, and anyone who goes into the corner with him pays the price. Don't expect to ever see his name on the Lady Byng.

THE INTANGIBLES

There are few better big-game players in NHL history than Messier, but the past is the past, and at 35 he is simply overtaxed by the amount of playing time he sees night after night. Messier *wants* to be on the ice, which makes it tough for a coach to tell him "No," (it's especially difficult, since Messier is the Rangers' unofficial assistant GM as well). But if Messier wants to bring New York another Stanley Cup, he'll have to pace himself.

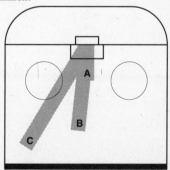

SERGIO MOMESSO

Yrs. of NHL service: 11
Born: Montreal, Que.; Sept. 4, 1965
Position: left wing
Height: 6-3
Weight: 215
Uniform no.: 32
Shoots: left

Career statistics:

GP	G	A	TP	PIM
670	151	190	341	1509

1992-93 statistics:

GP	G	A	TP	+/-	PIM	PP	SH	GW	GT	S	PCT
84	18	20	38	+11	200	4	0	1	0	146	12.3

1993-94 statistics:

GP	G	A	TP	+/-	PIM	PP	SH	GW	GT	S	PCT
68	14	13	27	-2	149	4	0	1	0	112	12.5

1994-95 statistics:

GP	G	A	TP	+/-	PIM	PP	SH	GW	GT	S	PCT
48	10	15	25	-2	65	6	0	1	0	82	12.2

1995-96 statistics:

GP	G	A	TP	+/-	PIM	PP	SH	GW	GT	S	PCT
73	11	12	23	-13	142	6	0	1	2	126	8.7

LAST SEASON

Acquired from Toronto with Bill Berg for Wayne
Presley and Nick Kypreos, Feb. 29, 1996.

THE FINESSE GAME

Momesso has the build of a power forward, but lacks
the hand skills to do too much damage in the scoring
column. He is big and strong and has enough speed to
drive defenders back, but he can't make much happen
with the extra room he gets.

He knows his game is to go to the net. He can also
use a heavy slap shot from the wing, but it is not very
accurate. When he does get it on target, he just about
knocks the goalie into the cage. Momesso uses his
power and balance well in front of the net to create
traffic and scrap for loose pucks. Teams frequently
use Momesso up front on the power play to create
screens.

He does a respectable job defensively. He's turned
into an average third-line winger. Expectations were
always there for Momesso to deliver more, but he
seems to have levelled off at the 15-goal mark.

THE PHYSICAL GAME

Momesso's great balance and size make him tough to
knock off the puck — and difficult for anyone to with-
stand one of his punishing hits. He is unpredictable,
which gets him plenty of room most nights. He could
go ballistic at any moment, and it's not a pretty sight.
Two drawbacks: the intensity isn't there every game,
and he takes bad penalties.

THE INTANGIBLES

Momesso became a more useful player when his work
ethic improved, but he lacks consistency with it,
which is why he's been changing jerseys so often
lately. Momesso tends to wear out his welcome
quickly. If he plays a game of controlled aggression,
he can be a valuable tempo-changer, but too often he
crosses the fine line between toughness and out-of-
control play. Other nights, he isn't there at all.

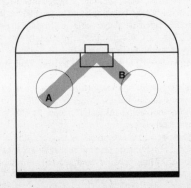

SERGEI NEMCHINOV

Yrs. of NHL service: 5
Born: Moscow, Russia; Jan. 14, 1964
Position: centre
Height: 6-0
Weight: 200
Uniform no.: 13
Shoots: left

Career statistics:

GP	G	A	TP	PIM
355	99	107	206	139

1992-93 statistics:

GP	G	A	TP	+/-	PIM	PP	SH	GW	GT	S	PCT
81	23	31	54	+15	34	0	1	3	0	144	16.0

1993-94 statistics:

GP	G	A	TP	+/-	PIM	PP	SH	GW	GT	S	PCT
76	22	27	49	+13	36	4	0	6	0	144	15.3

1994-95 statistics:

GP	G	A	TP	+/-	PIM	PP	SH	GW	GT	S	PCT
47	7	6	13	-6	16	0	0	3	0	67	10.4

1995-96 statistics:

GP	G	A	TP	+/-	PIM	PP	SH	GW	GT	S	PCT
78	17	15	32	+9	38	0	0	2	0	118	14.4

LAST SEASON

Missed two games with concussion. Missed two games with elbow injury.

THE FINESSE GAME

Defensively, Nemchinov is probably the Rangers' best forward. If there is a five-on-three against, this is the forward who is sent out for the draw. He backchecks well, coming back on his man, throwing him off-stride with a shoulder-check, collecting the puck and trying to do something with it.

He has the hand skills to play with almost any finesse player. Nemchinov is very fond of the backhand shot but isn't as accurate as he wants to be most of the time. Just as his strength powers his defensive game, it is critical to his offensive game as well. Nemchinov will win a battle for the puck along the boards, with his stick or his skates, muscle it into the scoring zone and create a chance. He is strong enough, also, to get away a shot when his stick is being held or when he is fending off a checker. He lacks only a finishing touch.

Nemchinov carries the puck in a classic fashion, well to the side, which makes him much more difficult to forecheck. He is unpredictable in whether he will shoot or pass, because the puck is always ready for either option and he does not telegraph his moves.

He is not a pretty skater and lacks acceleration. He doesn't have the skating ability usually associated with players out of the old Soviet system, but he is strong and balanced and is a dedicated chopper. Nemchinov's leg strength makes him sneaky-fast.

THE PHYSICAL GAME

Powerfully built, he forechecks with zest and drives through the boards and the corners. Linemates have to be alert, because Nemchinov will churn up loose pucks. He is very sneaky at holding an opponent's stick when the two players are tied up in a corner and his body shields the infraction from the officials. He takes every hit and keeps coming. Nemchinov is as mentally tough as any player in the league. He is enormously strong, and never stops competing.

Nemchinov gets checking assignments against behemoths such as Mario Lemieux, Eric Lindros and Joel Otto, and he more than holds his own. He always seems to pin an opponent's stick to the ice at the last second when a pass is arriving in a quality scoring area.

He blocks shots, hits and takes hits to make plays, and ties up his opposing centre on draws.

THE INTANGIBLES

Don't mistake his stoicism for a lack of emotion or intensity. Nemchinov is a quiet leader, a player of character who is committed to winning. Of his 15-20 goals per season, about half are scored in pressure situations. He is becoming more and more of a defensive specialist. His absence was most keenly felt when he was injured in the first round of the playoffs.

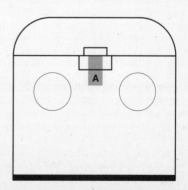

MIKE RICHTER

Yrs. of NHL service: 7
Born: Abingdon, Pa.; Sept. 22, 1966
Position: goaltender
Height: 5-10
Weight: 185
Uniform no.: 35
Catches: left

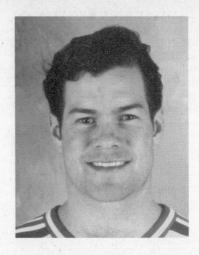

Career statistics:

GP	MIN	GA	SO	GAA	A	PIM
291	16418	817	14	2.99	7	20

1992-93 statistics:

GP	MIN	GAA	W	L	T	SO	GA	S	SAPCT	PIM
38	2105	3.82	13	19	3	1	134	2105	.886	2

1993-94 statistics:

GP	MIN	GAA	W	L	T	SO	GA	S	SAPCT	PIM
68	3710	2.57	42	12	6	5	159	1758	.910	2

1994-95 statistics:

GP	MIN	GAA	W	L	T	SO	GA	S	SAPCT	PIM
35	1993	2.92	14	17	2	2	97	884	.890	2

1995-96 statistics:

GP	MIN	GAA	W	L	T	SO	GA	S	SAPCT	PIM
41	2396	2.68	24	13	3	3	107	1221	.912	4

LAST SEASON

Missed 23 games with groin injuries. Ninth in NHL in GAA with second-best mark of his career. Sixth in NHL in save percentage.

THE PHYSICAL GAME

Richter has thighs the size of redwood trunks, which give him the explosive lateral movement that is the key to his success. He came back from his second groin injury of the season with this quality intact. He is agile, flexible and athletic, and he depends on his reflexes to reach second-chance shots off rebounds or slam-dunk one-timers off odd-man rushes. His motion isn't always all of one piece, however, and he will leave openings with a jerky, choppy movement.

He stays on his angle without charging out. He has worked hard at making his feet quicker, and as a result is much better down low, where he frustrates shooters by taking away the corners. Richter could play entire periods without productive use of his stick or gloves. He rarely catches shots, and hardly ever catches them cleanly.

Richter is starting to use his stick to play the puck more, but that is still not a natural part of his game, and while he is at last starting to use his stick for poke-checks, he still doesn't use it nearly enough as a defensive tool. Rather than use the poke-check, he concedes the pass across the crease and relies on his lateral movement to make the save.

He stands up well but leaves a lot of rebounds. His defense helps him out by scooping up the junk. Richter is getting better on shots through traffic but still has trouble with wraparounds and the occasional long shot. Richter seems to lose his concentration on the 50-footers, as if saying to himself, "Aw, he doesn't think he can beat me with that, does he?"

THE MENTAL GAME

Richter is such a marvellous athlete that it appears more than half his battle is mental. Gaining the role as number one goalie in the past two seasons has been important to his development, as was the successful comeback from his groin injury. When he plays on autopilot and when he lets his athletic skill run the show, Richter can win a game by himself. When he thinks too much, it all falls apart.

Richter used to be devastated by a bad goal, but he had learned to glide over the rough patches and will follow up a rare off night with a strong game. He still has inconsistent stretches where the battle is more mental than physical.

THE INTANGIBLES

Richter's solid work ethic has allowed him to improve his game to a point where he stands among the league's better goalies, but we still can't rank him among the elite.

LUC ROBITAILLE

Yrs. of NHL service: 10
Born: Montreal, Que.; Feb. 17, 1966
Position: left wing
Height: 6-1
Weight: 190
Uniform no.: 20
Shoots: left

Career statistics:

GP	G	A	TP	PIM
763	438	476	914	679

1992-93 statistics:

GP	G	A	TP	+/-	PIM	PP	SH	GW	GT	S	PCT
84	63	62	125	+18	100	24	2	8	1	265	23.8

1993-94 statistics:

GP	G	A	TP	+/-	PIM	PP	SH	GW	GT	S	PCT
83	44	42	86	-20	86	24	0	3	0	267	16.5

1994-95 statistics:

GP	G	A	TP	+/-	PIM	PP	SH	GW	GT	S	PCT
46	23	19	42	+10	37	5	0	3	1	109	21.1

1995-96 statistics:

GP	G	A	TP	+/-	PIM	PP	SH	GW	GT	S	PCT
77	23	46	69	+13	80	11	0	4	2	223	10.3

LAST SEASON

Acquired from Pittsburgh with Ulf Samuelsson for Petr Nedved and Sergei Zubov, Aug. 31, 1995. Third on team in assists and power play goals. Fourth on team in points. Not counting lockout season, failed to reach 40 goals for first time in career. Missed five games with stress fracture in ankle.

THE FINESSE GAME

Robitaille looked nothing like the premier left-winger he once was after joining the Rangers last season. Part of that may be attributed to the weight of a heavy contract. But the lack of a complementary centre was probably the biggest factor, because Robitaille is a pure shooter who has to have a good playmaker as a partner.

By the playoffs, Robitaille had turned into a defensive forward, which was a colossal waste. Robitaille has always been one of the best in the league at roofing a shot. Most of his goals come from in tight. He is so strong with his arms and stick that a defender will think he has him wrapped up, only to see the puck end up in the net after Robitaille has somehow gotten his hands free for a shot on net.

Robitaille works to get himself in the high percentage areas, and he doesn't waste any time with his shots. He unloads quickly, before a goalie has time to move, and his shots are not easily blocked because of his fast release. He simply buries his passes. The pucks just weren't there for him to tee up.

THE PHYSICAL GAME

Robitaille battles for the puck but not without it. He is not a combatant. He will get in the way with positional play but otherwise is not much involved.

THE INTANGIBLES

Robitaille needs to be a first-line player, and unless the Rangers break up the Adam Graves-Mark Messier combination (unlikely), Robitaille will be relegated to another role. He won't score 40 goals again unless the Rangers add a strong playmaking centre during the off-season. Robitaille took a lot of heat for the Rangers' playoff failure, along with Pat Verbeek. Now that Verbeek's gone, Robitaille will be under the gun, especially if he gets off to a slow start. If the Rangers do trade him, they will be forced to eat part of his contract.

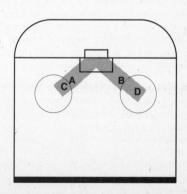

ULF SAMUELSSON

Yrs. of NHL service: 12
Born: Fagersta, Sweden; Mar. 26, 1964
Position: left defense
Height: 6-1
Weight: 195
Uniform no.: 5
Shoots: left

Career statistics:

GP	G	A	TP	PIM
814	43	245	288	2036

1992-93 statistics:

GP	G	A	TP	+/-	PIM	PP	SH	GW	GT	S	PCT
77	3	26	29	+36	249	0	0	1	0	96	3.1

1993-94 statistics:

GP	G	A	TP	+/-	PIM	PP	SH	GW	GT	S	PCT
80	5	24	29	+23	199	1	0	0	1	106	4.7

1994-95 statistics:

GP	G	A	TP	+/-	PIM	PP	SH	GW	GT	S	PCT
44	1	15	16	+11	113	0	0	0	0	47	2.1

1995-96 statistics:

GP	G	A	TP	+/-	PIM	PP	SH	GW	GT	S	PCT
74	1	18	19	+9	122	0	0	0	0	66	1.5

LAST SEASON

Acquired from Pittsburgh with Luc Robitaille for Sergei Zubov and Petr Nedved, Aug. 31, 1995. Missed two games with concussion. Missed two games with separated shoulder. Missed four games with elbow surgery.

THE FINESSE GAME

Samuelsson has wonderful skills that are often overshadowed by the more irritating aspects of his nature. He is a very good skater for his size, with flat-out speed and one-step quickness, agility, mobility and balance. He skates very well backwards. He reads plays well defensively and is always well positioned. He is tough to beat one-on-one and sometimes even two-on-one because of his anticipation.

He is not as effective offensively. He can't carry the puck at high tempo and is better off making the escape pass than trying to rush it up-ice himself. Although he likes trying to handle the puck himself, this is a mistake. He just doesn't read offensive plays well. He does have a nice shot but lacks poise and confidence in the attacking zone.

Samuelsson is an excellent penalty killer. He blocks shots and challenges aggressively.

THE PHYSICAL GAME

Samuelsson plays with so much extra padding that you wonder how he can even move. He looks like a kid whose overprotective parent has stuffed him into a snowsuit, with his arms sticking out at right angles. The protection does permit him to be absolutely fearless in shot-blocking, at which he is among the best in the league.

Samuelsson is a big hitter, sometimes too big. He will try to put someone through the wall when a simple take-out would do. He also needs to hit cleaner, but bringing his stick up on a hit is his most natural move, and he takes many unnecessary penalties because of this tendency. Considered by many to be the dirtiest player in the East, Samuelsson absorbs a lot of punishment in addition to dishing it out. Some of the physical wear and tear appears to be taking a toll on him.

THE INTANGIBLES

Samuelsson was a major disappointment in the playoffs against his old Pittsburgh teammates, but a high tempo game is not one where he excels. Samuelsson has just enough goon in him to distract the opponents, and enough talent to take advantage when the other team is too busy being enraged. He probably has a few seasons left as an effective defender.

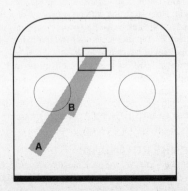

NIKLAS SUNDSTROM

Yrs. of NHL service: 1
Born: Ornskoldsvik, Sweden; June 6, 1975
Position: left wing
Height: 6-0
Weight: 190
Uniform no.: 24
Shoots: left

Career statistics:

GP	G	A	TP	PIM
82	9	12	21	14

1995-96 statistics:

GP	G	A	TP	+/-	PIM	PP	SH	GW	GT	S	PCT
82	9	12	21	+2	14	1	1	2	0	90	10.0

LAST SEASON

One of four Rangers and one of three NHL rookies to appear in all 82 games last season.

THE FINESSE GAME

Sundstrom is a puck magnet. He applies his skills to the defensive game, and when he forechecks, especially when killing penalties, he seldom fails to come up with the puck in a one-on-one battle. Sundstrom will occasionally fail to bear down when he gets control of the puck and doesn't always clear the zone.

Sundstrom is expected to become a very strong two-way player. Some onlookers in Sweden think he is more advanced than Peter Forsberg was at the same stage, but Sundstrom doesn't have Forsberg's elite shot and strength. Sundstrom is a passer more than a scorer. He has to learn to shoot the puck and drive to the net to add new facets to his game and make him less predictable. He reads plays very well. Defensively, he is aware and always makes the safe decision. He could become a more creative version of Sergei Nemchinov, although coach Colin Campbell has compared him to Doug Jarvis.

Sundstrom plays a smart game, and does a lot of little, subtle things well. One of his talents is lifting an opponent's blade to steal the puck. Sundstrom can play wing, but he is more effective as a centre.

THE PHYSICAL GAME

Sundstrom will not get much bigger, but he has to get stronger. He is a deceptively fast skater with good balance and a strong stride. Sundstrom has no mean streak. He will absorb hits to play the puck.

THE INTANGIBLES

Sundstrom showed steady progress during the season. This season, the Rangers will push him to use his offensive skills more, and if he becomes less shy about that, he could become a highly effective two-way forward.

OTTAWA SENATORS

Players' Statistics 1995-96

POS.	NO.	PLAYER	GP	G	A	PTS	+/-	PIM	PP	SH	GW	GT	S	PCT
R	11	*DANIEL ALFREDSSON	82	26	35	61	-18	28	8	2	3	1	212	12.3
C	19	ALEXEI YASHIN	46	15	24	39	-15	28	8		1		143	10.5
L	7	RANDY CUNNEYWORTH	81	17	19	36	-31	130	4		2		142	12.0
D	28	STEVE DUCHESNE	62	12	24	36	-23	42	7		2		163	7.4
C	76	RADEK BONK	76	16	19	35	-5	36	5		1		161	9.9
L	17	TOM CHORSKE	72	15	14	29	-9	21		2	1		118	12.7
D	4	SEAN HILL	80	7	14	21	-26	94	2		2		157	4.5
R	78	PAVOL DEMITRA	31	7	10	17	-3	6	2		1		66	10.6
C	91	ALEXANDRE DAIGLE	50	5	12	17	-30	24	1				77	6.5
C	13	TED DRURY	42	9	7	16	-19	54	1		1	1	80	11.3
R	22	*ANTTI TORMANEN	50	7	8	15	-15	28					68	10.3
R	20	*TRENT MCCLEARY	75	4	10	14	-15	68		1			58	6.9
C	10	ROB GAUDREAU	52	8	5	13	-19	15	1	1			76	10.5
D	94	STANISLAV NECKAR	82	3	9	12	-16	54	1				57	5.3
C	12	DAVID ARCHIBALD	44	6	4	10	-14	18			1		56	10.7
L	49	MICHEL PICARD	17	2	6	8	-1	10			1		21	9.5
D	2	LANCE PITLICK	28	1	6	7	-8	20					13	7.7
L	36	TROY MALLETTE	64	2	3	5	-7	171					51	3.9
D	21	DENNIS VIAL	64	1	4	5	-13	276					33	3.0
D	3	FRANK MUSIL	65	1	3	4	-10	85					37	2.7
D	27	*JANNE LAUKKANEN	23	1	2	3	-1	14	1				35	2.9
R	25	PAT ELYNUIK	29	1	2	3	2	16					27	3.7
R	14	JEAN-YVES ROY	4	1	1	2	3	2					6	16.7
L	29	PHIL BOURQUE	13	1	1	2	-3	14					12	8.3
D	6	CHRIS DAHLQUIST	24	1	1	2	-7	14					13	7.7
R	26	SCOTT LEVINS	27		2	2	-3	80					6	
G	1	DAMIAN RHODES	47		2	2	0	4						
D	18	*PATRICK TRAVERSE	5				-1	2					2	
D	27	JOE CIRELLA	6				-3	4					3	
D	24	DANIEL LAPERRIERE	6				2	4					12	
G	35	*MIKE BALES	20				0	2						

GP = games played; G = goals; A = assists; PTS = points; +/- = goals-for minus goals-against while player is on ice; PIM = penalties in minutes; PP = power play goals; SH = shorthanded goals; GW = game-winning goals; GT = game-tying goals; S = no. of shots; PCT = percentage of goals to shots; * = rookie

DANIEL ALFREDSSON

Yrs. of NHL service: 1
Born: Grums, Sweden; Dec. 11, 1972
Position: right wing
Height: 5-11
Weight: 187
Uniform no.: 11
Shoots: right

Career statistics:

GP	G	A	TP	PIM
82	26	35	61	28

1995-96 statistics:

GP	G	A	TP	+/-	PIM	PP	SH	GW	GT	S	PCT
82	26	35	61	-18	28	8	2	3	1	212	12.3

LAST SEASON

Won 1996 Calder Trophy. Led NHL rookies in points, assists and shots. Tied for first among rookies in power play goals. Second among NHL rookies in goals. Only rookie to lead his team in scoring. Also led team in goals, assists, shots and game-winning goals. Tied for team lead in power play goals and shorthanded goals. One of two Senators to appear in all 82 games. One of only four NHL rookies to score a hat trick.

THE FINESSE GAME

Alfredsson has a big time NHL shot. His release is already hair-trigger, and it will only get better. What stamps Alfredsson as more than a one-season wonder is his work ethic. He didn't make it to the NHL on cruise control. He had little support on a weak Ottawa team and had to accomplish much on his own.

An older rookie (he was 23 at the start of last season), Alfredsson is well schooled in the defensive aspects of the game and adapted easily to the "trap" system Ottawa used most of last season. Playing for three different coaches in his first NHL season must have been chaotic, but Alfredsson remained unruffled.

THE PHYSICAL GAME

Alfredsson has a very thick and powerful lower body to fuel his skating. He is fearless and takes a lot of abuse to get into the high scoring areas. Alfredsson will skate up the wall and cut to the middle of the ice. He might get nailed by the off-side defenseman, but on the next rush, Alfredsson will try it again. He won't be scared off, and on the next chance he may get the shot away and in.

THE INTANGIBLES

When Alexei Yashin failed to report for the first half of the season, the Senators were desperate for help from somewhere and they got it from the unheralded Alfredsson, who was the 133rd player drafted in 1994. With the exception of a little scoring slump in March

— more of a hiccup, really, given that it was the Swede's first experience with a full North American schedule — he was remarkably consistent. Alfredsson won't be a 40-goal scorer, but he should be a reliable 30-goal man every season.

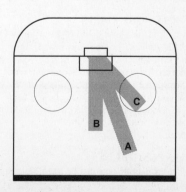

RADEK BONK

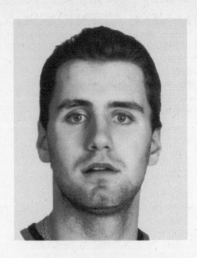

Yrs. of NHL service: 2
Born: Krnov, Czech Republic; Jan. 9, 1976
Position: centre
Height: 6-3
Weight: 215
Uniform no.: 76
Shoots: left

Career statistics:

GP	G	A	TP	PIM
118	19	27	46	64

1994-95 statistics:

GP	G	A	TP	+/-	PIM	PP	SH	GW	GT	S	PCT
42	3	8	11	-5	28	1	0	0	0	40	7.5

1995-96 statistics:

GP	G	A	TP	+/-	PIM	PP	SH	GW	GT	S	PCT
76	16	19	35	-5	36	5	0	1	0	161	9.9

LAST SEASON

Third on team in goals. Fifth on team in points. Missed one game with a hand injury. Failed on first career penalty shot attempt (vs. Daren Puppa, January 13, 1996).

THE FINESSE GAME

Because Bonk didn't set the hockey world on fire in his first two seasons, he was judged a washout at age 20. That's a bit hasty. Bonk won't be an elite forward, but he is improving and could be a useful second-line centre.

Bonk first must improve his skating. He's fine when he gets a good head of speed up, but he doesn't explode in his first two strides (the way Joe Sakic does, for example). He can't utilize his skills when he can't accelerate away from stick checks.

Bonk is a puck magnet; the puck always seems to end up on his stick in the slot. He scores the majority of his goals from work in tight, getting his stick free. He has a heavy shot but doesn't have a quick release. He is a smart and creative passer and plays well in advance of his years, with a great deal of poise.

Defensively, he needs to keep improving. He is decent on face-offs and can be used to kill penalties because of his anticipation.

THE PHYSICAL GAME

Bonk took off his face shield last season and that seemed to release his mean streak. Chippy play doesn't faze him a bit. Although he has good size, he does not show signs of becoming a power forward, but he is aggressive in his pursuit of the puck. He goes into the corners and wins many one-on-one battles because of his strength and hand skills. He is also getting smarter about when to hit, rather than just wasting energy.

THE INTANGIBLES

How hungry is Bonk now that he has a big contract?

That is one of the many questions about Bonk, along with his willingness to work on his weak areas (most players like to practise the skills they're best at). Frank Musil's addition was a good influence on Bonk. We won't give up on him yet. If Bonk had better talent around him, he might move up to the 20-25 goal range.

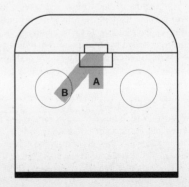

TOM CHORSKE

Yrs. of NHL service: 6
Born: Minneapolis, Minn.; Sept. 18, 1966
Position: left wing
Height: 6-1
Weight: 205
Uniform no.: 17
Shoots: right

Career statistics:

GP	G	A	TP	PIM
387	84	83	167	160

1992-93 statistics:

GP	G	A	TP	+/-	PIM	PP	SH	GW	GT	S	PCT
50	7	12	19	-1	25	0	0	1	0	63	11.1

1993-94 statistics:

GP	G	A	TP	+/-	PIM	PP	SH	GW	GT	S	PCT
76	21	20	41	+14	32	1	1	4	0	131	16.0

1994-95 statistics:

GP	G	A	TP	+/-	PIM	PP	SH	GW	GT	S	PCT
42	10	8	18	-4	16	0	0	2	0	59	16.9

1995-96 statistics:

GP	G	A	TP	+/-	PIM	PP	SH	GW	GT	S	PCT
72	15	14	29	-9	21	0	2	1	0	118	12.7

LAST SEASON

Acquired from New Jersey on waivers, Oct. 5, 1995. Missed one game with flu. Missed two games with back injury. Worst plus-minus on team for second consecutive season.

THE FINESSE GAME

Chorske has outstanding breakaway speed and considerable size — which make him a constant headscratcher among his coaches. On any given night, he will use his body along the boards and take headman passes to key a quick attack. But those nights are rare.

Chorske has too many skills to be a mere grinder, yet when the move to Ottawa gave him playing time on a first line, he never performed to those high levels of expectation. He does not play heads-up when he has the puck. He is always looking down at it, instead of at the goalie to find an opening or to a teammate for a pass. Breakaways or two-on-ones that involve him tend to get everyone excited until they realize, "Oh, it's Chorske." As one scout constantly mutters after his missed scoring opportunities, "American hands."

While that is an unfair slap (Pat LaFontaine and Jeremy Roenick might argue the assets of the American scoring touch), Chorske does lack the hand skills to make more of his speed. He works diligently in his checking role. With his quickness he gets many shorthanded scoring opportunities, but he doesn't bury as many as he should.

In addition to just being straight-line fast, Chorske is balanced and strong on his skates, getting great leg-drive for board and corner work. He is agile, but not when carrying the puck — then, his moves are pretty limited.

THE PHYSICAL GAME

Chorske came out of the college ranks and doesn't play a vicious game, but he is a solid hitter and won't back down. He will take the body in all zones and hits cleanly, but his physical work is inconsistent. Some nights it's there, some nights he could skate with the proverbial eggs in his pockets and not crack a shell. He takes very few bad penalties.

THE INTANGIBLES

With his speed and size, Chorske will always go into the books as a disappointment for barely netting more than 20 goals in a season, but that appears to be his limit. He is one of those players who will always be on the bubble, even with Ottawa, which was looking to trade him before new coach Jacques Martin took over.

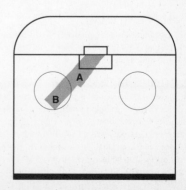

RANDY CUNNEYWORTH

Yrs. of NHL service: 13
Born: Etobicoke, Ont.; May 10, 1961
Position: left wing
Height: 6-0
Weight: 180
Uniform no.: 7
Shoots: left

Career statistics:

GP	G	A	TP	PIM
705	173	188	361	1118

1992-93 statistics:

GP	G	A	TP	+/-	PIM	PP	SH	GW	GT	S	PCT
39	5	4	9	-1	63	0	0	1	0	47	10.6

1993-94 statistics:

GP	G	A	TP	+/-	PIM	PP	SH	GW	GT	S	PCT
79	13	11	24	-1	100	0	1	2	0	154	8.4

1994-95 statistics:

GP	G	A	TP	+/-	PIM	PP	SH	GW	GT	S	PCT
48	5	5	10	-19	68	2	0	0	0	71	7.0

1995-96 statistics:

GP	G	A	TP	+/-	PIM	PP	SH	GW	GT	S	PCT
81	17	19	36	-31	130	4	0	2	0	142	12.0

LAST SEASON

Second on team in goals. Tied for second on team in game-winning goals. Tied for third on team in points. Missed one game with back spasms.

THE FINESSE GAME

Cunneyworth has good straight-ahead speed with a decent shot. He sprints. He hustles. He has had three injury-free seasons after a lot of physical woes, and he competes hard every night. Cunneyworth played on the first or second line all season. On a stronger team, he would be a perfect third-line checking winger, but the Senators ask him to do much more.

He has above-average hand skills and scores most of his goals from in tight around the net. He is a good passer and likes to work give-and-go plays, although at this stage of his career he is not a great finisher.

Cunneyworth is also an effective penalty killer and does everything asked of him. He is consistent in his effort.

THE PHYSICAL GAME

Cunneyworth will hit and agitate. He isn't big but he will check and use his body in any zone. He is very annoying to play against.

THE INTANGIBLES

Cunneyworth was sought after by a number of teams at the trade deadline to help in their playoff push, but the Senators realize they need a few veteran leaders to help their younger players through the team's chaos, and Cunneyworth is ideal in that role. He gave the Senators everything he had last season.

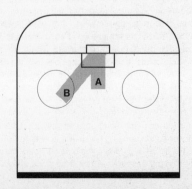

ALEXANDRE DAIGLE

Yrs. of NHL service: 3
Born: Laval, Que.; Feb. 7, 1975
Position: centre
Height: 6-0
Weight: 185
Uniform no.: 91
Shoots: left

Career statistics:

GP	G	A	TP	PIM
181	41	64	105	78

1993-94 statistics:

GP	G	A	TP	+/-	PIM	PP	SH	GW	GT	S	PCT
84	20	31	51	-45	40	4	0	2	0	168	11.9

1994-95 statistics:

GP	G	A	TP	+/-	PIM	PP	SH	GW	GT	S	PCT
47	16	21	37	-22	14	4	1	2	0	105	15.2

1995-96 statistics:

GP	G	A	TP	+/-	PIM	PP	SH	GW	GT	S	PCT
50	5	12	17	-30	24	1	0	0	0	77	6.5

LAST SEASON

Missed 31 games with forearm fracture.

THE FINESSE GAME

Daigle has NHL speed and acceleration, but he doesn't have an NHL body, NHL stick skills or an NHL shot. He was such a brilliant player in certain areas at the junior level that he never had to work at many parts of his game, and he seems unaware that he can't perform the same tricks in the big leagues.

He has fine, soft hands, but he has a tough time controlling the puck in traffic. His skating, his chief asset, is compromised because he gets slower when he's carrying the puck.

Daigle demonstrates a great enthusiasm for the game, but is impatient and stubborn. He has problems with teams that play a neutral zone trap. He has straight-on speed, but when the ice is closed off he looks bewildered because he is not seeking the best options.

A strong forechecker, Daigle is effective as a penalty killer not because of his defensive awareness, but because he wants the puck so desperately. He was making some headway before an injury ended his season, but his production was dismal and he spent part of the season on the fourth line.

THE PHYSICAL GAME

Daigle is feisty and will get involved in the offensive zone, but he has learned to stay away from taking dumb penalties. He could use his body better without getting creamed, but since he's not very big or strong he needs to stay out of the corners.

THE INTANGIBLES

If a game were decided on breakaways, Daigle's team would win more than its share. But there is more to hockey than that, and Daigle has to improve his game on so many levels that he won't be a front-line player unless he works exceptionally hard.

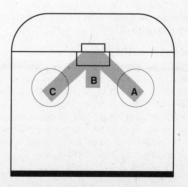

PAVOL DEMITRA

Yrs. of NHL service: 1
Born: Dubnica, Czech; Nov. 29, 1974
Position: left wing
Height: 6-0
Weight: 189
Uniform no.: 78
Shoots: left

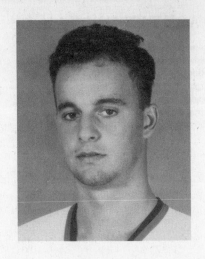

Career statistics:

GP	G	A	TP	PIM
59	12	14	26	10

1993-94 statistics:

GP	G	A	TP	+/-	PIM	PP	SH	GW	GT	S	PCT
12	1	1	2	-7	4	1	0	0	0	10	10.0

1994-95 statistics:

GP	G	A	TP	+/-	PIM	PP	SH	GW	GT	S	PCT
16	4	3	7	-4	0	1	0	0	0	21	19.0

1995-96 statistics:

GP	G	A	TP	+/-	PIM	PP	SH	GW	GT	S	PCT
31	7	10	17	-3	6	2	0	1	0	66	10.6

LAST SEASON

Second on team in plus-minus. Played 48 games with Prince Edward Island (AHL), scoring 28-53 — 81.

THE FINESSE GAME

DeMitra is a one-dimensional offensive player who spent part of the season in the minors to improve his defensive play. It hasn't improved drastically, but it was enough for DeMitra to get called up late in the season and see some regular ice time.

DeMitra is an exceptional puckhandler, and has a quick, deceptive shot. He's not shy about letting the puck go, either — DeMitra had seven shots on goal in one game and needs more nights like that. He likes to drag the puck into his skates and then shoot it through a defenseman's legs. The move gets the rearguard to move up a little bit, and DeMitra gets it by him on net.

He plays the off-wing, and will move to the middle on his forehand and throw the puck back against the grain.

THE PHYSICAL GAME

DeMitra is not very big, which will probably hurt his long-term chances of being a regular in the NHL. He needs to use his speed to stay out of situations where he will get crunched.

THE INTANGIBLES

DeMitra is one player who has to be grateful for expansion. He provides an offensive spark, but his overall game lacks too much to earn him a full-time role on a better team. He will get another chance with the Senators in training camp. If his conditioning and all-around game improve, he will get his share of ice time. He could be a sleeper, but we don't see many more than 20 goals a season in his future.

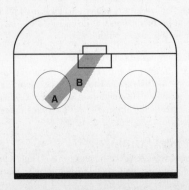

TED DRURY

Yrs. of NHL service: 3
Born: Boston, Mass.; Sept. 13, 1971
Position: centre
Height: 6-0
Weight: 185
Uniform no.: 13
Shoots: left

Career statistics:

GP	G	A	TP	PIM
126	18	25	43	111

1993-94 statistics:

GP	G	A	TP	+/-	PIM	PP	SH	GW	GT	S	PCT
50	6	12	18	-15	36	0	1	1	1	80	7.5

1994-95 statistics:

GP	G	A	TP	+/-	PIM	PP	SH	GW	GT	S	PCT
34	3	6	9	-3	21	0	0	0	0	31	9.7

1995-96 statistics:

GP	G	A	TP	+/-	PIM	PP	SH	GW	GT	S	PCT
42	9	7	16	-19	54	1	0	1	1	80	11.3

LAST SEASON

Missed 33 games with wrist injury. Missed seven games with shoulder separation.

THE FINESSE GAME

Drury is a cerebral player who is appreciated by coaches for his adaptability on the penalty kill. Drury will stick to the game plan. If a strong forecheck is needed, he will provide it. If the team has to key on a special opponent, a Brett Hull or a Jaromir Jagr, Drury will play it the way it is drawn on the chalkboard.

Drury is a shifty skater with decent speed. His forte is his passing ability. He isn't much of a finisher. He is an asset on the power play becuse of his effort and timing in moving the puck, and can stickhandle through traffic. Drury is a poor man's Craig Janney, but with better defensive instincts. He has superb hockey sense.

THE PHYSICAL GAME

Drury is underrated by opponents, who see a rather average-sized forward and may underestimate his wiry strength. Drury has been hit hard by injuries over the past two seasons (he had a broken kneecap in 1994-95), and if he can work his way back to NHL strength, he will play a determined game to stay at the NHL level.

THE INTANGIBLES

Drury will be given a lot of ice time in Ottawa and could be a 60-point man if he is able to recuperate from his wrist injury. Unfortunately for him, that's a big "if," given the delicacy of the surgery that was performed. His strength and flexibility could be affected.

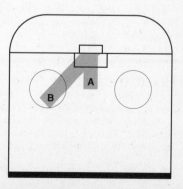

STEVE DUCHESNE

Yrs. of NHL service: 10
Born: Sept-Iles, Que.; June 30, 1965
Position: right defense
Height: 5-11
Weight: 195
Uniform no.: 28
Shoots: left

Career statistics:

GP	G	A	TP	PIM
687	169	366	535	632

1992-93 statistics:

GP	G	A	TP	+/-	PIM	PP	SH	GW	GT	S	PCT
82	20	62	82	+15	57	8	0	2	1	227	8.8

1993-94 statistics:

GP	G	A	TP	+/-	PIM	PP	SH	GW	GT	S	PCT
36	12	19	31	+1	14	8	0	1	0	115	10.4

1994-95 statistics:

GP	G	A	TP	+/-	PIM	PP	SH	GW	GT	S	PCT
47	12	26	38	+29	36	1	0	1	0	116	10.3

1995-96 statistics:

GP	G	A	TP	+/-	PIM	PP	SH	GW	GT	S	PCT
62	12	24	36	-23	42	7	0	2	0	163	7.4

LAST SEASON

Acquired from St. Louis for a second-round draft pick, August 5, 1995. Led team defensemen in scoring. Tied for second on team in assists and game-winning goals. Third on team in power play goals. Tied for third on team in points. Missed 20 games with ankle injury.

THE FINESSE GAME

Duchesne is a fluid, quick, smart skater who loves to join the attack. He often plays like a fourth forward. He is not afraid to gamble down deep, but he is such a good skater that he recovers quickly and is back in position in a flash. He does not waste time with the puck. He has sharp offensive sense; when the play is over he's out of there.

Duchesne has good poise and patience, and he can either drill a puck or take a little edge off it for his teammates to handle in front.

In the defensive zone, Duchesne uses his lateral mobility and quickness to maintain position. He is almost impossible to beat one-on-one in open ice. He helps his team out tremendously by being able to skate the puck out of danger or make a brisk headman pass. He is more interested in the puck than the man.

THE PHYSICAL GAME

Not only does Duchesne fail to knock anyone down in front of the net, most of the time he doesn't even tie them up effectively. He is not big or strong and he doesn't play tough. Positioning is the key to his defense, and he needs to play with a physical partner.

THE INTANGIBLES

Duchesne's production in only three-quarters of a season was impressive on this dreadful team. He'll be handy to have in the lineup as the Senators break in young defensemen Wade Redden and Chris Phillips this season. He has to bear the number one defenseman's role in Ottawa, which is tough, but Duchesne maintained a good attitude under difficult circumstances last season. He could net 50 points.

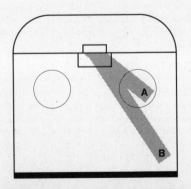

ROB GAUDREAU

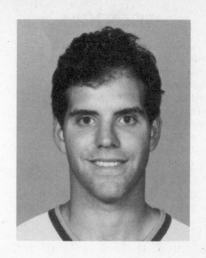

Yrs. of NHL service: 4
Born: Lincoln, R.I.; Jan. 20, 1970
Position: right wing
Height: 5-11
Weight: 185
Uniform no.: 10
Shoots: right

Career statistics:

GP	G	A	TP	PIM
231	51	54	105	69

1993-94 statistics:

GP	G	A	TP	+/-	PIM	PP	SH	GW	GT	S	PCT
84	15	20	35	-10	28	6	0	4	0	151	9.9

1994-95 statistics:

GP	G	A	TP	+/-	PIM	PP	SH	GW	GT	S	PCT
36	5	9	14	-16	8	0	0	0	0	65	7.7

1995-96 statistics:

GP	G	A	TP	+/-	PIM	PP	SH	GW	GT	S	PCT
52	8	5	13	-19	15	1	1	0	0	76	10.5

LAST SEASON

Missed three games with knee injury. Played three games with Prince Edward Island (AHL), scoring 2-0 — 2.

THE FINESSE GAME

Gaudreau is a very sleek, quick, up-and-down winger. He has nice scoring instincts and a good shot. He doesn't have a scary slapper; most of his goals come from going to the net and getting the shot away quickly. He is stocky and can keep his balance with the puck through traffic.

Gaudreau works both special teams. He handles the point on the power play on the second unit or will swing down low. He is a pure finisher. Defensively, his quickness enables him to step up and pick off passes or tip shots wide.

He takes pride in his defensive play and works hard at it. He played defense in his last year of college, so in a pinch can help out on the blueline. In five-on-five situations, he can be used as a checking winger against fast opponents, but not big ones.

THE PHYSICAL GAME

Gaudreau is small and gritty like Tony Granato, but lacks Granato's emotion. He will give up his body to make a play or score a goal.

THE INTANGIBLES

Gaudreau is a finesse player who will be on the bubble as Ottawa concentrates on its younger players. Gaudreau was a free agent after last season, and may not be back with the Senators. If he signs anywhere else, it will be as a third-line winger.

SEAN HILL

Yrs. of NHL service: 4
Born: Duluth, Minn.; Feb. 14, 1970
Position: right defense
Height: 6-0
Weight: 195
Uniform no.: 4
Shoots: right

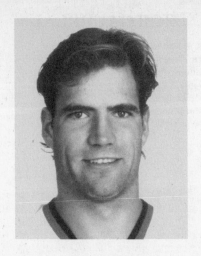

Career statistics:

GP	G	A	TP	PIM
224	17	54	71	256

1992-93 statistics:

GP	G	A	TP	+/-	PIM	PP	SH	GW	GT	S	PCT
31	2	6	8	-5	54	1	0	1	0	37	5.4

1993-94 statistics:

GP	G	A	TP	+/-	PIM	PP	SH	GW	GT	S	PCT
68	7	20	27	-12	78	2	1	1	0	165	4.2

1994-95 statistics:

GP	G	A	TP	+/-	PIM	PP	SH	GW	GT	S	PCT
45	1	14	15	-11	30	0	0	0	0	107	0.9

1995-96 statistics:

GP	G	A	TP	+/-	PIM	PP	SH	GW	GT	S	PCT
80	7	14	21	-26	94	2	0	2	0	157	4.5

LAST SEASON

Tied for team lead in game-winning goals. Second among team defensemen in scoring. Missed two games with back injury.

THE FINESSE GAME

A good skater, Hill is agile, strong and balanced, if not overly fast. He can skate the puck out of danger or make a smart first pass. He learned defense in the Montreal system but has since evolved into more of a specialty team player.

Hill has a good point shot and good offensive sense. He likes to carry the puck and start things off a rush, or he will jump into the play. He can handle power play time but is not exceptional. He is more suited to a second-unit role.

Hill's best quality is his competitiveness. He will hack and whack at puck carriers like an annoying terrier ripping and nipping your socks and ankles.

THE PHYSICAL GAME

For a smallish player, Hill gets his share of points, and he gets them by playing bigger than his size. He has a bit of a mean streak, and though he certainly can't overpower people, he is a solidly built player who doesn't get pushed around easily.

THE INTANGIBLES

A poor man's Al MacInnis, Hill brings a veteran composure to the Senators. He doesn't have elite skills, but can produce 25-30 points a season and will have better numbers if the team upgrades its skill level even slightly.

SHAWN MCEACHERN

Yrs. of NHL service: 4
Born: Waltham, Mass.; Feb. 28, 1969
Position: centre/left wing
Height: 6-1
Weight: 195
Uniform no.: 14
Shoots: left

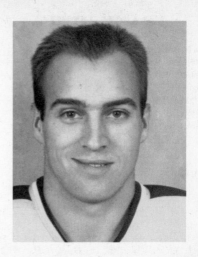

Career statistics:

GP	G	A	TP	PIM
301	85	101	186	136

1992-93 statistics:

GP	G	A	TP	+/-	PIM	PP	SH	GW	GT	S	PCT
84	28	33	61	+21	46	7	0	6	0	196	14.3

1993-94 statistics:

GP	G	A	TP	+/-	PIM	PP	SH	GW	GT	S	PCT
76	20	22	42	+14	34	0	5	1	0	159	12.6

1994-95 statistics:

GP	G	A	TP	+/-	PIM	PP	SH	GW	GT	S	PCT
44	13	13	26	+4	22	1	2	1	0	97	13.4

1995-96 statistics:

GP	G	A	TP	+/-	PIM	PP	SH	GW	GT	S	PCT
82	24	29	53	-5	34	3	2	3	0	238	10.1

LAST SEASON

Acquired by Boston from Pittsburgh with Kevin Stevens for Glen Murray and Bryan Smolinski, Aug. 2, 1995. Acquired from Boston for Trent McCleary, June 21, 1996. One of three Bruins to appear in all 82 games. Second on team in shots. Tied for second on team in game-winning goals.

THE FINESSE GAME

McEachern suffers from serious tunnel vision, which negates much of the advantage his speed brings to the lineup. He skates with his head down, looking at the ice instead of the play around him. He is strong and fast, with straightaway speed, but he tends to expend his energy almost carelessly and has to take short shifts.

McEachern's skating is what keeps him employed. He can shift speeds and direction smoothly without losing control of the puck. He can play both left wing and centre but is better on the wing. A very accurate shooter with a hard wrist shot, he has a quick release on his slap shot that he likes to drive after using his outside speed. He is strong on face-offs and is a smart penalty killer who pressures the puck carrier.

THE PHYSICAL GAME

Generally an open-ice player, McEachern will also pursue the puck with some diligence in the attacking zone. But he is light, and although he can sometimes build up momentum with his speed for a solid bump, he loses most of the close-in battles for the puck.

THE INTANGIBLES

McEachern is a versatile player who can fill a lot of roles with his speed, but his limited playmaking skills will prevent him from being much of a producer. He will get a lot of ice time in Ottawa, and may reach 60 points. He is bound to suffer some kind of depression after being dealt from his home state to the Senators.

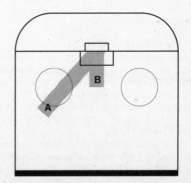

FRANK MUSIL

Yrs. of NHL service: 10
Born: Pardubice, Czechoslovakia; Dec. 17, 1964
Position: left defense
Height: 6-3
Weight: 215
Uniform no.: 3
Shoots: left

Career statistics:

GP	G	A	TP	PIM
671	33	94	127	1137

1992-93 statistics:

GP	G	A	TP	+/-	PIM	PP	SH	GW	GT	S	PCT
80	6	10	16	+28	131	0	0	0	0	87	6.9

1993-94 statistics:

GP	G	A	TP	+/-	PIM	PP	SH	GW	GT	S	PCT
75	1	8	9	+38	50	0	0	0	0	65	1.5

1994-95 statistics:

GP	G	A	TP	+/-	PIM	PP	SH	GW	GT	S	PCT
35	0	5	5	+6	61	0	0	0	0	18	0.0

1995-96 statistics:

GP	G	A	TP	+/-	PIM	PP	SH	GW	GT	S	PCT
65	1	3	4	-10	85	0	0	0	0	37	2.7

LAST SEASON

Acquired from Calgary for a fourth-round draft pick, Oct. 7, 1995. Missed six games with neck injury. Missed two games due to personal reasons. Missed seven games with foot injury. Missed one game with concussion.

THE FINESSE GAME

A strong skater with good lateral movement, Musil is tough to beat one-on-one because he surrenders nothing, and he won't be fooled by head fakes. Poised and confident, he has a relaxed look even when he is working hard.

Musil moves well with the puck and can even turn with it on his backhand, but he employs this skill only to skate the puck out of danger in the defensive zone and does not get involved in the attack. He is not very fast and does not overcommit in the offensive zone.

In the neutral zone, he will often step up and challenge. He can start a transition play when he takes the puck away, as he is a smooth passer. His offensive contributions are limited.

THE PHYSICAL GAME

Musil is strong but doesn't play the type of physical game he should on a consistent basis. If anything is lacking, it is his intensity. He can be a presence when he steps up his play. He finishes his checks and is not above adding a little spice by jabbing with his stick.

THE INTANGIBLES

Musil overcame personal tragedy (the death of his father) as well as a near-tragic throat cut (a skate blade sliced his neck close to the carotid artery) to act as a team leader and as a guiding influence on the Senators' Czech players. He does nothing fancy, but is a solid man to have on the blueline as well as in the dressing room. The Senators gave him a new two-year contract in March, proving that he figures in their short-term plans.

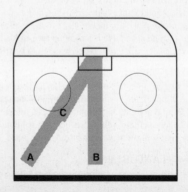

STANISLAV NECKAR

Yrs. of NHL service: 2
Born: Ceske Budejovice, Czechoslovakia; Dec. 22, 1975
Position: left defense
Height: 6-1
Weight: 196
Uniform no.: 94
Shoots: left

Career statistics:

GP	G	A	TP	PIM
130	4	12	16	91

1994-95 statistics:

GP	G	A	TP	+/-	PIM	PP	SH	GW	GT	S	PCT
48	1	3	4	-20	37	0	0	0	0	34	2.9

1995-96 statistics:

GP	G	A	TP	+/-	PIM	PP	SH	GW	GT	S	PCT
82	3	9	12	-16	54	1	0	0	0	57	5.3

LAST SEASON
One of two Senators to appear in all 82 games.

THE FINESSE GAME
Neckar understands the position of defenseman, but he is fundamentally unsound when it comes time to putting all of the components together. He has to use his body more in addition to learning body position.

His offensive skills are overrated, but the Senators give him a lot of time to work on them, including on the power play. He has a slow release on his point shot and doesn't do much that's creative other than put his head down and shoot. Neckar is not a very good puck-handler or passer.

Neckar is a polished skater, especially backwards. He is not often beaten wide. His forte will be defensive play.

THE PHYSICAL GAME
Neckar is not a good open-ice hitter, but is very strong along the boards and in the corners. He will fight if provoked, but he isn't very good at it. He needs to get much stronger. His cardiovascular conditioning is fine, and he can handle a lot of ice time (thrives on it, as a matter of fact), but he has to learn to stick and pin his man better.

THE INTANGIBLES
Expectations were high when Neckar came into training camp last season, off his promising rookie season, but he did not move forward. Three coaches in one season probably didn't help. Neckar may not even show up on time for training camp this season, as he is seeking a new contract. That's not a positive sign for a raw defenseman who has a lot of work ahead of him.

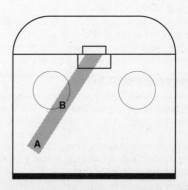

CHRIS PHILLIPS

Yrs. of NHL service: 0
Born: Fort McMurray, Alta.; Mar. 9, 1978
Position: defense
Height: 6-2
Weight: 200
Uniform no.: n.a.
Shoots: left

Career junior statistics:

GP	G	A	TP	PIM
61	10	30	40	97

1995-96 junior statistics:

GP	G	A	TP	+/P
61	10	30	40	97

LAST SEASON

Drafted first overall in 1996. Will be entering first NHL season. Named WHL Rookie of the Year. Named to WHL Central/East All-Star team.

THE FINESSE GAME

Lots of kids in this year's defenseman-heavy draft were being compared to Scott Stevens. Phillips may actually be the closest to him in style and leadership. He may even turn out to be better than advertised.

Phillips is a very good skater for his size. He has all of the attributes — decent speed, lateral mobility, balance and agility. Phillips skates well backwards and has a small turning radius. Carrying the puck doesn't slow him down much.

He will never post Ray Bourque numbers, but Phillips has a feel for the offensive part of the game. He will join the attack intelligently, and has a hard shot from the point as well as a good wrist shot when he goes in deep. One scout ranked his wrister as the best in the junior ranks last season. He is a heads-up passer and sees the ice well.

THE PHYSICAL GAME

Phillips is solidly built and there are very few question marks about his honest brand of toughness. He likes to hit, and he is mobile enough to catch a defender and drive with his legs to pack a wallop in his checks.

Phillips will eventually join Wade Redden, a teammate from the 1996 gold medal-winning Canadian Junior team, with Ottawa, and the future for the Senators may finally start looking less grim.

THE INTANGIBLES

Despite his considerable skills, Phillips ranks highest in this category. One scout said of him, "He's 18 years old, and I'm sure at his next birthday he'll be 28." Phillips cared for his ailing parents, choosing to delay his move to major junior by a year when he was just 16 to stay close to home to help. That is something that doesn't show up in the stats.

Phillips's maturity may accelerate his arrival in the NHL. If he does not start the season with the Senators, he will probably be there by season's end. He is expected to be a solid two-way defenseman whose emphasis will be defense, but he could still provide 40 points a season. Being the first player picked overall carries a lot of pressure, but Phillips has already handled real pressure in his life and coped well.

WADE REDDEN

Yrs. of NHL service: 0
Born: Lloydminster, Sask.; June 12, 1977
Position: left defense
Height: 6-2
Weight: 193
Uniform no.: n.a.
Shoots: left

Career junior statistics:

GP	G	A	TP	PIM
178	27	126	153	236

1995-96 junior statistics:

GP	G	A	TP	+/P
51	9	45	54	55

LAST SEASON

Acquired from Islanders with Damian Rhodes for Don Beaupre, Martin Straka and Bryan Berard, Jan. 23, 1996. Will be entering first NHL season.

THE FINESSE GAME

Redden has tried to pattern his game after Ray Bourque, and the young defenseman has a few things in common with the Boston great. He is a good skater who can change gears swiftly and smoothly, and his superb rink vision enables him to get involved in his team's attack. He has a high skill level. His shot is hard and accurate and he is a patient and precise passer. He worked both the power play and penalty-killing units for Brandon.

Scouts have been most impressed with Redden's poise. He plays older than his years and has a good grasp of the game. As he has been tested at higher and higher levels of competition he has elevated his game.

Redden has been given enthusiastic reviews for his work habits and attitude. He seems to be a player who is willing to learn in order to improve his game at the NHL level, and is a blue-chip prospect.

THE PHYSICAL GAME

Redden is not a big hitter, but he finishes his checks and stands up well. What he lacks in aggressiveness he makes up for with his competitive nature. He can handle a lot of ice time. He plays an economical game without a lot of wasted effort, is durable, and can skate all night long. He would move up a step if he dished it out instead of just taking it.

THE INTANGIBLES

Redden, who signed with the Senators during the off-season, has been a winner at the international and junior level, winning two gold medals with Canada in the last two World Junior Championships, and winning the WHL playoff crown with Brandon. How will he adjust to losing?

Redden is projected as a number two or three de-fenseman and a solid foundation player for the future, but his first few seasons in Ottawa will truly test his character.

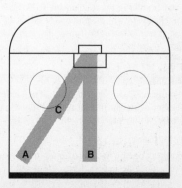

DAMIAN RHODES

Yrs. of NHL service: 2
Born: St. Paul, MN; May 28, 1969
Position: goaltender
Height: 6-0
Weight: 190
Uniform no.: 1
Catches: left

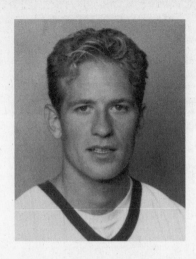

Career statistics:

GP	MIN	GA	SO	GAA	A	PIM
83	4780	215	2	2.70	2	10

1993-94 statistics:

GP	MIN	GAA	W	L	T	SO	GA	S	SAPCT	PIM
22	1213	2.62	9	7	3	0	53	541	.902	2

1994-95 statistics:

GP	MIN	GAA	W	L	T	SO	GA	S	SAPCT	PIM
13	760	2.68	6	6	1	0	34	404	.916	4

1995-96 statistics:

GP	MIN	GAA	W	L	T	SO	GA	S	SAPCT	PIM
47	2747	2.77	14	27	5	2	127	1342	.905	4

LAST SEASON

Acquired from N.Y. Islanders with Wade Redden for Don Beaupre, Martin Straka and Bryan Berard, Jan. 23, 1996. Career high in games and minutes played. Stopped penalty shot by Martin Straka (Apr. 3, 1996).

THE PHYSICAL GAME

Rhodes has sound fundamentals and his arrival in Ottawa — which had tried for more than a year to pry him away from Toronto — instantly upgraded the team's goaltending.

Rhodes makes great first saves and doesn't give up bad rebounds. He either guides the pucks to the corners or deadens the puck in front of him. That is an excellent survival skill for a goalie on a poor team, because the Senators' defense will tend to back in and collapse in front of the goalie, allowing the shooters to use the defensemen to screen their shots. Uncontrolled rebounds allow the shooter to drive in for the second chance, but Rhodes doesn't give away many. You have to beat him; he won't beat himself.

Rhodes was well-coached by Rick Wamsley in Toronto. He is a stand-up goalie who plays his angles well and is solid in his fundamentals. He gives his team a chance to win the game. The Senators won only 18 games last season. Ten of the wins came in Rhodes' 36 appearances.

THE MENTAL GAME

Ottawa doesn't look to be much better this season. How long can Rhodes stand the barrage before he suffers burnout? He came in with a great attitude but will have to be exceptionally resilient.

THE INTANGIBLES

Rhodes was one of the most improved players in 1994-95, when he put the heat on Felix Potvin in Toronto. Last season was tough for him personally, because of the death of his father, and that understandably affected his play while he was still with the Maple Leafs.

The trade to Ottawa gave him a fresh scene and the chance to prove himself as a numer one goalie for the first time in his career. The next challenge: getting a new contract from the cash-strapped Senators. Rhodes was a restricted free agent at the end of last season.

ANTTI TORMANEN

Yrs. of NHL service: 1
Born: Espoo, Finland; Sept. 19, 1970
Position: right wing
Height: 6-1
Weight: 198
Uniform no.: 22
Shoots: left

Career statistics:

GP	G	A	TP	PIM
50	7	8	15	28

1995-96 statistics:

GP	G	A	TP	+/-	PIM	PP	SH	GW	GT	S	PCT
50	7	8	15	-15	28	0	0	0	0	68	10.3

LAST SEASON

First NHL season. Played 22 games in AHL (6-11 —
17) with Prince Edward Island.

THE FINESSE GAME

Tormanen has very good speed for a player of his size,
but he is limited because he doesn't have great hockey
sense.

He is not a natural scorer, but he has a tremendously heavy slap shot. It's devastating. If it hits you,
it will hurt you. He scored an unbelievable goal
against New York's Mike Richter from outside the
blueline, and if that's all there was to making it in the
NHL, Tormanen would be a star.

But he won't score many like that. His slap shot
generally takes too long to unleash. His snap shot isn't
effective and he doesn't have good hands in tight. He
will have to be a role player of he's going to make it at
all in the NHL.

THE PHYSICAL GAME

Tormanen is not very good on the wall. He looks fearless because he really can absorb some serious hits
and he doesn't chicken out, but he doesn't distribute a
lot of hits. He hasn't shown he can fight through hold-
ups or interference, and that's a problem in his game
that can hold him back at the NHL level. He needs
more grit, but he's not a young rookie, and it's not
likely he will add it to his game at this late stage.

THE INTANGIBLES

Tormanen will never be an impact player. He did not
dominate games when he played in Finland or in the
minors, but he is in a weak organization where he can
earn some playing time. His future is as a checker who
can score 10-15 goals, but he will always be on the
bubble, even with the Senators.

ALEXEI YASHIN

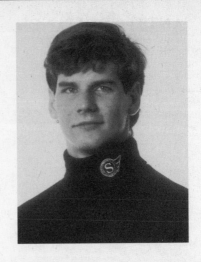

Yrs. of NHL service: 3
Born: Sverdlovsk, Russia; Nov. 5, 1973
Position: centre
Height: 6-3
Weight: 216
Uniform no.: 19
Shoots: right

Career statistics:

GP	G	A	TP	PIM
176	66	96	162	81

1993-94 statistics:

GP	G	A	TP	+/-	PIM	PP	SH	GW	GT	S	PCT
83	30	49	79	-49	22	11	2	3	0	232	12.9

1994-95 statistics:

GP	G	A	TP	+/-	PIM	PP	SH	GW	GT	S	PCT
47	21	23	44	-20	20	11	0	1	0	154	13.6

1995-96 statistics:

GP	G	A	TP	+/-	PIM	PP	SH	GW	GT	S	PCT
46	15	24	39	-15	28	8	0	1	0	143	10.5

LAST SEASON

Tied for team lead in power play goals. Second on team in assists and points. Missed 36 games in contract dispute.

THE FINESSE GAME

Yashin isn't a flashy skater, but he has drawn comparisons to Ron Francis in his quiet effectiveness. He is spectacular at times, but doesn't go all-out every shift. At times, it looks like he's pacing himself or is fatigued. He normally gets a lot of ice time and wasn't in great shape last year.

Yashin can be the best player on the ice one night, and the next you have to go back and check the videotape to see if he was dressed. He is a good friend of Alexei Kovalev, a player who has heard similar criticism in New York.

Yashin's skills rank with any of the new guard of players who have entered the league in the past two seasons. He has great hands and size. As he stickhandles in on the rush, he can put the puck through the legs of two or three defenders en route to the net. He has to learn, though, that he can go directly to the net and not wait for the defense to come to him, so that he can dazzle by using their legs as croquet wickets.

Basically, Yashin has to simply go to the net more and shoot. He has a devastating shot. He doesn't have breakaway speed, but he is powerful and balanced. He doesn't utilize his teammates well. They're not always the most talented bunch, but Mario Lemieux made a 50-goal scorer out of Warren Young, and Yashin hasn't shown signs of being able to make his teammates better.

THE PHYSICAL GAME

Yashin is big and rangy, and protects the puck well. He needs to show better second effort against the other team's top checkers because he isn't too willing to fight through the clutching and grabbing. He has little interest in defense.

THE INTANGIBLES

Yashin held out for a four-year, $13-million contract, but did little to start earning it last season. The argument is that he doesn't have much help, but if you set yourself up as the team's big money guy at age 22, then you had better back it up. Yashin's work ethic is deplorable. He reported to the team out of shape in December and must improve his attitude and conditioning to complement his skills.

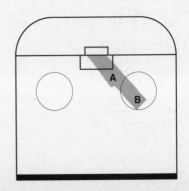

PHILADELPHIA FLYERS

Players' Statistics 1995-96

POS.	NO.	PLAYER	GP	G	A	PTS	+/-	PIM	PP	SH	GW	GT	S	PCT
C	88	ERIC LINDROS	73	47	68	115	26	163	15		4		294	16.0
L	10	JOHN LECLAIR	82	51	46	97	21	64	19		10	2	270	18.9
C	17	ROD BRIND'AMOUR	82	26	61	87	20	110	4	4	5	4	213	12.2
C	18	DALE HAWERCHUK	82	17	44	61	15	26	6		2		180	9.4
R	15	PAT FALLOON	71	25	26	51	14	10	9		2	1	170	14.7
D	37	ERIC DESJARDINS	80	7	40	47	19	45	5		2		184	3.8
C	11	DAN QUINN	63	13	32	45	-6	46	7				109	11.9
R	19	MIKAEL RENBERG	51	23	20	43	8	45	9		4		198	11.6
C	29	JOEL OTTO	67	12	29	41	11	115	6	1	1		91	13.2
R	26	JOHN DRUCE	77	13	16	29	-20	27					128	10.2
D	23	PETR SVOBODA	73	1	28	29	28	105					91	1.1
L	25	SHJON PODEIN	79	15	10	25	25	89		4	4		115	13.0
D	6	CHRIS THERIEN	82	6	17	23	16	89	3		1		123	4.9
R	9	ROB DIMAIO	59	6	15	21	0	58	1	1			49	12.2
D	24	KARL DYKHUIS	82	5	15	20	12	101	1				104	4.8
C	22	BOB CORKUM	76	9	10	19	3	34			3		126	7.1
R	20	TRENT KLATT	71	7	12	19	2	44			2		101	6.9
D	2	KERRY HUFFMAN	47	5	12	17	-18	69	3		1		91	5.5
D	5	KEVIN HALLER	69	5	9	14	18	92		2	2		89	5.6
D	28	KJELL SAMUELSSON	75	3	11	14	20	81			1	1	62	4.8
R	12	PATRIK JUHLIN	14	3	3	6	4	17	1				14	21.4
L	8	SHAWN ANTOSKI	64	1	3	4	-4	204					34	2.9
L	42	RUSS ROMANIUK	17	3		3	-2	17	1				13	23.1
C	22	JIM MONTGOMERY	5	1	2	3	1	9					4	25.0
L	18	*YANICK DUPRE	12	2		2	0	8			1		10	20.0
L	26	PHILIP CROWE	16	1	1	2	0	28					6	16.7
D	40	*ARIS BRIMANIS	17		2	2	-1	12					11	
D	21	DAN KORDIC	9	1		1	1	31					2	50.0
G	27	RON HEXTALL	53		1	1	0	28					1	
D	53	JASON BOWEN	2				0	2					2	
D	3	DARREN RUMBLE	5				0	4					7	
G	30	GARTH SNOW	26				0	18						

GP = games played; G = goals; A = assists; PTS = points; +/- = goals-for minus goals-against while player is on ice; PIM = penalties in minutes; PP = power play goals; SH = shorthanded goals; GW = game-winning goals; GT = game-tying goals; S = no. of shots; PCT = percentage of goals to shots; * = rookie

ROD BRIND'AMOUR

Yrs. of NHL service: 7
Born: Ottawa, Ont.; Aug. 9, 1970
Position: centre/left wing
Height: 6-1
Weight: 202
Uniform no.: 17
Shoots: left

Career statistics:

GP	G	A	TP	PIM
532	186	310	496	556

1992-93 statistics:

GP	G	A	TP	+/-	PIM	PP	SH	GW	GT	S	PCT
81	37	49	86	-8	89	13	4	4	1	206	18.0

1993-94 statistics:

GP	G	A	TP	+/-	PIM	PP	SH	GW	GT	S	PCT
84	35	62	97	-9	85	14	1	4	0	230	15.2

1994-95 statistics:

GP	G	A	TP	+/-	PIM	PP	SH	GW	GT	S	PCT
48	12	27	39	-4	33	4	1	2	0	86	14.0

1995-96 statistics:

GP	G	A	TP	+/-	PIM	PP	SH	GW	GT	S	PCT
82	26	61	87	+20	110	4	4	5	4	213	12.2

LAST SEASON

Led team in shorthanded goals. Second on team in game-winning goals and assists. Third on team in goals and points. One of five Flyers to appear in all 82 games. Has appeared in 239 consecutive games; fourth-longest current streak in NHL.

THE FINESSE GAME

Despite never playing on a set line or even in a set position, Brind'Amour has become ultrareliable and is one of the best two-way centres in the game. His biggest asset is that he is a complete player. He is not fancy and won't beat many players one-on-one in open ice, but he will outwork defenders along the boards and use a quick burst of speed to drive to the net. He's a playmaker in the mucking sense, with scoring chances emerging from his hard work and checking.

Brind'Amour has a long, powerful stride with a quick first step to leave a defender behind. He has the hand skills to go along with the hard work. He drives well into a shot on the fly, and he also has a quick-release snap shot and a strong backhand. His passes are crisp to either side.

Brind'Amour is as good without the puck as with it, because he will work ferociously for control. He is an excellent penalty killer and is the centre the Flyers send out if they are two men short.

THE PHYSICAL GAME

Brind'Amour appears to be sculpted from granite. He uses his size well and is a strong skater. He can muck with the best of them in the corners and along the boards. He will carry the puck through traffic in front of the net and battle for position for screens and tip-ins. He is among the hardest workers on the team, even in practice, and is always striving to improve his game.

THE INTANGIBLES

Brind'Amour can score 80-90 points a season while providing nearly mistake-free defense. He is the ideal second-line centre for the Flyers, and he would take a lot of pressure off the Legion of Doom Line if the Flyers could find two complementary wingers. Brind'Amour's name pops up in a lot of trade rumours because he is one of the first players other teams ask about.

BOB CORKUM

Yrs. of NHL service: 5
Born: Salisbury, Mass.; Dec. 18, 1967
Position: centre/right wing
Height: 6-2
Weight: 212
Uniform no.: 22
Shoots: right

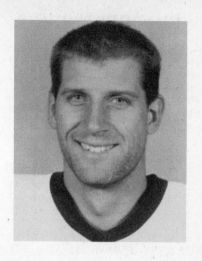

Career statistics:

GP	G	A	TP	PIM
292	52	55	107	138

1992-93 statistics:

GP	G	A	TP	+/-	PIM	PP	SH	GW	GT	S	PCT
68	6	4	10	-3	38	0	1	1	0	69	8.7

1993-94 statistics:

GP	G	A	TP	+/-	PIM	PP	SH	GW	GT	S	PCT
76	23	28	51	+4	18	3	3	0	1	180	12.8

1994-95 statistics:

GP	G	A	TP	+/-	PIM	PP	SH	GW	GT	S	PCT
44	10	9	19	-7	25	0	0	1	1	100	10.0

1995-96 statistics:

GP	G	A	TP	+/-	PIM	PP	SH	GW	GT	S	PCT
76	9	10	19	+3	34	0	0	3	0	126	7.1

LAST SEASON

Acquired from Anaheim for Chris Herperger and a seventh-round draft pick in 1997, Feb. 2, 1996. Missed three games with shoulder injury.

THE FINESSE GAME

Corkum has average skills but makes the most of them with his effort. He has good overall speed, balance and acceleration. He drives to the net for short-range shots and likes to use a strong wrist shot, though he doesn't get it away quickly. Corkum actually played some first-line centre in Anaheim's early days, by default, but with the Flyers he is in his appropriate role as a fourth-liner.

Corkum likes to use a short, sure pass. He will pass off rather than carry the puck. He anticipates well and will hit the open man. He is not terribly clever with the puck, but he makes the bread-and-butter play with confidence.

THE PHYSICAL GAME

Corkum stands tough in front of the net and works hard along the boards. He is a strong forechecker who likes to take the body. He relishes the physical game and makes big hits — anyone hit by Corkum knows it. He works hard and uses his size and strength well. He takes draws and kill penalties. His line (with Shawn Antoski and Trent Klatt) was an effective energy line for the Flyers in the playoffs.

THE INTANGIBLES

Corkum ran afoul of Mighty Ducks coach Ron Wilson, which led to his departure from a rather comfortable niche. The more talented Flyers may have room for him this season, but it will be limited to the fourth line.

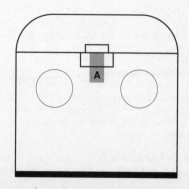

ERIC DESJARDINS

Yrs. of NHL service: 8
Born: Rouyn, Que.; June 14, 1969
Position: right defense
Height: 6-1
Weight: 200
Uniform no.: 37
Shoots: right

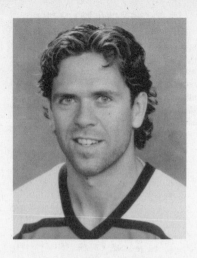

Career statistics:

GP	G	A	TP	PIM
519	55	195	250	408

1992-93 statistics:

GP	G	A	TP	+/-	PIM	PP	SH	GW	GT	S	PCT
82	13	32	45	+20	98	7	0	1	0	163	8.0

1993-94 statistics:

GP	G	A	TP	+/-	PIM	PP	SH	GW	GT	S	PCT
84	12	23	35	-1	97	6	1	3	0	193	6.2

1994-95 statistics:

GP	G	A	TP	+/-	PIM	PP	SH	GW	GT	S	PCT
43	5	24	29	+12	14	1	0	1	0	93	5.4

1995-96 statistics:

GP	G	A	TP	+/-	PIM	PP	SH	GW	GT	S	PCT
80	7	40	47	+19	45	5	0	2	0	184	3.8

LAST SEASON

Led team defensemen in scoring for second consecutive season. Career high in assists and points.

THE FINESSE GAME

Desjardins is an all-around defenseman who is solid in all areas without being exceptional in any single facet of the game. Defensively, he's stalwart. He has good defensive instincts and plays well positionally. He seldom loses his cool and doesn't run around getting caught up-ice.

Offensively, his game has improved but it's likely he has reached the top end. He is a very good skater with speed, balance and agility, and he is willing to join the attack. Desjardins works the left point on the power play and has an excellent one-timer, probably his best shot. He also moves the puck well, either breaking out of his own zone or sliding along the blueline and looking to move the puck in deep.

Desjardins is also a fine penalty killer because of his skating and his anticipation. He seldom drops down to the ice to block shots, but uses his stick or skate and stays on his feet to control the puck.

THE PHYSICAL GAME

Desjardins has worked hard to become stronger. He is very muscular and patrols the front of his net like a doberman. He makes take-out checks, and if his team needs a booming hit as a wake-up call, he will deliver the collision. He has a long fuse and does not fight. Desjardins plays hurt.

THE INTANGIBLES

Desjardins will consistently score in the 40-point range. He is a quiet leader, and although he isn't a dominating number one defenseman, he is a great player in the dressing room and improves any player he is paired with. Desjardins makes the game easy for his partners.

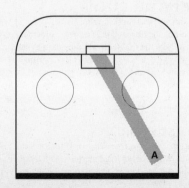

KARL DYKHUIS

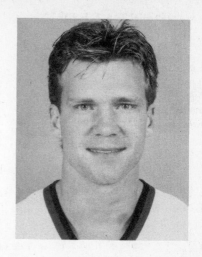

Yrs. of NHL service: 3
Born: Sept-Iles, Que.,; July 8, 1972
Position: right defense
Height: 6-3
Weight: 195
Uniform no.: 24
Shoots: left

Career statistics:

GP	G	A	TP	PIM
133	8	29	37	142

1992-93 statistics:

GP	G	A	TP	+/-	PIM	PP	SH	GW	GT	S	PCT
12	0	5	5	+2	0	0	0	0	0	10	0.0

1993-94 statistics:

P	G	A	TP	+/-	PIM	PP	SH	GW	GT	S	PC
					Did not play in NHL						

1994-95 statistics:

GP	G	A	TP	+/-	PIM	PP	SH	GW	GT	S	PCT
33	2	6	8	+7	37	1	0	1	0	46	4.3

1995-96 statistics:

GP	G	A	TP	+/-	PIM	PP	SH	GW	GT	S	PCT
82	5	15	20	+12	101	1	0	0	0	104	4.8

LAST SEASON

Career high in goals, assists and points. One of five Flyers to appear in all 82 games.

THE FINESSE GAME

Dykhuis has excellent mobility and quickness, with a quick shift of gears that allows him to get up the ice in a hurry. He learned the importance of keeping his feet moving from fellow Flyers defenseman Petr Svoboda. Dykhuis paid his dues in the minors (in Chicago's system) before getting his chance with the Flyers, and he is still learning the game.

Dykhuis's game has an edge on the offensive side, but he also uses his finesse skills well in his own end of the ice. He is one of the best defensemen on the team at moving the puck out of the zone. He is a heads-up passer.

Smart, with good hands for passing or drilling shots from the point, Dykhuis won't venture down low unless the decision to pinch is a sound one. He can kill penalties and play four-on-four.

THE PHYSICAL GAME

Although tall and rangy, Dykhuis isn't a heavyweight. He is strong and makes solid contact. He is such a good skater that he can break up a play, dig out the loose puck, and be off in just a stride or two to start an odd-man rush. The Flyers were unhappy with his physical play last season.

THE INTANGIBLES

Dykhuis took a step back in his development last season, which was a bit surprising given the price he paid to get a full-time job in the NHL.

PAT FALLOON

Yrs. of NHL service: 5
Born: Foxwarren, Man.; Sept. 22, 1972
Position: centre/right wing
Height: 5-11
Weight: 190
Uniform no.: 15
Shoots: right

Career statistics:

GP	G	A	TP	PIM
293	98	112	210	81

1992-93 statistics:

GP	G	A	TP	+/-	PIM	PP	SH	GW	GT	S	PCT
41	14	14	28	-25	12	5	1	1	0	131	10.7

1993-94 statistics:

GP	G	A	TP	+/-	PIM	PP	SH	GW	GT	S	PCT
83	22	31	53	-3	18	6	0	1	0	193	11.4

1994-95 statistics:

GP	G	A	TP	+/-	PIM	PP	SH	GW	GT	S	PCT
46	12	7	19	-4	25	0	0	3	0	91	13.2

1995-96 statistics:

GP	G	A	TP	+/-	PIM	PP	SH	GW	GT	S	PCT
71	25	26	51	+14	10	9	0	2	1	170	14.7

LAST SEASON

Acquired from San Jose for Martin Spanhel, a first-round draft pick and a fourth-round draft pick, Nov. 11, 1995. Tied for third on team in power play goals. Fifth on team in points.

THE FINESSE GAME

Falloon needs to play with people who can get him the puck. He had to go get it himself while in San Jose, which is one of the reasons why he is a much better player in Philadelphia. Playing right wing with Rod Brind'Amour, Falloon found a partner who would work to feed him.

Not a natural goal scorer, Falloon is opportunistic around the net, following up shots and pouncing on loose rebounds. He works to get open and always has his stick ready. He has soft hands and sharp instincts for the right play.

Falloon employs a smart array of shots, using a wrist or slap with confidence. He likes to cut against the grain from the right wing to the left and use the defenseman as a screen for a sneaky wrist shot. His major drawback is that he is a shade slow when carrying the puck; teammates who build up some speed for a charge across the blueline either have to put on the brakes or go offside.

He needs to work on his defensive game. He has shown progress and a willingness to improve.

THE PHYSICAL GAME

Falloon didn't know how bad his physical condition was in San Jose early this season until he came to the Flyers. He lost about 12 pounds under an intensive fitness regime and was a much more solid player.

Falloon is not physical, but he will go into traffic with the puck.

THE INTANGIBLES

Falloon isn't a franchise player, which he was expected to be in San Jose, but he does fit neatly into the role of a second-line winger with the Flyers. Assuming he starts out this season in peak condition, Falloon could easily have his best season ever. He will get second-unit power play time and scoop up the points while other teams are busy checking the Legion of Doom Line.

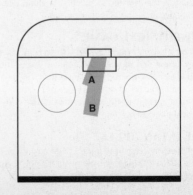

KEVIN HALLER

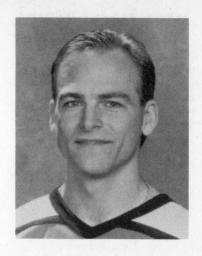

Yrs. of NHL service: 6
Born: Trochu, Alta.; Dec. 5, 1970
Position: left defense
Height: 6-2
Weight: 182
Uniform no.: 5
Shoots: left

Career statistics:

GP	G	A	TP	PIM
335	31	64	95	487

1992-93 statistics:

GP	G	A	TP	+/-	PIM	PP	SH	GW	GT	S	PCT
73	11	14	25	+7	117	6	0	1	0	126	8.7

1993-94 statistics:

GP	G	A	TP	+/-	PIM	PP	SH	GW	GT	S	PCT
68	4	9	13	+3	118	0	0	1	0	72	5.6

1994-95 statistics:

GP	G	A	TP	+/-	PIM	PP	SH	GW	GT	S	PCT
36	2	7	9	+16	48	0	0	0	0	26	7.7

1995-96 statistics:

GP	G	A	TP	+/-	PIM	PP	SH	GW	GT	S	PCT
69	5	9	14	+18	92	0	2	2	0	89	5.6

the poised Eric Desjardins. We keep expecting more from Haller point-wise. With his skill level, he should be contributing close to 40 points.

LAST SEASON

Missed 13 games with chest injury.

THE FINESSE GAME

Haller has good finesse skills, but over the past few seasons has paid a great deal more attention to his defensive play. While he still has trouble reading the rush, he is developing into a reliable two-way defenseman.

Haller still shines brightly on offense. An excellent skater with an easy stride, he makes skating look effortless, and he likes to carry the puck. Injuries affected his production last season. He will join the attack or even lead a rush. Haller can make a play. He is a good passer who spots the open receiver and can find a second option quickly.

He has a hard, low shot from the point that seems to get through traffic. He probably won't ever be among the NHL leaders in scoring by defensemen, but he can improve over the numbers he's put up the past few seasons.

THE PHYSICAL GAME

Haller is still a little light and needs to add more muscle, but he is playing tougher and mentally is more prepared to handle the rigors of a full season. He competes every night, and wants the responsibility of being on the ice in key situations. Haller can overcommit at times, especially when he is killing penalties, and tends to get a little too aggressive.

THE INTANGIBLES

Haller gets a lot of prime ice time as half of the team's top defense pairing, and benefits from playing with

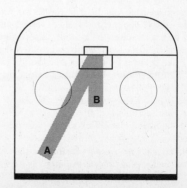

DALE HAWERCHUK

Yrs. of NHL service: 15
Born: Toronto, Ont.; Apr. 4, 1963
Position: centre
Height: 5-11
Weight: 190
Uniform no.: 18
Shoots: left

Career statistics:

GP	G	A	TP	PIM
1137	506	867	1375	728

1992-93 statistics:

GP	G	A	TP	+/-	PIM	PP	SH	GW	GT	S	PCT
81	16	80	96	-17	52	8	0	2	0	259	6.2

1993-94 statistics:

GP	G	A	TP	+/-	PIM	PP	SH	GW	GT	S	PCT
81	35	51	86	+10	91	13	1	7	0	227	15.4

1994-95 statistics:

GP	G	A	TP	+/-	PIM	PP	SH	GW	GT	S	PCT
23	5	11	16	-2	2	2	0	2	0	56	8.9

1995-96 statistics:

GP	G	A	TP	+/-	PIM	PP	SH	GW	GT	S	PCT
82	17	44	61	+15	26	6	0	2	0	180	9.4

LAST SEASON

Acquired from St. Louis for Craig MacTavish, Mar. 15, 1996. Fourth on team in points. One of five Flyers to appear in all 82 games.

THE FINESSE GAME

While he was in Mike Keenan's doghouse in St. Louis early in the season, Hawerchuk was relegated to special teams play. His acquisition by the Flyers freed Hawerchuk's considerable creativity again and he helped fill in for the injured Mikael Renberg on the Legion of Doom Line. Hawerchuk scored 20 points in 16 games with the Flyers.

Hawerchuk needs less space to turn than just about any NHL player, and he can do it quickly and with control of the puck. Shifty and smart, he lacks the breakaway speed to be a dynamic skater who can intimidate through power skating, but he can outwit most defenders because he's downright sneaky.

He is a terrific passer, which was especially important to linemate John LeClair. Hawerchuk sees all of his passing options, and if the lanes are closed down he'll dance down the ice with the puck himself. He has such a fine touch and is so confident that he will make bold feeds through a defender's legs and stick, or feather a fine backhander. Anyone playing with Hawerchuk has to be alert, because he will make a creative play out of what looks like a closed-off situation. He is excellent on draws, using his hand-eye coordination and quick stick to win most face-offs outright.

Hawerchuk runs a power play from the right point, keeping things in motion and avoiding chaos with his timing and control. He can also work down low, drawing defenders to him and slipping a pass to the open man. He is an intelligent player who hardly ever makes a mistake in a crucial situation.

THE PHYSICAL GAME

Hawerchuk doesn't go around slamming people or wasting his energy on futile battles in the corners. He doles himself out like a parent does an allowance, making the big hit when he's sure his team will control the puck, or else using his stick to whack at ankles for possession. However, he fails to use his body well on draws. If he does not win it cleanly, he will not always tie up the opposing centre as well as he should.

THE INTANGIBLES

At 33, Hawerchuk can't bear the brunt of first-line responsibility over the course of a full season, but he seems free from a hip ailment that threated his career a year ago and is an ideal second-line forward. Hawerchuk can provide 60-70 points in that role, assuming he again sees a big chunk of power play time.

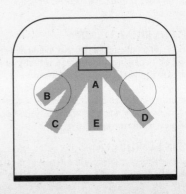

RON HEXTALL

Yrs. of NHL service: 10
Born: Brandon, Man.; May 3, 1964
Position: goaltender
Height: 6-3
Weight: 192
Uniform no.: 27
Catches: left

Career statistics:

GP	MIN	GA	SO	GAA	A	PIM
484	27733	1442	14	3.12	22	529

1992-93 statistics:

GP	MIN	GAA	W	L	T	SO	GA	S	SAPCT	PIM
54	2988	3.45	29	16	5	0	172	1529	.888	56

1993-94 statistics:

GP	MIN	GAA	W	L	T	SO	GA	S	SAPCT	PIM
65	3581	3.08	27	26	6	5	184	1801	.898	52

1994-95 statistics:

GP	MIN	GAA	W	L	T	SO	GA	S	SAPCT	PIM
31	1824	2.89	17	9	1	1	88	801	.890	13

1995-96 statistics:

GP	MIN	GAA	W	L	T	SO	GA	S	SAPCT	PIM
53	3102	2.17	31	13	7	4	112	1292	.913	28

LAST SEASON

Led NHL in goals-against average with career best. Fifth in NHL in save percentage. Fourth season with 30 or more wins. Missed nine games with hamstring injury.

THE PHYSICAL GAME

Hextall's puckhandling ability is still among the best in the NHL, and he's like a third defenseman. He can get overconfident and make the occasional bad pass, but he never loses his faith in his ability to whip the puck off the glass or find an open teammate with a pass. Hextall is a penalty-killing goalie, and his defense takes its cue from him when to get the puck and when to wheel off for a feed.

Hextall is not a great skater laterally. Teams that play a strong east-west game have the best success against him, and he has even more trouble going post-to-post with plays coming out from behind his net. The Flyers' team defense is so strong that Hextall doesn't have to worry about this tactic often.

Hextall is one of the most aggressive goalies in the NHL at challenging shooters. He comes well out to the top of his crease; some teams try to tempt him to come too far out so they can get him to overcommit. Hextall is quick down low, but has trouble on the glove side.

THE MENTAL GAME

Hextall is extremely competitive. He has matured and is a lot less hotheaded than he was in the past, but he will whack ankles and jump on heads if opponents are trespassing. Teams like to try to get Hextall off his game. They still think he's vulnerable mentally.

THE INTANGIBLES

No matter how fine his regular season was, Hextall still isn't a Stanley Cup champion. Unfair as it might be, it's impossible for a goalie to be considered great until he backstops his team to the Cup. Hextall is bound to be disappointed by the failure, and we don't think his 1999-97 numbers will be anywhere close to last season's stats.

JOHN LECLAIR

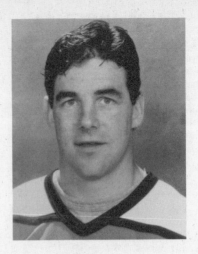

Yrs. of NHL service: 5
Born: St. Albans, VT.; July 5, 1969
Position: left wing
Height: 6-2
Weight: 219
Uniform no.: 10
Shoots: left

Career statistics:

GP	G	A	TP	PIM
343	125	139	264	165

1992-93 statistics:

GP	G	A	TP	+/-	PIM	PP	SH	GW	GT	S	PCT
72	19	25	44	+11	33	2	0	2	0	139	13.7

1993-94 statistics:

GP	G	A	TP	+/-	PIM	PP	SH	GW	GT	S	PCT
74	19	24	43	+17	32	1	0	1	0	153	12.4

1994-95 statistics:

GP	G	A	TP	+/-	PIM	PP	SH	GW	GT	S	PCT
46	26	28	54	+20	30	6	0	7	0	131	19.8

1995-96 statistics:

GP	G	A	TP	+/-	PIM	PP	SH	GW	GT	S	PCT
82	51	46	97	+21	64	19	0	10	2	270	18.9

LAST SEASON

Led team in game-winning goals for second consecutive season. Led team and tied for fifth in NHL in goals with career high. Led team and tied for fourth in NHL in power play goals. Led team in shooting percentage. Second on team in points with career high. Second on team in shots. Third on team in assists. One of five Flyers to appear in all 82 games.

THE FINESSE GAME

LeClair has a bullet shot (he finished second in the NHL's hardest-shot competition at the All-Star game) and can dominate with speed, size and hands. He is a strong skater who can drive the defense back when they see this big dude with the puck barrelling at them in overdrive.

LeClair sees the ice well and makes creative plays. He is not an instinctive scorer and has to work hard for what he achieves. A majority of his goals come from within 10 feet of the net. LeClair has a long reach. He can pass to either side and makes good use of the extra ice he gets, getting the puck free to a linemate if he attracts too much defensive attention.

LeClair was once a reluctant shooter — hard to believe when you see him in one of his grooves, where he just shoots, even if he doesn't know where the puck is going. It's usually on target. He seeks out the high percentage areas of the ice to fire from, and needs to play with forwards who will get him the puck. LeClair has worked to improve his release.

THE PHYSICAL GAME

LeClair can be a dominating physical forward, but he can just as easily be distracted by another team's tac-tics and play a chippy game that gets him nowhere. He was cutting a swath through the playoffs until he was slowed by an ankle injury.

THE INTANGIBLES

LeClair has long had his detractors, but his emergence as a 50-goal scorer has signalled his arrival as a power forward who has all of the skills and now has the desire to play a power game. LeClair has found the consistency that once eluded him.

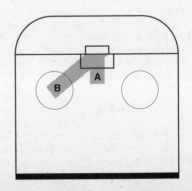

ERIC LINDROS

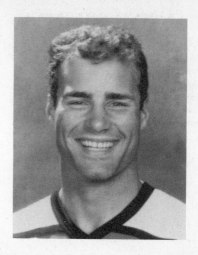

Yrs. of NHL service: 4
Born: London, Ont.; Feb. 28, 1973
Position: centre
Height: 6-5
Weight: 229
Uniform no.: 88
Shoots: right

Career statistics:

GP	G	A	TP	PIM
245	161	196	357	473

1992-93 statistics:

GP	G	A	TP	+/-	PIM	PP	SH	GW	GT	S	PCT
61	41	34	75	+28	147	8	1	5	1	180	22.8

1993-94 statistics:

GP	G	A	TP	+/-	PIM	PP	SH	GW	GT	S	PCT
65	44	53	97	+16	103	13	2	9	1	197	22.3

1994-95 statistics:

GP	G	A	TP	+/-	PIM	PP	SH	GW	GT	S	PCT
46	29	41	70	+27	60	7	0	4	1	144	20.1

1995-96 statistics:

GP	G	A	TP	+/-	PIM	PP	SH	GW	GT	S	PCT
73	47	68	115	+26	163	15	0	4	0	294	16.0

LAST SEASON

Finalist for 1996 Hart Trophy. Led team in points for second consecutive season. Sixth in NHL in scoring. Led team in assists. Second on team in goals, power play goals and plus-minus. Second on team in shooting percentage. Missed one game with calf injury. Missed seven games with knee injury.

THE FINESSE GAME

Lindros may be the best big skater the game has ever seen. He isn't the least bit clumsy, gets up to speed in just a few strides and can hurdle a defenseman to avoid a check, keeping his balance and the puck. His lone weakness is his knees. He wears braces on both knees, but still sustained an injury in the playoffs.

Lindros works for his goals. He is not a natural goal scorer rifling shots from the top of the circles, but drives down low and intimidates the defense and the goalie. He can take a pass with his soft hands and whistle a wrist or snap shot. He has strong arms and can roof the puck as well as anyone in the league. None of this comes easily — Lindros has worked hard on his shots and the results show. He uses a stick with a very stiff shaft and can get a lot of power on a one-handed shot.

He is a better finisher than playmaker, but he can make accurate passes off his forehand or backhand. He does just about everything well except kill penalties, but there are enough teammates to handle that.

Lindros is good on face-offs because he simply overpowers his opposite number.

THE PHYSICAL GAME

Lindros doesn't need to score to be effective, which is something he is still learning. He can dominate a game without getting on the scoreboard. There are still nights when he will float and not do much with or without the puck, although those nights are becoming rarer.

When there is a race to the puck in the corner, the opponent doesn't want to get there ahead of Lindros, because he knows he'll get smashed. So he slows to arrive at the same time, and Lindros has the hand skills and the muscle to win the battle for the puck. There are very few defensemen and no opposing centres able to match up to Lindros physically, not even Mark Messier or Mario Lemieux. His body slams make other players tentative. Instead of concerning themselves first with what to do with the puck, they are bracing themselves for the Lindros hit, and the puck goes bye-bye.

THE INTANGIBLES

Lindros was again among the league scoring leaders, a position he can expect to maintain this season, but because Lindros is still the focal point of a fairly thin team, he gets battered during the playoffs. The Flyers could use a talented gadfly like Claude Lemieux to wave the red cape at other teams and give Lindros some relief. He is still learning to be a team leader. Too bad Messier doesn't sell instructional videos.

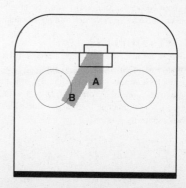

JANNE NIINIMAA

Yrs. of NHL service: 0
Born: Raahe, Finland; May 22, 1975
Position: defense
Height: 6-1
Weight: 196
Uniform no.: n.a.
Shoots: right

Career statistics (Finland):

GP	G	A	TP	PIM
136	15	33	48	139

1995-96 statistics (Finland):

GP	G	A	TP	+/-
49	5	15	20	79

LAST SEASON

Will be entering first NHL season. Fourth in scoring among defensemen for Jokerit (Finland).

THE FINESSE GAME

Niinimaa's skills are absolutely world class. He is a big, mobile skater who is an exceptional athlete. He ranks as the Flyers' best prospect since Peter Forsberg. Forsberg was traded away for Eric Lindros, but Niinimaa, a second-round draft pick in 1993, is a keeper.

Niinimaa will step into the league at age 21, a middle-aged rookie, if you will, and he has some learning to do defensively. Offensively, he is a big Phil Housley. He has terrific speed and agility, and loves to jump into the rush — even more importantly, he knows when to do so.

Niinimaa handles the puck well and doesn't slow down with it. His hockey sense is very good. He will have to learn to shoot more, but that is common with European players.

THE PHYSICAL GAME

Niinimaa will have to adjust to playing in the smaller North American rinks. He is not used to dealing with one-on-one battles, so he will have to learn to fight through those, and win. Niinimaa will also have to learn about body positioning. He won't be a big hitter, but he will have to learn to stick and pin his man.

THE INTANGIBLES

The Flyers are in desperate need of an offensive defenseman, and although it's a lot to dump on Niinimaa in his first NHL season, he is an elite, dynamic player who could step into that role. Pairing him with Eric Desjardins would be beneficial, and would accelerate the Finn's learning process.

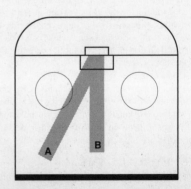

JOEL OTTO

Yrs. of NHL service: 11
Born: Elk River, Minn.; Oct. 29. 1961
Position: centre
Height: 6-4
Weight: 220
Uniform no.: 29
Shoots: right

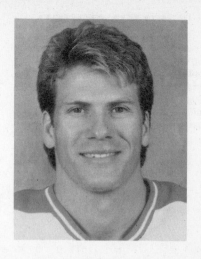

Career statistics:

GP	G	A	TP	PIM
797	179	290	469	1761

1992-93 statistics:

GP	G	A	TP	+/-	PIM	PP	SH	GW	GT	S	PCT
75	19	33	52	+2	150	6	1	4	1	115	16.5

1993-94 statistics:

GP	G	A	TP	+/-	PIM	PP	SH	GW	GT	S	PCT
81	11	12	23	-17	92	3	1	1	0	108	10.2

1994-95 statistics:

GP	G	A	TP	+/-	PIM	PP	SH	GW	GT	S	PCT
47	8	13	21	+8	130	0	2	2	1	46	17.4

1995-96 statistics:

GP	G	A	TP	+/-	PIM	PP	SH	GW	GT	S	PCT
67	12	29	41	+11	115	6	1	1	0	91	13.2

Otto's real value is in the playoffs, but unfortunately for the Flyers, he aggravated his knee injury in the post-season and wasn't as effective as he would have been if he were healthy.

LAST SEASON

Signed as free agent, July 31, 1995. Missed 13 games with recurring knee injury.

THE FINESSE GAME

Otto remains one of the game's best checking forwards. On draws, he doubles over his huge frame so that his head and shoulders prevent the opposing centre from seeing the puck drop. Helmets clash on Otto's face-offs. He has lost a little hand speed on the draws but is still among the best in the league.

Although he has the build to be a power centre, his production has always been a disappointment. In addition to bulk, power forwards have to have soft hands in deep for tips and rebounds, and Otto does not have the touch. The Flyers did give him some second-unit power play time, using his big body as a screen.

Otto is not very fast, but he is quite agile for a player of his size, and he is so strong and balanced on his skates that he has to be dynamited out of place. Even players close to his size bounce off him when they try to check him.

THE PHYSICAL GAME

A fierce and intelligent competitor, Otto is big, strong and involved. He knows he is a brute force, and he likes to make people scatter as he drives to the net. He also delivers bruising checks along the wall. He loves the hitting part of the game, and he has the work ethic to perform consistently to his own high level.

THE INTANGIBLES

The Flyers signed Otto largely to keep him from going to another Eastern team and checking Eric Lindros.

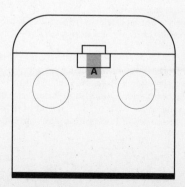

SHJON PODEIN

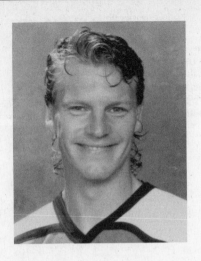

Yrs. of NHL service: 4
Born: Rochester, Minn.; Mar. 5, 1968
Position: left wing
Height: 6-2
Weight: 200
Uniform no.: 25
Shoots: left

Career statistics:

GP	G	A	TP	PIM
191	18	17	35	122

1992-93 statistics:

GP	G	A	TP	+/-	PIM	PP	SH	GW	GT	S	PCT
40	13	6	19	-2	25	2	1	1	0	64	20.3

1993-94 statistics:

GP	G	A	TP	+/-	PIM	PP	SH	GW	GT	S	PCT
28	3	5	8	+3	8	0	0	0	0	26	11.5

1994-95 statistics:

GP	G	A	TP	+/-	PIM	PP	SH	GW	GT	S	PCT
44	3	7	10	-2	33	0	0	1	0	48	6.3

1995-96 statistics:

GP	G	A	TP	+/-	PIM	PP	SH	GW	GT	S	PCT
79	15	10	25	+25	89	0	4	4	0	115	13.0

LAST SEASON

Tied for team lead in shorthanded goals. Third on team in plus-minus.

THE FINESSE GAME

Podein is a labourer. He works hard, loves his job and uses his size well. Podein started out as a centre, but he is better suited as a winger, because his hands aren't great. He is happiest in a dump-and-chase game, where he can use his straightaway speed to bore in on the puck carrier.

Podein is a mucker, not a fancy scorer. He gets most of his goals from digging around the net for rebounds and loose pucks. He doesn't have good hand skills or hockey sense.

Podein isn't an agile skater, but he is sturdy for work along the boards and he can work up a pretty good head of steam. Just don't ask him to turn.

THE PHYSICAL GAME

Podein is antagonistic, with a bit of a mean streak, and he tends to be a bit careless with his stick. He can take bad penalties because of that tendency.

THE INTANGIBLES

Podein played well on a checking line with Joel Otto. He is a high-energy player and penalty killer who can lift the bench with a strong shift. Podein has taken a long route to the NHL and will have to work to stay here. He can pop in 15-20 goals a season in his defensive role.

MIKAEL RENBERG

Yrs. of NHL service: 3
Born: Pitea, Sweden; May 5, 1972
Position: right wing
Height: 6-1
Weight: 218
Uniform no.: 19
Shoots: left

Career statistics:

GP	G	A	TP	PIM
181	87	95	182	101

1993-94 statistics:

GP	G	A	TP	+/-	PIM	PP	SH	GW	GT	S	PCT
83	38	44	82	+8	36	9	0	1	0	195	19.5

1994-95 statistics:

GP	G	A	TP	+/-	PIM	PP	SH	GW	GT	S	PCT
47	26	31	57	+20	20	8	0	4	0	143	18.2

1995-96 statistics:

GP	G	A	TP	+/-	PIM	PP	SH	GW	GT	S	PCT
51	23	20	43	+8	45	9	0	4	0	198	11.6

cult comeback from this kind of operation, and it may take at least half a season before Renberg can generate the kind of power that is essential to his game.

LAST SEASON

Tied for third on team in power play goals. Missed 31 games with recurring abdominal/pelvic muscle injury.

THE FINESSE GAME

Renberg isn't overwhelming in any single facet of his game. He is an average skater in terms of speed, but he has a long, strong stride with excellent balance and his anticipation gives him a head start on the defense.

He drives to the net. He is strong enough to shrug off a lot of checks or even shovel a one-handed shot or pass if one arm is tied up. He likes to come in on the off-wing, especially on the power play, and snap a strong shot off his back foot. He sees the ice well and is always looking for a teammate whom he can hit with a pass, but Renberg has to think "shoot" more often.

He can score in a lot of ways, but Renberg's best shots are his quick release wrists or snaps with little backswing. He is defensively aware and will be a solid two-way forward who can be on the ice in almost any situation.

THE PHYSICAL GAME

Renberg doesn't fight, but he has a bit of a nasty streak and he likes to hit hard. He won't be intimidated. Since he isn't a great skater, his adjustment to the smaller ice surfaces actually helped his game. Playing with John LeClair and Eric Lindros on the Legion of Doom Line has made him even braver.

Renberg just kept growing after his draft year and might actually play better a few pounds lighter, but he is very strong.

THE INTANGIBLES

Renberg underwent surgery after the season to correct his abdominal injury. Players frequently have a diffi-

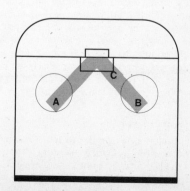

KJELL SAMUELSSON

Yrs. of NHL service: 10
Born: Tyngsryd, Sweden; Oct. 18, 1958
Position: right defense
Height: 6-6
Weight: 235
Uniform no.: 28
Shoots: right

Career statistics:

GP	G	A	TP	PIM
684	43	128	171	1112

1992-93 statistics:

GP	G	A	TP	+/-	PIM	PP	SH	GW	GT	S	PCT
63	3	6	9	+25	106	0	0	1	0	63	4.8

1993-94 statistics:

GP	G	A	TP	+/-	PIM	PP	SH	GW	GT	S	PCT
59	5	8	13	+18	118	1	0	0	0	57	8.8

1994-95 statistics:

GP	G	A	TP	+/-	PIM	PP	SH	GW	GT	S	PCT
41	1	6	7	+8	54	0	0	0	0	37	2.7

1995-96 statistics:

GP	G	A	TP	+/-	PIM	PP	SH	GW	GT	S	PCT
75	3	11	14	+20	81	0	0	1	1	62	4.8

LAST SEASON

Missed one game with neck injury. Missed two games with the flu.

THE FINESSE GAME

One NHL opponent said playing against Samuelsson is like playing in seaweed. He has the wingspan of a condor and is strong with his long stick, so that he can control the puck dangling miles away from his body after he has knocked it off the puck carrier's blade.

Samuelsson's enormous stride just eats up the ice. It doesn't look like he's moving fast, because he doesn't have to. He isn't very quick and doesn't get involved in the rush, but instead concentrates on his own zone. He makes the simple play, forcing the attacking player to the boards and taking him out of the play with a solid hit.

Samuelsson makes an excellent first pass out of the zone. This is one of his top skills. He will also just bank it off the boards if that is the safer play. He doesn't always look for the home-run pass and doesn't get pinned in while trying to make the perfect play. He doesn't amass many points, or many minuses, with his ultraconservative style. Samuelsson has a strong point shot but does not get it away very quickly. He won't be found deep, either, so don't expect to see him scrambling to get back into defensive position. He's already there.

THE PHYSICAL GAME

Samuelsson is a strong and nasty hitter for someone who looks so benign. In addition to using his body and powerful leg drive, he will rub his glove or elbow against an opponent's jaw or offer his stick for use as a dental device. He hits from behind. He also clutches and grabs, but does it in a smart veteran way, hanging on just long enough to provoke irritation but not long enough to merit a penalty. He will also yap to distraction.

He will pay the physical price to block shots and clear his crease.

THE INTANGIBLES

Samuelsson has great poise for pressure situations. He has started looking slower than ever, however, and needs to be paired with a mobile defense partner so he can continue to be effective in his plodding way.

PETR SVOBODA

Yrs. of NHL service: 12
Born: Most, Czechoslovakia; Feb. 14, 1966
Position: left defense
Height: 6-1
Weight: 174
Uniform no.: 23
Shoots: left

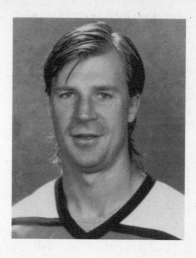

Career statistics:

GP	G	A	TP	PIM
757	45	270	315	1136

1992-93 statistics:

GP	G	A	TP	+/-	PIM	PP	SH	GW	GT	S	PCT
40	2	24	26	+3	59	1	0	1	0	61	3.3

1993-94 statistics:

GP	G	A	TP	+/-	PIM	PP	SH	GW	GT	S	PCT
60	2	14	16	+11	89	1	0	0	0	80	2.5

1994-95 statistics:

GP	G	A	TP	+/-	PIM	PP	SH	GW	GT	S	PCT
37	0	8	8	-5	70	0	0	0	0	39	0.0

1995-96 statistics:

GP	G	A	TP	+/-	PIM	PP	SH	GW	GT	S	PCT
73	1	28	29	+28	105	0	0	0	0	91	1.1

by Bureau in February. He has been plagued by nagging injuries during the past few seasons, and is starting his downslide.

LAST SEASON

Led team in plus-minus. Second among team defensemen in scoring. Missed two games with hamstring injury. Missed two games with shoulder injury. Missed one game with concussion.

THE FINESSE GAME

Svoboda was robbed of some of his skating power by knee surgery and injuries in recent seasons. He was never strong on his skates, but he had great quickness, balance and agility — and you can't hit what you can't catch (although he did get caught with one heavy check from Marc Bureau). Svoboda has very quick feet and is always in motion.

Svoboda has a long stride. Not a very solid player, he is lean and wiry, and his skating is economical.

He has excellent instincts. He can carry the puck well and join the rush. He has a quick release on his wrist and snap shots, and also a good one-timer that he uses on the power play on the second unit. He reads plays well offensively and defensively.

THE PHYSICAL GAME

Not one for physical play, he is still a feisty foe who will take the body and then use his stick to rap a player in the choppers or pull his skates out from under him. He ticks off a lot of people.

Svoboda is very lean and can't do much one-on-one in a close battle. He will ride an opponent out of the play well when he can use his skating to generate some power.

THE INTANGIBLES

Svoboda wasn't the same player after he was decked

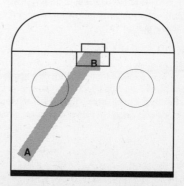

CHRIS THERIEN

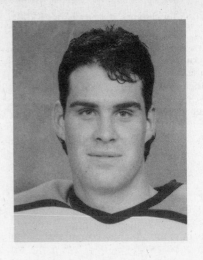

Yrs. of NHL service: 2
Born: Ottawa, Ont.; Dec. 14, 1971
Position: left defense
Height: 6-3
Weight: 230
Uniform no.: 6
Shoots: left

Career statistics:

GP	G	A	TP	PIM
130	9	27	36	127

1994-95 statistics:

GP	G	A	TP	+/-	PIM	PP	SH	GW	GT	S	PCT
48	3	10	13	+8	38	1	0	0	0	53	5.7

1995-96 statistics:

GP	G	A	TP	+/-	PIM	PP	SH	GW	GT	S	PCT
82	6	17	23	+16	89	3	0	1	0	123	4.9

LAST SEASON

Second NHL season. One of five Flyers to appear in all 82 games (consecutive games-played streak of 130).

THE FINESSE GAME

Therien played mistake-prone hockey last season, which is probably to be expected from a defenseman in only his second full season. Some of the errors came from trying too hard. Therien overcommitted in some coverage areas, especially when killing penalties. He is too hesitant, particularly in his physical play.

Therien likes to skate with the puck, and he has very good mobility for a big man. He concentrated on his own end of the ice last season, but he will become more involved in the attack. He can get up the ice in a hurry and has a good sense of offensive plays. Therien can play the point on the power play, and saw time on the second unit there last season.

THE PHYSICAL GAME

Therien is the strongest defenseman on the Flyers — so strong that he's the one teammate Eric Lindros can't mow down in practice. Therien doesn't always use his strength to his advantage, and was far too passive last season. He can dominate physically, but hasn't shown it's in his nature to do so. He simply has to get more aggressive.

THE INTANGIBLES

Therien needs to improve his defensive reads, so he will know when to step up for a hit or when to back off, and he will develop into a solid two-way defenseman. He figures to be among the Flyers' top four defensemen next season but he must be more consistent.

PHOENIX COYOTES

Players' Statistics 1995-96

POS.	NO.	PLAYER	GP	G	A	PTS	+/-	PIM	PP	SH	GW	GT	S	PCT
L	7	KEITH TKACHUK	76	50	48	98	11	156	20	2	6		249	20.1
C	29	CRAIG JANNEY	84	20	62	82	-33	26	7		2		91	22.0
C	10	ALEXEI ZHAMNOV	58	22	37	59	-4	65	5		2		199	11.1
D	27	TEPPO NUMMINEN	74	11	43	54	-4	22	6		3		165	6.7
D	44	NORM MACIVER	71	7	46	53	6	58	3				79	8.9
R	23	IGOR KOROLEV	73	22	29	51	1	42	8		5	1	165	13.3
C	16	ED OLCZYK	51	27	22	49	0	65	16		1		147	18.4
C	11	DALLAS DRAKE	69	19	20	39	-7	36	4	4	2	1	121	15.7
D	4	DAVE MANSON	82	7	23	30	8	205	3				189	3.7
D	20	OLEG TVERDOVSKY	82	7	23	30	-7	41	2				119	5.9
C	32	MIKE EASTWOOD	80	14	14	28	-14	20	2		3	1	94	14.9
C	14	MIKE STAPLETON	58	10	14	24	-4	37	3	1			91	11.0
L	34	DARRIN SHANNON	63	5	18	23	-5	28			1		74	6.8
L	17	KRIS KING	81	9	11	20	-7	151		1	2		89	10.1
D	5	*DERON QUINT	51	5	13	18	-2	22	2				97	5.2
C	18	*CHAD KILGER	74	7	10	17	-4	34			1		57	12.3
R	19	*SHANE DOAN	74	7	10	17	-9	101	1		3		106	6.6
D	28	CRAIG MUNI	72	1	7	8	-6	106					41	2.4
L	33	JIM MCKENZIE	73	4	2	6	-4	202					28	14.3
D	26	JEFF FINLEY	65	1	5	6	-2	81					27	3.7
C	15	RANDY GILHEN	22	2	3	5	1	12					26	7.7
R	21	DENIS CHASSE	60	3		3	-14	125	1		1		31	9.7
C	39	IAIN FRASER	12	1	1	2	1	4					12	8.3
D	55	*JASON DOIG	15	1	1	2	-2	28					7	14.3
R	22	*CRAIG MILLS	4		2	2	0							
D	3	BRENT THOMPSON	10		1	1	-2	21					7	
D	6	DALLAS EAKINS	18		1	1	-1	34					6	
G	37	TOM DRAPER	1				0							
C	12	ROB MURRAY	1				-1	2					1	
G	31	*SCOTT LANGKOW	1				0							
R	43	*RAVIL GUSMANOV	4				-3							6	
G	37	DOMINIC ROUSSEL	16				0	2						
R	30	ED RONAN	17				-3	16					13	
G	29	TIM CHEVELDAE	30				0							
G	35	N. KHABIBULIN	53				0	12						

GP = games played; G = goals; A = assists; PTS = points; +/- = goals-for minus goals-against while player is on ice; PIM = penalties in minutes; PP = power play goals; SH = shorthanded goals; GW = game-winning goals; GT = game-tying goals; S = no. of shots; PCT = percentage of goals to shots; * = rookie

SHANE DOAN

Yrs. of NHL service: 1
Born: Halkirk, Alberta; Oct. 10, 1976
Position: right wing
Height: 6-1
Weight: 215
Uniform no.: 19
Shoots: right

Career statistics:

GP	G	A	TP	PIM
74	7	10	17	101

1995-96 statistics:

GP	G	A	TP	+/-	PIM	PP	SH	GW	GT	S	PCT
74	7	10	17	-9	101	1	0	3	0	106	6.6

LAST SEASON

First NHL season. Missed five games with rib injury. Missed three games with back injury.

THE FINESSE GAME

Doan's game is speed. He is fast and strong, forechecking aggressively and intelligently along the wall and in the corners. Doan intimidates with his skating, because he gets in on a defenseman fast. Once he gains control of the puck, Doan will find the open man in front of the net. He isn't overly creative, but will thrive on the dump-and-chase play where he can just skate on his wing and race for the puck.

Doan has an acceptable wrist and slap shot, but he doesn't shoot much. He will become more of a threat if he gains some confidence in his shot.

Doan saw almost no special teams play last season, but he will develop into a good penalty killer and can probably handle second-unit power play time as well.

THE PHYSICAL GAME

Doan is strong and needs to show a little more aggressiveness. He seems to have a mean streak lurking under his exterior. He will lay some hard hits on people.

THE INTANGIBLES

Doan was the MVP of the 1995 Memorial Cup Tournament, so he has a history of stepping up in key situations. Doan's confidence was a little shaky last season, but he will play for a familiar coach, Don Hay, this season and that will help him. He has a very good attitude and work ethic. If he earns regular ice time on the third line, he could produce 15-20 goals.

DALLAS DRAKE

Yrs. of NHL service: 4
Born: Trail, B.C.; Feb. 4, 1969
Position: centre
Height: 6-0
Weight: 180
Uniform no.: 11
Shoots: left

Career statistics:

GP	G	A	TP	PIM
246	58	91	149	208

1992-93 statistics:

GP	G	A	TP	+/-	PIM	PP	SH	GW	GT	S	PCT
72	18	26	44	+15	93	3	2	5	0	89	20.2

1993-94 statistics:

GP	G	A	TP	+/-	PIM	PP	SH	GW	GT	S	PCT
62	13	27	40	-1	49	1	2	3	0	112	11.6

1994-95 statistics:

GP	G	A	TP	+/-	PIM	PP	SH	GW	GT	S	PCT
43	8	18	26	-6	30	0	0	1	0	66	12.1

1995-96 statistics:

GP	G	A	TP	+/-	PIM	PP	SH	GW	GT	S	PCT
69	19	20	39	-7	36	4	4	2	1	121	15.7

LAST SEASON

Led team in shorthanded goals. Missed two games with ear infection. Missed eight games with shoulder injury.

THE FINESSE GAME

Drake ended the season playing on the team's top line with Keith Tkachuk and Craig Janney, playing the grinder's role by going into the corners for the puck for his playmaking centre and power winger. This was a case of overachieving for Drake, who is better suited to a second-line role, but the chemistry worked.

Drake is an aggressive forechecker who is strong along the boards and in front of the net. He's on the small side, so he doesn't stand in and take a bashing, but he'll jump in and out of traffic to fight for the puck or bounce in on rebounds.

Drake is quick and powerful in his skating. He'll get outmuscled, but not outhustled. His scoring chances will come in deep.

THE PHYSICAL GAME

Drake gets noticed because he runs right over people. He is limited by his size, but he will give a team whatever he's got. He's feisty enough to get the other team's attention, and he works to keep himself in scoring position.

Good things invariably happen when Drake takes the body. He is a strong penalty killer and forechecker.

THE INTANGIBLES

Drake's grit and determination set him apart from some finesse players who take too many nights off.

We predicted 20 goals for Drake last season, and he would have exceeded that if he hadn't been injured.

New coach Don Hay will determine how Drake is used this season in Phoenix. If he retains his role on the number one line, expect his production to increase slightly. He received a new two-year contract in March, which assures him of his importance to the team. Drake suffered a knee ligament injury in the playoffs which may affect his start this season.

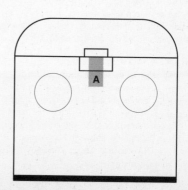

MIKE EASTWOOD

Yrs. of NHL service: 4
Born: Ottawa, Ont.; July 1, 1967
Position: centre
Height: 6-2
Weight: 190
Uniform no.: 32
Shoots: right

Career statistics:

GP	G	A	TP	PIM
204	31	43	74	109

1992-93 statistics:

GP	G	A	TP	+/-	PIM	PP	SH	GW	GT	S	PCT
12	1	6	7	-2	21	0	0	0	0	11	9.1

1993-94 statistics:

GP	G	A	TP	+/-	PIM	PP	SH	GW	GT	S	PCT
54	8	10	18	+2	28	1	0	2	0	41	19.5

1994-95 statistics:

GP	G	A	TP	+/-	PIM	PP	SH	GW	GT	S	PCT
49	8	11	19	-9	36	0	0	0	0	55	14.5

1995-96 statistics:

GP	G	A	TP	+/-	PIM	PP	SH	GW	GT	S	PCT
80	14	14	28	-14	20	2	0	3	1	94	14.9

LAST SEASON

Career high in goals, assists and points.

THE FINESSE GAME

With a little more spunk, Eastwood could be a strong third-line centre. His problem is a lack of consistency. He is a big, strong player that coaches always want to get more out of. He has some sparkling games but lacks the confidence and offensive contribution to become an effective everyday player.

Eastwood is sound defensively. He is good on draws and is alert and aware.

Deceptively quick as a skater, he doesn't always push himself hard and needs to be urged along by coaches. He kills penalties well. Eastwood received some power play time on the second unit last season, but will need to earn future ice time on the power play.

THE PHYSICAL GAME

Eastwood is strong and doesn't get knocked off the puck, but he doesn't have much presence on the ice and could initiate more contact. He has to work on his conditioning and off-ice strengthening.

THE INTANGIBLES

The next step is to wring more offense out of Eastwood. His numbers improved slightly last season, but given his size he should be producing in the 20-25 goal range. Eastwood was a restricted free agent at the end of last season. If he is re-signed by Phoenix, he could be on the bubble, although his position will improve if the Coyotes lose Alexei Zhamnov and don't acquire another quality centre.

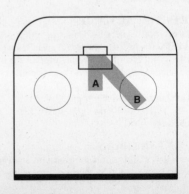

MIKE GARTNER

Yrs. of NHL service: 17
Born: Ottawa, Ont.; Oct. 29, 1959
Position: right wing
Height: 6-0
Weight: 190
Uniform no.: 11
Shoots: right

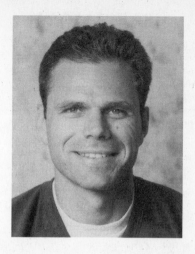

Career statistics:

GP	G	A	TP	PIM
1290	665	581	1245	1097

1992-93 statistics:

GP	G	A	TP	+/-	PIM	PP	SH	GW	GT	S	PCT
84	45	23	68	-4	59	13	0	3	1	323	13.9

1993-94 statistics:

GP	G	A	TP	+/-	PIM	PP	SH	GW	GT	S	PCT
81	34	30	64	+20	62	11	5	4	0	275	12.4

1994-95 statistics:

GP	G	A	TP	+/-	PIM	PP	SH	GW	GT	S	PCT
38	12	8	20	0	6	2	1	1	1	91	13.2

1995-96 statistics:

GP	G	A	TP	+/-	PIM	PP	SH	GW	GT	S	PCT
82	35	19	54	+5	52	15	0	4	1	275	12.7

LAST SEASON

Acquired from Toronto for a fourth-round draft pick, June 22, 1996. Led Maple Leafs in goals and power play goals. Second on team in plus-minus and game-winning goals. One of three Leafs to appear in all 82 games. Scored 1,200th career point.

THE FINESSE GAME

At 37, the ageless Gartner still has exceptional speed, and again won the fastest skater competition (for the fourth time!) at the NHL All-Star game skills competition. He has flawless technical form — great stride, deep knee bend and excellent posture, which add up to power and speed. He is a human skating machine. Carrying the puck doesn't slow him down and he can still pull away from pursuers, as his 16th season with 30 or more goals will attest.

Gartner may have to learn to add some more crafty moves to his patented drive wide down the wing. As he slows, he can hold up and wait for a trailing teammate, because he still pushes defensemen back with his speed and opens up the ice.

Ever alert to his offensive chances, Gartner is sometimes guilty of hanging a little at the redline, looking for the break into the attacking zone. He can accept a pass in full flight. He has a clever play he uses in which he treats the boards as an extra teammate, giving himself a little pass off the wall or setting up a linemate with a smart feed.

Gartner drives his shot off the wing on the fly or uses a strong wrist shot from closer range. If his lane to the net is blocked, he will curl around behind the net — still at good speed — for a wraparound try. He isn't much of a playmaker. His assists come from teammates smart enough to follow up on his play for rebounds.

THE PHYSICAL GAME

Gartner is wiry and strong. When he doesn't beat a checker cleanly to the outside, he will still manage to squeeze through along the boards and keep going forward with the puck, even if dragged to his knees.

He goes to the net and into the corners for the puck, and he has strong arms and wrists to reach into scrums and control it. He can flick a puck at the net one-handed. He seldom takes bad penalties. Even with a lot of miles on him, Gartner is very fit.

THE INTANGIBLES

We predicted another 30-goal season for Gartner last season, and he did it, but we don't know if we should push our luck. Aw, why not? He's still in the wild, wild Western Conference on a young, eager, quick team that will be playing in a new city and he can expect to feed off that energy.

Gartner threatened to retire after the trade — he was miffed because he was told the news by a fellow tourist while on vacation — but a contract extension delayed the rocking chair.

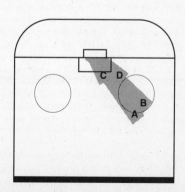

CRAIG JANNEY

Yrs. of NHL service: 8
Born: Hartford, Conn.; Sept. 26, 1967
Position: centre
Height: 6-1
Weight: 190
Uniform no.: 29
Shoots: left

Career statistics:

GP	G	A	TP	PIM
559	158	460	662	118

1992-93 statistics:

GP	G	A	TP	+/-	PIM	PP	SH	GW	GT	S	PCT
84	24	82	106	-4	12	8	0	6	0	137	17.5

1993-94 statistics:

GP	G	A	TP	+/-	PIM	PP	SH	GW	GT	S	PCT
69	16	68	84	-14	24	8	0	7	0	95	16.8

1994-95 statistics:

GP	G	A	TP	+/-	PIM	PP	SH	GW	GT	S	PCT
35	7	20	27	-1	10	3	0	1	0	40	17.5

1995-96 statistics:

GP	G	A	TP	+/-	PIM	PP	SH	GW	GT	S	PCT
84	20	62	82	-33	26	7	0	2	0	91	22.0

LAST SEASON

Acquired from San Jose for Darren Turcotte and a second-round draft pick, Mar. 18, 1996. Led team in assists. Led team and third in NHL in shooting percentage. One of three players on team to appear in all 82 games (one of two players in NHL to appear in 84, due to trade).

THE FINESSE GAME

Probably one of the top five passers in the NHL, Janney finds his target, and finds him in time to allow the shooter enough room to do something with the puck. He will draw the defender to him to open up ice, but by keeping the puck close to his body (he uses a very short stick) he makes it difficult for anyone fishing for the puck to knock it away. He then makes the pretty pass.

Janney is very creative and sees the ice and all of his options well. Get into the open and Janney will get the puck to you. He will usually disguise his intentions well enough so that the defense is caught napping. Linemates have to stay alert because he will turn what seems to be a dead play into a sudden scoring chance.

Janney's reluctance to shoot borders on the ridiculous. How can any first-line player have only 91 shots in 84 games? Ron Hextall probably had more shots on goal. Janney has an excellent release, and could tack on an extra 10 goals a year, but he would rather pass than shoot. He is patient with the puck and will wait for the goalie to commit. He has pinpoint accuracy, but he usually has to be wide open before he will take a shot.

No speed demon, Janney has slick moves that he puts on in a burst just when it appears he is about to come to a standstill. Defensively, he remains suspect.

THE PHYSICAL GAME

Janney isn't more of a scoring threat because he isn't strong enough to win the one-on-one battles in traffic. His conditioning has improved to handle all the ice time he usually gets.

The opponent's book is to hit Janney early and often. He will keep himself out of the trenches. He has fairly good size, but doesn't have the upper body strength to knock anyone off the puck or prevent the puck being stripped from him. He is not a coward, though, and will take a hit to make a play since he controls the puck until the last moment, waiting for the perfect play.

THE INTANGIBLES

Janney isn't known as one of the most amiable people in the league, but he hasn't missed the playoffs in his 10 NHL seasons, and since he's played on some pretty awful teams (St. Louis, San Jose, Winnipeg) that's a major accomplishment.

The trade to Winnipeg (now Phoenix) and his re-signing after last season by the Coyotes sets Janney up for what could be his best season ever. Keith Tkachuk is the perfect partner for Janney, a power forward with an excellent scoring touch. Janney scored 20 points in 13 games with the Jets, which projects to a 126-point season.

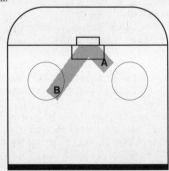

NIKOLAI KHABIBULIN

Yrs. of NHL service: 2
Born: Sverdlovsk, USSR; Jan. 13, 1973
Position: goaltender
Height: 6-1
Weight: 176
Uniform no.: 35
Catches: left

Career statistics:

GP	MIN	GA	SO	GAA	A	PIM
79	4253	228	2	3.22	1	16

1994-95 statistics:

GP	MIN	GAA	W	L	T	SO	GA	S	SAPCT	PIM
26	1339	3.41	8	9	4	0	76	723	.895	4

1995-96 statistics:

GP	MIN	GAA	W	L	T	SO	GA	S	SAPCT	PIM
53	2914	3.13	26	20	3	2	152	1656	.908	12

flaws in his game can easily be ironed out.

LAST SEASON

Career high in games played and wins. Missed 20 games with knee injury.

THE PHYSICAL GAME

Khabibulin plays goal like a shortstop. He gets down low and always gets his body behind the shot. Khabibulin stays on his feet and moves with the shooter. He may perform the best split save in the league. It's stunningly graceful and athletic, and his legs look about five feet long. He leaves only the tiniest five-hole because he also gets the paddle of his stick low down across the front of the crease. Shooters have to go upstairs on him, but he doesn't give away a lot of net high.

Khabibulin is solid in his fundamentals. He plays well out on the top of his crease, which is unusual for Russian goalies, who tend to stay deep in their net. He is aggressive but patient at the same time, and waits for the shooter to commit first.

Khabibulin needs to improve his work with the stick around the net and his puckhandling. He hates to move the puck, and he gets himself into trouble when he does because his clearing attempts are easily picked off. He gets run a lot, and it wouldn't hurt him to hack somebody's ankles now and then, just as a gentle reminder.

THE MENTAL GAME

Khabibulin proved last season that he has the desire and the temperament to be a number one goalie. He earned his teammates' respect and faith with a terrific playoffs. Khabibulin has the ability to steal games.

THE INTANGIBLES

Already the most successful Russian goalie in the NHL, Khabibulin has some upside because the team in front of him has to get better (there may be no one on the team happier about Phoenix signing shot-blocking defenseman Brad McCrimmon) and the

CHAD KILGER

Yrs. of NHL service: 1
Born: Cornwall, Ont.; Nov. 27, 1976
Position: centre
Height: 6-3
Weight: 204
Uniform no.: 18
Shoots: left

Career statistics:

GP	G	A	TP	PIM
74	7	10	17	34

1995-96 statistics:

GP	G	A	TP	+/-	PIM	PP	SH	GW	GT	S	PCT
74	7	10	17	-4	34	0	0	1	0	57	12.3

LAST SEASON

Acquired from Anaheim with Oleg Tverdosvky and a third-round draft pick for Teemu Selanne, Marc Chouinard and a fourth-round draft pick, Feb. 7, 1996. First NHL season.

THE FINESSE GAME

The first notion to dispense with is that Kilger can "replace" Selanne. The two players are totally dissimilar in style, as well as, of course, age and experience. Kilger will never be the sniper Selanne is, since his top skill is his playmaking.

Last season was a lost one for Kilger, who probably would have been better off with another year in junior where he could have played regularly. His skating definitely needs work.

Kilger plays an intelligent game and is poised for a youngster. He sees the ice well and is a good passer. The release on his shot is too slow for the NHL level right now. Kilger has a long reach which works to his advantage in dangling the puck away from defenders.

THE PHYSICAL GAME

Kilger is big, but needs to fill out and get stronger. He also has to play a little tougher. He doesn't play a very physical game for his size.

THE INTANGIBLES

Kilger scored a game-winning goal in the playoffs against Detroit, which gave him at least one pleasant memory from his first NHL season. Kilger is very raw, and we don't expect him to make much of an impact this season, although the Coyotes may not be very strong up the middle and he could challenge for some playing time.

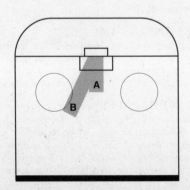

KRIS KING

Yrs. of NHL service: 8
Born: Bracebridge, Ont.; Feb. 18, 1966
Position: left wing
Height: 5-11
Weight: 210
Uniform no.: 17
Shoots: left

Career statistics:

GP	G	A	TP	PIM
567	55	65	120	1480

1992-93 statistics:

GP	G	A	TP	+/-	PIM	PP	SH	GW	GT	S	PCT
78	8	11	19	+4	203	0	0	1	0	74	10.8

1993-94 statistics:

GP	G	A	TP	+/-	PIM	PP	SH	GW	GT	S	PCT
83	4	8	12	-22	205	0	0	1	0	86	4.7

1994-95 statistics:

GP	G	A	TP	+/-	PIM	PP	SH	GW	GT	S	PCT
48	4	2	6	0	85	0	0	0	0	58	6.9

1995-96 statistics:

GP	G	A	TP	+/-	PIM	PP	SH	GW	GT	S	PCT
81	9	11	20	-7	151	0	1	2	0	89	10.1

LAST SEASON
Missed one game with rib injury.

THE FINESSE GAME
King is a checking winger, a role that can wear on a player night after night, but he brings enthusiasm and hustle to every shift. He has to play that way to stay in the NHL, and he knows it. He doesn't possess many skills. He will generate some scoring chances with his speed but can't do much with the puck at tempo. He's more intent on chasing the puck carrier. He will create turnovers but doesn't do much with the puck when he gets it. Most of his scoring chances will be garbage goals off the scrums in front from his hard work.

A superb crunch-time player, whether protecting a lead or needing a big play in overtime, he'll do his utmost to deliver. He is a gamer.

THE PHYSICAL GAME
King knows somebody's got to do the grunt work, and he's willing and able. He's relentless along the boards and in the corners, and anyone who has his back to King or his head down will pay the physical price. King takes no prisoners and will stand up for his teammates. He will fight if needed, but his reputation as a clean, hard checker is no secret.

THE INTANGIBLES
King brings sandpaper and leadership to a team in desperate need of both. Still, he is a third-line player who will find ice time harder to come by as the team gets deeper in talent. King suffered torn knee ligaments in the playoffs that will make this season even more of a struggle for him, but he has a huge heart.

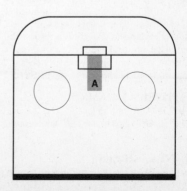

IGOR KOROLEV

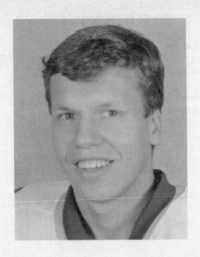

Yrs. of NHL service: 4
Born: Moscow, Russia; Sept. 6, 1970
Position: right wing
Height: 6-1
Weight: 187
Uniform no.: 23
Shoots: left

Career statistics:

GP	G	A	TP	PIM
265	40	84	124	112

1992-93 statistics:

GP	G	A	TP	+/-	PIM	PP	SH	GW	GT	S	PCT
74	4	23	27	-1	20	2	0	0	0	76	5.3

1993-94 statistics:

GP	G	A	TP	+/-	PIM	PP	SH	GW	GT	S	PCT
73	6	10	16	-12	40	0	0	1	0	93	6.5

1994-95 statistics:

GP	G	A	TP	+/-	PIM	PP	SH	GW	GT	S	PCT
45	8	22	30	+1	10	1	0	1	0	85	9.4

1995-96 statistics:

GP	G	A	TP	+/-	PIM	PP	SH	GW	GT	S	PCT
73	22	29	51	+1	42	8	0	5	1	165	13.3

LAST SEASON

Second on team in game-winning goals. Third on team in power play goals. Tied for third on team in goals with career high. Career high in assists and points. Missed three games with hip injury. Missed three games with fractured wrist.

THE FINESSE GAME

Korolev was a waiver draft pickup for the Jets in 1994, and he has proven to be the hockey equivalent of a flea market find. Korolev played most of the season with Alexei Zhamnov, moving from the left to the right wing after the trade of Teemu Selanne. Losing Selanne cost Korolev the room that his speedy ex-teammate used to merit, and Korolev was less effective because he had to work harder to get the puck. It didn't help that Zhamnov struggled with injuries and a contract hassle.

Korolev likes to trail the play, following up the speed of his linemates. He gets open and gets his chances, and he is a willing shooter. Unfortunately, he doesn't have a great shot, and has to work to get into the slot for his chances. His effort is inconsistent and as a result, he is a streaky scorer.

Korolev is a very good skater. He doesn't have exceptional speed, but he's quick and balanced.

THE PHYSICAL GAME

Korolev is solidly built to take hits. He doesn't initiate, but checkers often bounce off him because he is sturdy.

THE INTANGIBLES

Korolev played with Zhamnov in Russia, and they work well together, even if it's not exactly magic. Korolev's job on the number two line could easily be up for grabs unless he improves his intensity level.

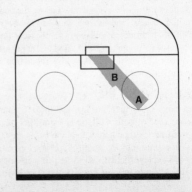

DAVE MANSON

Yrs. of NHL service: 10
Born: Prince Albert, Sask.; Jan. 27, 1967
Position: left defense
Height: 6-2
Weight: 202
Uniform no.: 4
Shoots: left

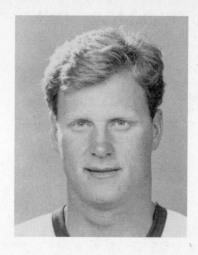

Career statistics:

GP	G	A	TP	PIM
688	83	205	288	2142

1992-93 statistics:

GP	G	A	TP	+/-	PIM	PP	SH	GW	GT	S	PCT
83	15	30	45	-28	210	9	1	1	1	244	6.1

1993-94 statistics:

GP	G	A	TP	+/-	PIM	PP	SH	GW	GT	S	PCT
70	4	17	21	-14	191	1	0	0	0	180	2.2

1994-95 statistics:

GP	G	A	TP	+/-	PIM	PP	SH	GW	GT	S	PCT
44	3	15	18	-20	139	2	0	1	0	104	2.9

1995-96 statistics:

GP	G	A	TP	+/-	PIM	PP	SH	GW	GT	S	PCT
82	7	23	30	+8	205	3	0	0	0	189	3.7

LAST SEASON

Led team in penalty minutes. Second on team in plus-minus. One of only three players on team to appear in all 82 games.

THE FINESSE GAME

Manson is his own worst enemy, making mental errors that keep him from stepping up into the ranks of the NHL's best defensemen. Although he was probably the most improved player on the team last season (and one of only three "plus" players among the regulars), Manson makes such low percentage plays as skating through his own crease under a heavy forecheck. Maybe skilled Russian defensemen can get away with that. Manson can't. He can be scary in his own end.

Manson has become more disciplined positionally, and is less likely to overcommit. Given that he was paired with the offensive-minded Norm Maciver much of the season, Manson was more aware of having to be the responsible half of the partnership.

Manson won the hardest-shot competition at the NHL All-Star game. He is smart and effective on the power play, because he will mix up his shot with a big fake and freeze. But there isn't much that's subtle about Manson. His game is power. He doesn't have much lateral mobility, so the shot isn't as effective as it would be in the hands of an Al MacInnis. He is not a bad skater for a big guy, though, and he will gamble down deep and is canny enough to use an accurate wrist shot when he is in close.

THE PHYSICAL GAME

Manson has become more disciplined, but still has a knack for taking bad penalties at the worst times. Manson can throw himself off his game. He will lose control and run after people. He patrols the front of his net well, can hit to hurt and intimidates players into getting rid of the puck faster than they want to. They flinch from even the threat of a Manson body check.

THE INTANGIBLES

Manson knows his shortcomings and wants to be a better player. Offensively, though, it's unlikely he will score more than 30-40 points. He is a key part of a team that is trying to get tougher. He plays through injuries and will be a part of the team leadership.

TEPPO NUMMINEN

Yrs. of NHL service: 8
Born: Tampere, Finland; July 3, 1968
Position: left defense
Height: 6-1
Weight: 190
Uniform no.: 27
Shoots: right

Career statistics:

GP	G	A	TP	PIM
547	53	212	265	215

1992-93 statistics:

GP	G	A	TP	+/-	PIM	PP	SH	GW	GT	S	PCT
66	7	30	37	+4	33	3	1	0	0	103	6.8

1993-94 statistics:

GP	G	A	TP	+/-	PIM	PP	SH	GW	GT	S	PCT
57	5	18	23	-23	28	4	0	1	0	89	5.6

1994-95 statistics:

GP	G	A	TP	+/-	PIM	PP	SH	GW	GT	S	PCT
42	5	16	21	+12	16	2	0	0	0	86	5.8

1995-96 statistics:

GP	G	A	TP	+/-	PIM	PP	SH	GW	GT	S	PCT
74	11	43	54	-4	22	6	0	3	0	165	6.7

LAST SEASON

Led team defensemen in scoring. Career high in assists and points. Matched career high in goals. Fourth on team in assists and points. Missed eight games with shoulder injury.

THE FINESSE GAME

Numminen's agility and anticipation make him look much faster than he is. He is graceful with a smooth change of direction, and he never telegraphs what he is about to do. His skating makes him valuable on the first penalty-killing unit. He will not get caught out of position and is seldom bested one-on-one.

Numminen is not afraid to give up the puck on a dump-and-chase rather than force a neutral zone play if he is under pressure. He would rather dish off than rush with the puck, and he is a savvy passer, moving the puck briskly and seldom overhandling it. He is not a finisher. He will join the play but not lead it. Most of his offense is generated from point shots or passes in deep.

He is uncannily adept at keeping the puck in at the point, frustrating opponents who try to clear it out around the boards.

THE PHYSICAL GAME

Numminen plays an acceptable physical game. He can be intimidated, which makes him a target for teams who want to neutralize his smart passing game. He'll employ his body as a last resort but would rather use his stick and gain the puck. He is even-tempered and not at all nasty.

THE INTANGIBLES

Numminen is the most underrated defenseman in hockey. Playing in Winnipeg all those seasons was part of the reason. Maybe he'll get more attention in that hockey hotbed, Phoenix.

Numminen has steadily improved, season by season. He is a complete if not an elite defenseman who is capable of playing a strong all-around game and scoring 50 points if he stays healthy.

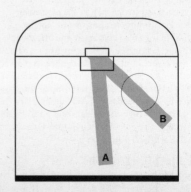

DERON QUINT

Yrs. of NHL service: 1
Born: Durham, NH; March 12, 1976
Position: left defense
Height: 6-1
Weight: 182
Uniform no.: 5
Shoots: left

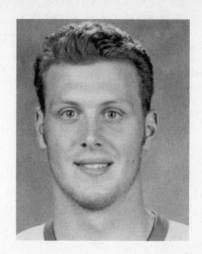

Career statistics:

GP	G	A	TP	PIM
51	5	13	18	22

1995-96 statistics:

GP	G	A	TP	+/-	PIM	PP	SH	GW	GT	S	PCT
51	5	13	18	-2	22	2	0	0	0	97	5.2

LAST SEASON

First NHL season. Tied for fourth in scoring among NHL rookie defensemen. Played part of season with Seattle (WHL).

THE FINESSE GAME

Quint has some NHL-level skills, starting with his skating. He has very good speed with a change of gears and can shift directions in a fluid motion. He also possesses a fine, accurate slap shot with a quick release. Quint can rush the puck end-to-end or start a rush with a smart pass and then join the attack.

The problem isn't in Quint's hands or feet, but in his head. He doesn't read the rush well and overcommits to plays. He has to learn to tune into odd-man rushes.

Quint would probably thrive if he were paired with the right defenseman, but there wasn't much to choose from in Winnipeg last season. Teppo Numminen, a vastly underrated rearguard, would make an ideal partner for Quint to learn from.

THE PHYSICAL GAME

Quint is finesse-oriented and needs to get more physically involved. He doesn't have great size for an NHL defenseman, but he is certainly big enough to bump and get in the way of people, though he is inconsistent with his body work. Quint also has a problem picking the right man to eliminate.

THE INTANGIBLES

Quint has some growing up to do, and if the Coyotes choose the right coach it will help him immensely. Conditioning has been a problem with him in the past two seasons. If he can mature and take a more professional approach to his career, this season could see him move into a full-time role as a top four defenseman with the Coyotes. Having Oleg Tverdovsky as a teammate will take some of the offensive heat off Quint, who was billed as the new Phil Housley. He has a long way to go to match that expectation.

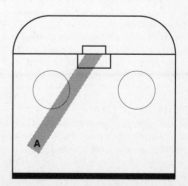

CLIFF RONNING

Yrs. of NHL service: 9
Born: Vancouver, B.C.; Oct. 1, 1965
Position: centre
Height: 5-8
Weight: 170
Uniform no.: 7
Shoots: left

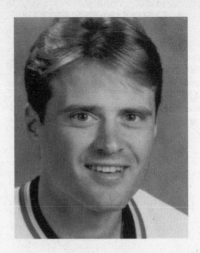

Career statistics:

GP	G	A	TP	PIM
546	166	287	453	229

1992-93 statistics:

GP	G	A	TP	+/-	PIM	PP	SH	GW	GT	S	PCT
79	29	56	85	+19	30	10	0	2	0	209	13.9

1993-94 statistics:

GP	G	A	TP	+/-	PIM	PP	SH	GW	GT	S	PCT
76	25	43	68	+7	42	10	0	4	1	197	12.7

1994-95 statistics:

GP	G	A	TP	+/-	PIM	PP	SH	GW	GT	S	PCT
41	6	19	25	-4	27	3	0	2	0	93	6.5

1995-96 statistics:

GP	G	A	TP	+/-	PIM	PP	SH	GW	GT	S	PCT
79	22	45	67	+16	42	5	0	1	1	187	11.8

LAST SEASON

Signed as free agent by Phoenix, July 2, 1996. Third on Vancouver in assists, points and plus-minus. Missed three games with groin injury.

THE FINESSE GAME

Ronning's forte is not scoring goals but creating chances for his wingers. He lets bigger linemates attract defenders so that he can dipsydoodle with the puck. He's quick, shifty and smart. He likes to work from behind the net, using the cage as a shield and daring defenders to chase him. Much of his game is a dare. He is a tempting target, and even smaller-sized defensemen fantasize about smashing Ronning to the ice, but he keeps himself out of the trouble spots by dancing in and out of openings and finding free teammates.

A quick thinker and unpredictable, Ronning can curl off the wall into the slot, pass to the corners or the point and jump to the net, or beat a defender wide to the top of the circle and feed a trailing teammate coming into the play late.

He puts a lot of little dekes into a compact area. He opens up the ice with his bursts of speed and his fakes. Unless the defense can force him along the wall and contain him, he's all over the ice trying to make things happen.

THE PHYSICAL GAME

No one asks jockeys to tackle running backs. Ronning is built for speed and deception. He is smart enough to avoid getting crunched and talented enough to compensate for his lack of strength. Ronning has skills and a huge heart.

He gets involved with his stick, hooking at a puck carrier's arm and worrying at the puck in a player's skates. He keeps the puck in his skates when he protects it, so that a checker will often have to pull Ronning down to get at the puck, which creates a power play.

THE INTANGIBLES

Tough in his own way, Ronning has excelled at a game that everyone told him he was too small to play. However, he is starting on the downside of his career, and it may be difficult for him to get ice time this season. Phoenix is deep up the middle, so he won't be asked to shoulder as much of a burden as he was in Vancouver.

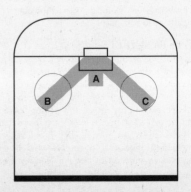

KEITH TKACHUK

Yrs. of NHL service: 4
Born: Melrose, Mass.; Mar. 28, 1972
Position: left wing
Height: 6-3
Weight: 215
Uniform no.: 7
Shoots: left

Career statistics:

GP	G	A	TP	PIM
308	144	145	289	792

1992-93 statistics:

GP	G	A	TP	+/-	PIM	PP	SH	GW	GT	S	PCT
83	28	23	51	-13	201	12	0	2	1	199	14.1

1993-94 statistics:

GP	G	A	TP	+/-	PIM	PP	SH	GW	GT	S	PCT
84	41	40	81	-12	255	22	3	3	1	218	18.8

1994-95 statistics:

GP	G	A	TP	+/-	PIM	PP	SH	GW	GT	S	PCT
48	22	29	51	-4	152	7	2	2	1	129	17.1

1995-96 statistics:

GP	G	A	TP	+/-	PIM	PP	SH	GW	GT	S	PCT
76	50	48	98	+11	156	20	2	6	0	249	20.1

LAST SEASON

Led team in goals, points, plus-minus, power play goals, game-winning goals and shots. Second on team in assists. Career high in goals, assists and points. Tied for second in NHL in power play goals. Missed three games with groin injury. Missed one game with concussion. Served two-game suspension.

THE FINESSE GAME

Tkachuk has joined the ranks of the league's top power forwards. He's at his best when he uses his power and scoring touch in tight. The scariest thing about him is how good he has become so young. Kevin Stevens, one of the NHL power-forward prototypes, didn't score 50 goals until he was 26 years old. Cam Neely was just shy of 25 in his first 50-goal season. Tkachuk had barely turned 24 in March of last season.

In front of the net, Tkachuk will bang and crash but he also has soft hands for picking pucks out of skates and flicking strong wrist shots. He can also kick at the puck with his skates without going down. He has a quick release. He looks at the net, not down at his stick — and finds the openings.

Tkachuk has improved his one-step quickness and agility. He is powerful and balanced, and often drives through bigger defensemen. The re-signing of set-up man Craig Janney is good news for Tkachuk, since the two connected well last season.

THE PHYSICAL GAME

Tkachuk is volatile and mean as a scorpion. He takes bad penalties, and since he has a reputation around the league for getting his stick up and retaliating for hits with a quick rabbit-punch to the head, referees keep a close eye on him. Tkachuk will have to avoid foolish penalties. He can be tough without buying a time share in the penalty box.

Tkachuk can dictate the physical tempo of a game with his work in the corners and along the boards.

THE INTANGIBLES

In last year's *HSR*, we wrote, "He will be in the 50-goal range in a season or two." Tkachuk did it despite the pressure of a huge front-loaded contract (U.S.$17.2 million, a free-agent offer sheet from Chicago that Winnipeg matched), injuries, a poor start, lack of a truly gifted playmaking centre and being captain of a lame duck team playing its last season in Winnipeg. If Janney and Tkachuk both stay healthy there is no reason why Tkachuk can't score 60.

OLEG TVERDOVSKY

Yrs. of NHL service: 2
Born: Donetsk, Ukraine; May 18, 1976
Position: defense
Height: 6-0
Weight: 185
Uniform no.: 20
Shoots: left

Career statistics:

GP	G	A	TP	PIM
118	10	32	42	55

1994-95 statistics:

GP	G	A	TP	+/-	PIM	PP	SH	GW	GT	S	PCT
36	3	9	12	-6	14	1	1	0	0	26	11.5

1995-96 statistics:

GP	G	A	TP	+/-	PIM	PP	SH	GW	GT	S	PCT
82	7	23	30	-7	41	2	0	0	0	119	5.9

LAST SEASON

Acquired from Anaheim with Chad Kilger for Teemu Selanne, February 7, 1996. One of three Jets to appear in all 82 games.

THE FINESSE GAME

Tverdovsky is an impressive talent. A weakness in the offensive zone is tough to find because this defenseman passes the puck well and shoots bullets. While he's clearly going to be primarily an offensive defenseman, Tverdovsky also settled down in his own zone after a stumbling start. If anything, he was guilty of trying to do too much instead of keeping the game simple. Once he realized that, he played a more solid all-around game.

Tverdovsky is such a good passer he doesn't feel the need to carry the puck all the time. And he doesn't just get the puck and go, he knows when to go. There are nights when he is simply brilliant but he hasn't achieved consistency yet.

Tverdovsky has Brian Leetch potential. He is an explosive skater and can carry the puck at high tempo. He works the point on the power play and kills penalties. He sees his options and makes his decisions at lightning speed. His creativity seemed stifled in Anaheim, yet he didn't produce well after the shock of the trade to Winnipeg (only eight assists in 31 games).

Of course, the price to pay with an "offenseman" are his defensive lapses, and Tverdovsky can make some world class errors.

THE PHYSICAL GAME

Some of Tverdovsky's defensive weaknesses can be attributed to the fact that he sometimes plays the puck instead of the man, or tries to poke-check without backing it up with his body. Physically, when he makes the right decision he can eliminate the man, and he looks to be improving in this area.

Tverdovsky is a devoted practice player who almost has to be wrestled off the ice. He loves to play and is enthusiastic and extremely competitive.

THE INTANGIBLES

This could be the season Tverdovsky starts to make some noise. He is becoming more and more acclimated to North American life and Phoenix should suit him better than Winnipeg, lifestyle-wise. He has a very outgoing personality and wants to succeed.

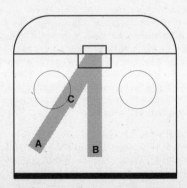

ALEXEI ZHAMNOV

Yrs. of NHL service: 4
Born: Moscow, Russia; Oct. 1, 1970
Position: centre
Height: 6-1
Weight: 195
Uniform no.: 10
Shoots: left

Career statistics:

GP	G	A	TP	PIM
235	103	164	267	205

1992-93 statistics:

GP	G	A	TP	+/-	PIM	PP	SH	GW	GT	S	PCT
68	25	47	72	+7	58	6	1	4	1	163	15.3

1993-94 statistics:

GP	G	A	TP	+/-	PIM	PP	SH	GW	GT	S	PCT
61	26	45	71	-20	62	7	0	1	1	196	13.3

1994-95 statistics:

GP	G	A	TP	+/-	PIM	PP	SH	GW	GT	S	PCT
48	30	35	65	+5	20	9	0	4	0	155	19.4

1995-96 statistics:

GP	G	A	TP	+/-	PIM	PP	SH	GW	GT	S	PCT
58	22	37	59	-4	65	5	0	2	0	199	11.1

talented but risky prospect.

LAST SEASON

Third on team in goals and points. Missed eight games with knee injury. Missed 16 games with recurring back problems.

THE FINESSE GAME

Zhamnov's back problems, which had disappeared in 1994-95, resurfaced last season and endanger his future as one of the league's budding elite forwards.

Zhamnov's game is puck control. He can carry it at top speed or work the give-and-go. The Russian is a crafty playmaker and is not too unselfish. He has an accurate if not overpowering shot. As well, he can blast off the pass, or manoeuvre until he has a screen and then wrist it. On the power play, he works the left point or, if used low, can dart in and out in front of the goalie, using his soft hands for a tip.

Defensively, he is very sound. He is a dedicated backchecker and never leaves the zone too quickly.

THE PHYSICAL GAME

Zhamnov will bump to prevent a scoring chance or go for a loose puck, but body work is not his forte. He is strong and fights his way through traffic in front of the net to get to a puck. He needs to do a better job of tying up the opposing centre on face-offs, since he wins few draws cleanly. Zhamnov quit smoking last season, which improved his stamina.

THE INTANGIBLES

Zhamnov once seemed poised for a 100-point season. Injuries and a contract hassle last season wiped out that prediction. The team has soured on Zhmanov, a Group 2 free agent, and will likely move him. He is a

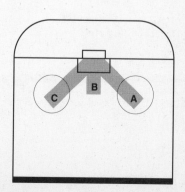

PITTSBURGH PENGUINS

Players' Statistics 1995-96

POS.	NO.	PLAYER	GP	G	A	PTS	+/-	PIM	PP	SH	GW	GT	S	PCT
C	66	MARIO LEMIEUX	70	69	92	161	10	54	31	8	8		338	20.4
R	68	JAROMIR JAGR	82	62	87	149	31	96	20	1	12	1	403	15.4
C	10	RON FRANCIS	77	27	92	119	25	56	12	1	4		158	17.1
C	93	PETR NEDVED	80	45	54	99	37	68	8	1	5	1	204	22.1
R	17	TOMAS SANDSTROM	58	35	35	70	4	69	17	1	2		187	18.7
D	56	SERGEI ZUBOV	64	11	55	66	28	22	3	2	1		141	7.8
C	20	BRYAN SMOLINSKI	81	24	40	64	6	69	8	2	1		229	10.5
R	8	KEVIN MILLER	81	28	25	53	-4	45	3	2	2	2	179	15.6
D	15	DMITRI MIRONOV	72	3	31	34	19	88	1		1	1	86	3.5
R	27	GLEN MURRAY	69	14	15	29	4	57			2		100	14.0
D	23	CHRIS JOSEPH	70	5	14	19	6	71			1		94	5.3
D	6	NEIL WILKINSON	62	3	14	17	12	120		1	1		59	5.1
L	51	*DAVE ROCHE	71	7	7	14	-5	130			1		65	10.8
D	2	CHRIS TAMER	70	4	10	14	20	153			1		75	5.3
D	36	J.J. DAIGNEAULT	57	4	7	11	-6	53	2				61	6.6
D	18	FRANCOIS LEROUX	66	2	9	11	2	161					43	4.7
L	16	*JOE DZIEDZIC	69	5	5	10	-5	68			3		44	11.4
C	76	*RICHARD PARK	56	4	6	10	3	36		1	1		62	6.5
C	26	DAVE MCLLWAIN	19	2	5	7	-5	6			1		20	10.0
R	14	BRAD LAUER	21	4	1	5	-5	6	1		1		29	13.8
D	4	COREY FOSTER	11	2	2	4	-2	2	1				8	25.0
C	12	*CHRIS WELLS	54	2	2	4	-6	59		1			25	8.0
C	52	*RUSTY FITZGERALD	21	1	2	3	7	12					15	6.7
G	35	TOM BARRASSO	49		3	3	0	18						
D	24	*IAN MORAN	51	1	1	2	-1	47					44	2.3
R	11	*ALEK STOJANOV	68	1	1	2	-13	130					20	5.0
R	44	ED PATTERSON	35		2	2	-5	38					17	
G	31	KEN WREGGET	37		2	2	0	8						
D	55	DRAKE BEREHOWSKY	1				1							
D	28	*GREG ANDRUSAK	2				-1						1	
D	33	*STEFAN BERGKVIST	2				0	2					4	
L	28	*JEFF CHRISTIAN	3				0	2						
C	9	LEN BARRIE	5				-1	18					5	
D	38	*PETER ALLEN	8				2	8					2	

GP = games played; G = goals; A = assists; PTS = points; +/- = goals-for minus goals-against while player is on ice; PIM = penalties in minutes; PP = power play goals; SH = shorthanded goals; GW = game-winning goals; GT = game-tying goals; S = no. of shots; PCT = percentage of goals to shots; * = rookie

TOM BARRASSO

Yrs. of NHL service: 13
Born: Boston, Mass.; Mar. 31, 1965
Position: goaltender
Height: 6-3
Weight: 211
Uniform no.: 35
Catches: right

Career statistics:

GP	MIN	GA	SO	GAA	A	PIM
597	34354	1962	23	3.43	43	395

1992-93 statistics:

GP	MIN	GAA	W	L	T	SO	GA	S	SAPCT	PIM
63	3702	3.01	43	14	5	4	186	1885	.901	24

1993-94 statistics:

GP	MIN	GAA	W	L	T	SO	GA	S	SAPCT	PIM
44	2482	3.36	22	15	5	2	139	1304	.893	42

1994-95 statistics:

GP	MIN	GAA	W	L	T	SO	GA	S	SAPCT	PIM
2	125	3.84	0	1	1	0	8	75	.893	0

1995-96 statistics:

GP	MIN	GAA	W	L	T	SO	GA	S	SAPCT	PIM
49	2799	3.43	29	16	2	2	160	1626	.902	18

LAST SEASON

Posted 10th season with 20 or more wins. Fourth among active goalies in career wins. Missed 12 games with groin and shoulder injuries.

THE PHYSICAL GAME

The Penguins tend to give up a lot of odd-man rushes and Barrasso makes the save, handling the puck quickly to get his team going on a counterattack. It's doubtful if he would have played as well in recent years if he had been with a more conservative team. Pittsburgh's flamboyance suits Barrasso, despite his inflated goals-against average.

One of the most impressive things about Barrasso is that although he is often on his knees, he is almost never on his side. He might be the best in the league at recovering from going down and will be back on his skates with his glove in position for the next shot. He surrenders a lot of long rebounds. Barrasso freezes the puck frequently and has one of the game's top face-off men, Ron Francis, always available for defensive zone draws.

Barrasso loves to handle the puck; he's like a third defenseman in both his willingness to leave the crease and his ability to pass. He is a good skater who is able to get to and control a lot of pucks that most goalies wouldn't dare try to reach. Staying on his feet more (a fundamental he has improved upon with experience) allows him to make the most of his skating skills. Most of the time he will use the boards for his passes, rather than make a risky play up the middle, but every so often he is vulnerable to the interception.

Because of Barrasso's range, teams have to adapt their attack. Hard dump-ins won't work, because he will stop them behind the net and zip the puck right back out for an alert counterattack by his teammates. Since he comes out around the post to his right better than his left, teams have to aim soft dumps to his left, making him more hesitant about making the play and giving the forecheckers time to get in on him. Barrasso's lone weakness appears to be shots low on the glove side.

THE MENTAL GAME

Barrasso is still one of the game's most intense competitors. He has battled through injuries and personal crises through the past few seasons and has lost little of his edge. He will whack guys in the ankle or get his body in the way for a subtle interference play. His concentration will slip, however, especially on long shots.

THE INTANGIBLES

The Penguins went to Barrasso as their number one goalie in the Eastern Conference Finals — although Ken Wregget had performed well while Barrasso was ailing — but the 55-foot deflected shot Barrasso allowed to Tom Fitzgerald in Game 7 may have been the last straw for the cantankerous goalie. Wregget makes less (U.S.$475,000 to Barrasso's U.S.$2.7 million) and is better liked by the Penguins and most of humanity than Barrasso is. His salary will make him difficult to unload, and his days as an elite goaltender are over, so the Pens may just be stuck with him.

RON FRANCIS

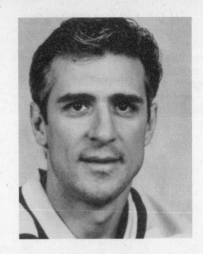

Yrs. of NHL service: 15
Born: Sault Ste. Marie, Ont.; Mar. 1, 1963
Position: centre
Height: 6-2
Weight: 200
Uniform no.: 10
Shoots: left

Career statistics:

GP	G	A	TP	PIM
1085	376	881	1257	793

1992-93 statistics:

GP	G	A	TP	+/-	PIM	PP	SH	GW	GT	S	PCT
84	24	76	100	+6	68	9	2	4	0	215	11.2

1993-94 statistics:

GP	G	A	TP	+/-	PIM	PP	SH	GW	GT	S	PCT
82	27	66	93	-3	62	8	0	2	1	216	12.5

1994-95 statistics:

GP	G	A	TP	+/-	PIM	PP	SH	GW	GT	S	PCT
44	11	48	59	+30	18	3	0	1	0	94	11.7

1995-96 statistics:

GP	G	A	TP	+/-	PIM	PP	SH	GW	GT	S	PCT
77	27	92	119	+25	56	12	1	4	0	158	17.1

LAST SEASON

Tied for NHL and team lead in assists with career high. Fourth in NHL and third on team in points with career high. Third 100-point season. Reached 1,200 points and 800 assists milestones. Served two-game suspension. Missed two games with hip flexor. Missed one game with back spasms.

THE FINESSE GAME

Petr Nedved and Jaromir Jagr owe much of their success last season to this cerebral centre, who appears ageless as long as he keeps his helmet on (it covers the grey better than Clairol). Once the Penguins lost Francis to a broken foot in the playoffs, their Stanley Cup hopes disappeared.

Francis is Dr. Draw. On rare nights when he is struggling with an opposing centre, he'll tinker with his changes in the neutral zone, then save what he has learned for a key draw deep in either zone. Just as a great scorer never shows a goalie the same move twice in a row, he never uses the same technique in succession. He has good hand-eye coordination and uses his body well at the dot. Pittsburgh goalies have no fear about freezing the puck because of Francis's superiority on face-offs. Few players win their draws as outright as Francis does on a consistent basis.

Francis can still put points on the board, as he proved last season at age 33. Technically, he is a choppy skater who gets where he has to be with a minimum amount of style. His understanding of the game is key because he has great awareness of his positioning. He gets loads of ice time (far too much), so he has learned to pace himself to conserve his energy. There are few useless bursts of speed.

While he focuses on a defensive role, Francis has the hands and the vision to come out of a defensive scramble into an attacking rush. He anticipates passes, blocks shots, then springs an odd-man breakout with a smart play. Jagr is always hanging and circling and looking for the opportunity, and Francis often finds him.

Francis doesn't have a screamingly hard shot, nor is he a flashy player. He works from the centre of the ice, between the circles, and has a quick release on a one-timer. He can kill penalties or work the point on the power play with equal effectiveness. He complements any kind of player.

THE PHYSICAL GAME

Not a big, imposing hitter, Francis will use his body to get the job done. He will bump and grind and go into the trenches. Back on defense, he can function as a third defenseman; on offense, you will find him going into the corners or heading for the front of the net for tips and rebounds. He is a strong and balanced skater with quickness, though he doesn't have a pretty stride.

Francis gets a lot of ice time but keeps himself in great shape. Still, he is a worn and weary player come playoff time and the Penguins urgently need to shore up their middle to give him a break.

THE INTANGIBLES

We predicted a 100-point season for Francis last season, but we have a feeling that this year the Penguins might pace their stars a little more during the regular season and let their younger forwards do something other than serve Tom Barrasso's penalties. If that's the case, then his production could be off by 20 points. His all-around game will be as invaluable as ever.

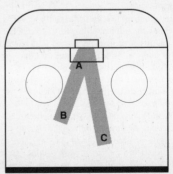

KEVIN HATCHER

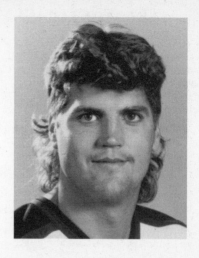

Yrs. of NHL service: 11
Born: Detroit, Mich.; Sept. 9, 1966
Position: right defense
Height: 6-4
Weight: 225
Uniform no.: 4
Shoots: right

Career statistics:

GP	G	A	TP	PIM
806	174	322	496	1125

1992-93 statistics:

GP	G	A	TP	+/-	PIM	PP	SH	GW	GT	S	PCT
83	34	45	79	-7	114	13	1	6	0	329	10.3

1993-94 statistics:

GP	G	A	TP	+/-	PIM	PP	SH	GW	GT	S	PCT
72	16	24	40	-13	108	6	0	3	0	217	7.4

1994-95 statistics:

GP	G	A	TP	+/-	PIM	PP	SH	GW	GT	S	PCT
47	10	19	29	-4	66	3	0	2	1	138	7.2

1995-96 statistics:

GP	G	A	TP	+/-	PIM	PP	SH	GW	GT	S	PCT
74	15	26	41	-24	58	7	0	3	2	237	6.3

LAST SEASON

Acquired from Dallas for Sergei Zubov, June 22, 1996. Led Stars defensemen in points. Third on team in assists. Fourth on team in points. Second on team in shots. Tied for third on team in game-winning goals. Served four-game suspension.

THE FINESSE GAME

Hatcher is not among the game's elite defensemen, but he is solidly in the second flight. Hatcher has good anticipation in his own zone for picking off passes, which he then carries up the middle to start a counter-attack. He has the speed and strength to elude checkers in the neutral zone, and he's solid enough on his skates that he seldom goes off-course or loses the puck if bumped. He can finish in close offensively. And he is smart about jumping into the play, but also clever enough to make the best play the situation dictates. He will drive it deep or take a shot from the point if a shot is open. Hatcher moves to the left point on the power play to open up his forehand for one-timers.

Hatcher has the puck so much during a game that there are times when he'll turn the puck over or carry it dangerously in front of his own net, but he makes a far greater number of intelligent plays than mistakes. He makes decisions quickly in all zones. If the heat is on him in his own zone, he is aware of his teammates' positions on the ice and makes the smart outlet pass or bangs the puck off the glass. He is constantly looking to see which attackers might be bearing in on him, but he is poised under pressure.

He is sometimes slow with his first step but achieves top speed quite quickly for a big skater, and should fit in well with the Penguins' open style.

THE PHYSICAL GAME

Hatcher was very tame last season in Dallas and who wants a finesse defenseman this big? Why is a player of his size getting a four-game suspension for a slashing incident? He's not very brave.

THE INTANGIBLES

Hatcher may have an 80-point season in him. But he has yet to prove he can be a dominating defenseman. His points will be inflated thanks to the strength of his new Penguins teammates, but he is only a legitimate 50-point man at best.

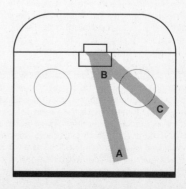

JAROMIR JAGR

Yrs. of NHL service: 6
Born: Kladno, Czechoslovakia; Feb. 15, 1972
Position: right wing
Height: 6-2
Weight: 208
Uniform no.: 68
Shoots: left

Career statistics:

GP	G	A	TP	PIM
441	219	319	538	331

1992-93 statistics:

GP	G	A	TP	+/-	PIM	PP	SH	GW	GT	S	PCT
81	34	60	94	+30	61	10	1	9	0	242	14.0

1993-94 statistics:

GP	G	A	TP	+/-	PIM	PP	SH	GW	GT	S	PCT
80	32	67	99	+15	61	9	0	6	2	298	10.7

1994-95 statistics:

GP	G	A	TP	+/-	PIM	PP	SH	GW	GT	S	PCT
48	32	38	70	+23	37	8	3	7	0	192	16.7

1995-96 statistics:

GP	G	A	TP	+/-	PIM	PP	SH	GW	GT	S	PCT
82	62	87	149	+31	96	20	1	12	1	403	15.4

LAST SEASON

Second in NHL in scoring with career high. Second in NHL in goals with career high. Third on team in assists with career high. Set NHL record for points and assists in a season by a right wing. Led NHL in shots with club record. Second on team in power play goals and plus-minus. Only Penguin to appear in all 82 games.

THE FINESSE GAME

Jagr creates a terrible quandary for opposing coaches, because there is simply no defense for him. He can't be shadowed, because there is not a player on earth who can stay with him, and when he beats his shadow he creates an odd-man situation. Teams have to concentrate on playing positionally and trying to cut down his passing lanes, but Jagr plays with such talented cohorts that this is a prayer more than a tactic.

Jagr is as close to a perfect skater as there is in the NHL. He keeps his body centred over his skates, giving him a low centre of gravity and making it very tough for anyone to knock him off the puck. He has a deep knee bend, for quickness and power. His strokes are long and sure, he has control over his body and exceptional lateral mobility. He dazzles with his footwork and handles the puck at high tempo.

He brings sheer joy and a dynamic energy to the game every night. Jagr lives and loves to play hockey. His long hair flowing out from beneath his helmet, Jagr is poetry is motion with his beautifully effortless skating style. Playing with the more defensive-minded Ron Francis as his safety valve last season again gave the flashy Czech even more freedom to freewheel, and no one does it like Jagr, while creative new linemate Petr Nedved proved a scoring or play-making threat.

With his Lemieux-like reach, he can dangle the puck while he's gliding and swooping. Jagr will fake the backhand and go to his forehand in a flash. He is powerful enough to drag a defender with him to the net and push off a strong one-handed shot. He has a big slap shot and can drive it on the fly or fire it with a one-timer off a pass.

One of the reasons for Jagr's wicked shots are his barely legal sticks. He gets them illegally curved on order from the factory, and sharp-eyed opposing coaches (or their equipment managers) should keep a lookout for those he hasn't doctored to NHL specifications. He will shoot from the most ridiculous angles and generate great scoring chances from the shot.

THE PHYSICAL GAME

Considering how often he gets pounded and how much ice time he logs, Jagr's durability over the past three seasons is remarkable. Earlier in his career, he could be intimidated physically, and he still doesn't like to get hit but he's not as wimpy as he used up be. He's confident, almost cocky, and he's tough to catch — impossible to hit in open ice.

THE INTANGIBLES

Last season we said Jagr hadn't maxed out and was capable of a 60-goal season. Let's up the ante. With or without Mario Lemieux in the lineup next season, Jagr has the capability to flirt with 70 goals and 160 points.

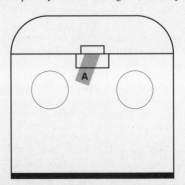

CHRIS JOSEPH

Yrs. of NHL service: 8
Born: Burnaby, B.C.; Sept. 10, 1969
Position: right defense
Height: 6-2
Weight: 210
Uniform no.: 23
Shoots: right

Career statistics:

GP	G	A	TP	PIM
340	32	86	118	442

1992-93 statistics:

GP	G	A	TP	+/-	PIM	PP	SH	GW	GT	S	PCT
33	2	10	12	-9	48	1	0	0	0	49	4.1

1993-94 statistics:

GP	G	A	TP	+/-	PIM	PP	SH	GW	GT	S	PCT
76	11	20	31	-21	136	8	0	0	0	179	6.1

1994-95 statistics:

GP	G	A	TP	+/-	PIM	PP	SH	GW	GT	S	PCT
33	5	10	15	+3	46	0	0	0	0	73	6.8

1995-96 statistics:

GP	G	A	TP	+/-	PIM	PP	SH	GW	GT	S	PCT
70	5	14	19	+6	71	0	0	1	0	94	5.3

LAST SEASON

Missed four games with knee injury. Missed one game with flu.

THE FINESSE GAME

Joseph has good skating skills forward and backward. He can skate and stickhandle with the puck or pass it out of the defensive zone. He joins the rush effectively because of his speed. It sounds like all of the ingredients for a top offensive defenseman, but several key components are lacking, mostly in his helmet.

Joseph's offensive reads and sense of pace are off. He started losing ice time late in the season, and only got back in the lineup when some injuries gave him a chance.

He has the hand skills to beat players one-on-one, but he doesn't choose his spots for pinching or rushing wisely. He has a decent point shot, but isn't a great power play quarterback. Joseph doesn't see the ice well and often tries to force plays that result in turnovers.

THE PHYSICAL GAME

Joseph plays much smaller than his size. Strength and aggressiveness would help him clear out his crease, but he has to play with a bigger defenseman.

THE INTANGIBLES

This could be the last season for Joseph to prove himself. He will be on the bubble in Pittsburgh as a fifth or even sixth defenseman, and if he doesn't have a strong training camp, he will have a real uphill climb to get back into the lineup.

MARIO LEMIEUX

Yrs. of NHL service: 11
Born: Montreal, Que.; Oct. 5, 1965
Position: centre
Height: 6-4
Weight: 210
Uniform no.: 66
Shoots: right

Career statistics:

GP	G	A	TP	PIM
669	563	809	1372	672

1992-93 statistics:

GP	G	A	TP	+/-	PIM	PP	SH	GW	GT	S	PCT
60	69	91	160	+55	38	16	6	10	0	286	24.1

1993-94 statistics:

GP	G	A	TP	+/-	PIM	PP	SH	GW	GT	S	PCT
22	17	20	37	-2	32	7	0	4	0	92	18.5

1994-95 statistics:

P	G	A	TP	+/-	PIM	PP	SH	GW	GT	S	PC
					Did not play in NHL						

1995-96 statistics:

GP	G	A	TP	+/-	PIM	PP	SH	GW	GT	S	PCT
70	69	92	161	+10	54	31	8	8	0	338	20.4

LAST SEASON

Won Hart Trophy for third time in 1996. Led the NHL in scoring for the fifth time with his third-highest career total and 12th highest in league history. Ninth season with 100 or more points. Tied for NHL lead in assists. Led NHL in power play goals. Led NHL in shorthanded goals. Scored 500th NHL goal, reaching milestone faster than any NHL player except Wayne Gretzky. Scored five goals in one game (Mar. 26, 1996). Missed two games with back injury. Missed one game with flu.

THE FINESSE GAME

The single biggest sports story last season was the return of Mario Lemieux, who conquered cancer (Hodgkin's disease), a near-crippling back injury, and the NHL.

Lemieux tried to reserve his strength during the season, but if he was on cruise control half the time, who could tell? Lemieux always seems to have some new move ready to dazzle and amaze, as if he spends his idle hours reinventing the game. He is one of those rare athletes who can seize a game by the throat, as if to say, "Enough fooling around. I want to win this thing." He then goes out and does what has to be done, whether it is breaking a goalie's heart with a shorthanded breakaway or calmly sneaking into the slot to bury a power play rebound. Lemieux can score a hat trick and barely cover 100 feet of ice.

Lemieux was probably a half step slower last season, but his first stride to the puck is so huge and effortless that he can still make defensemen look silly. Step up to challenge Lemieux, and he will use his long reach to pull the puck through a defender's legs. Back off him and he will use the open ice to wheel and send a perfect pass to a breaking teammate.

His shots are accurate, and he never telegraphs where they are going, which makes him nearly unstoppable on a breakaway. With his long, strong reach, he can flick off a shot when he looks out of position and off balance. The goalie will position himself for Lemieux's body, but the shot comes from so far away that the netminder is at his mercy.

Lemieux can do everything at high tempo. He is an excellent skater, and his vision of the ice is so acute he seems to be watching from one of those overhead cameras hanging from the centre ice scoreboard. He knows where everyone is and where they're going. This makes him as dangerous killing penalties as he is on the power play.

THE PHYSICAL GAME

When healthy, Lemieux is the most dominant player in the NHL. Lindros may catch him one day, or maybe Peter Forsberg, but neither has reached Mario's elite level yet. The physical toll showed on Lemieux last season, however, as he was not able to challenge one-on-one as in the past, nor did he recover quickly from long shifts. He took only nine non-injury days off last season, and may be spelled more this season.

THE INTANGIBLES

Even as he accepted his Hart Trophy, Lemieux had the public guessing about whether he will return this season. It seems too cruel to deprive the sport of this awesome talent, and we fervently hope he will be well enough to be lured back to the ice for another crack at the Stanley Cup.

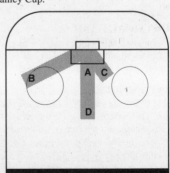

DMITRI MIRONOV

Yrs. of NHL service: 4
Born: Moscow, Russia; Dec. 25, 1965
Position: left defense
Height: 6-3
Weight: 215
Uniform no.: 15
Shoots: right

Career statistics:

GP	G	A	TP	PIM
247	25	94	119	234

1992-93 statistics:

GP	G	A	TP	+/-	PIM	PP	SH	GW	GT	S	PCT
59	7	24	31	-1	40	4	0	1	1	105	6.7

1993-94 statistics:

GP	G	A	TP	+/-	PIM	PP	SH	GW	GT	S	PCT
76	9	27	36	+5	78	3	0	0	2	147	6.1

1994-95 statistics:

GP	G	A	TP	+/-	PIM	PP	SH	GW	GT	S	PCT
33	5	12	17	+6	28	2	0	0	0	68	7.4

1995-96 statistics:

GP	G	A	TP	+/-	PIM	PP	SH	GW	GT	S	PCT
72	3	31	34	+19	88	1	0	1	1	86	3.5

LAST SEASON

Career high in assists. Missed eight games with shoulder injury.

THE FINESSE GAME

Mironov can do phenomenal things with the puck, but the problem is getting an involved game out of him every night. He teases with glimpses of the kind of player he can be. If Mironov is suited for any team, it's the Penguins, because he loves to get involved in the attack.

Mironov understands the game well. He can shoot bullets, but is often reluctant to let fire. He can work the puck up the ice, handle the point on the power play, sees the ice well and is a good passer, but he does none of those things with authority.

Mironov is especially tentative in his own end. He has to play with a real rock of a defenseman as his partner, because he is high-risk and can be beaten one-on-one.

THE PHYSICAL GAME

Mironov has a long reach and is big, but he plays very soft and doesn't use either attribute to his best advantage. He gives up easily on plays in his own end. He likes to step up and challenge in the neutral zone, but doesn't take the body well and often lets the opponent get by him.

THE INTANGIBLES

Mironov seemed much happier playing on the Penguins' laissez-faire defense, but if the team clamps down on its freewheeling style, Mironov will have to evolve into a better player or lose his grip on the number four defenseman role. He is running out of options, since he doesn't produce well enough to be a strictly one-way defenseman. If Mironov scored 55 or 60 points, a team could live with his flaws.

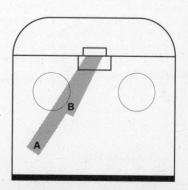

IAN MORAN

Yrs. of NHL service: 1
Born: Cleveland, Ohio; Aug. 24, 1972
Position: right defense
Height: 5-11
Weight: 195
Uniform no.: 24
Shoots: right

Career statistics:

GP	G	A	TP	PIM
51	1	1	2	47

1995-96 statistics:

GP	G	A	TP	+/-	PIM	PP	SH	GW	GT	S	PCT
51	1	1	2	-1	47	0	0	0	0	44	2.3

LAST SEASON

Missed 21 games with recurring shoulder injuries and season-ending surgery.

THE FINESSE GAME

Moran posted good numbers in the college ranks and was billed as an offensive defenseman, but hasn't been able to translate his skills to the NHL level yet. Moran has very good hockey sense, which is probably his chief asset.

His skating is quite good. He is strong and mobile, and handles the puck well. He makes good outlet passes from his own zone or joins the rush.

Moran has spent the last two seasons learning the defensive part of the game and is being groomed as a two-way defenseman. His shot isn't NHL calibre yet, either. He needs a quicker release.

THE PHYSICAL GAME

Players from the college and international ranks (Moran played on the 1994 U.S. national team) tend to be a little shy about developing their defensive game, but Moran picked up 94 penalty minutes with Cleveland (IHL) in 1994-95 to indicate an aggressive side.

Moran isn't big by NHL defensemen standards, but he is solidly built and willing to hit.

THE INTANGIBLES

Because the Penguins generally tend to play only their top four defensemen, youngsters like Moran have had trouble getting ice time to develop, and his shoulder injury forced a layoff. It's unlikely Moran will start the season in the top four, but he's a "high five" and has some offensive upside.

GLEN MURRAY

Yrs. of NHL service: 4
Born: Halifax, N.S.; Nov. 1, 1972
Position: right wing
Height: 6-2
Weight: 210
Uniform no.: 27
Shoots: right

Career statistics:

GP	G	A	TP	PIM
217	43	35	78	159

1992-93 statistics:

GP	G	A	TP	+/-	PIM	PP	SH	GW	GT	S	PCT
27	3	4	7	-6	8	2	0	1	0	28	10.7

1993-94 statistics:

GP	G	A	TP	+/-	PIM	PP	SH	GW	GT	S	PCT
81	18	13	31	-1	48	0	0	4	2	114	15.8

1994-95 statistics:

GP	G	A	TP	+/-	PIM	PP	SH	GW	GT	S	PCT
35	5	2	7	-11	46	0	0	2	0	64	7.8

1995-96 statistics:

GP	G	A	TP	+/-	PIM	PP	SH	GW	GT	S	PCT
69	14	15	29	+4	57	0	0	2	0	100	14.0

in Boston and the same problem dogged him in Pittsburgh. He will have to scramble to find his spot in training camp and he might be the odd man out unless he comes into camp smoking.

LAST SEASON

Acquired from Boston with Bryan Smolinski for Kevin Stevens and Shawn McEachern, Aug. 1, 1995. Missed 10 games with shoulder injury.

THE FINESSE GAME

Murray is a lumbering skater who often looked out of place with the fleet, European-style Penguins. He needs a good old dump-and-chase game on a line with a playmaker who can get him the puck and set him up in the slot. Murray was also stuck on his off (left) wing when he did get ice time, which put him on his backhand. Murray is not that gifted. He needs to be on the right side, jamming in his forehand shots.

Murray has good size and a good short game. He has a quick release, and like a lot of great goal scorers he just plain shoots. He doesn't even have to look at the net because he feels where the shot is going. He protects the puck well with his body.

Murray is a little fragile confidence-wise. He opened his Pittsburgh career with only one goal in his first 11 games, and although he enjoyed the occasional streak, he never looked comfortable.

THE PHYSICAL GAME

On nights when he's playing well, Murray is leaning on people and making his presence felt. He likes to bang, but on some nights he doesn't want to pay the price and prefers to rely on his shot. When he sleepwalks, he is useless. When he's ready to rock-and-roll, he is effective.

THE INTANGIBLES

Murray is an enigma. He has trouble finding his role

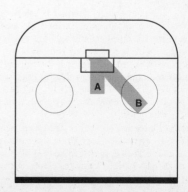

PETR NEDVED

Yrs. of NHL service: 6
Born: Liberec, Czechoslovakia; Dec. 9, 1971
Position: centre
Height: 6-3
Weight: 195
Uniform no.: 93
Shoots: left

Career statistics:

GP	G	A	TP	PIM
367	125	141	266	254

1992-93 statistics:

GP	G	A	TP	+/-	PIM	PP	SH	GW	GT	S	PCT
84	38	33	71	+20	96	2	1	3	0	149	25.5

1993-94 statistics:

GP	G	A	TP	+/-	PIM	PP	SH	GW	GT	S	PCT
19	6	14	20	+2	8	2	0	0	1	63	9.5

1994-95 statistics:

GP	G	A	TP	+/-	PIM	PP	SH	GW	GT	S	PCT
46	11	12	23	-1	26	1	0	3	0	123	8.9

1995-96 statistics:

GP	G	A	TP	+/-	PIM	PP	SH	GW	GT	S	PCT
80	45	54	99	+37	68	8	1	5	1	204	22.1

LAST SEASON

Acquired from New York Rangers with Sergei Zubov for Ulf Samuelsson and Luc Robitaille, Aug. 31, 1995. Third on team in goals with career high. Led team and tied for third in NHL in plus-minus. Fourth on team in points with career high. Career high in assists. Led team and second in NHL in shooting percentage. Third on team in game-winning goals. Recorded first career hat trick (a four-goal game). Missed two games with thigh injury.

THE FINESSE GAME

There aren't many players who made as dramatic an offensive improvement last season as Nedved did, and we doubt that he would have done it with any team other than the Penguins. Pittsburgh is a team that is a little less uptight about those pesky defensive liabilities, although the playoffs and the subsequent trade of high-risk defenseman Sergei Zubov may signal an end to that laissez-faire era.

Tall but slightly built, Nedved can handle the puck well in traffic or in open ice at tempo. He uses his forehand and backhand equally well for a pass or a shot. He sees the ice very well and has a creative mind. Nedved played both center and wing, but was most often on the left side with Ron Francis and Jaromir Jagr. It was a dream job for him because Francis is a conscientious two-way player and Jagr opens up a lot of ice.

Nedved made use of the time and space. He may have the best wrist shot in the NHL, with a hair-trigger release and radar-like accuracy. Nedved likes to go high on the glove side, picking the corner. Although he lacks a big slap shot, Nedved has the vision to handle the power play from the point.

Nedved will pay the price occasionally along the boards if he's not the inside man, the guy who will get hit. If there's a chance of contact, he generally won't be the first to the puck.

THE PHYSICAL GAME

Good on attacking-zone draws, he knows his way around a face-off. He has good hand quickness and cheats well. On offensive-zone draws, he turns his body so he is almost facing the boards. He improved enough to take some defensive-zone draws (probably learning from Francis). That is about it for his defensive contribution, although he can kill penalties because of his quickness and anticipation.

THE INTANGIBLES

Nedved played well in Pittsburgh because he was afraid Mario Lemieux would kill him if he didn't. That's a bit of an exaggeration, but let's just say that Nedved was more respectful of No. 66 in Pittsburgh than he was of No. 11 (Mark Messier) in New York. Messier disliked Nedved intensely and was one of the major reasons why Nedved was traded. Nedved is a Group 2 free agent but he would be foolish to sign anywhere other than Pittsburgh, even for less cash. If he goes elsewhere, expect his point totals to tumble.

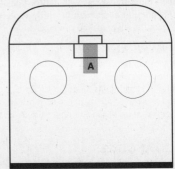

DAVE ROCHE

Yrs. of NHL service: 1
Born: Lindsay, Ont.; June 13, 1975
Position: left wing
Height: 6-4
Weight: 224
Uniform no.: 51
Shoots: left

Career statistics:

GP	G	A	TP	PIM
71	7	7	14	130

1995-96 statistics:

GP	G	A	TP	+/-	PIM	PP	SH	GW	GT	S	PCT
71	7	7	14	-5	130	0	0	1	0	65	10.8

LAST SEASON

First NHL season. Missed three games with ankle injury. Missed two games with ear infection. Missed two games with shoulder injury.

THE FINESSE GAME

Roche is a diamond in the rough. Actually, at this stage, he's still carbon, but he is a power forward in progress, and if he can step up his game, he'll supply one of the ingredients the Penguins have been missing up front.

A 100-point scorer at the junior level (twice), Roche spent last season with Pittsburgh in a part-time role when he would have been better served getting a lot of ice time and developing his game in the minors. Like a lot of big men, Roche is something of a plodder. He needs to apply himself to his skating to develop that quick, strong stride that power forwards use around the net.

Roche hasn't developed an NHL-calibre release yet, either, but he is fresh out of junior and it takes at least a season for all but the elite players to adjust to the NHL pace.

THE PHYSICAL GAME

Roche is big, and tough. He had 17 fighting majors last season (we weren't even aware he was given that many shifts all season), and has established a reputation around the league. Now he has to back up his game with his skills.

THE INTANGIBLES

Roche has an excellent work ethic and will have to utilize it to bring his game up to the NHL level. We don't think he'll explode this season, but if he is going to make an impact, he'll have to show some gradual improvement, at least.

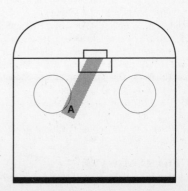

TOMAS SANDSTROM

Yrs. of NHL service: 12
Born: Jakobstad, Finland; Sept. 4, 1964
Position: right wing
Height: 6-2
Weight: 200
Uniform no.: 17
Shoots: left

Career statistics:

GP	G	A	TP	PIM
774	352	413	765	1018

1992-93 statistics:

GP	G	A	TP	+/-	PIM	PP	SH	GW	GT	S	PCT
39	25	27	52	+12	57	8	0	3	1	134	18.7

1993-94 statistics:

GP	G	A	TP	+/-	PIM	PP	SH	GW	GT	S	PCT
78	23	35	58	-7	83	4	0	3	1	193	11.9

1994-95 statistics:

GP	G	A	TP	+/-	PIM	PP	SH	GW	GT	S	PCT
47	21	23	44	+1	42	4	1	3	1	116	18.1

1995-96 statistics:

GP	G	A	TP	+/-	PIM	PP	SH	GW	GT	S	PCT
58	35	35	70	+4	69	17	1	2	0	187	18.7

LAST SEASON

Third on team in power play goals. Fourth on team in goals. Missed nine games with ankle surgery. Missed 15 games with shoulder separation.

THE FINESSE GAME

For three-quarters of the season, Sandstrom was in heaven on earth as Mario Lemieux's right-hand man. Lemieux made a 50-goal scorer out of Warren Young, for crying out loud, and the much more skilled Sandstrom was on a pace to hit that mark for the first time in his career. Then the injury hex hit Sandstrom, as it usually does.

Sandstrom is one of the few players in the league who can release a shot when the puck is in his feet. He uses a short backswing and surprises goalies with the shot's velocity and accuracy. He can beat a netminder in a number of ways, but this shot is unique. Sandstrom is also smart enough to know that when you play with Mario, all you have to do is work to get yourself open and be ready for the puck.

Sandstrom combines size, speed, strength and skill. He doesn't react well to change. He wants a regular role and lots of ice time, but injuries (his own and his team's) have made a set lineup almost impossible in recent seasons. One thing is certain: Sandstrom needs to play to keep his legs going.

His skating is impressive for someone of his dimensions. Quick and agile, he intimidates with his speed. He has a superb passing touch and shoots well on the fly or off the one-timer.

THE PHYSICAL GAME

Wildly abrasive, Sandstrom will give facials with his gloves, make late hits, get his stick up and take the body. Usually he hits and runs, resulting in angry opponents chasing him around the ice.

Sandstrom will also pay an honest physical price along the boards and in front of the net. He wants the puck and will scrap to control it.

THE INTANGIBLES

Sandstrom's move up to a second-line winger with the Penguins has revitalized his career. If he is able to hold on to the number two role, Sandstrom may enjoy another season at a good scoring clip, but some players are just fragile, and Sandstrom is a sure bet to get banged up at least once next season.

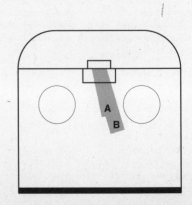

BRYAN SMOLINSKI

Yrs. of NHL service: 3
Born: Toledo, Ohio; Dec. 27, 1971
Position: centre/right wing
Height: 6-1
Weight: 200
Uniform no.: 20
Shoots: right

Career statistics:

GP	G	A	TP	PIM
217	74	76	150	186

1992-93 statistics:

GP	G	A	TP	+/-	PIM	PP	SH	GW	GT	S	PCT
9	1	3	4	+3	4	0	0	0	0	10	10.0

1993-94 statistics:

GP	G	A	TP	+/-	PIM	PP	SH	GW	GT	S	PCT
83	31	20	51	+4	82	4	3	5	0	179	17.3

1994-95 statistics:

GP	G	A	TP	+/-	PIM	PP	SH	GW	GT	S	PCT
44	18	13	31	-3	31	6	0	5	0	121	14.9

1995-96 statistics:

GP	G	A	TP	+/-	PIM	PP	SH	GW	GT	S	PCT
81	24	40	64	+6	69	8	2	1	0	229	10.5

LAST SEASON

Acquired from Boston with Glen Murray for Kevin Stevens and Shawn McEachern, Aug. 1, 1995. Tied for second on team in shorthanded goals. Career highs in assists and points. Missed one game with bruised knee.

THE FINESSE GAME

Smolinski can play either centre or wing, but the Penguins used him predominantly on the right side to make use of his size and grit. He brings a centre's vision to the wing. Some scouts have compared him to a budding Jean Ratelle for his crafty play. He has a quick release and an accurate shot, and works to get himself into quality shooting areas. Confidence is a big factor, and Smolinski has a history of being a streaky player, although he was quite consistent last season. His play away from the puck has improved to where he can contribute even when the points aren't forthcoming.

His skating is adequate, but it could improve with some lower body work. He has good balance and lateral movement but is not very quick. He has a railroad-track skating base.

Smolinski has the smarts to be an asset on both specialty teams, and he has really stepped up as a penalty killer. He has good defensive awareness, and his play away from the puck is sound. He is good in tight with the puck.

THE PHYSICAL GAME

Smolinski has a thick, blocky build, and when he hits people, he can crunch. He doesn't have much of an aggressive nature on a nightly basis. It shows up spo-

radically, and on those nights Smolinski is at his most effective.

THE INTANGIBLES

Smolinski gets a little lost at times because of the Penguins' penchant for overplaying their stars. His skills aren't world class, but they are certainly good enough to merit more ice time than he received last season. Confidence is a factor in his game. With the right amount of playing time, he should again be in the 60-70 point range.

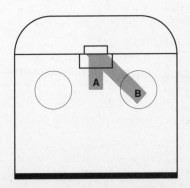

CHRIS TAMER

Yrs. of NHL service: 2
Born: Dearborn, Mich.; Nov. 17, 1970
Position: left defense
Height: 6-2
Weight: 185
Uniform no.: 2
Shoots: left

Career statistics:

GP	G	A	TP	PIM
118	6	10	16	244

1993-94 statistics:

GP	G	A	TP	+/-	PIM	PP	SH	GW	GT	S	PCT
12	0	0	0	+3	9	0	0	0	0	10	0.0

1994-95 statistics:

GP	G	A	TP	+/-	PIM	PP	SH	GW	GT	S	PCT
36	2	0	2	0	82	0	0	0	0	26	7.7

1995-96 statistics:

GP	G	A	TP	+/-	PIM	PP	SH	GW	GT	S	PCT
70	4	10	14	+20	153	0	0	1	0	75	5.3

LAST SEASON

Missed five games with abdominal injury. Missed five games with wrist injury. Missed two games with fractured jaw.

THE FINESSE GAME

If there were an award given to the most improved defenseman in the NHL last season, Tamer would be a finalist, if not the winner. As Sergei Zubov's partner, Tamer had plenty of practice with odd-man rushes and serving as the conservative, stay-at-home defenseman, which just happens to be his forte. Tamer has limited skating and stick skills but is smart enough to stay within his limitations and play a positional game.

Tamer was only a second-year NHLer last season, but played a poised game and learned from his mistakes. He does the little things well, chipping a puck off the boards or angling an attacker to the wall.

Tamer is smart enough when he is shooting from the point to make sure his shot doesn't get blocked (he learned this because Zubov was usually in deep as a fourth forward, and unless Ron Francis was on the ice, no forward dropped back to help). Tamer will take someting off his shot, or put it wide so the forwards could attack the puck off the end boards.

THE PHYSICAL GAME

Tamer doesn't nail people, but he has some strength and will use it to push people out of the crease and battle in the corners. He doesn't have a good skating base to be a punishing open-ice hitter. He will defend himself or stick up for a teammate. He doesn't have a serious nasty side, although he is often guilty of late hits.

Tamer is a well-conditioned athlete and can handle a lot of ice time. He kills penalties well and blocks shots.

THE INTANGIBLES

Tamer is a fixture among the team's top four defensemen. He will never be a star, but he will give solid support and can complement a more offensive player. His point production will be low, but he is an intelligent defenseman who will only get better.

KEVIN TODD

Yrs. of NHL service: 5
Born: Winnipeg, Man.; May 4, 1968
Position: centre
Height: 5-10
Weight: 180
Uniform no.: 12
Shoots: left

Career statistics:

GP	G	A	TP	PIM
291	57	105	162	169

1992-93 statistics:

GP	G	A	TP	+/-	PIM	PP	SH	GW	GT	S	PCT
55	9	14	23	-9	26	0	0	3	0	87	10.3

1993-94 statistics:

GP	G	A	TP	+/-	PIM	PP	SH	GW	GT	S	PCT
47	8	14	22	-3	24	4	0	1	0	65	12.3

1994-95 statistics:

GP	G	A	TP	+/-	PIM	PP	SH	GW	GT	S	PCT
33	3	8	11	-5	12	0	0	1	0	34	8.8

1995-96 statistics:

GP	G	A	TP	+/-	PIM	PP	SH	GW	GT	S	PCT
74	16	27	43	+6	38	0	2	4	0	132	12.1

LAST SEASON

Led Kings in plus-minus. Tied for second on team in game-winning goals. Second on team in shorthanded goals. Fifth on team in points. Missed eight games with a back injury. Signed as a free agent by Pittsburgh.

THE FINESSE GAME

Not an impressive skater, Todd gets his goals in tight because his wide-based stance allows him to dig in despite his small stature. He is like a terrier, wiry and tough, and he competes for rebounds. He isn't overly creative, but he keeps goalies guessing because he is just as likely to shoot as pass. He presses on the attack on a strong forecheck that the Kings favoured last season. Todd loves a basic game.

Todd can win draws on his forehand or backhand. He is built so low to the ice that it gives him an edge, but he can be outmuscled by a bigger, stronger centre. Todd has had to pay his dues to get his shot at the NHL and he wants to pay the price to stay there.

THE PHYSICAL GAME

Todd is small, but works tirelessly along the boards and the corners, often squirting free because bigger defenders tend to aim high with their checks and he is able to duck under and maintain his balance. He is not intimidated and will take abuse in pursuit of the puck. He'll strike back, too.

THE INTANGIBLES

Coach Larry Robinson thought Todd was his team's MVP last season, so it's surprising that the Kings let him go to the Penguins. He won't be the team MVP in

Pittsburgh, but don't expect him to coast. He doesn't know how. A higher skill level would mean more production, but Todd is likely to account for 40-50 points in a second- or third-line role.

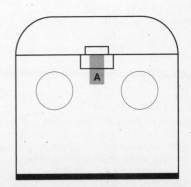

NEIL WILKINSON

Yrs. of NHL service: 7
Born: Selkirk, Man.; Aug. 15, 1967
Position: left defense
Height: 6-3
Weight: 190
Uniform no.: 6
Shoots: right

Career statistics:

GP	G	A	TP	PIM
379	14	63	77	719

1992-93 statistics:

GP	G	A	TP	+/-	PIM	PP	SH	GW	GT	S	PCT
59	1	7	8	-50	96	0	1	0	0	51	2.0

1993-94 statistics:

GP	G	A	TP	+/-	PIM	PP	SH	GW	GT	S	PCT
72	3	9	12	+2	114	1	0	0	0	72	4.2

1994-95 statistics:

GP	G	A	TP	+/-	PIM	PP	SH	GW	GT	S	PCT
40	1	4	5	-26	75	0	0	0	0	25	4.0

1995-96 statistics:

GP	G	A	TP	+/-	PIM	PP	SH	GW	GT	S	PCT
62	3	14	17	+12	120	0	1	1	0	59	5.1

LAST SEASON

Acquired from Winnipeg for Norm Maciver, Dec. 28, 1995. Missed 13 games with broken foot. Missed three games with shoulder injury. Missed two games with bruised heel.

THE FINESSE GAME

Wilkinson is solid in most areas of the game, though nothing really stands out. He carries the puck, but wouldn't be categorized as a rushing defenseman. He will play back, but his defensive reads are in serious need of improvement. He does not complete easy passes and doesn't have much of a shot.

Wilkinson is an average skater and has some difficulty with his foot speed when backskating. He is vulnerable to outside speed. He has to learn to angle his man to the boards.

He has a good attitude and will try anything the coaching staff asks, but he is a high-risk defenseman.

THE PHYSICAL GAME

Wilkinson is tall and gives the impression that he will be more of a bruiser, but he isn't that solid and his checks aren't that jarring. He will play tough and help his teammates. He is not a great fighter, but he will give it a go if provoked. Because he isn't a good skater, he can't hit a moving target.

THE INTANGIBLES

The Penguins acquired Wilkinson to add some toughness to their lineup, and he figures in among their top four defensemen this season. He can complement a more adventurous rearguard like Dmitri Mironov.

SAN JOSE SHARKS

Players' Statistics 1995-96

POS.	NO.	PLAYER	GP	G	A	PTS	+/-	PIM	PP	SH	GW	GT	S	PCT
R	11	OWEN NOLAN	81	33	36	69	-33	146	16	1	2		207	15.9
L	39	JEFF FRIESEN	79	15	31	46	-19	42	2				123	12.2
C	9	DARREN TURCOTTE	68	22	21	43	5	30	2	1	4		167	13.2
C	14	RAY WHITNEY	60	17	24	41	-23	16	4	2	2		106	16.0
D	33	*MARCUS RAGNARSSON	71	8	31	39	-24	42	4				94	8.5
C	13	JAMIE BAKER	77	16	17	33	-19	79	2	6			117	13.7
R	22	ULF DAHLEN	59	16	12	28	-21	27	5		2	1	103	15.5
D	3	DOUG BODGER	73	4	24	28	-24	68	3				121	3.3
C	18	CHRIS TANCILL	45	7	16	23	-12	20		1			93	7.5
R	42	*SHEAN DONOVAN	74	13	8	21	-17	39		1	2		73	17.8
D	38	MICHAL SYKORA	79	4	16	20	-14	54	1				80	5.0
D	47	YVES RACINE	57	1	19	20	-10	54					51	2.0
R	25	*VIKTOR KOZLOV	62	6	13	19	-15	6	1				107	5.6
L	36	JEFF ODGERS	78	12	4	16	-4	192			1	1	84	14.3
R	23	ANDREI NAZAROV	42	7	7	14	-15	62	2		1		55	12.7
L	37	*VILLE PELTONEN	31	2	11	13	-7	14					58	3.4
R	43	*JAN CALOUN	11	8	3	11	4		2				20	40.0
C	16	*DODY WOOD	32	3	6	9	0	138		1			33	9.1
D	4	JAY MORE	74	2	7	9	-32	147					67	3.0
D	44	VLASTIMIL KROUPA	27	1	7	8	-17	18					11	9.1
D	2	JIM KYTE	57	1	7	8	-12	146					32	3.1
D	40	MIKE RATHJE	27		7	7	-16	14					26	
R	48	*ALEXEI YEGOROV	9	3	2	5	-5	2	2				10	30.0
D	41	TOM PEDERSON	60	1	4	5	-9	40	1		1		59	1.7
G	30	CHRIS TERRERI	50		5	5	0	4						
R	21	DAVE BROWN	37	3	1	4	4	46					8	37.5
D	28	SERGEI BAUTIN	1				-1	2						
G	29	*GEOFF SARJEANT	4				0	2						
G	32	ARTURS IRBE	22				0	4						
G	31	WADE FLAHERTY	24				0								

GP = games played; G = goals; A = assists; PTS = points; +/- = goals-for minus goals-against while player is on ice; PIM = penalties in minutes; PP = power play goals; SH = shorthanded goals; GW = game-winning goals; GT = game-tying goals; S = no. of shots; PCT = percentage of goals to shots; * = rookie

DOUG BODGER

Yrs. of NHL service: 12
Born: Chemainus, B.C.; June 18, 1966
Position: left defense
Height: 6-2
Weight: 210
Uniform no.: 3
Shoots: left

Career statistics:

GP	G	A	TP	PIM
835	93	384	477	848

1992-93 statistics:

GP	G	A	TP	+/-	PIM	PP	SH	GW	GT	S	PCT
81	9	45	54	+14	87	6	0	0	1	154	5.8

1993-94 statistics:

GP	G	A	TP	+/-	PIM	PP	SH	GW	GT	S	PCT
75	7	32	39	+8	76	5	1	1	0	144	4.9

1994-95 statistics:

GP	G	A	TP	+/-	PIM	PP	SH	GW	GT	S	PCT
44	3	17	20	-3	47	2	0	0	0	87	3.4

1995-96 statistics:

GP	G	A	TP	+/-	PIM	PP	SH	GW	GT	S	PCT
73	4	24	28	-24	68	3	0	0	0	121	3.3

LAST SEASON

Acquired from Buffalo in three-way deal that sent Pat Falloon to Philadelphia, Nov. 17, 1995. Second among team defensemen in scoring. Missed three games with sprained knee.

THE FINESSE GAME

Bodger is a smooth skater with good quickness, and he can make tight pivots while carrying the puck. He's among the better-skating defensemen in the league, though he lacks the dynamite speed of the more charismatic defensemen. It is Bodger who will collect the puck from the goalie behind the net, let his teammates wheel back and get ready to attack, then move out with the puck. He can either carry up, or feed one of the forwards with a smooth pass and then jump into the play. Bodger sees his passing options well and is very smart with the puck.

A natural on the point on the power play, he works the left point. He has a big slapper that he keeps down for tips and scrambles in front. His best shot is a one-timer off a feed.

Bodger has great poise with the puck. He gives his team a sense of control when he is quarterbacking.

THE PHYSICAL GAME

Bodger takes the body when he absolutely must, but he is not by nature a hitter. He has never used his size as well as he should. Because his hand skills are so good, he prefers to position himself and try to poke- or sweep-check. He's a strong one-on-one defender because of his skating, but he will not clear people out from in front of his net as well as he should. He is aggressive stepping up into the neutral zone and challenges on penalty killing as well.

THE INTANGIBLES

Bodger has become an effective two-way defenseman and will play a key role in the development of some of the Sharks' younger defensemen this season. San Jose's management rewarded him with a new three-year deal, and he can be expected to see prime ice time. A solid, two-way performer, Bodger may score in the 35-40 point range.

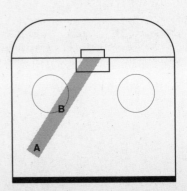

JAN CALOUN

Yrs. of NHL service: 0
Born: Usti-Nad-Labem, Czech.; Dec. 20, 1972
Position: right wing
Height: 5-11
Weight: 185
Uniform no.: 43
Shoots: right

Career statistics:

GP	G	A	TP	PIM
11	8	3	11	0

1995-96 statistics:

GP	G	A	TP	+/-	PIM	PP	SH	GW	GT	S	PCT
11	8	3	1	+4	0	2	0	0	0	20	40.0

LAST SEASON

Will be entering first NHL season. Led Kansas City
(IHL) last season with 38-30 — 68 in 61 games.

THE FINESSE GAME

Caloun scored goals on his first four NHL shots last
season, which pretty much sums up what he does best.

Caloun has a slippery way of getting his scoring
chances. He gets around people in tight places, and
when he gets a chance, he buries it. He isn't a great
skater, which is why he has spent the past two seasons
in the minors, but he is able to use his lower body
strength to work his way through the high traffic areas
to retrieve the puck or get free for a pass. He just
doesn't have top-end speed. If he did, he would be a
sure thing.

Caloun has wonderful offensive instincts. His
shots are quick and accurate, and he anticipates the
action. But right now, Caloun doesn't bring much else
to the table. He simply scores.

THE PHYSICAL GAME

Caloun is small but solidly built. He will take a hit to
make a play. He is not intimidated and will churn
around the net for his scoring chances.

THE INTANGIBLES

There are a legion of minor-league scorers who just
haven't had that extra skating step to put their scoring
skills to use at the NHL level, and Caloun may be one
of those players. The Sharks think otherwise, and he
should be ready to step in this season, but if they can't
find a spot for him on the top two lines, then Caloun
will struggle trying to get ice time.

ULF DAHLEN

Yrs. of NHL service: 9
Born: Ostersund, Sweden; Jan. 12, 1967
Position: centre/right wing
Height: 6-2
Weight: 195
Uniform no.: 22
Shoots: left

Career statistics:

GP	G	A	TP	PIM
613	217	230	447	176

1992-93 statistics:

GP	G	A	TP	+/-	PIM	PP	SH	GW	GT	S	PCT
83	35	39	74	-20	6	13	0	6	0	223	15.7

1993-94 statistics:

GP	G	A	TP	+/-	PIM	PP	SH	GW	GT	S	PCT
78	25	44	69	-1	10	15	0	5	1	190	13.2

1994-95 statistics:

GP	G	A	TP	+/-	PIM	PP	SH	GW	GT	S	PCT
46	11	23	34	-2	11	4	1	4	0	85	12.9

1995-96 statistics:

GP	G	A	TP	+/-	PIM	PP	SH	GW	GT	S	PCT
59	16	12	28	-21	27	5	0	2	1	103	15.5

LAST SEASON

Second on team in power play goals. Missed 20 games with broken foot.

THE FINESSE GAME

Dahlen is an intelligent hockey player who sees the ice well. He has great puck skill, although he does not move the puck quickly. He is extremely effective down low on the power play and is a good possession player. He lures defenders to him and opens up ice for his teammates. Dahlen scores goals that are tough to defend against — wraparounds and jam-ins — and those are the kind of goals that frustrate a goaltender. His real gift is puck protection and finding the open man.

Dahlen is an unusual skater, slow but with some deceptive moves. He has good balance and strength and always protects the puck with his body. Along the boards, it's almost impossible to beat him to the puck. It doesn't matter what the size or speed of the opponent is, Dahlen won't surrender the puck. He is one of the best board and corner men in the league as long as the puck is on his blade.

Dahlen has good hands and scores all of his goals from 10 inches to 10 feet away from the net. He slides out once in a while, but he is usually willing to pay the price to stay in the heavy traffic zone.

THE PHYSICAL GAME

Hitting Dahlen is like hitting a fire hydrant. It takes two or three checks to knock him down. Dahlen doesn't initiate. While he is willing to do just about anything to protect the puck when he has control, he will not win many one-on-one fights to strip the puck away from an opponent. He lacks the aggressiveness to bump his game up a notch.

THE INTANGIBLES

Losing Dahlen for a quarter of the season only added to the Sharks' woes. They might be going through a youth movement, but they want to keep some character older players on hand, and Dahlen is one of those. The Swede is the kind of versatile, veteran player that a lot of teams will be asking about at the next trade deadline if San Jose is not contending.

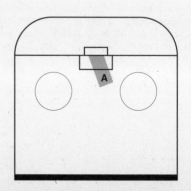

SHEAN DONOVAN

Yrs. of NHL service: 1
Born: Timmins, Ont.; Jan. 22, 1975
Position: right wing
Height: 6-2
Weight: 190
Uniform no.: 42
Shoots: right

Career statistics:

GP	G	A	TP	PIM
88	13	8	21	45

1994-95 statistics:

GP	G	A	TP	+/-	PIM	PP	SH	GW	GT	S	PCT
14	0	0	0	-6	6	0	0	0	0	13	0.0

1995-96 statistics:

GP	G	A	TP	+/-	PIM	PP	SH	GW	GT	S	PCT
74	13	8	21	-17	39	0	1	2	0	73	17.8

LAST SEASON

First NHL season. Led team in shooting percentage. Missed two games with flu. Played four games with Kansas City (IHL), scoring no points.

THE FINESSE GAME

Donovan has big-league speed. His quickness and powerful stride allow him to shift directions with agility. And he doesn't waste energy. He knows where he is supposed to be positioned and reads plays well. He has good anticipation, which stamps him as a strong penalty killer, although he is not a real short-handed scoring threat yet because of his lack of moves on a breakaway.

Donovan showed a more promising finishing touch last season, getting his goals in limited ice time. He may never be a great point-getter because of his lack of scoring or playmaking touch, but it will not be for lack of effort. He is a diligent worker, and may develop into one of the top defensive forwards in the NHL. He isn't fazed by facing some of the league's better forwards, either.

THE PHYSICAL GAME

Donovan is always busy making his hits, and brings a lot of energy to a game, much in the manner of Dave Lowry. Donovan doesn't have much of a mean streak, nor will he agitate. He takes the body, but doesn't punish people. He is well-conditioned and has good stamina.

THE INTANGIBLES

Of all the players the Sharks have tested for skating speed over the years, Donovan ranks right at the top with noted NHL speedster Mike Gartner. His scoring touch is something new, and there is the possibility of Donovan developing into one of those prized checking forwards who can pot 20-25 goals in a season. He has a great attitude and is one of those special character players every dressing room needs.

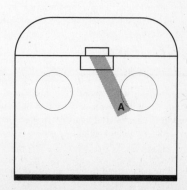

JEFF FRIESEN

Yrs. of NHL service: 2
Born: Meadow Lake, Sask.; Aug. 5, 1976
Position: left wing/centre
Height: 6-0
Weight: 185
Uniform no.: 39
Shoots: left

Career statistics:

GP	G	A	TP	PIM
127	30	41	71	56

1994-95 statistics:

GP	G	A	TP	+/-	PIM	PP	SH	GW	GT	S	PCT
48	15	10	25	-8	14	5	1	2	0	86	17.4

1995-96 statistics:

GP	G	A	TP	+/-	PIM	PP	SH	GW	GT	S	PCT
79	15	31	46	-19	42	2	0	0	0	123	12.2

LAST SEASON

Second NHL season. Second on team in assists and points. One of five players to score on a penalty shot last season.

THE FINESSE GAME

Friesen was an offensive-minded fellow as a junior, but he was retooled two seasons ago to think like a checker. As a result, he has become a more well-rounded player with a rapidly maturing game.

Friesen is a fast, strong skater, handles the puck well and has the size to go with those qualities. He is a better finisher than playmaker. He has a quick, strong release on his snap or wrist shot. He needs to play with someone to get him the puck, and worked well with the playmaking Ray Whitney in their time together. Friesen is shifty with a smooth change of speed.

He never seems to get rattled or forced into making bad plays. In fact, he's the one who forces opponents into panic moves with his pressure. He will draw penalties by keeping his feet moving as he drives to the net or digs for the puck along the boards. He is strong on face-offs.

THE PHYSICAL GAME

Friesen has a future as a winger who will get a lot of ice time against other team's top lines, and he will need to get stronger and maintain his conditioning in order to compete at that level.

THE INTANGIBLES

Friesen went through the "sophomore slump" early last season, disagreed with ex-coach Kevin Constantine, and was benched by subsequent ex-coach Jim Wiley, but overcame all of it to finish well. We said in last year's *HSR* that Friesen would be an unlikely candidate for the slump, but the rap on him as a junior was his work ethic and that's what appeared to plague him.

We were encouraged by Friesen's late play and figure he will resume his positive ways to become a 55-60 point scorer.

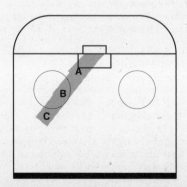

TODD GILL

Yrs. of NHL service: 11
Born: Cardinal, Ont.; Nov. 9, 1965
Position: right defense
Height: 6-0
Weight: 180
Uniform no.: 23
Shoots: left

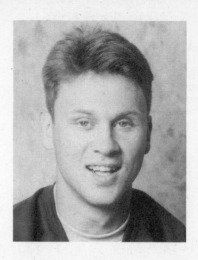

Career statistics:

GP	G	A	TP	PIM
639	59	208	267	922

1992-93 statistics:

GP	G	A	TP	+/-	PIM	PP	SH	GW	GT	S	PCT
69	11	32	43	+4	66	5	0	2	0	113	9.7

1993-94 statistics:

GP	G	A	TP	+/-	PIM	PP	SH	GW	GT	S	PCT
45	4	23	27	+8	44	2	0	1	0	74	5.4

1994-95 statistics:

GP	G	A	TP	+/-	PIM	PP	SH	GW	GT	S	PCT
47	7	25	32	-8	64	3	1	2	0	82	8.5

1995-96 statistics:

GP	G	A	TP	+/-	PIM	PP	SH	GW	GT	S	PCT
74	7	18	25	-15	116	1	0	2	0	109	6.4

THE INTANGIBLES

Gill is a respected competitor who will add some stability to the Sharks' blueline and some character to the room. His top end now is probably 30 points. His first concern will be team defense.

LAST SEASON

Acquired by San Jose for Jamie Baker and a fifth-round draft pick, June 14, 1996. Missed four games with pulled hamstring. Missed four games with back spasms.

THE FINESSE GAME

Gill wants to be a leader on the team, and he is an excellent veteran addition to a young team like San Jose that is trying to right itself. He is a gamer, and a player who knows his limitations and seldom tries to do what he can't.

Gill has sufficient offensive skills to get involved in the attack. He has good hockey sense and can do some things with the puck, like making a short, smart pass or taking a well-timed point shot. Gill doesn't like the puck to linger in his own zone. He will carry it out and make smart plays. He has faith in his partners and lets them and the puck do the work.

He isn't afraid to venture deep and use a wrist or snap shot from the left circle. Once in a while he will brave the front of the net (though he has to be darned sure when he tries it). He is smart and talented enough to work the point on the power play on the second unit.

THE PHYSICAL GAME

Gill is a tough defenseman with a ton of heart and spunk. He's on the slight side for an NHL defenseman, and has to be mindful of conditioning and nutrition to keep up with the grind. And grind is what he has to do to be effective. He will drop the gloves and go if he has to, and he stands up for his teammates, taking on the biggest guy on the ice.

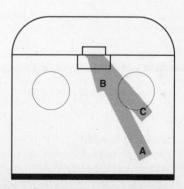

AL IAFRATE

Yrs. of NHL service: 10
Born: Dearborn, Mich.; Mar. 21, 1966
Position: left defense
Height: 6-4
Weight: 235
Uniform no.: 43
Shoots: left

Career statistics:

GP	G	A	TP	PIM
740	144	295	439	1182

1992-93 statistics:

GP	G	A	TP	+/-	PIM	PP	SH	GW	GT	S	PCT
81	25	41	66	+15	169	11	1	4	0	289	8.7

1993-94 statistics:

GP	G	A	TP	+/-	PIM	PP	SH	GW	GT	S	PCT
79	15	43	58	+16	163	6	0	4	0	299	5.0

1994-95 statistics:
Did not play in NHL

1995-96 statistics:
Did not play in NHL

LAST SEASON
Acquired by San Jose for Jeff Odgers, June 21, 1996. Missed last two seasons with knee injuries.

THE FINESSE GAME
If you really want to know what's going on with Iafrate, don't read the rest of this page. You would do just as well calling a psychic hotline.

Iafrate has sought his own medical opinions and took the Bruins to arbitration on a salary grievance (he won) before the Sharks gambled on trading for him.

We can only assess the pre-surgery Iafrate, and wonder whether he will return to his former frightening self. He has a big-time slap shot, he can leave a defender flat-footed with his skating, and he has one of the spookiest stares in the NHL. Iafrate can play an all-out offensive game, which is his strength, or settle back and provide some solid defense.

It's unlikely Iafrate will be the skater he was before missing two years of activity. Before the surgeries, he was fast and agile for a large man. He is capable of rushing end to end but is better at jumping up into the play. He moves the puck quickly out of his own zone, often taking it himself. He can stickhandle and uses all of the ice.

Iafrate can play either point on the power play. He has a deadly one-timer. His point shot is intimidating, and he will fake the shot, freeze the defense, then move around for a snap shot or slide the puck in deep. There isn't much he can't do as far as finesse skills are concerned.

THE PHYSICAL GAME
For a big guy, Iafrate does not hit with much intensity. He can, but he is more intent on playing the offensive game. He does not enjoy the one-on-one battles. He will be a booming open-ice hitter when the spirit moves him, but just as often he will be wiped out along the boards. Of course, his conditioning will be a huge question mark, but Iafrate was skating late last season.

THE INTANGIBLES
Iafrate seemed enthusiastic about the trade to San Jose, but he is the riskiest of propositions.

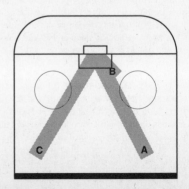

VIKTOR KOZLOV

Yrs. of NHL service: 1
Born: Togliatti, Russia; Feb. 14, 1975
Position: right wing
Height: 6-5
Weight: 225
Uniform no.: 25
Shoots: right

Career statistics:

GP	G	A	TP	PIM
78	8	13	21	8

1994-95 statistics:

GP	G	A	TP	+/-	PIM	PP	SH	GW	GT	S	PCT
16	2	0	2	-5	2	0	0	0	0	23	8.7

1995-96 statistics:

GP	G	A	TP	+/-	PIM	PP	SH	GW	GT	S	PCT
62	6	13	19	-15	6	1	0	0	0	107	5.6

LAST SEASON

Second NHL season. Played 15 games with Kansas City (IHL), scoring 4-7 — 11.

THE FINESSE GAME

Kozlov was schooled at centre last season, and towards the end of the season was being given more freedom to play his creative game. The new coaches in San Jose are said to be very high on Kozlov's ability, and may just decide to put him with the team's two most suitable forwards and turn him loose.

Kozlov is very coachable, and maybe a little too tractable. If he spoke up and demanded some more playing time, or a better playing situation, he might have been deemed a more assertive player, but that's not Kozlov's nature.

He is a beautiful skater for his size. He has the moves of a 150-pounder, with quickness and agility. Kozlov has learned to come off the boards much quicker, and is shooting with more authority. He has also learned to make a move and then take a shot, and not look for the pass. But when passing is the best option, Kozlov can do that as well. He has a keen sense of timing and pace.

Kozlov won't float and he has defensive principles. He won't hang at the red line.

THE PHYSICAL GAME

Kozlov's new physique has enabled him to be a lot sturdier in contact. He will still have to prove he has a taste for the North American style.

Kozlov has a long reach but doesn't care to play the body defensively, although offensively he will work with the puck to get in front of the net and into scoring position. He needs to develop lower body strength.

THE INTANGIBLES

Kozlov may yet be a season away from being the kind of impact player San Jose still hopes he will be. This year should be the one that shows which direction he is heading in, since a lot of young Sharks players will be given their chance to shine. Expect him to get plenty of ice time early.

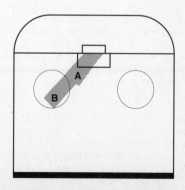

ANDREI NAZAROV

Yrs. of NHL service: 2
Born: Chelyabinsk, Soviet Union; May 22, 1974
Position: right wing
Height: 6-5
Weight: 230
Uniform no.: 23
Shoots: right

Career statistics:

GP	G	A	TP	PIM
69	10	12	22	156

1993-94 statistics:

GP	G	A	TP	+/-	PIM	PP	SH	GW	GT	S	PCT
1	0	0	0	0	0	0	0	0	0	0	0.0

1994-95 statistics:

GP	G	A	TP	+/-	PIM	PP	SH	GW	GT	S	PCT
26	3	5	8	-1	94	0	0	0	0	19	15.8

1995-96 statistics:

GP	G	A	TP	+/-	PIM	PP	SH	GW	GT	S	PCT
42	7	7	14	-15	62	2	0	1	0	55	12.7

figures in San Jose's plans this year, however, and if he shows even a hint of improvement he'll stick.

LAST SEASON

First NHL season. Played 27 games with Kansas City (IHL), scoring 4-6 — 10 with 118 penalty minutes.

THE FINESSE GAME

The Sharks envision plopping this giant in front of their net on the power play and wishing the opposing goalie good luck. Nazarov doesn't have the skating to be a real power forward as yet, but he can handle some second-unit power play time in addition to what will probably be his role as a third- or fourth-line winger.

He needs a lot of work on his skating (which has improved) but he has fairly good hand skills for scooping up rebounds around the net. He was productive in limited ice time. Nazarov needs to be a regular player and get the ice time to be allowed to improve, because of his fairly high technical level.

Nazarov is smart and understands the game well. He is aware of his limitations and won't try to do too much.

THE PHYSICAL GAME

How scary is the spectre of Nazarov? One scout says of him, "He's sick." Nazarov is rattlesnake-mean and he has a short fuse. He will fight anyone, and has a long reach that makes him tough for even some of the league's best fighters to cope with. He will protect his teammates. Anyone checked by Nazarov does not get back into the play quickly. He could star in a lot of very ugly highlight tapes.

THE INTANGIBLES

Nazarov started last season with the Sharks, but with the team in a tailspin, he struggled and was sent to the minors to rebuild his game. He'll have to do more than fight to stay in the NHL, and he may start this season in the minors to add some polish to his game. Nazarov

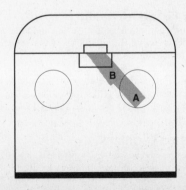

BERNIE NICHOLLS

Yrs. of NHL service: 15
Born: Haliburton, Ont.; June 24, 1961
Position: centre
Height: 6-1
Weight: 185
Uniform no.: 92
Shoots: right

Career statistics:

GP	G	A	TP	PIM
992	457	677	1134	1199

1992-93 statistics:

GP	G	A	TP	+/-	PIM	PP	SH	GW	GT	S	PCT
69	13	47	60	-13	80	5	0	1	0	132	9.8

1993-94 statistics:

GP	G	A	TP	+/-	PIM	PP	SH	GW	GT	S	PCT
61	19	27	46	+24	86	3	0	1	1	142	13.4

1994-95 statistics:

GP	G	A	TP	+/-	PIM	PP	SH	GW	GT	S	PCT
48	22	29	51	+4	32	11	2	5	0	114	19.3

1995-96 statistics:

GP	G	A	TP	+/-	PIM	PP	SH	GW	GT	S	PCT
59	19	41	60	+11	60	6	0	2	2	100	19.0

LAST SEASON

Third on team in assists. Missed 22 games with spleen injury. Signed as a free agent with San Jose, July 30, 1996.

THE FINESSE GAME

A loose and loopy personality off the ice, Nicholls exhibits some of those same tendencies on the ice. Sometimes this is a plus, as Nicholls can be wonderfully inventive with the puck, especially when creating plays from behind the net. The downside comes on nights when it looks like his mind is elsewhere. Bad penalties and baffling decisions follow.

Nicholls is an excellent passer, equally deft on the forehand to his left wing or the backhand to his right wing. He has vision and touch. He is best down low. He will not plant himself in front of the net, being a bit too frail for that, but he will linger on the fringes and then move through the goalie's line of sight, either screening or picking a puck out of mid-air for a redirect. He has quick reactions for picking caroms off the goalie's pads.

Nicholls has turned into an excellent penalty killer. He blocks shots better than many defensemen. Although he is not fast, he does pay attention to his positioning.

THE PHYSICAL GAME

Nicholls is strong for his size and has a real nasty streak. When playing with the right bodyguard, he becomes an outrageous opponent. He needles, nettles and intimidates with his words (but he's so funny it's a wonder he doesn't just leave opponents doubled over in laughter). Nicholls is erratic on face-offs. He is fairly quick with his hands, but gets overpowered by bigger centres.

THE INTANGIBLES

The Sharks are thin in the middle and Nicholls could be very useful as a number two or three centre who can add pop to their power play.

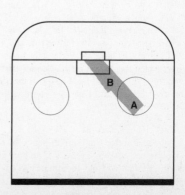

OWEN NOLAN

Yrs. of NHL service: 6
Born: Belfast, N. Ireland; Sept. 22, 1971
Position: right wing
Height: 6-1
Weight: 200
Uniform no.: 11
Shoots: right

Career statistics:

GP	G	A	TP	PIM
334	144	137	291	672

1992-93 statistics:

GP	G	A	TP	+/-	PIM	PP	SH	GW	GT	S	PCT
73	36	41	77	-1	185	15	0	4	1	241	14.9

1993-94 statistics:

GP	G	A	TP	+/-	PIM	PP	SH	GW	GT	S	PCT
6	2	2	4	+2	8	0	0	0	0	15	13.3

1994-95 statistics:

GP	G	A	TP	+/-	PIM	PP	SH	GW	GT	S	PCT
46	30	19	49	+21	46	13	2	8	0	137	21.9

1995-96 statistics:

GP	G	A	TP	+/-	PIM	PP	SH	GW	GT	S	PCT
81	33	36	69	-33	146	16	1	2	0	207	15.9

LAST SEASON

Acquired from Colorado for Sandis Ozolinsh, Oct. 26, 1995. Led team in goals, assists, points, power play goals and shots. Worst plus-minus on team. Missed one game for disciplinary reasons. Missed two games with flu.

THE FINESSE GAME

Nolan rips one-timers from the circle with deadly speed and accuracy. He is a pure shooter with good hands. His game suffers when he tries to get too fancy and ventures away from a meat-and-potatoes game. When that happens, he holds onto the puck too long and tries to make plays instead of shooting. Nobody knows where Nolan's shot is headed, except Nolan. He has an amazing knack for letting the puck go at just the right moment. He has a little move in tight to the goal with a forehand to backhand, and around the net he is about as good as anyone in the game.

Nolan is a strong skater with good balance and fair agility. He is quick straight ahead but won't split the defense when carrying the puck. He's better without the puck, driving into open ice for the pass and quick shot. Defensively, he has improved tremendously.

Nolan ended the season playing on an effective line with Ray Whitney and Jeff Freisen. If the Sharks can improve the supporting cast a little, it will take some of the pressure off him.

THE PHYSICAL GAME

Nolan had a season free from serious injury (he had a bad shoulder two seasons ago) and if he becomes a consistent physical forward then the Sharks won't look so bad for having sent Ozolinsh to win a Stanley Cup in Colorado.

THE INTANGIBLES

Nolan is not by nature an outgoing guy, and when he was thrust into the role of a leader in San Jose, it took some time to get used to the notion. The Sharks clearly have faith in him, as they signed him to a two-year deal worth U.S.$4.6 million after last season. Nolan can be a bit volatile emotionally, but he may grow into the job. Maturity will only make him a better player. He is capable of a 50-goal season if he approaches the game like a true professional.

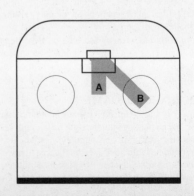

MARCUS RAGNARSSON

Yrs. of NHL service: 1
Born: Ostervala, Sweden; Aug. 13, 1971
Position: left defense
Height: 6-1
Weight: 200
Uniform no.: 33
Shoots: left

Career statistics:

GP	G	A	TP	PIM
71	8	31	39	42

1995-96 statistics:

GP	G	A	TP	+/-	PIM	PP	SH	GW	GT	S	PCT
71	8	31	39	-24	42	4	0	0	0	94	8.5

LAST SEASON

First NHL season. Named to NHL All-Rookie team. Led NHL rookie defensemen in scoring and tied for seventh among all rookie scorers. Third among rookies and tied for second on team in assists. Fifth on team in points. Missed three games with hamstring injury. Missed two games with concussion.

THE FINESSE GAME

Ragnarsson has a lot of poise, hand skills and skating ability. He has very quick feet and moves the puck well. He makes a good first pass and also makes some good decisions at the blueline to get the puck through.

He controlled a lot of the breakout for San Jose, and made smart choices in the neutral zone. He was given a lot of responsibility on the power play, and while he is not in the elite class of quarterbacks, he has a decent point shot and isn't afraid to shoot.

The pressure of playing so much in his own zone on a poor team wore on Ragnarsson, especially since the ice time and travel was so much tougher than he was used to in Europe. He had a slower second half for that reason.

THE PHYSICAL GAME

Ragnarsson is built solidly and will play a physical game, although finesse is his forte. He has a taste for hitting, though, and anyone not expecting a solid hit from him will be rudely surprised. He may become even more physical as he matures.

THE INTANGIBLES

Ragnarsson was one the team's few pleasant surprises last season, and expectations will be high for him to build on his strong rookie year. The Sharks are a very young team, which could make things especially hard on the defense corps. Ragnarsson is capable of a 70-point season, but if the Sharks struggle it might not happen until another year down the line.

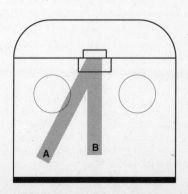

MIKE RATHJE

Yrs. of NHL service: 3
Born: Mannville, Alta.; May 11, 1974
Position: left defense
Height: 6-6
Weight: 220
Uniform no.: 40
Shoots: left

Career statistics:

GP	G	A	TP	PIM
116	3	23	26	102

1993-94 statistics:

GP	G	A	TP	+/-	PIM	PP	SH	GW	GT	S	PCT
47	1	9	10	-9	59	1	0	0	0	30	3.3

1994-95 statistics:

GP	G	A	TP	+/-	PIM	PP	SH	GW	GT	S	PCT
42	2	7	9	-1	29	0	0	0	0	38	5.3

1995-96 statistics:

GP	G	A	TP	+/-	PIM	PP	SH	GW	GT	S	PCT
27	0	7	7	-16	14	0	0	0	0	26	0.0

LAST SEASON

Played 36 games with Kansas City (IHL), scoring 6-11 — 17. Missed five games for personal reasons. Missed 12 games with shoulder injury.

THE FINESSE GAME

A stay-at-home defenseman, Rathje is a cornerstone for a new and improved defense. He will become even more effective once he learns to use his reach and eliminate more of the ice.

He has the ability to get involved in the attack but is prized primarily for his defense. He helps get the puck out of the zone quickly. He can either carry the puck out and make a smart headman pass, then follow the play, or make the safe move and chip the puck out along the wall.

Rathje has great poise for a young player. He will probably have to be paired with a more offensive defenseman, though he does a nice job on the right point on the power play. He combines his lateral mobility with a good low shot to get the puck on the net without being blocked.

He has to improve his defensive reads, but that should come with experience. Adding Todd Gill to the team's roster will help him.

THE PHYSICAL GAME

Rathje has good size and he is adding more muscle. He's only 22, but has built himself up to about 6-5, 220. What Rathje has to learn is controlled aggression. He has a tendency to try to do too much, which is a happier problem than the reverse. He has a little bit of mean in him, and he likes to hit, but he doesn't eliminate as well as he should; he has to concentrate on the takeout instead of the knockout. He has unbelievable strength and good mobility for his size.

THE INTANGIBLES

Some family problems prevented Rathje from having his head completely in the game last season, and the losing atmosphere around the Sharks' dressing room didn't help. He benefited from a stint in Kansas City working with Don Jackson, and the potential exists for Rathje to step up and prove himself as a blue-chip prospect.

Rathje had a terrific playoffs against Calgary in 1994, and he seems to have brought his confidence back to that level. He has a big upside, and could finish the season as one of the team's top two defensemen.

MICHAL SYKORA

Yrs. of NHL service: 2
Born: Pardubice, Czech Republic; July 5, 1973
Position: left defense
Height: 6-5
Weight: 225
Uniform no.: 38
Shoots: left

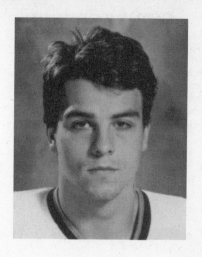

Career statistics:

GP	G	A	TP	PIM
117	5	24	29	78

1993-94 statistics:

GP	G	A	TP	+/-	PIM	PP	SH	GW	GT	S	PCT
22	1	4	5	-4	14	0	0	0	0	22	4.5

1994-95 statistics:

GP	G	A	TP	+/-	PIM	PP	SH	GW	GT	S	PCT
16	0	4	4	+6	10	0	0	0	0	6	0.0

1995-96 statistics:

GP	G	A	TP	+/-	PIM	PP	SH	GW	GT	S	PCT
79	4	16	20	-14	54	1	0	0	0	80	5.0

LAST SEASON

Games played and point totals career high.

THE FINESSE GAME

Sykora was a middle-round steal (123rd overall) in the 1992 draft for the Sharks. He has very good finesse skills, which he can use offensively or defensively.

Sykora is a strong skater forwards or backwards. He has a heavy, hard shot, but hasn't quite adjusted to NHL speed in his offensive decision-making process. He headmans the puck well out of his own zone and doesn't panic under pressure. He's confident in his puckhandling skills in his own end of the ice.

Sykora is an intelligent player who plays a good transition game. He will probably see second-unit power play time.

THE PHYSICAL GAME

Sykora was a bit weedy at the start of his NHL career and had to pay some dues in the minors to develop better upper body strength. He has a long reach that he uses to tie up attackers along the boards. He plays well positionally.

THE INTANGIBLES

Sykora has quietly been developing into a top four defenseman for the Sharks. Although he has been concentrating on his defensive play, he was a scorer at the junior level and may have some upside to post better numbers.

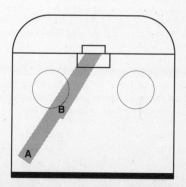

CHRIS TERRERI

Yrs. of NHL service: 7
Born: Providence, RI; Nov. 15, 1964
Position: goaltender
Height: 5-8
Weight: 160
Uniform no.: 30
Catches: left

Career statistics:

GP	MIN	GA	SO	GAA	A	PIM
314	17247	914	6	3.18	11	29

1992-93 statistics:

GP	MIN	GAA	W	L	T	SO	GA	S	SAPCT	PIM
48	2672	3.39	19	21	3	2	151	1324	.886	6

1993-94 statistics:

GP	MIN	GAA	W	L	T	SO	GA	S	SAPCT	PIM
44	2340	2.72	11	4	2	2	106	1141	.907	4

1994-95 statistics:

GP	MIN	GAA	W	L	T	SO	GA	S	SAPCT	PIM
15	734	2.53	3	7	2	0	31	309	.900	0

1995-96 statistics:

GP	MIN	GAA	W	L	T	SO	GA	S	SAPCT	PIM
50	2726	3.61	16	29	1	0	164	1414	.884	4

LAST SEASON

Acquired from New Jersey for a second-round draft pick, November 15, 1995. Missed 12 games with arm injury.

THE MENTAL GAME

Terreri adjusted from being a number two goalie in New Jersey behind Martin Broduer to being the main man every night. Not every goalie can do that, but Terreri had been there before and he shifted gears to handle the responsibility.

Terreri is very competitive and can easily get down after a bad goal. Out of self-preservation, he had to develop a thicker hide in San Jose and learned to shake off some of the bad nights. His goaltending was one of the few bright spots for San Jose last season.

THE INTANGIBLES

Terreri hadn't been a number one goalie for two seasons when he was acquired by the Sharks, and he is too small and has too active a style to maintain a high level of play over the long haul. The Sharks started him in 24 consecutive games and that is too heavy a workload.

He was disappointed by the trade from New Jersey, but turned out to be one of the leaders in the Sharks' dressing room. He figures to be the number one goalie again this season, but he'll need to be used more judiciously by the new coaching staff.

DARREN TURCOTTE

Yrs. of NHL service: 7
Born: Boston, Mass.; Mar. 2, 1968
Position: centre
Height: 6-0
Weight: 180
Uniform no.: 9
Shoots: left

Career statistics:

GP	G	A	TP	PIM
459	163	183	346	239

1992-93 statistics:

GP	G	A	TP	+/-	PIM	PP	SH	GW	GT	S	PCT
71	25	28	53	-3	40	7	3	3	1	213	11.7

1993-94 statistics:

GP	G	A	TP	+/-	PIM	PP	SH	GW	GT	S	PCT
32	4	15	19	-13	17	0	0	0	0	60	6.7

1994-95 statistics:

GP	G	A	TP	+/-	PIM	PP	SH	GW	GT	S	PCT
47	17	18	35	+1	22	3	1	3	0	121	14.0

1995-96 statistics:

GP	G	A	TP	+/-	PIM	PP	SH	GW	GT	S	PCT
68	22	21	43	+5	30	2	1	4	0	167	13.2

LAST SEASON

Acquired from Winnipeg with a second-round draft pick in 1996 for Craig Janney, March 18, 1996. Led Jets in plus-minus and game-winning goals. Second on team in goals. Third on team in assists. Missed six games with thumb injury. Missed one game with hand injury.

THE FINESSE GAME

Turcotte is much better on special teams than at even strength, though he is a capable five-on-five player. With the extra open ice — even when his team is shorthanded — he makes things happen. Turcotte is a fine skater who appears to hover over the ice. He takes long, fluid strides that cover a lot of territory and creates space with his speed, driving the defenders back and daring them to come up to challenge him.

Turcotte kills penalties aggressively. He forces the play and when he gets a turnover he springs down-ice on a break. He makes point men nervous, and teams who use forwards at the point are especially vulnerable to his pressure.

On the power play, Turcotte works down low but can drop back to handle the point if the defenseman comes in deep. He has a fine snap shot, as well as a good wrister and one-timer. He has sharp hand-eye coordination and is skilled on draws. Turcotte is a centre who likes to shoot rather than pass.

THE PHYSICAL GAME

Turcotte will take a hit to make a play but he is not a physical player. He will go into traffic with the puck and has the hand skills to control the puck in a crowd.

THE INTANGIBLES

Turcotte will be asked to perform a number one centre's role in San Jose, but he is really better suited as a number two. Still, he will benefit from the ice time, especially on the power play, and should rebound to a 70-point season.

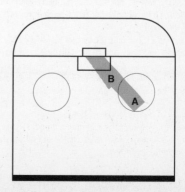

RAY WHITNEY

Yrs. of NHL service: 4
Born: Fort Saskatchewan, Alta.; May 8, 1972
Position: left wing/centre
Height: 5-9
Weight: 160
Uniform no.: 14
Shoots: right

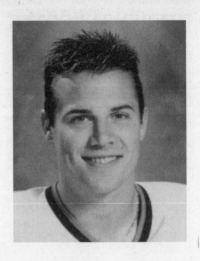

Career statistics:

GP	G	A	TP	PIM
188	48	71	119	48

1992-93 statistics:

GP	G	A	TP	+/-	PIM	PP	SH	GW	GT	S	PCT
26	4	6	10	-14	4	1	0	0	0	24	16.7

1993-94 statistics:

GP	G	A	TP	+/-	PIM	PP	SH	GW	GT	S	PCT
61	14	26	40	+2	14	1	0	0	1	82	17.1

1994-95 statistics:

GP	G	A	TP	+/-	PIM	PP	SH	GW	GT	S	PCT
39	13	12	25	-7	14	4	0	1	0	67	19.4

1995-96 statistics:

GP	G	A	TP	+/-	PIM	PP	SH	GW	GT	S	PCT
60	17	24	41	-23	16	4	2	2	0	106	16.0

LAST SEASON

Third on team in goals with career high. Fourth on team in points with career high. Missed 17 games with wrist injury. Missed five games with groin injury.

THE FINESSE GAME

Despite losing his friend and junior teammate Pat Falloon to an early-season trade, the Sharks' many personnel moves ended up being the best thing to happen to Whitney. He was moved from left wing to centre, which is his best position, and played his most successful hockey on a line with Jeff Friesen and Owen Nolan.

Whitney is small but determined. Nifty and crafty, he compensates for a lack of quickness with his keen anticipation. He jumps into the right spot simply by knowing it's the right place to be before the defender is aware, and that makes him appear quicker than he really is. In traffic, he is steady on his skates and handles the puck well. He has exceptionally good hands and can lift a backhand shot when he is practically on top of the goalie.

He does a lot of nice things just inside the blueline, carrying in and wheeling to hit a trailing teammate or throwing the puck in deep if that is the better play. He would rather pass than shoot, but he has a deceptive shot, and he can contribute to a power play.

THE PHYSICAL GAME

Whitney plays a smart, small man's game. He doesn't head into too many areas where he'll get crunched, but darts in and out of holes.

THE INTANGIBLES

Depending on how Whitney is used by new coach Al Sims, he could continue to progress toward becoming a 20-25 goal scorer on a second line. He and Darren Turcotte will vie for the prime centre ice time, and neither is a big-time number one centre, so Whitney should get his share.

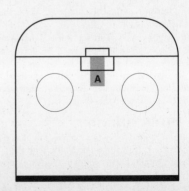

ANDREI ZYUZIN

Yrs. of NHL service: 0
Born: Ufa, Russia; Jan. 21, 1978
Position: left defense
Height: 6-1
Weight: 187
Uniform no.: n.a.
Shoots: left

Career statistics (Russia):				
GP	G	A	TP	PIM
71	9	3	12	40

1995-96 statistics (Russia):				
GP	G	A	TP	+/P
41	6	3	9	24

LAST SEASON

Drafted second overall. Named best player in 1996 European Junior Tournament.

THE FINESSE GAME

Zyuzin rose a few notches in the scouting rankings with a superb performance for bronze medalist Russia in the 1996 World Junior Championship. He is an offensive-minded defenseman with the kind of speed and anticipation that will prevent him from being too much of a liability on defense, because of his ability to recover and position himself.

Zyuzin could well prove to be the kind of player who can dictate the tempo of a game, or break it wide open with one end-to-end rush, à la Brian Leetch. At the moment, he doesn't seem to possess the exceptional lateral movement along the blueline that sets Leetch apart from most of his NHL brethren, but Zyuzin has a big upside.

He is a fast skater with quick acceleration and balance. Zyuzin handles the puck well at a high tempo. He will pass or shoot, and is a smart playmaker but one who will not pass up a golden scoring opportunity. He has a hard point shot and will become a good power play quarterback.

THE PHYSICAL GAME

Zyuzin is not a physical player. He has adequate size, but will need a streak of Chris Chelios-like aggressiveness to make the best use of his ability. Zyuzin does have a desire to excel, and if it means stepping up his game physically, he will probably be able to make that transition.

THE INTANGIBLES

Zyuzin has been compared to Oleg Tverdovsky, who is about to bloom in his third NHL season. Scouts have called him everything from the next Ray Bourque to a complete defenseman, but he will need more bulk before he can fulfill those lofty expectations. Zyuzin will need at least one year's grace in North America (he speaks almost no English) before becoming an impact player. Scouts are high on his character and his drive to be a successful NHLer. San Jose has had a streak of bad luck with its Russian draft picks. Zyuzin may break the spell.

ST. LOUIS BLUES

Players' Statistics 1995-96

POS.	NO.	PLAYER	GP	G	A	PTS	+/-	PIM	PP	SH	GW	GT	S	PCT
C	99	WAYNE GRETZKY	80	23	79	102	-13	34	6	1	3	1	195	11.8
R	16	BRETT HULL	70	43	40	83	4	30	16	5	6		327	13.1
D	2	AL MACINNIS	82	17	44	61	5	88	9	1	1	1	317	5.4
L	9	SHAYNE CORSON	77	18	28	46	3	192	13			2	150	12.0
L	14	GEOFF COURTNALL	69	24	16	40	-9	101	7	1	1	2	228	10.5
R	28	BRIAN NOONAN	81	13	22	35	2	84	3	1	6		131	9.9
L	13	YURI KHMYLEV	73	8	21	29	-17	40	5	1	1	1	136	5.9
R	27	STEPHEN LEACH	73	11	17	28	-7	108	1		2		157	7.0
L	32	STEPHANE MATTEAU	78	11	15	26	-8	87	4		2	1	109	10.1
D	44	CHRIS PRONGER	78	7	18	25	-18	110	3	1	1		138	5.1
D	5	IGOR KRAVCHUK	66	7	16	23	-19	34	3		1		173	4.0
C	20	ADAM CREIGHTON	61	11	10	21	0	78	2		3	1	98	11.2
C	25	PETER ZEZEL	57	8	13	21	-2	12	2		1		87	9.2
C	15	MIKE HUDSON	59	5	12	17	2	55					59	8.5
R	36	GLENN ANDERSON	32	6	8	14	-11	33	2		1		71	8.5
C	23	CRAIG MACTAVISH	68	5	9	14	-9	70			1	1	58	8.6
D	34	MURRAY BARON	82	2	9	11	3	190					86	2.3
R	12	ROB PEARSON	27	6	4	10	4	54	1		1		51	11.8
D	22	CHARLIE HUDDY	64	5	5	10	-12	65	2		1		70	7.1
D	35	*CHRISTER OLSSON	26	2	8	10	-6	14	2				32	6.3
D	33	KEN SUTTON	38		8	8	-13	43					41	
L	18	TONY TWIST	51	3	2	5	-1	100			1		12	25.0
C	37	*ROMAN VOPAT	25	2	3	5	-8	48	1		1		33	6.1
D	26	JAY WELLS	76		3	3	-8	67					24	
L	17	BASIL MCRAE	18	1	1	2	-5	40					5	20.0
R	21	PAUL BROTEN	17	1	1	2	-1	4					11	
L	7	GREG GILBERT	17	1	1	2	-1	8					9	
G	31	GRANT FUHR	79		1	1	0	8						
R	41	*ALEXANDER VASILEVSKI	1				-1							
L	33	FRED KNIPSCHEER	1				0	2					2	
D	6	*JAMIE RIVERS	3				-1	2					5	
G	30	JON CASEY	9				0							
G	29	BRUCE RACINE	11				0	2						

GP = games played; G = goals; A = assists; PTS = points; +/- = goals-for minus goals-against while player is on ice; PIM = penalties in minutes; PP = power play goals; SH = shorthanded goals; GW = game-winning goals; GT = game-tying goals; S = no. of shots; PCT = percentage of goals to shots; * = rookie

MURRAY BARON

Yrs. of NHL service: 6
Born: Prince George, B.C., June 1, 1967
Position: left defense
Height: 6-3
Weight: 210
Uniform no.: 34
Shoots: left

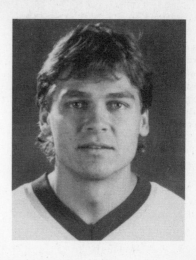

Career statistics:

GP	G	A	TP	PIM
401	22	43	65	645

1992-93 statistics:

GP	G	A	TP	+/-	PIM	PP	SH	GW	GT	S	PCT
53	2	2	4	-5	59	0	0	1	0	42	4.8

1993-94 statistics:

GP	G	A	TP	+/-	PIM	PP	SH	GW	GT	S	PCT
77	5	9	14	-14	123	0	0	0	0	73	6.8

1994-95 statistics:

GP	G	A	TP	+/-	PIM	PP	SH	GW	GT	S	PCT
39	0	5	5	+9	93	0	0	0	0	28	0.0

1995-96 statistics:

GP	G	A	TP	+/-	PIM	PP	SH	GW	GT	S	PCT
82	2	9	11	+3	190	0	0	0	0	86	2.3

has played his best hockey in the past two seasons. His point totals will barely break into double digits, but Baron will be one of the Blues' top three defensemen again next season.

LAST SEASON

Second on team in penalty minutes with career high. One of two Blues to appear in all 82 games.

THE FINESSE GAME

Baron looked like a new player last season: tougher, more intelligent and consistent. He was easily the steadiest defenseman on the team.

A strong skater with some agility, Baron jumps into the play rather than leading a rush, but he doesn't do much creatively. Baron concentrates on defense. He can lug the puck at a pretty good clip, but does little more than stop inside the blueline and fire a shot from the point. His shot is merely average. You rarely find Baron gambling in deep. He seldom works on specialty teams.

Baron has developed more poise defensively and is now less likely to get rid of the puck in a panic. Instead, he will make a safe, if unspectacular, play. He was paired with the offensive-minded Al MacInnis late in the season, and Baron was content to let MacInnis handle the flashy stuff.

THE PHYSICAL GAME

Baron has stepped up his physical play over the past two seasons. Once noted for being a rather timid player for his size, he is doing a better job of clearing out the front of his crease. He even got into a couple of fights and stood up for his teammates, which endears him to coach Mike Keenan and results in more ice time.

THE INTANGIBLES

Baron is 29, and qualifies as a late bloomer since he

SHAYNE CORSON

Yrs. of NHL service: 10
Born: Barrie, Ont.; Aug. 13, 1966
Position: centre/left wing
Height: 6-1
Weight: 200
Uniform no.: 9
Shoots: left

Career statistics:

GP	G	A	TP	PIM
689	192	278	470	1496

1992-93 statistics:

GP	G	A	TP	+/-	PIM	PP	SH	GW	GT	S	PCT
80	16	31	47	-19	209	9	2	1	0	164	9.8

1993-94 statistics:

GP	G	A	TP	+/-	PIM	PP	SH	GW	GT	S	PCT
64	25	29	54	-8	118	11	0	3	1	171	14.6

1994-95 statistics:

GP	G	A	TP	+/-	PIM	PP	SH	GW	GT	S	PCT
48	12	24	36	-17	86	2	0	1	0	131	9.2

1995-96 statistics:

GP	G	A	TP	+/-	PIM	PP	SH	GW	GT	S	PCT
77	18	28	46	+3	192	13	0	0	2	150	12.0

LAST SEASON

Signed as free agent, July 28, 1995. Led team in penalty minutes. Second on team in power play goals. Third on team in plus-minus. Fourth on team in points. Missed five games with broken jaw.

THE FINESSE GAME

Corson makes a lot of things happen by overpowering people around the net. Like Bob Probert in his prime, he has surprising scoring ability for a player who is considered a mucker. People give Corson an extra foot or two because of his muscle, which allows him extra time to pick up loose pucks out of scrums and jam his shots in tight, or lift shots over a goalie's stick.

Corson gets a lot of rebound goals if he plays on a line with people who throw the puck to the net, because he will go barrelling in for it. He's free to play that style more on the left wing than at centre, but he also has some nice playmaking abilities when put in the middle. He won't do anything too fancy but is intelligent enough to play a basic short game. Corson can win draws outright on his backhand.

Corson is a powerful skater but not very fast or agile. He has good balance for his work along the boards. He has all the attributes of a power forward.

He does his dirty work in front of the net for screens and deflections and has the hands to guide hard point shots. He is wildly inaccurate with any shots other than at close range, so on the off nights when he is not winning his duels around the net, he is a non-factor.

THE PHYSICAL GAME

Corson is tremendous along the wall. He has grit, and plays tough and hard every shift. He is dangerous because of his short fuse. Opponents never known when he will go off, and since he's strong and can throw punches, few people want to be around when he does. He inspires fear. He hits to hurt, and because he is so unpredictable he earns himself plenty of room on the ice. Corson has become more consistently smart and aggressive.

THE INTANGIBLES

We expected Corson to leave Edmonton after the 1994-95 season, but he fell well short of the predicted 35-40 goals. There were a lot of reasons, starting with the pressure he felt in St. Louis replacing the popular Brendan Shanahan. Corson scored only three goals in his first 25 games with the Blues, then got caught up in more controversy as he was given the captaincy when it was stripped from Brett Hull (then given to Wayne Gretzky).

Corson is due for a big bounce-back season, assuming the Blues find someone to replace Gretzky at centre. Corson had a very strong playoffs, which is a positive sign for this season.

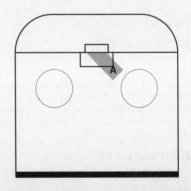

GEOFF COURTNALL

Yrs. of NHL service: 12
Born: Victoria, B.C.; Aug. 18, 1962
Position: left wing
Height: 6-1
Weight: 190
Uniform no.: 14
Shoots: left

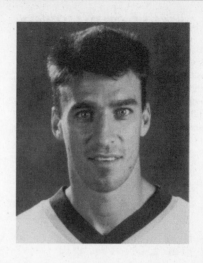

Career statistics:

GP	G	A	TP	PIM
857	312	352	664	1253

1992-93 statistics:

GP	G	A	TP	+/-	PIM	PP	SH	GW	GT	S	PCT
84	31	46	77	+27	167	9	0	11	0	214	14.5

1993-94 statistics:

GP	G	A	TP	+/-	PIM	PP	SH	GW	GT	S	PCT
82	26	44	70	+15	123	12	1	2	0	264	9.8

1994-95 statistics:

GP	G	A	TP	+/-	PIM	PP	SH	GW	GT	S	PCT
45	16	18	34	+2	81	7	0	1	0	144	11.1

1995-96 statistics:

GP	G	A	TP	+/-	PIM	PP	SH	GW	GT	S	PCT
69	24	16	40	-9	101	7	1	1	2	228	10.5

LAST SEASON

Second on team in goals. Fifth on team in points. Missed 13 games with fractured thumb.

THE FINESSE GAME

Throughout his NHL career, Courtnall has been a streaky scorer. When he's hot he uses a variety of shots to pepper the net. He can score off the backhand, muscle a close-range shot to the top shelf, use a snap shot off the wing on the fly, or wrist in a rebound.

He finds the holes and is a textbook give-and-go player. He makes the first pass, burns for the opening, then rips a one-timer from the circle to complete the play. But when he's cold, he's frigid, as he was at the start of the season, when coach Mike Keenan sat him at the end of the bench on several occasions.

Courtnall has good hands for passing, making especially nice touch passes to breaking teammates on a give-and-go. He has sharp hand-eye coordination to play up front on the power play. He doesn't stand in front of the net to take punishment, but instead times his moves in for deflections with his stick.

THE PHYSICAL GAME

Courtnall is a good-sized forward who has never had much of a physical element to his game. He goes to his stick first when he is trying to intimidate an opponent or battle along the boards for the puck. He will sometimes use his body, but not consistently. If opponents come at him hard enough early in the game, Courtnall will mail in the rest of the game.

THE INTANGIBLES

Injuries prevented Courtnall from hitting the 30-mark

we expected he would nail with the change to St. Louis. Courtnall needs a coach to stay after him, and Keenan does that. Consistency continues to elude him, but he has the skill for another 30-goal season.

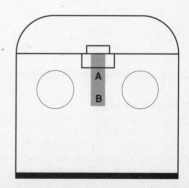

ADAM CREIGHTON

Yrs. of NHL service: 12
Born: Burlington, Ont.; June 2, 1965
Position: centre
Height: 6-5
Weight: 225
Uniform no.: 20
Shoots: left

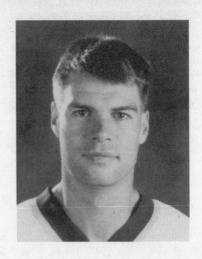

Career statistics:

GP	G	A	TP	PIM
689	186	214	400	1064

1992-93 statistics:

GP	G	A	TP	+/-	PIM	PP	SH	GW	GT	S	PCT
83	19	20	39	-19	110	7	1	0	0	168	11.3

1993-94 statistics:

GP	G	A	TP	+/-	PIM	PP	SH	GW	GT	S	PCT
53	10	10	20	-7	37	2	0	1	0	77	13.0

1994-95 statistics:

GP	G	A	TP	+/-	PIM	PP	SH	GW	GT	S	PCT
48	14	20	34	+17	74	3	0	1	0	81	17.3

1995-96 statistics:

GP	G	A	TP	+/-	PIM	PP	SH	GW	GT	S	PCT
61	11	10	21	0	78	2	0	3	1	98	11.2

fast to begin with. Creighton will still get his playing time and a modest amount of points (30 or so) as long as the Blues' depth problems continue.

LAST SEASON

Tied for third on team in game-winning goals. Missed 19 games with broken jaw. Missed two games with bruised ankle.

THE FINESSE GAME

Creighton has never been much of an impact player despite his imposing reach because he doesn't have the same sense of timing or strength in his hands and wrist that the similarly built Dave Andreychuk possesses. Creighton will get his share of points simply by being around the front of the net, but he doesn't position himself well offensively or use the long wraparound from behind the net that would be so effective.

Creighton has become a "tweener," not quite a third-line checking centre, because he lacks the speed, and a borderline fourth-line centre, who will complement some mucking wingers, although he's not really tough enough or energetic enough to produce one of those change-of-tempo shifts.

THE PHYSICAL GAME

Creighton isn't very well-balanced for a big skater, which allows smaller players to take advantage of him. He lacks a mean streak, although he can take some hits to keep a play going.

THE INTANGIBLES

Creighton is one of the many veterans rescued and resuscitated by coach Mike Keenan in St. Louis. He doesn't have a whole lot of hockey life left, but he's one of those big, gangly players whose loss of speed doesn't mean a whole lot because he was never that

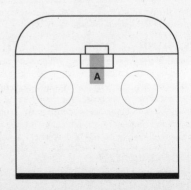

GRANT FUHR

Yrs. of NHL service: 15
Born: Spruce Grove, Alta.; Sept. 28, 1962
Position: goaltender
Height: 5-9
Weight: 190
Uniform no.: 31
Catches: right

Career statistics:

GP	MIN	GA	SO	GAA	A	PIM
675	38012	2259	17	3.57	42	114

1992-93 statistics:

GP	MIN	GAA	W	L	T	SO	GA	S	SAPCT	PIM
58	3359	3.30	24	24	6	1	185	1729	.893	20

1993-94 statistics:

GP	MIN	GAA	W	L	T	SO	GA	S	SAPCT	PIM
32	1726	3.68	13	12	3	2	106	907	.883	16

1994-95 statistics:

GP	MIN	GAA	W	L	T	SO	GA	S	SAPCT	PIM
17	878	4.03	2	9	3	0	59	464	.873	2

1995-96 statistics:

GP	MIN	GAA	W	L	T	SO	GA	S	SAPCT	PIM
79	4365	2.87	30	28	16	3	209	2157	.903	8

LAST SEASON

Signed as a free agent, July 14, 1995. Set NHL record for games played by a goalie. Best goals-against average of career. Led NHL in shots faced. Finalist for 1996 Masterton Trophy. Missed three games with knee injury. Became 11th goalie in NHL history to reach 300-win milestone. Stopped Dave Hannan on penalty shot (Oct. 25, 1995). Third season with 30 or more wins.

THE PHYSICAL GAME

Fuhr has never been a fitness freak, and after two seasons as a bit player showed up in the St. Louis training camp looking like he was wearing his pads under his street clothes. Coach Mike Keenan put him on a training regimen that knocked off about 15 pounds in three weeks (Iron Mike can get into Richard Simmons' line of work when he's done coaching) and Fuhr was a new man — and showed signs of being the old goalie he was in his Edmonton glory days.

Fuhr probably never got enough credit when the Oilers were winning all those Stanley Cups, but he was always spectacularly quick. Injuries and age have conspired to slow him down a bit, but his reflexes are still superb. He is a great skater with outstanding balance. He catches with his right hand, which is disconcerting to some shooters, and his strength is his glove side.

Fuhr recovers well for second shots and is so efficient about it that he never seems to be scrambling or panicky. He controls his rebounds well. He isn't overly active with his stick.

THE MENTAL GAME

Fuhr has always possessed a very laid-back demeanour, and that calm gives his defense confidence. But the cool exterior masks a very determined personality. Fuhr maintains his concentration well through screens and scrambles. He doesn't allow many soft goals because his attention doesn't waver.

Fuhr is very smart. He reads plays coming at him as well as any top defenseman, and is a master of the read and react.

THE INTANGIBLES

No one would have believed this story at the start of last season. That the aging and overweight Fuhr would be able to return to iron-man status and win respect as one of the most consistent goalies for one of the worst defensive teams in the league is nothing short of remarkable, but that was the Fuhr saga. He would have started all 82 games if he hadn't suffered a knee injury. A lot of the games in the streak were bogus since Fuhr was pulled early, and he will be better off if he keeps to a 60-game schedule. He is still an effective goalie, if not an elite one.

BRETT HULL

Yrs. of NHL service: 9
Born: Belleville, Ont.; Aug. 9, 1964
Position: right wing
Height: 5-10
Weight: 201
Uniform no.: 16
Shoots: right

Career statistics:

GP	G	A	TP	PIM
658	485	348	833	262

1992-93 statistics:

GP	G	A	TP	+/-	PIM	PP	SH	GW	GT	S	PCT
80	54	47	101	-27	41	29	0	2	1	390	13.8

1993-94 statistics:

GP	G	A	TP	+/-	PIM	PP	SH	GW	GT	S	PCT
81	57	40	97	-3	38	25	3	6	1	392	14.5

1994-95 statistics:

GP	G	A	TP	+/-	PIM	PP	SH	GW	GT	S	PCT
48	29	21	50	+13	10	9	3	6	0	200	14.5

1995-96 statistics:

GP	G	A	TP	+/-	PIM	PP	SH	GW	GT	S	PCT
70	43	40	83	+4	30	16	5	6	0	327	13.1

LAST SEASON

Led team in goals and power play goals for third consecutive season. Led team in shots, shorthanded goals and shooting percentage. Tied for team lead in game-winning goals. Second on team in points and plus-minus. Third on team in assists. Missed seven games with recurring groin injury. Missed four games with hamstring injury. Missed penalty shot (third failed attempt of career).

THE FINESSE GAME

Despite his war with Mike Keenan, Hull was the Blues' best all-around forward last season. Hull's game is evolving. He plays well in all three zones, but he'll never be mistaken for Doug Gilmour, because he is a shooter first. His shot is seldom blocked because he gets it away so quickly that the defense doesn't have time to react. Hull's shots have tremendous velocity, especially his one-timers from the tops of the circles in.

Hull is always working to get himself in position for a pass. On the power play, he will be in open ice, constantly moving, and he can fire off any kind of shot accurately. He usually moves to his off-wing on the power play.

Hull is an underrated playmaker who can thread a pass through traffic right onto the tape of a teammate. He will find the open man because he has soft hands, good vision, and because the opponent usually plays off him a bit to give Hull some room. He has become a serviceable penalty killer as well and is a shorthanded threat.

THE PHYSICAL GAME

Hull is compact and when he wants to hit, it's a solid check. He is not as physically involved as he was when he was scoring goals at an absurd rate, but he will bump people. Hull's conditioning has improved, and he routinely played up to 30 minutes a game.

THE INTANGIBLES

Would Keenan, already reviled for trading away the popular Brendan Shanahan and Curtis Joseph and alienating Wayne Gretzky, dare trade this St. Louis icon? Don't be shocked if he does. Hull would thrive on a competing team with actual centres (he didn't play much with Gretzky). He won't score 86 again, but he could flirt with 60.

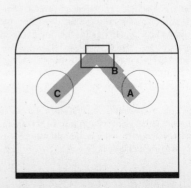

YURI KHMYLEV

Yrs. of NHL service: 4
Born: Moscow, Russia; Aug. 9, 1964
Position: left wing
Height: 6-1
Weight: 190
Uniform no.: 13
Shoots: right

Career statistics:

GP	G	A	TP	PIM
261	63	88	151	131

1992-93 statistics:

GP	G	A	TP	+/-	PIM	PP	SH	GW	GT	S	PCT
68	20	19	39	+6	28	0	3	3	0	122	16.4

1993-94 statistics:

GP	G	A	TP	+/-	PIM	PP	SH	GW	GT	S	PCT
72	27	31	58	+13	49	11	0	4	0	171	15.8

1994-95 statistics:

GP	G	A	TP	+/-	PIM	PP	SH	GW	GT	S	PCT
48	8	17	25	+8	14	2	1	1	0	71	11.3

1995-96 statistics:

GP	G	A	TP	+/-	PIM	PP	SH	GW	GT	S	PCT
73	8	21	29	-17	40	5	1	1	1	136	5.9

LAST SEASON

Acquired from Buffalo with a fifth-round draft pick for Jean-Luc Grand-Pierre and a second- and third-round draft pick, Mar. 20, 1996.

THE FINESSE GAME

Khmylev is a strong skater with outstanding balance. If his stick is tied up, he'll keep the puck going with his feet and make smart "soccer" passes. He doesn't worry much about the offensive zone, but he has a nice wrist shot and will work through traffic with the puck. He employs his long reach as a defensive weapon, to reach in around puck carriers to knock the puck free.

Khmylev kills penalties and is highly effective and aggressive. When a defenseman gambles deep, he will be the forward who drops back to cover the point.

Well-schooled in the eastern European system where the left winger is the most defensively responsible member of his line, Khmylev can be teamed with offensive players to act as a safety valve for their more freewheeling style. Or he can serve on a checking line. He has the skating and hand skills to complement almost anyone, but he won't dazzle with one-on-one play. He's primarily a support player.

THE PHYSICAL GAME

Khmylev is a tough, grinding winger who makes big checks. He will step up and create turnovers, and will bounce off checks and keep going. He is better suited to North American play than many Canadians and Americans.

THE INTANGIBLES

Khmylev has become more defense-oriented, which means he probably won't get ice time on a top line (as he once did in Buffalo with Pat LaFontaine), and his point totals will shrink as a result.

IGOR KRAVCHUK

Yrs. of NHL service: 4
Born: Ufa, Russia; Sept. 13, 1966
Position: right defense
Height: 6-1
Weight: 200
Uniform no.: 5
Shoots: left

Career statistics:

GP	G	A	TP	PIM
256	37	90	127	115

1992-93 statistics:

GP	G	A	TP	+/-	PIM	PP	SH	GW	GT	S	PCT
55	10	17	27	+3	32	4	0	0	0	143	7.0

1993-94 statistics:

GP	G	A	TP	+/-	PIM	PP	SH	GW	GT	S	PCT
81	12	38	50	-12	16	5	0	2	0	197	6.1

1994-95 statistics:

GP	G	A	TP	+/-	PIM	PP	SH	GW	GT	S	PCT
36	7	11	18	-15	29	3	1	0	0	93	7.5

1995-96 statistics:

GP	G	A	TP	+/-	PIM	PP	SH	GW	GT	S	PCT
66	7	16	23	-19	34	3	0	1	0	173	4.0

LAST SEASON

Acquired from Edmonton with Ken Sutton for Jeff Norton and Donald Dufresne, Jan. 4, 1996. Missed four games with knee injury. Missed six games with leg bruise.

THE FINESSE GAME

Kravchuk is a big defenseman who does a lot of little things well. There is no one facet of his game that stands out from the rest, but there are no serious flaws, either. Kravchuk's skills are subtle. He has good offensive instincts, but his sound defensive game is the basis for his world-class skills.

An exceptionally mobile skater, he can pivot like a figure skater with the puck and accelerate quickly. He likes to jump into the play and keeps the puck moving. Kravchuk sees the ice well. He is able to carry the puck out of the defensive zone to alleviate pressure on his goalie, something no other Oiler defenseman does well. But he will sometimes make a mistake in joining the rush too soon, and he often gets caught when there's a turnover. He is over-aggressive offensively.

Kravchuk plays the point on the second power play unit and will freeze a defenseman with a fake slap shot before sliding a pass down low. He can also fire, and he has the moves to beat a defender in open ice.

Kravchuk is an intelligent penalty killer and utilizes his skating well. He is strong in four-on-four team play.

THE PHYSICAL GAME

Kravchuk has some strength but he is a pusher, not a hitter. He will tie up his man in front of the net, or lean with his stick on top of an opponent's to keep that player from doing something with the puck, but Kravchuk won't wipe anyone out. It won't hurt to keep him paired with a more physical partner.

THE INTANGIBLES

Kravchuk is a two-way defenseman who will produce 10-15 goals a season when healthy. He fits in as a number three or four defenseman on the Blues, because his skills aren't enough to carry the role of a number one.

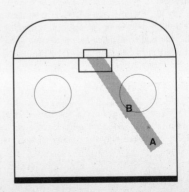

STEPHEN LEACH

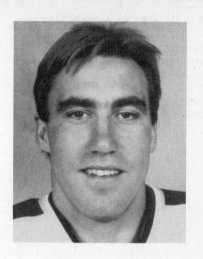

Yrs. of NHL service: 10
Born: Cambridge, Mass.; Jan. 16, 1966
Position: right wing
Height: 5-11
Weight: 197
Uniform no.: 27
Shoots: right

Career statistics:

GP	G	A	TP	PIM
553	121	141	262	845

1992-93 statistics:

GP	G	A	TP	+/-	PIM	PP	SH	GW	GT	S	PCT
78	31	29	60	-8	147	12	0	4	0	243	12.8

1993-94 statistics:

GP	G	A	TP	+/-	PIM	PP	SH	GW	GT	S	PCT
42	5	10	15	-10	74	1	0	1	1	89	5.6

1994-95 statistics:

GP	G	A	TP	+/-	PIM	PP	SH	GW	GT	S	PCT
35	5	6	11	-3	68	1	0	1	0	82	6.1

1995-96 statistics:

GP	G	A	TP	+/-	PIM	PP	SH	GW	GT	S	PCT
73	11	17	28	-7	108	1	0	2	0	157	7.0

LAST SEASON

Acquired from Boston for Kevin Sawyer and Steve Staios, Mar. 8, 1996.

THE FINESSE GAME

Leach is a dedicated forechecker whose game has become more defense-oriented in recent years. A serious knee injury in 1993-94 signalled the start of that trend.

Leach's shot, once very heavy and quickly released, has become less of an effective weapon for him, although he still rifles one once in awhile with his old velocity. He doesn't have a great touch or soft hands, but likes to churn things up with his pressure in the offensive zone to force the puck lose.

Defense was once considered Leach's weakness. He can't be called a true checking winger yet, but he has improved his reads.

THE PHYSICAL GAME

When healthy, Leach adds grit and power to a lineup. He fits in well with a finesse player or two on his line, since he will do the dirty work and let his partners pick up the pieces and convert the loose pucks. A linemate would be wise to trail in Leach's wake.

THE INTANGIBLES

Leach's age and injury history make him a bit of a question mark, but he was well received in St. Louis after his trade, and he needed a change of scenery from his Boston hometown. He is not likely to be more than a third-line player with the Blues.

AL MACINNIS

Yrs. of NHL service: 14
Born: Inverness, N.S.; July 11, 1963
Position: right defense
Height: 6-2
Weight: 195
Uniform no.: 2
Shoots: right

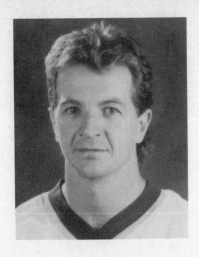

Career statistics:

GP	G	A	TP	PIM
917	238	673	911	1084

1992-93 statistics:

GP	G	A	TP	+/-	PIM	PP	SH	GW	GT	S	PCT
50	11	43	54	+15	61	7	0	4	0	201	5.5

1993-94 statistics:

GP	G	A	TP	+/-	PIM	PP	SH	GW	GT	S	PCT
75	28	54	82	+35	95	12	1	5	0	324	8.6

1994-95 statistics:

GP	G	A	TP	+/-	PIM	PP	SH	GW	GT	S	PCT
32	8	20	28	+19	43	2	0	0	0	110	7.3

1995-96 statistics:

GP	G	A	TP	+/-	PIM	PP	SH	GW	GT	S	PCT
82	17	44	61	+5	88	9	1	1	1	317	5.4

LAST SEASON

Led team defensemen and tied for 10th among NHL defensemen in scoring. Led team in plus-minus. Second on team in assists and shots. Third on team in points. One of two Blues to appear in all 82 games.

THE FINESSE GAME

What makes his shot so good is that MacInnis knows the value of a change-up, and he won't always fire with the same velocity. If there is traffic in front, he will take a little off his shot to make it more tippable (and so he doesn't break too many teammates' ankles). One-on-one, of course, MacInnis will fire the laser and can just about knock a goalie into the net.

MacInnis knows when to jump into the play and when to back off. He can start a rush with a rink-wide pass, then be quick enough to burst up-ice and be in position for a return pass. Because his shot is such a formidable weapon, he can freeze the opposition by faking a big wind-up, then quickly dish a pass in low to an open teammate. Even when he merely rings the puck off the boards, he's a threat, since there is so much on the shot the goaltender has to be careful to stop it.

MacInnis skates well with the puck. He is not very mobile, but he gets up to speed in a few strides and can hit his outside speed to beat a defender one-on-one. He will gamble and is best paired with a defensively alert partner.

He has improved his defensive play and is very smart against a two-on-one.

THE PHYSICAL GAME

MacInnis was able to shake his shoulder problems of the previous two seasons but still wasn't much of a physical defenseman. He will use his finesse skills in a defensive posture, always looking for the counterattack. He reads defenses alertly, and positions himself to tie up attackers rather than try to knock them down. He gets caught fishing for the puck instead of taking the body, and this is an especially dangerous habit at his own blueline. In his own way, he is a tough competitor who will pay the price to win.

THE INTANGIBLES

MacInnis ended the season in a slump and joined the mob in the Mike Keenan doghouse. It's impossible to predict what the free-spending Blues will do in the off-season, but it wouldn't surprise us if they move MacInnis. He could be among the top 10 defensemen in scoring again, but at 33, he is at the stage of his career where his point totals will tail off rather than rise.

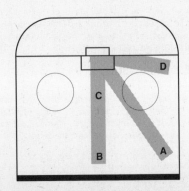

CRAIG MACTAVISH

Yrs. of NHL service: 16
Born: London, Ont.; Aug. 15, 1958
Position: centre
Height: 6-1
Weight: 195
Uniform no.: 23
Shoots: left

Career statistics:

GP	G	A	TP	PIM
1043	211	263	474	858

1992-93 statistics:

GP	G	A	TP	+/-	PIM	PP	SH	GW	GT	S	PCT
82	10	20	30	-16	110	0	3	3	0	101	9.9

1993-94 statistics:

GP	G	A	TP	+/-	PIM	PP	SH	GW	GT	S	PCT
78	20	13	33	-14	91	1	0	2	1	122	16.4

1994-95 statistics:

GP	G	A	TP	+/-	PIM	PP	SH	GW	GT	S	PCT
45	3	9	12	+2	23	0	0	0	0	38	7.9

1995-96 statistics:

GP	G	A	TP	+/-	PIM	PP	SH	GW	GT	S	PCT
68	5	9	14	-9	70	0	0	1	1	58	8.6

Cup rings, he is especially valuable to a team looking for a good influence on its younger players — too bad the Blues don't have any.

LAST SEASON

Acquired from Philadelphia for Dale Hawerchuk, Mar. 15, 1996. Played in 1,000th NHL game. Missed eight games with ankle injury.

THE FINESSE GAME

MacTavish plays the whole ice well, but is exceptional in the 25 feet from the attacking slot to the lane behind the net. He is relentless, smart, strong, tough and quick. He can create a turnover or he can finish a scoring chance. He also matches up defensively against all but the fastest centres in the league.

MacTavish is among the best in the NHL at face-offs. That is, he is among the best in the league at cheating on face-offs. MacTavish always seems to have his body turned a little more than he should, or doesn't have his stick on the ice the way he is supposed to. Subtle enough to not get caught, effective enough to give him an edge.

MacTavish plays a basic offensive game, just getting the puck and moving it quickly. He can rag the puck when he's killing penalties, but he seldom over-handles.

THE PHYSICAL GAME

MacTavish's competitive fire still burns. He gives his all and his durability is amazing given the way he sacrifices every night. He forechecks tenaciously, and he will drive to the net dragging a defender with him.

THE INTANGIBLES

How much hockey is left in MacTavish at age 38? Not much. If a team can afford to carry a defensive specialist, MacTavish is the man. Given his four Stanley

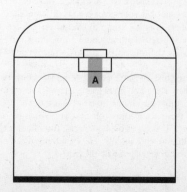

STEPHANE MATTEAU

Yrs. of NHL service: 5
Born: Rouyn-Noranda, Que.; Sept. 2, 1969
Position: left wing
Height: 6-3
Weight: 215
Uniform no.: 32
Shoots: left

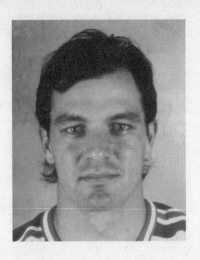

Career statistics:

GP	G	A	TP	PIM
377	69	84	153	424

1992-93 statistics:

GP	G	A	TP	+/-	PIM	PP	SH	GW	GT	S	PCT
79	15	18	33	+6	98	2	0	4	0	95	15.8

1993-94 statistics:

GP	G	A	TP	+/-	PIM	PP	SH	GW	GT	S	PCT
77	19	19	38	+15	57	3	0	2	1	135	14.1

1994-95 statistics:

GP	G	A	TP	+/-	PIM	PP	SH	GW	GT	S	PCT
41	3	5	8	-8	25	0	0	0	0	37	8.1

1995-96 statistics:

GP	G	A	TP	+/-	PIM	PP	SH	GW	GT	S	PCT
78	11	15	26	-8	87	4	0	2	1	109	10.1

LAST SEASON

Acquired from N.Y. Rangers for Ian Laperriere, Dec. 28, 1995.

THE FINESSE GAME

Matteau has never clearly defined himself as a physical player or an offensive player, which means Matteau is inconsistent even in his inconsistency. It's the kind of dilemma that drives coaches batty . . . unless of course you are Mike Keenan, in which case you just keep trading for him and live with the flaws.

Matteau's most valuable asset is his ability to get to the boards, hurry a defenseman into a turnover, then get to the front of the net for a deflection or to set a screen. The problem is, you might see that play out of him once in a game, then maybe not again for a week or more. He is mentally fragile. He gets down on himself, which leads to catastrophic slumps, and this just a year after his self-esteem had to be at an all-time high. Some players need a pat on the back, some need a kick in the pants. Matteau needs both at different times.

Matteau is not going to overpower goalies with many shots. His goals come from short range — rebounds, deflections, backhands, wraparounds. More often, though, he's the player causing a distraction and getting cross-checked while a teammate converts the garbage. He shows good hustle and works hard to get into scoring position in front of the net, but he doesn't have the touch to finish off the play. When he wants to, he will skate through a check. Too often, it takes too little to stop his legs. He's got a big reach and a reasonably quick wit with the puck.

THE PHYSICAL GAME

Matteau is big enough to make himself useful, strong enough to make himself a force, fast enough to be intimidating, but he's also inconsistent enough to make you understand why so many teams have given up on him.

He finishes his checks, hard at times, but tends to use his size in more subtle ways. He makes the defenseman tie him up in front of the net, which leaves openings down low for teammates. He does a decent job along the boards, shielding the puck and kicking it to his stick.

THE INTANGIBLES

Matteau came into the Rangers training camp 15 pounds overweight and didn't start to get in shape until the second half (seven of his 11 goals came in the last 41 games, after his trade to St. Louis). But he had a dismal playoffs, and that is supposed to be his time to shine.

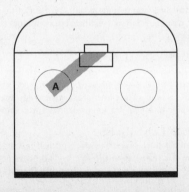

JOE MURPHY

Yrs. of NHL service: 9
Born: London, Ont.; Oct. 16, 1967
Position: right wing
Height: 6-1
Weight: 190
Uniform no.: 17
Shoots: left

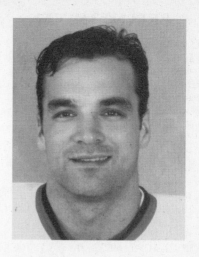

Career statistics:

GP	G	A	TP	PIM
522	166	178	344	518

1992-93 statistics:

GP	G	A	TP	+/-	PIM	PP	SH	GW	GT	S	PCT
19	7	10	17	-3	18	5	0	1	0	43	16.3

1993-94 statistics:

GP	G	A	TP	+/-	PIM	PP	SH	GW	GT	S	PCT
81	31	39	70	+1	111	7	4	4	0	222	14.0

1994-95 statistics:

GP	G	A	TP	+/-	PIM	PP	SH	GW	GT	S	PCT
40	23	18	41	+7	89	7	0	3	0	120	19.2

1995-96 statistics:

GP	G	A	TP	+/-	PIM	PP	SH	GW	GT	S	PCT
70	22	29	51	-3	86	8	0	3	0	212	10.4

LAST SEASON

Third on Chicago in power play goals. Missed eight games with strained back.

THE FINESSE GAME

Murphy is a goal scorer, and when he's on his game there aren't many better. He has an explosive burst of speed and can take the puck to the net. Murphy has great hands. He is creative off the forecheck and has confidence with the puck. He is sometimes too selfish and single-minded when he has made the decision to shoot, even when a better option to pass suddenly presents itself. He needs a centre who can get him the puck at the right times, and didn't always have that last year in Chicago.

Murphy has a lot of zip on his slap and wrist shots. He gets both away quickly and through a crowd, and he's been a high-percentage shooter through much of his career.

Murphy is fairly keen defensively and can kill penalties and take defensive-zone draws. He has become a more consistent player but remains below the elite level.

THE PHYSICAL GAME

Murphy makes preemptive hits when going for the puck in the corners — which is a nice way of saying he takes a lot of interference calls. He will use his size and strength in front of the net to establish position, and he'll fight along the wall and in the corners. He's not a big banger or crasher, but he does have a nasty streak.

THE INTANGIBLES

Murphy became an unrestricted free agent after last season and was signed by the Blues, an organization noted for overpaying mediocre talent. He will have his moments of brilliance but consistency has never been his strong suit. He has the ability to notch 30-35 goals, but he has never done it in nine NHL seasons. He did have a good playoff, leading Chicago in goals with six, and he has a knack for scoring the occasional big goal (he has four career overtime winners in the play-offs). He's always a potential game-breaker, but the key to Murphy is "potential," and he's never fulfilled his.

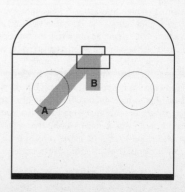

BRIAN NOONAN

Yrs. of NHL service: 7
Born: Boston, Mass.; May 29, 1965
Position: right wing
Height: 6-1
Weight: 200
Uniform no.: 28
Shoots: right

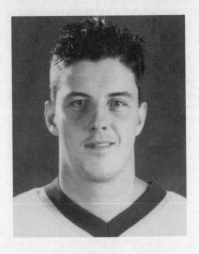

Career statistics:

GP	G	A	TP	PIM
467	94	122	216	422

1992-93 statistics:

GP	G	A	TP	+/-	PIM	PP	SH	GW	GT	S	PCT
63	16	14	30	+3	82	5	0	3	0	129	12.4

1993-94 statistics:

GP	G	A	TP	+/-	PIM	PP	SH	GW	GT	S	PCT
76	18	23	41	+7	69	10	0	6	1	160	11.3

1994-95 statistics:

GP	G	A	TP	+/-	PIM	PP	SH	GW	GT	S	PCT
45	14	13	27	-3	26	7	0	1	0	95	14.7

1995-96 statistics:

GP	G	A	TP	+/-	PIM	PP	SH	GW	GT	S	PCT
81	13	22	35	+2	84	3	1	6	0	131	9.9

LAST SEASON

Tied for the team lead in game-winning goals.

THE FINESSE GAME

Noonan's strongest attribute is his willingness to go into the corners for the puck, win a battle for it, and come out and do something with it by either finding a man at the point with a pass or taking it to the net himself. He might also draw a penalty.

Noonan has good-enough hands and moves to win the blueline almost every time he attacks it with the puck. Defensemen seem to have a difficult time reading him, so they retreat, which buys him an extra 10 feet of ice in which to make a decision. He also varies his attacks to the blueline, which adds an unpredictable element, but he doesn't always identify the best passing option when he gains the line.

No speedster, and often seeming to be moving in slow motion, Noonan doesn't have the world's smallest turning radius. He is reliable defensively, however, and is smart enough to maximize what little speed he has by changing gears a lot. He doesn't always skate at top speed, but can get an extra step by cranking up the pace just at the moment a defenseman has to make the pivot from backskating to frontskating.

Noonan is crafty with his hands, and clever with his shot, which is never overpowering but often unstoppable due to its unpredictability. He also knows his defensive responsibilities and can kill a penalty, although he's no shorthanded scoring threat. Noonan is a third-line player, but he makes a team better because of his honest effort. He never cheats on his shifts.

THE PHYSICAL GAME

Noonan is a cruiserweight who uses his skating strength and balance and is difficult to knock down. He favours what might be called a flying hip check, where he throws himself into an onrushing opponent at the sideboards.

He has become more consistent at finishing his checks. He pins his target to the wall and keeps him out of the play. He also plays the gut-check areas on offense. Noonan goes to the front of the net and gives up his body on tips and screens. He is a short-game player who pays the price to be in the right spot. He makes good use of his weight with a quiet strength.

THE INTANGIBLES

Noonan is a poker-faced guy who doesn't show much emotion and who doesn't really draw a lot of attention to himself. He keeps the game basic, nothing really fancy, but he has a nice amount of smarts and savvy. Noonan is a humble kid from a large family who made it to the NHL on hard work, and he will have to keep at it to have a regular job. He is willing to get involved physically and will always be found along the walls and in the corners. In short, Noonan is the perfect Mike Keenan player. He doesn't score often (he had a 0-for-21 streak last season), but tends to score at key moments.

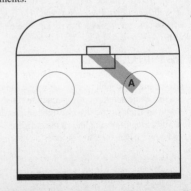

CHRIS PRONGER

Yrs. of NHL service: 3
Born: Dryden, Ont.; Oct. 10, 1974
Position: left defense
Height: 6-5
Weight: 210
Uniform no.: 44
Shoots: left

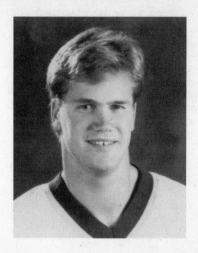

Career statistics:

GP	G	A	TP	PIM
202	17	52	69	192

1993-94 statistics:

GP	G	A	TP	+/-	PIM	PP	SH	GW	GT	S	PCT
81	5	25	30	-3	113	2	0	0	0	174	2.9

1994-95 statistics:

GP	G	A	TP	+/-	PIM	PP	SH	GW	GT	S	PCT
43	5	9	14	-12	54	3	0	1	0	94	5.3

1995-96 statistics:

GP	G	A	TP	+/-	PIM	PP	SH	GW	GT	S	PCT
78	7	18	25	-18	110	3	1	1	0	138	5.1

LAST SEASON

Second among team defensemen in scoring. Served four-game suspension in slashing incident.

THE FINESSE GAME

Pronger has been touted as a young Larry Robinson, and although he has a long way and a handful of Stanley Cup rings to go before he can live up to that comparison, there are similarities. Pronger is lanky, almost weedy, with a powerful skating stride for angling his man to the boards for a take-out. He blends his physical play with good offensive instincts and skills.

He also handles the puck well when skating and is always alert for passing opportunities. His vision shows in his work on the power play. He patrols the point smartly, using a low, tippable shot. Like many tall defensemen, Pronger doesn't get his slap shot away quickly, but he compensates with a snap shot that he uses liberally.

Pronger not only jumps into the rush, he knows when to, which is an art. He'll back off if the opportunity is not there. Pronger knows he has a green light under coach Mike Keenan. He makes unique plays that make him stand out, great breakout passes and clever feeds through the neutral zone. He is also wise enough to dump-and-chase rather than hold onto the puck and force a low-percentage pass. Pronger focused more on his defensive role last season, but there is a considerable upside to his offense.

Disciplined away from the puck and alert defensively, Pronger shows good anticipation, going where the puck is headed before it's shot there. He is very confident with the puck in his own end.

THE PHYSICAL GAME

Pronger bulked up 20 pounds at the start of last sea-son, but it wasn't healthy weight. He must learn to take care of his body through conditioning, rest and nutrition, and get stronger. A healthy, energetic Pronger will finish every check with enthusiasm, and show something of a nasty streak with his stick (as evident by his suspension). He makes his stand between the blueline and the top of the circle, forcing the forward to react. His long reach helps to make that style effective. He also uses his stick and reach when killing penalties.

Pronger was once notorious for being soft on the puck, but he has become stronger.

THE INTANGIBLES

Pronger needed a good dose of tough love, and after showing up at training camp out of shape, he got the proper handling from the strict Keenan. In the second half of the season, Pronger looked like the kind of player the Hartford Whalers had hoped for when they drafted him second overall in 1993 — only his progress is coming with the Blues.

If Keenan stays in St. Louis, watch for Pronger to continue along the path towards becoming a dominating defenseman and a force to build a team around. When Scotty Bowman coached a young Robinson in Montreal, he never gave him an inch to breathe. Pronger needs the same constant prodding.

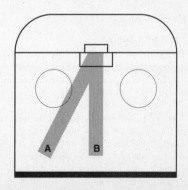

JAMIE RIVERS

Yrs. of NHL service: 0
Born: Ottawa, Ont.; March 16, 1975
Position: defense
Height: 6-0
Weight: 190
Uniform no.: 6
Shoots: left

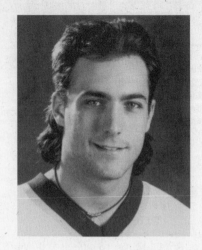

Career statistics:

GP	G	A	TP	PIM
3	0	0	0	2

1995-96 statistics:

GP	G	A	TP	+/-	PIM	PP	SH	GW	GT	S	PCT
3	0	0	0	-1	2	0	0	0	0	5	0.0

LAST SEASON

Will be entering first NHL season. Played 75 games with Worcester (AHL), scoring 7-45 — 52, second in team scoring.

THE FINESSE GAME

Rivers handled his first pro season very capably, proving he was able to adjust his shot to the pace of the game and keep up with the skating tempo. The next step is the question mark.

There is no doubt Rivers has a big-league shot. It is low, hard and accurate from the left point, and he shoots off the pass with a fine one-timer. He skates well with the puck. He has good acceleration to start his team on the attack and is an accurate passer. Rivers reads plays well offensively but has to be more intelligent about when to jump into the attack and when to back off.

Rivers played some forward in junior, evidence of his hockey sense and hand skills. He has some defensive weaknesses, not unusual for a young player who has relied on his scoring.

THE PHYSICAL GAME

Rivers isn't very big and doesn't make very good use of what size he has because he isn't very strong. Improvement in this department will be absolutely necessary before he wins an NHL job. Rivers won't be intimidated and has a quiet toughness to him.

THE INTANGIBLES

Just when you thought the Blues had traded away all of their young prospects, along comes an actual product of the St. Louis system who has an actual chance of playing for the team this season. If he doesn't get traded for Bryan Trottier first.

Rivers is an offensive defenseman who may emerge by next season as the team's primary power play quarterback. He'll get some playing time this season to learn the game, and who better to study than Al MacInnis?

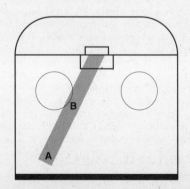

TAMPA BAY LIGHTNING

Players' Statistics 1995-96

POS.	NO.	PLAYER	GP	G	A	PTS	+/-	PIM	PP	SH	GW	GT	S	PCT
C	19	BRIAN BRADLEY	75	23	56	79	-11	77	9		5		189	12.2
D	44	ROMAN HAMRLIK	82	16	49	65	-24	103	12		2	3	281	5.7
R	29	ALEXANDER SELIVANOV	79	31	21	52	3	93	13		5	2	215	14.4
R	85	PETR KLIMA	67	22	30	52	-25	68	8		3	2	164	13.4
C	12	JOHN CULLEN	76	16	34	50	1	65	8		3		152	10.5
L	23	BRIAN BELLOWS	79	23	26	49	-14	39	13		4		190	12.1
C	77	CHRIS GRATTON	82	17	21	38	-13	105	7		3		183	9.3
L	7	ROB ZAMUNER	72	15	20	35	11	62		3	4		152	9.9
L	15	PAUL YSEBAERT	55	16	15	31	-19	16	4	1	1		135	11.9
L	11	SHAWN BURR	81	13	15	28	4	119	1		2		122	10.7
D	2	BILL HOULDER	61	5	23	28	1	22	3			1	90	5.6
L	34	MIKAEL ANDERSSON	64	8	11	19	0	2			1		104	7.7
L	24	JASON WIEMER	66	9	9	18	-9	81	4		1		89	10.1
L	28	PATRICK POULIN	46	7	9	16	7	16	1			1	51	13.7
D	4	CORY CROSS	75	2	14	16	4	66					57	3.5
C	22	*AARON GAVEY	73	8	4	12	-6	56	1	1	2		65	12.3
D	95	MICHEL PETIT	54	4	8	12	-11	135			1		68	5.9
D	5	IGOR ULANOV	64	3	9	12	11	116			1		37	8.1
D	27	DAVID SHAW	66	1	11	12	5	64					90	1.1
R	14	JOHN TUCKER	63	3	7	10	-8	18	1				53	5.7
R	20	RUDY POESCHEK	57	1	3	4	-2	88					36	2.8
D	6	ADRIEN PLAVSIC	7	1	2	3	5	6					4	25.0
C	18	*DAYMOND LANGKOW	4		1	1	-1						4	
D	5	*DREW BANNISTER	13		1	1	-1	4					10	
G	93	DAREN PUPPA	57		1	1	0	4						
L	9	*JEFF TOMS	1				0						1	
G	35	*DEREK WILKINSON	4				0	2						
C	25	*ALAN EGELAND	5				0	2					1	
G	30	J.C. BERGERON	12				0							
D	26	CHRIS LIPUMA	21				-7	13					8	
G	1	JEFF REESE	26				0							

GP = games played; G = goals; A = assists; PTS = points; +/- = goals-for minus goals-against while player is on ice; PIM = penalties in minutes; PP = power play goals; SH = shorthanded goals; GW = game-winning goals; GT = game-tying goals; S = no. of shots; PCT = percentage of goals to shots; * = rookie

BRIAN BELLOWS

Yrs. of NHL service: 14
Born: St. Catharines, Ont.; Sept. 1, 1964
Position: left wing
Height: 5-11
Weight: 210
Uniform no.: 23
Shoots: left

Career statistics:

GP	G	A	TP	PIM
1032	446	500	946	664

1992-93 statistics:

GP	G	A	TP	+/-	PIM	PP	SH	GW	GT	S	PCT
82	40	48	88	+4	44	16	0	5	0	260	15.5

1993-94 statistics:

GP	G	A	TP	+/-	PIM	PP	SH	GW	GT	S	PCT
77	33	38	71	+9	36	13	0	2	1	251	13.1

1994-95 statistics:

GP	G	A	TP	+/-	PIM	PP	SH	GW	GT	S	PCT
41	8	8	16	-7	8	1	0	1	0	110	7.3

1995-96 statistics:

GP	G	A	TP	+/-	PIM	PP	SH	GW	GT	S	PCT
79	23	26	49	-14	39	13	0	4	0	190	12.1

LAST SEASON

Tied for team lead in power play goals. Second on team in goals. Tied for third on team in game-winning goals. Appeared in 1,000th NHL game. Missed one game with groin injury. Missed one game with hip injury. Missed one game with shoulder injury.

THE FINESSE GAME

Although you won't notice him much in open ice, Bellows is scary around the net. A power play specialist, he has great hands and instincts in deep. He is not as big as the prototypical power forward, but he plays that style in driving to the crease. He is nimble in traffic and can handle the puck in a scrum. He has good balance for scrapping in front. He works down low on the first power play unit.

Bellows moves and shoots the puck quickly — he doesn't like to fool around with it. He has a strong one-timer and powerful wrist shot. Once in a while he'll score from a drive off the wing, but most of his goals come from in close.

Bellows's five-on-five play improves when he is teamed with the kind of centre who will get the puck to him and who is defensively alert.

THE PHYSICAL GAME

Bellows plays bigger than his size. He will bump and crash and work the boards in the offensive zone, but he is better as a finisher in front of the net. When he has the right linemate, he can concentrate on scoring.

THE INTANGIBLES

Bellows had a nice comeback season, and was a contributor to Tampa Bay's successful run to the playoffs, although he wasn't 100 per cent and came up empty in the post-season. Bellows' days as a scoring leader are over, but he can chip in 45-50 points as a second-line forward and power play specialist. The Lightning will have to make a decision on him, however, if they want to promote some young forwards.

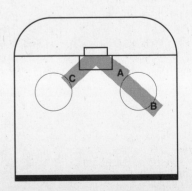

BRIAN BRADLEY

Yrs. of NHL service: 10
Born: Kitchener, Ont.; Jan. 21, 1965
Position: centre
Height: 5-10
Weight: 177
Uniform no.: 19
Shoots: right

Career statistics:

GP	G	A	TP	PIM
602	173	299	472	506

1992-93 statistics:

GP	G	A	TP	+/-	PIM	PP	SH	GW	GT	S	PCT
80	42	44	86	-24	92	16	0	6	1	205	20.5

1993-94 statistics:

GP	G	A	TP	+/-	PIM	PP	SH	GW	GT	S	PCT
78	24	40	64	-8	56	6	0	2	0	180	13.3

1994-95 statistics:

GP	G	A	TP	+/-	PIM	PP	SH	GW	GT	S	PCT
46	13	27	40	-6	42	3	0	2	0	111	11.7

1995-96 statistics:

GP	G	A	TP	+/-	PIM	PP	SH	GW	GT	S	PCT
75	23	56	79	-11	77	9	0	5	0	189	12.2

LAST SEASON

Led team in assists and points for fourth consecutive season. Has led Tampa Bay in scoring in each of the team's four years of existence. Tied for team lead in game-winning goals. Second on team in goals. Missed one game with toe injury. Missed five games with knee injuries. Missed one game with hip pointer.

THE FINESSE GAME

Bradley is an above-average skater with good speed, a nice shot and passing skills. He prefers shooting to passing. He has a neat move where he drives wide to the right wing, then uses a little delay and a half-snap to handcuff the goalie. Bradley is patient with the puck and will draw defenders to him to open up ice for a teammate.

Bradley will work low around the net and likes to use his backhand in tight. He has always had a nose for the net, but he doesn't have a big cannon. He has the quickness to jump into holes and the good hockey sense to work give-and-gos. He opens up some room for his linemates with his stickhandling, and he will also drive to the net with the puck.

Bradley is used on the point on the power play, more for his common sense with the puck than his shot. He puts low, tippable shots towards the goal.

THE PHYSICAL GAME

Bradley is a small centre and doesn't play a physical game. He uses fairly good leg drive and will force people to drag him down and take penalties. His deceptive change of speed has defenders thinking they've got him covered, until he squirts out of their grasp. Bradley played gritty hockey down the stretch,

and his knee injury cost the Lightning a valuable performer in the playoffs.

THE INTANGIBLES

Bradley remained the Lightning's number one centre last season, and continued to be the team's go-to-guy. Until one of the younger centres (Chris Gratton, or more likely, Aaron Gavey) is ready to dethrone him, Bradley will be the top man in the middle again as the season opens. Assuming he gets the same kind of ice time, Bradley should snare 60-70 points. He is the only original member from the 1992 expansion draft left on Tampa Bay.

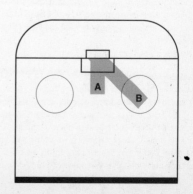

SHAWN BURR

Yrs. of NHL service: 11
Born: Sarnia, Ont,; July 1, 1966
Position: left wing
Height: 6-1
Weight: 200
Uniform no.: 11
Shoots: left

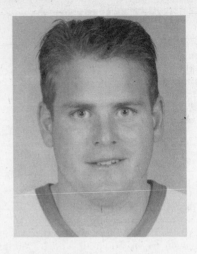

Career statistics:

GP	G	A	TP	PIM
740	161	229	390	884

1992-93 statistics:

GP	G	A	TP	+/-	PIM	PP	SH	GW	GT	S	PCT
80	10	25	35	+18	74	1	1	2	0	99	10.1

1993-94 statistics:

GP	G	A	TP	+/-	PIM	PP	SH	GW	GT	S	PCT
51	10	12	22	+12	31	0	1	1	0	64	15.6

1994-95 statistics:

GP	G	A	TP	+/-	PIM	PP	SH	GW	GT	S	PCT
42	6	8	14	+13	60	0	0	3	0	65	9.2

1995-96 statistics:

GP	G	A	TP	+/-	PIM	PP	SH	GW	GT	S	PCT
81	13	15	28	+4	119	1	0	2	0	122	10.7

LAST SEASON

Acquired from Detroit with third-round draft pick for Marc Bergevin, Aug. 17, 1995. Led team in plus-minus. Second on team in penalty minutes. Missed one game with elbow injury.

THE FINESSE GAME

Burr found a more comfortable niche with the Lightning as a third-line checking winger than he had in Detroit. Burr is an aggressive forechecker. His skating isn't the best, but he is a diligent enough plugger to stick with all but the fastest NHL forwards. He goes hard to the nets and along the boards, trying to make up with energy what he lacks in acceleration.

Burr is a smart hockey player, which makes him a natural in the defensive role, either as a checker or as the safety valve on a scoring line. He creates turnovers with his aggressive checking, but lacks the finishing touch to bury his chances. He was a scorer at the junior and minor-league level, but that touch has not manifested itself in the majors. Most of Burr's scoring chances come from scrums around the net. His shot scares no one.

Burr is a solid penalty-killer who can take defensive-zone draws.

THE PHYSICAL GAME

Burr has to be involved every night, using his muscle along the boards and in front of the net. He makes puck carriers rush their passes because he sticks to them tenaciously. Because he is not a very good skater and has limited range, he does not hit in open ice. He is scrappy and can be very annoying to play against.

THE INTANGIBLES

Burr is respected for his honest defensive work despite his lack of production, but he has to bring a lot to the ice when he only scores 10 goals a year. Burr's exit from Detroit was clinched when he was accused of handing a stick back to Devils defenseman Scott Niedermayer in a 1995 Stanley Cup finals game after a clash behind the net, only to have Niedermayer go down ice and score a goal.

Both Niedermayer and Burr say the stick just bounced up into Niedermayer's hands, but Detroit was so unhappy with the incident that Burr's No. 11 was airbrushed off the back of his jersey on the cover photo of the Red Wings' 1995-96 media guide. Of course, Burr himself was erased from the Detroit picture.

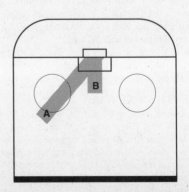

CORY CROSS

Yrs. of NHL service: 2
Born: Lloydminster, Alta.; Jan. 3, 1971
Position: left defense
Height: 6-5
Weight: 212
Uniform no.: 4
Shoots: left

Career statistics:

GP	G	A	TP	PIM
123	3	19	22	113

1993-94 statistics:

GP	G	A	TP	+/-	PIM	PP	SH	GW	GT	S	PCT
5	0	0	0	-3	6	0	0	0	0	5	0.0

1994-95 statistics:

GP	G	A	TP	+/-	PIM	PP	SH	GW	GT	S	PCT
43	1	5	6	-6	41	0	0	1	0	35	2.9

1995-96 statistics:

GP	G	A	TP	+/-	PIM	PP	SH	GW	GT	S	PCT
75	2	14	16	+4	66	0	0	0	0	57	3.5

LAST SEASON

Second NHL season. Missed one game with foot injury.

THE FINESSE GAME

Cross may have been the most improved player on the Lightning last season. His most impressive asset is his intelligence. He is smart enough to recognize the mistakes he makes and learn from them. He is highly skilled, a fine skater who can either lug the puck out of his zone or start things with a pass and then jump up into the play. He has a good shot and will make wise pinches to keep the puck in the zone.

Cross was the first player taken in the 1992 supplemental draft and shot his way up the Lightning depth chart. He may be good enough with the puck to merit more power play time on the point on the second unit. Cross is adjusting to the pace and the grind of the NHL, but he seems to meet every challenge head on.

THE PHYSICAL GAME

Cross did not play in a physical environment at the collegiate level, and is just learning that he is supposed to hit people hard. He has taken a real shine to NHL play, showing a latent aggressive streak. He is a solid skater with good size, and is still discovering how truly big and powerful he is. He can get his stick up at times. Cross can develop even more upper body strength.

THE INTANGIBLES

Cross continues to quietly develop into a very effective NHL defenseman. He is probably the number three man on the depth chart now.

AARON GAVEY

Yrs. of NHL service: 1
Born: Sudbury, Ont; Feb. 22, 1974
Position: centre
Height: 6-1
Weight: 175
Uniform no.: 22
Shoots: left

Career statistics:

GP	G	A	TP	PIM
73	8	4	12	56

1995-96 statistics:

GP	G	A	TP	+/-	PIM	PP	SH	GW	GT	S	PCT
73	8	4	12	-6	56	1	1	2	0	65	12.3

LAST SEASON

First full NHL season. Missed six games with facial laceraton. Missed one game with ankle injury.

THE FINESSE GAME

Gavey filled in down the stretch and in the playoffs when the Lightning's veteran centres were injured, and he looked right at home. Although he is being groomed as a two-way centre, he could be a Ron Francis type who plays intelligent defense but also has terrific offensive ability.

Gavey has a very good shot, a strong wrist or snap. He is also very good on face-offs, and may already be the best on the team. Gavey received more ice time and power play time late in the season, and every time the bar was raised, he cleared it with room to spare. He has met every challenge so far and is ready for more.

He reads plays with exceptional intelligence for a young player. His defensive game is advanced for his age. Gavey is a key first-unit penalty killer and was put on the ice when the team was two men down.

THE PHYSICAL GAME

Gavey needs to get stronger. He is a weedy 6-1 and needs to bulk up a little — not much, or it will throw his overall game off. But he won't succeed at the NHL level without more strength. He is very competitive and intense and plays to the last second of a period.

Gavey came back from a ghastly injury in February in which he suffered 120 stitches in his face, and played gutsy hockey after his return.

THE INTANGIBLES

Gavey has performed well in pressure situations, whether it's the Memorial Cup or the World Junior Championships or the Stanley Cup. He may develop into one of the top Tampa Bay forwards this season. We haven't seen his best yet. It would be wrong to peg Gavey as a second-line centre, because he has the skills to be a number one.

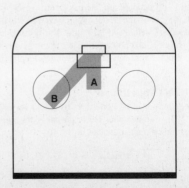

CHRIS GRATTON

Yrs. of NHL service: 3
Born: Brantford, Ont.; July 5, 1975
Position: centre
Height: 6-4
Weight: 218
Uniform no.: 77
Shoots: left

Career statistics:

GP	G	A	TP	PIM
212	37	70	107	317

1993-94 statistics:

GP	G	A	TP	+/-	PIM	PP	SH	GW	GT	S	PCT
84	13	29	42	-25	123	5	1	2	1	161	8.1

1994-95 statistics:

GP	G	A	TP	+/-	PIM	PP	SH	GW	GT	S	PCT
46	7	20	27	-2	89	2	0	0	0	91	7.7

1995-96 statistics:

GP	G	A	TP	+/-	PIM	PP	SH	GW	GT	S	PCT
82	17	21	38	-13	105	7	0	3	0	183	9.3

LAST SEASON

One of two Lightning players to appear in all 82 games. Career high in goals. Third on team in penalty minutes.

THE FINESSE GAME

Gratton was supposed to be a power centre, but he is clearly overmatched at the position. One of the major reasons is his lack of foot speed, which really hurts him despite a lot of coaching in this area. Tampa Bay even kept its strength coach, Chris Reichart, on the bench during games, and his sole responsibility was to keep Gratton positive and pumped up.

Gratton's game is meat and potatoes. He's a grinder and needs to work hard every shift, every night, to make an impact. He has a hard shot, which he needs to use more. He gets his goals from digging around the net, and there's some Cam Neely in him, but he lacks the long, strong stride that Neely uses in traffic. He has good hand-eye coordination and can pick passes out of midair for a shot.

Gratton is an unselfish playmaker. He's not the prettiest of passers, but he has some poise with the puck and knows when to pass and when to shoot. He has shown an ability to win face-offs, and works diligently in his own end.

THE PHYSICAL GAME

Gratton is a hard-working sort who doesn't shy from contact, but he has to initiate more. If his skating improves, he will be able to establish a more physical presence. He doesn't generate enough speed from leg drive to be much of a checker. He won't be an NHL impact player until he does.

THE INTANGIBLES

Gratton is among the disappointments from the top draft picks of 1993 (he went third, after Alexandre Daigle and Chris Pronger). Last year it was time for Gratton to step up, but he had a mediocre regular season, followed by a dismal playoffs (two assists in six games). He's a very likeable guy, but his lack of confidence and his skill deficiencies will prevent him from ever becoming the number one centre the Lightning had envisioned.

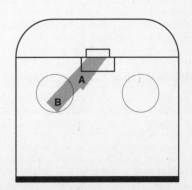

ROMAN HAMRLIK

Yrs. of NHL service: 4
Born: Gottwaldov, Czech.; Apr. 12, 1974
Position: left defense
Height: 6-2
Weight: 202
Uniform no.: 44
Shoots: left

Career statistics:

GP	G	A	TP	PIM
261	37	93	130	395

1992-93 statistics:

GP	G	A	TP	+/-	PIM	PP	SH	GW	GT	S	PCT
67	6	15	21	-21	71	1	0	1	0	113	5.3

1993-94 statistics:

GP	G	A	TP	+/-	PIM	PP	SH	GW	GT	S	PCT
64	3	18	21	-14	135	0	0	0	0	158	1.9

1994-95 statistics:

GP	G	A	TP	+/-	PIM	PP	SH	GW	GT	S	PCT
48	12	11	23	-18	86	7	1	2	0	134	9.0

1995-96 statistics:

GP	G	A	TP	+/-	PIM	PP	SH	GW	GT	S	PCT
82	16	49	65	-24	103	12	0	2	3	281	5.7

LAST SEASON

Tied for lead among NHL defensemen in power play goals. Led team defensemen in scoring for second consecutive season. Led team in shots for second consecutive season. Second on team in assists and points. Third on team in power play goals. One of two Lightning players to appear in all 82 (consecutive games-played streak of 130 games).

THE FINESSE GAME

Hamrlik is drawing comparisons to Ray Bourque and Chris Chelios for his marathon ice time and his desire to control a game. He is very close to becoming the NHL's next star defenseman. He has all the tools. He is a fast, strong skater forwards and backwards. Although he still needs to improve his reads, he's getting better.

He is a mobile defenseman with a solid shot and good passing skills, but he is not very creative. Right now, the young Czech thinks he can just overpower people, and he frequently can, but he could also learn to outsmart them and not make the game so difficult. Hamrlik loves to get involved offensively. He plays nearly the full two minutes of a power play on the point, but he won't hesitate to jump into the play low. He has an excellent shot with a quick release.

He has adjusted to the NHL pace because of his strong skating. He makes fewer high-risk plays and saw more ice time as a result. Hamrlik benefited from playing with the veteran Michel Petit most of last season, and another veteran, David Shaw, proved helpful in his progress. Petit gives Hamrlik the confidence to take some chances. The pair faced other teams' top lines game after game. Defensively, Hamrlik runs into problems when he is trying to move the puck out of his zone and when forced to handle the puck on his backhand, but that is about the only way the opposition can cope with him.

THE PHYSICAL GAME

Hamrlik is aggressive and likes physical play, although he is not a huge, splashy hitter. He is in great shape, and routinely plays 27-30 minutes a night . . . or wants to, but that became a major source of contention in the playoffs.

THE INTANGIBLES

Hamrlik's public feud with head coach Terry Crisp and the departure of assistant coach Wayne Cashman makes for a very uneasy truce in Tampa. Hamrlik, who hasn't missed a game in two seasons, suddenly developed the "flu" in the playoffs after complaining that his ice time was being reduced (from 30 to about 23 minutes) and implying that Crisp was anti-Czech. Crisp had his contract renewed after the season, and Hamrlik is in the second year of a five-year, U.S.$8.5-million deal, so the power struggle is on. The Lightning can hardly afford to part with a player of his rare ability, and how this issue is handled may decide the team's fate for the season.

We predicted a 20-goal, 50-point season for Hamrlik last year, and he exceeded that. He will be among the top 10 defensemen in scoring, maybe even top five, depending on the resolution of the rift.

BILL HOULDER

Yrs. of NHL service: 9
Born: Thunder Bay, Ont.; Mar. 11, 1967
Position: left defense
Height: 6-3
Weight: 218
Uniform no.: 2
Shoots: left

Career statistics:

GP	G	A	TP	PIM
293	30	84	114	140

1992-93 statistics:

GP	G	A	TP	+/-	PIM	PP	SH	GW	GT	S	PCT
15	3	5	8	+5	6	0	0	0	1	29	10.3

1993-94 statistics:

GP	G	A	TP	+/-	PIM	PP	SH	GW	GT	S	PCT
80	14	25	39	-18	40	3	0	3	0	187	7.5

1994-95 statistics:

GP	G	A	TP	+/-	PIM	PP	SH	GW	GT	S	PCT
41	5	13	18	+16	20	1	0	0	0	59	8.5

1995-96 statistics:

GP	G	A	TP	+/-	PIM	PP	SH	GW	GT	S	PCT
61	5	23	28	+1	22	3	0	0	1	90	5.6

LAST SEASON

Signed a free agent, Aug. 1, 1995. Missed seven games with recurring groin injury. Missed four games with rib injury.

THE FINESSE GAME

Houlder has a big shot, but otherwise his overall skills are average. Although he struggles as a skater, especially in his turns, he has a decent first step to the puck and is strong on his skates.

He makes smart options with his passes. He does not like to carry the puck but is a stay-at-home type who is aware he is limited by his range; he will make a pass to a teammate or chip the puck out along the wall rather than try to carry it past a checker.

Houlder's offensive input is minimal (he can get 5-10 goals a year) and is mostly limited to point shots, though he will get brave once in a while and gamble to the top of the circle. Most of his goals come from 60 feet out with some traffic in front. He can play on the second units on power play and penalty killing, but is best in five-on-five situations.

THE PHYSICAL GAME

Houlder is a gentle giant. There is always the expectation with bigger players that they will make monster hits, but we have the feeling that a lot of them were big as youngsters and were told by their parents not to go around picking on smaller kids. Houlder is definitely among the big guys who don't hit to hurt. If he did get involved he would be a dominating defenseman, but that's not about to happen at this stage of his career.

He will take out his man with quiet efficiency. He has to angle the attacker to the boards because of his lack of agility. He is vulnerable to outside speed when he doesn't close off the lane.

THE INTANGIBLES

Houlder was limited last season by a groin injury that flared up during training camp and never really healed. He is a reliable fifth or sixth defenseman, but doesn't have much upside at this stage of his career.

PETR KLIMA

Yrs. of NHL service: 11
Born: Chomutov, Czechoslovakia; Dec. 23, 1964
Position: left wing
Height: 6-0
Weight: 190
Uniform no.: 85
Shoots: right

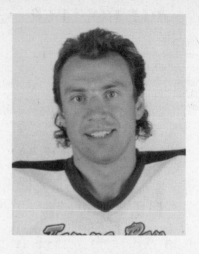

Career statistics:

GP	G	A	TP	PIM
738	310	298	558	655

1992-93 statistics:

GP	G	A	TP	+/-	PIM	PP	SH	GW	GT	S	PCT
68	32	16	48	-15	100	13	0	2	0	175	18.3

1993-94 statistics:

GP	G	A	TP	+/-	PIM	PP	SH	GW	GT	S	PCT
75	28	77	55	-15	76	10	0	2	0	167	16.8

1994-95 statistics:

GP	G	A	TP	+/-	PIM	PP	SH	GW	GT	S	PCT
47	13	13	26	-13	26	4	0	3	0	75	17.3

1995-96 statistics:

GP	G	A	TP	+/-	PIM	PP	SH	GW	GT	S	PCT
67	22	30	52	-25	68	8	0	3	2	164	13.4

LAST SEASON

Tied for third on team in points. Missed seven games with shoulder separation. Missed three games with shoulder injury.

THE FINESSE GAME

Talented and exasperating, Klima on one night will make a careless play and be indifferent to defense. On another, he will be dazzling. Few of his goals, however, are crunch-time tallies.

There are a lot of things he can do. He can score in a variety of ways and in a variety of areas on the ice. Klima is a great one-on-one player but doesn't use his teammates well. He has elite speed with the puck and without it. He is flashy and blessed with great offensive instincts, but needs open ice. Klima plays the left point on the power play, but he will inexplicably carry the puck back deep to regroup even when he isn't under real pressure.

Klima is an expert at drawing penalties. He keeps his legs pumping, grasps an opponent's stick and jumps into the air before falling to the ice. Is it a dive? Sure, but a penalty for diving has been so infrequently called in the past two seasons it might just as well be eliminated from the rule book. He will also take cheap shots with his stick or an elbow and tends to take these penalties at inopportune moments.

THE PHYSICAL GAME

Klima is inconsistent in the application of his body. Some nights he will check, and hard, or sneak up from behind a player and hound him until he strips the puck away. He uses his feet well and keeps the puck alive along the boards. But on even more nights, he'll do

none of those things. Klima has paid better attention to his conditioning, but isn't a fanatic.

THE INTANGIBLES

The Lightning need a 40-goal season from this sniper, but they will never get it. While Klima seems to have cleaned up his act, he remains one of the most erratic performers in the NHL, just as capable of a brilliant streak as he is of a month-long goal drought. This could be the season Tampa Bay finally improves enough for some younger forwards to challenge Klima for ice time. He has had things pretty much his own way for three seasons.

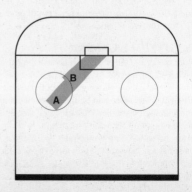

DAYMOND LANGKOW

Yrs. of NHL service: 0
Born: Edmonton, Alberta; Sept. 27, 1976
Position: centre
Height: 5-10
Weight: 170
Uniform no.: 18
Shoots: left

Career statistics:

GP	G	A	TP	PIM
4	0	1	1	0

1995-96 statistics:

GP	G	A	TP	+/-	PIM	PP	SH	GW	GT	S	PCT
4	0	1	1	-1	0	0	0	0	0	4	0.0

LAST SEASON

Will be entering first NHL season. Played 48 games for Tri-City (WHL), scoring 30-61 — 91.

THE FINESSE GAME

Langkow is the complete package. The only problem is, it's such a darned small package.

Small men can succeed in the NHL, however, and it appears that Langkow can be one of them. He has terrific hockey sense, which is probably his chief asset, to go along with his stickhandling ability and shot. He is a fine passer with good vision and is patient with the puck. He is not shy about shooting and possesses a good wrist shot and slap shot.

Langkow has good speed, spies his options quickly, and works hard. He knows what's going to happen before it does, which is the mark of an elite playmaker. He will harass opponents on the forecheck and create turnovers. Langkow could become a very good two-way forward. His defensive awareness is above average for a young player.

THE PHYSICAL GAME

Langkow has a little sandpaper in his game, which gives him an edge over small forwards who rely only on their finesse skills. Langkow doesn't mind aggravating people. He won't be intimidated, either, and does his scoring in the trenches despite getting hit. He has a high pain threshhold.

THE INTANGIBLES

Langkow's small size is a drawback, especially since the one major team weakness exposed by Philadelphia during the playoffs was the Lightning's lack of size. Langkow will get his chance in training camp, but it would sure help his cause if Tampa Bay can acquire or graduate a big winger or two.

Langkow was a captain in junior, and is determined to be an NHL player. He played for Canada in the 1996 World Junior Tournament, winning a gold medal, and was second on the team in scoring.

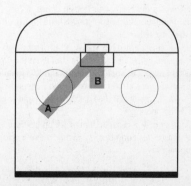

PATRICK POULIN

Yrs. of NHL service: 4
Born: Vanier, Que.; Apr. 23, 1973
Position: left wing
Height: 6-1
Weight: 210
Uniform no.: 28
Shoots: left

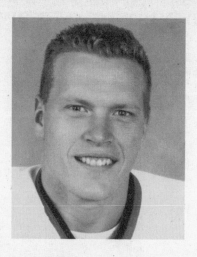

Career statistics:

GP	G	A	TP	PIM
240	56	69	125	159

1992-93 statistics:

GP	G	A	TP	+/-	PIM	PP	SH	GW	GT	S	PCT
81	20	31	51	-19	37	4	0	2	0	160	12.5

1993-94 statistics:

GP	G	A	TP	+/-	PIM	PP	SH	GW	GT	S	PCT
67	14	14	28	-8	51	2	0	3	0	96	14.6

1994-95 statistics:

GP	G	A	TP	+/-	PIM	PP	SH	GW	GT	S	PCT
45	15	15	30	+13	53	4	0	2	0	77	19.5

1995-96 statistics:

GP	G	A	TP	+/-	PIM	PP	SH	GW	GT	S	PCT
46	7	9	16	+7	16	1	0	0	1	51	13.7

LAST SEASON

Acquired from Chicago with Igor Ulanov for Enrico Ciccone and an exchange of second-round draft picks on Mar. 20, 1996. Missed 19 games with sprained ankle. Missed two games with back spasms. Missed eight games with flu.

THE FINESSE GAME

Poulin has all of the tools — size, strength, speed, shot, hands — to be an elite player, but Chicago became the latest team to be frustrated by Poulin's inability to combine all of those qualities on a nightly basis.

Poulin is intelligent and attentive, but he is also high maintenance, since he gets down on himself and needs to be shored up mentally. As he matures, he has to take more of the burden upon himself to motivate his game. It's not an uncommon tendency for a player who starred at the junior level with little effort, as Poulin did, to try to cruise on talent alone his first season or two in the NHL, but Poulin is not in that elite group of athletes and he has shown little improvement over the past season.

Possessing explosive speed, Poulin can peel off the wing and barrel in with a rifle shot from the circle. He has an excellent shot with a quick release, and his wrist shot is very strong; however, he does not skate well with the puck. He has a fluid stride and a good eye for the openings.

Poulin needs a great deal of work on his defensive game, but he has good hockey instincts and a grasp of positional play.

THE PHYSICAL GAME

Poulin is large in stature but not in on-ice presence. He does not use his body well, doesn't finish his checks and doesn't create the openings a player of his ability should. Floating should be something Poulin does in the pool, not on the ice. Coaches keep hoping Poulin will become a Kevin Stevens type, but he lacks that aggressive streak. He doesn't drive to the net or fight through checks.

THE INTANGIBLES

We have been one of Poulin's biggest supporters since draft day, but now that he is on his third NHL team in four seasons and shows little sign of waking up, we have to conclude that he will never develop the mental toughness to enhance his skills. Poulin did little down the stretch and in the playoffs for the Lightning. He's a 15-goal scorer in the body of a 40-goal scorer.

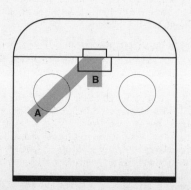

DAREN PUPPA

Yrs. of NHL service: 10
Born: Kirkland Lake, Ont.; Mar. 23, 1965
Position: goaltender
Height: 6-3
Weight: 205
Uniform no.: 93
Catches: right

Career statistics:

GP	MIN	GA	SO	GAA	A	PIM
379	21098	1072	17	3.05	17	34

1992-93 statistics:

GP	MIN	GAA	W	L	T	SO	GA	S	SAPCT	PIM
32	1785	3.23	17	7	4	1	96	938	.898	0

1993-94 statistics:

GP	MIN	GAA	W	L	T	SO	GA	S	SAPCT	PIM
63	3653	2.71	22	33	6	4	165	1637	.899	2

1994-95 statistics:

GP	MIN	GAA	W	L	T	SO	GA	S	SAPCT	PIM
36	2013	2.68	14	19	2	1	90	946	.905	2

1995-96 statistics:

GP	MIN	GAA	W	L	T	SO	GA	S	SAPCT	PIM
57	3189	2.46	29	16	9	5	131	1605	.918	4

LAST SEASON

Finalist for 1996 Vezina Trophy. Career high in wins. Career best in goals-against average. Tied for third in NHL in shutouts. Second in NHL in save percentage. Missed 12 games with knee injury. Missed one game with forearm injury. Missed one game with groin injury. Missed one game with back spasms. Missed one game for personal reasons.

THE PHYSICAL GAME

Considering all the nagging injuries that Puppa suffered last season, his performance looks even more remarkable. A big player, with big pads, Puppa stands up well to make himself look even bigger in the nets. He tries to stay on his feet and play his angles, and he challenges shooters. He plays a butterfly style, and even when he drops to his knees there is still a lot of torso blocking the net.

Puppa has a good glove. He catches right-handed, which is an advantage (much like left-handed tennis players and pitchers have) because shooters are used to looking at left-gloved goalies. His weakness is high stick-side (as with most goalies), but shooters who think they are going stick-side on him are actually shooting to his glove side.

He is very good on low shots, though he gets in trouble when he drops down too early, and flounders. Puppa occasionally gets into a bad habit of staying too deep in his net and playing a passive game. He has to be aggressive to be sucessful.

Puppa moves in and out of his net well. He will set picks or interfere with the opposition trying to get in, and he helps his defensemen by holding up forwards (illegal, but he gets away with it). He does not handle the puck well, however, and since he isn't playing behind a mobile defense corps, it would really help his cause if he could improve in this area. He uses his stick well around the net to knock away loose pucks and cut off passes near the crease.

THE MENTAL GAME

Finally getting recognition around the league as a quality netminder has meant a great deal to Puppa, who toiled for years in Buffalo and Toronto as a backup. Confidence is a major part of any goalie's game, and Puppa has become less fragile mentally and much more resilient.

THE INTANGIBLES

Puppa rebounded from criticism to play a big role in getting Tampa Bay into the playoffs for the first time in the team's history. He is the key to the hockey club. The Lightning doesn't win unless Puppa is one of the best players on the ice every night. He outplayed a number of quality goalies — including John Vanbiesbrouck — in the final weeks of the season. Unfortunately, Puppa probably gets less respect in Tampa than he does around the rest of the league.

ALEXANDER SELIVANOV

Yrs. of NHL service: 2
Born: Moscow, Russia; March 23, 1971
Position: right wing
Height: 6-1
Weight: 187
Uniform no.: 29
Shoots: left

Career statistics:

GP	G	A	TP	PIM
122	41	27	68	107

1994-95 statistics:

GP	G	A	TP	+/-	PIM	PP	SH	GW	GT	S	PCT
43	10	6	16	-2	14	4	0	3	0	94	10.6

1995-96 statistics:

GP	G	A	TP	+/-	PIM	PP	SH	GW	GT	S	PCT
79	31	21	52	+3	93	13	0	5	2	215	14.4

LAST SEASON

Led team in goals in second NHL season. Led team in shooting percentage. Tied for team lead in power play goals and game-winning goals. Second on team in shots. Tied for third on team in points.

THE FINESSE GAME

Selivanov is very clever with the puck. He can beat people one-on-one with his speed and puckhandling, but needs to learn to use his teammates better. Once he does, he will be much more productive. Selivanov loves to score, and he works to get himself in position for a quality shot. He needs to play with a creative centre who will get the puck to him, because he can finish.

Selivanov tends to take very long shifts, which drives his coaches crazy, but that is a common tendency with Russian players. Communication was also a problem, but that is improving. He is strong on the puck but has some defensive lapses. It's not as much of a liability with him as it is with many young players.

Selivanov has an excellent release on his shot and is one of many NHL players who gets away with playing with an illegal curve on his stick. He's a lefthand shot who plays right wing, and playing with a straighter stick would help him receive passes and handle the puck on his backhand.

THE PHYSICAL GAME

Selivanov is wiry but he is not terribly strong or aggressive. He is not intimidated but he will probably need at least one bodyguard on his line. He is quick and smart enough to stay out of trouble.

THE INTANGIBLES

Selivanov exceeded our expectations in last year's *HSR* of 20-25 goals, and there is still more upside to his game because of his tremendous creativity. He has also become more comfortable with North American life after bouts of homesickness in his rookie year. Last season was no fluke.

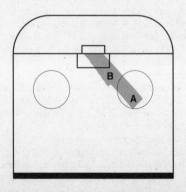

IGOR ULANOV

Yrs. of NHL service: 5
Born: Krasnokamsk, USSR; Oct. 1, 1969
Position: left defense
Height: 6-1
Weight: 205
Uniform no.: 5
Shoots: left

Career statistics:

GP	G	A	TP	PIM
243	8	53	61	501

1992-93 statistics:

GP	G	A	TP	+/-	PIM	PP	SH	GW	GT	S	PCT
56	2	14	16	+6	124	0	0	0	0	26	7.7

1993-94 statistics:

GP	G	A	TP	+/-	PIM	PP	SH	GW	GT	S	PCT
74	0	17	17	-11	165	0	0	0	0	46	0.0

1994-95 statistics:

GP	G	A	TP	+/-	PIM	PP	SH	GW	GT	S	PCT
22	1	4	5	+1	29	0	0	0	0	13	7.7

1995-96 statistics:

GP	G	A	TP	+/-	PIM	PP	SH	GW	GT	S	PCT
64	3	9	12	+11	116	0	0	1	0	37	8.1

THE INTANGIBLES

Ulanov is too unreliable to be much more than a fifth defenseman. He is scary when he plays like a head-hunter, but gets too involved in running around instead of playing his game.

LAST SEASON

Acquired by Chicago from Washington for a third-round draft pick, Oct. 17, 1995. Acquired from Chicago with Patrick Poulin for Enrico Ciccone, Mar. 20, 1996.

THE FINESSE GAME

Ulanov's skills are magnified by the kind of tough physical game he is capable of playing. A player who can skate and handle the puck as well as he can, or level you with a hit, is going to command a lot of space. Ulanov knows what to do with that space once he gets it. He loves to join the attack. He has good first-step quickness, with agility and balance.

He anticipates well. He will break up a rush at his own blueline and start a quick counterattack. Ulanov has very good puck skills, but he is not a real offensive defenseman because he does not finish and has only a modest point shot. He starts breakouts with a smart, short pass. He can carry the puck although he would rather have a teammate lug it.

THE PHYSICAL GAME

Ulanov is inconsistent in his physical play. He is a punishing open-ice hitter — just ask Eric Lindros, who was flipped by an Ulanov submarine check in the playoffs — and has a real nasty streak. Some nights he won't hesitate to make a vicious hit right in front of the opponent's bench. But in the same game he'll lose an attacker by failing to make a simple take-out check, leaving his defense partner outnumbered. He raises the temperature of the opposition by raising his stick, too.

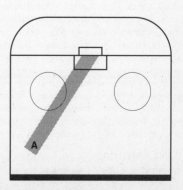

JASON WIEMER

Yrs. of NHL service: 2
Born: Kimberley, B.C.; Apr. 14, 1976
Position: left wing
Height: 6-1
Weight: 215
Uniform no.: 24
Shoots: left

Career statistics:

GP	G	A	TP	PIM
102	10	13	23	125

1994-95 statistics:

GP	G	A	TP	+/-	PIM	PP	SH	GW	GT	S	PCT
36	1	4	5	-2	44	0	0	0	0	10	10.0

1995-96 statistics:

GP	G	A	TP	+/-	PIM	PP	SH	GW	GT	S	PCT
66	9	9	18	-9	81	4	0	1	0	89	10.1

LAST SEASON

Second NHL season. Missed one game with jaw injury.

THE FINESSE GAME

The youngest player on the Lightning last season, Wiemer was unable to find a steady role until late in the year.

Wiemer is a budding power forward in the Brendan Shanahan/Owen Nolan mode. He has the build and the touch for standing in the traffic areas and picking pucks out of scrambles. He also has a touch of mean that merits him some room and time to execute. His release has improved and he will have an NHL shot.

Wiemer's major shortcoming is his skating, but his foot speed is improving and shouldn't hold him back from being an impact player. He is very strong and well balanced for work around the net. He doesn't play a creative game, but relies on his strength and his reach.

THE PHYSICAL GAME

Wiemer didn't come into his first NHL camp (in 1994) in great shape. He suffered a broken ankle during the lockout season and it basically set his development back a year. He is starting to get the idea that what he does off-ice and in the off-season will pay dividends (remember, this is a young guy).

Wiemer relishes body contact and will usually initiate checks to intimidate. He is very strong and can hit to hurt. He drives to the net and pushes defenders back, and isn't shy about dropping his gloves or raising his elbows. While he works best as a finisher, he can also function as the grinder on a line since he will scrap along the boards and in the corners for the puck. He can complement almost any linemate.

THE INTANGIBLES

Wiemer will have to earn his coaches' confidence with a strong training camp. It will probably take another season or two for Wiemer to start hitting his stride, and he will need to get quality ice time this season (not just token fourth-line shifts) to improve.

PAUL YSEBAERT

Yrs. of NHL service: 6
Born: Sarnia, Ont.; May 15, 1966
Position: left wing
Height: 6-1
Weight: 190
Uniform no.: 15
Shoots: left

Career statistics:

GP	G	A	TP	PIM
401	131	147	278	179

1992-93 statistics:

GP	G	A	TP	+/-	PIM	PP	SH	GW	GT	S	PCT
80	34	28	62	+19	42	3	3	8	1	186	18.3

1993-94 statistics:

GP	G	A	TP	+/-	PIM	PP	SH	GW	GT	S	PCT
71	14	21	35	-7	26	3	0	1	0	151	9.3

1994-95 statistics:

GP	G	A	TP	+/-	PIM	PP	SH	GW	GT	S	PCT
44	12	16	28	+3	18	0	0	1	0	93	12.9

1995-96 statistics:

GP	G	A	TP	+/-	PIM	PP	SH	GW	GT	S	PCT
55	16	15	31	-19	16	4	1	1	0	135	11.9

he does is spectacular, but he will seldom cost a team a game and his point production will be in the 50-point range as he has become more defense-minded.

LAST SEASON

Missed 24 games with torn groin muscle.

THE FINESSE GAME

Ysebaert thrives on his skating, which made last season a nightmare because of the injury he suffered halfway through the season. When healthy, Ysebaert accelerates in a heartbeat and has the speed and balance to beat defenders wide. He has a wide scoring stance, which makes him tough to knock off the puck even though he's not overly strong.

He has a good array of shots and will work diligently for his scoring opportunities around the net. He goes to the net hard with the puck, but last season he showed more of a tendency to hurry his shots and to not work to get into the high-percentage scoring areas. He has a quick release, and his shot is heavy.

Ysebaert needs someone to open up a bit of ice so he can use his skating to jump into the holes. He can kill penalties and contribute shorthanded.

THE PHYSICAL GAME

Ysebaert has worked on his upper body strength and has increased confidence in his ability to win battles along the wall. He might still get outmuscled by bigger defenders, but he'll scrap for the puck with great enthusiasm. He isn't much of a fighter, but he won't be intimidated, either.

THE INTANGIBLES

Ysebaert has made himself into a solid all-around player, but needs to recover fully from his injury to be effective. His attitude and consistent effort is a bonus for Tampa Bay. Ysebaert can show the way. Nothing

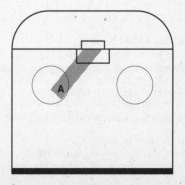

ROB ZAMUNER

Yrs. of NHL service: 4
Born: Oakville, Ont.; Sept. 17, 1969
Position: left wing
Height: 6-2
Weight: 202
Uniform no.: 7
Shoots: left

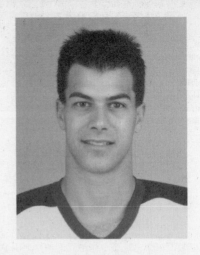

Career statistics:

GP	G	A	TP	PIM
267	46	62	108	204

1992-93 statistics:

GP	G	A	TP	+/-	PIM	PP	SH	GW	GT	S	PCT
84	15	28	45	-25	74	1	0	0	2	183	8.2

1993-94 statistics:

GP	G	A	TP	+/-	PIM	PP	SH	GW	GT	S	PCT
59	6	6	12	-9	42	0	0	1	0	109	5.5

1994-95 statistics:

GP	G	A	TP	+/-	PIM	PP	SH	GW	GT	S	PCT
43	9	6	15	-3	24	0	3	1	0	74	12.2

1995-96 statistics:

GP	G	A	TP	+/-	PIM	PP	SH	GW	GT	S	PCT
72	15	20	35	+11	62	0	3	4	0	152	9.9

of the lineup, because few players try as hard as he does. His leap to 15 goals last season (after missing the start of the year with a knee injury) was a real plus. Zamuner was one of the team's best performers in the playoffs. He's a gamer.

LAST SEASON

Career high in goals. Led team in shorthanded goals for second consecutive season. Missed 10 games with knee injury.

THE FINESSE GAME

Zamuner doesn't have great speed, but he compensates for it in other ways, including all-out effort. He is a complementary player, a grinder who can also handle the puck and has some good hand skills. Zamuner isn't quite good enough to play as a third-line checking winger because of his lack of speed, and has to be spotted cautiously by his coaches. Lacking speed, he plays well positionally and takes away the attacker's angles to the net.

Zamuner was a good scorer at the minor league level but has not been able to make the same impact in the NHL. He has a decent touch for scoring or passing, but it is average at best. He is a shorthanded threat because of his anticipation and work ethic. He has a knack for scoring key goals, and was big for the Lightning in the playoff stretch run.

THE PHYSICAL GAME

Zamuner had problems in the past with fitness, until he realized what a big edge he could have with better conditioning. He has good size and uses it effectively. He is pesky and annoying to play against. On many nights, he will be the most physically active forward on the Lightning, adding a real spark with his effort.

THE INTANGIBLES

Zamuner is a tough guy to keep in the lineup, because of his marginal skating. He's a tough guy to keep out

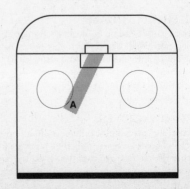

TORONTO MAPLE LEAFS

Players' Statistics 1995-96

POS.	NO.	PLAYER	GP	G	A	PTS	+/-	PIM	PP	SH	GW	GT	S	PCT
C	13	MATS SUNDIN	76	33	50	83	8	46	7	6	7	1	301	11.0
C	93	DOUG GILMOUR	81	32	40	72	-5	77	10	2	3		180	17.8
D	55	LARRY MURPHY	82	12	49	61	-2	34	8		1	2	182	6.6
L	17	WENDEL CLARK	71	32	26	58	-5	76	8		3	1	237	13.5
R	11	MIKE GARTNER	82	35	19	54	5	52	15		4	1	275	12.7
D	72	MATHIEU SCHNEIDER	78	13	41	54	-20	103	7		1		191	6.8
C	15	DAVE GAGNER	73	21	28	49	-19	103	7		3		215	9.8
C	21	KIRK MULLER	51	13	19	32	-13	57	7		1		102	12.7
D	23	TODD GILL	74	7	18	25	-15	116	1		2		109	6.4
D	4	DAVE ELLETT	80	3	19	22	-10	59	1	1			153	2.0
R	9	MIKE CRAIG	70	8	12	20	-8	42	1		1		108	7.4
L	8	*TODD WARRINER	57	7	8	15	-11	26	1				79	8.9
R	18	WAYNE PRESLEY	80	6	8	14	3	85	1	1	2		113	5.3
R	28	TIE DOMI	72	7	6	13	-3	297			1		61	11.5
D	26	DIMITRI YUSHKEVICH	69	1	10	11	-14	54	1				96	1.0
L	32	NICK KYPREOS	61	4	5	9	1	107			1		49	8.2
C	18	PETER WHITE	27	5	3	8	-14		1				34	14.7
C	25	PAUL DIPIETRO	20	4	4	8	-3	4	1				23	17.4
D	34	JAMIE MACOUN	82		8	8	2	87					74	
C	12	*BRANDON CONVERY	11	5	2	7	-7	4	3		1		16	31.3
R	37	*MARK KOLESAR	21	2	2	4	0	14					10	20.0
R	20	*ZDENEK NEDVED	7	1	1	2	-1	6					7	14.3
G	33	DON BEAUPRE	41		2	2	0	31						
D	40	*KELLY FAIRCHILD	1		1	1	1	2					1	
D	2	ROB ZETTLER	29		1	1	-1	48					11	
D	38	*DAVID HARLOCK	1				0							
L	52	*SEAN HAGGERTY	1				0							
R	36	*JAMIE HEWARD	5				-1						8	
D	3	MATT MARTIN	13				-1	14					3	
G	29	FELIX POTVIN	69				0	4						

GP = games played; G = goals; A = assists; PTS = points; +/- = goals-for minus goals-against while player is on ice; PIM = penalties in minutes; PP = power play goals; SH = shorthanded goals; GW = game-winning goals; GT = game-tying goals; S = no. of shots; PCT = percentage of goals to shots; * = rookie

JAMIE BAKER

Yrs. of NHL service: 5
Born: Ottawa, Ont.; Aug. 31, 1966
Position: centre
Height: 6-0
Weight: 190
Uniform no.: 13
Shoots: left

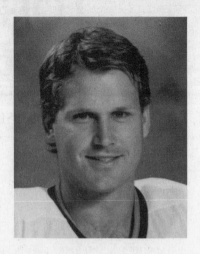

Career statistics:

GP	G	A	TP	PIM
332	63	65	128	233

1991-92 statistics:

GP	G	A	TP	+/-	PIM	PP	SH	GW	GT	S	PCT
52	7	10	17	-5	32	3	0	1	0	77	9.1

1992-93 statistics:

GP	G	A	TP	+/-	PIM	PP	SH	GW	GT	S	PCT
76	19	29	48	-20	54	10	0	2	0	160	11.9

1993-94 statistics:

GP	G	A	TP	+/-	PIM	PP	SH	GW	GT	S	PCT
65	12	5	17	+2	38	0	0	2	0	68	17.6

1994-95 statistics:

GP	G	A	TP	+/-	PIM	PP	SH	GW	GT	S	PCT
43	7	4	11	-7	22	0	1	0	0	60	11.7

1995-96 statistics:

GP	G	A	TP	+/-	PIM	PP	SH	GW	GT	S	PCT
77	16	17	33	-19	79	2	6	0	0	117	13.7

LAST SEASON

Acquired by Toronto with a fifth-round draft pick in 1996 for Todd Gill, June 14, 1996. Led San Jose in shorthanded goals. Missed three games with concussion.

THE FINESSE GAME

Baker plays a largely defensive role, but he also has the skills to pop in some points even when he is working as a checker. In fact, that's what makes Baker a "tweener" — between defense and offense — because he always looks like he has the ability to deliver more than he shows on the stat sheet.

Baker does his best work in the corners. He hustles and is always quickly onto the puck carrier on the forecheck. He reads offensive plays nicely, so if he is able to force a turnover, he knows where to make the pass and whether or not to head to the net. He protects the puck well along the boards and while skating. This is his biggest asset.

Baker will keep the puck alive with his stick even when he's been knocked flat to the ice. He won't just cough it up. He's a better playmaker than scorer, but he can finish around the net when given the chance. He passes off his forehand or backhand, and is effective down low. He has a choppy stride but can move quickly for the first step or two.

Baker is average on draws. He is a determined and aggressive penalty killer and a shorthanded threat. He is a reliable man to have on the ice at crunch time.

THE PHYSICAL GAME

Baker has good size and has added some strength to make himself a more effective hitter, but continued work in the muscle department would help his career. He goes full out, regardless of the score.

THE INTANGIBLES

Baker is a character guy who always gives the maximum effort with his modest skills. He is an intelligent player who won't hurt a team, and he can score 30 points or so as a checking forward.

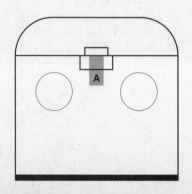

WENDEL CLARK

Yrs. of NHL service: 11
Born: Kelvington, Sask.; Oct. 25, 1966
Position: left wing
Height: 5-11
Weight: 195
Uniform no.: 17
Shoots: left

Career statistics:

GP	G	A	TP	PIM
571	282	190	596	1464

1992-93 statistics:

GP	G	A	TP	+/-	PIM	PP	SH	GW	GT	S	PCT
66	17	22	39	+2	193	2	0	5	1	146	11.6

1993-94 statistics:

GP	G	A	TP	+/-	PIM	PP	SH	GW	GT	S	PCT
64	46	30	76	+10	115	21	0	8	0	275	16.7

1994-95 statistics:

GP	G	A	TP	+/-	PIM	PP	SH	GW	GT	S	PCT
37	12	18	30	-1	45	5	0	0	0	95	12.6

1995-96 statistics:

GP	G	A	TP	+/-	PIM	PP	SH	GW	GT	S	PCT
71	32	26	58	-5	76	8	0	3	1	237	13.5

LAST SEASON

Acquired by the Islanders from Colorado for Claude Lemieux, October 3, 1995. Acquired from the Islanders with Mathieu Schneider and D. J. Smith for Kenny Jonsson, Darby Hendrickson, Sean Haggerty and a first-round draft pick, March. 13, 1996. Tied for third on team in goals and power play goals.

THE FINESSE GAME

Clark is an accurate shooter. He uses a slightly shorter stick than he did early in his career and keeps his hands higher on the stick, like Brett Hull. His shots are more accurate that way. He can still overpower a goalie from the blueline, even with his wrist shot, which has tremendous power.

Not a clever player, Clark rarely passes the puck. His effectiveness depends on him charging down the ice, wreaking havoc and letting his teammates trail in his wake, picking through the debris to make a play. When Clark gets the puck, he has to shoot in. He gets into trouble when he makes plays.

Clark is not a smart player positionally, either. Although a strong skater, he's not agile, fast or mobile. When he's playing well, he uses his leg drive like a linebacker in football to hit hard.

THE PHYSICAL GAME

Clark is just plain mean. He hits when it's least expected, often well away from the play. And he's a big, big hitter who hurts. He's a strong forechecker, though, but he gets frustrated when his scoring touch deserts him and he'll run around and take bad penalties.

THE INTANGIBLES

If there is any deal that could cost GM Cliff Fletcher his job, this is the one. Clark is a leader, true, but he is brittle and pushing 30 and his best seasons are behind him. He gives everything he's got but who knows how much is left? If the Leafs ever allow anyone under age 30 to play, Clark will be a leader by example. Because of the battering his body has taken over the years, just getting ready for a game is usually an ordeal.

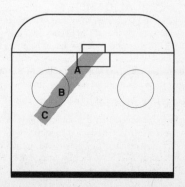

MIKE CRAIG

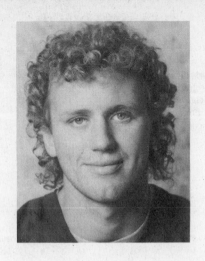

Yrs. of NHL service: 6
Born: London, Ont.; June 6, 1971
Position: right wing
Height: 6-0
Weight: 180
Uniform no.: 9
Shoots: right

Career statistics:

GP	G	A	TP	PIM
355	64	84	148	486

1992-93 statistics:

GP	G	A	TP	+/-	PIM	PP	SH	GW	GT	S	PCT
70	15	23	38	-11	106	7	0	0	0	131	11.5

1993-94 statistics:

GP	G	A	TP	+/-	PIM	PP	SH	GW	GT	S	PCT
72	13	24	37	-14	139	3	0	2	0	150	8.7

1994-95 statistics:

GP	G	A	TP	+/-	PIM	PP	SH	GW	GT	S	PCT
37	5	5	10	-21	12	1	0	1	0	61	8.2

1995-96 statistics:

GP	G	A	TP	+/-	PIM	PP	SH	GW	GT	S	PCT
70	8	12	20	-8	42	1	0	1	0	108	7.4

LAST SEASON

Missed one game with sprained ankle.

THE FINESSE GAME

Craig is a choppy skater, but he chops with enthusiasm. Almost everything he does he does with great intensity, Tony Granato-style.

Craig has good hands and tenacity. He can play well with top offensive people because he will do the grunt work for them in the corners and along the boards. With his nice touch, he produces goals when he goes to the front of the net. His wrist shot is especially effective, accurate and quickly unleashed. The problem with Craig continues to be his inconsistency, which is why he had trouble getting into the lineup and why he played on the fourth line when he did.

His short game is his greatest asset. He is smart and poised through traffic. He can play the power play down low.

THE PHYSICAL GAME

Craig needs to play bigger than he is. He has to continue gaining more strength so he can hold that game through a full schedule — either that or he has to learn to pace himself better, because he tends to wear down in the second half. That wasn't as much of a problem last year since he didn't get much ice time.

THE INTANGIBLES

Craig will continue to have trouble getting ice time this season and that will make it hard to improve his game. It is the beginning of a downward spiral. He has too much talent to let his game slip away, but he has to find the tenacity to earn a spot.

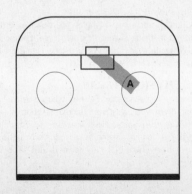

TIE DOMI

Yrs. of NHL service: 6
Born: Windsor, Ont.; Nov. 1, 1969
Position: right wing
Height: 5-10
Weight: 200
Uniform no.: 28
Shoots: right

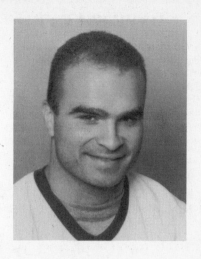

Career statistics:

GP	G	A	TP	PIM
326	27	36	63	1620

1992-93 statistics:

GP	G	A	TP	+/-	PIM	PP	SH	GW	GT	S	PCT
61	5	10	15	+1	344	0	0	0	0	40	12.5

1993-94 statistics:

GP	G	A	TP	+/-	PIM	PP	SH	GW	GT	S	PCT
81	8	11	19	-8	347	0	0	1	0	98	8.2

1994-95 statistics:

GP	G	A	TP	+/-	PIM	PP	SH	GW	GT	S	PCT
40	4	5	9	-5	159	0	0	0	0	46	8.7

1995-96 statistics:

GP	G	A	TP	+/-	PIM	PP	SH	GW	GT	S	PCT
72	7	6	13	-3	297	0	0	1	0	61	11.5

THE INTANGIBLES

Domi can play with controlled aggression, but the knowledge that he could snap at any moment makes opponents leery of him, and he earns some time and space. His key role, though, is to make some of his skilled teammates braver.

LAST SEASON

Third in NHL and led team in penalty minutes. Served eight-game suspension.

THE FINESSE GAME

Finesse? Should that be discussed in context with this rock-hard (some might say rock-headed) right-winger?

Yes, indeed, because Domi has some skills that elevate him above the level of a mere goon. He is a pretty nifty skater, and in a role as a third-line checker will often be in quickly on the opposing goalie behind the net, trying to force a bad pass or a turnover by the netminder. He barrels in on defensemen, too (the obstruction crackdown is ideal for forecheckers like Domi).

When he gets the puck, he has the presence of mind to try to do something useful. Bang-bang reaction plays, whether shots or passes, are his strong suit. He shouldn't think too much. Domi has a short-range shot. He will wallow into the activity around the crease. He is surprisingly good with his feet, and if his stick is tied up or dropped, he will attempt to kick the puck to a teammate.

THE PHYSICAL GAME

Short but burly, Domi is one of the most eager fighters in the NHL. He talks trash and builds up some of his upcoming "bouts" as if he were Don King, which doesn't exactly endear him to the NHL hierarchy (he was slapped with an eight-game suspension for a sucker-punch on the Rangers' Ulf Samuelsson).

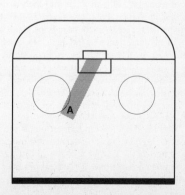

DAVE ELLETT

Yrs. of NHL service: 12
Born: Cleveland, Ohio; Mar. 30, 1964
Position: left defense
Height: 6-2
Weight: 205
Uniform no.: 4
Shoots: left

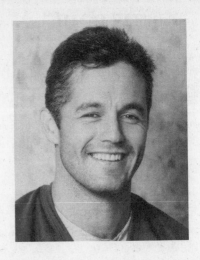

Career statistics:

GP	G	A	TP	PIM
865	142	366	508	841

1992-93 statistics:

GP	G	A	TP	+/-	PIM	PP	SH	GW	GT	S	PCT
70	6	34	40	+19	46	4	0	1	0	186	3.2

1993-94 statistics:

GP	G	A	TP	+/-	PIM	PP	SH	GW	GT	S	PCT
68	7	36	43	+6	42	5	0	1	1	146	4.8

1994-95 statistics:

GP	G	A	TP	+/-	PIM	PP	SH	GW	GT	S	PCT
33	5	10	15	-6	26	3	0	1	0	84	6.0

1995-96 statistics:

GP	G	A	TP	+/-	PIM	PP	SH	GW	GT	S	PCT
80	3	19	22	-10	59	1	1	0	0	153	2.0

LAST SEASON

Missed one game with sprained knee. Missed one game with flu.

THE FINESSE GAME

Ellett is a very sound player for someone who was labelled as an offensive defenseman early in his career. He is used in all situations: power play, penalty killing, four-on-four, protecting a lead or helping his team come from behind.

His game has always been powered by his fine skating. He is a graceful mover. His lateral mobility is not great, which is why he's not an elite point man on the power play. He has been on the second unit since the addition of Mathieu Schneider. He sometimes has trouble getting his shot through.

Ellett started using a shorter stick a few seasons ago and his shots were more accurate and more quickly released. His hand skills are fine, too, but instead of using his skills to jump into the offense at every opportunity, he conserves his energy for the defensive part of the ice. He understands the game and is aware of his importance to the team. He is not expected to go end to end, but instead to be steady and move the puck. He is a good passer with a soft touch, and uses his skills to get to the puck, get turned, make the first pass and watch the forwards go.

THE PHYSICAL GAME

Ellett uses his skills to keep himself out of physical situations. By getting to the puck and moving it briskly out of the corner, he can avoid getting crunched. He doesn't have a physical presence and doesn't clear out the front of his net as well as he

should for a player of his size. He will tie up players with his long reach.

THE INTANGIBLES

Versatile and a good team player, the classy Ellett has developed into a solid two-way defenseman. He turned his considerable finesse skills to defense first and became a much better all-around defenseman. We anticipated a gradual decline in his production, but he tailed off sharply last season and that is probably his future.

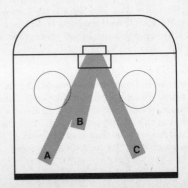

DOUG GILMOUR

Yrs. of NHL service: 13
Born: Kingston, Ont.; June 25, 1963
Position: centre
Height: 5-11
Weight: 180
Uniform no.: 93
Shoots: left

Career statistics:

GP	G	A	TP	PIM
981	346	695	1041	890

1992-93 statistics:

GP	G	A	TP	+/-	PIM	PP	SH	GW	GT	S	PCT
83	32	95	127	+32	100	15	3	2	2	211	15.2

1993-94 statistics:

GP	G	A	TP	+/-	PIM	PP	SH	GW	GT	S	PCT
83	27	84	111	+25	105	10	1	3	1	167	16.2

1994-95 statistics:

GP	G	A	TP	+/-	PIM	PP	SH	GW	GT	S	PCT
44	10	23	33	-5	26	3	0	1	1	73	13.7

1995-96 statistics:

GP	G	A	TP	+/-	PIM	PP	SH	GW	GT	S	PCT
81	32	40	72	-5	77	10	2	3	0	180	17.8

LAST SEASON

Led team in shooting percentage for second consecutive year. Second on team in points and power play goals. Tied for third on team in points. Scored 1,000th career point.

THE FINESSE GAME

A superior leader on ice (he is rather quiet in the dressing room), Gilmour is on the verge of losing that fine edge in skills and determination that placed him among the league's elite. He sees a lot of ice time and battles through injuries, and is looking truly worn down.

Gilmour is one of those rare individuals who feels he owes his team and teammates every dollar of his salary. For a team to have its best player possess that attitude is invaluable. The mark of a great player is that he takes his team upwards with him.

A creative playmaker, he is one of those rare NHL players who has eschewed the banana blade for a nearly straight model, so he can handle the puck equally well on his forehand or backhand and control the puck. He will bring people right in on top of him before he slides a little pass to a teammate, creating time and space. He is very intelligent and has great anticipation. He loves to set up from behind the net and intimidates because he plays with such supreme confidence.

Gilmour is a set-up man who needs finishers around him and doesn't shoot much. When he does, he won't use a big slapper, but instead scores from close range either as the trailer or after losing a defender with his subtle dekes and moves. He's not a smooth, gifted skater, but he is nimble and quick.

Gilmour ranks as one of the best face-off men in the NHL and routinely beats big, stronger centres on draws. In his own end, he is very sound positionally.

THE PHYSICAL GAME

Gilmour plays with passion and savvy, challenging bigger opponents regardless of where or when he plays. He puts life into the Leafs with his relentless work ethic. Although he's listed at 185 pounds, he plays at around 165 during the season and can lose up to seven pounds in a single playoff game. Gilmour needs to keep the weight off. His play is effortless at a lighter weight.

The only drawback to Gilmour's competiveness is that he can become so fierce and intense that he loses his focus. He does not turn the other cheek. He goes into the trenches because that's where the puck is, and that's what he hungers for.

THE INTANGIBLES

Gilmour provides never-say-die leadership. He often responds with a big shift after his team has been scored upon and will ignite the Leafs and the crowd with an inspirational bump or goal. He will do everything he can to win a game, but the reservoir is only so deep. Gilmour will be 33 when the season starts, and unless his persistent back problems are healed, he will not be the 100-point performer of two and three seasons ago.

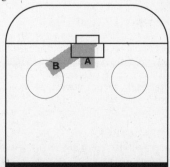

NICK KYPREOS

Yrs. of NHL service: 7
Born: Toronto, Ont.; June 6, 1966
Position: left wing
Height: 6-0
Weight: 207
Uniform no.: 32
Shoots: left

Career statistics:

GP	G	A	TP	PIM
407	43	42	85	1148

1992-93 statistics:

GP	G	A	TP	+/-	PIM	PP	SH	GW	GT	S	PCT
75	17	10	27	-5	325	0	0	2	0	81	21.0

1993-94 statistics:

GP	G	A	TP	+/-	PIM	PP	SH	GW	GT	S	PCT
56	3	5	8	-16	139	0	0	1	0	34	8.8

1994-95 statistics:

GP	G	A	TP	+/-	PIM	PP	SH	GW	GT	S	PCT
40	1	3	4	0	93	0	0	0	0	34	8.8

1995-96 statistics:

GP	G	A	TP	+/-	PIM	PP	SH	GW	GT	S	PCT
61	4	5	9	+1	107	0	0	1	0	49	8.2

LAST SEASON

Acquired from N.Y. Rangers with Wayne Presley for Bill Berg and Sergio Momesso, Feb. 29, 1996.

THE FINESSE GAME

If Kypreos isn't going to come out decking people, there is little point in giving him a sweater. His offensive contributions are going to be limited to slam-ins from five feet away on the third rebound. He won't carry the puck, but he will go into the corner and try to win it. Even if he just keeps the puck alive for someone to come along and pick up, he has done his job.

Kypreos may handle some checking roles, but he is not fast enough to keep up with a quick offensive line and that kind of thinking doesn't come naturally to him. He's an up-and-down wing who wants to forecheck.

Kypreos has a history of uneven emotional involvement in a game, and has to be consistent on a nightly basis. That's not always easy to do when you get limited ice time.

THE PHYSICAL GAME

Kypreos is a hard, even vicious hitter. He couldn't care less if his hit is dirty or not, and he can throw the kind of checks that can intimidate a team right out of the game during the regular season. It's a little different in the playoffs, but that alone is enough of a commodity to keep him in the lineup. Kypreos has a physical presence and makes his teammates a little braver.

THE INTANGIBLES

Kypreos played the fourth line after his arrival in Toronto, and can be the kind of high-energy part-timer who makes his teammates a little braver. The Maple Leafs thought enough of him to re-sign him after the season.

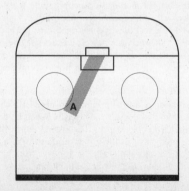

JAMIE MACOUN

Yrs. of NHL service: 13
Born: Newmarket, Ont.; Aug. 17, 1961
Position: left defense
Height: 6-2
Weight: 200
Uniform no.: 34
Shoots: left

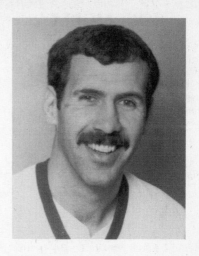

Career statistics:

GP	G	A	TP	PIM
912	74	255	329	1014

1992-93 statistics:

GP	G	A	TP	+/-	PIM	PP	SH	GW	GT	S	PCT
77	4	15	19	+3	55	2	0	1	0	114	3.5

1993-94 statistics:

GP	G	A	TP	+/-	PIM	PP	SH	GW	GT	S	PCT
82	3	27	30	-5	115	1	0	1	0	122	2.5

1994-95 statistics:

GP	G	A	TP	+/-	PIM	PP	SH	GW	GT	S	PCT
46	2	8	10	-6	75	1	0	0	0	84	2.4

1995-96 statistics:

GP	G	A	TP	+/-	PIM	PP	SH	GW	GT	S	PCT
82	0	8	8	+2	87	0	0	0	0	74	0.0

THE INTANGIBLES

Macoun was given a two-year, $2-million contract extension. The Leafs' defense is very creaky, and until there are some young challengers for jobs, Macoun will remain in the top four or five.

LAST SEASON

One of only three Leafs to appear in all 82 games. One of only four Leaf regulars to be a plus player.

THE FINESSE GAME

Macoun is a master at keeping the game simple and supplying veteran calm — although his occasional panic attacks in his own end have been known to rattle a defensive partner now and then. He moves the puck ahead well and quickly out of the zone. He plays a sound positional game and doesn't get suckered into chasing people behind the net. He is a solid penalty killer who reads the rush well.

Macoun is primarily known for his work in the defensive zone, but every now and then he will find a little patch of ice open before him and he can do some smart things with the puck because of his nice offensive skills. He can handle the point on a second-unit power play, using a low shot that he gets away quickly and puts on net.

He can still be turned to the outside and burned by a forward driving wide, so he has to be careful not to overcommit.

THE PHYSICAL GAME

At age 35, Macoun can skate until you think his legs would fall off, but they don't, because of the attention he pays to conditioning. When he is at the top of his game, he can be a force. He plays the man, not the puck, and anyone in his territory pays a price. Macoun plays with a little mean streak and will get his stick up and tick people off.

KIRK MULLER

Yrs. of NHL service: 12
Born: Kingston, Ont.; Feb. 8, 1966
Position: centre
Height: 6-0
Weight: 200
Uniform no.: 21
Shoots: left

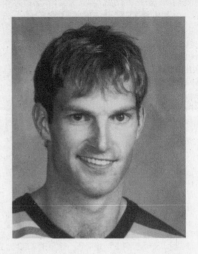

Career statistics:

GP	G	A	TP	PIM
886	305	502	807	935

1992-93 statistics:

GP	G	A	TP	+/-	PIM	PP	SH	GW	GT	S	PCT
80	37	57	94	+8	77	12	0	4	0	231	16.0

1993-94 statistics:

GP	G	A	TP	+/-	PIM	PP	SH	GW	GT	S	PCT
76	23	34	57	-1	96	9	2	3	0	168	13.7

1994-95 statistics:

GP	G	A	TP	+/-	PIM	PP	SH	GW	GT	S	PCT
45	11	16	27	-18	47	4	1	2	1	97	11.3

1995-96 statistics:

GP	G	A	TP	+/-	PIM	PP	SH	GW	GT	S	PCT
51	13	19	32	-13	57	7	0	1	0	102	12.7

LAST SEASON

Acquired from N.Y. Islanders with Don Beaupre for future considerations (Damian Rhodes and Ken Belanger), Jan. 23, 1996. Missed 29 games in contract dispute.

THE FINESSE GAME

Muller's reputation took a pounding from his badly handled Islanders tenure. For most of his career, Muller has been extolled for his leadership. He is a gritty player who makes the most of his skills — which are above average, but well shy of world class — by exerting himself to the utmost.

Muller plays at his best with linemates who have keen enough hockey sense to pounce on the pucks he works free with his efforts along the wall. He does not have a clever passing touch. He is a sturdy player through traffic and has some speed, but he won't dazzle. He doesn't give up until the buzzer sounds, and he takes nothing for granted.

Muller is not an especially gifted playmaker or shooter. None of his plays will make highlight films. Their ooh and ahh factor is low, but the result is in the net one way or another. It helps if he plays with at least one winger with a good burst of speed.

Muller is defensively strong and can shut down the opposing team's top centres. He can work both special teams.

THE PHYSICAL GAME

Muller blocks shots. He ties up players along the boards and uses his feet to kick the puck to a teammate. Ditto for his work on face-offs. Strong on his skates, he uses his skateblades almost as well as his stickblade.

THE INTANGIBLES

Muller scored 25 points in 36 games with Toronto despite missing a lot of playoff time in the first half of the season. He is in the garden spot (pun intended) in Toronto as the number two centre behind Gilmour, and should score 55-60 points. He is a versatile player who can take some of the load off Gilmour.

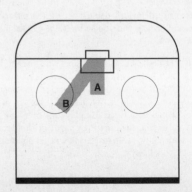

LARRY MURPHY

Yrs. of NHL service: 16
Born: Scarborough, Ont.; Mar. 8, 1961
Position: right defense
Height: 6-2
Weight: 210
Uniform no.: 55
Shoots: right

Career statistics:

GP	G	A	TP	PIM
1234	245	755	1006	928

1992-93 statistics:

GP	G	A	TP	+/-	PIM	PP	SH	GW	GT	S	PCT
83	22	63	85	+45	73	6	2	2	0	230	9.6

1993-94 statistics:

GP	G	A	TP	+/-	PIM	PP	SH	GW	GT	S	PCT
84	17	56	73	+10	44	7	0	4	0	236	7.2

1994-95 statistics:

GP	G	A	TP	+/-	PIM	PP	SH	GW	GT	S	PCT
48	13	25	38	+12	18	4	0	3	0	124	10.5

1995-96 statistics:

GP	G	A	TP	+/-	PIM	PP	SH	GW	GT	S	PCT
82	12	49	61	-2	34	8	0	1	2	182	6.6

LAST SEASON

Led team defensemen in scoring for fourth consecutive season. Tied for 10th among NHL defensemen in scoring. Second on team in assists. Third on team in points. Tied for third on team in power play goals. One of three Maple Leafs to appear in all 82 games. Became fourth NHL defenseman to score 1,000 career points.

THE FINESSE GAME

Murphy seems to score the quietest points of any of the offensive-oriented NHL defensemen. He is big, but not physical. He is skilled, but not flashy.

Murphy has become a fairly sound two-way defenseman, but he is still the player the Maple Leafs want to collect the puck behind his goal line and start the attack. Murphy has never been a great skater. He actually has a rather choppy stride, but his feet are quick enough to mark him as a fairly agile skater.

He can either rush the puck out of his zone or make the nice first pass that gives his team the jump on the opponents. Murphy is smart and poised. He will not force bad passes up the middle but he will use the boards if that's the safest play. His pinches are well timed, and he has the reach to prevent a lot of pucks from getting by him at the point.

Murphy's shot selection is intelligent. He loves to shoot, but he won't fire blindly. He will use a low wrist shot rather than a big slap to keep the puck on net. Murphy's positional play is where he has shown the most improvement. He reads plays well and seldom seems to be floundering on the ice.

THE PHYSICAL GAME

Murphy does not play a physical game. He will bump his man in front but doesn't make strong takeouts. He prefers to position his body and force the shooter to make a play while he himself goes for the puck or stick. It is the weakest part of his game, and is just adequate.

THE INTANGIBLES

Age (35) and ice time have started to catch up with Murphy. He will be a key man on the point for the Maple Leafs' power plays (he works on the first unit with Mathieu Schneider), and can continue to contribute as a two-way defenseman, but his even-strength points should continue to decline.

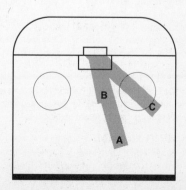

FELIX POTVIN

Yrs. of NHL service: 4
Born: Anjou, Que.; June 23, 1971
Position: goaltender
Height: 6-1
Weight: 183
Uniform no.: 29
Catches: left

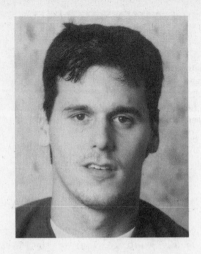

Career statistics:
GP	MIN	GA	SO	GAA	A	PIM
223	13027	607	7	2.80	5	16

1992-93 statistics:
GP	MIN	GAA	W	L	T	SO	GA	S	SAPCT	PIM
48	2781	2.50	25	25	7	2	116	1286	.910	4

1993-94 statistics:
GP	MIN	GAA	W	L	T	SO	GA	S	SAPCT	PIM
66	3883	2.89	34	22	9	3	187	2010	.907	4

1994-95 statistics:
GP	MIN	GAA	W	L	T	SO	GA	S	SAPCT	PIM
36	2144	2.91	15	13	7	0	104	1120	.907	4

1995-96 statistics:
GP	MIN	GAA	W	L	T	SO	GA	S	SAPCT	PIM
69	4009	2.87	30	26	11	2	192	2135	.910	4

LAST SEASON

Goals-against average has been below 3.00 in each of his four NHL seasons. Posted 100th career win.

THE PHYSICAL GAME

Potvin is a goalie whose technique is flawed, but whenever the coaches try to improve it, Potvin struggles. He plays very deep in his net. His skates are in the paint at all times. But when his goalie coach, Rick Wamsley, tried to teach him to come out of his net more, Potvin lost track of his angle.

So Potvin has to be Potvin, and that means he has to rely on his reflexes night after night. That means there will be some exceptional games, some average games and some truly awful nights.

Potvin is excellent on low shots. His style is similar to his idol, Patrick Roy's, in that Potvin likes to butterfly and flirt with leaving a five-hole for shooters. The best place to beat Potvin is high, but shooters see that tempting gap and go for it, and Potvin snaps the pads shut.

Potvin allows very few bad rebounds. He either controls them into the corners or deadens them in front of him. He isn't shy about hanging on for a face-off because the Maple Leafs have a good corps of centres.

Potvin is still weak with his stick. He doesn't use it well around the net to break up passes and hates to come out of his net to try to move the puck.

THE MENTAL GAME

While Potvin's game is up and down, he has matured over the past few seasons and keeps himself on a fairly even keel. His teammates have faith in him.

THE INTANGIBLES

Potvin was a Group 2 free agent at the end of last season, and his contract haggle, if prolonged, could affect the start of his season (as it did Martin Brodeur, who like Potvin is a client of agent Gilles Lupien). Potvin needs to prove he can win the big ones, but he is still fairly young and he hasn't played behind very powerful teams in his Toronto tenure.

MATHIEU SCHNEIDER

Yrs. of NHL service: 7
Born: New York, N.Y.; June 12, 1969
Position: left defense
Height: 5-11
Weight: 189
Uniform no.: 72
Shoots: left

Career statistics:

GP	G	A	TP	PIM
454	79	183	262	447

1992-93 statistics:

GP	G	A	TP	+/-	PIM	PP	SH	GW	GT	S	PCT
60	13	31	44	+8	91	3	0	2	0	169	7.7

1993-94 statistics:

GP	G	A	TP	+/-	PIM	PP	SH	GW	GT	S	PCT
75	20	32	52	+15	62	11	0	4	0	193	10.4

1994-95 statistics:

GP	G	A	TP	+/-	PIM	PP	SH	GW	GT	S	PCT
43	8	21	29	-8	79	3	0	2	0	118	6.8

1995-96 statistics:

GP	G	A	TP	+/-	PIM	PP	SH	GW	GT	S	PCT
78	13	41	54	-20	103	7	0	1	0	191	6.8

LAST SEASON

Acquired from N.Y. Islanders with Wendel Clark and D.J. Smith for Kenny Jonsson, Darby Hendrickson, Sean Haggerty and a first-round draft pick, Mar. 13, 1996. Second among Leafs defensemen in scoring. Third on team in assists.

THE FINESSE GAME

Schneider has developed into a good two-way defenseman. He has the offensive skills to get involved in the attack and work the point on the power play; his major concern is his solid positional play. He makes fewer high-risk plays as he has gained more experience.

A talented skater, strong, balanced and agile, he lacks breakaway speed but is quick with his first step and changes directions smoothly. He can carry the puck but does not lead many rushes. He gets the puck out of the corner quickly. Schneider makes good defensive decisions.

Schneider has improved his point play, doing more with the puck than just drilling shots. He handles the puck well and looks for the passes down low. Given the green light, he is likely to get involved down low more often. He has the skating ability to recover quickly when he takes a chance.

THE PHYSICAL GAME

Schneider plays with determination, but he lacks the size and strength to be an impact defenseman physically. His goal is to play a containment game and move the puck quickly and intelligently out of the zone, which he does well. He is matched against other teams' top scoring lines and always tries to do the job.

He is best when paired with a physical defenseman. Schneider has a tendency to hit high and gets penalties because of it.

THE INTANGIBLES

Schneider was happy to get back into a hockey city with his trade to Toronto. He will be one of the Maple Leafs' top two defensemen and will get a lot of ice time. Schneider scored seven points in 13 games after the trade, but didn't have a great playoffs (four assists). His production should be in the 45-50 points range.

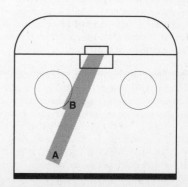

MATS SUNDIN

Yrs. of NHL service: 6
Born: Bromma, Sweden; Feb. 13, 1971
Position: right wing/centre
Height: 6-4
Weight: 215
Uniform no.: 13
Shoots: right

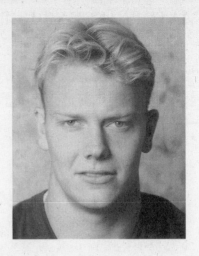

Career statistics:

GP	G	A	TP	PIM
447	191	273	464	379

1992-93 statistics:

GP	G	A	TP	+/-	PIM	PP	SH	GW	GT	S	PCT
80	47	67	114	+21	96	13	4	9	1	215	21.9

1993-94 statistics:

GP	G	A	TP	+/-	PIM	PP	SH	GW	GT	S	PCT
84	32	53	85	+1	60	6	2	4	0	226	14.2

1994-95 statistics:

GP	G	A	TP	+/-	PIM	PP	SH	GW	GT	S	PCT
47	23	24	47	-5	14	9	0	4	1	173	13.3

1995-96 statistics:

GP	G	A	TP	+/-	PIM	PP	SH	GW	GT	S	PCT
76	33	50	83	+8	46	7	6	7	1	301	11.0

LAST SEASON

Led team in points and game-winning goals for second consecutive season. Led team in assists, plus-minus, shorthanded goals and shots. Third on team in goals. Missed four games with knee injury. Missed one game with tonsillitis.

THE FINESSE GAME

Sundin is a big skater who looks huge as he uses an ultralong stick that gives him a broad wingspan. For a big man, he is an agile skater, and his balance has improved. He has good lower body strength, supplying drive for battles along the boards. He doesn't stay checked. He is evasive, and once he is on the fly he is hard to stop. Sundin is less effective when carrying the puck. His best play is to get up a head of steam, jump into the holes and take a quick shot. He also likes to use his reach, curling around behind the net for a stuff-in goal.

Sundin can take bad passes in stride, either kicking an errant puck up onto his stick or reaching behind to corral it. He has played centre and wing, but makes a much better winger. He isn't a clever stickhandler. Sundin's game is power and speed.

In open ice, Sundin doesn't look fast, but he has ground-eating strides that allow him to cover in two strides what other skaters do in three or four. He is quick, too, and can get untracked in a heartbeat.

His shot is excellent. He can use a slap shot, one-timer, wrister, or backhand. The only liability to his reach is that he will dangle the puck well away from his body and he doesn't always control it, which makes him vulnerable to a poke-check.

THE PHYSICAL GAME

Sundin is big and strong. He has shown better attention to off-ice work to improve his strength. His conditioning is excellent — he can skate all night. He has even shown a touch of mean, but mostly with his stick, not his fists.

THE INTANGIBLES

The Maple Leafs are indecisive about whether Sundin should be a centre or a wing. With the arrival of Kirk Muller, Sundin played mostly alongside Doug Gilmour on the right wing, and that is where he should stick. Is a 100-point season in Sundin's future? Like everyone else in Toronto, we're starting to doubt it.

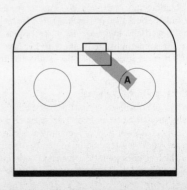

TODD WARRINER

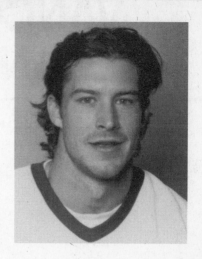

Yrs. of NHL service: 1
Born: Blenheim, Ont.; Jan. 3, 1974
Position: left wing
Height: 6-1
Weight: 188
Uniform no.: 8
Shoots: left

Career statistics:

GP	G	A	TP	PIM
62	7	8	15	0

1994-95 statistics:

GP	G	A	TP	+/-	PIM	PP	SH	GW	GT	S	PCT
5	0	0	0	-3	0	0	0	0	0	1	0.0

1995-96 statistics:

GP	G	A	TP	+/-	PIM	PP	SH	GW	GT	S	PCT
57	7	8	15	-11	26	1	0	0	0	79	8.9

LAST SEASON

First NHL season. Played 11 games with St. John's (AHL), scoring 5-6 — 11.

THE FINESSE GAME

Warriner's best asset is his shot. He releases it quickly from the circles, and while he doesn't have blinding speed he is slick enough to jump into holes, accept a pass, and throw it quickly on net. Warriner knows the element of surprise is more important than winding up for a blast. On the flip side, however, he has to learn to take his time with his shot when he does have the room. He has a tendency to panic and get rid of the puck when there might be a better play.

Teaming with Kirk Muller after the centre's acquisition seemed to help Warriner, because Muller is a very unselfish player. Warriner could also take a cue from Muller's work ethic. Warriner has relied on his natural ability through most levels of the sport, but will need to push himself to succeed at the NHL level.

Warriner's defensive game needs to improve, but he is a clever player who should be able to grasp the intricacies of a well-rounded game.

THE PHYSICAL GAME

Warriner is a little on the light side and will need to add some muscle, since he lacks the top-shelf finesse skills to play a perimeter game.

THE INTANGIBLES

The crumbling Leafs will have to give some of their younger players a chance at playing larger roles this season, and Warriner — while not a scintillating prospect — certainly has paid his dues and will be given his shot, probably on the second line. The rest is up to him.

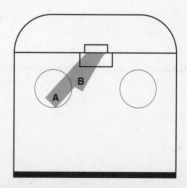

VANCOUVER CANUCKS

Players' Statistics 1995-96

POS	NO.	PLAYER	GP	G	A	PTS	+/-	PIM	PP	SH	GW	GT	S	PCT
R	89	ALEXANDER MOGILNY	79	55	52	107	14	16	10	5	6	3	292	18.8
R	16	TREVOR LINDEN	82	33	47	80	6	42	12	1	2		202	16.3
C	7	CLIFF RONNING	79	22	45	67	16	42	5		1	1	187	11.8
R	9	RUSS COURTNALL	81	26	39	65	25	40	6	4	4	2	205	12.7
L	23	MARTIN GELINAS	81	30	26	56	8	59	3	4	5	1	181	16.6
R	22	MARKUS NASLUND	76	22	33	55	20	42	4		5		144	15.3
D	21	JYRKI LUMME	80	17	37	54	-9	50	8		2	2	192	8.9
L	10	ESA TIKKANEN	58	14	30	44	1	36	8	1	2		95	14.7
C	14	JESSE BELANGER	72	20	21	41	-5	14	8		2		151	13.2
R	26	MIKE SILLINGER	74	14	24	38	-18	38	7	1	2		159	8.8
D	3	BRET HEDICAN	77	6	23	29	8	83	1				113	5.3
D	44	DAVE BABYCH	53	3	21	24	-5	38	3				69	4.3
D	27	LEIF ROHLIN	56	6	16	22	0	32	1				72	8.3
C	17	MIKE RIDLEY	37	6	15	21	-3	29	2		1		32	18.8
C	42	JOSEF BERANEK	61	6	14	20	-11	60			1		131	4.6
C	15	JIM DOWD	66	5	15	20	-9	23					76	6.6
D	6	*ADRIAN AUCOIN	49	4	14	18	8	34	2				85	4.7
L	96	PAVEL BURE	15	6	7	13	-2	8	1	1			78	7.7
D	24	*SCOTT WALKER	63	4	8	12	-7	137			1	1	45	8.9
D	5	DANA MURZYN	69	2	10	12	9	130					68	2.9
D	2	FRANTISEK KUCERA	54	3	6	9	2	20			1		77	3.9
L	29	GINO ODJICK	55	3	4	7	-16	181					59	5.1
R	25	JIM SANDLAK	33	4	2	6	-3	6		1	1		44	9.1
R	36	*BRIAN LONEY	12	2	3	5	2	6				1	19	10.5
R	28	JOEY KOCUR	45	1	3	4	-7	68					20	5.0
R	19	TIM HUNTER	60	2		2	-8	122			1		26	7.7
D	34	JASSEN CULLIMORE	27	1	1	2	4	21			1		12	8.3
D	32	*DEAN MALKOC	41		2	2	-10	136					8	
G	31	*COREY HIRSCH	41		2	2	0	2						
G	1	KIRK MCLEAN	45		2	2	0	6						
L	14	*LARRY COURVILLE	3	1		1	1				1		2	50.0
R	14	*LONNY BOHONOS	3		1	1	1						3	

GP = games played; G = goals; A = assists; PTS = points; +/- = goals-for minus goals-against while player is on ice; PIM = penalties in minutes; PP = power play goals; SH = shorthanded goals; GW = game-winning goals; GT = game-tying goals; S = no. of shots; PCT = percentage of goals to shots; * = rookie

ADRIAN AUCOIN

Yrs. of NHL service: 1
Born: Ottawa, Ont.; July 3, 1973
Position: right defenseman
Height: 6-2
Weight: 210
Uniform no.: 6
Shoots: right

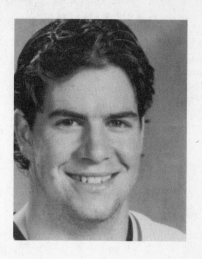

Career statistics:

GP	G	A	TP	PIM
50	5	14	19	34

1994-95 statistics:

GP	G	A	TP	+/-	PIM	PP	SH	GW	GT	S	PCT
1	1	0	1	+1	0	0	0	0	0	2	50.0

1995-96 statistics:

GP	G	A	TP	+/-	PIM	PP	SH	GW	GT	S	PCT
49	4	14	18	+8	34	2	0	0	0	85	4.7

LAST SEASON

First NHL season. Tied for fourth among rookie defensemen in scoring. Played 29 games with Syracuse (AHL), scoring 5-13 — 18.

THE FINESSE GAME

Aucoin was a low draft pick (117th overall in 1992), but by playing with the Canadian national team and in the 1994 Olympics, he has upgraded his offensive skills and developed into a promising offensive defenseman.

Aucoin is a mobile, agile skater who moves well with the puck. He doesn't have breakaway speed, but he jumps alertly into the play. On the power play, he smartly switches off with a forward to cut in deep, and he has good hands for shots in tight. He also has a good point shot, though it is not elite.

Aucoin's overall game still needs work. He was a fourth or fifth defenseman last season.

THE PHYSICAL GAME

Aucoin is a good-sized defenseman who often plays smaller. He needs to be more assertive around the net to earn himself more ice time. Aucoin has no mean streak to speak of, and opponents know he can be pushed around.

THE INTANGIBLES

It would have been nice for Aucoin if he had been able to gradually work his way up to a responsible role as one of the top two point men on Vancouver's power play. Instead, after Jeff Brown's rancorous departure, Aucoin was all but crowned the new king of the power play, and he wasn't quite ready for the throne.

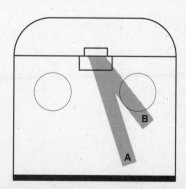

PAVEL BURE

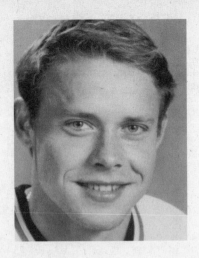

Yrs. of NHL service: 5
Born: Moscow, Russia; Mar. 31, 1971
Position: right wing
Height: 5-10
Weight: 187
Uniform no.: 96
Shoots: left

Career statistics:

GP	G	A	TP	PIM
283	180	153	333	240

1992-93 statistics:

GP	G	A	TP	+/-	PIM	PP	SH	GW	GT	S	PCT
83	60	50	110	+35	69	13	7	9	0	407	14.7

1993-94 statistics:

GP	G	A	TP	+/-	PIM	PP	SH	GW	GT	S	PCT
76	60	47	107	+1	86	25	4	9	0	374	16.0

1994-95 statistics:

GP	G	A	TP	+/-	PIM	PP	SH	GW	GT	S	PCT
44	20	23	43	-8	47	6	2	2	0	198	10.1

1995-96 statistics:

GP	G	A	TP	+/-	PIM	PP	SH	GW	GT	S	PCT
15	6	7	13	-2	8	1	1	0	0	78	7.7

LAST SEASON

Missed 67 games with reconstructive knee surgery.

THE FINESSE GAME

Bure was injured just 15 games into the season, and since the surgery will impact on his greatest skill, his skating, the Canucks will be holding their collective breath to see if he has lost an iota of his old speed.

Every time Bure touches the puck, fans in his home rink move to the edge of their seats. The Russian Rocket's quickness — and his control of the puck at supersonic speed — means anything is possible. He intimidates with his skating, driving back defenders who must play off him or risk being deked out of their skates at the blueline. He opens up tremendous ice for his teammates and will leave a drop pass or, more often, try to do it himself.

Bure's major weakness is his failure to use his teammates better. He will attempt to go through a team one-on-five rather than use his support. Of course, once in a while he can actually do it. That's the scary part. He has great balance and agility and he seems to move equally well with the puck or without it. The puck doesn't slow him down a fraction.

Bure doesn't do much defensively. He prefers to hang out at centre ice, and when he is going through a slump he doesn't do the other little things that can make a player useful until the scoring starts to click again. He is a shorthanded threat because of his breakaway speed and anticipation.

His explosive skating comes from his thick, powerful thighs, which look like a speed skater's.

THE PHYSICAL GAME

During his rehab, Bure bulked up his upper body, which should enhance the physical aspect of his play. Bure has a little nasty edge to him, and will make solid hits for the puck, although he doesn't apply himself as enthusiastically in a defensive role.

THE INTANGIBLES

The arrival of Mogilny and the reunion of the two former Soviet national junior linemates was highly anticipated, but the magic was missing in the brief weeks that the two old pals got to play together. Odds are the Canucks will play them on two lines, except on the power play.

Bure was skating at the end of last season and is expected to play in the World Cup. He is a fitness devotee, and should be in excellent condition to start the season.

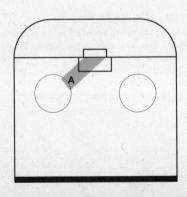

RUSS COURTNALL

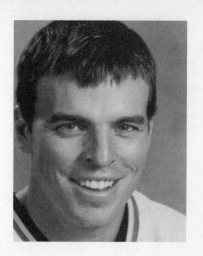

Yrs. of NHL service: 12
Born: Duncan, B.C.; June 2, 1965
Position: right wing
Height: 5-11
Weight: 183
Uniform no.: 9
Shoots: right

Career statistics:

GP	G	A	TP	PIM
853	268	404	672	485

1992-93 statistics:

GP	G	A	TP	+/-	PIM	PP	SH	GW	GT	S	PCT
84	36	43	79	+1	49	14	2	3	2	294	12.2

1993-94 statistics:

GP	G	A	TP	+/-	PIM	PP	SH	GW	GT	S	PCT
84	23	57	80	+6	59	5	0	4	0	231	10.0

1994-95 statistics:

GP	G	A	TP	+/-	PIM	PP	SH	GW	GT	S	PCT
45	11	24	35	+2	17	2	2	2	0	132	8.3

1995-96 statistics:

GP	G	A	TP	+/-	PIM	PP	SH	GW	GT	S	PCT
81	26	39	65	+25	40	6	4	4	2	205	12.7

LAST SEASON

Led team in plus-minus. Tied for second on team in shorthanded goals. Third on team in game-winning goals.

THE FINESSE GAME

Courtnall has jackrabbit speed. He goes straight down the runway, creating fear in the opposition and opening up a lot of room for his teammates. He pushes people back with sheer velocity.

He uses his speed intelligently and puts a lot of pucks in the net or works the give-and-go. He often follows a great play with a good one, and can slip a puck into a tiny hole off the rush. Once a fairly selfish player, he now uses his teammates well. He needs to play on a line with slick skaters, or else he tends to get too far ahead of the play.

Defensively aware, Courtnall uses his speed well defensively and is a shorthanded threat.

THE PHYSICAL GAME

Courtnall is scrappy for his size, although he played more uninterested games than usual last season. While he tends to stick to the open ice where he can flash and dash, he will make a hit to drive to the net. For the most part, though, he avoids scrums and corner work.

THE INTANGIBLES

Courtnall had an off-season last year (as nearly everyone on the team did), and played all three forward positions on different lines without finding a comfortable spot. He was benched in November by ex-coach Rick Ley and never got untracked. He may be on the trade block as the Canucks look to dump salaries.

MARTIN GELINAS

Yrs. of NHL service: 7
Born: Shawinigan, Que.; June 5, 1970
Position: left wing
Height: 5-11
Weight: 195
Uniform no.: 23
Shoots: left

Career statistics:

GP	G	A	TP	PIM
449	117	110	227	285

1992-93 statistics:

GP	G	A	TP	+/-	PIM	PP	SH	GW	GT	S	PCT
65	11	12	23	+3	30	0	0	1	0	93	11.8

1993-94 statistics:

GP	G	A	TP	+/-	PIM	PP	SH	GW	GT	S	PCT
64	14	14	28	-8	34	3	0	1	2	107	13.1

1994-95 statistics:

GP	G	A	TP	+/-	PIM	PP	SH	GW	GT	S	PCT
46	13	10	23	+8	36	1	0	4	0	75	17.3

1995-96 statistics:

GP	G	A	TP	+/-	PIM	PP	SH	GW	GT	S	PCT
81	30	26	56	+8	59	3	4	5	1	181	16.6

LAST SEASON

Third on team in goals with career high. Tied for second on team in game-winning goals and shorthanded goals. Fifth on team in points with career high. Second on team in shooting percentage. Career high in assists.

THE FINESSE GAME

At age 25, Gelinas finally put his game together last season. He has fine finesse skills and broke into the league as a one-way player, but gradually added a defensive aspect to his game. As he did, he seemed to lose his scoring touch. He has achieved equilibrium.

Gelinas is very quick; handling the puck doesn't slow him down. He's creative, and he likes to use all of the ice so he can play with forwards who like a more European style. But Gelinas can also play a grinding game on the dump-and-chase. Much of his scoring is generated by his forechecking. He is strong along the boards and in front of the net. He is not a natural scorer, but he has good instincts and works hard for his chances. He is a good penalty killer.

THE PHYSICAL GAME

Gelinas is a small player and seems to get himself into situations where he just gets flattened. He isn't intimidated, but he does get wiped out of the play and he has to be smarter about jumping in and out of holes, paying the price only when necessary.

THE INTANGIBLES

Gelinas was on hockey's scrap heap when Quebec put him on waivers two seasons ago; he was just 23 and had a Stanley Cup ring (from Edmonton). We said last season that Gelinas had the skills, but not the consistency for a 25-goal season, but he summoned up the work ethic to move up to the role of number one left wing (in the absence of Pavel Bure, who would have played right wing with Alexander Mogilny on the right). If he maintains his consistency, he could net another 25-30. Gelinas has to prove himself to a new coach in Vancouver, but he's used to that by now.

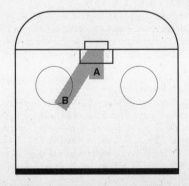

BRET HEDICAN

Yrs. of NHL service: 4
Born: St. Paul, Minn.; Aug. 10, 1970
Position: left defense
Height: 6-2
Weight: 195
Uniform no.: 3
Shoots: left

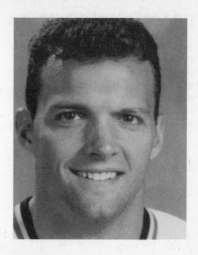

Career statistics:

GP	G	A	TP	PIM
237	9	54	63	190

1992-93 statistics:

GP	G	A	TP	+/-	PIM	PP	SH	GW	GT	S	PCT
42	0	8	8	-2	30	0	0	0	0	40	0.0

1993-94 statistics:

GP	G	A	TP	+/-	PIM	PP	SH	GW	GT	S	PCT
69	0	12	12	-7	64	0	0	0	0	88	0.0

1994-95 statistics:

GP	G	A	TP	+/-	PIM	PP	SH	GW	GT	S	PCT
45	2	11	13	-3	34	0	0	0	0	56	3.6

1995-96 statistics:

GP	G	A	TP	+/-	PIM	PP	SH	GW	GT	S	PCT
77	6	23	29	+8	83	1	0	0	0	113	5.3

LAST SEASON

Second among team defensemen in scoring. Career high in points. Missed three games with back injury. Missed two games with charley horse.

THE FINESSE GAME

Hedican is a confident puck carrier. He happily uses his speed with the puck to drive down the wing and create trouble in the offensive zone. He also varies the attack. He seems to prefer the left wing boards but will also take the right wing route to try to make plays off the backhand. Teammate Alexander Mogilny "doctored" some of Hedican's sticks during the season, and that boosted his scoring touch.

Hedican is a good enough stickhandler to try one-on-one moves. He is eager to jump into the play and shows signs of becoming an "offenseman," a defender who is down the attacking boards and into the corners as much as he is at the blueline, although he does not have elite ability.

Skating is his key asset. He has a nice, deep knee bend and his fluid stride provides good acceleration; each stride eats up lots of ice. His steady balance allows him to go down to one knee and use his stick to challenge passes from the corners. He uses quickness, range and reach to make a confident stand at the defensive blueline.

Hedican knows that if an attacker beats him, he will be able to keep up with him and steer him to bad ice. He is the perfect guy to pick up the puck behind the net and get it to the redline and start the half-court game. He doesn't always just put his head down and go. He will move up the middle and look for a pass to a breaking wing.

THE PHYSICAL GAME

Hedican has decent size but not a great deal of strength or toughness. He won't bulldoze people in front of the net, preferring to tie people up and go for the puck. He is more of a stick checker than a body checker, but will sometimes body a player off the puck at the blueline, control it and make a smart first pass. His preference is to use body positioning to nullify an opponent rather than initiate hard body contact.

THE INTANGIBLES

Hedican's numbers are improving gradually from season to season, but we doubt he'll ever surpass the 50-point mark. He is developing into a solid two-way defenseman and can be expected to improve sharply over the next few seasons as he gains confidence and experience. He won't lead the team in scoring, but don't be surprised if he's first or second among team defensemen.

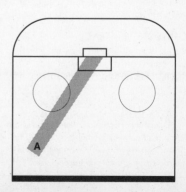

FRANTISEK KUCERA

Yrs. of NHL service: 6
Born: Prague, Czechoslovakia; Feb. 3, 1968
Position: left defense
Height: 6-2
Weight: 205
Uniform no.: 2
Shoots: left

Career statistics:

GP	G	A	TP	PIM
350	21	75	96	225

1992-93 statistics:

GP	G	A	TP	+/-	PIM	PP	SH	GW	GT	S	PCT
71	5	14	19	+7	59	1	0	1	0	117	4.3

1993-94 statistics:

GP	G	A	TP	+/-	PIM	PP	SH	GW	GT	S	PCT
76	5	16	21	-3	48	3	0	0	0	122	4.1

1994-95 statistics:

GP	G	A	TP	+/-	PIM	PP	SH	GW	GT	S	PCT
48	3	17	20	+3	30	0	0	1	0	73	4.1

1995-96 statistics:

GP	G	A	TP	+/-	PIM	PP	SH	GW	GT	S	PCT
54	3	6	9	+2	20	0	0	1	0	77	3.9

LAST SEASON

Acquired from Hartford with Jim Dowd and a second-round draft pick for Jeff Brown and a third-round draft pick. Missed 19 games with shoulder injury.

THE FINESSE GAME

Kucera is a reliable defenseman as long as he isn't asked to do too much. He is fine in the role of a fourth or fifth defenseman who gives a team some depth. Kucera tends to wear down if he gets much more than 18 minutes of ice time a night.

Kucera is a strong and mobile skater who is hard to beat one-on-one in open ice. He reads plays well defensively and can also make a neat outlet pass and get involved in the attack as he moves up. He sometimes overhandles the puck at the offensive blueline because he doesn't like to just dump the puck in and will try to make a play.

Kucera's skills are adequate to play on a second power play unit. His shoulder separation last season affected his play.

THE PHYSICAL GAME

Kucera plays much smaller than his generous size, and as a result is often viewed as an underachiever by his coaches. He loses many one-on-one battles in tight.

THE INTANGIBLES

Unless he suddenly becomes stronger and commits to playing a more physical game, Kucera will be on the bubble in Vancouver, which hopes to work some younger defensemen into the lineup.

TREVOR LINDEN

Yrs. of NHL service: 8
Born: Medicine Hat, Alta.; Apr. 11, 1970
Position: centre/right wing
Height: 6-4
Weight: 210
Uniform no.: 16
Shoots: right

Career statistics:

GP	G	A	TP	PIM
611	231	276	507	493

1992-93 statistics:

GP	G	A	TP	+/-	PIM	PP	SH	GW	GT	S	PCT
84	33	39	72	+19	64	8	0	3	0	209	15.8

1993-94 statistics:

GP	G	A	TP	+/-	PIM	PP	SH	GW	GT	S	PCT
84	32	29	61	+6	73	10	2	3	0	234	13.7

1994-95 statistics:

GP	G	A	TP	+/-	PIM	PP	SH	GW	GT	S	PCT
48	18	22	40	-5	40	9	0	1	3	129	14.0

1995-96 statistics:

GP	G	A	TP	+/-	PIM	PP	SH	GW	GT	S	PCT
82	33	47	80	+6	42	12	1	2	0	202	16.3

LAST SEASON

Longest active consecutive games-played streak at 454. Only Canuck to appear in all 82 games. Led team in power play goals for second consecutive year. Second on team in goals, assists and points. Career high in points. Matched career high in goals.

THE FINESSE GAME

Linden would be much more effective as a winger than a centre, but the Canucks are very weak up the middle and need a centre with good size to match up against many of the NHL's power centres, so he is pretty much stuck. Not a graceful skater, at times Linden looks very awkward, and he's not as strong on his skates as a player of his size should be. Despite his heavy feet his agility is satisfactory, but he lacks first-step quickness and doesn't have the all-out speed to pull away from a checker. He has a big turning radius.

Linden has improved his release, but it is not quick. He has a long reach, but unlike, say, Dave Andreychuk (who is built along similar lines), his short game is not as effective as it should be.

Linden is unselfish and makes quick, safe passing decisions that help his team break smartly up the ice, often creating odd-man rushes. He has improved tremendously in his defensive coverage.

THE PHYSICAL GAME

Linden is big but doesn't always play tough, and so doesn't make good use of his size. He will attack the blueline and draw the attention of both defensemen, but will pull up rather than try to muscle through and earn a holding penalty. There are people he should nullify who still seem able to get away from him. He does not skate through the physical challenges along the boards.

If only he would keep his feet moving, Linden would be so much more commanding. Instead, he can be angled off the play fairly easily because he will not battle for better ice. He uses his body more to defend than to help create offense. He will use his range to cut down the ice on a player, then merely stick out his stick to slow him down, rather than throw a shoulder into him.

When Linden is throwing his weight around, he drives to the net and drags a defender or two with him, opening up a lot of ice for his teammates. He creates havoc in front of the net on the power play, planting himself for screens and deflections. When the puck is at the side boards, he's smart enough to move up higher, between the circles, and force the penalty killers to make a decision. If the defenseman on that side steps up to cover him, space will open behind the defenseman; if a forward collapses to cover him, a point shot will open up.

THE INTANGIBLES

Linden is very likable and is a team leader. He received a fat contract as a result of his Group 2 free agent status, but didn't slack off. He faces other team's top checking attention night after night. Linden won't be a 100-point scorer. His 80 points last season is about his top end. He had a good playoffs, but wasn't strong enough to drag everyone else with him.

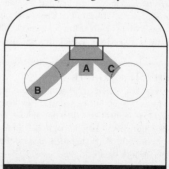

JYRKI LUMME

Yrs. of NHL service: 8
Born: Tampere, Finland; July 16, 1966
Position: right defense
Height: 6-1
Weight: 205
Uniform no.: 21
Shoots: left

Career statistics:

GP	G	A	TP	PIM
514	65	215	280	364

1992-93 statistics:

GP	G	A	TP	+/-	PIM	PP	SH	GW	GT	S	PCT
74	8	36	44	+30	55	3	2	1	0	123	6.5

1993-94 statistics:

GP	G	A	TP	+/-	PIM	PP	SH	GW	GT	S	PCT
83	13	42	55	+3	50	1	3	3	0	161	8.1

1994-95 statistics:

GP	G	A	TP	+/-	PIM	PP	SH	GW	GT	S	PCT
36	5	12	17	+4	26	3	0	1	0	78	6.4

1995-96 statistics:

GP	G	A	TP	+/-	PIM	PP	SH	GW	GT	S	PCT
80	17	37	54	-9	50	8	0	2	2	192	8.9

LAST SEASON

Led team defensemen in scoring. Tied for third on team in power play goals. Missed two games with flu.

THE FINESSE GAME

Lumme is one of the Canucks' more mobile defenseman, an accomplished puck carrier who can rush the puck out of danger and make a smart first pass to start the attack. He likes to gamble a bit offensively, but he has the good skating ability to be able to wheel back into a defensive mode. He became a lower-risk defenseman last season.

He plays the right point on the power play. His shot isn't overpowering, but he keeps it low and on net and times it well. He has very good hands and is adept at keeping the puck in. He also uses his lateral mobility to slide along the blueline into the centre to quarterback the power play. Lumme will also glide to the top of the circle for a shot.

Defensively, he uses his hand skills for sweep- and poke-checks. He will challenge at the blueline to try to knock the puck free, but he doesn't always follow through with his body if the poke-check fails.

Lumme is a strong penalty killer because of his range and anticipation.

THE PHYSICAL GAME

Lumme is all finesse. He will take a hit to protect the puck or make a play, but he won't throw himself at anybody. Other teams like to key on Lumme, because if he gets hit often and hard enough, he can be taken out of a game early, depriving the Canucks of a valuable component of their offense.

THE INTANGIBLES

The trade of Jeff Brown placed more offensive responsibility on Lumme. He is not a number one defenseman because his all-around skills aren't good enough, but he's just a cut below the NHL's best rearguards. Lumme has improved defensively, but his key value remains his open-ice play and his involvement in the attack.

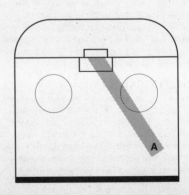

KIRK MCLEAN

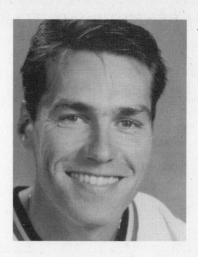

Yrs. of NHL service: 9
Born: Willowdale, Ont.; June 26, 1966
Position: goaltender
Height: 6-0
Weight: 195
Uniform no.: 1
Catches: left

Career statistics:

GP	MIN	GA	SO	GAA	A	PIM
449	26096	1423	19	3.27	18	52

1992-93 statistics:

GP	MIN	GAA	W	L	T	SO	GA	S	SAPCT	PIM
54	3261	3.39	28	21	5	3	184	1615	.886	16

1993-94 statistics:

GP	MIN	GAA	W	L	T	SO	GA	S	SAPCT	PIM
52	3128	2.99	23	26	3	3	156	1430	.891	2

1994-95 statistics:

GP	MIN	GAA	W	L	T	SO	GA	S	SAPCT	PIM
40	2374	2.75	18	12	10	1	109	1140	.904	4

1995-96 statistics:

GP	MIN	GAA	W	L	T	SO	GA	S	SAPCT	PIM
45	2645	3.54	15	21	9	2	156	1292	.879	6

LAST SEASON

Missed 18 games with knee injury.

THE PHYSICAL GAME

McLean endured his worst season since 1990-91. His knee injury was a contributing factor, as was the play of rookie Corey Hirsch during McLean's absence.

McLean stays on his feet more than any goalie in the NHL. He has great lateral movement. Maybe because of his soccer training, his movement and balance are advanced. He is smooth, almost casual, in his post-to-post moves.

McLean makes himself look big in the net because of his positioning and stand-up play. He is very solid technically and has good reflexes. His solid foundation means few bad stretches of play. He will blow the occasional angle, especially on the stick side, but he has a great deal of confidence in his game and does not rattle easily. His bad streaks are usually caused by playing too deep in the net and being passive.

He's good up high, with a quick glove hand. He is strong on his stick and uses it well around the net for jabbing at puckhandlers or breaking up passes. He makes shooters try to be too perfect. McLean does not waste any motion, which makes him seem downright lethargic at times, but the lack of dramatics should not detract from appreciation of his overall technical skill. There's nothing objectionable about making the job easier, the job is tough enough without adding unnecessary flourishes. He does not showboat.

McLean handles the puck well, again, without much excitement, but enough to help out his team defensively. He is smart with the puck on his forehand and backhand, and recognizes when to move it and when to leave it for his defense.

THE MENTAL GAME

The key to McLean is to fluster him early. He is a big goalie, who usually needs to handle some shots to get into the flow of the game, and he tends to get better as the game moves along.

THE INTANGIBLES

McLean is going into the third year of a U.S.$12.5-million contract, which will give the Canucks trouble in moving him if they want to give the number one job to Hirsch. Hirsch supplanted McLean in the Vancouver net for the playoffs, but McLean is mentally tough and will battle in training camp to regain his spot.

ALEXANDER MOGILNY

Yrs. of NHL service: 7
Born: Khabarovsk, Russia; Feb. 18, 1969
Position: right wing
Height: 5-11
Weight: 190
Uniform no.: 89
Shoots: left

Career statistics:

GP	G	A	TP	PIM
460	266	285	551	219

1992-93 statistics:

GP	G	A	TP	+/-	PIM	PP	SH	GW	GT	S	PCT
77	76	51	127	+7	40	27	0	11	0	360	21.1

1993-94 statistics:

GP	G	A	TP	+/-	PIM	PP	SH	GW	GT	S	PCT
66	32	47	79	+8	22	17	0	7	1	258	12.4

1994-95 statistics:

GP	G	A	TP	+/-	PIM	PP	SH	GW	GT	S	PCT
44	19	28	47	0	36	12	0	2	1	148	12.8

1995-96 statistics:

GP	G	A	TP	+/-	PIM	PP	SH	GW	GT	S	PCT
79	55	52	107	+14	16	10	5	6	3	292	18.8

LAST SEASON

Led team in points for fourth consecutive season. Led team in goals, assists, game-winning goals, short-handed goals and shooting percentage. Second on team in power play goals. Second highest goal and point totals of career. Missed three games with hamstring injury.

THE FINESSE GAME

Skating is the basis of Mogilny's game. He has a burst of speed from a standstill. He hits his top speed in just a few strides. When he streaks down the ice, there is a good chance you'll see something new, something you didn't expect. He is unbelievably quick. Mogilny may hate to fly in a plane but he loves to fly over the ice.

His anticipation sets him apart from other players who are merely fast. He won't skate deeply into his own defensive zone, instead awaiting a turnover and a chance to get a jump on the defenseman, with a preferred move to the outside — but he is not afraid to go inside either, so a defenseman intent on angling him to the boards could just as easily get burned inside.

Mogilny can beat you in so many ways. He has a powerful and accurate wrist shot from the tops of the circles in. He shoots without breaking stride. He can work a give-and-go that is a thing of beauty. He one-times with the best of them. And everything is done at racehorse speed.

THE PHYSICAL GAME

The major knock on Mogilny is that, as good as he is, there always seems to be something left in the tank, that Mogilny doesn't push himself to the limit. He also suffers from a lack of consistency (he had a slump with only one goal in a 13-game stretch), and no one is ever sure which Mogilny is going to show up. There are nights when he is invisible on the ice, and that is unpardonable for a player of his ability and importance.

Mogilny intimidates with his speed but will also add a physical element. He has great upper body strength and will drive through a defender to the net.

THE INTANGIBLES

Mogilny didn't get to play with his old friend Pavel Bure after all, due to Bure's knee injury. Given the Canucks' lack of depth, the two might be split up when Bure does return this season, to divert checking attention. Mogilny should score 50 again, but with his skill level he should hit 60. There were rumours that the Canucks might look to trade Mogilny.

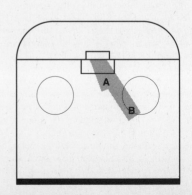

JOHN NAMESTNIKOV

Yrs. of NHL service: 1
Born: Novgorod, USSR; Oct. 9, 1971
Position: right defense
Height: 5-11
Weight: 190
Uniform no.: 2
Shoots: right

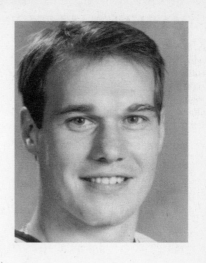

Career statistics:

GP	G	A	TP	PIM
33	0	8	8	14

1993-94 statistics:

GP	G	A	TP	+/-	PIM	PP	SH	GW	GT	S	PCT
17	0	5	5	-2	10	0	0	0	0	11	0.0

1994-95 statistics:

GP	G	A	TP	+/-	PIM	PP	SH	GW	GT	S	PCT
16	0	3	3	+2	4	0	0	0	0	18	0.0

1995-96 statistics:

P	G	A	TP	+/-	PIM	PP	SH	GW	GT	S	PC
Did not play in NHL											

LAST SEASON

Will be entering first full NHL season. Played with Syracuse (AHL) and led team defensemen in scoring.

THE FINESSE GAME

Namestnikov skates well and moves the puck well, but to survive in the NHL he had to add an offensive element or become a slightly larger version of Curt Giles. He was given prime ice time in the minors, and has become more involved in the attack. He has the hand skills to make nice passes out of his zone, but isn't overly creative. Namestnikov has an average NHL point shot.

He reads and reacts quickly to the rush, and can be paired with a more eager partner because he will make a smart pass out of the zone and then stay back to take care of business while his partner goes up-ice. He is a good penalty killer.

THE PHYSICAL GAME

Despite his small stature, Namestnikov is a willing and earnest open-ice hitter. His skating gives him the impetus to put more oomph in his checks. He has trouble with attackers down low, where he can be overpowered, but he is a human torpedo when he gets some room. He likes to step up, and while he's not a fighter, he is tough as nails. Namestnikov's face is always festooned with fresh cuts from crashing into people.

THE INTANGIBLES

Namestnikov has been on the verge of breaking into the Canucks lineup for the past two seasons. He will get another chance under a new head coach this season, probably as a fourth or fifth defenseman who will add some gritty play.

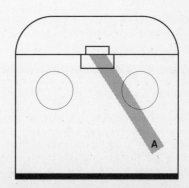

MARKUS NASLUND

Yrs. of NHL service: 3
Born: Bonassund, Sweden; July 30, 1973
Position: left/right wing
Height: 5-11
Weight: 195
Uniform no.: 22
Shoots: left

Career statistics:

GP	G	A	TP	PIM
161	28	42	70	71

1993-94 statistics:

GP	G	A	TP	+/-	PIM	PP	SH	GW	GT	S	PCT
71	4	7	11	-3	27	1	0	0	0	80	5.0

1994-95 statistics:

GP	G	A	TP	+/-	PIM	PP	SH	GW	GT	S	PCT
14	2	2	4	0	2	0	0	0	0	13	15.4

1995-96 statistics:

GP	G	A	TP	+/-	PIM	PP	SH	GW	GT	S	PCT
76	22	33	55	+20	42	4	0	5	0	144	15.3

LAST SEASON
Acquired from Pittsburgh for Alex Stojanov, Mar. 20, 1996.

THE FINESSE GAME
Naslund is a pure sniper. He has excellent snap and wrist shots, and can score in just about every way imaginable, including the backhand in tight. He has quick hands and an accurate touch.

Naslund needs to play with people who will get him the puck. He will not play aggressively and dig in the corners for the puck, and is a little shy in traffic. He is a fine skater who can keep up with the fastest linemates, and since Vancouver does have some team speed, he fit in well there in his brief stint. Naslund had three goals in 10 games with the Canucks, but all three came in one game.

Naslund has good hockey sense and has developed some defensive responsibilty, although he is primarily a one-way winger.

THE PHYSICAL GAME
Naslund is erratic in his physical play. Some nights he will play a little bigger, and make something of a pest out of himself, but other nights he will be invisible. He needs to be involved on a nightly basis.

THE INTANGIBLES
Naslund and Peter Forsberg were born 10 days apart, but they are a world apart in NHL accomplishment. Naslund, a former first-round draft pick (by Pittsburgh in 1991), has never lived up to the hype that surrounded his first few seasons in the NHL. He had trouble breaking into Pittsburgh's deep roster, but the Canucks must have seen something they liked, because they traded a physical player (Stojanov) for this unaggressive player at a time when they desperately needed some grit. Look for the Canucks to experiment with Naslund on a line with Pavel Bure during training camp.

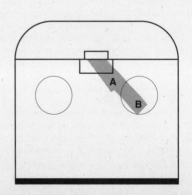

GINO ODJICK

Yrs. of NHL service: 6
Born: Maniwaki, Que.; Sept. 7, 1970
Position: left wing
Height: 6-3
Weight: 210
Uniform no.: 29
Shoots: left

Career statistics:

GP	G	A	TP	PIM
339	38	42	80	1575

1992-93 statistics:

GP	G	A	TP	+/-	PIM	PP	SH	GW	GT	S	PCT
75	4	13	17	+3	370	0	0	1	0	79	5.1

1993-94 statistics:

GP	G	A	TP	+/-	PIM	PP	SH	GW	GT	S	PCT
76	16	13	29	+13	271	4	0	5	0	121	13.2

1994-95 statistics:

GP	G	A	TP	+/-	PIM	PP	SH	GW	GT	S	PCT
23	4	5	9	-3	109	0	0	0	0	35	11.4

1995-96 statistics:

GP	G	A	TP	+/-	PIM	PP	SH	GW	GT	S	PCT
55	3	4	7	-16	181	0	0	0	0	59	5.1

with the fans in Vancouver, and the coaches can't help but love the effort he puts into his game and his career. If he continues to work at the little parts of his game, he will make a big impact for seasons to come. His skating remains a major flaw, and his recurring abdominal injury is also a concern.

LAST SEASON

Missed 24 games with torn abdominal muscle. Missed one game with knee injury. Led team in penalty minutes.

THE FINESSE GAME

Odjick is a goon who knows that goons are facing extinction in the NHL. To preserve his job, he has added important elements to become more than a one-dimensional player.

His abdominal injury, which has plagued him for the past two seasons, robbed him of most of the strength and toughness that are his hallmarks. He had improved his skating since dropping some weight, and conditioning must continue to be a priority.

Odjick's scoring chances come from in tight. He works tirelessly around the net for loose pucks, slamming and jamming. He could use a little more patience, since he gets a lot of room for his first move, but his theory seems to be that three whacks at the puck (which he can get easily) are worth one finesse move (which he might not be able to make anyway).

THE PHYSICAL GAME

Odjick takes cheap penalties. He aggravates, hits late and hits from behind, yet is a legitimate tough guy when the gloves come off. He protects his teammates. He is also strong enough to simply run over people en route to the net.

THE INTANGIBLES

Odjick scored three goals in the playoffs, which was more than more skilled players like Russ Courtnall or Martin Gelinas produced. Odjick is a huge favourite

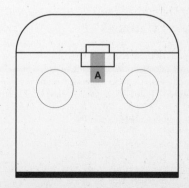

MATTIAS OHLUND

Yrs. of NHL service: 0
Born: Pitea, Sweden; Sept. 9, 1976
Position: defense
Height: 6-3
Weight: 209
Uniform no.: n.a.
Shoots: left

Career statisics (Sweden):

GP	G	A	TP	PIM
72	10	20	30	60

1995-96 statistics (Sweden):

GP	G	A	TP	+/P
38	4	10	14	26

LAST SEASON

Will be entering first NHL season. Fourth among team defensemen in scoring for Lulea.

THE FINESSE GAME

Ohlund has a high skill level and a big body to go with it. Because he is such a wonderful skater, and has a long reach, he is difficult to beat one-on-one. Ohlund isn't fooled by dekes. He plays the crest and maintains his position.

Ohlund makes a good first pass out of the defensive zone, like Kjell Samuelsson, but his skating and puckhandling skills are better than Samuelsson's. He gets involved in the attack by moving up into the rush, but he won't get caught deep very often. Defense is his priority.

Ohlund just keeps growing, but unlike many young skaters who experience sudden growth spurts, he has stayed balanced in his skating. He was a regular in the Swedish Elite League at age 19.

THE PHYSICAL GAME

Ohlund is big and powerful, and at least at the international level has played a physical game, clearing out the front of the net and working the boards and corners. Ohlund will probably be more of a finesse defenseman at the NHL level, at least the Canucks aren't expecting him to batter people.

THE INTANGIBLES

The Canucks have waited for Ohlund to complete a commitment in Sweden, and were hopeful of signing him to a contract during the off-season. Ohlund can step right into a Canucks lineup that is thin in all areas. His Swedish Elite League team (Lulea) won its championship, so there could be at least one player in camp coming off an upbeat season.

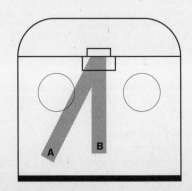

DAVID ROBERTS

Yrs. of NHL service: 2
Born: Alameda, Calif.; May 28, 1970
Position: left wing
Height: 6-0
Weight: 185
Uniform no.: 15
Shoots: left

Career statistics:

GP	G	A	TP	PIM
54	9	15	24	28

1993-94 statistics:

GP	G	A	TP	+/-	PIM	PP	SH	GW	GT	S	PCT
1	0	0	0	0	2	0	0	0	0	1	0.0

1994-95 statistics:

GP	G	A	TP	+/-	PIM	PP	SH	GW	GT	S	PCT
19	6	5	11	+2	10	3	0	2	1	41	14.6

1995-96 statistics:

GP	G	A	TP	+/-	PIM	PP	SH	GW	GT	S	PCT
34	3	10	13	-7	18	1	0	1	0	47	6.4

LAST SEASON

Signed as free agent by Vancouver, July 10, 1996. Split season between St. Louis and Edmonton. Played 22 games with Worcester (AHL), scoring 8-17 — 25.

THE FINESSE GAME

Roberts has great skills and skating ability. He is another graduate of the U.S. Olympic program, which has produced some excellent pro players despite having little success in the Games.

Because he has also played defense, and can drop back in a pinch to play that position, Roberts is highly aware defensively and is a complete player. He could see more ice time with the Canucks than he did in St. Louis, because he has good vision and a fine shot from the point. Understandably, he ranks behind Steve Duchesne and Al MacInnis in that department, but give him time and he will be a very capable power play quarterback. He is very creative.

Roberts handles the puck at high speed and doesn't get cornered with it. He has the sense to escape and use other players to open up ice. The Oilers used Roberts as a third-line left-winger.

THE PHYSICAL GAME

Roberts is a finesse player, but has great heart. He will finish his checks. He won't dominate physically and he's not mean, but he's not afraid, either.

THE INTANGIBLES

Roberts has a lot of upside, and showed some zest in his brief stint with the Oilers (scoring six points in six games). The Canucks are a quick team, which suits Roberts's game, but he will have a tough time breaking into the top six forwards with Vancouver if Pavel Bure comes back healthy.

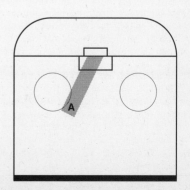

ESA TIKKANEN

Yrs. of NHL service: 11
Born: Helsinki, Finland; Jan. 25, 1965
Position: left wing
Height: 6-1
Weight: 190
Uniform no.: 10
Shoots: left

Career statistics:

GP	G	A	TP	PIM
721	218	348	546	949

1992-93 statistics:

GP	G	A	TP	+/-	PIM	PP	SH	GW	GT	S	PCT
81	16	24	40	-24	94	2	4	3	0	202	7.9

1993-94 statistics:

GP	G	A	TP	+/-	PIM	PP	SH	GW	GT	S	PCT
83	22	32	54	+5	114	5	3	4	0	257	8.6

1994-95 statistics:

GP	G	A	TP	+/-	PIM	PP	SH	GW	GT	S	PCT
43	12	23	35	+13	22	5	2	1	1	107	11.2

1995-96 statistics:

GP	G	A	TP	+/-	PIM	PP	SH	GW	GT	S	PCT
58	14	30	44	+1	36	8	1	2	0	95	14.7

LAST SEASON

Acquired from St. Louis by New Jersey for third-round draft pick, Nov. 1, 1995. Acquired from New Jersey for second-round pick, Nov. 23, 1995. Tied for third on team in power play goals.

THE FINESSE GAME

Tikkanen can play all three forward positions and applies all his considerable finesse skills to the defensive aspects of the game. Once a consistent 30-goal scorer, he's unlikely to hit that mark again, though he can provide 20 and some solid two-way play . . . if his suspect knee remains intact.

Although Tikkanen's lost a step, he still has some speed, which he uses most effectively killing penalties, and he is an aggressive forechecker, creating offensive chances off his work in the offensive zone. He blocks shots, hooks, holds and bumps, and if assigned to shadow a specific player will hound that mark relentlessly. The bigger the name, the bigger his game.

Tikkanen has accomplished enough offensive skills to work on the power play as well, from either the point or by working the puck down low. All eight of his power play goals were scored in 35 games with the Canucks last season. He has confidence in his puckhandling ability and sees the ice well. Despite taking chances low, he will be the first forward back to help out on defense. He likes to work out from behind the net, curl in front and shoot. Tikkanen also has a laser blast that he likes to go high with on the goalie's left side.

He is a choppy skater but chugs hard and gets to where he has to go.

THE PHYSICAL GAME

Tikkanen plays a grinding game. He cycles and works the boards and corners eagerly. The size of the opponent is of no concern: he will hurl his body at the biggest guy on the ice. Tikkanen is in your face — and also in your armpit or crawling up your back. He is as annoying as a mosquito and almost impossible to swat, since he is a master at the hit and run. One of the funniest sights in hockey is Tikkanen's wounded-victim look after he has goaded an opponent into taking a bad penalty. He often starts a war that one of his teammates ends up fighting. Tikkanen yaps constantly, which really drives his opponents nuts because he speaks some otherworldly gibberish that not even other Finns can translate.

THE INTANGIBLES

Tikkanen will probably require a complete knee replacement when his hockey career is done, yet he paid his own insurance policy premiums last season in order to play for Vancouver. Tikkanen is this close to being done, but some remarkable drive keeps him going, and he may last one more season. He provides grit, leadership and life, and Vancouver is lacking in all three of those areas.

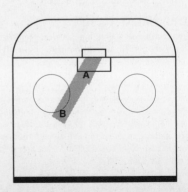

WASHINGTON CAPITALS

Players' Statistics 1995-96

POS	NO.	PLAYER	GP	G	A	PTS	+/-	PIM	PP	SH	GW	GT	S	PCT
C	20	MICHAL PIVONKA	73	16	65	81	18	36	6	2	5		168	9.5
R	12	PETER BONDRA	67	52	28	80	18	40	11	4	7	3	322	16.1
C	90	JOE JUNEAU	80	14	50	64	-3	30	7	2	2		176	8.0
L	21	TODD KRYGIER	76	15	33	48	-1	82	3	1		1	181	8.3
C	22	STEVE KONOWALCHUK	70	23	22	45	13	92	7	1	3		197	11.7
R	9	KEITH JONES	68	18	23	41	8	103	5		2		155	11.6
D	55	SERGEI GONCHAR	78	15	26	41	25	60	4		4		139	10.8
D	3	SYLVAIN COTE	81	5	33	38	5	40	3		2		212	2.4
C	32	DALE HUNTER	82	13	24	37	5	112	4		3	2	128	10.2
C	14	PAT PEAKE	62	17	19	36	7	46	8		3		129	13.2
D	6	CALLE JOHANSSON	78	10	25	35	13	50	4				182	5.5
L	10	KELLY MILLER	74	7	13	20	7	30		2	1		93	7.5
R	16	*STEFAN USTORF	48	7	10	17	8	14			1		39	17.9
D	24	MARK TINORDI	71	3	10	13	26	113	2				82	3.7
L	27	CRAIG BERUBE	50	2	10	12	1	151	1		1		28	7.1
D	2	*KEN KLEE	66	8	3	11	-1	60		1	2		76	10.5
C	36	MIKE EAGLES	70	4	7	11	-1	75					70	5.7
D	29	JOE REEKIE	78	3	7	10	7	149					52	5.8
C	11	*JEFF NELSON	33		7	7	3	16					21	
L	18	*ANDREW BRUNETTE	11	3	3	6	5				1		16	18.8
D	4	JIM JOHNSON	66	2	4	6	-3	34					49	4.1
D	19	*BRENDAN WITT	48	2	3	5	-4	85			1		44	4.5
R	34	*MARTIN GENDRON	20	2	1	3	-5	8					22	9.1
C	23	KEVIN KAMINSKI	54	1	2	3	-1	164					17	5.9
C	41	*JASON ALLISON	19		3	3	-3	2					18	
D	15	STEVE POAPST	3	1		1	-1				1		2	50.0
D	28	ERIC CHARRON	18		1	1	-3	22					13	
D	26	STEWART MALGUNAS	30		1	1	-10	32					13	
G	30	JIM CAREY	71	1	1		0	6						
D	38	*NOLAN BAUMGARTNER	1				-1							
L	8	*RICHARD ZEDNIK	1				0							
G	37	OLAF KOLZIG	18				0	2						

GP = games played; G = goals; A = assists; PTS = points; +/- = goals-for minus goals-against while player is on ice; PIM = penalties in minutes; PP = power play goals; SH = shorthanded goals; GW = game-winning goals; GT = game-tying goals; S = no. of shots; PCT = percentage of goals to shots; * = rookie

NOLAN BAUMGARTNER

Yrs. of NHL service: 0
Born: Calgary, Alta.; Mar. 23, 1976
Position: defense
Height: 6-1
Weight: 200
Uniform no.: 38
Shoots: right

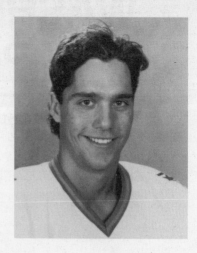

Career statistics:

GP	G	A	TP	PIM
1	0	0	0	0

1995-96 statistics:

GP	G	A	TP	+/-	PIM	PP	SH	GW	GT	S	PCT
1	0	0	0	-1	0	0	0	0	0	0	0.0

LAST SEASON

Will be entering first NHL season.

THE FINESSE GAME

Washington has mined a number of fine defensemen through the years; Baumgartner appears to be another prospect in that long line. He looks like he has the ability to become a two-way defenseman.

Although he is a good-sized defenseman, Baumgartner's assets are his skills and his hockey sense more than his body work. He is a smooth skater with good lateral mobility, and he's able to shift directions easily. He has the talent and intelligence to jump into the play, and is adept at lugging the puck. He's a good passer.

Baumgartner likes to pinch aggressively, which will fit into the Caps system, and if he can combine his lateral skating with his hard shot, he could become a second-unit power-play point man.

THE PHYSICAL GAME

Baumgartner needs to improve his strength to compete at the NHL level. He could probably use a little AHL seasoning to adjust to the professional game, but he has strong competitive instincts. He battles for the puck and is more likely to make a mistake by trying too hard than by being afraid to make a play. He has confidence in his skills. Baumgartner will fight for control along the boards and in the corners.

THE INTANGIBLES

Baumgartner ranked just below the top flight of Washington defensemen at season's end; he even made one playoff game appearance. If the team makes no player moves during the off-season, he will probably start the year in the minors, but expect to see him in a Caps uniform if any of the older defensemen are dealt. He has all of the ingredients in skill and attitude.

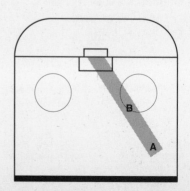

PETER BONDRA

Yrs. of NHL service: 6
Born: Luck, Ukraine; Feb. 7, 1968
Position: right wing
Height: 6-1
Weight: 200
Uniform no.: 12
Shoots: left

Career statistics:

GP	G	A	TP	PIM
391	187	148	335	263

1992-93 statistics:

GP	G	A	TP	+/-	PIM	PP	SH	GW	GT	S	PCT
83	37	48	85	+8	70	10	0	7	0	239	15.5

1993-94 statistics:

GP	G	A	TP	+/-	PIM	PP	SH	GW	GT	S	PCT
69	24	19	43	+22	40	4	0	2	0	200	12.0

1994-95 statistics:

GP	G	A	TP	+/-	PIM	PP	SH	GW	GT	S	PCT
47	34	9	43	+9	24	12	6	3	1	177	19.2

1995-96 statistics:

GP	G	A	TP	+/-	PIM	PP	SH	GW	GT	S	PCT
67	52	28	80	+18	40	11	4	7	3	322	16.1

LAST SEASON

Fourth in NHL in goals. Led team in goals for second consecutive season with career high. Led team in power play goals for second consecutive season. Led team in shorthanded goals for second consecutive season. Second on team in points. Tied for third on team in plus-minus. Missed four games with groin injury. Missed five games with shoulder separation. Missed six games to contract dispute.

THE FINESSE GAME

Bondra's speed is exceptional and he is intelligent on the ice offensively. He accelerates quickly and smoothly and drives defenders back because they have to play off his speed. If he gets hooked to the ice he doesn't stay down, but jumps back to his skates and gets involved in the play again, often after the defender has forgotten about him. He has excellent balance and quickness.

He cuts in on the off-wing and shoots in stride. He has a very good backhand shot and likes to cut out from behind the net and make things happen in tight. He mixes up his shots. He will fire quickly — not many European players have this good a slap shot — or drive in close and deke and wrist a little shot.

Bondra had never killed penalties until 1994-95, and he has become a real shorthanded threat with 13 SHG over the past two seasons. He makes other teams' power plays jittery because of his anticipation and breakaway speed.

Bondra has become a more confident player. His best scoring chances come from feeds from Michal Pivonka, and the two work as if they had radar.

Bondra also follows up his shots to the net and is quick to pounce on rebounds.

THE PHYSICAL GAME

Bondra isn't strong, but he will lean on people. He has improved his off-ice conditioning and handled a lot of ice time last season. He doesn't seem to tire. Bondra is much more determined in fighting through checks.

THE INTANGIBLES

We dearly wish we could take credit for this one, but it was Caps GM David Poile who steadfastly insisted that Bondra would be a 50-goal scorer. We merely repeated his prediction in last year's *HSR*, and voila! Poile's patience and vision pays off. Bondra would have actually been on a 60-goal pace if he hadn't missed the start of the season and been hit with some injuries. As long as his set-up man Pivonka stays healthy, Bondra should be even more productive this season.

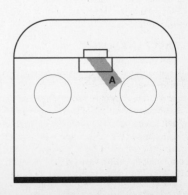

JIM CAREY

Yrs. of NHL service: 2
Born: Dorchester, Mass.; May 31, 1974
Position: goaltender
Height: 6-2
Weight: 205
Uniform no.: 30
Catches: left

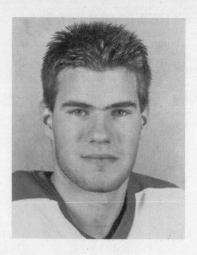

Career statistics:

GP	MIN	GA	SO	GAA	A	PIM
99	5673	210	13	2.22	1	6

1994-95 statistics:

GP	MIN	GAA	W	L	T	SO	GA	S	SAPCT	PIM
28	1604	2.13	18	6	3	4	57	654	.913	0

1995-96 statistics:

GP	MIN	GAA	W	L	T	SO	GA	S	SAPCT	PIM
71	4069	2.26	35	24	9	9	153	1631	.906	6

LAST SEASON

Won 1996 Vezina Trophy. Led NHL in shutouts. Second in NHL in goals-against average with career best in second NHL season. Second in NHL in wins.

THE PHYSICAL GAME

When someone has had the kind of phenomenal success Carey has had during the regular season, it's hard to find fault with him. But we'll try.

It's no secret, really, because teams like New Jersey (whom Carey hasn't beaten in five tries) and Pittsburgh (who have flirted with playoff disaster with Carey and the Caps for the past two seasons, but prevailed) have already pounced on the weakest aspect of his game, which is his terrible lateral movement. Teams that play a strong east-west game against him and get him moving from post to post are able to pick him apart.

Carey is great straight on. If you come down the wing and blast, he will stop you. He's great in tight because of his dynamic reflexes. But Carey is a big man and doesn't look as big as he should in the net.

He is also very poor handling the puck, and creates his own problems when he is forced to do too much. Carey solves this by trying to do as little as possible outside his net. He is starting to use his stick better around the goal to break up plays but he could also improve in this area.

THE MENTAL GAME

Carey was an intense competitor during the regular season, but suffered another playoff disaster as the Caps failed to get by the first round for the fourth time in five years. Carey has only been here for the last two (both first-round losses), and doesn't deserve all of the blame. But he did not make the big saves early in the Pittsburgh series to give his team any chance. A goalie, no matter how fine his regular season, is never judged a winner until he wears a ring. Just ask Ron Hextall.

THE INTANGIBLES

Can this goalie be saved? Only if the Caps make a top-notch goalie coach (think Jacques Caron, Francois Allaire, Billy Smith) an off-season priority. Carey's flaws are fixable, and the fine-tuning can be done without ruining his strengths.

SYLVAIN COTE

Yrs. of NHL service: 11
Born: Quebec City, Que.; Jan. 19, 1966
Position: left defense
Height: 5-11
Weight: 185
Uniform no.: 3
Shoots: right

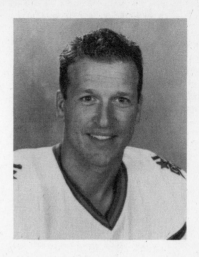

Career statistics:

GP	G	A	TP	PIM
749	89	201	290	371

1992-93 statistics:

GP	G	A	TP	+/-	PIM	PP	SH	GW	GT	S	PCT
77	21	29	50	+28	34	8	2	3	0	206	10.2

1993-94 statistics:

GP	G	A	TP	+/-	PIM	PP	SH	GW	GT	S	PCT
84	16	35	51	+30	66	3	2	2	0	212	7.5

1994-95 statistics:

GP	G	A	TP	+/-	PIM	PP	SH	GW	GT	S	PCT
47	5	14	19	+2	53	1	0	2	0	124	4.0

1995-96 statistics:

GP	G	A	TP	+/-	PIM	PP	SH	GW	GT	S	PCT
81	5	33	38	+5	40	3	0	2	0	212	2.4

LAST SEASON

Tied for third on team in assists. Second among team defensemen in scoring.

THE FINESSE GAME

Cote is a solid two-way defenseman. He has good puckhandling skills and can make a pass to his forehand or backhand side with confidence. He overhandles the puck at times, especially in his defensive zone, and when he gets into trouble he seems to struggle with his forehand clearances off the left wing boards.

Cote can do everything in stride. Carrying the puck does not slow him down and he can rush end to end. He is gifted in all of the skating areas — fine agility, good balance, quick stops and starts. He likes to bring the puck up on the power play. He gets a lot on his shot from the point, which causes rebounds, and is the source of most of his assists.

His hockey sense has improved. He can lead a rush or come into the play as a trailer, but he knows enough not to force and to play more conservatively when the situation dictates.

He still needs to improve his defensive reads, but he is working hard at it and his skating helps cover up for most of his lapses. His instincts lag well behind his skill level. Cote can be beaten one-on-one, but it takes a good player to do it.

THE PHYSICAL GAME

Cote is one of the underrated members of the Washington defense corps. He doesn't have great size, but he is a solid hitter who finishes his checks. He isn't mean, however. He will occasionally fall into the trap of playing the puck instead of the man.

THE INTANGIBLES

Cote is ideally a number three or number four defenseman, and when the Caps' blueliners are healthy (as they were so infrequently last season) he can play that role behind the top pairing of Mark Tinordi and Sergei Gonchar. That keeps him away from the other team's top lines, and Cote can certainly do an adequate job against a number two unit. At 30, he should be good for another season of close to 40 points.

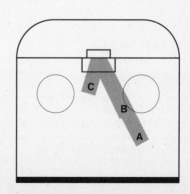

MIKE EAGLES

Yrs. of NHL service: 10
Born: Sussex, N.B.; Mar. 7, 1963
Position: centre
Height: 5-10
Weight: 190
Uniform no.: 36
Shoots: left

Career statistics:

GP	G	A	TP	PIM
670	66	110	176	805

1992-93 statistics:

GP	G	A	TP	+/-	PIM	PP	SH	GW	GT	S	PCT
84	8	18	26	-1	131	1	0	1	0	67	11.9

1993-94 statistics:

GP	G	A	TP	+/-	PIM	PP	SH	GW	GT	S	PCT
73	4	8	12	-20	96	0	1	0	0	53	7.5

1994-95 statistics:

GP	G	A	TP	+/-	PIM	PP	SH	GW	GT	S	PCT
40	3	4	7	-11	48	0	0	0	0	28	10.7

1995-96 statistics:

GP	G	A	TP	+/-	PIM	PP	SH	GW	GT	S	PCT
70	4	7	11	-1	75	0	0	0	0	70	5.7

LAST SEASON

Missed 11 games with broken finger.

THE FINESSE GAME

Eagles is the prototypical defensive centre. He is on the puck in a hurry when forechecking, creating turnovers and forcing bad passes. He has never had the touch to convert these chances into scoring attempts, but he can create chaos for the opponents.

Eagles always hustles and hits. If any points come, they are a bonus. He usually concentrates on shutting down the opposing centre on draws. He blocks shots and kills penalties. He can't match up against some of the league's power forwards, but he can keep up with the fleet ones.

THE PHYSICAL GAME

Eagles drives other players to distraction with his dogged pursuit, and he will get the stick up or give a facial massage with his glove. He's no angel. Despite his relatively small size, Eagles never fails to finish his checks.

THE INTANGIBLES

Eagles is a steady, veteran checker, and a coach knows just what he's getting in terms of effort every night. Eagles will always be on the bubble because there is so little offense to complement the rest of his game, but Washington is an organization that prizes intelligence and a strong work ethic. Unless the Devils acquire Miroslav Satan, Eagles will be the only NHL player whose name matches his team's logo.

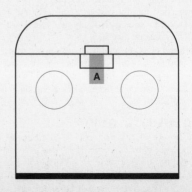

SERGEI GONCHAR

Yrs. of NHL service: 2
Born: Chelyabinsk, USSR; Apr. 13, 1974
Position: left defense
Height: 6-2
Weight: 212
Uniform no.: 55
Shoots: left

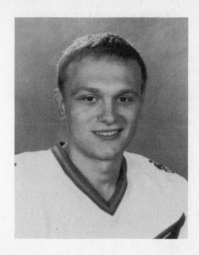

Career statistics:

GP	G	A	TP	PIM
109	17	31	48	82

1994-95 statistics:

GP	G	A	TP	+/-	PIM	PP	SH	GW	GT	S	PCT
31	2	5	7	+4	22	0	0	0	0	38	5.3

1995-96 statistics:

GP	G	A	TP	+/-	PIM	PP	SH	GW	GT	S	PCT
78	15	26	41	+25	60	4	0	4	0	139	10.8

LAST SEASON

Led Capitals defensemen in scoring. Second on team in plus-minus. Missed two games with groin pull. Missed two games with flu.

THE FINESSE GAME

It's difficult to believe that Gonchar was known as a defensive defenseman when he played in Russia. He sees the ice well and passes well, but he never put up any big offensive numbers before coming into the NHL, which made his rapid development last season a surprise, even to the Caps.

Gonchar jumps up into the play willingly and intelligently. He has a natural feel for the flow of a game, and makes tape-to-tape feeds through people and under pressure. The Caps quickly realized this while he was in their farm system at the start of the 1994-95 season, and gave Gonchar a green light. He saw first-unit power play time on the point, and is growing into the role after some struggles. He doesn't have the blazing speed that elite defensemen have when carrying the puck, but he is very heads-up. Gonchar is better after the team has set up in the zone.

Gonchar has a good shot but there isn't a lot on it. He doesn't push the puck forward and step into it like Al MacInnis. Most of the time he is content with getting it on the net, and he is not reluctant to shoot.

THE PHYSICAL GAME

Gonchar is very strong on his skates and has worked hard on his off-ice conditioning. His defense is based more on reads and positional play than a physical element, but he has a bit of an aggressive streak. He was known as a very aggressive player by Russian standards, but he won't run people. Gonchar will probably become a little more assertive as he gains confidence.

Gonchar has logged a lot of ice time the past two seasons and has a tendency to pace himself, which is why at times he appears a bit passive. Gonchar was teamed with Mark Tinordi much of last season against other teams' top lines, and did a very intelligent job. He is an effective penalty killer.

THE INTANGIBLES

Gonchar has a big upside, even given the distance he has already covered since coming to North America. He won't be in the top 10 scorers among defensemen, but he may provide 50-55 points backed up by a solid defensive game.

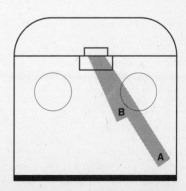

PHIL HOUSLEY

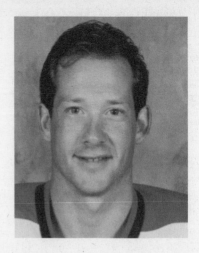

Yrs. of NHL service: 14
Born: St. Paul, Minn.; Mar. 9, 1964
Position: right defense
Height: 5-10
Weight: 185
Uniform no.: 6
Shoots: left

Career statistics:

GP	G	A	TP	PIM
990	274	676	950	614

1992-93 statistics:

GP	G	A	TP	+/-	PIM	PP	SH	GW	GT	S	PCT
80	18	79	97	-14	52	6	0	2	0	249	7.2

1993-94 statistics:

GP	G	A	TP	+/-	PIM	PP	SH	GW	GT	S	PCT
26	7	15	22	-5	12	4	0	1	1	60	11.7

1994-95 statistics:

GP	G	A	TP	+/-	PIM	PP	SH	GW	GT	S	PCT
43	8	35	43	+17	18	3	0	0	0	135	5.9

1995-96 statistics:

GP	G	A	TP	+/-	PIM	PP	SH	GW	GT	S	PCT
81	17	51	68	-6	30	6	0	1	0	205	8.3

LAST SEASON

Signed as a free agent by Washington, July 22, 1996. Acquired from Calgary with Dan Keczmer for Tommy Albelin, Cale Hulse and Jocelyn Lemieux, Feb. 26, 1996. One of two defensemen to lead his team in scoring. Led team and was sixth among NHL defensemen in assists. Fifth among defensemen in points. Missed three games with flu.

THE FINESSE GAME

Among the best-skating defensemen in the NHL, Housley, like Paul Coffey, takes a lot of heat for his defensive shortcomings, but his offensive skills are extraordinary.

Housley's skating fuels his game. He can accelerate in a heartbeat, and his edges are deep and secure, giving him the ability to avoid checks with gravity-defying moves. Everything he does is at high tempo. He intimidates with his speed and skills, forcing defenders back and opening up more ice for himself and his teammates. Like Mike Gartner, Housley can continue to be an effective offensive weapon because he has barely lost a step over the years.

He has an excellent grasp of the ice. On the power play he is a huge threat. His shots are low, quick and heavy, either beating the goalie outright or setting up a rebound for the forwards down deep. He will also set up low on the power play, and he doesn't mind shooting from an impossible angle that can catch a goalie napping on the short side.

Housley has great anticipation and can break up a rush by picking off a pass and turning the play into a counterattack. He is equally adept with a long head-man or a short cup-and-saucer pass over a defender's stick.

THE PHYSICAL GAME

Housley is not the least bit physical. Who wants a player as gifted as Housley risking life and limb in routine plays along the boards when there are a dozen less gifted players who could do it for him? He is not strong enough to shove anyone out of the zone, so his defensive play is based on his pursuit of the puck. He is likely to avoid traffic areas unless he feels he can get in and out with the puck quickly enough.

Success on a rush, even a two-on-one, against Housley is no guarantee, since he is a good enough skater to position himself well and break up the play with his stick.

THE INTANGIBLES

Housley hoped last season's trade to the Devils would give him a shot at the Stanley Cup, but the team failed to make the playoffs despite his contribution of 16 points in 22 games. As an unrestricted free agent, Housley chose to sign with the Caps, whose power play (ranked 22nd last season) will get an immediate boost from his offense. He will get first-unit power play time, possibly with the talented Sergei Gonchar, and may be good for another 65-point season.

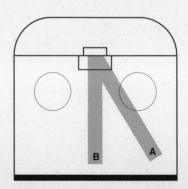

DALE HUNTER

Yrs. of NHL service: 16
Born: Petrolia, Ont.; July 31, 1960
Position: centre
Height: 5-10
Weight: 198
Uniform no.: 32
Shoots: left

Career statistics:

GP	G	A	TP	PIM
1181	299	638	947	3218

1992-93 statistics:

GP	G	A	TP	+/-	PIM	PP	SH	GW	GT	S	PCT
84	20	59	79	+3	198	10	0	2	0	120	16.7

1993-94 statistics:

GP	G	A	TP	+/-	PIM	PP	SH	GW	GT	S	PCT
52	9	29	38	-4	131	1	0	1	0	61	14.8

1994-95 statistics:

GP	G	A	TP	+/-	PIM	PP	SH	GW	GT	S	PCT
45	8	15	23	-4	101	3	0	1	0	73	11.0

1995-96 statistics:

GP	G	A	TP	+/-	PIM	PP	SH	GW	GT	S	PCT
82	13	24	37	+5	112	4	0	3	2	128	10.2

LAST SEASON

Only Capital to appear in all 82 games. Second to Tiger Williams (3,966) on all-time PIM list.

THE FINESSE GAME

Hunter is a crafty player, especially down low. He doesn't skate well enough to be very effective in open ice, but when the Caps have control of the offensive zone, he digs in deep, setting screens and picks and driving to the net. He is not a big player, but he forces teams to pay attention with his effort.

Hunter is skilled on face-offs. He gets low to the ice, then moves forward and drives back the opposing centre. He never fails to bump his opposite number. He turns his body and grinds it out. He uses his helmet to bump the chin and chest of the opposing centre. And he works at buying time for his linemates by creating time and space with his puck control.

Hunter is a complete player. At this stage of his career he should have settled into a nice role-playing position. Last season, the Caps again needed him full-time due to injuries. Hunter can be more effective by being spotted. His days as a big point producer are over, but he still produces key points. Of his 13 goals, five won or tied games last season.

THE PHYSICAL GAME

Hunter knows only one way to play the game. He gets shots in, hits, harasses and does whatever it takes to win. This has been his hallmark from the first day he pulled on an NHL jersey. Look at the few great moments in the Capitals' history — notably their drive to the Stanley Cup semifinals in 1990 — and Hunter has always been a key-player. The size of the opponent doesn't matter to him. He has a low, low centre of gravity that makes it a pain to hit him, and he will take or make a hit to make a play. He is grating.

THE INTANGIBLES

Love him or hate him, you have to respect Hunter for the leadership and work ethic he shows from shift to shift. He is a fine example for the team's younger players, not for sportmanship certainly, but for paying the price to be a successful NHL player. Hunter can still perform well in a limited role. He is getting older, but he keeps himself in good physical condition, and can contribute 35 points while providing defense.

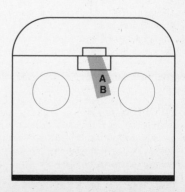

CALLE JOHANSSON

Yrs. of NHL service: 9
Born: Göteborg, Sweden; Feb. 14, 1967
Position: left defense
Height: 5-11
Weight: 200
Uniform no.: 6
Shoots: left

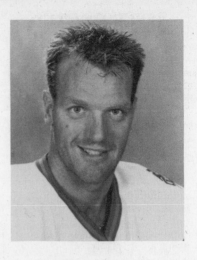

Career statistics:

GP	G	A	TP	PIM
645	71	292	363	371

1992-93 statistics:

GP	G	A	TP	+/-	PIM	PP	SH	GW	GT	S	PCT
77	7	38	45	+3	56	6	0	0	1	133	5.3

1993-94 statistics:

GP	G	A	TP	+/-	PIM	PP	SH	GW	GT	S	PCT
84	9	33	42	+3	59	4	0	1	0	141	6.4

1994-95 statistics:

GP	G	A	TP	+/-	PIM	PP	SH	GW	GT	S	PCT
46	5	26	31	-6	35	4	0	2	0	112	4.5

1995-96 statistics:

GP	G	A	TP	+/-	PIM	PP	SH	GW	GT	S	PCT
78	10	25	35	+13	50	4	0	0	0	182	5.5

LAST SEASON

Missed four games with wrist injury.

THE FINESSE GAME

Johansson has tremendous legs, notably big, strong thighs that generate the power for his shot and his explosive skating. He makes every move look easy. He is agile, mobile and great at moving up the ice with the play. Speed, balance and strength allow him to chase a puck behind the net, pick it up without stopping and make an accurate pass. He is confident, even on the backhand, and likes to have the puck in key spots.

He is smart offensively. He moves the puck with a good first pass, then has enough speed and instinct to jump up and be ready for a return pass. He keeps the gap tight as the play enters the attacking zone, which opens up more options: he is available to the forwards if they need him for offense, and closer to the puck if it is turned over to the opposition.

Johansson has a low accurate shot that can be tipped. He is unselfish to a fault, often looking to pass when he should use his shot.

He has good defensive instincts and reads plays well. His skating gives him the confidence (maybe overconfidence) to gamble and challenge the puck carrier. He has a quick stick for poke- and sweep-checks.

THE PHYSICAL GAME

Johansson is not an aggressive player, but he is strong and knows what he has to do with his body in the defensive zone. This part of the game has not come naturally, but Johansson has worked at it. He is still not an impact player defensively, although he wins his share of the one-on-one battles because he gets so much power from his legs.

THE INTANGIBLES

Johansson has taken a back seat to Sergei Gonchar as the team's number one offensive defenseman and will probably see his points decline again slightly to the 30-35 point range next season. Still, Johansson does so many things well that his position among the team's top four defensemen is secure. A wrist injury forced him to miss the playoffs and his absence was felt against the Penguins.

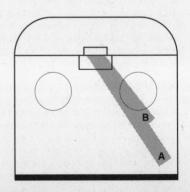

KEITH JONES

Yrs. of NHL service: 4
Born: Brantford, Ont.; Nov. 8, 1968
Position: right wing
Height: 6-2
Weight: 200
Uniform no.: 9
Shoots: left

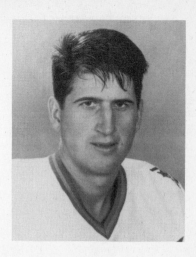

Career statistics:

GP	G	A	TP	PIM
244	60	65	122	441

1992-93 statistics:

GP	G	A	TP	+/-	PIM	PP	SH	GW	GT	S	PCT
71	12	14	26	+18	124	0	0	3	0	73	16.4

1993-94 statistics:

GP	G	A	TP	+/-	PIM	PP	SH	GW	GT	S	PCT
68	16	19	35	+4	149	5	0	1	0	97	16.5

1994-95 statistics:

GP	G	A	TP	+/-	PIM	PP	SH	GW	GT	S	PCT
40	14	6	20	-2	65	1	0	4	0	85	16.5

1995-96 statistics:

GP	G	A	TP	+/-	PIM	PP	SH	GW	GT	S	PCT
68	18	23	41	+8	103	5	0	2	0	155	11.6

LAST SEASON

Third on team in goals with career high. Missed 14 games with recurring groin injury.

THE FINESSE GAME

Jones is a spark plug. He likes to make things happen by driving to the front of the net and taking a defenseman with him. His skating is adequate, and he uses quick bursts of speed to power himself to and through the traffic areas.

He has decent hands, is an eager finisher and plays well at both ends of the ice. He keeps the game simple and does his job. He isn't very creative, but his efforts churn up loose pucks for teammates smart enough to trail in his wake. Jones is the antithesis of a natural scorer, because everything he accomplishes is through effort.

Jones was ready to step up to play a larger role last season, but injuries slowed him down mid-season and never allowed him to fully contribute.

THE PHYSICAL GAME

Jones is energetic and uses his size well. He needs more experience, but is tough and willing to pay a physical price. The Caps could use a couple more players like him. He isn't the biggest player on the ice, but there are nights when you come away thinking he is.

Jones finishes every check in every zone, and sometimes runs around a bit, but he is becoming more responsible defensively.

THE INTANGIBLES

Jones was a scorer at the college level and plays with grit and determination. He improves season by season, and has grown into his role as a two-way winger who can get 15-20 goals a season and act as a catalyst. He loves the game and knows what he has to do to stay in the lineup. Jones was a Group 2 free agent during the off-season but is expected to re-sign with the Caps. He'll probably get a substantial raise but he's one athlete that won't be spoiled by a bigger paycheck.

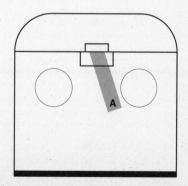

JOE JUNEAU

Yrs. of NHL service: 4
Born: Pont-Rouge, Que.; Jan. 5, 1968
Position: centre/left wing
Height: 6-0
Weight: 195
Uniform no.: 90
Shoots: right

Career statistics:

GP	G	A	TP	PIM
296	75	186	313	116

1992-93 statistics:

GP	G	A	TP	+/-	PIM	PP	SH	GW	GT	S	PCT
84	32	70	102	+23	33	9	0	3	3	229	14.0

1993-94 statistics:

GP	G	A	TP	+/-	PIM	PP	SH	GW	GT	S	PCT
74	19	66	85	+11	41	6	0	2	1	164	11.6

1994-95 statistics:

GP	G	A	TP	+/-	PIM	PP	SH	GW	GT	S	PCT
44	5	38	43	-1	8	3	0	0	0	1	7.1

1995-96 statistics:

GP	G	A	TP	+/-	PIM	PP	SH	GW	GT	S	PCT
80	14	50	64	-3	30	7	2	2	2	0	8.0

LAST SEASON

Second on team in assists. Third on team in points. Tied for third on team in power play goals. Missed two games with flu.

THE FINESSE GAME

Juneau plays at centre, but he seems to gravitate to the left wing and generates most of his scoring chances from there. He varies his play selection. He will take the puck to the net on one rush, then pull up at the top of the circle and hit the trailer late on the next rush.

While the circles are his office, he is not exclusively a perimeter player. Juneau will go into traffic. He is bigger than he looks on the ice. His quick feet and light hands make him seem smaller, because he is so crafty with the puck.

Laterally, Juneau is among the best skaters in the NHL. He has an extra gear that allows him to pull away from people. He does not have breakaway speed, but he has great anticipation and gets the jump on a defender with his first few steps.

Juneau doesn't shoot the puck enough and gets a little intimidated when there is a scramble for a loose puck in front of the net. He is not always willing to sacrifice his body that way. He shoots a tad prematurely. When he could wait and have the goalie down and out, he unloads quickly, because he hears footsteps. His best shot is a one-timer from the left circle.

Defensively Juneau has improved in recent years. He can kill penalties and is excellent on draws.

THE PHYSICAL GAME

Juneau has improved his toughness and willingness to take a hit to make a play — probably dressing room osmosis — but he is still something of a featherweight. He skates in a hunched-over position, like a human letter C, and a hit that would otherwise be clean catches him in the face. He plays with a huge protective shield that doesn't appear to get in his way too much unless the puck is right in his feet.

THE INTANGIBLES

Would somebody please get this man a winger? After all, Michal Pivonka has Peter Bondra to pass to, and Juneau has . . . well, certainly no one to make magic with. Juneau is a smart playmaker who could make some winger very happy. If the Caps find him the right partner, they will have a powerful second line, but last season Juneau looked lost.

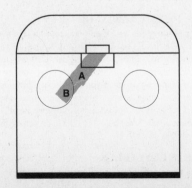

STEVE KONOWALCHUK

Yrs. of NHL service: 4
Born: Salt Lake City, Utah; Nov. 11, 1972
Position: centre
Height: 6-1
Weight: 195
Uniform no.: 22
Shoots: left

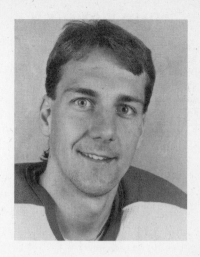

Career statistics:

GP	G	A	TP	PIM
215	50	57	107	185

1992-93 statistics:

GP	G	A	TP	+/-	PIM	PP	SH	GW	GT	S	PCT
36	4	7	11	+4	16	1	0	1	0	34	11.8

1993-94 statistics:

GP	G	A	TP	+/-	PIM	PP	SH	GW	GT	S	PCT
62	12	14	26	+9	33	0	0	0	0	63	19.0

1994-95 statistics:

GP	G	A	TP	+/-	PIM	PP	SH	GW	GT	S	PCT
46	11	14	25	+7	44	3	3	3	0	88	12.5

1995-96 statistics:

GP	G	A	TP	+/-	PIM	PP	SH	GW	GT	S	PCT
70	23	22	45	+13	92	7	1	3	0	197	11.7

sleepers of the season and is a quality person to have on the ice or in the locker room.

LAST SEASON

Second on team in goals with career high. Third on team in power play goals. Fifth on team in points with career high. Career high in assists. Missed 12 games with fractured left hand. Scored first career hat trick.

THE FINESSE GAME

Konowalchuk is just the kind of player coach Jim Schoenfeld loves, and the heir to Dave Poulin as a willing guy who will play any role asked of him. He's a digger who has to work hard for his goals, and an intelligent and earnest player who uses every ounce of energy on every shift.

There is nothing fancy about his offense. He just lets his shot rip and drives to the net. He doesn't have the moves and hand skills to beat a defender one-on-one, but he doesn't care. He'll go right through him. Konowalchuk's release on his shot is improving.

Konowalchuk is reliable and intelligent defensively. On the draw, he ties up the opposing centre if he doesn't win the puck drop outright. He uses his feet along the boards as well as his stick.

THE PHYSICAL GAME

Konowalchuk is very strong. He has some grit in him, too, and will aggravate opponents with his constant effort. He doesn't take bad penalties, but often goads rivals into retaliating. He is very fit and can handle a lot of ice time.

THE INTANGIBLES

Konowalchuk exceeded our expectations with his production last season and as he gains confidence he is becoming a better player. He could be one of the

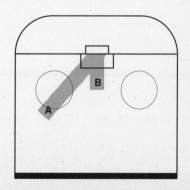

TODD KRYGIER

Yrs. of NHL service: 7
Born: Chicago Heights, Mich.; Oct. 12, 1965
Position: left wing
Height: 6-0
Weight: 185
Uniform no.: 21
Shoots: left

Career statistics:

GP	G	A	TP	PIM
451	93	120	213	466

1992-93 statistics:

GP	G	A	TP	+/-	PIM	PP	SH	GW	GT	S	PCT
77	11	12	23	-13	60	0	2	0	1	133	8.3

1993-94 statistics:

GP	G	A	TP	+/-	PIM	PP	SH	GW	GT	S	PCT
66	12	18	30	-4	60	0	1	3	0	146	8.2

1994-95 statistics:

GP	G	A	TP	+/-	PIM	PP	SH	GW	GT	S	PCT
35	11	11	22	+1	10	1	0	1	0	90	12.2

1995-96 statistics:

GP	G	A	TP	+/-	PIM	PP	SH	GW	GT	S	PCT
76	15	33	48	-1	82	3	1	0	1	181	8.3

winger who will never score more than 20 goals. Krygier ran into problems with coach Ron Wilson in Anaheim, which was the reason for his departure from the Ducks.

LAST SEASON
Acquired from Anaheim for Mike Torchia, Mar. 8, 1996. Third on team in assists.

THE FINESSE GAME
Krygier may be too fast for his own good. He has blazing speed and anticipation, which gets him his share of breakaways and odd-man rushes. But when it comes time to shoot or move the puck to a teammate, he can't do it. He has to slow down in order to do something constructive with the puck, and because his hand skills aren't great, he loses the advantage his speed gives him.

Most of his goals come with his hard wrist shot, but he doesn't beat many goalies cleanly. He needs someone screening in front, but he doesn't know how to time his plays to use an opposing defenseman in that manner.

Krygier plays with enthusiasm, and is a strong penalty killer. His speed allows him to backcheck and badger the puck carrier from behind, lifting the stick and stealing the puck.

THE PHYSICAL GAME
Krygier is not strong on the puck. He intimidates with his speed, but unless he is racing for a puck in open ice he is not likely to scrap for it. He will bump an opponent, but without much ferocity.

THE INTANGIBLES
Krygier is a known quantity, as the Caps knew when they reacquired him for some help down the stretch and into the playoffs. His speed and work ethic will guarantee him employment. Ideally, he is a third-line

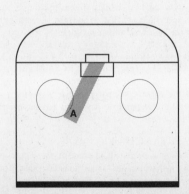

KELLY MILLER

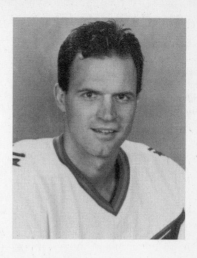

Yrs. of NHL service: 11
Born: Lansing, Mich.; Mar. 3, 1963
Position: left wing/right wing
Height: 5-11
Weight: 196
Uniform no.: 10
Shoots: left

Career statistics:

GP	G	A	TP	PIM
842	162	256	418	409

1992-93 statistics:

GP	G	A	TP	+/-	PIM	PP	SH	GW	GT	S	PCT
84	18	27	45	-2	32	3	0	3	0	144	12.5

1993-94 statistics:

GP	G	A	TP	+/-	PIM	PP	SH	GW	GT	S	PCT
84	14	25	39	+8	32	0	1	3	0	138	10.1

1994-95 statistics:

GP	G	A	TP	+/-	PIM	PP	SH	GW	GT	S	PCT
48	10	13	23	+5	6	2	0	1	0	70	14.3

1995-96 statistics:

GP	G	A	TP	+/-	PIM	PP	SH	GW	GT	S	PCT
74	7	13	20	+7	30	0	2	1	0	93	7.5

THE INTANGIBLES

Miller has become more and more a strictly defensive entity, as his diminishing point totals indicate. He remains one of the game's most intelligent penalty killing and checking forwards, night after night.

LAST SEASON

Missed eight games with abdominal/groin strain, ending consecutive games-played streak at 322.

THE FINESSE GAME

If a team doesn't have complete control of the puck in the zone, Miller will come in hard. If they have control, he backs off to the neutral zone. He's smart enough to know the difference, instead of plunging in with a wild forecheck and expending useless energy. Miller is one of the top defensive wingers in the game because of his reads.

Miller has never produced the kind of offensive numbers that his skills indicate he could, and now those numbers are dwindling even more. He has the skating ability, hockey sense and hands to score maybe 30 goals, but he'll never do it because he's always thinking defense. Miller drives to the net on occasion and has a quick release on his shot.

Defensively, there is no weak part to Miller's game. A complete player, he is always in motion. He creates a lot of scoring chances from turnovers. He reads plays when he forechecks, and either goes to the net or finds a teammate in front with a good short pass. He is one of the best penalty killers around.

THE PHYSICAL GAME

Miller is not very big, but he is strong and durable. Until last year, he had never missed more than four games in a single season since he was a rookie. His stamina allows him to forecheck hard all night, and he drives opponents batty because he is always on them. There is never a moment's peace when Miller is on the ice.

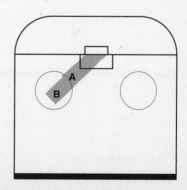

PAT PEAKE

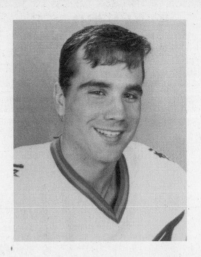

Yrs. of NHL service: 3
Born: Rochester, Mich.; May 28, 1973
Position: centre
Height: 6-1
Weight: 195
Uniform no.: 14
Shoots: right

Career statistics:

GP	G	A	TP	PIM
129	28	41	69	97

1993-94 statistics:

GP	G	A	TP	+/-	PIM	PP	SH	GW	GT	S	PCT
49	11	18	29	+1	39	3	0	1	1	91	12.1

1994-95 statistics:

GP	G	A	TP	+/-	PIM	PP	SH	GW	GT	S	PCT
18	0	4	4	-6	12	0	0	0	0	30	0.0

1995-96 statistics:

GP	G	A	TP	+/-	PIM	PP	SH	GW	GT	S	PCT
62	17	19	36	+7	46	8	0	3	0	129	13.2

LAST SEASON

Second on team in power play goals. Missed 10 games with throat injury. Missed three games with shoulder injury. Missed one game with kidney stone. Missed five games with knee injury.

THE FINESSE GAME

If Peake ever gets to play a complete season, we might know where he really stacks up among the Class of '91, which ranks as one of the best in ages with alumni such as Eric Lindros, Pat Falloon, Scott Niedermayer, Scott Lachance and Peter Forsberg.

Peake's run of bad luck, however, has slowed his progress. He has worked to improve his skating (he even attended a power skating school during the 1995 off-season) and he didn't look out of place last season.

He has flashed the talent to dominate games. He also has polished playmaking skills and can pass equally well to either side. Peake has a hard shot and loves to score. He has good hockey vision and creativity.

The Capitals' power play was at its most effective last season when Peake was healthy and working the puck off the half-boards. He has all of the ingredients — grit, hand skills, intelligence and hockey sense — to be a very good player.

THE PHYSICAL GAME

Peake is a finesse player who is competitive, but he will have to learn to pay the physical price necessary in the NHL. He adjusted to the NHL pace to move and shoot the puck and isn't intimidated. He will need to get stronger as he works during the off-season to rehabilitate his latest injury.

THE INTANGIBLES

Peake's list of injuries and illnesses since his last year of junior (1993) are astounding. A broken ankle, mononucleosis, kidney stones and a fractured thyroid (throat) cartilage. And, in the 1996 playoffs, a broken heel that had to be pieced back together like a mosaic.

The latest injury, which will keep him off the ice until November, has to be demoralizing. To Peake's credit, he keeps coming back, but there are some players who just seem brittle and injury-prone; Peake could be the poster boy for *E.R.*

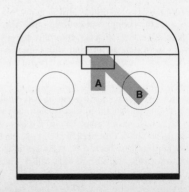

MICHAL PIVONKA

Yrs. of NHL service: 10
Born: Kladno, Czechoslovakia; Jan. 28, 1966
Position: centre/left wing
Height: 6-2
Weight: 195
Uniform no.: 20
Shoots: left

Career statistics:

GP	G	A	TP	PIM
702	186	390	576	424

1992-93 statistics:

GP	G	A	TP	+/-	PIM	PP	SH	GW	GT	S	PCT
69	21	53	74	+14	66	6	1	5	0	147	14.3

1993-94 statistics:

GP	G	A	TP	+/-	PIM	PP	SH	GW	GT	S	PCT
82	14	36	50	+2	38	5	0	4	0	138	10.1

1994-95 statistics:

GP	G	A	TP	+/-	PIM	PP	SH	GW	GT	S	PCT
46	10	23	33	+3	50	4	2	2	0	80	12.5

1995-96 statistics:

GP	G	A	TP	+/-	PIM	PP	SH	GW	GT	S	PCT
73	16	65	81	+18	36	6	2	5	0	168	9.5

LAST SEASON

Led team in assists and points, both career highs. Second on team in game-winning goals. Tied for third on team in plus-minus. Missed first three games of the season with a suspension as the result of a 1995 playoff incident. Missed six games in contract dispute.

THE FINESSE GAME

Pivonka has marvellous skills. On the power play and in four-on-four situations, he takes full advantage of the extra ice. He skates well, with quickness and breakaway speed. He moves the puck quickly and jumps into the play for a give-and-go. His acceleration is outstanding.

He shoots well in stride (a trait of many Europeans), but he is too shy about shooting, usually looking to make the pass first. This worked well last season, as his linemate and favourite receiver was Peter Bondra. Pivonka's stick is always on the ice. It's a small detail, but it allows him to pick up pucks that bounce off other players' sticks or skates.

Pivonka makes a lot of little dekes in tight, forcing a goalie to move his feet, and then he finds the opening.

THE PHYSICAL GAME

Last season, both mentally and physically, Pivonka developed into the kind of consistent, on-ice leader the Caps had been waiting for. He isn't aggressive enough to physically dominate a game, but when the style is a little more wide-open, Pivonka excels because of his elite skills. He is also less likely to be intimidated.

THE INTANGIBLES

Last season we predicted an 80-point season for Pivonka. He nailed it and now that he has the confidence, there is no reason why he can't surpass that total this year. The key is his alliance with Bondra.

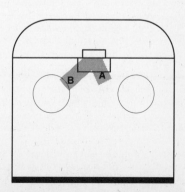

MARK TINORDI

Yrs. of NHL service: 8
Born: Deer River, Alta.; May 9, 1966
Position: left defense
Height: 6-4
Weight: 213
Uniform no.: 24
Shoots: left

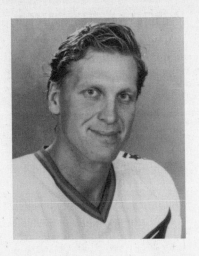

Career statistics:

GP	G	A	TP	PIM
512	42	127	169	1249

1992-93 statistics:

GP	G	A	TP	+/-	PIM	PP	SH	GW	GT	S	PCT
69	15	27	42	-1	157	7	0	2	0	122	12.3

1993-94 statistics:

GP	G	A	TP	+/-	PIM	PP	SH	GW	GT	S	PCT
61	6	18	24	+6	143	1	0	0	0	112	5.4

1994-95 statistics:

GP	G	A	TP	+/-	PIM	PP	SH	GW	GT	S	PCT
42	3	9	12	-5	71	2	0	1	0	71	4.2

1995-96 statistics:

GP	G	A	TP	+/-	PIM	PP	SH	GW	GT	S	PCT
71	3	10	13	+26	113	2	0	0	0	82	3.7

LAST SEASON

Led team in plus-minus. Missed 11 games with concussion.

THE FINESSE GAME

Tinordi can play both sides and with any partner. He can be the point man on the power play and he can kill penalties. You can use him in the first minute and in the last minute, when you're trying to protect a lead.

Tinordi doesn't have much in the way of finesse skills, but oh, how he loves to go to the net. He starts out at the point on the power play but doesn't hesitate to crash down low. He is an impact player and a major force on the ice.

Tinordi has an effective point shot: low, hard and accurate. He also sees the play well and moves his passes crisply. He intimidates when he moves low and bulls his way to the net. He is poised with the puck and will use a wrist shot in deep.

An above-average skater, Tinordi is mobile for his large size. He lacks one-step quickness, but once in gear he has a long stride with good balance and mobility. He can use his long reach well around the net or to take the puck away from a defender. He is a strong penalty killer with good hockey sense.

THE PHYSICAL GAME

Tinordi plays with the throttle wide open and doesn't recognize any other playing style. One of the reasons why he is so susceptible to getting hurt is that he is more concerned with making the play than with protecting himself, and he ends up in vulnerable situations. A little less reckless abandon would help keep him in one piece, but we're not sure if Tinordi knows

how to play that way. He usually ends up missing a big chunk of playing time each season with some serious ailment.

As honest and tough as they come, Tinordi commands respect on the ice. He has too short a fuse, though in recent years he has done a better job of curbing his temper, realizing he is more important to his team on the ice than in the penalty box. He is competitive and fearless.

THE INTANGIBLES

Last season, Tinordi was paired with rookie Sergei Gonchar and was content to let the talented youngster carry much of the attack. If that pairing continues, expect Tinordi's point totals to diminish while he concentrates on defense. He could score 25 goals and have a great season, or five goals and still have a great season. He's that useful in that many ways. He is a crunch-time player. Too bad he's the one who so often ends up crunched.

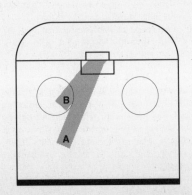

STEFAN USTORF

Yrs. of NHL service: 1
Born: Kaufbeuren, Germany; Jan. 3, 1974
Position: right wing
Height: 6-0
Weight: 185
Uniform no.: 16
Shoots: left

Career statistics:

GP	G	A	TP	PIM
48	7	10	17	14

1995-96 statistics:

GP	G	A	TP	+/-	PIM	PP	SH	GW	GT	S	PCT
48	7	10	17	+8	14	0	0	1	0	39	17.9

LAST SEASON

First NHL season. Led team in shooting percentage. Played eight games with Portland, scoring 1-4 — 5. Missed three games with flu. Missed eight games with separated shoulder. Missed one game with pulled hamstring.

THE FINESSE GAME

Ustorf is a very talented player who hasn't found a role in the NHL. He was a gifted scorer on the international level, but that was in a finesse-oriented game. He has had a hard time adjusting to the North American style of play on a smaller ice surface.

Ustorf is a very fast skater, which is the strength of his game. He is creative with the puck, but sometimes seems to think that style points count for something in the standings. If he makes a nice play, he is happy, even if it doesn't result in a goal. He needs to learn to demand more from himself.

He makes smart plays but needs to improve his shot. His snap shot is his best weapon — he may not have taken a slap shot all season — and has a good wrist shot, but needs to shoot more. Ustorf played wing most of last season but could be moved to centre, which will open up his game.

Ustorf was scheduled to play for Germany in the World Cup, and if he has a good tournament it could give him a boost to a strong NHL season.

THE PHYSICAL GAME

Ustorf has a very lean build and will need to improve his strength. He doesn't go into a lot of high traffic areas and isn't very assertive.

THE INTANGIBLES

Ustorf will be a bubble player unless he adds some other elements to his game to become a better all-around player. He certainly has the skills to become a good penalty killer, and was given some shorthanded ice time by the Caps late in the season, so that is a role he could grow into. He could have been making a lot of money playing in Germany, but gave it up to play in the minors in 1994-95, which indicates he has a desire to succeed and become an NHL regular. With sufficient ice time, he could prove to be a sleeper. He's a potential 60-point scorer.

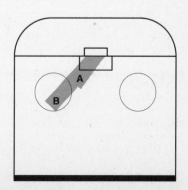

ALEXANDRE VOLCHKOV

Yrs. of NHL service: 0
Born: Moscow, Russia; Sept. 25, 1977
Position: right wing
Height: 6-1
Weight: 194
Uniform no.: n.a.
Shoots: left

Career junior statistics:

GP	G	A	TP	PIM
47	37	27	64	36

1995-96 junior statistics:

GP	G	A	TP	+/P
47	37	27	64	36

LAST SEASON

Drafted fourth overall. Will be entering first NHL season. Led Barrie (OHL) in scoring despite missing 21 games with a fractured ankle.

THE FINESSE GAME

Volchkov can play all three forward positions with equal skill, and as a left-handed shooter, he could help the Capitals at their weakest position, left wing. He is the kind of player who wants to be on the ice when the game is at a critical juncture; he has the skill to have a say in the outcome.

Volchkov dominated games at the junior level. He is aggressive and confident. He prefers to do the scoring himself, and has a long reach that frustrates defenders. He has very strong hands and wrists for shots in tight and on the backhand.

He is also an intelligent playmaker but is a little bit selfish with the puck, unlike many Russian players. He can kill penalties or work on the power play. Volchkov is a sound skater with mobility, quickness and speed.

THE PHYSICAL GAME

Volchkov is a burly sort who will battle for the puck in the high-traffic areas around the net. He has the strength to bowl people over but isn't a mean hitter. He will absorb a lot of abuse to protect the puck and has a long fuse. Plenty of players will try to intimidate him in his first NHL season but it's not likely he will be scared off on those nights when he's in the mood to play.

THE INTANGIBLES

Volchkov was considered to be the most NHL-ready of the 1996 draft crop. He may also prove to be the least predictable of the top dozen prospects. Islanders coach and GM Mike Milbury, who bypassed Volchkov in favour of Jean-Pierre Dumont, called the Russian winger, "A wild card. He's a potential 50-goal scorer with a potentially fatal flaw." That flaw is Volchkov's inconsistency.

Scouts liked the fact that Volchkov left Russia to play last season in the OHL, because that gave him a year to acclimate himself to North American life. His father, Alexander, played for the Soviet Union in the 1972 Summit Series, so Volchkov has the right bloodlines, and he could step right in to start the season with the Capitals.

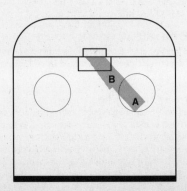

BRENDAN WITT

Yrs. of NHL service: 1
Born: Humboldt, Sask.; Feb. 20, 1975
Position: left defense
Height: 6-1
Weight: 205
Uniform no.: 19
Shoots: left

Career statistics:

GP	G	A	TP	PIM
48	2	3	5	85

1995-96 statistics:

GP	G	A	TP	+/-	PIM	PP	SH	GW	GT	S	PCT
48	2	3	5	-4	85	0	0	1	0	44	4.5

LAST SEASON

First NHL season. Missed 34 games with broken wrist.

THE FINESSE GAME

Witt's skill level proved to be very high, especially considering the season he spent away from the game (see Intangibles). It may have helped that he is a defensive defenseman, and that may be the easiest position to come back to after a long layoff. That should help him again after missing almost half the season with a broken wrist.

Witt's skating is capable, although he needs to improve his agility. His turning and passing are a little bit raw, but he does not overhandle the puck and by making simple plays keeps himself out of serious trouble. He skates well backwards and has decent lateral mobility.

Witt will get involved somewhat in the attack, but the extent of his contribution will be a hard point shot. He won't gamble low and can't run a power play. He won't ever be an offensive force.

THE PHYSICAL GAME

Witt has a strong physical presence on the ice, but he needs to get even stronger. He was turned by some players in one-on-one battles against bigger players, and a defensive defenseman can't allow that to happen. Witt blocks shots fearlessly.

Witt is naturally aggressive and intimidating. If he can pick up where he left off after the injury, he will be a factor again, although he is lacking experience.

THE INTANGIBLES

Witt missed an entire season (1994-95) after refusing to sign with the Capitals and refusing to play for his junior team. The expected resentment was simmering in the dressing room, but never boiled over as Witt was quickly accepted by his teammates because of his commitment to the team. He is a potential Rod Langway.

PLAYER INDEX

Player Index